Hits That Missed

Missed

The UK
Bubbling Under Chart
1954-1961

Colin Driscoll

MUSIC MENTOR BOOKS
York, England

British Library Cataloguing-in-Publication Data
A catalogue record for this book is available from the British Library.

ISBN-13: 978-0-9562679-9-3

Published worldwide by Music Mentor Books *(Proprietor: G.R. Groom-White)*
69 Station Road, Upper Poppleton, York YO26 6PZ, North Yorkshire, England.
Telephone: +44 (0)1904 330308 *Email:* music.mentor@lineone.net

Illustrations courtesy of Terry Kay, *Now Dig This,*
Music Mentor archive and author's collection.

Cover by It's Great To Be Rich, York.

Printed and bound in Great Britain by Bonacia Ltd, Peterborough.

This book is dedicated to my family
and all pop chart enthusiasts.

Also, to all would-be authors – believe.

Contents

ALL KINDS OF MUSIC BUBBLED UNDER...

Introduction

The period between the summer of 1954 and the spring of 1961 was a time of great upheaval in popular music in the British Isles, witnessing the emergence of trad jazz, skiffle and rock'n'roll (and to a lesser extent calypso, folk and C&W), a renaissance of Irish and Scottish music, and a gradual fading of the influence of operatic balladeers, crooners and the big band sounds of the post-war period. However, it was rock'n'roll that would ultimately have the biggest and most far-reaching impact.

This book picks up the story in June 1954, when Johnnie Ray's interpretation of the Drifters' 'Such A Night' was sitting at the top of the UK hit parade, but it would be the autumn of that year before real rock'n'roll began to make a breakthrough – initially via white cover versions of R&B records. The first of these, 'Sh-Boom' by the Crew-Cuts (originally by the Chords), entered the charts that October. It was followed in December by a reworking of Joe Turner's 'Shake, Rattle And Roll' by Bill Haley & His Comets, and in January 1955 by the anthem of the new era, 'Rock Around The Clock', also by Haley. Over the next eighteen months or so, black American music continued to make its presence increasingly felt in the UK pop mainstream via more white cover versions like the Crew-Cuts' 'Earth Angel' (Penguins), the Hilltoppers' 'Only You' (Platters), and Pat Boone's 'Ain't That A Shame' (Fats Domino) and 'I'll Be Home' (Flamingos), but it was Haley who led the pack with exciting rockers like 'Mambo Rock', 'Rock-A-Beatin' Boogie' and 'See You Later, Alligator'. Then, Elvis Presley's 'Heartbreak Hotel' exploded in May 1956, after which the music scene was never the same again.

Presley and other American rock'n'rollers – among them Fats Domino, Chuck Berry, Gene Vincent, Buddy Holly, Little Richard, Larry Williams, Jerry Lee Lewis, Ricky Nelson and Eddie Cochran – dominated popular music until the Beatles stormed the British charts in 1963. However, the UK also fielded a vast array of home-grown talent ranging from rockers like Tommy Steele, Marty Wilde and Cliff Richard to pop singers like Alma Cogan, Ruby Murray, Petula Clark, Frankie Vaughan, Dickie Valentine and Jimmy Young, to singing groups like the Stargazers, the Beverley Sisters and the King Brothers – all of whom were capable of rivalling the biggest American stars in the hit parade. Of course, it wasn't rock'n'roll all the way, and there was always room for a balladeer with a decent song, or a dance band with a good tune.

Against this musical backdrop, the UK pop charts developed. The first of these was a Top 12 published in November 1952 by the *New Musical Express*. By 1958, the *New Musical Express*, *Disc*, *Melody Maker* and *Record Mirror* were all publishing their own Top 20s. In March 1960, the music trade paper *Record Retailer* launched its Top 50 singles chart.

Unlike America, however, notable records which 'bubbled under' the charts but did not become hits went unrecorded in the British music press and unrecognised by history. At last, all that is about to change with the publication of this book. I hope you enjoy the nostalgia trip. If you can't find your favourite tune here, it didn't bubble.

Acknowledgements

It would have been impossible to produce a book such as this without the support of many other people. I am indebted to Bill Dean-Myatt, Chris Hamilton, Conor Long (Glenside Records), Ted McGraw, the Mitchell Library, Glasgow and the National Library of Scotland for their assistance with numerous queries pertaining to Irish and Scottish records, and to Julian Barker, Dave Cooper (The Record Collector's Shop, Trowbridge), Ray Darby, Max Hooley (Maxvinyl), Peter Miles, Pete Oakman, Ray Pallett (*Memory Lane* magazine), Dave Penny, John Poole, Alan Ross (Jazz House Records) and the British Library's National Sound Archive for their help with a host of other matters.

Colin Driscoll
October 2018

About the *UK Bubbling Under Chart*

In June 1959, the US music industry periodical *Billboard* launched the 'Bubbling Under The Hot 100' chart, listing new releases heading for America's national pop chart. Many of these never broke through, of course, and it is enlightening to look back and discover which classic recordings ground to a premature halt – not least because many non-charting 'bubblers' ultimately outsold faster-selling but shorter-lived 'hits'. Often overlooked by music writers and researchers, they are the missing pieces of the jigsaw which help complete our understanding of rock and pop history. There *was* life outside the 'Hot 100'!

Sadly, no similar chart was ever published in the UK. However, between June 1954 and March 1961 *Record Mirror*[*] regularly published 'Top Tens' of local best-sellers submitted by record shops from all over the country, and it occurred to me that it should be possible to compile a retrospective 'Bubbling Under' chart based on these. Indeed, with up to fifty such returns appearing most weeks, the size of the sample was larger than those used to produce most other charts at the time.

I compiled the *UK Bubbling Under Chart* by ranking all the weekly returns using a simple marking system (10 points for each dealer's No.1, 9 points for each No.2, and so on), after which I aggregated the scores for the week and filtered out any current or former chart hits. The *UK Bubbling Under Chart* therefore includes the pre-chart history of records which went on to become hits, as well as details of all those 'strong sellers with hit potential' that never made it. For the purposes of this book, any record which appeared in charts published by *Disc*, *Melody Maker*, *New Musical Express*, *Record Mirror* or *Record Retailer* qualifies as a hit.

Unlike the *Billboard* 'Bubbling Under' chart, whose positions follow on from the 'Hot 100', the *UK Bubbling Under Chart* starts at No.1. There are a several reasons for this. Firstly, the *UK Bubbling Under Chart* was compiled from a different data source, and therefore does not dovetail exactly with *Record Mirror* or any other chart. Secondly, the size of UK charts varied during the period in question, which would have resulted in different starting positions for the *UK Bubbling Under Chart* at different times. Thirdly, dealers sometimes included EPs and LPs in their returns, and these are also included in the *UK Bubbling Under Chart* along with singles.

This notwithstanding, I hope it will prove to be a useful resource for music fans and researchers for years to come.

---

[*] *Record & Show Mirror* from August 1959.

Technical Notes

1 Terminology

In this book, records which appear in the *UK Bubbling Under Chart* are referred to as 'bubblers', or are said to have 'bubbled' or 'bubbled under'. Any references to 'entering the charts' or 'charting' refer to the hit parade.

2 Layout

This book consists of two main sections: 'Artists A-Z' and 'The Weekly *Bubbling Under* Charts'.

'Artists A-Z' lists all the singles and albums which appear in the *UK Bubbling Under Chart* in chronological order under each artist's name. For the benefit of researchers, flip sides and track listings of medleys, EPs and LPs have also been included. (I have said 'flip sides' rather than 'B' sides', as in many cases the titles reported by dealers as selling more strongly were 'B' sides, rather than the official 'A' sides.)

Titles which bubbled under are shown in **bold**. In some instances, both sides were listed by dealers, constituting a double-sided bubbler. Where this occurs, the stronger-selling side is listed first.

The 'Weekly *Bubbling Under* Charts' section is a month-by-month listing of all the weekly charts from 19 June 1954 to 25 March 1961. These include the pre-chart history of records which went on to become hits, as well as all those bubblers that didn't. The symbol ★ indicates the date when a record charted.

For reasons of space, some artists' names and song titles have been abbreviated in the *Bubbling Under* charts. Song titles are shown exactly as they appeared on the label, which in some cases may differ in styling/spelling from the US originals.

3 Catalogue numbers

78 r.p.m. numbers are quoted for singles which bubbled under before the end of 1957, as this was the most common format at the time. 45 r.p.m. numbers are used from January 1958 onwards.

Several labels including London and Columbia used the same catalogue numbers for 78s and 45s, but with a '45-' prefix to identify the latter format. For clarity and ease of reference, these prefixes have been omitted.

4 Reliability of source data

Every effort has been made to ensure that the information included in this book is as complete and accurate as possible, but some details may have been missed or misinterpreted. In the dealer returns, some records were only vaguely described and a considerable amount of detective work was required to pin down the correct details. For example, one quoted the title of a Nat 'King' Cole record as 'Kiss Me Deadly'. In fact, the song was 'I'd Rather Have The Blues' from the film *Kiss Me Deadly*.

5   Hits not listed in the *Guinness Book of British Hit Singles*

The following bubblers went on to become hits, but are not listed in Guinness because they did not appear in the charts used by that publication (*NME* up to March 1960, *Record Retailer* thereafter). The month and year they charted in is shown on the left, followed by the periodical(s) in whose chart(s) they appeared.

D	=	*Disc*
MM	=	*Melody Maker*
NME	=	*New Musical Express*
RM	=	*Record Mirror*

6/60	NME	Marke Anthony - **Why Didn't You Tell Me**
5/58	MM	Frankie Avalon - **Dede Dinah**
11/59	D	Shirley Bassey - **Count On Me**
6/58	RM	Chuck Berry - **Johnny B. Goode**
11/55	RM	Eve Boswell - **Blue Star**
10/56	RM	Marlon Brando / Jean Simmons - **GUYS AND DOLLS** 🔲
8/60	MM, RM	Brook Brothers - **Please Help, Me I'm Falling**
12/60	RM	Johnny Carson - **You Talk Too Much**
12/60	NME, RM	Pete Chester & The Consulates - **Ten Swingin' Bottles**
2/55	RM	Alma Cogan - **The Naughty Lady Of Shady Lane** / **Mambo Italiano**
11/55	RM	Nat 'King' Cole - **Love Is A Many Splendored Thing**
3/58	MM	Edric Connor - **Manchester United Calypso**
11/55	RM	Billy Cotton & His Band - **The Dam Busters March**
11/58	RM	Crickets - **It's So Easy**
3/58	RM	Jim Dale - **Don't Let Go**
10/60	NME	Sammy Davis Jr. - **Eee-O Eleven**
3/57	MM	Jill Day - **I Dreamed**
5/59	MM	Craig Douglas - **Come Softly To Me**
10/59	RM	Craig Douglas - **The Riddle Of Love**
8/58	RM	Charlie Drake - **Hello My Darlings**
2/56	RM	Robert Earl - **With Your Love**
3/56	RM	Robert Earl - **My September Love**
4/59	RM	Duane Eddy - **The Lonely One**
7/60	MM, NME	Johnny Ferguson - **Angela Jones**
4/60	NME	Ernie Fields & His Orchestra - **Chattanooga Choo Choo**
10/60	NME	Flee-Rakkers - **Sunday Date**
11/55	RM	Fontane Sisters - **Seventeen**
1/56	RM	Stan Freberg - **The Yellow Rose Of Texas**
12/60	RM	Iain Gregory - **Time Will Tell**
1/55	RM	Ronnie Harris and the Coronets - **Don't Go To Strangers**
12/55	RM	Julius LaRosa - **Suddenly There's A Valley**
6/60	MM, RM	Josh MacRae - **Talking Army Blues**
2/61	RM	Josh MacRae - **Messing About On The River**
12/58	RM	Martinas & His Music - **Cha Cha Momma Brown**
7/60	NME	Valerie Masters - **Banjo Boy**
9/60	RM	Ian Menzies & His Clyde Valley Stompers - **The Fish Man**
12/55	RM	Ruby Murray - **The Very First Christmas Of All**
10/60	MM	Ray Peterson - **Tell Laura I Love Her**

2/59	MM	Playmates - **Beep Beep**
1/56	RM	Joan Regan - **Croce di Oro**
10/59	MM	Johnny Restivo - **The Shape I'm In**
4/56	MM	Jackie Riggs - **The Great Pretender**
8/58	MM	Jimmie Rodgers - **Secretly**
12/60	NME	Marion Ryan - **It's You That I Love**
12/56	RM	Jimmy Shand & His Band - **Sing With Jimmy Shand [M]**
7/58	RM	Frank Sinatra - **SINATRA! EP**
2/58	RM	Southlanders - **Put A Light In The Window**
4/58	RM	Tommy Steele - **Princess**
5/59	MM	Dodie Stevens - **Pink Shoe Laces**
3/56	RM	Gale Storm - **I Hear You Knocking**
9/60	RM	Vince Taylor & His Playboys - **I'll Be Your Hero / Jet Black Machine**
7/58	MM	Art & Dotty Todd - **Chanson d'Amour**
2/58	MM, RM	Nick Todd - **At The Hop**
11/55	RM	Mitchell Torok - **Caribbean**
9/57	MM	Frankie Vaughan - **These Dangerous Years**
2/58	MM, RM	Billy Vaughn & His Orchestra - **Raunchy**
2/61	RM	Lawrence Welk & His Orchestra - **Calcutta**
7/60	NME	Marty Wilde - **Angry**

Artists A–Z

This section lists in chronological order under each artist's name all their singles and albums which appear in the *UK Bubbling Under Chart*. Records released under a pseudonym are listed under the artist's main/usual name.

Additionally, there are separate entries for Original Broadway Cast, Original London Cast, Original Soundtrack and Various Artists releases. Soundtrack albums are listed in the Original Soundtrack section except where the entire album is by a single artist. Where this is the case, the album is listed under the artist's name instead, with **[OST]** after the title.

Both sides of singles are listed, and each re-entry is shown separately.

Titles which bubbled under are shown in bold. Where both sides of a single bubbled under, the stronger-selling side is listed first. 'Flipped' after a re-entry indicates that the other side was previously listed as the stronger-selling side.

Records which subsequently became hits are marked ★. For extra clarity, the hit sides of singles are underlined, as the sides which charted were not always the ones that bubbled under.

[M] after a title indicates that the recording was a medley.

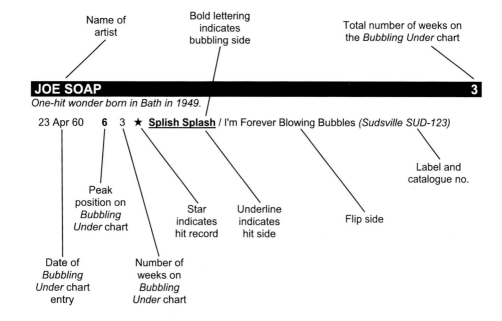

2.19 SKIFFLE GROUP   2
Quartet from Kent. Winners of the First National Skiffle Contest in June 1957.

  27 Apr 57 **12** 1   **Freight Train Blues** / Railroad Bill *(Esquire 10-497)*
  11 May 57 **4** 1   **Freight Train Blues** / Railroad Bill *(Esquire 10-497)* ***re-entry***

751st U.S.A.F. BAND   3
The only American military band based in the UK. They bubbled under with this swinging march recorded live at the 1955 S.S.A.F.A. Searchlight Tattoo at White City Stadium, London.

  17 Dec 55 **13** 1   **St. Louis Blues March** *(H.M.V. B-10937)*
                       Flip is 'The Commonwealth On The March' by the Massed Bands
    7 Jan 56 **6** 2   **St. Louis Blues March** *(H.M.V. B-10937)* ***re-entry***

SHIRLEY ABICAIR   2
Zither-strumming folk singer, actress, children's TV personality and author from Melbourne, Australia.

  21 Apr 56 **8** 2   **Willie Can** / Happy Trails *(Parlophone R-4150)*

ADAM SINGERS   1
The Adam Singers were formed in 1954 by Stargazer Cliff Adams, and specialised in well-known melodies from bygone decades. Their popular Sunday night BBC radio show, 'Sing Something Simple', stayed on the air for an amazing 42 years until Adams' death in 2001.

  10 Oct 59 **15** 1   **Morgen** / Two Blue Pigeons *(Pye International 7N.25033)*
                       Both sides by the Adam Singers with the Cliff Adams Orchestra

See also Cliff Adams Orchestra
         Stargazers

CLIFF ADAMS ORCHESTRA   1
Best known for his vocal work (see previous entry), this haunting instrumental by Cliff Adams was used in the classic 'You're never alone with a Strand' TV commercial in which a man walking along a dark and desolate London street stops to light up a cigarette.

  23 Apr 60 **6** 1 ★ <u>**The Lonely Man Theme**</u> / Trigger Happy *(Pye International 7N.25056)*

See also Adam Singers
         Stargazers

MARIE ADAMS
See Johnny Otis Show

ADDRISI BROTHERS   1
Dick and Don Addrisi were more successful as songwriters than singers, although they did enjoy some chart success in the 1970s. Don tragically died of cancer in 1984, aged just 45.

  21 Nov 59 **12** 1   **It's Love** / Back To The Old Salt Mine *(Columbia DB-4370)*

ADRIANO   1
Lincoln-born accordionist Jack Emblow was a ubiquitous presence on the British music scene for many years, both as a sessionman and as leader of his own sextet. He also made solo recordings as 'Adriano'.

  19 Dec 59 **6** 1   **The Happy Hobo** / Folies Begère *(Parlophone R-4602)*

ALYN AINSWORTH & His Orchestra   1
Conductor/arranger from Bolton who served apprenticeships with Oscar Rabin and Geraldo before becoming leader of the BBC's Northern Dance Orchestra in the late '50s.

  30 May 59 **11** 1   **Bedtime For Drums** / The Cobbler's Song *(Parlophone R-4533)*

LAUREL AITKEN 1

Ska pioneer born Lorenzo Aitken in Cuba in 1927. Produced by future Island label boss Chris Blackwell, 'Boogie In My Bones' was the first Jamaican pop record to be released in the UK..

25 Jun 60 **11** 1   **Boogie In My Bones** / Little Sheila *(Starlite ST.45-011)*

ALFI & HARRY

See David Seville

RICHARD ALLAN 9

British balladeer and former amateur boxing champion who recorded three singles before disappearing into obscurity.

5 Mar 60   **4**   2   ★ **As Time Goes By** / **Only One** *(Parlophone R-4634)*
27 Aug 60   **3**   6   **Doctor In Love** / Everyday *(Parlophone R-4673)*
           Both sides as by Richard Allen
7 Jan 61   **15**   1   **Poetry In Motion** / Don't Ever Say You're Gonna Leave Me
           (Parlophone R-4711)

JERRY ALLEN 1

Discovered by the comedian Tommy Trinder, singing organist Jerry Allen was a regular on ATV's popular mid-'50s lunchtime music show, 'Lunchbox'.

15 Jan 55   **27**   1   **S'posin'** / When I Needed You Most *(Decca F-10428)*
           Both sides by Jerry Allen with his Trio and the Allentones

STEVE ALLEN 2

American actor, comedian, musician, composer and TV show host born in New York in 1921.

18 Feb 56   **9**   1   **What Is A Wife?** / Memories Of You *(Vogue Coral Q-72126)*
6 Dec 58   **15**   1   **Almost In Your Arms** / Hula Hoop *(London HLD-8742)*

LYNNE ALLISON 2

British singer whose 'Mama From The Train' competed with Patti Page's version in the UK.

19 Jan 57   **7**   1   **Mama From The Train** / Song Of The Sparrow *(Columbia DB-3867)*
2 Feb 57   **16**   1   **Mama From The Train** / Song Of The Sparrow *(Columbia DB-3867)*
           re-entry

BRUNO AMADUCCI *(conductor)*

See Fernando Corena

AMES BROTHERS 5

Old-style singing quartet from Malden, Massachusetts who enjoyed immense popularity in the States throughout the '50s, though they only managed one hit in the UK.

15 Jan 55   **5**   3   ★ **The Naughty Lady Of Shady Lane** / Addio *(H.M.V. B-10800)*
12 Oct 57   **5**   1   **Tammy** / Rockin' Shoes *(R.C.A. RCA-1015)*
23 Nov 57   **12**   1   **Melodie d'Amour** / So Little Time *(R.C.A. RCA-1021)*

EAMONN ANDREWS 2

Boxing commentator and radio/TV presenter born in Dublin in 1922. By the time he recorded the spoken narrative below, the affable Irishman was already a household name in the UK thanks to hosting shows like 'What's My Line?' and 'This Is Your Life'.

7 Jan 56   **1**   2   ★ **The Shifting Whispering Sands (Parts 1 & 2)** *(Parlophone R-4106)*

JULIE ANDREWS   1

Talented British star of stage and screen born Julia Wells, whose later triumphs included 'Mary Poppins' and 'The Sound of Music'.

16 Aug 58   **6**   1   **I Could Have Danced All Night** *(Julie Andrews and Philippa Bevans)* / Without You *(Julie Andrews) (Philips PB-846)*

See also Original Broadway Cast (MY FAIR LADY)

MICKY ANDREWS   1

Singer/impressionist who trod the boards of variety theatres up and down the UK. The bubbler below was the last and most successful of his four releases.

2 Oct 54   **31**   1   **I Can't Believe That You're In Love With Me** / Try Again
(Columbia DB-3517)
Both sides with the Jackie Brown Quintet and the Coronets

ANDREWS SISTERS   1

Singing trio Patti, Maxene and LaVerne Andrews were hugely popular in the USA from the late 1930s until the early 1950s, often recording with Bing Crosby as well as in their own right. This reissue of their 1945 US chart-topper was the closest they got to the UK charts.

27 Apr 57   **14**   1   **Rum And Coca-Cola** / No, Baby *(Capitol CL-14705)*

JOHNNY ANGEL   10

Singer/songwriter James Ouckama from British Guiana recording under a pseudonym presumably inspired by the 1945 film noir (Shelley Fabares didn't record her 'Johnny Angel' hit until 1962).

20 Aug 60   **12**   1   **You're Thrilling** / Too Young To Go Steady *(Parlophone R-4679)*
3 Sep 60   **6**   1   **You're Thrilling** / Too Young To Go Steady *(Parlophone R-4679)*
        1st re-entry
17 Sep 60   **3**   8   **You're Thrilling** / Too Young To Go Steady *(Parlophone R-4679)*
        2nd re-entry

PAUL ANKA   13

Highly successful singer/songwriter and teen idol born in Ottawa, Canada in 1941. He racked up 14 UK hits between 1957 and 1962.

19 Apr 58   **2**   6   ★ **Crazy Love** / **Let The Bells Keep Ringing** *(Columbia DB-4110)*
11 Oct 58   **10**   1   ★ **Midnight** / Verboten! *(Columbia DB-4172)*
24 Jan 59   **9**   1   ★ **My Heart Sings** / That's Love *(Columbia DB-4241)*
30 May 59   **8**   1   **I Miss You So** / Late Last Night *(Columbia DB-4286)*
17 Oct 59   **7**   2   ★ **Put Your Head On My Shoulder** / Don't Ever Leave Me
        (Columbia DB-4355)
16 Jan 60   **8**   2   ★ **It's Time To Cry** / Something Has Changed Me *(Columbia DB-4390)*

ANNETTE   1

Former Walt Disney Mouseketeer and future beach movie starlet Annette Funicello scored 10 hits in the USA between 1959 and 1961. 'O Dio Mio' came close to being her first UK chart success.

9 Apr 60   **2**   1   **O Dio Mio** / It Took Dreams *(Top Rank JAR-343)*

BILLIE ANTHONY   7

Singer and dancer born Philomena McGeachie Levy in Glasgow in 1932. Despite her popularity, she only managed one hit.

25 Sep 54   **1**   3   ★ **This Ole House** / What A Dream *(Columbia DB-3519)*
26 Mar 55   **24**   1   **Tweedle Dee** / Shake The Hand Of A Stranger *(Columbia DB-3592)*
25 Jun 55   **23**   2   **Something's Gotta Give** / **Boom Boom Boomerang**
        (Columbia DB-3627)
23 Feb 57   **8**   1   **I Dreamed** / The Charge Of The Light Brigade *(Columbia DB-3874)*

MARKE ANTHONY 1

British one-hit wonder whose real name was Anthony Bloom. Curiously, he never recorded a follow-up.

18 Jun 60 **13** 1 ★ <u>**Why Didn't You Tell Me**</u> / Foolishly *(Decca F-11242)*

RAY ANTHONY & His Orchestra 6

Popular American trumpeter/bandleader born Raymond Antonini in Bentleyville, Pennsylvania.

16 Jul 55 **14** 1 **Sluefoot** / Something's Gotta Give *(Capitol CL-14306)*
30 Jul 55 **19** 3 **Sluefoot** / Something's Gotta Give *(Capitol CL-14306)*
                    re-entry
26 Nov 55 **13** 1 **Hernando's Hideaway** / The Bunny Hop *(Capitol CL-14354)*
14 Jan 56 **20** 1 **Hernando's Hideaway** / The Bunny Hop *(Capitol CL-14354)*
                    re-entry

APPLEJACKS 1

Not to be confused with the mid-'60s hitmakers from Solihull, these Applejacks were Dave Appel's studio band at Cameo-Parkway Records in Philadelphia.

23 Jan 60 **5** 1 **Circle Dance** / Love Scene *(Top Rank JAR-273)*

CHARLIE APPLEWHITE 1

Baritone crooner from Fort Worth, Texas who came to fame as a regular on Milton Berle's TV show in the mid-'50s. A near-fatal plane crash in 1961 effectively ended his career.

17 Sep 55 **10** 1 ★ <u>**Blue Star**</u> / A Prayer Was Born *(Brunswick 05416)*

AQUATONES 7

Doo-wop quartet from New York fronted by the operatically trained Lynne Nixon.

21 Jun 58 **5** 3 **You** / She's The One For Me *(London HLO-8631)*
26 Jul 58 **5** 4 **You** / She's The One For Me *(London HLO-8631)* *re-entry*

TONI ARDEN 2

Toni Arden aka Antoinette Ardizzone from New York sang with several name bands before going solo in 1946. Although she had six hits in the USA, 'Beware' was her biggest success in the UK.

30 Jul 55 **16** 2 **Beware** / I'll Step Aside *(H.M.V. B-10893)*

LOUIS ARMSTRONG 37

Legendary influential jazz trumpeter, singer and movie star born in New Orleans in 1901.

19 Jun 54 **1** 7 **Basin Street Blues (Parts 1 & 2)** *(Brunswick 05303)*
                    Both sides by Louis Armstrong & The All Stars
14 Aug 54 **21** 1 **Basin Street Blues (Parts 1 & 2)** *(Brunswick 05303)* *re-entry*
28 Aug 54 **30** 1 **MUSIC FEATURED IN 'THE GLEN MILLER STORY'**
                    (Brunswick OE-9006) **EP**
                    Louis Armstrong & The All Stars
                    Basin Street Blues (Parts 1 & 2) / Otchi-Tchor-Ni-Ya / Struttin' With Some Barbecue / Margie
16 Oct 54 **29** 1 **PERIOD – 1926** *(Columbia 33SX-1029)* **LP**
                    Louis Armstrong & His Hot Five
                    Muskrat Ramble / Heebie Jeebies / Gut Bucket Blues / Skid-Dat-De-Dat / Yes! I'm In The Barrel / Cornet Chop Suey / Struttin' With Some Barbecue / I'm Not Rough / The Last Time / Got No Blues / Hotter Than That / Ory's Creole Trombone
16 Oct 54 **40** 1 **The Whiffenpoof Song** / Bye And Bye *(Brunswick 05235)*
                    Both sides by Louis Armstrong with Gordon Jenkins & His Chrous and Orchestra
23 Oct 54 **17** 3 **Skokiaan (Vocal)** / Skokiaan (Instrumental) *(Brunswick 05332)*
                    Both sides by Louis Armstrong with orchestra conducted by Sy Oliver

20 Nov 54	**15**	2	**1927** *(Columbia 33S-1041)* 🔲LP
			Louis Armstrong & His Hot Seven
			Potato Head Blues / Wild Man Blues / S.O.L. Blues / Gully Low Blues / Melancholy Blues / Weary Blues / Twelfth Street Rag / Willie The Weeper / Keyhole Blues / That's When I'll Come Back To You / Alligator Crawl / Chicago Breakdown
20 Nov 54	**42**	1	**Skokiaan (Vocal)** / Skokiaan (Instrumental) *(Brunswick 05332)*
			re-entry
8 Jan 55	**26**	1	**MUSKRAT RAMBLE** *(Columbia SEG-7514)* 🔲EP
			Louis Armstrong & His Hot Five
			Muskrat Ramble / Cornet Chop Suey / Gut Bucket Blues / Yes! I'm In The Barrel
10 Mar 56	**2**	5	★ <u>Theme from 'The Threepenny Opera'</u> / Back O' Town Blues
			(Philips PB-574)
			Both sides by Louis Armstrong & The All Stars
19 May 56	**1**	3	★ <u>TAKE IT SATCH!</u> *(Philips BBE-12035)* 🔲EP
			Louis Armstrong & His All-Stars
			Tiger Rag / Mack The Knife / The Faithful Hussar / Back O' Town Blues
24 Nov 56	**9**	1	**Now You Has Jazz** *(Bing Crosby and Louis Armstrong)* / High Society Calypso *(Louis Armstrong & His Band)* *(Capitol CL-14643)*
8 Dec 56	**5**	4	**Now You Has Jazz** *(Bing Crosby and Louis Armstrong)* / High Society Calypso *(Louis Armstrong & His Band)* *(Capitol CL-14643)* **1st re-entry**
8 Dec 56	**7**	1	**ELLA AND LOUIS** *(H.M.V. CLP-1098)* 🔲LP
			Ella Fitzgerald and Louis Armstrong
			Can't We Be Friends / Isn't This A Lovely Day / Moonlight In Vermont / They Can't Take That Away From Me / Under The Blanket Of Blue / Tenderly / A Foggy Day / Stars Fell On Alabama / Cheek To Cheek / The Nearness Of You / April In Paris
5 Jan 57	**4**	1	**ELLA AND LOUIS** *(H.M.V. CLP-1098)* 🔲LP *re-entry*
12 Jan 57	**2**	1	**Now You Has Jazz** *(Bing Crosby and Louis Armstrong)* / High Society Calypso *(Louis Armstrong & His Band)* *(Capitol CL-14643)* **2nd re-entry**
26 Jan 57	**3**	1	**Now You Has Jazz** *(Bing Crosby and Louis Armstrong)* / High Society Calypso *(Louis Armstrong & His Band)* *(Capitol CL-14643)* **3rd re-entry**
28 Sep 57	**5**	1	**Now You Has Jazz** *(Bing Crosby and Louis Armstrong)* / High Society Calypso *(Louis Armstrong & His Band)* *(Capitol CL-14643)* **4th re-entry**
12 Oct 57	**7**	1	**Now You Has Jazz** *(Bing Crosby and Louis Armstrong)* / High Society Calypso *(Louis Armstrong & His Band)* *(Capitol CL-14643)* **5th re-entry**

See also Original Soundtrack (THE FIVE PENNIES)
Original Soundtrack (HIGH SOCIETY)

EDDY ARNOLD   6
Hugely successful country singer from Henderson, Tennessee. He was managed by Colonel Tom Parker early on in his career.

3 Dec 60	**15**	1	**Just Out Of Reach** / Before This Day Ends *(R.C.A. RCA-1212)*
7 Jan 61	**5**	1	**Before This Day Ends** / **Just Out Of Reach** *(R.C.A. RCA-1212)* **1st re-entry (flipped)**
28 Jan 61	**8**	2	**Before This Day Ends** / **Just Out Of Reach** *(R.C.A. RCA-1212)* **2nd re-entry**
18 Feb 61	**10**	2	**Before This Day Ends** / **Just Out Of Reach** *(R.C.A. RCA-1212)* **3rd re-entry**

IRVING ASHBY
See Norman Granz' Jazz At The Philharmonic
Gene Norman's 'Just Jazz'

JOHNNY ASHCROFT   3

Popular country singer and TV host from Down Under. Reputedly the first-ever Australian country-rock song, 'Little Boy Lost' was inspired by a real event, when a youngster named Steven Walls went missing in the bush. Happily, he was found alive and well after four days.

16 Jul 60	**11**	1	**Little Boy Lost** / My Love Is A River *(H.M.V. POP-759)*
			Both sides with the Norman Gilmour Sextet and the Emitrons
13 Aug 60	**17**	1	**Little Boy Lost** / My Love Is A River *(H.M.V. POP-759)* **1st re-entry**
24 Sep 60	**14**	1	**Little Boy Lost** / My Love Is A River *(H.M.V. POP-759)* **2nd re-entry**

LYS ASSIA   2

Swiss songstress born Rosel Mina Schärer in Rupperswil in 1924. She won the very first Eurovision Song Contest in 1956 with the ballad 'Refrain'.

| 26 Nov 55 | **25** | 2 | **Arrivederci Darling** / I'll Be Waiting *(Decca F-10635)* |
| | | | *Both sides by Lys Assia and the Johnston Brothers* |

CHET ATKINS   4

Virtuoso country guitarist with a unique picking style who was one of the chief architects of the pop-oriented 'Nashville Sound'.

7 Nov 59	**6**	1		**Boo Boo Stick Beat** / Django's Castle *(R.C.A. RCA-1153)*
5 Dec 59	**14**	1		**Boo Boo Stick Beat** / Django's Castle *(R.C.A. RCA-1153)* **re-entry**
5 Mar 60	**5**	1	★	**Teensville** / One Mint Julep *(R.C.A. RCA-1174)*
25 Feb 61	**8**	1	★	**THE OTHER CHET ATKINS** *(R.C.A. Victor RD-27194)* **LP**

Begin The Beguine / Sabrosa / Yours (Quiéreme Mucho) / Siboney / The Streets Of Laredo / Delicado / Peanut Vendor / El Relicario / Maria Elena / Marcheta / Tzena, Tzena, Tzena / Poinciana (Song Of The Tree)

ATMOSPHERES   2

Short-lived instrumental group formed by six high school students from Dallas, Texas.

| 28 Nov 59 | **20** | 1 | **The Fickle Chicken** / Kabalo *(London HLW-8977)* |
| 19 Dec 59 | **12** | 1 | **The Fickle Chicken** / Kabalo *(London HLW-8977)* **re-entry** |

WINIFRED ATWELL   31

Superb piano technician who was capable of playing classical pieces or rags and boogie-woogies with equal ease. After moving to Britain from her native Trinidad in 1946, she quickly found a niche as one of the nation's most popular entertainers.

26 Jun 54	**9**	4	★	**The Story Of Three Loves** / Moonlight Fiesta *(Philips PB-234)*
26 Jun 54	**17**	1		**The Charleston** / Dill Pickles *(Philips PB-266)*
7 Aug 54	**7**	2		**The Charleston** / Dill Pickles *(Philips PB-266)* **1st re-entry**
4 Sep 54	**2**	2		**Dixieland** / Play, Play, Play *(Philips PB-300)*
				Winifred Atwell also sings vocals on both sides
4 Sep 54	**30**	2		**The Charleston** / **Dill Pickles** *(Philips PB-266)* **2nd re-entry**
2 Oct 54	**35**	1		**Vendetta** / Asia Minor *(Philips PB-332)*
23 Oct 54	**1**	3		**Vendetta** / Asia Minor *(Philips PB-332)* **re-entry**
26 Feb 55	**17**	1		**The Black Mask Waltz** / **Song Of The Sea** *(Decca F-10448)*
19 Mar 55	**21**	2		**Song Of The Sea** / The Black Mask Waltz *(Decca F-10448)*
				re-entry (flipped)
28 Apr 56	**1**	3	★	**Port-au-Prince** / Startime *(Decca F-10727)*
14 Jul 56	**15**	1	★	**The Left Bank** / Rampart Street Rock *(Decca F-10762)*
6 Oct 56	**18**	1		**Bumble Boogie** / St. Louis Blues *(Decca F-10785)*
20 Oct 56	**10**	1	★	**Make It A Party (Parts 1 & 2) [M]** *(Decca F-10796)*

Who Were You With Last Night? – Hello! Hello! Who's Your Lady Friend? – Yes, Sir, That's My Baby – Don't Dilly Dally On The Way – Beer Barrel Polka / After The Ball – Peggy O'Neil – Meet Me Tonight In Dreamland – I Belong To Glasgow – Down At The Old Bull And Bush

| 30 Nov 57 | **12** | 1 | ★ | **Let's Have A Ball (Parts 1 & 2) [M]** *(Decca F-10956)* |

Music! Music! Music! – This Ole House – Heartbreaker – The Woody Woodpecker / Last Train To San Fernando – Bring A Little Water Sylvie – Puttin' On The Style – Don't You Rock Me Daddy-O

8 Feb 58	10	1	**Raunchy** / Dugga Dugga Boom Boom *(Decca F-10987)*
8 Mar 58	1	1	**Raunchy** / Dugga Dugga Boom Boom *(Decca F-10987)* *re-entry*
28 Jun 58	17	1	**Streets Of Sorrento** / The Hope Waltz *(Decca F-10924)*
21 Nov 59	10	1	★ <u>**Piano Party (Parts 1 & 2)**</u> **[M]** *(Decca F-11183)*

Baby Face – Comin' Thro' The Rye – Annie Laurie – Little Brown Jug – Let Him Go, Let Him Tarry – Put Your Arms Around Me Honey / I'll Be With You In Apple Blossom Time – Shine On Harvest Moon – Blue Skies – I'll Never Say 'Never Again' Again – I'll See You In My Dreams

| 5 Mar 60 | 12 | 1 | **Tops In Pops (Parts 1 & 2) [M]** *(Decca F-11208)* |

Staccato'sTheme – Oh! Carol – Why / Seven Little Girls Sitting In The Back Seat – Way Down Yonder In New Orleans – What Do You Want To Make Those Eyes At Me For?

| 19 Mar 60 | 3 | 1 | **Tops In Pops (Parts 1 & 2) [M]** *(Decca F-11208)* *re-entry* |

See also Various Artists (All Star Hit Parade)

FRANKIE AVALON   13

Young trumpeter from Philadelphia who became a singing teen idol and film star, appearing in a string of beach movies with Annette in the mid-'60s.

26 Apr 58	4	2	★ <u>**Dede Dinah**</u> / Ooh La La *(H.M.V. POP-453)*
17 May 58	5	1	★ <u>**Dede Dinah**</u> / Ooh La La *(H.M.V. POP-453)* *re-entry*
4 Oct 58	2	1	★ <u>**Ginger Bread**</u> / Blue Betty *(H.M.V. POP-517)*
28 Mar 59	8	2	★ <u>**Venus**</u> / I'm Broke *(H.M.V. POP-603)*
31 Oct 59	6	3	**Just Ask Your Heart** / Two Fools *(H.M.V. POP-658)*
9 Jan 60	6	1	★ <u>**Why**</u> / Swingin' On A Rainbow *(H.M.V. POP-688)*
19 Mar 60	9	1	★ <u>**Don't Throw Away All Those Teardrops**</u> / Talk, Talk, Talk *(H.M.V. POP-727)*
16 Apr 60	5	1	★ <u>**Don't Throw Away All Those Teardrops**</u> / Talk, Talk, Talk *(H.M.V. POP-727)* *re-entry*
14 May 60	9	1	**The Faithful Kind** / Gee Whiz – Whilikins – Golly Gee *(H.M.V. POP-742)*

AVON SISTERS   1

Pop duo formed by sisters-in-law Elaine Murtagh and Valerie Murtagh (née Jenkins).

| 7 Feb 59 | 12 | 1 | **Jerri-Lee (I Love Him So)** / Baby-O *(Columbia DB-4236)* |

See also Avons

AVONS   1

A few months after their 'Jerri Lee' bubbled under, the Avon Sisters teamed up with former Nat Gonella band vocalist Ray Adams to enjoy several hits as 'The Avons'.

| 18 Jun 60 | 13 | 1 | ★ <u>**We're Only Young Once**</u> / I Keep Dreaming *(Columbia DB-4461)* |

See also Avon Sisters

JOHNNY BACHELOR   2

Rockabilly artist with a novel sound created by an overactive echo chamber. 'Mumbles' was actually a demo of a song Bachelor made to pitch to Elvis Presley, but it was released on spec by Era Records. Unfortunately, he was drafted in the same week, so was unable to promote it. Despite this, it proved to be a strong regional seller in the US – and very nearly a UK hit.

| 19 Mar 60 | 4 | 1 | **Mumbles** / Arabella Jean *(London HLN-9074)* |
| 2 Apr 60 | 6 | 1 | **Mumbles** / Arabella Jean *(London HLN-9074)* *re-entry* |

BACHELORS   1

This British group – not to be confused with Ireland's more famous 'I Wouldn't Trade You For The World' trio – briefly caused a stir with this Johnny Kidd cover.

| 6 Jun 59 | 16 | 1 | **Please Don't Touch** / Ding Ding *(Parlophone R-4547)* |

THE REFRESHING VOICE OF

Harry
Belafonte

MAKES A GREAT NEW HIT OF

SCARLET
RIBBONS

coupling

HOLD'EM JOE

POP 360 (45 & 78)

Shirley
Abicair

*A lush new voice
for 1957*

Lynne
Allison

INTRODUCES

Song of the sparrow

with

Mama from the train

(A KISS, A KISS)

DB3867 (on 78 & 45 r.p.m.)

COLUMBIA ⊙
RECORDS

*No. 10
in the U.S. Hit Parade*

CHUCK
BERRY

JOHNNY B. GOODE

HLM 8629

45/78

LONDON
RECORDS

Johnny Bond

JIM BACKUS 1

Jim Backus was a prolific American radio, TV and movie performer, and the voice of the short-sighted cartoon character Mr. Magoo.

11 Oct 58 **16** 1 **Delicious (The Laughing Song)** *(Jim Backus & Friend)* /
I Need A Vacation *(Jim Backus) (London HLJ-8674)*

ARTHUR BAIRD SKIFFLE GROUP featuring Jack Taylor 1

Scottish skiffle trio comprising Arthur Baird (guitar, banjo and violin), Jim Scott (tub bass) and Jack Taylor (washboard). Both sides of their single were recorded live at St. Andrew's Hall, Glasgow on 30 June 1956.

17 Nov 56 **11** 1 **Union Maid** / Union Train *(Beltona BL-2669)*

CHET BAKER QUARTET 2

Cool jazz trumpeter/singer from Yale, Oklahoma who played with Charlie Parker and Gerry Mulligan.

26 Jun 54 **4** 1 **Winter Wonderland** / This Time The Dream's On Me *(Vogue V-2232)*
19 Feb 55 **15** 1 **CHET BAKER QUARTET** *(Vogue EPV-1007)* **EP**
Winter Wonderland / Imagination / This Time The Dream's On Me / Maid In Mexico

LaVERN BAKER 3

The exuberant LaVern Baker was one of the most copied R&B divas of the 1950s. She chalked up a string of hits in the USA, but in Britain her success was limited to these two bubblers.

3 Oct 59 **18** 1 **So High, So Low** / If You Love Me *(London HLE-8945)*
31 Dec 60 **12** 1 **Bumble Bee** / My Turn Will Come *(London HLK-9252)*
14 Jan 61 **20** 1 **Bumble Bee** / My Turn Will Come *(London HLK-9252)* *re-entry*

HANK BALLARD & THE MIDNIGHTERS 1

Pioneering black doo-wop group from Detroit with an exciting vocal style and dynamic dance routines. Although their original recording of 'The Twist' became a Top Ten R&B hit in the States, it was soon eclipsed by the immense success of Chubby Checker's cover version.

10 Sep 60 **9** 1 **The Twist** / Teardrops On Your Letter *(Parlophone R-4688)*

CHRIS BARBER'S JAZZ BAND 38

Influential Dixieland jazz trombonist/bandleader born in Welwyn Garden City in 1930. He also featured ragtime, swing and blues in his repertoire and pioneered skiffle with Lonnie Donegan.

13 Nov 54 **9** 6 **White Christmas** / On A Christmas Day *(Vocal: Lonnie Donegan)*
(Columbia DC-672)
11 Dec 54 **11** 5 **NEW ORLEANS JOYS** *(Decca LF-1198)* **LP**
Chris Barber's Jazz Band / Lonnie Donegan's Skiffle Group
Bobby Shaftoe *(Chris Barber's Jazz Band)* / Chimes Blues *(Chris Barber's Jazz Band)* / Rock Island Line *(Lonnie Donegan's Skiffle Group)* / The Martinique *(Chris Barber's Jazz Band)* / New Orleans Blues *(Chris Barber's Jazz Band)* / John Henry *(Lonnie Donegan's Skiffle Group)* / Merrydown Rag *(Chris Barber's Jazz Band)* / Stevedore Stomp *(Chris Barber's Jazz Band)*
1 Jan 55 **16** 1 **Merrydown Rag** / Chimes Blues *(Decca F-10417)*
22 Jan 55 **18** 2 **CHRIS BARBER PLAYS SPIRITUALS** *(Columbia SEG-7568)* **EP**
Sing On / Lawd, You've Been So Good To Me / Precious Lord, Take My Hand *(Vocal: Lonnie Donegan)* / God Leads His Dear Children
22 Jan 55 **22** 1 **NEW ORLEANS JOYS** *(Decca LF-1198)* **LP** *re-entry*
12 Feb 55 **1** 2 **CHRIS BARBER PLAYS SPIRITUALS** *(Columbia SEG-7568)* **EP**
re-entry
26 Mar 55 **13** 2 **Reckless Blues** / I Hate A Man Like You *(Decca Jazz F-10472)*
Both sides by Ottilie Patterson with Chris Barber's Jazz Band
2 Apr 55 **8** 1 **Bobby Shafto** / The Martinique *(Decca Jazz F-10492)*
23 Apr 55 **7** 1 **Bobby Shafto** / The Martinique *(Decca Jazz F-10492)*
1st re-entry
28 May 55 **12** 1 **The Martinique** / Bobby Shafto *(Decca Jazz F-10492)*
2nd re-entry (flipped)

15 Oct 55	**26**	1	**Precious Lord, Lead Me On** / **Tiger Rag** *(Tempo A-116)*
2 Jun 56	**17**	1	**The World Is Waiting For The Sunrise** *(Chris Barber's Jazz Band)* / St. Louis Blues *(Chris Barber's Jazz Band with Ottilie Patterson)* *(Decca Jazz FJ-10724)*
30 Jun 56	**19**	1	**CHRIS BARBER PLAYS (VOL. 2)** *(Pye Nixa NJT-502)* 🄻🄿 Whistling Rufus / Big House Blues / April Showers / One Sweet Letter From You / Hushabye / We Shall Walk Through The Valley
15 Sep 56	**10**	2	**Whistlin' Rufus** *(Chris Barber's Jazz Band)* / Hushabye *(Monty Sunshine Quartet)* *(Pye Nixa NJ-2011)*
6 Oct 56	**15**	1	**Whistlin' Rufus** *(Pye Nixa NJ-2011)* **re-entry**
6 Oct 56	**15**	1	**JAZZ AT THE ROYAL FESTIVAL HALL** *(Decca Jazz DFE-6238)* 🄴🄿 *Chris Barber's Jazz Band with Bertie King* Merrydown Blues / Skokiaan / I'd Love It / It's Tight Like That
2 Feb 57	**12**	1	**THE CHRIS BARBER SKIFFLE GROUP** *(Pye Nixa NJE-1025)* 🄴🄿 *Chris Barber's Skiffle Group* Can't You Line 'em *(Vocal: Dick Bishop)* / Doin' My Time *(Vocal: Johnny Duncan)* / Where Could I Go? *(Vocal: Johnny Duncan)* / Gypsy Davy *(Vocal: Dick Bishop)*
2 Feb 57	**16**	1	**CHRIS BARBER PLAYS (VOL. 3)** *(Pye Nixa NJT-505)* 🄻🄿 Thriller Rag / Texas Moaner / Sweet Georgia Brown / Bugle Call Rag / Petite Fleur / Wabash Blues
16 Feb 57	**9**	1	**THE CHRIS BARBER SKIFFLE GROUP** *(Pye Nixa NJE-1025)* 🄴🄿 **re-entry**
19 Jul 58	**7**	1	**When The Saints Go Marching In (Parts 1 & 2)** *(Pye Nixa 7NJ-2023)* *Both sides by Chris Barber's Jazz Band (Vocal: Ottilie Patterson)*
29 Aug 59	**8**	2	★ <u>Lonesome</u> *(Chris Barber's Jazz Band featuring Monty Sunshine)* / There'll Be A Hot Time In Old Town Tonight *(Chris Barber's Jazz Band featuring Ottillie Patterson)* *(Columbia DB-4333)*
26 Sep 59	**12**	1	★ <u>Lonesome</u> *(Chris Barber's Jazz Band featuring Monty Sunshine)* / There'll Be A Hot Time In Old Town Tonight *(Chris Barber's Jazz Band featuring Ottillie Patterson)* *(Columbia DB-4333)* **re-entry**
14 May 60	**13**	1	**Bill Bailey, Won't You Please Come Home** / Wild Cat Blues *(Pye Nixa 7NJ-2030)* *Both sides by Chris Barber's Jazz Band featuring Monty Sunshine*
17 Sep 60	**15**	1	**Bohemia Rag** / Swanee River *(Columbia DB-4501)*

See also Dickie Bishop & The Sidekicks
Lonnie Donegan
Johnny Duncan & The Blue Grass Boys

SIR JOHN BARBIROLLI *(conductor)*

See Hallé Orchestra
London Philharmonic Orchestra

BOBBY BARE   5

Bobby Bare's first hit, 'The All American Boy', was famously miscredited to Bill Parsons. Although the follow-up stalled, he went on to become an immensely successful country singer and songwriter.

21 Feb 59	**1**	2	★ <u>The All American Boy</u> / Rubber Dolly *(London HL-8798)* *Both sides as by Bill Parsons & His Orchestra*
21 Mar 59	**2**	2	★ <u>The All American Boy</u> / Rubber Dolly *(London HL-8798)* **re-entry**
19 Mar 60	**10**	1	**I'm Hanging Up My Rifle** / That's Where I Want To Be *(Top Rank JAR-310)*

RICHARD BARRETT   2

One of the first successful independent black record producers in the USA, Richard Barrett was also a songwriter and performer in his own right, initially as lead singer with the Valentines (1954-57). 'Smoke Gets In Your Eyes' was his first solo release.

19 Apr 58	**15**	1	**Smoke Gets In Your Eyes** / Remember Me *(M.G.M. MGM-976)* *Both sides as by Dickie Barrett*
18 Apr 59	**16**	1	**Come Softly To Me** / Walking Through Dreamland *(H.M.V. POP-609)* *Both sides by Richard Barrett with the Chantels*

JOHN BARRY 9

Composer/arranger born John Barry Prendergast. After initially dabbling with rock'n'roll, he went on to become one of the world's leading film score writers.

19 Apr 58	**4**	1	**Big Guitar** / Rodeo *(Parlophone R-4418)*
			Both sides by the John Barry Seven
10 Jan 59	**2**	1	**Farrago** / **Bee's Knees** *(Parlophone R-4488)*
			Both sides by the John Barry Seven
24 Jan 59	**4**	1	**Farrago** / **Bee's Knees** *(Parlophone R-4488)* ***1st re-entry***
7 Feb 59	**17**	1	**Farrago** / **Bee's Knees** *(Parlophone R-4488)* ***2nd re-entry***
28 Mar 59	**3**	2	**Long John** / Snap 'n Whistle *(Parlophone R-4530)*
			Both sides by the John Barry Seven
18 Apr 59	**18**	1	**Long John** / Snap 'n Whistle *(Parlophone R-4530)* ***re-entry***
20 Feb 60	**15**	1	★ <u>**Hit And Miss**</u> / Rockin' Already *(Columbia DB-4414)*
			Both sides by the John Barry Seven Plus Four
9 Jul 60	**12**	1	★ <u>**Blueberry Hill**</u> / **Never Let Go** *(Columbia DB-4480)*
			Both sides by John Barry & His Orchestra

See also Keith Kelly

MARGARET BARRY 1

Raw-voiced street singer/banjoist born into a travelling family in Cork, Ireland. She moved to London in the early '50s and teamed up with fiddler Michael Gorman to become a permanent fixture on the capital's thriving Irish music scene.

8 Feb 58	**10**	1	**If You Ever Go To Ireland** / The Blarney Stone *(Topic TRC-99)*

COUNT BASIE 3

Born in Red Bank, New Jersey in 1904, William 'Count' Basie was an influential jazz pianist, bandleader and composer. He established the Kansas City Seven in the late 1930s, when he recorded with a small section of his Big Band. The original members were Buck Clayton, Freddie Green, Jo Jones, Walter Page, Dicky Wells and Lester Young.

6 Nov 54	**35**	2	**COUNT BASIE / LESTER YOUNG** *(Oriole/Mercury MG-25015)* 🔲**LP**
			Count Basie & His Kansas City Seven: Lester Leaps Again / After Theatre Jump / Destination K.C. / *Lester Young Quartet:* I Never Knew / Just You, Just Me / Afternoon Of A Basie-ite / Sometimes I'm Happy
18 Dec 54	**34**	1	**COUNT BASIE / LESTER YOUNG** *(Oriole/Mercury MG-25015)* 🔲**LP**
			re-entry

See also Buck Clayton

SHIRLEY BASSEY 15

Singer from Cardiff's Tiger Bay who rapidly became one of Britain's most successful female chart artists. The recordings below date from the early days of her long and illustrious career.

17 Aug 57	**4**	1	★ <u>**Fire Down Below**</u> / <u>**You, You Romeo**</u> *(Philips PB-723)*
16 Nov 57	**10**	1	**Puh-leeze! Mister Brown** / Take My Love, Take My Love
			(Philips PB-757)
30 Nov 57	**5**	1	**Puh-leeze! Mister Brown** / Take My Love, Take My Love
			(Philips PB-757) ***re-entry***
4 Oct 58	**7**	1	★ **Hands Across The Sea** / <u>**As I Love You**</u> *(Philips PB-845)*
13 Dec 58	**5**	1	★ <u>**As I Love You**</u> / Hands Across The Sea *(Philips PB-845)*
			re-entry (flipped)
20 Dec 58	**6**	1	★ <u>**Kiss Me, Honey Honey, Kiss Me**</u> / There's Never Been A Night
			(Philips PB-860)
25 Apr 59	**1**	1	**Crazy Rhythm** / Love For Sale *(Philips PB-917)*
6 Jun 59	**22**	1	**Love For Sale** / Crazy Rhythm *(Philips PB-917)* ***re-entry (flipped)***
3 Oct 59	**23**	1	★ <u>**Count On Me**</u> / **If You Love Me** *(Columbia DB-4344)*
24 Oct 59	**15**	3	★ <u>**Count On Me**</u> / **If You Love Me** *(Columbia DB-4344)* ***re-entry***
19 Mar 60	**1**	2	★ <u>**With These Hands**</u> / The Party's Over *(Columbia DB-4421)*
9 Jul 60	**14**	1	★ <u>**As Long As He Needs Me**</u> / So In Love *(Columbia DB-4490)*

ART BAXTER & HIS ROCK'N'ROLL SINNERS   1
Jazz singer born Arthur Gomm in Canterbury in 1926. An early convert to rock'n'roll, he appeared with his Bill Haley-styled combo in the first British rocksploitation flick, 'Rock You Sinners' (1957).

8 Dec 56	4	1	**Rock And Roll Rag** / Jingle Rock *(Philips PB-652)*

LES BAXTER & His Orchestra and Chorus   30
One of the progenitors of the '50s 'exotica' movement, singer/pianist/saxophonist Les Baxter rose to become Capitol's chief arranger. 'Unchained Melody' was his only UK hit.

18 Sep 54	12	6	**The High And The Mighty** / Venezuela *(Capitol CL-14147)* *Both sides by Les Baxter with His Orchestra and Chorus*
16 Oct 54	24	6	**I Love Paris** *(Les Baxter with His Chorus and Orchestra)* / Manhattan *(Les Baxter & His Orchestra) (Capitol CL-14166)*
13 Nov 54	5	3	**The High And The Mighty** / Venezuela *(Capitol CL-14147)* **1st re-entry**
4 Dec 54	17	1	**I Love Paris** / Manhattan *(Capitol CL-14166)* **1st re-entry**
11 Dec 54	30	3	**The High And The Mighty** / Venezuela *(Capitol CL-14147)* **2nd re-entry**
15 Jan 55	23	1	**I Love Paris** / Manhattan *(Capitol CL-14166)* **2nd re-entry**
7 May 55	9	1	★ <u>**Unchained Melody**</u> / **The Medic Theme** *(Capitol CL-14257)* *Both sides by Les Baxter, His Chorus & Orchestra*
18 Jun 55	14	1	**Earth Angel** / Happy Baby *(Capitol CL-14239)* *Both sides by Les Baxter & The Bombers*
22 Oct 55	25	1	**Wake The Town And Tell The People** / I'll Never Stop Loving You *(Capitol CL-14344)* *Both sides by Les Baxter, His Chorus & Orchestra*
10 Mar 56	8	3	**Poor John** / Theme from 'Helen Of Troy' *(Capitol CL-14533)* *Both sides by Les Baxter, His Chorus & Orchestra*
7 Apr 56	2	2	**Poor John** / Theme from 'Helen Of Troy' *(Capitol CL-14533)* **1st re-entry**
28 Apr 56	6	2	**Poor John** / Theme from 'Helen Of Troy' *(Capitol CL-14533)* **2nd re-entry**

E.C. BEATTY   1
Country/rock'n'roll singer born Erson Calvin Beatty Jr. in Charlotte, North Carolina in 1927.

28 Nov 59	26	1	**Ski King** / I'm A Lucky Man *(Felsted AF-127)*

BEAU-MARKS   1
Four-piece rock'n'roll band from Montreal, led by guitarist Ray Hutchinson. Unusually for the time, they wrote their own material. 'Clap Your Hands' was their only US hit.

11 Jun 60	11	1	**Clap Your Hands** / Daddy Said *(Top Rank JAR-377)*

BOB BECKHAM   1
Country singer/songwriter from Oklahoma. Not related to footballer David (as far as is known).

6 Aug 60	8	1	**Mais Oui** / Only The Broken Hearted *(Brunswick 05835)*

HARRY BELAFONTE   10
Born in New York to black immigrant parents, singer Harry Belafonte made the calypso internationally popular during the late '50s. As a prominent civil rights activist and anti-apartheid campaigner, he also played an important part in breaking down racial barriers in the USA.

6 Apr 57	13	1	**CALYPSO** *(H.M.V. 7EG-8211)* **EP** Banana Boat (Day-O) / Will His Love Be Like His Rum? / Jamaica Farewell / Dolly Dawn
8 Jun 57	1	1	★ <u>**Island In The Sun**</u> / Cocoanut Woman *(R.C.A. RCA-1007)*
29 Jun 57	11	1	**Mama Looka Boo Boo** / Don't Ever Love Me *(H.M.V. POP-339)*
27 Jul 57	10	1	★ <u>**Scarlet Ribbons**</u> / Hold 'em Joe *(H.M.V. POP-360)*

| 29 Nov 58 | **4** | 2 | ★ **The Son Of Mary** / I Heard The Bells On Christmas Day (*R.C.A. RCA-1084*) |
| 6 Dec 58 | **7** | 4 | **Silent Night** / **The Twelve Days Of Christmas** (*R.C.A. RCA-1085*) |

BELL SOUNDS   1

New York sessionmen who backed Fabian and Frankie Avalon on recording dates at Bell Sound Studios. The two instrumentals below were released as a one-off single by the Philadelphia-based Chancellor label.

| 26 Dec 59 | **16** | 1 | **Marching Guitars** / Chloe (*H.M.V. POP-685*) |

BOYD BENNETT & HIS ROCKETS   10

Rockabilly singer/songwriter and saxophonist born in Muscle Shoals, Alabama in 1924.

29 Oct 55	**2**	6	★ **Seventeen** / Little Ole You-All (*Parlophone R-4063*)
17 Dec 55	**12**	1	★ **Seventeen** / Little Ole You-All (*Parlophone R-4063*) **re-entry**
26 May 56	**9**	2	**Blue Suede Shoes** / Oo-Oo-Oo (*Parlophone R-4167*)
18 Aug 56	**9**	1	**Honolulu Rock-A-Roll-A** / Seven Nights To Rock (*Parlophone R-4195*) *Both sides by Moon Mullican with Boyd Bennett & His Rockets*

DICKIE BENNETT   1

Former warehouseman Dickie Bennett was a high-kicking song-and-dance man with a swinging style. He appeared, somewhat incongruously, in the first-ever British rock'n'roll movie, 'Rock You Sinners' (1957).

| 10 Mar 56 | **11** | 1 | **Dungaree Doll** / Can't We Be Partners (*Decca F-10697*) |

TONY BENNETT   18

Quality singer born Anthony Dominick Benedetto in 1926, responsible for memorable hits like 'Rags To Riches', 'Stranger In Paradise' and 'I Left My Heart In San Francisco'.

9 Apr 55	**6**	1	★ **Stranger In Paradise** / Take Me Back Again (*Philips PB-420*)
21 May 55	**17**	1	★ **Close Your Eyes** / It's Too Soon To Know (*Philips PB-445*)
11 Jun 55	**31**	1	★ **Close Your Eyes** / It's Too Soon To Know (*Philips PB-445*) **1st re-entry**
25 Jun 55	**12**	2	★ **Close Your Eyes** / It's Too Soon To Know (*Philips PB-445*) **2nd re-entry**
23 Jul 55	**5**	8	★ **Close Your Eyes** / It's Too Soon To Know (*Philips PB-445*) **3rd re-entry**
20 Oct 56	**10**	1	**Happiness Street** / From The Candy Store On The Corner To The Chapel On The Hill (*Philips PB-628*)
17 Aug 57	**8**	1	**One For My Baby** / No Hard Feelings (*Philips PB-710*)
24 Aug 57	**6**	2	**In The Middle Of An Island** / I Am (*Philips PB-724*)

MARIE BENSON   6

Australian jazz and pop singer. Original female lead of top UK vocal group, the Stargazers.

23 Apr 55	**26**	2	**Our Old Pi-anna** / I'm So Lonely, Lonely, Lonely Tonight (*Philips PB-431*)
14 May 55	**20**	1	**Our Old Pi-anna** / I'm So Lonely, Lonely, Lonely Tonight (*Philips PB-431*) **1st re-entry**
11 Jun 55	**20**	1	**Our Old Pi-anna** / I'm So Lonely, Lonely, Lonely Tonight (*Philips PB-431*) **2nd re-entry**
26 Nov 55	**8**	2	**Twenty Tiny Fingers** / I Wish We Were Sweethearts Again (*Philips PB-512*)

DICK BENTLEY

See Joy Nichols

BROOK BENTON 13

Smooth black balladeer and songwriter born Benjamin Peay in Lugoff, South Carolina in 1931.

30 May 59	8	1	★ **Endlessly** / So Close *(Mercury AMT-1043)*
13 Jun 59	16	1	★ **Endlessly** / So Close *(Mercury AMT-1043)* **re-entry**
19 Sep 59	8	1	**Thank You Pretty Baby** / With All Of My Heart *(Mercury AMT-1061)*
3 Oct 59	4	2	**Thank You Pretty Baby** / With All Of My Heart *(Mercury AMT-1061)* **re-entry**
21 Nov 59	4	1	**So Many Ways** / I Want You Forever *(Mercury AMT-1068)*
13 Feb 60	3	1	**So Many Ways** / I Want You Forever *(Mercury AMT-1068)* **re-entry**
4 Jun 60	20	1	**The Ties That Bind** / Hither And Thither And Yon *(Mercury AMT-1097)*
9 Jul 60	12	1	**A Rockin' Good Way** *(Dinah Washington and Brook Benton)* / I Believe *(Brook Benton and Dinah Washington) (Mercury AMT-1099)*
13 Aug 60	17	1	**The Ties That Bind** / Hither And Thither And Yon *(Mercury AMT-1097)* **re-entry**
1 Oct 60	3	1	★ **Kiddio** / The Same One *(Mercury AMT-1109)*
10 Dec 60	23	1	★ **Fools Rush In** / Someday You'll Want Me To Want You *(Mercury AMT-1121)*
7 Jan 61	7	1	★ **Fools Rush In** / Someday You'll Want Me To Want You *(Mercury AMT-1121)* **re-entry**

ELMER BERNSTEIN & Orchestra 10

American composer/arranger responsible for many memorable movie themes. 'Clark Street' came from the soundtrack of 'The Man With The Golden Arm' (1955).

7 Apr 56	5	2	**Clark Street (Parts 1 & 2)** *(Brunswick 05544)*
28 Apr 56	4	1	**Clark Street (Parts 1 & 2)** *(Brunswick 05544)* **1st re-entry**
12 May 56	2	6	**Clark Street (Parts 1 & 2)** *(Brunswick 05544)* **2nd re-entry**
14 Jul 56	15	1	**Clark Street (Parts 1 & 2)** *(Brunswick 05544)* **3rd re-entry**

CHUCK BERRY 16

Hugely influential black rock'n'roller born in St. Louis, Missouri. His career as a UK hitmaker didn't really take off until 1963, when Pye struck a distribution deal with Chess Records in Chicago.

1 Jun 57	4	3	★ **School Day** / Deep Feeling *(Columbia DB-3951)*
8 Feb 58	4	4	**Rock And Roll Music** / Blue Feeling *(London HLM-8531)*
5 Apr 58	1	2	★ **Sweet Little Sixteen** / Reelin' And Rockin' *(London HLM-8585)*
31 May 58	3	1	★ **Johnny B. Goode** / Around And Around *(London HLM-8629)*
13 Sep 58	4	1	**Vacation Time** / Beautiful Delilah *(London HL-8677)*
2 May 59	3	1	**Almost Grown** / Little Queenie *(London HLM-8853)*
12 Mar 60	1	3	**Too Pooped To Pop** / Let It Rock *(London HLM-9069)*
27 Aug 60	16	1	**Bye Bye Johnny** / Mad Lad *(London HLM-9159)*

PHILIPPA BEVANS 1

Stage and screen actress from London. She appeared in the original Broadway production of 'My Fair Lady' and also on the Original Cast album from which the single below was taken.

| 16 Aug 58 | 6 | 1 | **I Could Have Danced All Night** *(Julie Andrews and Philippa Bevans) (Philips PB-846)* Flip is 'Without You' by Julie Andrews |

BEVERLEY SISTERS 15

Real sisters, Joy, Teddie and Babs were the UK's top girl group of the '50s.

2 Oct 54	15	1	**Val De Ri, Val De Ra** / We Like To Do Things Like That *(Philips PB-239)*
27 Nov 54	10	2	**The Mama Doll Song** / Sisters *(Philips PB-370)*
8 Jan 55	9	1	**The Mama Doll Song** / Sisters *(Philips PB-370)* **re-entry**
19 Feb 55	15	1	**The Naughty Lady Of Shady Lane** / Where Were You Last Night? *(Philips PB-395)*

8 Oct 55	22	1	**Humming Bird** / Have You Ever Been Lonely? *(Decca F-10603)*
5 Nov 55	12	1	**Humming Bird** / Have You Ever Been Lonely? *(Decca F-10603)* **re-entry**
31 Mar 56	14	2	★ <u>**Willie Can**</u> / We've Started Courtin' *(Decca F-10705)*
20 Oct 56	8	1	**Born To Be With You** / It's Easy *(Decca F-10770)*
15 Dec 56	1	3	**Come Home To My Arms** / Doodle Doo Doo *(Decca F-10813)*
9 Mar 57	4	1	**Greensleeves** / I'll See You In My Dreams *(Decca F-10853)*
14 Nov 59	23	1	★ <u>**Little Donkey**</u> / And Kings Came A-Calling *(Decca F-11172)*

See also Various Artists (MY FAIR LADY)

BIG BEN ACCORDION BAND   3

A creation of UK Columbia producer Norrie Paramor, this was a less successful variation on his Big Ben Banjo Band project (see below).

27 Oct 56	2	2	**Rock'n'Roll No. 1 (Parts 1 & 2) [M]** *(Columbia DB-3835)*
			(We're Gonna) Rock Around The Clock – See You Later Alligator – The Saints Rock'n'Roll / Blue Suede Shoes – Rock Island Line – Why Do Fools Fall In Love?
17 Nov 56	5	1	**Rock'n'Roll No. 1 (Parts 1 & 2) [M]** *(Columbia DB-3835)* **re-entry**

See also Big Ben Banjo Band
         Norrie Paramor & His Orchestra

BIG BEN BANJO BAND   36

Formed in 1954 by UK Columbia producer Norrie Paramor, the Big Ben Banjo Band found immediate success with the medley 'Let's Get Together No. 1' and continued to record prolifically until the early 1970s.

20 Nov 54	1	3	★ <u>**Let's Get Together No. 1 (Parts 1 & 2) [M]**</u> *(Columbia DB-3549)*
			I'm Just Wild About Harry – April Showers – Rock-A-Bye Your Baby – Swanee / The Darktown Strutters' Ball – For Me And My Gal – Oh! You Beautiful Doll – Yes Sir! That's My Baby
27 Nov 54	1	8	**Let's Get Together No. 2 (Parts 1 & 2) [M]** *(Columbia DB-3554)*
			California, Here I Come – Back Home In Tennessee – Carolina In The Morning – Are You From Dixie? / Waiting For The Robert E. Lee – Coal Black Mammy – When The Red Red Robin – Toot Toot Tootsie (Goodbye)
19 Mar 55	21	1	**There's No Business Like Show Business (Parts 1 & 2) [M]** *(Columbia DB-3584)*
			There's No Business Like Show Business – If You Believe – Heat Wave / Alexander's Rag Time Band – After You Get What You Want, You Don't Want It – When The Midnight Choo-Choo Leaves For Alabam!
14 May 55	2	9	**The Crazy Otto Rag** / Hey Mr. Banjo *(Columbia DB-3620)*
			Both sides by the Big Ben Banjo Band with the Coronets
13 Aug 55	2	5	**Alabama Jubilee** / Sweet Georgia Brown *(Columbia DB-3641)*
13 Aug 55	5	2	**The Crazy Otto Rag** / Hey Mr. Banjo *(Columbia DB-3620)* **1st re-entry**
3 Sep 55	21	1	**The Crazy Otto Rag** / Hey Mr. Banjo *(Columbia DB-3620)* **2nd re-entry**
8 Oct 55	22	1	**Alabama Jubilee** / Sweet Georgia Brown *(Columbia DB-3641)* **1st re-entry**
29 Oct 55	37	1	**Alabama Jubilee** / Sweet Georgia Brown *(Columbia DB-3641)* **2nd re-entry**
12 Nov 55	3	4	★ <u>**Let's Get Together Again (Parts 1 & 2) [M]**</u> *(Columbia DB-3676)*
			I'm Looking Over A Four-Leaf Clover – By The Light Of The Silvery Moon – Oh, Susanna – Baby Face / I'm Sitting On Top Of The World – My Mammy – Dixie's Land – Margie
10 Jan 59	11	1	**Be Happy** / Philadelphia U.S.A. *(Columbia DB-4233)*

See also Big Ben Accordion Band
         Norrie Paramor & His Orchestra

BIG BOPPER   5

Singer, songwriter and radio personality born Jiles Perry Richardson. He scored a transatlantic hit with 'Chantilly Lace' before tragically perishing in the same plane crash that killed Buddy Holly and Ritchie Valens on 3 February 1959. The follow-up deserved to do better.

22 Nov 58	8	3	★ **Chantilly Lace** / Purple People Eater Meets Witchdoctor
			(Mercury AMT-1002)
31 Jan 59	3	2	**Big Bopper's Wedding** / Little Red Riding Hood *(Mercury AMT-1017)*

THE BIG SOUND OF DON RALKE   2

Prolific composer, arranger and producer born in Battle Creek, Michigan in 1920.

16 Apr 60	4	1	**77 Sunset Strip** *(Warner Bros. WB-2)*
			Flip is '77 Sunset Strip Cha-Cha' by Pete Candoli & His Orchestra
15 Oct 60	9	1	**77 Sunset Strip** *(Warner Bros. WB-2)* **re-entry**

MR. ACKER BILK'S PARAMOUNT JAZZ BAND   5

Somerset-born jazz clarinettist Bernard Bilk was one of the leading lights of the UK 'trad' boom, chalking up 11 hits in the early '60s including the unforgettable 'Stranger On The Shore'.

23 Jun 56	8	1	**Where The River Shannon Flows** / Dippermouth Blues *(Tempo A-134)*
			Both sides by Acker Bilk's Paramount Jazz Band
2 May 59	13	1	★ **MR. ACKER BILK SINGS** *(Pye Nixa NJE-1067)* **EP**
			Mr. Acker Bilk's Paramount Jazz Band
			Carry Me Back / Jump In The Line / Louisian-i-ay / Higher Ground
24 Oct 59	23	1	★ **ACKER'S AWAY** *(Columbia SEG-7940)* **EP**
			Mr. Acker Bilk & His Paramount Jazz Band
			Acker's Away / Blues For Jimmy / Lastic / East Coast Trot
26 Dec 59	13	1	★ **Summer Set** / Acker's Away *(Columbia DB-4382)*
			Both sides by Mr. Acker Bilk & His Paramount Jazz Band
21 May 60	12	1	**Marching Through Georgia** / Delia Gone *(Pye 7NJ-2029)*
			Mr. Acker Bilk's Paramount Jazz Band

BILLY & LILLIE   2

Black pop duo who recorded for the Swan label in Philadelphia. Ford was also a trumpeter and bandleader. 'La Dee Dah', went gold in the States and only just missed out in the UK.

29 Mar 58	1	2	**La Dee Dah** *(Billy & Lillie with Billy Ford's Thunderbirds)*
			(London HLU-8564)
			Flip is 'The Monster' by Billy Ford's Thunderbirds

BILLY'S BANJO BAND   1

Ensemble formed by bandleader Geoff Love, doubtless inspired by the success of the Big Ben Banjo Band (qv).

17 Dec 55	19	1	**Join In The Chorus (Parts 1 & 2) [M]** *(H.M.V. POP-139)*
			Alabamy Bound – On The Mississippi – The Trolley Song / Lily Of Laguna – My
			Mammy – Shine On Harvest Moon

UMBERTO BINDI   1

Singer/songwriter from Bogliasco, Genoa. 'Il Nostro Concerto' was a huge hit, topping the Italian hit parade for several months. He later co-wrote Cilla Black's 'You're My World' ('Il Mio Mondo').

| 5 Nov 60 | 3 | 1 | ★ **Il Nostro Concerto** / Un Giorno, Un Mese, Un Anno *(Oriole CB-1577)* |

DICKIE BISHOP & THE SIDEKICKS   2

Guitarist who joined Chris Barber's band in January 1956. He took over on banjo following Lonnie Donegan's departure in April, but left seven months later to pursue his own solo ambitions.

| 30 Mar 57 | 7 | 2 | **Cumberland Gap** / No Other Baby *(Decca F-10869)* |

See also Chris Barber's Jazz Band

JEANNE BLACK   4

Country singer born in Pomona, California in 1937. 'He'll Have To Stay' was an 'answer' to Jim Reeves' 1960 C&W chart-topper, 'He'll Have To Go'.

28 May 60   **4**   4   ★ <u>**He'll Have To Stay**</u> *(Jeanne Black) /*
                                Under Your Spell Again *(Jeanne & Janie) (Capitol CL-15131)*

BILL BLACK'S COMBO   6

Instrumental outfit led by Elvis Presley's former bass player. Black died of a brain tumour in October 1965, aged 39, but his combo continued recording until the late 1970s.

19 Dec 59   **6**   1   **Smokie (Parts 1 & 2)** *(Felsted AF-129)*
 9 Apr 60   **9**   1   ★ <u>**White Silver Sands**</u> / The Wheel *(London HLU-9090)*
15 May 60   **6**   3   ★ <u>**White Silver Sands**</u> / The Wheel *(London HLU-9090)* ***re-entry***
28 Jan 61   **4**   1   **Blue Tango** / Willie *(London HLU-9267)*

BILLY BLAND   2

R&B singer/songwriter born in Wilmington, North Carolina in 1932. 'Let The Little Girl Dance' was a huge R&B and pop hit in the States, and rightly made the UK charts too.

16 Apr 60   **5**   1   ★ <u>**Let The Little Girl Dance**</u> / Sweet Thing *(London HL-9096)*
 7 May 60   **9**   1   ★ <u>**Let The Little Girl Dance**</u> / Sweet Thing *(London HL-9096)* ***re-entry***

ARCHIE BLEYER & His Orchestra & Chorus   7

Bandleader, arranger and founder of Cadence Records, whose biggest stars were Andy Williams and the Everly Brothers. Although Bleyer had a couple of hits under his own name in the States, he wasn't so lucky in the UK.

15 Jan 55   **27**   2   **The Naughty Lady Of Shady Lane** /
                                While The Vesper Bells Were Ringing *(London HL-8111)*
19 Feb 55   **10**   2   **The Naughty Lady Of Shady Lane** /
                                While The Vesper Bells Were Ringing *(London HL-8111)* ***re-entry***
 1 Oct 55   **7**   3   **Hernando's Hideaway** / S'il Vous Plait *(London HLA-8176)*

RAY BLOCH & His Orchestra   2

German-born composer and pianist most famous for being arranger and orchestra leader for the Ed Sullivan and Jackie Gleason TV shows.

19 May 56   **12**   1   **Donkey Tango** / Vicki *(Vogue Coral Q-72131)*
                                Both sides by Ray Bloch & His Orchestra
 7 Jul 56   **15**   1   **The Carousel Waltz** / You'll Never Walk Alone *(Vogue Coral Q-72165)*
                                Both sides by Ray Bloch & His Orchestra and Chorus

ENID BLYTON   1

The best-selling English children's author reads stories with assistance from actor Ian Hockridge and instrumental accompaniments by Philip Green.

27 Apr 57   **18**   1   **Noddy Is Naughty** / Noddy's Adventure With His Car *(H.M.V. BD-1299)*
                                'Noddy Is Naughty' consists of two stories, 'Stamp! Stamp! Stamp! and 'The Wobbly
                                Man'.

BOBBEJAAN   3

Belgian singer whose real name was Modest Schoepen. He was responsible for introducing country music to the masses of Western Europe and became one of the first Europeans to perform on the 'Grand Ole Opry'.

21 Jan 61   **10**   1   **I'm Cryin' In My Beer** / A Little Bit Of Heaven *(Palette PG-9009)*
25 Feb 61   **3**   2   **I'm Cryin' In My Beer** / A Little Bit Of Heaven *(Palette PG-9009)*
                                re-entry

BOBBETTES 3

Black female doo-wop quintet from Harlem, New York. Their bouncy 'Mr. Lee' shot to No. 6 in the Billboard 'Top 100', but didn't quite catch on in Britain.

9 Nov 57   **7**   3   **Mr. Lee** / Look At The Stars *(London HLE-8477)*

KARL BOHN *(conductor)*

See Hilde Gueden

JOHNNY BOND 4

Country singer/songwriter born Cyrus Bond in Enville, Oklahoma in 1915. 'Hot Rod Jalopy' was a remake of his big US hit, 'Hot Rod Lincoln', which could not be played on the BBC because it mentioned the names of certain cars and might therefore have been construed as advertising.

24 Sep 60   **5**   3   **Hot Rod Jalopy** / Five-Minute Love Affair *(London HLU-9189)*
5 Nov 60   **10**   1   **Hot Rod Jalopy** / Five-Minute Love Affair *(London HLU-9189)* ***re-entry***

U.S. BONDS 5

Singer Gary Anderson was reputedly rechristened 'U.S. Bonds' by label boss Frank Guida in the hope that his record would be confused with a public service announcement promoting the sale of Government bonds, and thereby receive more airplay. It is not known to what extent this stratagem was responsible for its massive success.

26 Nov 60   **8**   4   ★ <u>**New Orleans**</u> / Please Forgive Me *(Top Rank JAR-527)*
14 Jan 61   **4**   1   ★ <u>**New Orleans**</u> / Please Forgive Me *(Top Rank JAR-527)* ***re-entry***

ISSY BONN 6

Amply proportioned English music hall comedian/singer born Benjamin Levine. He was extremely popular in the 1930s and '40s.

28 Aug 54   **18**   1   **Mom-e-le** / My Friend *(Columbia DB-3504)*
25 Sep 54   **33**   1   **Mom-e-le / My Friend** *(Columbia DB-3504)* ***1st re-entry***
23 Oct 54   **12**   1   **My Friend** / Mom-e-le *(Columbia DB-3504)* ***2nd re-entry (flipped)***
6 Nov 54   **20**   2   **My Friend** / Mom-e-le *(Columbia DB-3504)* ***3rd re-entry***
21 Jan 56   **9**   1   **When You Lose The One You Love** / A Little Boy's Prayer
                      (Columbia DB-3683)

BONNIE LOU 6

Bonnie Lou aka Mary Jo Kath from Indiana started out as a country singer, but soon switched to rockabilly and rock'n'roll. Her third release, 'Tennessee Wig Walk', was a hit on both sides of the Atlantic in 1953-54.

6 Nov 54   **27**   1   **Wait For Me, Darling** / Blue Tennessee Rain *(Parlophone R-3895)*
27 Nov 54   **58**   2   **Wait For Me, Darling** / Blue Tennessee Rain *(Parlophone R-3895)*
                      re-entry
11 Dec 54   **43**   1   **Two Step – Side Step** / Please Don't Laugh When I Cry
                      (Parlophone R-3931)
9 Apr 55   **12**   1   **A Rusty Old Halo** / Danger! Heartbreak Ahead *(Parlophone R-4012)*
5 Apr 58   **8**   1   **La Dee Dah** / Let The School Bell Ring Ding-A-Ling
                      Both sides by Bonnie Lou and Rusty York (Parlophone R-4409)

PAT BOONE 30

It's hard to imagine nowadays, but this clean-cut pop singer and matinée idol was Elvis Presley's main rival until the early '60s. Ironically, his pallid interpretations of R&B hits helped to popularise rock'n'roll with the mass white audience in America.

24 Sep 55   **23**   1   ★ <u>**Ain't That A Shame**</u> / Tennessee Saturday Night *(London HLD-8172)*
24 Oct 55   **3**   2   ★ <u>**Ain't That A Shame**</u> / Tennessee Saturday Night *(London HLD-8172)*
                      re-entry
7 Apr 56   **2**   2   ★ <u>**I'll Be Home**</u> / **Tutti Frutti** *(London HLD-8253)*
23 Jun 56   **21**   1   ★ <u>**Long Tall Sally**</u> / Just As Long As I'm With You *(London HLD-8291)*

7 Jul 56	**1**	3	★ <u>**Long Tall Sally**</u> / Just As Long As I'm With You *(London HLD-8291)*
			re-entry
22 Sep 56	**10**	1	**Rich In Love** / Two Hearts, Two Kisses *(London HLD-8316)*
6 Oct 56	**14**	1	**Rich In Love** / Two Hearts, Two Kisses *(London HLD-8316)* ***re-entry***
6 Apr 57	**3**	3	★ <u>**Why Baby Why**</u> / I'm Just Waiting For You *(London HLD-8404)*
21 Sep 57	**10**	1	★ <u>**Remember You're Mine**</u> / <u>**There's A Gold Mine In The Sky**</u>
			(London HLD-8479)
30 Nov 57	**10**	1	★ <u>**April Love**</u> / When The Swallows Come Back To Capistrano
			(London HLD-8512)
22 Mar 58	**1**	2	★ <u>**A Wonderful Time Up There**</u> / <u>It's Too Soon To Know</u>
			(London HLD-8574)
21 Jun 58	**10**	1	★ <u>**Sugar Moon**</u> / Cherie, I Love You *(London HLD-8640)*
15 Nov 58	**6**	1	★ <u>**Gee, But It's Lonely**</u> / For My Good Fortune *(London HLD-8739)*
29 Nov 58	**4**	1	★ <u>**For My Good Fortune**</u> / <u>Gee, But It's Lonely</u> *(London HLD-8739)*
			re-entry (flipped)
4 Apr 59	**5**	1	★ <u>**With The Wind And The Rain In Your Hair**</u> /
			<u>**There's Good Rockin' Tonight**</u> *(London HLD-8824)*
14 Nov 59	**4**	6	**A Fool's Hall Of Fame** / Brightest Wishing Star *(London HLD-8974)*
12 Mar 60	**6**	1	**New Lovers** / Words *(London HLD-9067)*
18 Jun 60	**12**	1	★ <u>**Walking The Floor Over You**</u> / Spring Rain *(London HLD-9138)*

See also Original Soundtrack (APRIL LOVE)

EARL BOSTIC & His Orchestra   19

Popular black alto saxophonist from Tulsa, Oklahoma who straddled jazz and R&B. His signature tune, 'Flamingo' – a No. 1 R&B hit in the USA – remains an all-time classic.

7 Aug 54	**27**	1	**Jungle Drums** / Danube Waves *(Parlophone R-3881)*
21 Aug 54	**24**	1	**Flamingo** / Sleep *(Vogue V-2145)*
11 Sep 54	**16**	1	**Flamingo** / Sleep *(Vogue V-2145)* ***1st re-entry***
11 Sep 54	**34**	1	**Blue Skies** / **Mambolino** *(Parlophone R-3892)*
25 Sep 54	**30**	1	**Blue Skies** / **Mambolino** *(Parlophone R-3892)* ***re-entry***
9 Oct 54	**29**	1	**Offshore** / What! No Pearls *(Parlophone R-3818)*
6 Nov 54	**41**	1	**Mambostic** / These Foolish Things *(Parlophone R-3932)*
11 Dec 54	**31**	1	**Memories** / The Very Thought Of You *(Parlophone R-3782)*
11 Dec 54	**31**	1	**These Foolish Things** / Mambostic *(Parlophone R-3932)*
			re-entry (flipped)
18 Dec 54	**34**	1	**Flamingo** / Sleep *(Vogue V-2145)* ***2nd re-entry***
25 Dec 54	**43**	1	**EARL BOSTIC, HIS ALTO SAX AND HIS ORCHESTRA**
			(Vogue LDE-100) **LP**
			Flamingo / Sleep / I'm Getting Sentimental Over You / Moonglow / Ain't Misbehavin' /
			Linger Awhile / Lover Come Back To Me / Seven Steps
8 Jan 55	**22**	3	**Flamingo** / Sleep *(Vogue V-2145)* ***3rd re-entry***
8 Jan 55	**32**	1	**FLAMINGO** *(Parlophone GEP-8506)* **EP**
			Flamingo / Swing Low Sweet Boogie / I Can't Give You Anything But Love / The
			Moon Is Low
5 Feb 55	**21**	1	**Flamingo** / Sleep *(Vogue V-2145)* ***4th re-entry***
30 Apr 55	**16**	1	**Deep Purple** / Smoke Rings *(Parlophone R-3838)*
7 May 55	**16**	1	**Melody Of Love** / Sweet Lorraine *(Parlophone R-4003)*
23 Jul 55	**25**	1	**Night And Day** / Embraceable You *(Parlophone R-4028)*

EVE BOSWELL   11

Hungarian-born Ewa Keleti moved to South Africa with her parents in 1939, where as 'Eve Boswell' she became a popular singing star. She came to Britain in 1949, hitting the charts six years later with the catchy 'Pickin' A Chicken'.

5 Nov 55	**23**	2	★ <u>**Blue Star**</u> / <u>Pickin' A Chicken</u> *(Parlophone R-4082)*
31 Mar 56	**5**	3	**Cookie** / It's Almost Tomorrow *(Parlophone R-4143)*
5 May 56	**7**	2	**Cookie** / It's Almost Tomorrow *(Parlophone R-4143)* ***re-entry***
7 Jul 56	**11**	1	**Down By The Sugar Cane** / Keeping Cool With Lemonade
			(Parlophone R-4181)
22 Sep 56	**7**	1	**Come Back My Love** / Saries Marais *(Parlophone R-4189)*
13 Jul 57	**2**	1	**Sugar Candy** / With All My Heart *(Parlophone R-4328)*
13 Jul 57	**8**	1	**Chantez, Chantez** / She Said *(Parlophone R-4299)*

SIR ADRIAN BOULT *(conductor)*

See Kathleen Ferrier
　　　Philharmonic Promenade Orchestra

JIMMY BOWEN with the Rhythm Orchids   1

Buddy Knox's partner in the Rhythm Orchids, Jimmy Bowen had several US hits in 1957-58, starting with 'I'm Stickin' With You', but failed to register in the UK. He subsequently moved into record production and label management, becoming immensely successful at both.

26 Apr 58　**12**　1　　**Cross Over** / It's Shameful *(Columbia DB-4027)*

BOWHILL COLLIERY & DISTRICT PIPE BAND   3

Popular Scottish band from Fife. They won the World Pipe Band Championship in 1947.

10 Sep 55　**16**　1　　**Selection of Marches [M]** / My Home – Donald Dhu **[M]**
　　　　　　　　　　　(Parlophone F-3400)
　　　　　　　　　　　Selection of Marches: Scotland The Brave – Jeanie's Black E'ee – The Rowan Tree
　1 Oct 55　**23**　1　　**Selection of Marches [M]** / My Home – Donald Dhu **[M]**
　　　　　　　　　　　(Parlophone F-3400) **1st re-entry**
　3 Dec 55　**19**　1　　**Selection of Marches [M]** / My Home – Donald Dhu **[M]**
　　　　　　　　　　　(Parlophone F-3400) **2nd re-entry**

BOY SCOUT ASSOCIATION   1

This unusual single features extracts from the Boy Scout Association's Royal Albert Hall pageant, 'Boy Scout' by Ralph Reader, with musical backings by Geoff Love & His Orchestra.

12 Feb 55　**11**　1　　**Boy Scout (Parts 1 & 2)** *(Philips PB-151)*

JIMMY BOYD   2

Thirteen-year-old Jimmy Boyd shot to the top of the US charts in 1952 with the delightful 'I Saw Mommy Kissing Santa Claus'. Sadly, 'Rudolph' came a poor second.

　4 Dec 54　**39**　2　　**Rudolph The Red-Nosed Reindeer** / I Said A Prayer For Santa Claus
　　　　　　　　　　　(Philips PB-358)

OWEN BRADLEY QUINTET   3

Legendary Nashville pianist and bandleader who in his time produced Buddy Holly, Brenda Lee, Gene Vincent, Conway Twitty and many others.

29 Mar 58　**1**　2　　**Big Guitar** / Sentimental Dream *(Brunswick 05736)*
　3 May 58　**15**　1　　**Big Guitar** / Sentimental Dream *(Brunswick 05736)* **re-entry**

MARLON BRANDO   1

Famous movie actor and director born in Omaha, Nebraska in 1924.

　6 Oct 56　**2**　1　★　**GUYS AND DOLLS [OST]** *(Brunswick OE-9241)* **EP**
　　　　　　　　　　　A Woman In Love *(Marlon Brando and Jean Simmons)* / I'll Know *(Marlon Brando and Jean Simmons)* / Luck Be A Lady *(Marlon Brando)* / If I Were A Bell *(Jean Simmons)*

JOHNNY BRANDON   6

Pre-rock'n'roll singer from London who struck it lucky in 1955 with the self-penned 'Tomorrow' and 'Don't Worrry'. He emigrated to New York in the mid-'50s and switched to writing musicals.

19 Feb 55　**3**　3　★　**Tomorrow** / High As A Mountain *(Polygon P-1131)*
　　　　　　　　　　　Both sides by Johnny Brandon with the Phantoms
25 Jun 55　**30**　1　★　**Don't Worry** / Strike It Lucky *(Polygon P-1163)*
　　　　　　　　　　　Both sides by Johnny Brandon with the Phantoms
15 Oct 55　**26**　1　　**Anyone Can Be A Millionaire** / Love And Kisses *(Polygon P-1174)*
　　　　　　　　　　　Both sides by Johnny Brandon with the Phantoms
22 Oct 55　**20**　1　　**Home** / I'm Burning My Bridges Behind Me *(Polygon P-1187)*

See also Original London Cast (LOVE FROM JUDY)

ROSSANO BRAZZI   1

Italian singer and actor famed for his appearance in the 1954 blockbuster 'Three Coins In The Fountain' and for his role as Emile de Becque in 'South Pacific' (1958).

19 Nov 55	**14**	1	**Summertime In Venice** / Believe In Me *(H.M.V. B-10920)*

ROSE BRENNAN   2

Dublin-born resident singer with Joe Loss & His Orchestra, who eventually scored a hit in 1961 with 'Tall Dark Stranger'.

7 Apr 56	**14**	1	**Band Of Gold** / My Believing Heart *(H.M.V. POP-180)*
16 Mar 57	**13**	1	**Without Love** / Tra La La *(H.M.V. POP-302)*

TONY BRENT   46

Crooner born Reginald Bretagne in Bombay, India. He moved to the UK in 1947 after getting married and enjoyed a successful chart career from 1952 onwards. He relocated to Australia in 1961.

7 Aug 54	**2**	14	**Sway / Three Coins In The Fountain** *(Columbia DB-3496)*
11 Sep 54	**8**	5	**The Magic Tango** / I Understand Just How You Feel *(Columbia DB-3514)*
6 Nov 54	**23**	2	**Tell Me, Tell Me / Nicolette** *(Columbia DB-3532)*
29 Jan 55	**31**	1	**It's A Woman's World** / Give Me The Right To Be Wrong *(Columbia DB-3556)*
19 Mar 55	**23**	3	**When I Leave The World Behind** / I Need *(Columbia DB-3428)*
23 Apr 55	**12**	1	**Open Up Your Heart** *(Tony Brent and Anne Warren)* / Hearts Of Stone *(Tony Brent and the Coronets) (Columbia DB-3579)*
30 Apr 55	**5**	5	**How Important Can It Be?** / Letter To Virginia *(Columbia DB-3610)*
11 Jun 55	**13**	2	**When I Leave The World Behind** / I Need *(Columbia DB-3428)* **1st re-entry**
2 Jul 55	**13**	1	**When I Leave The World Behind** / I Need *(Columbia DB-3428)* **2nd re-entry**
16 Jul 55	**14**	2	**Mirror, Mirror / Love And Kisses** *(Columbia DB-3638)*
14 Jan 56	**1**	4	**With Your Love** / On A Little Balcony In Spain *(Columbia DB-3675)*
3 Mar 56	**6**	3	**With Your Love** / On A Little Balcony In Spain *(Columbia DB-3675)* **1st re-entry**
31 Mar 56	**11**	1	**With Your Love** / On A Little Balcony In Spain *(Columbia DB-3675)* **2nd re-entry**
21 Sep 57	**8**	1	**Deep Within Me** / Why Ask For The Moon *(Columbia DB-3987)*
17 Oct 59	**16**	1	**Forever, My Darling** / Worried Mind *(Columbia DB-4357)*

BERNARD BRESSLAW   1

Cockney-born comedy actor, star of ITV's 'The Army Game' and numerous 'Carry On' films.

21 Mar 59	**6**	1	**Charlie Brown** / The Teenager's Lament *(H.M.V. POP-599)*

TERESA BREWER   13

Chirpy singer from Toledo, Ohio who kicked off her career in 1950 with 'Music! Music! Music!'.

15 Jan 55	**48**	1	★ <u>**Let Me Go, Lover**</u> *(Teresa Brewer and the Lancers)* / Baby, Baby, Baby *(Teresa Brewer) (Vogue Coral Q-72043)*
7 Jul 56	**19**	1	★ <u>**A Sweet Old Fashioned Girl**</u> / Goodbye John *(Vogue Coral Q-72172)*
16 Feb 57	**7**	1	★ **When I Leave The World Behind** / <u>Nora Malone</u> *(Vogue Coral Q-72224)*
23 Mar 57	**13**	1	★ <u>Nora Malone</u> / When I Leave The World Behind *(Vogue Coral Q-72224)* **1st re-entry (flipped)**
6 Apr 57	**6**	2	★ <u>Nora Malone</u> / When I Leave The World Behind *(Vogue Coral Q-72224)* **2nd re-entry**
13 Apr 57	**17**	1	**I'm Drowning My Sorrows** / How Lonely Can One Be *(Vogue Coral Q-72239)*
27 Apr 57	**1**	2	★ <u>Nora Malone</u> / When I Leave The World Behind *(Vogue Coral Q-72224)* **3rd re-entry**

29 Nov 58	15	1	**The Hula Hoop Song** / So Shy *(Coral Q-72340)*
7 Mar 59	6	1	**The One Rose** / Satellite *(Coral Q-72354)*
21 Mar 59	13	1	**The One Rose** / Satellite *(Coral Q-72354)* *re-entry*
18 Apr 59	16	1	**Fair Weather Sweetheart** / Heavenly Lover *(Coral Q-72364)*

BROOK BROTHERS   24

Real brothers from Winchester, Ricky and Geoff Brook were the UK's answer to the Everly Brothers. They had five hits between 1961 and 1963, of which 'Warpaint' was the biggest.

7 May 60	2	1	**Green Fields** / How Will It End *(Top Rank JAR-349)*
			Both sides as by the Brooks Brothers
4 Jun 60	14	1	**Green Fields** / How Will It End *(Top Rank JAR-349)* **1st re-entry**
16 Jul 60	11	2	**Green Fields** / How Will It End *(Top Rank JAR-349)* **2nd re-entry**
23 Jul 60	4	1	★ **Please Help Me, I'm Falling** / **When Will I Be Loved**
			Both sides as by the Brooks Brothers (Top Rank JAR-409)
6 Aug 60	9	1	★ **Please Help Me, I'm Falling** / When Will I Be Loved
			Both sides as by the Brooks Brothers (Top Rank JAR-409) *re-entry*
29 Oct 60	4	2	**Say The Word** / Everything But Love *(Pye 7N.15298)*
19 Nov 60	1	13	**Say The Word** / **Everything But Love** *(Pye 7N.15298)* *re-entry*
25 Feb 61	1	3	★ **Warpaint** / Sometimes *(Pye 7N.15333)*

DONNIE BROOKS   5

Dallas native John Dee Abohosh recorded as Johnny Jordan, Dick Bush and Johnny Faire before finally settling on Donnie Brooks.

13 Aug 60	5	3	**Mission Bell** / Do It For Me *(London HLN-9168)*
7 Jan 61	12	1	**Doll House** / Round Robin *(London HLN-9253)*
21 Jan 61	8	1	**Doll House** / Round Robin *(London HLN-9253)* *re-entry*

NORMAN BROOKS   8

Canadian Al Jolson soundalike, born Norman Joseph Arie in Montreal in 1928.

| 18 Sep 54 | 5 | 8 | ★ **A Sky Blue Shirt And A Rainbow Tie** / This Waltz With You |
| | | | *(London L-1228)* |

BROTHER SISTERS   3

American girl group who took on the Shepherd Sisters, the Kaye Sisters and Petula Clark with this song and lost.

| 23 Nov 57 | 5 | 1 | **Alone** / Pass Me The Mustard *(Mercury MT-186)* |
| 7 Dec 57 | 3 | 2 | **Alone** / Pass Me The Mustard *(Mercury MT-186)* *re-entry* |

BROTHERS & GIRLS

See Howard Keel
Original Soundtrack (SEVEN BRIDES FOR SEVEN BROTHERS (PART 1))

BROTHERS FOUR   2

Folk group formed by four male students at the University of Washington, Seattle.

| 23 Apr 60 | 2 | 2 | ★ **Greenfields** / East Virginia *(Philips PB-1009)* |

AL BROWN'S TUNETOPPERS featuring Cookie Brown   1

Band from New York who scored a one-off hit in the States with this catchy number. The dance calls were by Cookie Brown.

| 4 Jun 60 | 21 | 1 | **The Madison** / Mo' Madison *(Top Rank JAR-374)* |

BOOTS BROWN & HIS BLOCKBUSTERS   5

See Shorty Rogers

CLIFFORD BROWN 14

Influential and respected jazz trumpeter/composer from Wilmington, Delaware. He was tragically killed in a car crash in 1956, aged just 25.

19 Jun 54	6	3	**CLIFFORD BROWN & ART FARMER WITH THE SWEDISH ALL STARS (VOL. 2)** *(Esquire EP-3)* EP Falling In Love With Love / Lover Come Back To Me
19 Jun 54	8	1	**Salute To The Bandbox (Parts 1 & 2)** *(Vogue V-2239)* *Both sides by the Gigi Gryce–Clifford Brown Sextet*
3 Jul 54	3	5	**Salute To The Bandbox (Parts 1 & 2)** *(Vogue V-2239)* *1st re-entry*
14 Aug 54	4	3	**Salute To The Bandbox (Parts 1 & 2)** *(Vogue V-2239)* *2nd re-entry*
25 Dec 54	36	2	**Salute To The Bandbox (Parts 1 & 2)** *(Vogue V-2239)* *3rd re-entry*

See also Swedish-American All Stars

JOE BROWN & THE BRUVVERS 3

One of Britain's top guitarists in the late '50s/early '60s and a stalwart of early TV pop shows, though his choice of repertoire occasionally let him down...

| 20 Feb 60 | 5 | 1 | ★ **The Darktown Strutters' Ball** / Swagger *(Decca F-11207)* |
| 2 Jul 60 | 5 | 2 | **Jellied Eels** / Dinah *(Decca F-11246)* |

LES BROWN & HIS BAND OF RENOWN 1

Saxophonist, clarinettist and big band leader from Pennsylvania, who in 1945 launched Doris Day to stardom with 'Sentimental Journey'.

| 5 Feb 55 | 37 | 1 | **CONCERT AT THE LONDON PALLADIUM (VOL. 2)** *(Vogue Coral LVA-9002)* LP
Midnight Sun / Begin The Beguine / Happy Hooligan / I Would Do Anything For You *(Vocal: Stumpy Brown)* / Laura / Jersey Bounce / From This Moment On / Crazy Legs / Flying Home / One O'Clock Jump / Cherokee / Sentimental Journey *(Vocal: Jo Ann Greer)* / Closing Announcement by Les Brown (Sentimental Journey) |

NAPPY BROWN 9

R&B singer with a unique style, born Napoleon Brown Goodson Culp in Charlotte, North Carolina in 1929.

| 22 Oct 55 | 7 | 7 | **Don't Be Angry** / It's Really You *(London HL-8145)* |
| 6 Apr 57 | 13 | 2 | **Little By Little** / I'm Getting Lonesome *(London HLC-8384)* |

RAY BROWN

See Norman Granz
Oscar Peterson

RUTH BROWN 2

Black singer/songwriter from Portsmouth, Virginia who introduced pop sensibilities into R&B with immense success. In 1963, Cliff Richard had a Top Five hit with a version of her 'Lucky Lips'.

| 10 Jan 59 | 6 | 1 | **This Little Girl's Gone Rockin'** / Why Me *(London HLE-8757)* |
| 7 Feb 59 | 9 | 1 | **This Little Girl's Gone Rockin'** / Why Me *(London HLE-8757)*
re-entry |

BROWNS 8

Country-flavoured close harmony trio from Sparkman, Arkansas consisting of Jim Ed Brown and his sisters Maxine and Bonnie.

5 Sep 59	7	1	★ **The Three Bells** / Heaven Fell Last Night *(R.C.A. RCA-1140)*
26 Dec 59	5	4	**Scarlet Ribbons** / Blue Bells Ring *(R.C.A. RCA-1157)*
7 May 60	7	1	**The Old Lamplighter** / Teen-Ex *(R.C.A. RCA-1176)* *Both sides by the Browns featuring Jim Edward Brown*
30 Jul 60	17	1	**Lonely Little Robin** / Margo *(R.C.A. RCA-1193)* *Both sides by the Browns featuring Jim Edward Brown*

| 4 Feb 61 | **22** | 1 | **Send Me The Pillow You Dream On** /
You're So Much A Part Of Me *(R.C.A. RCA-1218)*
Both sides by the Browns featuring Jim Edward Brown |

DAVE BRUBECK · 8

Progressive 'cool jazz' pianist and composer born in Concord, California in 1920.

11 Sep 54	**20**	1	**Singing In The Rain** / Perfidia *(Vogue V-2264)* *Both sides by the Dave Brubeck Trio*
25 Sep 54	**15**	3	**Perfidia / Singing In The Rain** *(Vogue V-2264)* **re-entry (flipped)**
20 Nov 54	**34**	1	**DAVE BRUBECK QUARTET** *(Vogue EPV-1063)* **EP** Me And My Shadow / At A Perfume Counter / Frenesi / Mam'selle
4 Dec 54	**51**	1	**DAVE BRUBECK TRIO** *(Vogue LDE-090)* **LP** You Stepped Out Of A Dream / Lullaby In Rhythm / Singing In The Rain / I'll Remember April / Body And Soul / Let's Fall In Love / Laura / Indiana
15 Jan 55	**42**	1	**DAVE BRUBECK QUARTET** *(Vogue EPV-1063)* **EP** *re-entry*
22 Jan 55	**22**	1	**DAVE BRUBECK QUARTET (VOL. 2)** *(Vogue LDE-104)* **LP** This Can't Be Love / Look For The Silver Lining / Fine Romance / Just One Of Those Things / Stardust / Lulu's Back In Town / Alice In Wonderland / All The Things You Are
22 Feb 58	**12**	1	**JAZZ AT THE BLACKHAWK** *(Vogue LAE-12094)* **LP** *Dave Brubeck Quartet featuring Paul Desmond* Jeepers Creepers / On A Little Street In Singapore / The Trolley Song (Rehearsal) / The Trolley Song / I May Be Wrong / Blue Moon / My Heart Stood Still / Let's Fall In Love

ALLAN BRUCE · 1

Scottish balladeer who recorded several unsuccessful singles for Fontana.

| 13 Aug 60 | **14** | 1 | **In All The World** / Simple, Simple, Simple *(Fontana H-250)* |

ANITA BRYANT · 2

Pop singer and former Miss Oklahoma, who later became an outspoken critic of gay rights.

| 21 May 60 | **7** | 1 | ★ <u>**Paper Roses**</u> / Mixed Emotions *(London HLL-9114)* |
| 17 Sep 60 | **20** | 1 | ★ <u>**My Little Corner Of The World**</u> / Just In Time *(London HLL-9171)* |

MARIE BRYANT · 4

Daughter of New Orleans bandleader and long-time Apollo Theater MC, Willie Bryant. The suggestive 'Tomato' was one of several calypsos she recorded while resident in Britain between 1952 and 1954.

18 Sep 54	**29**	2	**Tomato** / Rhumboogie Anna *(Lyragon J-701)*
27 Nov 54	**65**	1	**Tomato** / Rhumboogie Anna *(Lyragon J-701)* **1st re-entry**
15 Jan 55	**48**	1	**Tomato** / Rhumboogie Anna *(Lyragon J-701)* **2nd re-entry**

RAY BRYANT TRIO · 1

Philadelphia-born jazz pianist/composer of the hard bop persuasion. (In case you were wondering, Parts 1 & 3 were released on Philips PB-1003 in March 1960.)

| 27 Feb 60 | **5** | 1 | **Little Susie (Parts 2 & 4)** *(Pye International 7N.25052)* |

TEDDY BUCKNER · 1

Louis Armstrong-styled Dixieland jazz trumpeter from Sherman, Texas.

| 19 May 56 | **17** | 1 | **When The Saints Go Marching In** / West End Blues *(Vogue V-2375)* |

DORSEY BURNETTE · 1

Older brother of Johnny Burnette (see below) and former member of the Johnny Burnette Trio. He died of a heart attack in 1979, aged just 46.

| 9 Apr 60 | **4** | 1 | **Tall Oak Tree** / Juarez Town *(London HLN-9047)* |

JOHNNY BURNETTE   5

Younger brother of Dorsey Burnette (see above) and former member of the Johnny Burnette Trio. He drowned in 1964 at the age of 30 after his unlit fishing boat was struck by a cabin cruiser.

27 Aug 60   **3**   5   ★   <u>**Dreamin'**</u> / Cincinnatti Fireball *(London HLG-9172)*

JOHNNY BURNETTE TRIO   1

Johnny Burnette formed the Rock'n'Roll Trio with his brother Dorsey and friend Paul Burlison, but didn't achieve chart success until he went solo. Even so, both sides of this bubbler have long been acknowledged as rockabilly classics.

27 Apr 57   **18**   1   **Lonesome Train** / Honey Hush *(Vogue Coral Q-72277)*

SMILEY BURNETTE   1

No relation to Dorsey and Johnny, singer/songwriter Lester Alvin Burnett from Summum, Illinois could reputedly play over 100 musical instruments, and was also a successful comedy actor in films and TV for three decades. He died of leukaemia in 1967.

27 Nov 54   **72**   1   **Rudolph The Red-Nosed Reindeer** / Grandaddy Frog
                         (Capitol CL-13388)

RAY BURNS   20

English band vocalist born Reuben Klot. He enjoyed short-lived solo success in 1955 with 'Mobile' and 'That's How A Love Song Was Born'.

15 Jan 55   **3**   2   ★   <u>**Mobile**</u> / These Are The Things We'll Share *(Columbia DB-3563)*
26 Feb 55   **6**   2   **Goin' Co'tin'** *(Ronnie Harris, Diana Decker, Ray Burns and Ruby Murray)* /
                         Spring, Spring, Spring *(Ruby Murray, Ray Burns, Diana Decker and*
                         Ronnie Harris) (Columbia DB-3567)
30 Apr 55   **16**   3   **Spring, Spring, Spring** *(Ruby Murray, Ray Burns, Diana Decker and*
                         Ronnie Harris) / **Goin' Co'tin'** *(Ronnie Harris, Diana Decker, Ray*
                         Burns and Ruby Murray) (Columbia DB-3567) **re-entry (flipped)**
9 Jul 55   **3**   5   ★   <u>**That's How A Love Song Was Born**</u> / The Voice *(Columbia DB-3640)*
                         Both sides by Ray Burns with the Coronets
8 Oct 55   **2**   8   **Blue Star** / Memory *(Columbia DB-3670)*

FRED BUSCAGLIONE & HIS ASTERNOVAS   2

Italian singer/actor who was immensely popular during the late '50s for his characterisation of a humorous mobster with a predilection for whiskey and women. He died in a car crash in 1960, aged just 39.

3 Oct 59   **21**   1   **Guarda Che Luna** / Pity Pity *(Cetra SP-4011)*
3 Oct 59   **23**   1   **Carina** / Love In Portofino *(Cetra SP-4010)*

LOU BUSCH & His Orchestra   2

Pianist, songwriter and record producer born Louis Bush in Louisville, Kentucky in 1910 (he added the 'c' to his surname to make it sound more exotic). He also enjoyed some success as a honky-tonk pianist, recording under the alias 'Joe "Fingers" Carr'.

14 Jan 56   **9**   2   ★   <u>**Zambesi**</u> / Rainbow's End *(Capitol CL-14504)*

SAM BUTERA & THE WITNESSES

See Louis Prima

JERRY BUTLER   3

Black singer born in Sunflower, Mississippi in 1939. He sang lead on the Impressions' first two hits, then went solo in 1958 and became a major R&B star.

31 Dec 60   **7**   3   **He Will Break Your Heart** / Thanks To You *(Top Rank JAR-531)*

Popular entertainer born Walter William Bygraves in Rotherhithe, London. He first came to national attention as the tutor 'Big 'ead' on the BBC radio comedy show 'Educating Archie'.

3 Jul 54	**8**	6	**Friends And Neighbours** *(Max Bygraves and the Tanner Sisters)* / Chip Chopper Charlie *(Max Bygraves)* *(H.M.V. B-10703)*
14 Aug 54	**4**	4	★ **Gilly Gilly Ossenfeffer Katzenellen Bogen By The Sea** / Third Little Turning *(H.M.V. B-10734)*
21 Aug 54	**24**	2	**Friends And Neighbours** *(Max Bygraves and the Tanner Sisters)* / Chip Chopper Charlie *(Max Bygraves)* *(H.M.V. B-10703)* **1st re-entry**
2 Oct 54	**35**	1	**Friends And Neighbours** *(Max Bygraves and the Tanner Sisters)* / Chip Chopper Charlie *(Max Bygraves)* *(H.M.V. B-10703)* **2nd re-entry**
27 Nov 54	**1**	8	★ **Mister Sandman** / Do You Love Old Santa Claus *(H.M.V. B-10821)*
5 Mar 55	**11**	4	**Tomorrow** / C-R-A-Z-Y Music *(H.M.V. B-10842)*
9 Apr 55	**7**	2	**Tomorrow** / C-R-A-Z-Y Music *(H.M.V. B-10842)* **1st re-entry**
30 Apr 55	**20**	1	**Tomorrow** / C-R-A-Z-Y Music *(H.M.V. B-10842)* **2nd re-entry**
14 May 55	**26**	1	**Tomorrow** / C-R-A-Z-Y Music *(H.M.V. B-10842)* **3rd re-entry**
28 May 55	**36**	1	**The Pendulum Song** / I'm Singing A Song For The Old Folks *(H.M.V. B-10876)*
11 Jun 55	**21**	3	**The Pendulum Song** / I'm Singing A Song For The Old Folks *(H.M.V. B-10876)* **1st re-entry**
9 Jul 55	**26**	1	**The Pendulum Song** / I'm Singing A Song For The Old Folks *(H.M.V. B-10876)* **2nd re-entry**
29 Oct 55	**7**	2	★ **Meet Me On The Corner** / The Little Laplander *(H.M.V. POP-116)*
28 Jan 56	**4**	1	★ **The Ballad of Davy Crockett** / A Good Idea – Son *(H.M.V. POP-153)*
10 Mar 56	**24**	1	**Nothin' To Do** / Lift Boy *(H.M.V. POP-185)*
5 May 56	**2**	3	★ **Out Of Town** / Fingers Crossed *(H.M.V. POP-164)*
19 May 56	**3**	7	**Seventeen Tons** / Try Another Cherry Tree *(H.M.V. POP-208)*
9 Jun 56	**10**	1	**Nothin' To Do** / Lift Boy *(H.M.V. POP-185)* **re-entry**
15 Dec 56	**1**	3	**That Dear Old Gentleman** / The Feather Song *(H.M.V. POP-262)*
23 Mar 57	**4**	2	★ **Heart** / In A Shanty In Old Shanty Town *(Decca F-10862)*
19 Apr 58	**1**	2	★ **Tulips From Amsterdam** *(Max Bygraves)* / **You Need Hands** *(Max Bygraves with the Clarke Brothers)* *(Decca F-11004)*
9 Aug 58	**12**	1	★ **Gotta Have Rain** / **Little Train** *(Decca F-11046)*
13 Dec 58	**5**	3	★ **My Ukelele** / Come To Our Coming Out Party *(Decca F-11077)*
28 Mar 59	**4**	1	**Napoli – Napoli** / Old Tymes Square *(Decca F-11119)*
5 Dec 59	**3**	2	★ **Jingle Bell Rock** / Who Made The Morning *(Decca F-11176)*
5 Mar 60	**6**	1	★ **Fings Ain't Wot They Used T' Be** / When The Thrill Has Gone *(Decca F-11214)*
31 Dec 60	**5**	1	**When You Come To The End Of A Lollipop** / Underneath The Arches *(Decca F-11308)*

EDWARD BYRNES 1

Actor born Edward Byrne Breitenberger in New York in 1933. His most famous role was as the continually hair-combing amateur sleuth Gerald 'Kookie' Kookson III in the TV series '77 Sunset Strip'. The tie-in record sold over a million copies.

30 Apr 60	**7**	1	★ **Kookie Kookie (Lend Me Your Comb)** *(Edward Byrnes and Connie Stevens)* / You're The Top *(Edward Byrnes)* *(Warner Bros. WB-5)*

RED CALLENDER

See Gene Norman's 'Just Jazz'

EDDIE CALVERT 20

Trumpet player from Preston, Lancashire who had a string of hits in the mid-'50s starting with 'Oh, Mein Papa' in 1953. He later moved to South Africa, where he died in 1978.

19 Jun 54	**10**	1	**Midnight** / Margot's Minuet *(Columbia DB-3444)*
7 Aug 54	**23**	1	**Midnight** / Margot's Minuet *(Columbia DB-3444)* **re-entry**

25 Sep 54	**39**	1	**Faraway** / Donna *(Columbia DB-3462)*
2 Oct 54	**2**	5	**My Son, My Son** / Sherpa Song *(Columbia DB-3507)*
13 Nov 54	**10**	1	**My Son, My Son** / Sherpa Song *(Columbia DB-3507)* **1st re-entry**
27 Nov 54	**28**	1	**My Son, My Son** / Sherpa Song *(Columbia DB-3507)* **2nd re-entry**
19 Mar 55	**1**	3	★ **Cherry Pink (And Apple Blossom White)** / Roses Of Picardy *(Columbia DB-3581)*
30 Apr 55	**5**	2	★ **Stranger In Paradise** / Sincerely *(Columbia DB-3594)*
2 Jul 55	**14**	1	★ **John And Julie** / Heart Of The Sunset *(Columbia DB-3624)*
7 Jan 56	**20**	2	**The Holy City** / O My Beloved Daddy *(Columbia DB-3674)*
14 Jun 58	**5**	1	★ **Little Serenade** / Fanfare Tango *(Columbia DB-4105)*
24 Jan 59	**6**	1	**Trumpet Cha Cha Cha** / Cha Cha In The Rain *(Columbia DB-4221)*

JIM CAMERON & His Band   3
Very popular Scottish dance band from Kirriemuir led by fiddler Jim Cameron, which unusually also featured a cornet player, Dod Michie.

16 Oct 54	**29**	2	**Grand March [M]** / Triumph *(Beltona BL-2596)*
			Grand March: Scotland The Brave – The Meeting Of The Waters
27 Nov 54	**32**	1	**Grand March [M]** / Triumph *(Beltona BL-2596)* **re-entry**

GWEN CAMPBELL   1
Operatic-voiced singer who recorded duets with Jan Rosol and Gerry Gray, both on Polygon.

11 Dec 54	**43**	1	**I Love Paris** *(Jan Rosol and Gwen Campbell) (Polygon P-1136)*
			Flip is 'C'est Magnifique' by Jan Rosol

JEAN CAMPBELL   1
Once described by Tony Bennett as 'Britain's Jo Stafford', Glaswegian singer Jean Campbell worked with the Gibson Trio, Cyril Stapleton, the Keynotes and the Coronets, but this was the closest she got to a her big break as a solo artist.

11 Jun 55	**20**	1	**Dance With Me Henry (The Wallflower)** / Two Hearts, Two Kisses *(Parlophone R-4026)*

MURRAY CAMPBELL   1
22-year-old trumpeter from Devon discovered by Frankie Vaughan.

7 Sep 57	**9**	1	**Mandolin Serenade** / Gypsy Trumpet *(Philips PB-718)*
			Both sides with Wally Stott & His Orchestra

FREDDY CANNON   13
Exciting rock'n'roll singer born Frederick Picariello Jr. in Revere, Massachusetts in 1936.

20 Jun 59	**1**	8	★ **Tallahassee Lassie** / You Know *(Top Rank JAR-135)*
5 Dec 59	**13**	3	★ **Way Down Yonder In New Orleans** / Fractured *(Top Rank JAR-247)*
			Both sides as by Freddie Cannon
27 Feb 60	**3**	1	★ **California Here I Come** / **Indiana** *(Top Rank JAR-309)*
			Both sides as by Freddie Cannon
14 May 60	**3**	1	★ **The Urge** / **Jump Over** *(Top Rank JAR-369)*

PADDY CARNEY   4
One of many Irish balladeers who specialised in sentimental songs.

14 Apr 56	**9**	1	**An Irish Mother's Prayer** / They Can't Change The Name Of Ireland *(Decca (Irish Series) MU-12)*
5 May 56	**10**	1	**An Irish Mother's Prayer** / They Can't Change The Name Of Ireland *(Decca (Irish Series) MU-12)* **1st re-entry**
14 Jul 56	**13**	1	**They Can't Change The Name Of Ireland** / An Irish Mother's Prayer *(Decca (Irish Series) MU-12)* **2nd re-entry (flipped)**
27 Apr 57	**18**	1	**They Can't Change The Name Of Ireland** / An Irish Mother's Prayer *(Decca (Irish Series) MU-12)* **3rd re-entry**

RENATO CAROSONE 2

Italian pianist and internationally popular bandleader born in Naples in 1920. He abruptly quit music in 1960, at the height of his career, to pursue painting and other interests.

14 Jun 58   **16**   1   ★ <u>**Torero – Cha Cha Cha**</u> *(Renato Carosone and His Sextet)* / Il Piccolo Montanaro *(Renato Carosone and His Quartet)* *(Parlophone R-4433)*

28 Jun 58   **6**   1   ★ <u>**Torero – Cha Cha Cha**</u> *(Renato Carosone and His Sextet)* / Il Piccolo Montanaro *(Renato Carosone and His Quartet)* *(Parlophone R-4433)* **re-entry**

CATHY CARR 11

Singer/dancer born Angelina Helen Catherine Cordovano in New York in 1936. Her cover of Otis Williams & The Charms' R&B hit went all the way to No. 2 in the Billboard 'Top 100' pop chart.

19 May 56   **2**   5   **Ivory Tower** / Please, Please Believe Me *(London HLH-8274)*
30 Jun 56   **2**   2   **Ivory Tower** / Please, Please Believe Me *(London HLH-8274)* **1st re-entry**
4 Aug 56   **4**   3   **Ivory Tower** / Please, Please Believe Me *(London HLH-8274)* **2nd re-entry**
1 Sep 56   **12**   1   **Ivory Tower** / Please, Please Believe Me *(London HLH-8274)* **3rd re-entry**

RONNIE CARROLL 10

Singer from Belfast born Ronald Cleghorn. He enjoyed great popularity from the mid-'50s to the mid-'60s, and represented the UK in the Eurovision Song Contest in 1962 and 1963.

10 Mar 56   **24**   1   **Last Love** / My Believing Heart *(Philips PB-553)*
27 Oct 56   **4**   1   **It Only Hurts For A Little While** / Love Me As Though There Were No Tomorrow *(Philips PB-623)*
9 Mar 57   **2**   3   ★ <u>**The Wisdom Of A Fool**</u> / **Without Love** *(Philips PB-667)*
22 Jun 57   **8**   1   **Around The World** / Let There Be You *(Philips PB-695)*
6 Jul 57   **5**   2   **Around The World** / Let There Be You *(Philips PB-695)* **re-entry**
5 Sep 59   **7**   1   **The Wonder Of You** / **Wonderful You** *(Philips PB-944)*
1 Oct 60   **20**   1   **Chain Gang** / Move Two Mountains *(Philips PB-1060)*

JOHNNY CARSON 17

English singer born Derek Clarkson. He made a handful of records in the early '60s, but didn't enjoy nearly as much success as his cousin, Cliff Richard.

25 Jun 60   **5**   2   **Fraülein** / I Wish It Were You *(Fontana H-243)*
9 Jul 60   **4**   7   **The Train Of Love** / First Proposal *(Fontana H-259)*
3 Sep 60   **6**   3   **The Train Of Love** / First Proposal *(Fontana H-259)* **1st re-entry**
1 Oct 60   **18**   1   **The Train Of Love** / First Proposal *(Fontana H-259)* **2nd re-entry**
19 Nov 60   **2**   4   ★ <u>**You Talk Too Much**</u> / Now And Always *(Fontana H-277)*

BENNY CARTER

See Norman Granz
    Gene Norman's 'Just Jazz'

JOHNNY CASH 42

Influential country singer/songwriter born in Kingsland, Arkansas in 1932. Amazingly, the Man In Black had to wait until 1965 for his first UK hit, but many of his early releases were serious contenders.

22 Mar 58   **14**   1   **Give My Love To Rose** / **Home Of The Blues** *(London HLS-8514)* Both sides by Johnny Cash & The Tennessee Two
5 Apr 58   **1**   1   **Ballad Of A Teenage Queen** / Big River *(London HLS-8586)* Both sides by Johnny Cash & The Tennessee Two

19 Apr 58	1	5	**Ballad Of A Teenage Queen** / Big River *(London HLS-8586)*
			1st re-entry
31 May 58	10	3	**Ballad Of A Teenage Queen** / Big River *(London HLS-8586)*
			2nd re-entry
26 Jul 58	6	4	**Guess Things Happen That Way** /
			Come In, Stranger *(London HLS-8656)*
			Both sides by Johnny Cash & The Tennessee Two
11 Oct 58	7	1	**The Ways Of A Woman In Love** /
			You're The Nearest Thing To Heaven *(London HLS-8709)*
			Both sides by Johnny Cash & The Tennessee Two
25 Oct 58	11	1	**I Walk The Line** / Get Rhythm *(London HL-8358)*
15 Nov 58	4	1	**All Over Again** / **What Do I Care** *(Philips PB-874)*
7 Mar 59	5	1	**Don't Take Your Guns To Town** / I Still Miss Someone *(Philips PB-897)*
28 Mar 59	12	1	**JOHNNY CASH SINGS HANK WILLIAMS** *(London RE-S-1193)* **EP**
			I Can't Help It / Hey, Good Lookin' / You Win Again / I Could Never Be Ashamed
25 Apr 59	2	2	**Luther Played The Boogie** / **Thanks A Lot** *(London HLS-8847)*
9 May 59	6	1	**COUNTRY BOY** *(London RE-S-1212)* **EP**
			Country Boy / If The Good Lord's Willing / The Rock Island Line / I Heard That
			Lonesome Whistle
6 Jun 59	5	2	**Frankie's Man, Johnny** / **You Dreamer You** *(Philips PB-928)*
19 Sep 59	3	4	**I Got Stripes** / **Five Feet High And Rising** *(Philips PB-953)*
19 Sep 59	10	3	**Katy Too** / I Forgot To Remember To Forget *(London HLS-8928)*
7 Nov 59	3	1	**You Tell Me** / **Goodbye, Little Darlin', Goodbye** *(London HLS-8979)*
26 Dec 59	3	1	**Little Drummer Boy** / I'll Remember You *(Philips PB-979)*
12 Mar 60	2	1	**Straight A's In Love** / I Love You Because *(London HLS-9070)*
30 Apr 60	1	2	**Seasons Of My Heart** / **Smiling Bill McCall** *(Philips PB-1017)*
17 Sep 60	11	1	**Down The Street To 301** / Story Of A Broken Heart
			(London HLS-9182)
8 Oct 60	4	1	**NOW, THERE WAS A SONG!** *(Philips BBL-73580)* **LP**
			Seasons Of My Heart / I Feel Better All Over / I Couldn't Keep From Crying / Time
			Changes Everything / My Shoes Keep Walking Back To You / I'd Just Be Fool
			Enough (To Fall) / Transfusion Blues / Why Do You Punish Me (For Loving You) /
			I Will Miss You When You Go / I'm So Lonesome I Could Cry / Just One More /
			Honky-Tonk Girl
8 Oct 60	10	1	**Down The Street To 301** / Story Of A Broken Heart
			(London HLS-9182) *1st re-entry*
22 Oct 60	7	1	**Loading Coal** / Going To Memphis *(Philips PB-1075)*
10 Dec 60	8	1	**RIDE THIS TRAIN** *(Philips BBL-7417)* **LP**
			Loading Coal / Slow Rider / Lumberjack / Dorraine Of Ponchartrain / Going To
			Memphis / When Papa Played The Dobro / Boss Jack / Old Doc Brown
10 Dec 60	21	1	**Down The Street To 301** / Story Of A Broken Heart
			(London HLS-9182) *2nd re-entry*

CARMEN CAVALLARO   6

Billed as 'The Poet of the Piano', Carmen Cavallaro was the forerunner of later flashy classically-styled pop pianists like Liberace and Bobby Crush. He was born in New York in 1913.

25 Aug 56	4	1	**To Love Again** / Brazil *(Brunswick 05576)*
15 Sep 56	3	1	**To Love Again** / Brazil *(Brunswick 05576)* *re-entry*
17 Nov 56	15	1	**Autumn Concerto** / La Gondola *(Brunswick 05609)*
15 Dec 56	7	3	**Autumn Concerto** / La Gondola *(Brunswick 05609)* *re-entry*

CENTRAL BAND OF THE ROYAL AIR FORCE   12

Leading military band frequently present at British state ceremonial events. 'The Dam Busters', conducted by Wing Commander A.E. Sims, OBE, was their first recording.

| 23 Jul 55 | 19 | 3 | ★ **The Dam Busters – March** / Lilliburlero *(H.M.V. B-10877)* |
| 20 Aug 55 | 1 | 9 | ★ **The Dam Busters – March** / Lilliburlero *(H.M.V. B-10877)* *re-entry* |

43

FRANK CHACKSFIELD & His Orchestra · 15

Celebrated UK bandleader and musical director who also managed to break through in America. His biggest successes were 'Terry's Theme from "Limelight"' (1953) and 'Ebb Tide' (1954).

28 Aug 54	**13**	1	**Smile** / Piper In The Heather *(Decca F-10354)*
11 Sep 54	**12**	3	**Smile** / Piper In The Heather *(Decca F-10354)* **1st re-entry**
9 Oct 54	**4**	3	**Smile** / Piper In The Heather *(Decca F-10354)* **2nd re-entry**
9 Apr 55	**30**	1	**Blue Mirage** / Lady From Luxembourg *(Decca F-10467)*
10 Mar 56	**18**	1	**Love Is A Many Splendoured Thing** / Lights Of Vienna *(Decca F-10639)*
4 Aug 56	**3**	4	★ **The Donkey Cart** / The Banks Of The Seine *(Decca F-10743)*
29 Sep 56	**6**	2	**Fanagalo** / Soft Summer Breeze *(Decca F-10786)* *Both sides as by the Frank Chacksfield Tunesmiths*

CHAMPS · 10

Los Angeles-based instrumental rock'n'roll outfit chiefly remembered for their Latin-flavoured hit 'Tequila', featuring the sax of Chuck Rio (Danny Flores).

29 Mar 58	**3**	1	★ **Tequila** / Train To Nowhere *(London HLU-8580)*
19 Jul 58	**3**	2	**El Rancho Rock** / Midnighter *(London HL-8655)*
15 Nov 58	**6**	2	**Chariot Rock** / Subway *(London HL-8715)*
4 Apr 59	**3**	1	**Gone Train** / Beatnik *(London HLH-8811)*
18 Apr 59	**18**	1	**Gone Train** / Beatnik *(London HLH-8811)* **re-entry**
30 May 59	**2**	1	**Caramba** / Moonlight Bay *(London HLH-8864)*
20 Feb 60	**3**	1	★ **Too MuchTequila** / Twenty Thousand Leagues *(London HLH-9052)*
12 Mar 60	**9**	1	★ **Too MuchTequila** / Twenty Thousand Leagues *(London HLH-9052)* **re-entry**

JEFF CHANDLER · 6

Rugged film and TV actor born Ira Grossel in Brooklyn, New York. He died in 1961, aged 42, from surgical malpractice following a baseball injury.

14 Aug 54	**10**	1	**I Should Care** / More Than Anyone *(Brunswick 05264)*
28 Aug 54	**10**	3	**I Should Care** / More Than Anyone *(Brunswick 05264)* **1st re-entry**
25 Sep 54	**30**	1	**I Should Care** / More Than Anyone *(Brunswick 05264)* **2nd re-entry**
19 Feb 55	**36**	1	**Always** / Everything Happens To Me *(Brunswick 05380)*

CHANTELS · 1

Black female singing quintet from the Bronx discovered by Richard Barrett, one of the first successful independent black record producers in the USA.

18 Apr 59	**16**	1	**Come Softly To Me** / Walking Through Dreamland *(H.M.V. POP-609)* *Both sides by Richard Barrett with the Chantels*

PAUL CHAPLAIN & HIS EMERALDS · 1

Rockin' quartet who recorded for the tiny Harper label in New York.

15 Oct 60	**2**	1	**Shortnin' Bread** / Nicotine *(London HLU-9205)*

GRADY CHAPMAN · 1

Former lead singer of the Robins trying his luck as solo artist.

3 Sep 60	**16**	1	**Sweet Thing** / I Know What I Want *(Mercury AMT-1107)*

RAY CHARLES · 3

Blind singer and pianist from Albany, Georgia born Ray Charles Robinson. He enjoyed phenomenal success with his unique blend of R&B and gospel, and later country music and blues.

22 Aug 59	**3**	1	**What'd I Say? (Parts 1 & 2)** *(London HLE-8917)*
4 Feb 61	**16**	1	**Ruby** / Hardhearted Hannah *(H.M.V. POP-825)*
25 Feb 61	**18**	1	**Ruby** / Hardhearted Hannah *(H.M.V. POP-825)* **re-entry**

CHARMS 2

R&B doo-wop quintet from Cincinnati led by Otis Williams.

23 Apr 55	**7**	1	**Hearts Of Stone** / Ko Ko Mo *(Parlophone R-3988)*
1 Mar 58	**8**	1	**Come On, Come On, Come On** /
			Ring Around My Finger *(Parlophone R-4397)*
			Both sides by Tiny Topsy and the Charms

CHUBBY CHECKER 7

Generously proportioned chicken-plucker Ernest Evans from Spring Gulley, South Carolina adopted a stage name inspired by Fats Domino and became King of the Twist.

29 Aug 59	**10**	1	**The Class** / Schooldays, Oh Schooldays *(Top Rank JAR-154)*
17 Sep 60	**8**	1	★ **The Twist** / Toot *(Columbia DB-4503)*
26 Nov 60	**9**	3	**The Hucklebuck** / **Whole Lotta Shakin' Goin' On** *(Columbia DB-4541)*
31 Dec 60	**11**	2	**The Hucklebuck** / **Whole Lotta Shakin' Goin' On** *(Columbia DB-4541)*
			re-entry

DON CHERRY 1

Big band singer born in Wichita Falls, Texas in 1924, whose big hits were 'Thinking Of You' (1950) and 'Band Of Gold' (1955). A keen competitive amateur golfer, he went pro in 1962.

| 19 May 56 | **5** | 1 | **Wild Cherry** / I'm Still A King To You *(Philips PB-581)* |

PETE CHESTER & THE CONSULATES 4

British instrumental group led by drummer Pete Chester, son of comedian Charlie Chester.

| 26 Nov 60 | **1** | 4 | ★ **Ten Swingin' Bottles** / Whole Lotta Shakin' On The Range |
| | | | *(Pye 7N.15305)* |

See also Five Chestnuts

CHIMES 1

Doo-wop group from Brooklyn, New York formed by Lenny Cocco in 1957.

| 18 Feb 61 | **7** | 1 | **Once In A While** / Summer Night *(London HLU-9283)* |

CHIPMUNKS

See David Seville

CHORDETTES 5

Smooth female quartet from Sheboygan, Wisconsin who registered on both sides of the Atlantic with 'Mr. Sandman', 'Born To Be With You' and 'Lollipop'.

10 Sep 55	**22**	1	**Humming Bird** / Lonely Lips *(London HLA-8169)*
24 Sep 55	**7**	1	**Humming Bird** / Lonely Lips *(London HLA-8169)* **re-entry**
18 Aug 56	**6**	1	★ **Born To Be With You** / Love Never Changes *(London HLA-8302)*
5 Apr 58	**1**	2	★ **Lollipop** / Baby, Come-A-Back-A *(London HLA-8584)*

CHORUS AND ORCHESTRA SINFONICA DELL'EIAR 1

Turin-based symphony orchestra founded in 1931 by Italy's public service broadcaster, EIAR. The recordings below date from 1941, three years before EIAR became RAI and the orchestra was merged with three others to form the Orchestra Sinfonica Nazionale della RAI.

23 Oct 54	**49**	1	**Nabucco (Act 3)** *(Cond. Ugo Tansini)* /
			I Lombardi Alla Prima Crociata (Act 4) *(Cond. Gino Marinuzzi)*
			(Parlophone Odeon BSP-3001)

KEITH CHRISTIE

See Jo Hunter etc.

EUGENE CHURCH   1

R&B singer born in St. Louis, Missouri in 1938. He recorded for a variety of labels between 1956 and 1963, but found greatest success on Class, for whom he recorded 'Pretty Girls Everywhere' and 'Miami'. He subsequently pursued a career in gospel music.

17 Oct 59	**14**	1	**Miami** / I Ain't Goin' For That *(London HL-8940)*

DENNIS CLANCY   2

Internationally popular Scottish tenor from Dundee who also performed with accordionist Arthur Spink as the 'Twa Braw Lads'.

12 Nov 60	**2**	2	**A Hundred Thousand Welcomes** / The Tartan *(Waverley SLP-507)* Both sides by Dennis Clancy with Johnstone's Scottish Accordion Band

JIMMY CLANTON   3

Teen idol from Baton Rouge, Louisiana, who debuted in 1958 with 'Just A Dream'.

16 Jan 60	**5**	1	**Go, Jimmy, Go** / I Trusted You *(Top Rank JAR-269)*
11 Jun 60	**8**	1	★ **Another Sleepless Night** / I'm Gonna Try *(Top Rank JAR-382)*
9 Jul 60	**7**	1	★ **Another Sleepless Night** / I'm Gonna Try *(Top Rank JAR-382)* **re-entry**

DEE CLARK   5

Black singer born in Blytheville, Arkansas and raised in Chicago. He had a string of R&B and pop hits in the late '50s and early '60s, including the million-selling 'Raindrops' (1961).

29 Aug 59	**1**	2	★ **Just Keep It Up** / Whispering Grass *(London HL-8915)*
24 Oct 59	**16**	1	**Hey Little Girl** / If It Wasn't For Love *(Top Rank JAR-196)*
7 Nov 59	**20**	2	**Hey Little Girl** / If It Wasn't For Love *(Top Rank JAR-196)* **re-entry**

PETULA CLARK   24

Child actor and singing star born in Epsom, Surrey in 1932. She went on to become one of the most successful British female recording artists of all time.

9 Oct 54	**11**	3	**Smile** / Somebody *(Polygon P-1128)*
15 Jan 55	**21**	3	★ **Majorca** / Fascinating Rhythm *(Polygon P-1146)*
12 Feb 55	**24**	1	★ **Majorca** / Fascinating Rhythm *(Polygon P-1146)* **re-entry**
5 Mar 55	**18**	1	**Somebody** / Smile *(Polygon P-1128)* **1st re-entry (flipped)**
19 Mar 55	**16**	1	**Somebody** / Smile *(Polygon P-1128)* **2nd re-entry**
28 May 55	**6**	1	**Crazy Otto Rag** (Petula Clark, the Radio Revellers, Joe 'Mr. Piano' Henderson and Friends) / **The Pendulum Song** (Petula Clark and the Radio Revellers) *(Polygon P-1169)*
11 Jun 55	**11**	2	**Crazy Otto Rag** / **The Pendulum Song** *(Polygon P-1169)* **re-entry**
19 Nov 55	**1**	1	★ **Suddenly There's A Valley** / With Your Love *(Pye Nixa N.15013)*
3 Mar 56	**17**	2	**Memories Are Made Of This** / Band Of Gold *(Pye Nixa N.15040)*
31 Mar 56	**9**	4	**Memories Are Made Of This** / Band Of Gold *(Pye Nixa N.15040)* **re-entry**
20 Jul 57	**7**	1	★ **With All My Heart** / Gonna Find Me A Bluebird *(Pye Nixa N.15096)*
22 Feb 58	**1**	1	★ **Baby Lover** / Little Blue Man *(Pye Nixa 7N.15126)*
26 Sep 59	**9**	1	**Adonis** / If I Had My Way *(Pye Nixa 7N.15220)*
15 Oct 60	**15**	1	**Cinderella Jones** / All Over Now *(Pye 7N.15281)*
21 Jan 61	**15**	1	★ **Sailor** / My Heart *(Pye 7N.15324)*

SANFORD CLARK   8

Rockabilly singer from Tulsa, Oklahoma whose classic debut recording, 'The Fool', hit the US Top Ten in 1956.

17 Oct 59	**16**	1	**New Kind Of Fool** / Run, Boy Run *(London HLW-8959)*
16 Jan 60	**11**	1	**Son-Of-A-Gun** / I Can't Help It *(London HLW-9026)*
13 Feb 60	**1**	2	**Son-Of-A-Gun** / I Can't Help It *(London HLW-9026)* **re-entry**
16 Apr 60	**2**	1	**Go On Home** / Pledging My Love *(London HLW-9095)*

Another smash hit by

MAX BYGRAVES

Try another Cherry Tree

(with Children's chorus)
Coupled with his comedy number
"Seventeen Tons"
Orchestra conducted by
FRANK CORDELL
POP208 5/7d. inc. tax. Also on 7″

'HIS MASTER'S VOICE" RECORD

THE GRAMOPHONE COMPANY LTD. (RECORD DIVISION) · 8-11 GREAT CASTLE STREET · LONDON · W.1

DAVE BRUBECK Quartet

ME AND MY SHADOW
AT A PERFUME COUNTER
FRENESI
MAM'SELLE

EPV 1063

vogue RECORDS

RONNIE CARROLL

"THE WISDOM OF A FOOL"

PB 667

coupled with "WITHOUT LOVE"

from **PHILIPS**

The Records of the Century

Another Smash Hit to follow 'Dark Moon'

Tony Brent

sings

Deep Within Me

COLUMBIA RECORDS

(Regd. Trade Mark of
Columbia Graphophone Co. Ltd.)

and

WHY ASK FOR THE MOON

DB3987 (45 & 78 r.p.m.)

E.M.I. RECORDS LTD. (Controlled by Electric & Musical Industries Ltd.), 8-11 Great Castle St., London W.1

Brook Brothers

30 Apr 60	**6**	1	**Go On Home** / Pledging My Love *(London HLW-9095)* ***1st re-entry***
28 May 60	**5**	1	**Go On Home** / Pledging My Love *(London HLW-9095)* ***2nd re-entry***
25 Jun 60	**14**	1	**Go On Home** / Pledging My Love *(London HLW-9095)* ***3rd re-entry***

KENNY CLARKE

See Paul Quinichette etc.

BUCK CLAYTON   1

Mainstream jazz trumpeter born Wilbur Clayton in Parsons, Kansas in 1928. He was associated for many years with Count Basie.

14 Jul 56	**15**	1	**JUMPIN' AT THE WOODSIDE** *(Philips BBL-7087)* 🔲
			Rock-A-Bye Basie / Jumpin' At The Woodside / Blue And Sentimental / Broadway

See also Count Basie
Norman Granz' Jazz At The Philharmonic

BUZZ CLIFFORD   1

Pop singer born Reese Clifford in Berwyn, Illinois. 'Baby Sittin' Boogie' was a big novelty hit on both sides of the Atlantic, but further success eluded him and he eventually turned to songwriting.

25 Feb 61	**13**	1	★ **Baby Sittin' Boogie** / Driftwood *(Fontana H-297)*

BETTY CLOONEY   2

Younger sister of Rosemary Clooney, with whom she performed as the Clooney Sisters from 1946 to 1949. After Rosemary went solo, Betty became a TV presenter and nightclub singer. They briefly reunited in 1954 for this recording of 'Sisters'.

8 Jan 55	**13**	2	**Sisters** *(Rosemary Clooney and Betty Clooney) (Philips PB-359)*
			Flip is 'Love – You Didn't Do Right By Me' by Rosemary Clooney

GAIL CLOONEY   1

Half-sister of Rosemary and Betty Clooney who decided not to pursue a show-business career.

23 Apr 55	**23**	1	**Open Up Your Heart** / The Lord Is Counting On You *(Philips PB-409)*
			Both sides by Little Sister Gail and Big Sister Rosemary Clooney

ROSEMARY CLOONEY   25

Older sister of Betty Clooney, with whom she performed as the Clooney Sisters from 1946 to 1949. Propelled to solo stardom in 1951 by her novelty recording 'Come On-A My House', she became one of the leading pop and jazz singers of the post-war era.

21 Aug 54	**34**	1	**Man And Woman** *(Rosemary Clooney and Guy Mitchell)* /
			Good Intentions *(Rosemary Clooney) (Philips PB-255)*
2 Oct 54	**11**	1	★ **This Ole House** / My Baby Sends Me *(Philips PB-336)*
8 Jan 55	**13**	2	**Sisters** *(Rosemary Clooney and Betty Clooney)* /
			Love – You Didn't Do Right By Me *(Rosemary Clooney)*
			(Philips PB-359)
8 Jan 55	**26**	1	**Count Your Blessings Instead Of Sheep** /
			Gee, I Wish I Was Back In The Army *(Philips PB-375)*
23 Apr 55	**9**	2	★ **Where Will The Dimple Be?** / Brahms' Lullaby *(Philips PB-428)*
23 Apr 55	**23**	1	**Open Up Your Heart** / The Lord Is Counting On You *(Philips PB-409)*
			Both sides by Little Sister Gail and Big Sister Rosemary Clooney
14 May 55	**10**	1	★ **Where Will The Dimple Be?** / Brahms' Lullaby *(Philips PB-428)*
			re-entry
8 Oct 55	**22**	4	**Go On By** / Sailor Boys Have Talk To Me In English *(Philips PB-499)*
12 Nov 55	**18**	2	**Go On By** / Sailor Boys Have Talk To Me In English *(Philips PB-499)*
			1st re-entry
24 Dec 55	**9**	2	**C-H-R-I-S-T-M-A-S** / Winter Wonderland *(Philips PB-530)*
4 Feb 56	**6**	1	**Go On By** / Sailor Boys Have Talk To Me In English *(Philips PB-499)*
			2nd re-entry

11 Feb 56	6	1	**Memories Of You** *(Benny Goodman Trio with Rosemary Clooney)* / It's Bad For Me *(Benny Goodman Sextet with Rosemary Clooney)* *(Philips PB-547)*
25 Feb 56	2	2	**Memories Of You** *(Benny Goodman Trio with Rosemary Clooney)* / It's Bad For Me *(Benny Goodman Sextet with Rosemary Clooney)* *(Philips PB-547)* ***1st re-entry***
31 Mar 56	19	1	**Memories Of You** *(Benny Goodman Trio with Rosemary Clooney)* / It's Bad For Me *(Benny Goodman Sextet with Rosemary Clooney)* *(Philips PB-547)* ***2nd re-entry***
21 Jun 58	2	3	**I Could Have Danced All Night** / I've Grown Accustomed To Your Face *(Philips PB-800)*

CLOVERS   1

Popular black vocal group from Washington, DC, whose hitmaking career stretched from 1951 to 1959. 'Love Potion No. 9' was their last US chart success.

10 Oct 59	10	1	**Love Potion No. 9** / Stay Awhile *(London HLT-8949)*

CLUB QUINTET   1

Studio group featured in the 1960 film, 'The Awakening'.

12 Nov 60	14	1	**Caravelle** / Bluer Than Blue *(Top Rank JAR-362)*

CLYDE VALLEY STOMPERS   46

Popular Scottish jazz band fronted by trombonist Ian Menzies and vocalist Mary McGowan.

1 Sep 56	1	4	**Keep Right On To The End Of The Road** / Uist Tramping Song *(Beltona BL-2648)*
8 Sep 56	2	2	**Old Rustic Bridge By The Mill** / I Love A Lassie *(Beltona BL-2649)*
15 Sep 56	2	5	**Pearly Gates** *(Vocal: Mary McGowan)* / Old Time Religion *(Vocal: Mary McGowan)* *(Beltona BL-2650)*
12 Jan 57	7	1	**Pearly Gates** *(Vocal: Mary McGowan)* / **Old Time Religion** *(Vocal: Mary McGowan)* *(Beltona BL-2650)* ***1st re-entry***
26 Jan 57	9	1	**Pearly Gates** *(Vocal: Mary McGowan)* / **Old Time Religion** *(Vocal: Mary McGowan)* *(Beltona BL-2650)* ***2nd re-entry***
1 Jun 57	3	2	**Milenberg Joys** *(Vocal: Mary McGowan)* / **Bill Bailey, Won't You Please Come Home** *(Vocal: Mary McGowan)* *(Decca Jazz F-10897)*
22 Jun 57	1	14	**Milenberg Joys** *(Vocal: Mary McGowan)* / **Bill Bailey, Won't You Please Come Home** *(Vocal: Mary McGowan)* *(Decca Jazz F-10897)* ***1st re-entry***
9 Nov 57	2	2	**Milenberg Joys** *(Vocal: Mary McGowan)* / **Bill Bailey, Won't You Please Come Home** *(Vocal: Mary McGowan)* *(Decca Jazz F-10897)* ***2nd re-entry***
9 Nov 57	10	1	**Pearly Gates** *(Vocal: Mary McGowan)* / Old Time Religion *(Vocal: Mary McGowan)* *(Beltona BL-2650)* ***3rd re-entry***
21 Dec 57	9	2	**Milenberg Joys** *(Vocal: Mary McGowan)* / **Bill Bailey, Won't You Please Come Home** *(Vocal: Mary McGowan)* *(Decca Jazz F-10897)* ***3rd re-entry***
18 Jan 58	7	1	**Milenberg Joys** *(Vocal: Mary McGowan)* / **Bill Bailey, Won't You Please Come Home** *(Vocal: Mary McGowan)* *(Decca Jazz F-10897)* ***4th re-entry***
8 Feb 58	15	1	**Milenberg Joys** *(Vocal: Mary McGowan)* / **Bill Bailey, Won't You Please Come Home** *(Vocal: Mary McGowan)* *(Decca Jazz F-10897)* ***5th re-entry***
16 Jul 60	1	10	★ <u>**The Fish Man**</u> / Salty Dog *(Vocal: Fiona Duncan)* *(Pye 7NJ-2031)* *Both sides as by Ian Menzies & His Clyde Valley Stompers*

See also Various Artists (SCOTS TRADITIONAL JAZZ CONCERT)

COASTERS 17

Black vocal group who specialised in humorous songs by Leiber & Stoller. 'Sorry But I'm Gonna Have To Pass' became a minor UK hit in 1994 after being featured in a Volkswagen TV commercial.

17 Aug 57	3	3	★ **Searchin'** / Young Blood *(London HLE-8450)*
14 Sep 57	4	1	★ **Searchin'** / Young Blood *(London HLE-8450)* *re-entry*
26 Jul 58	4	1	★ **Yakety Yak** / Zing! Went The Strings Of My Heart *(London HLE-8665)*
8 Nov 58	10	1	**Sorry But I'm Gonna Have To Pass** / The Shadow Knows *(London HLE-8729)*
14 Mar 59	2	2	★ **Charlie Brown** / Three Cool Cats *(London HLE-8819)*
20 Jun 59	2	8	**Along Came Jones** / That Is Rock And Roll *(London HLE-8882)*
24 Oct 59	1	1	★ **Poison Ivy** / I'm A Hog For You *(London HLE-8938)*

ERIC COATES (conductor)

See Concert Orchestra

EDDIE COCHRAN 17

Pioneering rocker born in Albert Lea, Minnesota in 1938. He was killed in a car crash at the age of 21 while on tour in the UK in 1960.

6 Apr 57	9	1	**20 Flight Rock** / Dark Lonely Street *(London HLU-8386)*
27 Apr 57	12	1	**20 Flight Rock** / Dark Lonely Street *(London HLU-8386)* *1st re-entry*
8 Jun 57	10	1	**20 Flight Rock** / Dark Lonely Street *(London HLU-8386)* *2nd re-entry*
22 Jun 57	8	1	**20 Flight Rock** / Dark Lonely Street *(London HLU-8386)* *3rd re-entry*
17 Aug 57	9	1	**20 Flight Rock** / Dark Lonely Street *(London HLU-8386)* *4th re-entry*
4 Oct 58	3	3	★ **Summertime Blues** / Love Again *(London HLU-8702)*
31 Jan 59	1	5	★ **C'mon Everybody** / Don't Ever Let Me Go *(London HLU-8792)*
26 Sep 59	1	3	★ **Somethin' Else** / Boll Weevil Song *(London HLU-8944)*
16 Jan 60	4	1	★ **Hallelujah, I Love Her So** / Little Angel *(London HLW-9022)*

ALMA COGAN 90

Dubbed 'The Girl With A Giggle In Her Voice', chirpy Alma Cogan was renowned for her fabulous gowns and was the highest-paid British female entertainer of her era. She tragically died from cancer in 1966, aged just 34.

19 Jun 54	18	1	**Make Love To Me** / Said The Little Moment *(H.M.V. B-10677)*
3 Jul 54	1	5	★ **Little Things Mean A Lot** / Canoodlin' Rag *(H.M.V. B-10717)*
10 Jul 54	20	5	**Make Love To Me** / Said The Little Moment *(H.M.V. B-10677)* *re-entry*
21 Aug 54	5	1	★ **Little Things Mean A Lot** / Canoodlin' Rag *(H.M.V. B-10717)* *re-entry*
21 Aug 54	24	1	**The Little Shoemaker** / Chiqui-Chaqui *(H.M.V. B-10698)*
4 Sep 54	10	1	**The Little Shoemaker** / Chiqui-Chaqui *(H.M.V. B-10698)* *re-entry*
27 Nov 54	42	1	★ **I Can't Tell A Waltz From A Tango** / Christmas Cards *(H.M.V. B-10786)*
27 Nov 54	50	1	**Skokiaan** / This Ole House *(H.M.V. B-10761)*
12 Feb 55	1	1	★ **The Naughty Lady Of Shady Lane** / **Mambo Italiano** *(H.M.V. B-10832)*
19 Feb 55	4	6	**Softly, Softly** / **Paper Kisses** *(H.M.V. B-10828)*
23 Apr 55	3	4	**Tweedle-Dee** / More Than Ever Now *(H.M.V. B-10848)*
7 May 55	5	9	**Chee-Chee-Oo-Chee** / Tika Tika Tok *(H.M.V. B-10862)*
14 May 55	17	2	★ **Dreamboat** / Irish Mambo *(H.M.V. B-10872)*
28 May 55	36	1	**Tweedle-Dee** / More Than Ever Now *(H.M.V. B-10848)* *1st re-entry*
11 Jun 55	31	1	**Tweedle-Dee** / More Than Ever Now *(H.M.V. B-10848)* *2nd re-entry*
18 Jun 55	25	1	**Where Will The Dimple Be** / Keep Me In Mind *(H.M.V. B-10887)*
20 Aug 55	19	1	**Where Will The Dimple Be** / Keep Me In Mind *(H.M.V. B-10887)* *re-entry*
27 Aug 55	13	2	★ **The Banjo's Back In Town** / Go On By *(H.M.V. B-10917)*
3 Sep 55	26	1	**Give A Fool A Chance** / Got'n Idea *(H.M.V. B-10896)*
17 Sep 55	19	1	★ **The Banjo's Back In Town** / Go On By *(H.M.V. B-10917)* *re-entry*
29 Oct 55	12	2	**Hernando's Hideaway** / Blue Again *(H.M.V. B-10929)*
26 Nov 55	28	1	★ **Never Do A Tango With An Eskimo** / Twenty Tiny Fingers *(H.M.V. POP-129)*
3 Dec 55	29	1	**Hernando's Hideaway** / Blue Again *(H.M.V. B-10929)* *re-entry*

10 Dec 55	6	2	★	Never Do A Tango With An Eskimo / Twenty Tiny Fingers
				(H.M.V. POP-129) re-entry
7 Jan 56	1	3		Love And Marriage / Sycamore Tree (H.M.V. POP-163)
4 Feb 56	2	3		Love And Marriage / Sycamore Tree (H.M.V. POP-163) 1st re-entry
3 Mar 56	4	4		Love And Marriage / Sycamore Tree (H.M.V. POP-163) 2nd re-entry
17 Mar 56	3	2	★	Willie Can / Lizzie Borden (H.M.V. POP-187)
14 Apr 56	21	1		Don't Ring-a Da Bell / Bluebell (H.M.V. POP-189)
28 Apr 56	10	3		Don't Ring-a Da Bell / Bluebell (H.M.V. POP-189) 1st re-entry
26 May 56	1	6		Don't Ring-a Da Bell / Bluebell (H.M.V. POP-189) 2nd re-entry
23 Jun 56	8	1	★	The Birds And The Bees / Why Do Fools Fall In Love?
				(H.M.V. POP-223)
7 Jul 56	6	1	★	Why Do Fools Fall In Love? / The Birds And The Bees
				(H.M.V. POP-223) re-entry (flipped)
13 Oct 56	1	2		Mama Teach Me To Dance / I'm In Love Again (H.M.V. POP-239)
27 Oct 56	8	1	★	In The Middle Of The House / Two Innocent Hearts
				(H.M.V. POP-261)
12 Jan 57	6	1	★	You, Me And Us / Three Brothers (H.M.V. POP-284)
23 Mar 57	15	1	★	Whatever Lola Wants / Lucky Lips (H.M.V. POP-317)
17 May 58	19	1		Stairway Of Love / Comes Love (H.M.V. POP-482)
26 Jul 58	17	1		Fly Away Lovers / Sorry, Sorry, Sorry (H.M.V. POP-500)
16 Aug 58	11	1		Fly Away Lovers / Sorry, Sorry, Sorry (H.M.V. POP-500) re-entry
11 Apr 59	2	2		Pink Shoe Laces / The Universe (H.M.V. POP-608)
21 Nov 59	2	4	★	The Train Of Love (Alma Cogan) /
				The 'I Love You' Bit (Alma Cogan with Ocher Nebbish)
				(H.M.V. POP-760)

COZY COLE   1

Jazz drummer born William Randolph Cole in East Orange, New Jersey in 1909. He obviously had a sense of humour, as the follow-up to his hit was called 'Turvy'.

29 Nov 58	9	1	★	Topsy (Parts 1 & 2) (London HL-8750)

NAT 'KING' COLE   78

Popular jazz pianist from Montgomery, Alabama who made a seamless transition to smooth-voiced pop balladeer in the late '40s. A heavy smoker, he died of lung cancer in 1965 at the age of 45. His daughter, Natalie Cole, also became a successful singer.

19 Jun 54	4	1		SINGS FOR TWO IN LOVE (Capitol LC-6627) LP
				Love Is Here To Stay / A Handful Of Stars / This Can't Be Love / A Little Street
				Where Old Friends Meet / There Goes My Heart / Dinner For One, Please James /
				Almost Like Being In Love / Tenderly
19 Jun 54	21	1		Sleeping Beauty / Lovelight (Capitol CL-14126)
28 Aug 54	1	2	★	Smile / Make Her Mine (Capitol CL-14149)
23 Oct 54	7	7		There Goes My Heart / I Am In Love (Capitol CL-14172)
27 Nov 54	3	7		Hold My Hand / If I Give My Heart To You (Capitol CL-14203)
11 Dec 54	14	3		Papa Loves Mambo / Teach Me Tonight (Capitol CL-14207)
18 Dec 54	4	8		Unbelievable / Hajji Baba (Capitol CL-14155)
18 Dec 54	24	1		There Goes My Heart / I Am In Love (Capitol CL-14172) re-entry
15 Jan 55	12	3		Papa Loves Mambo / Teach Me Tonight (Capitol CL-14207)
				1st re-entry
5 Feb 55	17	1	★	A Blossom Fell / Alone Too Long (Capitol CL-14235)
12 Feb 55	30	1		Teach Me Tonight / Papa Loves Mambo (Capitol CL-14207)
				2nd re-entry (flipped)
19 Feb 55	3	1	★	A Blossom Fell / Alone Too Long (Capitol CL-14235) re-entry
5 Mar 55	15	2		Hajji Baba / Unbelievable (Capitol CL-14155) re-entry (flipped)
5 Mar 55	15	1		Teach Me Tonight / Papa Loves Mambo (Capitol CL-14207)
				3rd re-entry
2 Apr 55	15	1		Papa Loves Mambo / Teach Me Tonight (Capitol CL-14207)
				4th re-entry (flipped)
16 Apr 55	5	3		The Sand And The Sea / Darling Je Vous Aime Beaucoup
				(Capitol CL-14251)

21 May 55	8	2	**Long, Long Ago** (Nat 'King' Cole and Dean Martin) /
			Open Up The Doghouse (Dean Martin and Nat 'King' Cole)
			(Capitol CL-14215)
11 Jun 55	25	2	**Open Up The Doghouse** (Dean Martin and Nat 'King' Cole) /
			Long, Long Ago (Nat 'King' Cole and Dean Martin)
			(Capitol CL-14215) **re-entry (flipped)**
16 Jul 55	18	1	**I'd Rather Have The Blues** / Annabelle (Capitol CL-14317)
13 Aug 55	8	2	★ <u>My One Sin</u> / Don't Hurt The Girl (Capitol CL-14327)
29 Oct 55	26	1	★ <u>Love Is A Many Splendored Thing</u> / Autumn Leaves
			(Capitol CL-14364)
20 Oct 56	10	1	**My Dream Sonata** / I Just Found Out About Love (Capitol CL-14632)
19 Jan 57	7	1	**To The Ends Of The Earth** / Toyland (Capitol CL-14661)
2 Mar 57	3	5	**You Are My First Love** / Ballerina (Capitol CL-14688)
13 Apr 57	15	1	**NIGHT LIGHTS** (Capitol EAP1-801) **EP**
			Night Lights / Nothing Ever Changes My Love For You / To The Ends Of The Earth /
			My Dream Sonata
29 Jun 57	8	1	★ **It's All In The Game** / <u>When Rock And Roll Came To Trinidad</u>
			(Capitol CL-14733)
14 Sep 57	4	1	★ <u>My Personal Possession</u> (Nat 'King' Cole and the Four Knights) /
			Send For Me (Nat 'King' Cole) (Capitol CL-14765)
5 Oct 57	3	2	★ <u>My Personal Possession</u> (Nat 'King' Cole and the Four Knights) /
			Send For Me (Nat 'King' Cole) (Capitol CL-14765) **re-entry**
15 Feb 58	1	1	**Angel Smile** / Back In My Arms (Capitol CL-14820)
21 Jun 58	1	6	**Looking Back** / Just For The Fun Of It (Capitol CL-14882)
2 Aug 58	16	1	**Come Closer To Me** / Nothing In The World (Capitol CL-14898)
16 Aug 58	18	1	**Looking Back** / Just For The Fun Of It (Capitol CL-14882) **re-entry**
28 Feb 59	8	1	**Madrid** / Give Me Your Love (Capitol CL-14987)
4 Apr 59	14	1	**Madrid** / Give Me Your Love (Capitol CL-14987) **re-entry**
9 May 59	4	1	★ <u>You Made Me Love You</u> / I Must Be Dreaming (Capitol CL-15017)
27 Aug 60	16	2	**My Love** / Steady (Capitol CL-15144)
			Both sides by Nat 'King' Cole and Stan Kenton (vocal)
28 Jan 61	11	1	★ <u>The World In My Arms</u> / The Very Thought Of You (Capitol CL-15178)

GLENDA COLLINS   1

Talented teenage pop vocalist from London touted by Decca as their answer to Helen Shapiro.
She later recorded for legendary producer Joe Meek, but sadly never got that elusive hit.

| 17 Dec 60 | 8 | 1 | **Take A Chance** / Crazy Guy (Decca F-11280) |

TOMMY COLLINS   2

Philosophical country singer/songwriter from Oklahoma born Leonard Raymond Sipes.

5 Apr 58	6	1	**Think It Over, Boys** / All Of The Monkeys Ain't In The Zoo
			(Capitol CL-14838)
25 Oct 58	6	1	**It Tickles** / Let Down (Capitol CL-14894)

JERRY COLONNA   11

Madcap singer, songwriter and comedian from Boston, Massachusetts with bulging eyes and an
enormous handlebar moustache. His unique singing style, once described as a 'comic caterwaul',
can be heard to good effect on the records below.

10 Jul 54	20	4	**Ebb Tide** / The Velvet Glove (Brunswick 05243)
23 Oct 54	5	2	**Ebb Tide** / The Velvet Glove (Brunswick 05243) **1st re-entry**
20 Nov 54	23	1	**Sweet Adeline** / Down By The Old Mill Stream (Brunswick 05125)
30 Apr 55	21	2	**Let Me Go, Lover** / I Want To Love You Cara Mia (Parlophone R-4007)
			Both sides by Jerry Colonna and the Three Lovers
28 May 55	12	1	**Let Me Go, Lover** / I Want To Love You Cara Mia (Parlophone R-4007)
			re-entry
9 Jul 55	19	1	**Ebb Tide** / The Velvet Glove (Brunswick 05243) **2nd re-entry**

COLUMBIA PICTURES ORCHESTRA   1

In addition to supplying a wide variety of musical backings for every kind of film, Columbia's in-house orchestra recorded extensively under the leadership of Morris Stoloff, the studio's Musical Director from 1936 to 1962.

| 19 May 56 | 12 | 1 | ★ **Moonglow _and_ Theme from 'Picnic'** *(Cond. Morris Stoloff)* / Theme from 'Picnic' *(Cond. George Duning) (Brunswick 05553)* |

KEN COLYER'S JAZZMEN   14

Influential New Orleans-style jazz trumpeter and skiffle pioneer born in Great Yarmouth, Norfolk in 1928. The first line-up of his band included Chris Barber, Monty Sunshine and Lonnie Donegan.

11 Dec 54	30	3	**BACK TO THE DELTA** *(Decca LF-1196)* **LP**
			Ken Colyer's Jazzmen: Sing On / Lord, Lord, Lord, You Sure Been Good To Me / Faraway Blues / Moose March / *Ken Colyer's Skiffle Group:* Midnight Special / Casey Jones / K.C. Moan / *Ken Colyer's Jazzmen:* Saturday Night Function / Shim-Me-Sha-Wabble
15 Jan 55	15	2	**BACK TO THE DELTA** *(Decca LF-1196)* **LP** *re-entry*
3 Sep 55	8	1	**Red Wing** / It Looks Like A Big Time Tonight *(Decca Jazz F-10565)*
10 Sep 55	22	1	**The Entertainer** / If You Ever Cease To Love *(Decca Jazz F-10519)*
17 Sep 55	11	2	**Red Wing** / It Looks Like A Big Time Tonight *(Decca Jazz F-10565)* *re-entry*
24 Sep 55	23	1	**If You Ever Cease To Love** / The Entertainer *(Decca Jazz F-10519)* *re-entry (flipped)*
12 Nov 55	31	1	**Take This Hammer** / Down By The Riverside *(Decca Jazz F-10631)* *Both sides by Ken Colyer's Skiffle Group*
24 Mar 56	14	1	**Down By The Riverside** / Take This Hammer *(Decca Jazz F-10631)* *1st re-entry (flipped)*
28 Apr 56	10	1	**Take This Hammer** / Down By The Riverside *(Decca Jazz F-10631)* *2nd re-entry (flipped)*
30 Jun 56	10	1	**Mule Skinner** / Down Bound Train *(Decca Jazz F-10751)* *Both sides by Ken Colyer's Skiffle Group*

PERRY COMO   32

Smooth balladeer born Pierino Como in Canonsburg, Pennsylvania. Thanks to his professionalism and relaxed, romantic style, he enjoyed a long and successful career as a singer and TV personality.

23 Oct 54	38	1	★ **Papa Loves Mambo** / There Never Was A Night So Beautiful *(H.M.V. B-10776)*
13 Nov 54	8	4	★ **Papa Loves Mambo** / There Never Was A Night So Beautiful *(H.M.V. B-10776)* *re-entry*
19 Mar 55	3	5	**Ko Ko Mo** / You'll Always Be My Lifetime Sweetheart *(H.M.V. B-10841)*
30 Apr 55	10	1	**Ko Ko Mo** / You'll Always Be My Lifetime Sweetheart *(H.M.V. B-10841)* *1st re-entry*
11 Jun 55	13	1	**You'll Always Be My Lifetime Sweetheart** / Ko Ko Mo *(H.M.V. B-10841)* *2nd re-entry (flipped)*
29 Oct 55	37	1	★ **Tina Marie** / Home For The Holidays *(H.M.V. POP-103)*
19 Nov 55	1	5	★ **Tina Marie** / Home For The Holidays *(H.M.V. POP-103)* *re-entry*
14 Apr 56	6	1	★ **Juke Box Baby** / The Things I Didn't Do *(H.M.V. POP-191)*
14 Jul 56	1	3	**SO SMOOTH** *(H.M.V. 7EG-8171)* **EP**
			No Other Love / You Do Something To Me / One For My Baby / In The Still Of The Night
20 Apr 57	1	5	**Round And Round** / **My House Is Your House** *(H.M.V. POP-328)*
1 Jun 57	2	1	**The Girl With The Golden Braids** / My Little Baby *(R.C.A. RCA-1001)*
1 Jun 57	10	1	**Round And Round** / My House Is Your House *(H.M.V. POP-328)* *re-entry*
3 May 58	11	1	★ **Kewpie Doll** / Dance Only With Me *(R.C.A. RCA-1055)*
1 Nov 58	2	1	★ **Love Makes The World Go 'round** / **Mandolins In The Moonlight** *(R.C.A. RCA-1086)*
20 Feb 60	15	1	★ **Delaware** / I Know What God Is *(R.C.A. RCA-1170)*

BOBBY COMSTOCK & THE COUNTS 2

A native of Ithaca, New York, Bobby Comstock ran a slick blues-rock combo that often backed other artists on tour. He launched his career with these rocked-up versions of country classics.

21 Nov 59	**21**	1	**Tennessee Waltz** / Sweet Talk *(Top Rank JAR-223)*
26 Mar 60	**4**	1	**Jambalaya** / Let's Talk It Over *(London HLE-9080)*

CONCERT ORCHESTRA, cond. Eric Coates 12

Nottinghamshire-born Coates composed numerous epic themes including 'The Dam Busters March' and 'By The Sleepy Lagoon', the signature tune for BBC Radio's 'Desert Island Discs'.

22 Oct 55	**2**	5	**The Dam Busters March** / Sound And Vision *(Pye Nixa N.15003)*
3 Dec 55	**29**	1	**The Dam Busters March** / Sound And Vision *(Pye Nixa N.15003)* **1st re-entry**
17 Dec 55	**1**	5	**The Dam Busters March** / Sound And Vision *(Pye Nixa N.15003)* **2nd re-entry**
19 May 56	**9**	1	**The Dam Busters March** / Sound And Vision *(Pye Nixa N.15003)* **3rd re-entry**

CONCERTGEBOUW ORCHESTRA OF AMSTERDAM, cond. Erich Kleiber 3

Symphony orchestra founded in 1888 and considered to be one of the world's finest. They now have almost one thousand recordings to their name.

19 Jun 54	**2**	2	**BEETHOVEN – SYMPHONY NO. 5 IN C MINOR, OP. 67** *(Decca LXT-2851)* **LP** First Movement: Allegro Con Brio / Second Movement: Andante Con Moto / Third Movement: Scherzo (Allegro) / Fourth Movement: Allegro
25 Sep 54	**25**	1	**BEETHOVEN – SYMPHONY NO. 5 IN C MINOR, OP. 67** *(Decca LXT-2851)* **LP** *re-entry*

RAY CONNIFF 3

Choirmaster, orchestra leader and arranger born in Attleboro, Massachusetts in 1916. He became a prolific MOR album artist in the '60s.

30 Jul 60	**14**	1	**Smoke Gets In Your Eyes** / Paradise *(Philips PB-1048)* Both sides by Ray Conniff & His Orchestra and Chorus
12 Nov 60	**11**	1	**Here Comes Santa Claus** / Winter Wonderland *(Philips PB-1071)* Both sides by the Ray Conniff Singers
14 Jan 61	**20**	1	**Smoke Gets In Your Eyes** / Paradise *(Philips PB-1048)* *re-entry*

EDRIC CONNOR 6

Pioneering calypso singer, actor and folklorist born in Trinidad in 1913. He was based in the UK from 1944 until his death from a stroke in 1968.

6 Apr 57	**1**	6	★ <u>**Manchester United Calypso**</u> / Yorumba Highlife *(Oriole CB-1362)*

See also Original London Cast (SUMMER SONG)

RUSS CONWAY 17

Pianist born Trevor Stanford in Bristol in 1925. He was enormously popular in the late '50s and early '60s, and also accompanied stars like Gracie Fields and Joan Regan.

27 Jul 57	**3**	1	**Soho Fair** / The Spotlight Waltz *(Columbia DB-3971)*
2 Nov 57	**6**	3	**The Red Cat** / Late Extra *(Columbia DB-3999)*
7 Dec 57	**8**	2	**Piano Pops No. 1 (Parts 1 & 2) [M]** *(Columbia DB-4015)* Love Letters In The Sand – In The Middle Of An Island – Bye Bye Love / Around The World – Tammy – We Will Make Love
29 Mar 58	**8**	1	**Piano Pops No. 3 (Parts 1 & 2) [M]** *(Columbia DB-4097)* Love Me Forever – April Love – Magic Moments / The Story Of My Life – Sugartime – Mandy (The Pansy)
26 Jul 58	**14**	2	★ <u>**Got A Match**</u> / Toby's Walk *(Columbia DB-4166)*

| 20 Dec 58 | 1 | 2 | 'My Fair Lady' Pops (Parts 1 & 2) [M] *(Columbia DB-4191)* |

'My Fair Lady' Pops (Parts 1 & 2) [M] *(Columbia DB-4191)*
On The Street Where You Live – With A Little Bit Of Luck – I Could Have Danced All Night / Wouldn't It Be Loverly – Get Me To The Church On Time – I've Grown Accustomed To Her Face

10 Jan 59   3   1   ★ **The World Outside** / Love Like Ours *(Columbia DB-4234)*

14 Feb 59   7   1   ★ **Side Saddle** / Pixilated Penguin *(Columbia DB-4256)*

9 May 59   1   1   ★ **Roulette** / Trampolina *(Columbia DB-4298)*

14 Nov 59   6   1   ★ **More And More Party Pops (Parts 1 & 2) [M]** *(Columbia DB-4373)*
The Sheik Of Araby – Who Were You With Last Night – Any Old Iron / Tiptoe Through The Tulips – If You Were The Only Girl In The World – When I Leave The World Behind

19 Mar 60   10   1   ★ **MY CONCERTO FOR YOU** *(Columbia 33SX-1214)* **LP**
My Concerto For You / The Way To The Stars / Dream Of Olwen / Dusk / The Lonely Melody / The Warsaw Concerto / Autumn Concerto / Forgotten Dreams / Cornish Rhapsody / Jeannie / Till / La Mer

19 Nov 60   21   1   ★ **PARTY TIME** *(Columbia 33SX-1279)* **LP**
The Dark Town Strutters' Ball / Oh, Johnny! Oh, Johnny! Oh! / You Were Meant For Me / Toot, Toot, Tootsie! (Goo'bye) / When The Red, Red Robin Comes Bob, Bob, Bobbin' Along / Give My Regards To Broadway / Miss Annabelle Lee / Rock-A-Bye Your Baby With A Dixie Melody / Put Your Arms Around Me, Honey / Rolling Round The World / Painting The Clouds With Sunshine / Down Yonder / A Gal In Calico / I'm Sitting On Top Of The World / Carolina In The Morning / Swanee

SAM COOKE   5

Pioneering and hugely successful black singer/songwriter from Clarksdale, Mississippi who racked up over forty Billboard 'Hot 100' hits. He was shot dead in a motel in 1964 at the age of 29.

23 Nov 57   8   1   ★ **You Send Me** / Summertime *(London HLU-8506)*

4 Jan 58   2   2   ★ **You Send Me** / Summertime *(London HLU-8506)*
re-entry

2 Jul 60   10   1   ★ **Wonderful World** / Along The Navajo Trail *(H.M.V. POP-754)*

21 Jan 61   20   1   **Sad Mood** / Love Me *(R.C.A. RCA-1221)*

BOB COOPER SEXTET   8

West Coast jazz saxophonist born in Pittsburgh, Pennsylvania in 1925. He joined Stan Kenton's band in 1945 and ended up marrying their singer, June Christy.

4 Dec 54   10   3   **KENTON PRESENTS JAZZ – BOB COOPER** *(Capitol KPL-102)* **LP**
Group Activity / Excursion / Polka Dots And Moonbeams / The Way You Look Tonight / Solo Plight / Lisbon Lady / When The Sun Comes Out / She Didn't Say Yes

1 Jan 55   16   2   **KENTON PRESENTS JAZZ – BOB COOPER** *(Capitol KPL-102)* **LP**
1st re-entry

22 Jan 55   10   3   **KENTON PRESENTS JAZZ – BOB COOPER** *(Capitol KPL-102)* **LP**
2nd re-entry

See also Howard Rumsey's Lighthouse All Stars

TERENCE COOPER   1

Actor born in Carnmoney, Northern Ireland in 1933. He is perhaps most famous for appearing in the James Bond parody, 'Casino Royale' (1967), though he starred in many New Zealand TV series during the '70s and '80s. He later opened a curry restaurant in Auckland.

3 Oct 59   23   1   **Lovely Lover** / Kind Fate *(Decca F-11165)*
Both sides by Stephanie Voss and Terence Cooper

See also Original London Cast (LOCK UP YOUR DAUGHTERS)

COWBOY COPAS 8

Lloyd 'Cowboy' Copas was killed in the 1963 plane crash that also claimed the lives of fellow country music stars Patsy Cline and Hawkshaw Hawkins. 'Alabam', his biggest US hit, topped the Billboard C&W chart in the spring of 1960.

| 26 Nov 60 | **11** | 3 | **Alabam** / I Can *(Melodisc 45/1566)* |
| 7 Jan 61 | **4** | 5 | **Alabam** / I Can *(Melodisc 45/1566)* ***re-entry*** |

HÉLÈNE CORDET 4

French actress and sometime girlfriend of the Duke of Edinburgh who hosted the early '50s Saturday evening TV cabaret spectacular, 'Café Continental'.

| 10 Jul 54 | **20** | 4 | **Ki Ri** / Hold Me Close *(Planet E-1011)* |

FERNANDO CORENA with ORCHESTRA DEI POMMERIGGI MUSICALI DI MILANO, *cond.* Bruno Amaducci 1

Celebrated Swiss bass opera singer who enjoyed a long and successful residency at New York's Metropolitan Opera from 1954 to 1978.

| 27 Nov 54 | **59** | 1 | **CIMAROSA – IL MAESTRO DI CAPPELLA** *(Decca LW-5112)* **LP** |
| | | | Intermezzo Giocoso for Basso-Buffo and Orchestra (Parts 1 and 2) |

DON CORNELL 13

Smooth baritone born Luigi Varlaro in New York in 1919. He was a top headliner in the late '40s and '50s.

5 Feb 55	**7**	3	**S'posin'** / I Was Lucky *(Vogue Coral Q-2037)*
12 Mar 55	**1**	5	**No Man Is An Island** / All At Once *(Vogue Coral Q-72058)*
16 Apr 55	**18**	1	★ <u>**Stranger In Paradise**</u> / The Devil's In Your Eyes *(Vogue Coral Q-72073)*
11 Jun 55	**24**	1	**Unchained Melody** / Most Of All *(Vogue Coral Q-72080)*
29 Oct 55	**35**	1	**Love Is A Many Splendoured Thing** / The Bible Tells Me So *(Vogue Coral Q-72104)*
24 Dec 55	**4**	2	**Love Is A Many Splendoured Thing** / The Bible Tells Me So *(Vogue Coral Q-72104)* ***re-entry***

LYN CORNELL 3

Pop and jazz singer from Liverpool. Originally a member of the Vernons Girls, she left to pursue a solo career in 1960. She subsequently recorded with the Carefrees in 1964 ('We Love You Beatles') and formed a duo called the Pearls with former Vernons Girl Ann Simmons in the 1970s.

7 May 60	**6**	1	**Like Love** / Demon Lover *(Decca F-11227)*
15 Oct 60	**12**	1	★ <u>**Never On Sunday**</u> / Swain Kelly *(Decca F-11277)*
17 Dec 60	**20**	1	**The Angel And The Stranger** / Xmas Stocking *(Decca F-11301)*

CORO MIXTO 4

Brazilian choir with a song from the 1953 cult film 'O Cangaceiro' (The Bandit). Their name should properly be spelt 'Côro Misto' (Portugese for 'mixed chorus/choir'), rather than 'Coro Mixto', which is Spanish.

| 28 Aug 54 | **6** | 4 | **Mulher Rendeira** *(H.M.V. JO-377)* |
| | | | The flip, 'Lua Bonita' by Zé do Norte, also bubbled under |

CORONETS 31

Mixed vocal quintet formed by Mike Sammes and Bill Shepherd. As well as recording in their own right, they also sang backing vocals for other UK artists. Following Shepherd's departure in 1956, Sammes expanded the group and created the even more successful Mike Sammes Singers.

| 2 Oct 54 | **31** | 1 | **I Can't Believe That You're In Love With Me** / Try Again *(Columbia DB-3517)* |
| | | | Both sides by Micky Andrews with the Jackie Brown Quintet and the Coronets |

15 Jan 55	42	1	★ **Don't Go To Strangers** / Surprisingly *(Columbia DB-3555)*
			Both sides by Ronnie Harris and the Coronets
14 May 55	2	9	**The Crazy Otto Rag** / **Hey Mr. Banjo** *(Columbia DB-3620)*
			Both sides by the Big Ben Banjo Band with the Coronets
9 Jul 55	3	5	★ **That's How A Love Song Was Born** / The Voice *(Columbia DB-3640)*
			Both sides by Ray Burns with the Coronets
13 Aug 55	5	2	**The Crazy Otto Rag** / **Hey Mr. Banjo** *(Columbia DB-3620)*
			1st re-entry
3 Sep 55	21	1	**The Crazy Otto Rag** / **Hey Mr. Banjo** *(Columbia DB-3620)*
			2nd re-entry
22 Oct 55	4	5	★ **Twenty Tiny Fingers** / **Meet Me On The Corner** *(Columbia DB-3671)*
10 Dec 55	12	1	**Make It A Party (Parts 1 & 2) [M]** *(Columbia DB-3678)*
			Who Were You With Last Night – Daddy Wouldn't Buy Me A Bow-Wow – John
			Brown's Body – Any Old Iron / Don't Dilly Dally On The Way – Dear Old Pals –
			Just Like The Ivy – Knees Up Mother Brown
24 Dec 55	26	1	**Make It A Party (Parts 1 & 2) [M]** *(Columbia DB-3678)* **re-entry**
18 Feb 56	4	2	**Lizzie Borden** / My Believing Heart *(Columbia DB-3728)*
10 Mar 56	13	2	**Lizzie Borden** / My Believing Heart *(Columbia DB-3728)* **1st re-entry**
31 Mar 56	8	1	**Lizzie Borden** / My Believing Heart *(Columbia DB-3728)* **2nd re-entry**

See also Jean Campbell
Knightsbridge Chorale
Original Soundtrack (IT'S GREAT TO BE YOUNG)

BOB CORT SKIFFLE GROUP — 4

Early exponent of skiffle who hailed from Loughborough. His 'Six-Five Special' was used as the theme for early episodes of the groundbreaking BBC TV pop show before Don Lang took over.

26 Jan 57	3	1	**Don't You Rock Me Daddy-O** / It Takes A Worried Man To Sing
			A Worried Blues *(Decca Jazz FJ-10831)*
16 Mar 57	18	1	**It Takes A Worried Man To Sing A Worried Blues** /
			Don't You Rock Me Daddy-O *(Decca Jazz FJ-10831)*
			re-entry (flipped)
1 Jun 57	5	1	**Six-Five Special** / Roll Jen Jenkins *(Decca F-10892)*
			Both sides by the Bob Cort Skiffle
6 Jul 57	4	1	**School Day** / Ain't It A Shame *(Decca F-10905)*
			Both sides by the Bob Cort Skiffle

DAVE 'BABY' CORTEZ — 3

Organist from Detroit born David Cortez Clowney. He scored eight instrumental hits in the States including the chart-topping 'Happy Organ', which just failed to break through for him in the UK.

23 May 59	1	1	**The Happy Organ** / Love Me As I Love You *(London HLU-8852)*
6 Jun 59	2	2	**The Happy Organ** / Love Me As I Love You *(London HLU-8852)*
			re-entry

DON COSTA & His Orchestra and Chorus — 3

Boston-born arranger and producer who worked with Paul Anka, the Ames Brothers and later Frank Sinatra.

28 Nov 59	10	1	**I Walk The Line** / Cat Walk *(London HLT-8992)*
2 Jan 60	4	1	**I Walk The Line** / Cat Walk *(London HLT-8992)*
			re-entry
8 Oct 60	1	1	★ **Never On Sunday** / The Sound Of Love *(London HLT-9195)*

BILLY COTTON & His Band — 13

Top British bandleader, singer and entertainer, whose popular Sunday lunchtime radio show (which always commenced with his famous war cry, 'Wakey, wakey!') ran from 1949 until 1968.

24 Sep 55	13	1	**Yellow Rose Of Texas** *(Vocal: The Bandits)* /
			Domani *(Vocal: Alan Breeze and the Bandits)* *(Decca F-10602)*
8 Oct 55	2	2	**Yellow Rose Of Texas** / Domani *(Decca F-10602)* **1st re-entry**

29 Oct 55	15	1	★ **The Dam Busters March** /
			Bring Your Smile Along *(Vocal: Alan Breeze and the Bandits)*
			(Decca F-10630)
29 Oct 55	15	1	**Yellow Rose Of Texas** / Domani *(Decca F-10602)* *2nd re-entry*
12 Nov 55	12	3	**Yellow Rose Of Texas** / Domani *(Decca F-10602)* *3rd re-entry*
31 Dec 55	5	2	**Yellow Rose Of Texas** / Domani *(Decca F-10602)* *4th re-entry*
3 Mar 56	13	3	**Robin Hood** *(Vocal: Doreen Stephens, Alan Breeze and the Bandits)* /
			Happy Trails *(Vocal: Doreen Stephens and Alan Breeze)*
			(Decca F-10682)

WARREN COVINGTON

See Tommy Dorsey Orchestra

NOËL COWARD   1

Flamboyant playwright, actor, singer, composer and wit born in Teddington, Middlesex in 1899.

20 Oct 56	2	1	**AT LAS VEGAS** *(Philips BBL-7108)* 🔲
			Medley: I'll See You Again – Dance, Little Lady – Poor Little Rich Girl – A Room
			With A View – Someday I'll Find You – I'll Follow My Secret Heart – If Love Were
			All – Play, Orchestra, Play / Uncle Harry / Loch Lomond / A Bar On The Piccola
			Marina / World Weary / Nina / Mad Dogs And Englishmen / Matelot / Alice Is At It
			Again / A Room With A View / Let's Do It / The Party's Over Now

COWBOY CHURCH SUNDAY SCHOOL   4

One of American radio's first singing cowboys, Stuart Hamblen underwent a religious conversion in 1949 at a Billy Graham crusade and switched to Christian broadcasting with his radio show, 'The Cowboy Church of the Air'. In 1955, he produced this unusual inspirational record, which featured the speeded-up voices of his wife and daughters to resemble small children singing. It made the Top Ten in the States.

30 Apr 55	28	1	**Open Up Your Heart** / The Lord Is Counting On You
			(Brunswick 05371)
28 May 55	12	1	**Open Up Your Heart** / The Lord Is Counting On You
			(Brunswick 05371) *1st re-entry*
11 Jun 55	20	2	**Open Up Your Heart** / The Lord Is Counting On You
			(Brunswick 05371) *2nd re-entry*

MICHAEL COX   3

Singer from Liverpool discovered by 'Oh Boy!' producer Jack Good. He triumphed in 1960 with 'Angela Jones' and 'Along Came Caroline', then went on to become a record star in Sweden.

24 Sep 60	5	2	★ **Along Came Caroline** / Lonely Road *(H.M.V. POP-789)*
4 Mar 61	19	1	**Teenage Love** *(Michael Cox and the Hunters)* /
			Linda *(Michael Cox and the Dave Lee Group)* *(H.M.V. POP-830)*

See also Hunters

BILLY 'CRASH' CRADDOCK   1

Gene Vincent's cousin from Greensboro, North Carolina. Although he was unsuccessful as a rock'n'roller, he broke through as a country rocker in the '70s and '80s.

| 7 Jan 61 | 19 | 1 | **Good Time Billy** / Heavenly Love *(Philips PB-1092)* |

FLOYD CRAMER   3

Country pianist from Shreveport, Louisiana who played on Elvis Presley's early RCA sessions and later became one of the architects of the 'Nashville Sound'.

| 5 Apr 58 | 4 | 2 | **Flip, Flop And Bop** / Sophisticated Swing *(R.C.A. RCA-1050)* |
| 11 Feb 61 | 6 | 1 | **Last Date** / Sweetie Baby *(R.C.A. RCA-1211)* |

CRAZY OTTO   15

German ragtime pianist born Fritz Schulz-Reichel in Meiningen in 1912.

8 Oct 55	1	8	**Glad Rag Doll** / Smiles *(Polydor BM-6003)*
17 Dec 55	3	3	**Glad Rag Doll** / Smiles *(Polydor BM-6003)* **1st re-entry**
14 Jan 56	6	2	**Glad Rag Doll** / Smiles *(Polydor BM-6003)* **2nd re-entry**
22 Oct 60	16	1	**Glad Rag Doll** / Answer Me *(Polydor NH-66634)* **reissue**
10 Dec 60	14	1	**A Merry Christmas from Crazy Otto (Parts 1 & 2) [M]**
			(Polydor NH-66637)
			Sleigh Ride – Winter Wonderland – White Christmas / Rudolph The Red-Nosed
			Reindeer – I Saw Mummy Kissing Santa Claus – Jingle Bells

CRESTS   3

Racially integrated doo-wop group from New York. Their lead, Johnny Maestro (né Mastrangelo), later formed the Brooklyn Bridge.

28 Feb 59	4	1	**16 Candles** / Beside You *(London HL-8794)*
17 Oct 59	5	1	**The Angels Listened In** / I Thank The Moon *(London HL-8954)*
13 Aug 60	14	1	**Trouble In Paradise** / Always You *(H.M.V. POP-768)*

CREW-CUTS   16

Tame white vocal group from Toronto, Canada who described their style as 'rhythm and barbershop harmony'. Like Pat Boone, they covered many R&B hits.

21 Aug 54	3	6	★ Sh-Boom / I Spoke Too Soon *(Mercury MB-3140)*
26 Mar 55	1	3	★ Earth Angel / Ko Ko Mo *(Mercury MB-3202)*
28 May 55	5	1	**Two Hearts, Two Kisses** / Unchained Melody *(Mercury MB-3222)*
11 Jun 55	5	2	**Two Hearts, Two Kisses** / Unchained Melody *(Mercury MB-3222)*
			1st re-entry
2 Jul 55	9	3	**Two Hearts, Two Kisses** / Unchained Melody *(Mercury MB-3222)*
			2nd re-entry
3 Sep 55	5	1	**Unchained Melody** / Two Hearts, Two Kisses *(Mercury MB-3222)*
			3rd re-entry (flipped)

BERNARD CRIBBINS   1

Actor, comedian and voice-over artist born in Oldham, Lancashire in 1928.

28 Jan 61	11	1	**Folk Song** *(Bernard Cribbins)* /
			My Kind Of Someone *(Bernard Cribbins and Joyce Blair)*
			(Parlophone R-4712)

CRICKETS   5

Rock'n'roll group from Lubbock, Texas led by singer/songwriter/guitarist Buddy Holly. When Holly left in late 1958, he was replaced by Sonny Curtis and the Crickets carried on (see below).

21 Sep 57	10	1	★ That'll Be The Day / I'm Lookin' For Someone To Love
			(Vogue Coral Q-72279)
8 Mar 58	1	1	★ Maybe Baby / Tell Me How *(Coral Q-72307)*
8 Nov 58	1	2	★ It's So Easy / Lonesome Tears *(Coral Q-72343)*

See also Buddy Holly

CRICKETS (post-Holly)   10

Buddy Holly's former backing group, who continued to enjoy success in their own right after his death in February 1959.

18 Apr 59	4	1	★ Love's Made A Fool Of You / Someone, Someone *(Coral Q-72365)*
28 Nov 59	14	3	★ When You Ask About Love / Deborah *(Coral Q-72382)*
9 Jan 60	5	1	★ When You Ask About Love / Deborah *(Coral Q-72382)* **re-entry**
7 May 60	2	3	★ Baby My Heart / More Than I Can Say *(Coral Q-72395)*
14 Jan 61	13	2	**Don'tCha Know** / Peggy Sue Got Married *(Coral Q-72417)*

TONY CROMBIE & HIS ROCKETS   1

Acclaimed jazz drummer, bandleader and composer born Anthony Kronenberg. He briefly switched to rock'n'roll in the mid-'50s after being prevailed upon by promoter Jeffrey Kruger. 'Teach You To Rock' is widely regarded as the first British rock'n'roll record.

13 Oct 56   **4**   1   ★ **Teach You To Rock** / Short'nin' Bread Rock *(Columbia DB-3822)*

BING CROSBY   33

Crooner from Tacoma, Washington born Harry Lillis Crosby. He was a hugely influential vocal stylist and one of the biggest music and film stars of the mid-twentieth century.

Date	Pos	Wks		Title
3 Jul 54	9	1		**Young At Heart** / **Oh Baby Mine I Get So Lonely** *(Brunswick 05277)*
14 Aug 54	26	1		**Back In The Old Routine** / If There's Anybody Here *(Brunswick 05304)*
				Both sides by Bing Crosby and Donald O'Connor
21 Aug 54	24	1		**Young At Heart** / **Oh Baby Mine I Get So Lonely** *(Brunswick 05277)*
				re-entry
20 Nov 54	14	3	★	**Count Your Blessings Instead Of Sheep** /
				What Can You Do With A General *(Brunswick 05339)*
27 Nov 54	9	3		**White Christmas** / Snow *(Brunswick 05354)*
				Both sides by Bing Crosby, Danny Kaye, Peggy Lee and Trudy Stevens. This re-recording of Bing's famous hit was featured in the film 'White Christmas'.
18 Dec 54	39	2	★	**Count Your Blessings Instead Of Sheep** /
				What Can You Do With A General *(Brunswick 05339)* **re-entry**
25 Dec 54	37	1		**White Christmas** / Snow *(Brunswick 05354)* **1st re-entry**
8 Jan 55	12	2		**White Christmas** / Snow *(Brunswick 05354)* **2nd re-entry**
16 Apr 55	5	2	★	**Stranger In Paradise** / Who Gave You The Roses *(Brunswick 05410)*
7 Apr 56	3	1	★	**In A Little Spanish Town** / Ol' Man River *(Brunswick 05543)*
17 Nov 56	9	1	★	**True Love** *(Bing Crosby and Grace Kelly)* /
				Well Did You Evah? *(Bing Crosby and Frank Sinatra)* *(Capitol CL-14645)*
24 Nov 56	9	1		**Now You Has Jazz** *(Bing Crosby and Louis Armstrong)*
				Flip is 'High Society Calypso' by Louis Armstrong & His Band (Capitol CL-14643)
8 Dec 56	5	4		**Now You Has Jazz** *(Bing Crosby and Louis Armstrong)* *(Capitol CL-14643)* **1st re-entry**
12 Jan 57	2	1		**Now You Has Jazz** *(Bing Crosby and Louis Armstrong)* *(Capitol CL-14643)* **2nd re-entry**
26 Jan 57	3	1		**Now You Has Jazz** *(Bing Crosby and Louis Armstrong)* *(Capitol CL-14643)* **3rd re-entry**
18 May 57	11	1	★	**Around The World** *(Brunswick 05674)*
				Flip is 'Around The World' by Victor Young & His Orchestra
28 Sep 57	5	1		**Now You Has Jazz** *(Bing Crosby and Louis Armstrong)* *(Capitol CL-14643)* **4th re-entry**
12 Oct 57	7	1		**Now You Has Jazz** *(Bing Crosby and Louis Armstrong)* *(Capitol CL-14643)* **5th re-entry**
16 Nov 57	10	1	★	**MERRY CHRISTMAS (VOL. 1)** *(Brunswick OE-9069)* **EP**
				Silent Night, Holy Night / Adeste Fidelis / White Christmas / God Rest Ye Merry Gentlemen
7 Dec 57	6	2		**Man On Fire** / Seven Nights A Week *(Capitol CL-14761)*
5 Apr 58	15	1		**Man On Fire** / Seven Nights A Week *(Capitol CL-14761)* *re-entry*
2 May 59	6	1		**Gigi** / The Next Time It Happens *(Brunswick 05770)*

See also Original Soundtrack (HIGH SOCIETY)

SIMON CRUM

See Ferlin Husky

61

XAVIER CUGAT & His Orchestra   6

Spanish-born violinist and bandleader who moved to Cuba as a child. He is chiefly remembered for infusing Latin rhythms into American pop music, and for his succession of sexy wives.

9 Apr 55	**4**	1	**Cherry Pink And Apple Blossom White** / The Americano (Philips PB-413)
30 Apr 55	**21**	1	**Cherry Pink And Apple Blossom White** / The Americano (Philips PB-413) **1st re-entry**
14 May 55	**5**	4	**Cherry Pink And Apple Blossom White** / The Americano (Philips PB-413) **2nd re-entry**

ALAN DALE   1

Pop singer and former TV host born Aldo Sigismondi in New York in 1925. In 1956, he played the part of a rock'n'rol singer in the film 'Don't Knock The Rock', and also sang the title song.

| 27 Aug 55 | **18** | 1 | **Sweet And Gentle** / You Still Mean The Same To Me (Vogue Coral Q-72089) |

JIM DALE   8

Actor, comedian and singer/songwriter born James Smith in Rothwell, Northamptonshire in 1935. He first came to national prominence as a rock'n'roll singer on '6.5 Special', but is now chiefly remembered for his appearances in the 'Carry On' films.

20 Jul 57	**10**	1	**Piccadilly Line** / I Didn't Mean It (Parlophone R-4329)
7 Dec 57	**1**	4	★ **Crazy Dream** / **Just Born** (Parlophone R-4376)
22 Feb 58	**1**	2	★ **Sugartime** / **Don't Let Go** (Parlophone R-4402)
25 Oct 58	**6**	1	**Tread Softly Stranger** / Jane Belinda (Parlophone R-4424)

See also Various Artists (Top Ten Special)

DALIDA   3

Singer born in Egypt to Italian parents (her real name was Iolanda Gigliotti). She moved to Paris in 1954 to pursue a film career, but became a fixture on the French music scene from the late '50s onwards. She committed suicide in 1987 after enduring a string of personal tragedies.

15 Oct 60	**7**	2	**Never On Sunday** (H.M.V. POP-793)
			Flip is 'Parle Doucement' by Milko Papayaki & His Orchestra
5 Nov 60	**5**	1	**Never On Sunday** (H.M.V. POP-793) **re-entry**

TONI DALLI   6

Italian tenor Antonio d'Alessandro aka Toni Dalli came to the UK aged 15 and found both fame and fortune. He later moved to Spain, where he ran a large Italian restaurant in Marbella.

5 Apr 58	**15**	1	**If You Loved Me** / **Just Say I Love Her** (Columbia DB-4096)
26 Apr 58	**8**	3	**If You Loved Me** / **Just Say I Love Her** (Columbia DB-4096) **re-entry**
1 Nov 58	**4**	1	**More Than Ever** / Santa Lucia (Columbia DB-4195)
13 Dec 58	**3**	1	**Catari, Catari** / The Man Who Plays The Mandolino (Columbia DB-4173)

DAMITA JO   1

Pop and soul singer born Damita Jo DeBlanc in Austin, Texas. The bubbler below was an 'answer' to the Drifters' 'Save The Last Dance For Me'.

| 17 Dec 60 | **16** | 1 | **I'll Save The Last Dance For You** / Forgive (Mercury AMT-1116) |

VIC DAMONE   6

Sinatra-styled balladeer born Vito Farinola. His hitmaking career began in the late 1940s.

| 4 Jun 55 | **13** | 1 | **Hello Mrs. Jones** / Foolishly (Mercury MB-3219) |
| 3 Sep 55 | **17** | 1 | **Why, Oh Why?** (Tony Martin, Vic Damone, Russ Tamblyn [actually Rex Dennis], Jane Powell, Debbie Reynolds and Ann Miller) / Chiribiribee (Kay Armen, Jane Powell, Tony Martin, Debbie Reynolds, Vic Damone and Russ Tamblyn [actually Rex Dennis]) (M.G.M. MGM-837) |

16 Nov 57	10	1	★ **An Affair To Remember** / The Legend Of The Bells *(Philips PB-745)*
30 Nov 57	12	1	★ **An Affair To Remember** / The Legend Of The Bells *(Philips PB-745)*
			re-entry
14 Mar 59	2	1	**Gigi** / Separate Tables *(Philips PB-889)*
28 Mar 59	10	1	**Gigi** / Separate Tables *(Philips PB-889)* *re-entry*

See also Various Artists (KISMET)

BILLY DANIELS   13

Energetic showman from Jacksonville, Florida discovered by bandleader Erskine Hawkins. One of the first black singers to perform in a white pop style, he rose to fame with 'That Old Black Magic', a huge hit for him in 1950.

26 Jun 54	19	1	**It's A Good Day** / I'll Never Know Why *(Mercury MB-3127)*
14 Aug 54	6	3	**Smile** / Mom-e-le *(Mercury MB-3142)*
11 Sep 54	4	7	**Smile** / Mom-e-le *(Mercury MB-3142)* *re-entry*
30 Oct 54	26	1	**Bye Bye Blackbird** / She's Funny That Way *(Mercury MB-3144)*
12 May 56	12	1	**That Old Black Magic** / I Concentrate On You *(Oriole CB-1095)*

JOHNNY DANKWORTH & His Orchestra   1

Legendary British jazz saxophonist/clarinettist and partner of jazz singer Cleo Laine. He was born in Woodford, Essex in 1927 and formed his Big Band in 1953.

| 18 Feb 61 | 2 | 1 | ★ **African Waltz** / Moanin' *(Columbia DB-4590)* |

DANNY & THE JUNIORS   4

Singing quartet from Philadelphia fronted by Danny Rapp. Sadly, their great follow-up to their big hit, 'At The Hop', just missed the UK charts.

11 Jan 58	6	1	★ **At The Hop** / Sometimes *(H.M.V. POP-436)*
5 Apr 58	4	3	**Rock And Roll Is Here To Stay** / School Boy Romance
			(H.M.V. POP-467)

DANTE & THE EVERGREENS   2

Los Angeles quartet led by Don 'Dante' Drowty who rushed out a cover of 'Alley-Oop' that successfully stole some of the thunder from the Hollywood Argyles' original. Despite this, both versions were big hits in the US.

| 9 Jul 60 | 4 | 1 | **Alley-Oop** / The Right Time *(Top Rank JAR-402)* |
| 6 Aug 60 | 11 | 1 | **Alley-Oop** / The Right Time *(Top Rank JAR-402)* *re-entry* |

BOBBY DARIN   7

Versatile singer/songwriter born Walden Robert Cassotto. Plagued throughout his career by heart problems stemming from a childhood illness, he died of a heart attack in 1973, aged 37.

26 Jul 58	15	1	★ **Splish Splash** / Judy Don't Be Moody *(London HLE-8666)*
8 Nov 58	7	1	★ **Queen Of The Hop** / Lost Love *(London HLE-8737)*
22 Nov 58	10	1	★ **Queen Of The Hop** / Lost Love *(London HLE-8737)* *1st re-entry*
20 Dec 58	10	2	★ **Queen Of The Hop** / Lost Love *(London HLE-8737)* *2nd re-entry*
7 Mar 59	6	1	**Plain Jane** / While I'm Gone *(London HLE-8815)*
5 Nov 60	10	1	**Somebody To Love** / I'll Be There *(London HLK-9215)*

JAMES DARREN   1

Actor and singer from Philadelphia born James Ercolani in 1936. His biggest hit was 'Goodbye Cruel World', which reached No. 3 in the Billboard 'Hot 100' in 1961.

| 23 Jul 60 | 18 | 1 | ★ **Because They're Young** / Let There Be Love |
| | | | *(Pye International 7N.25059)* |

DANNY DAVIS 10

Singer/guitarist from Stoke-on-Trent who went on to front the Marauders beat group.

18 Jun 60	8	1	**You're My Only Girl** / Love Me *(Parlophone R-4657)*
2 Jul 60	6	1	**You're My Only Girl** / Love Me *(Parlophone R-4657)*
			1st re-entry
16 Jul 60	4	7	**You're My Only Girl** / **Love Me** *(Parlophone R-4657)*
			2nd re-entry
10 Sep 60	9	1	**Love Me** / You're My Only Girl *(Parlophone R-4657)*
			3rd re-entry (flipped)

SAMMY DAVIS JR. 46

New York-born dancer, actor, impressionist, comedian, multi-instrumentalist and singer whose private life was as colourful as his career.

11 Dec 54	35	1		**Because Of You (Parts 1 & 2)** *(Brunswick 05326)*
26 Mar 55	29	1		**The Birth Of The Blues** / Love *(Brunswick 05383)*
2 Apr 55	18	2		**Six Bridges To Cross** / Glad To Be Unhappy *(Brunswick 05389)*
14 May 55	26	3		**Because Of You (Parts 1 & 2)** *(Brunswick 05326)* *1st re-entry*
11 Jun 55	5	1		**Because Of You (Parts 1 & 2)** *(Brunswick 05326)* *2nd re-entry*
25 Jun 55	2	5	★	**Something's Gotta Give** / **Love Me Or Leave Me** *(Brunswick 05428)*
25 Jun 55	17	1		**Because Of You (Parts 1 & 2)** *(Brunswick 05326)* *3rd re-entry*
9 Jul 55	3	14		**Because Of You (Parts 1 & 2)** *(Brunswick 05326)* *4th re-entry*
3 Sep 55	1	4	★	**That Old Black Magic** / Give A Fool A Chance *(Brunswick 05450)*
24 Sep 55	23	1	★	**Hey There** / My Funny Valentine *(Brunswick 05469)*
22 Oct 55	17	1		**Because Of You (Parts 1 & 2)** *(Brunswick 05326)* *5th re-entry*
14 Jan 56	11	1		**Back Track** / It's Bigger Than You And Me *(Brunswick 05478)*
11 Feb 56	2	1		**Back Track** / It's Bigger Than You And Me *(Brunswick 05478)* *re-entry*
3 Mar 56	13	2	★	**In A Persian Market** / Man With The Golden Arm *(Brunswick 05518)*
24 Mar 56	1	4	★	**In A Persian Market** / **Man With The Golden Arm** *(Brunswick 05518)*
				re-entry
18 Aug 56	10	1		**Adelaide** / I'll Know *(Brunswick 05583)*
24 Nov 56	5	1		**Frankie And Johnny** / Circus *(Brunswick 05611)*
25 May 57	3	1		**Too Close For Comfort** / Jacques d'Iraque *(Brunswick 05668)*
24 Sep 60	11	1	★	**Eee-O Eleven** / Ain't That A Kick In The Head? *(H.M.V. POP-777)*

SKEETER DAVIS 3

Born Mary Frances Penick, Skeeter Davis was one half of the successful Davis Sisters duo until her partner, Betty Jack Davis, was killed in a car crash in 1953. After quitting the music business for several years, she resurfaced in the late '50s to pursue a solo career as a country/pop singer.

| 18 Feb 61 | 3 | 3 | **My Last Date** / Someone I'd Like To Forget *(R.C.A. RCA-1222)* |

BOBBY DAY 2

R&B singer born Robert Byrd in Forth Worth, Texas in 1930. He initially sang lead with the Hollywood Flames, then went solo in 1957.

| 1 Nov 58 | 6 | 1 | ★ | **Rockin' Robin** / Over And Over *(London HL-8726)* |
| 18 Feb 61 | 7 | 1 | | **Over And Over** / Gee Whiz *(Top Rank JAR-538)* |

See also Hollywood Flames

DORIS DAY 69

Blonde-haired singer born Doris Kappelhoff in Cincinnati, Ohio. She began her hitmaking career in 1945 and became the clean-cut darling of the matinée set during the late '50s and early '60s.

19 Jun 54	11	2		**The Blue Bells Of Broadway** / I Speak To The Stars *(Philips PB-295)*
10 Jul 54	4	5		**The Blue Bells Of Broadway** / I Speak To The Stars *(Philips PB-295)*
				1st re-entry
7 Aug 54	10	3	★	**The Black Hills Of Dakota** / Just Blew In From The Windy City *(Philips PB-287)*
7 Aug 54	27	1		**Kiss Me Again, Stranger** / Choo Choo Train *(Philips PB-264)*
18 Sep 54	4	2	★	**If I Give My Heart To You** / Anyone Can Fall In Love *(Philips PB-325)*

18 Sep 54	15	1	The Blue Bells Of Broadway / I Speak To The Stars *(Philips PB-295)*
			2nd re-entry
9 Oct 54	12	4	I Speak To The Stars / The Blue Bells Of Broadway *(Philips PB-295)*
			3rd re-entry (flipped)
22 Jan 55	50	1	The Blue Bells Of Broadway / I Speak To The Stars *(Philips PB-295)*
			4th re-entry (flipped)
19 Feb 55	2	2	★ Ready, Willing And Able / You My Love *(Philips PB-402)*
12 Mar 55	4	4	★ Ready, Willing And Able / You My Love *(Philips PB-402)* *re-entry*
7 May 55	16	1	Hold Me In Your Arms / There's A Rising Moon *(Philips PB-401)*
28 May 55	18	2	Two Hearts, Two Kisses / Foolishly Yours *(Philips PB-451)*
25 Jun 55	6	3	Two Hearts, Two Kisses / Foolishly Yours *(Philips PB-451)*
			1st re-entry
30 Jul 55	16	2	Two Hearts, Two Kisses / Foolishly Yours *(Philips PB-451)*
			2nd re-entry
27 Aug 55	24	1	You Made Me Love You / Mean To Me *(Philips PB-489)*
3 Sep 55	13	1	★ Love Me Or Leave Me / Sam, The Accordion Man *(Philips PB-479)*
10 Sep 55	12	1	LOVE ME OR LEAVE ME [OST] *(Philips BBL-7047)* 🅛🅟
			It All Depends On You / You Made Me Love You (I Didn't Want To Do It) / Stay On The Right Side, Sister / Mean To Me / Everybody Loves My Baby (But My Baby Don't Love Nobody But Me) / Sam, The Old Accordion Man / Shaking The Blues Away / Ten Cents A Dance / I'll Never Stop Loving You / Never Look Back / At Sundown / Love Me Or Leave Me
10 Sep 55	16	1	You Made Me Love You / Mean To Me *(Philips PB-489)* *1st re-entry*
1 Oct 55	8	1	★ I'll Never Stop Loving You / Ten Cents A Dance *(Philips PB-497)*
8 Oct 55	12	1	You Made Me Love You / Mean To Me *(Philips PB-489)* *2nd re-entry*
15 Oct 55	4	1	★ I'll Never Stop Loving You / Ten Cents A Dance *(Philips PB-497)*
			re-entry
10 Dec 55	18	1	Ooh Bang Jiggilly Jang / Ol' Saint Nicholas *(Philips PB-532)*
31 Dec 55	2	5	Ooh Bang Jiggilly Jang / Ol' Saint Nicholas *(Philips PB-532)* *re-entry*
4 Feb 56	3	3	Jimmy Unknown / Love's Little Island *(Philips PB-542)*
3 Mar 56	1	3	Jimmy Unknown / Love's Little Island *(Philips PB-542)* *1st re-entry*
14 Apr 56	14	1	Jimmy Unknown / Love's Little Island *(Philips PB-542)* *2nd re-entry*
21 Apr 56	8	4	Let It Ring / By The Light Of The Silvery Moon *(Philips PB-560)*
9 Jun 56	10	1	Let It Ring / By The Light Of The Silvery Moon *(Philips PB-560)*
			re-entry
16 Jun 56	12	2	★ Whatever Will Be, Will Be / We'll Love Again *(Philips PB-586)*
26 Jan 57	5	2	Julie / I've Gotta Sing Away These Blues *(Philips PB-634)*
26 Apr 58	1	2	★ A Very Precious Love / Teacher's Pet *(Philips PB-799)*
24 May 58	3	3	★ A Very Precious Love / Teacher's Pet *(Philips PB-799)* *re-entry*
31 Oct 59	20	2	The Tunnel Of Love / Run Away, Skidaddle, Skidoo *(Philips PB-949)*

See also Original Soundtrack (YOUNG AT HEART)

JILL DAY   2
Singer and actress from Brighton, born Yvonne Page. She made the front pages in 1956 after fainting on set during the live TV comedy thriller 'Double Cross'.

5 May 56	7	1	A Tear Fell / Holiday Affair *(H.M.V. POP-199)*
2 Feb 57	12	1	★ I Dreamed / Give Her My Love When You Meet Her *(H.M.V. POP-288)*

DAY BROTHERS   2
British teen duo whose solitary release is now quite collectable.

19 Nov 60	19	1	Angel / Just One More Kiss *(Oriole CB-1575)*
10 Dec 60	25	1	Angel / Just One More Kiss *(Oriole CB-1575)* *re-entry*

DE CASTRO SISTERS   7
Raised in a mansion in Havana, Cuba, Peggy, Cherie and Babette De Castro were a singing trio who patterned themselves after the Andrews Sisters.

25 Dec 54	5	7	★ Teach Me Tonight / It's Love *(London HL-8104)*

DIANA DECKER   6

American-born dance band singer who moved to the UK at the age of four. She had a one-off hit in 1953 with the cute 'Poppa Piccolino', but subsequently achieved greater success as a stage and TV actress.

14 Aug 54	**26**	1	**Kitty In The Basket** / **Never Never Land** *(Columbia DB-3489)*
26 Feb 55	**6**	2	**Goin' Co'tin'** *(Ronnie Harris, Diana Decker, Ray Burns and Ruby Murray)* / Spring, Spring, Spring *(Ruby Murray, Ray Burns, Diana Decker and Ronnie Harris) (Columbia DB-3567)*
30 Apr 55	**16**	3	**Spring, Spring, Spring** *(Ruby Murray, Ray Burns, Diana Decker and Ronnie Harris)* / **Goin' Co'tin'** *(Ronnie Harris, Diana Decker, Ray Burns and Ruby Murray) (Columbia DB-3567)* **re-entry (flipped)**

TOMMY DEE   1

Radio deejay in San Bernadino, California whose real name was Thomas Donaldson. He wrote and recorded 'Three Stars' as a tribute to Buddy Holly, Ritchie Valens and the Big Bopper, who had recently perished in a plane crash on 3 February 1959. His record sold over one million copies in the USA, but in the UK it was Ruby Wright's cover version that became a hit.

6 Jun 59	**12**	1	**Three Stars** *(Tommy Dee with Teen Jones and Orchestra)* / I'll Never Change *(Teen Jones) (Melodisc 45/1516)*

DEEP RIVER BOYS   11

Slick black vocal outfit from Hampton, Virginia who spent a great deal of time in the UK and Scandinavia. They could turn their hand to harmony ballads or uptempo novelties with equal ease.

5 Feb 55	**37**	1	**Shake, Rattle And Roll** / St. Louis Blues *(H.M.V. B-10790)*
12 Nov 55	**1**	5	**Rock Around The Clock** / Adam Never Had No Mammy *(H.M.V. POP-113)*
24 Dec 55	**4**	2	**Rock Around The Clock** / Adam Never Had No Mammy *(H.M.V. POP-113)* **re-entry**
27 Oct 56	**6**	1	★ **That's Right** / Honey Honey (Comic Folk-Song) *(H.M.V. POP-263)*
10 Nov 56	**3**	2	★ **That's Right** / Honey Honey (Comic Folk-Song) *(H.M.V. POP-263)* **re-entry**

ERIC DELANEY & His Band   29

Voted 'Britain's Best Young Swing Drummer' at the age of 16, Eric Delaney cut his teeth with George Shearing, Ambrose and Geraldo before becoming a celebrity bandleader specialising in uptempo dance music. He was awarded a silver disc for sales of the non-charting 'Oranges And Lemons'.

2 Oct 54	**25**	1	**Oranges And Lemons** / Delaney's Delight *(Mercury MB-3143)*
23 Oct 54	**49**	1	**Oranges And Lemons** / Delaney's Delight *(Mercury MB-3143)* **1st re-entry**
20 Nov 54	**34**	1	**Oranges And Lemons** / Delaney's Delight *(Mercury MB-3143)* **2nd re-entry**
8 Jan 55	**18**	3	**Truckin'** / Sweet Georgia Brown *(Mercury MB-3168)*
8 Jan 55	**52**	1	**Oranges And Lemons** / **Delaney's Delight** *(Mercury MB-3143)* **3rd re-entry**
22 Jan 55	**8**	6	**Oranges And Lemons** / **Delaney's Delight** *(Mercury MB-3143)* **4th re-entry**
5 Feb 55	**56**	1	**Truckin'** / Sweet Georgia Brown *(Mercury MB-3168)* **1st re-entry**
12 Mar 55	**14**	1	**Oranges And Lemons** / **Delaney's Delight** *(Mercury MB-3143)* **5th re-entry**
9 Apr 55	**17**	8	**Roamin' In The Gloamin'** / Ting-A-Ling *(Mercury MB-3213)*
16 Apr 55	**22**	1	**Oranges And Lemons** / **Delaney's Delight** *(Mercury MB-3143)* **6th re-entry**
11 Jun 55	**24**	2	**Roamin' In The Gloamin'** / Ting-A-Ling *(Mercury MB-3213)* **re-entry**
20 Aug 55	**14**	1	**Oranges And Lemons** / Delaney's Delight *(Mercury MB-3143)* **7th re-entry**
2 Jun 56	**14**	1	**Cockles And Mussels** / Say Si Si *(Pye Nixa N.15046)* Both sides as by the Eric Delaney Band
30 Nov 57	**7**	1	**Truckin'** / Sweet Georgia Brown *(Mercury MB-3168)* **2nd re-entry**

JOHNNY DeLITTLE   1

Talented Welsh singer and actor born Brian King in Penrhiwceiber, Cynon Valley. Despite being a protégé of John Barry, chart success eluded him.

4 Feb 61 **22** 1   **Not Guilty** / They *(Columbia DB-4578)*

DELL-VIKINGS   7

Racially integrated doo-wop quintet formed by U.S.A.F. personnel stationed in Pittsburgh, Pennsylvania. Sadly, neither of their US Top Ten hits made the charts in the UK.

11 May 57 **9** 2   **Come Go With Me** / How Can I Find True Love *(London HLD-8405)*
22 Jun 57 **5** 2   **Come Go With Me** / How Can I Find True Love *(London HLD-8405)*
                       re-entry
7 Sep 57   **4** 2   **Whispering Bells** / Little Billy Boy *(London HLD-8464)*
5 Oct 57   **4** 1   **Whispering Bells** / Little Billy Boy *(London HLD-8464)* *re-entry*

DELTA SKIFFLE GROUP   1

Skiffle outfit from Glasgow. The second of their three releases bubbled under.

11 Jan 58 **6** 1   **K.C. Moan** / Pick A Bale Of Cotton *(Esquire 10-507)*

TERRY DENE   6

Early British rock'n'roller born Terence Williams, whose promising career was prematurely cut short by a nervous breakdown and a disproportionate amount of negative publicity.

25 May 57 **9** 1 ★ **A White Sport Coat (And A Pink Carnation)** /
                       The Man In The Phone Booth *(Decca F-10895)*
19 Oct 57 **5** 1   **Teenage Dream** / Come And Get It *(Decca F-10938)*
2 Nov 57   **4** 1   **Teenage Dream** / Come And Get It *(Decca F-10938)* *re-entry*
3 May 58   **11** 1   **The Golden Age** / C'min And Be Loved *(Decca F-10977)*
10 May 58 **3** 1 ★ **Stairway Of Love** / Lover, Lover! *(Decca F-11016)*
3 Sep 60   **18** 1   **Love Me Or Leave Me** / Geraldine *(Oriole CB-1562)*

JACKIE DENNIS   1

Kilt-wearing teenage pop singer from Leith near Edinburgh who had a UK Top Five hit in early 1958 with 'La Dee Dah'.

21 Jun 58 **10** 1 ★ **The Purple People Eater** / You-Oo *(Decca F-11033)*

WILLIE DENNIS

See J.J. Johnson etc.

JOHNNY DESMOND   11

Singer from Detroit, born Giovanni DeSimone. Immensely popular during the '40s and early '50s, he performed with the Bob Crosby, Gene Krupa and Glenn Miller bands.

20 Nov 54 **34** 1   **The High And The Mighty** / Got No Time *(Vogue Coral Q-2019)*
8 Oct 55   **4** 4   **The Yellow Rose Of Texas** / You're In Love With Someone
                       (Vogue Coral Q-72099)
12 Nov 55 **6** 4   **The Yellow Rose Of Texas** / You're In Love With Someone
                       (Vogue Coral Q-72099) *re-entry*
7 Jan 56   **2** 2   **Sixteen Tons** / Ballo Italiano *(Vogue Coral Q-72115)*

LORRAE DESMOND   6

Award-winning singer, lyricist, actress and cabaret entertainer born Beryl Hunt in Mittagong, New South Wales in 1932. She came to Britain at the age of 16 and stayed.

11 Dec 54 **18** 1   **I Can't Tell A Waltz From A Tango** /
                       For Better, For Worse *(Decca F-10404)*
                       Both sides by Lorrae Desmond and the Johnston Brothers
21 May 55 **6** 2   **Where Will The Dimple Be** / Don't *(Decca F-10510)*
                       Both sides by Lorrae Desmond with the Melodaires

11 Jun 55	**20**	1	**Where Will The Dimple Be** / Don't *(Decca F-10510)* ***re-entry***
24 Aug 57	**3**	1	**Kansas City Special** / Preacher, Preacher *(Parlophone R-4320)*
			Both sides by Lorrae Desmond and the Rebels
14 Sep 57	**11**	1	**Kansas City Special** / Preacher, Preacher *(Parlophone R-4320)*
			re-entry

JIMMY DEUCHAR QUARTET   5

Dundee-born jazz trumpeter and arranger, who played with both Johnny Dankworth and Jack Parnell.

3 Jul 54	**15**	5	**THE JIMMY DEUCHAR QUARTET WITH VICTOR FELDMAN**
			(Esquire EP-53) **EP**
			They Can't Take That Away From Me / Close As Pages In A Book / Folks Who Live On The Hill / Thou Swell

See also Jo Hunter etc.

DIAMOND ACCORDION BAND

See Fred Hanna Band

DIAMONDS   10

White doo-wop group from Toronto who specialised in covering R&B tunes. Their interpretation of the Gladiolas' 'Little Darlin' ' was a Top Five UK hit in 1957.

1 Feb 58	**4**	5	**The Stroll** / Land Of Beauty *(Mercury 7MT-195)*
22 Nov 58	**15**	1	**Walking Along** / Eternal Lovers *(Mercury AMT-1004)*
10 Jan 59	**6**	2	**Walking Along** / Eternal Lovers *(Mercury AMT-1004)* ***1st re-entry***
31 Jan 59	**4**	2	**Walking Along** / Eternal Lovers *(Mercury AMT-1004)* ***2nd re-entry***

VIC DICKENSON

See Gene Norman's 'Just Jazz'

BO DIDDLEY   3

Black rock'n'roll singer/guitarist born Ellas McDaniel in McComb, Mississippi. Although he pioneered the thumping 'Bo Diddley' beat, his three bubblers were stylistically very different.

10 Oct 59	**7**	1	**Crackin' Up** / The Great Grandfather *(London HLM-8913)*
7 Nov 59	**10**	1	**Say Man** / The Clock Strikes Twelve *(London HLM-8975)*
14 May 60	**1**	1	**Road Runner** / My Story *(London HLM-9112)*

MARK DINNING   1

Younger brother of 1940s hitmakers the Dinning Sisters, born Max Dinning in Manchester, Oklahoma in 1933. Sadly, his addiction to alcohol put paid to a promising career.

| 20 Feb 60 | **8** | 1 | ★ **Teen Angel** / Bye Now Baby *(M.G.M. MGM-1053)* |

DION   2

Former lead singer of Dion & The Belmonts born Dion DiMucci in New York in 1939.

| 7 Jan 61 | **4** | 2 | ★ **Lonely Teenager** / Little Miss Blue *(Top Rank JAR-521)* |

See also Dion & The Belmonts

DION & THE BELMONTS   6

Top vocal group of the late '50s and early '60s, fronted by Dion DiMucci until 1960 (see above). They named themselves after the area where they lived: Belmont Avenue in the Bronx.

5 Jul 58	**18**	1	**I Wonder Why** / Teen Angel *(London HLH-8646)*
30 May 59	**1**	3	★ **A Teenager In Love** / I've Cried Before *(London HLU-8874)*
5 Mar 60	**8**	2	**Where Or When** / That's My Desire *(London HLU-9030)*

See also Dion

REGINALD DIXON   1

Organist born in Sheffield in 1904. He became a national institution thanks to a 40-year residency at the Tower Ballroom, Blackpool, from 1930 until 1970.

16 Jul 55   **18**   1   **Dancing At The Tower No. 16 (Parts 1 & 2) [M]** *(Columbia FB-3744)*
                                Foxtrots: It May Sound Silly – My World Stood Still – Stranger In Paradise /
                                Quicksteps: I'm In Favour Of Friendship – Dreamboat – The Crazy Otto Rag

CARL DOBKINS JR.   4

Singer from Cincinnati, Ohio who launched his career with the poppy 'My Heart Is An Open Book', but could also lay down some very passable rockabilly when the occasion demanded.

15 Aug 59   **5**   1   **My Heart Is An Open Book** / My Pledge To You *(Brunswick 05804)*
29 Aug 59   **2**   2   **My Heart Is An Open Book** / My Pledge To You *(Brunswick 05804)*
                             re-entry
23 Jan 60   **12**   1   ★   <u>**Lucky Devil**</u> / In My Heart *(Brunswick 05817)*
                             Both sides by Carl Dobkins

KEN DODD   7

Much-loved zany Liverpool comedian and singer who brought 'Tears' and 'Happiness' to millions.

25 Jun 60   **8**   1   ★   <u>**Love Is Like A Violin**</u> / The Treasure In My Heart *(Decca F-11248)*
26 Nov 60   **16**   4   **Dream That I Love You** / Jealous Of You *(Decca F-11293)*
31 Dec 60   **16**   2   **Dream That I Love You** / Jealous Of You *(Decca F-11293)* ***re-entry***

BILL DOGGETT COMBO   1

Jazz and R&B organist from Philadelphia who unexpectedly shot to No. 2 in the Billboard 'Top 100' in 1956 with this guitar-and-sax-led instrumental. The featured sax player was Clifford Scott.

12 Jan 57   **2**   1   **Honky Tonk (Parts 1 & 2)** *(Parlophone R-4231)*

RALPH DOLLIMORE

See Jo Hunter etc.

FATS DOMINO   51

Corpulent New Orleans singer/pianist with over 60 US pop hits to his name. Curiously, he never had a No. 1 record on either side of the Atlantic.

23 Jun 56   **18**   1   ★   **My Blue Heaven** / <u>I'm In Love Again</u> *(London HLU-8280)*
 7 Jul 56   **1**   3   ★   <u>**I'm In Love Again**</u> / My Blue Heaven *(London HLU-8280)*
                             re-entry (flipped)
29 Sep 56   **4**   2   **When My Dream Boat Comes Home** / So Long *(London HLU-8309)*
24 Nov 56   **8**   1   ★   <u>**Blueberry Hill**</u> / I Can't Go On *(London HLU-8330)*
12 Jan 57   **5**   2   ★   <u>**Ain't That A Shame**</u> / La La *(London HLU-8173)*
12 Jan 57   **7**   1   ★   <u>**Honey Chile**</u> / Don't You Know *(London HLU-8356)*
 9 Feb 57   **2**   2   ★   <u>**Blue Monday**</u> / What's The Reason I'm Not Pleasing You
                             (London HLP-8377)
 2 Mar 57   **1**   4   ★   <u>**Blue Monday**</u> / What's The Reason I'm Not Pleasing You
                             (London HLP-8377) ***re-entry***
13 Apr 57   **11**   1   ★   <u>**I'm Walkin'**</u> / I'm In The Mood For Love *(London HLP-8407)*
 6 Jul 57   **2**   2   ★   <u>**Valley Of Tears**</u> / It's You I Love *(London HLP-8449)*
21 Sep 57   **3**   3   **When I See You** / **What Will I Tell My Heart** *(London HLP-8471)*
21 Dec 57   **5**   2   **Wait And See** / I Still Love You *(London HLP-8519)*
15 Feb 58   **9**   1   **Wait And See** / I Still Love You *(London HLP-8519)*
                             1st re-entry
22 Mar 58   **3**   1   ★   <u>**The Big Beat**</u> / I Want You To Know *(London HLP-8575)*
26 Apr 58   **6**   1   **Wait And See** / I Still Love You *(London HLP-8519)*
                             2nd re-entry
14 Jun 58   **2**   3   ★   <u>**Sick And Tired**</u> / No, No *(London HLP-8628)*
26 Jul 58   **2**   1   **Little Mary** / The Prisoner's Song *(London HLP-8663)*
10 Jan 59   **1**   5   **Whole Lotta Loving** / Coquette *(London HLP-8759)*
21 Mar 59   **9**   1   **Telling Lies** / When The Saints Go Marching In *(London HLP-8822)*

19 Sep 59	1	5	★ **I Want To Walk You Home** / **I'm Gonna Be A Wheel Some Day**
			(London HLP-8942)
12 Dec 59	6	1	★ **Be My Guest** / I've Been Around *(London HLP-9005)*
25 Jun 60	11	1	**Tell Me That You Love Me** / Before I Grow Too Old
			(London HLP-9133)
15 Oct 60	3	3	★ **Three Nights A Week** / Put Your Arms Around Me, Honey
			(London HLP-9198)
17 Dec 60	7	3	★ **My Girl Josephine** / Natural Born Lover *(London HLP-9244)*
11 Mar 61	5	1	**Ain't That Just Like A Woman** / What A Price *(London HLP-9301)*

LONNIE DONEGAN   38

Born in Glasgow but raised in London, the energetic singer/guitarist Anthony 'Lonnie' Donegan ruled the UK charts in pre-Beatles days as the King of Skiffle.

11 Dec 54	11	5	**NEW ORLEANS JOYS** *(Decca LF-1198)* **LP**
			Chris Barber's Jazz Band / Lonnie Donegan's Skiffle Group
			Bobby Shaftoe (Chris Barber's Jazz Band) / Chimes Blues (Chris Barber's Jazz Band) / Rock Island Line (Lonnie Donegan's Skiffle Group) / The Martinique (Chris Barber's Jazz Band) / New Orleans Blues (Chris Barber's Jazz Band) / John Henry (Lonnie Donegan's Skiffle Group) / Merrydown Rag (Chris Barber's Jazz Band) / Stevedore Stomp (Chris Barber's Jazz Band)
22 Jan 55	22	1	**NEW ORLEANS JOYS** *(Decca LF-1198)* **LP** *re-entry*
22 Oct 55	12	2	**BACKSTAIRS SESSION** *(Polygon Jazz Today JTE-107)* **EP**
			Lonnie Donegan Skiffle Group
			Midnight Special / New Burying Ground / It Takes A Worried Man (To Sing A Worried Song) / When The Sun Goes Down
26 Nov 55	19	1	★ **Rock Island Line** / John Henry *(Decca Jazz F-10647)*
			Both sides by the Lonnie Donegan Skiffle Group
17 Dec 55	1	3	★ **Rock Island Line** / John Henry *(Decca Jazz F-10647)* *re-entry*
3 Mar 56	17	3	**Diggin' My Potatoes** / **Bury My Body** *(Decca Jazz FJ-10695)*
			Both sides by the Lonnie Donegan Skiffle Group
31 Mar 56	19	1	**Midnight Special** / When The Sun Goes Down *(Pye Nixa NJ-2006)*
			Both sides by Lonnie Donegan's Skiffle Group
14 Apr 56	14	1	**Diggin' My Potatoes** / Bury My Body *(Decca Jazz FJ-10695)*
			1st re-entry
14 Apr 56	14	1	★ **Lost John** / **Stewball** *(Pye Nixa N.15036)*
			Both sides by the Lonnie Donegan Skiffle Group
5 May 56	7	1	**BACKSTAIRS SESSION** *(Pye Nixa NJE-1014)* **EP**
			reissue
2 Jun 56	10	1	**BACKSTAIRS SESSION** *(Pye Nixa NJE-1014)* **EP**
			reissue / 1st re-entry
2 Jun 56	14	1	**Diggin' My Potatoes** / Bury My Body *(Decca Jazz FJ-10695)*
			2nd re-entry
30 Jun 56	1	1	★ **SKIFFLE SESSION** *(Pye Nixa NJE-1017)* **EP**
			Lonnie Dogengan Skiffle Group
			Railroad Bill / Stackalee / The Ballad Of Jesse James / Ol' Riley
30 Jun 56	5	1	**BACKSTAIRS SESSION** *(Pye Nixa NJE-1014)* **EP**
			reissue / 2nd re-entry
7 Jul 56	15	1	**Diggin' My Potatoes** / Bury My Body *(Decca Jazz FJ-10695)*
			3rd re-entry
2 Feb 57	1	2	**LONNIE DONEGAN HIT PARADE** *(Pye Nixa NEP-24031)* **EP**
			Lonnie Donegan & His Skiffle Group
			Lost John / Stewball / Bring A Little Water, Sylvie / Dead Or Alive
5 Jul 58	23	1	**DONEGAN ON STAGE** *(Pye Nixa NEP-24075)* **EP**
			Lonnie Donegan & His Skiffle Group
			Mule-Skinner Blues (Blue Yodel No. 8) / Old Hannah / On A Monday /Glory
13 Sep 58	2	1	★ **Lonesome Traveller** /
			Times Are Gettin' Hard Boys *(Pye Nixa 7N.15158)*
			Both sides by Lonnie Donegan & His Skiffle Group
25 Apr 59	1	2	**RELAX WITH LONNIE** *(Pye Nixa NEP-24107)* **EP**
			Lonnie Donegan
			Bewildered / Kevin Barry / It Is No Secret / My Laggan Love

14 Nov 59	3	3	★ San Miguel / Talking Guitar Blues *(Pye Nixa 7N.15237)*
			Both sides by Lonnie Donegan & His Skiffle Group
23 Jul 60	5	2	Kevin Barry / My Laggan Love *(Pye Nixa 7N.15219)*
			Both sides by Lonnie Donegan
25 Feb 61	1	3	Beneath The Willow / Leave My Woman Alone *(Pye 7N.15330)*
			Both sides by Lonnie Donegan

See also Chris Barber's Jazz Band
Miki & Griff

DICKY DOO & THE DON'TS   2
Novelty vocal group from Philadelphia fronted by Gerry Granahan.

| 19 Apr 58 | 5 | 2 | Click Clack / Did You Cry *(London HLU-8589)* |

See also Fireflies

ANTÁL DORATI *(conductor)*
See London Philharmonic Orchestra
Minneapolis Symphony Orchestra

HAROLD DORMAN   1
Rock'n'roll singer/songwriter born in Drew, Mississippi in 1926. The lushly produced 'Mountain Of Love' was a sizeable pop hit in the US, but sadly he was unable to repeat his success.

| 14 May 60 | 5 | 1 | Mountain Of Love / To Be With You *(Top Rank JAR-357)* |

TOMMY DORSEY ORCHESTRA starring Warren Covington   3
Trombonist who led the top band in the USA throughout most of the swing era. Following his death in 1956, his older brother Jimmy stepped in as leader, but died himself a year later – at which point trombone ace Warren Covington took over.

11 Oct 58	4	1	★ Tea For Two Cha Cha / My Baby Just Cares For Me
			(Brunswick 05757)
13 Dec 58	7	1	I Want To Be Happy Cha Cha / Spooky Takes A Holiday
			(Brunswick 05769)
28 Mar 59	12	1	Dinah – Cha Cha / I Still Get Jealous – Cha Cha *(Brunswick 05784)*

ELIZABETH DOUBLEDAY   3
Classical soprano drafted in to partner Mario Lanza on RCA's re-recording of this duet from MGM's 'The Student Prince' (1954). Ann Blyth, who sang the female part in the film, was unable to record for RCA due to contractual reasons.

7 May 55	13	1	Summertime In Heidelberg *(Mario Lanza and Elizabeth Doubleday)*
			(H.M.V. DA-2070)
			Flip is 'Gaudeamus Igitur' by Mario Lanza

See also Mario Lanza

CRAIG DOUGLAS   18
Pop singer from Newport, Isle of Wight, born Terence Perkins. His third single, 'Only Sixteen', topped the UK charts in the summer of 1959, outselling Sam Cooke's original.

25 Apr 59	15	1	★ Come Softly To Me / Golden Girl *(Top Rank JAR-110)*
6 Jun 59	7	1	★ A Teenager In Love / The 39 Steps *(Top Rank JAR-133)*
17 Oct 59	16	1	★ Wish It Were Me / The Riddle Of Love *(Top Rank JAR-204)*
16 Jan 60	1	1	★ Pretty Blue Eyes / Sandy *(Top Rank JAR-268)*
16 Apr 60	5	1	★ The Heart Of A Teenage Girl / New Boy *(Top Rank JAR-340)*
23 Jul 60	3	3	★ Oh! What A Day / Why Why Why *(Top Rank JAR-406)*
22 Oct 60	2	7	Where's The Girl / My Hour Of Love *(Top Rank JAR-515)*
25 Feb 61	3	3	The Girl Next Door / Hey Mister Conscience *(Top Rank JAR-543)*

CHARLIE DRAKE 4

Diminutive red-haired comedian from London, born Charles Springall. He had a brief but relatively successful recording career in the late '50s/early '60s with novelties like 'Splish Splash', 'Mr. Custer' and the unforgettable 'My Boomerang Won't Come Back'.

2 Aug 58	16	1	★ <u>Hello, My Darlings</u> / <u>Splish Splash</u>	*(Parlophone R-4461)*
17 Jan 59	7	1	**Tom Thumb's Tune** / Goggle Eye Ghee	*(Parlophone R-4496)*
15 Oct 60	1	2	★ <u>Mr. Custer</u> / Glow Worm	*(Parlophone R-4701)*

DREAM WEAVERS 1

Vocal group formed at Florida University by Gene Adkinson (baritone) and Wade Buff (lead).

28 Jan 56	2	1	★ <u>It's Almost Tomorrow</u> / You've Got Me Wondering	*(Brunswick 05515)*

DRIFTERS 8

Long-lasting black vocal group from New York with ever-changing personnel. Ben E. King and Clyde McPhatter were just two of the great singers that passed through their ranks.

15 Aug 59	8	1	**There Goes My Baby** / Oh My Love	*(London HLE-8892)*
28 Nov 59	2	1	★ <u>Dance With Me</u> / True Love, True Love	*(London HLE-8988)*
26 Dec 59	1	2	★ <u>Dance With Me</u> / True Love, True Love	*(London HLE-8988)* **re-entry**
2 Apr 60	5	1	**This Magic Moment** / Baltimore	*(London HLE-9081)*
22 Oct 60	1	1	★ <u>Save The Last Dance For Me</u> / Nobody But Me	*(London HLK-9201)*
25 Feb 61	11	2	★ <u>I Count The Tears</u> / Sadie My Lady	*(London HLK-9287)*

See also Ben E. King
Clyde McPhatter

JIMMIE DRIFTWOOD 2

James Morris was a popular country guitarist, as well as a prolific songwriter responsible for the likes of 'Battle Of New Orleans' and 'Tennessee Stud'. He changed his name to Jimmie Driftwood in the 1950s.

18 Feb 61	9	2	**COUNTRY GUITAR (VOL. 13)** *(R.C.A. RCX-191)* `EP`
			Unfortunate Man / Fair Rosamond's Bower / Old Joe Clark / I'm Too Young To Marry / Zelma Lee

BETTY DRIVER 4

Actress and singer born in Leicester in 1920. She later became famed for her hotpot at the Rovers Return on Coronation Street.

10 Jul 54	23	4	**I Know You're Mine** / Let's Gather Round The Old Parlour Piano *(Planet E-1012)*

FRANK D'RONE 2

Acclaimed jazz singer/guitarist born Frank Caldarone in Brockton, Massachusetts in 1932. He had a minor hit in the UK in 1960 with 'Strawberry Blonde'.

21 Dec 57	6	2	**My Special Angel** / Once In A Million Years *(Mercury MT-183)*

JOHNNY DUNCAN & THE BLUE GRASS BOYS 13

Country singer/guitarist from Oliver Springs, Tennessee who joined Chris Barber's Jazz Band and espoused skiffle. After a year, he branched out on his own and briefly became a star when his debut release made No. 2 in the UK charts.

6 Jul 57	2	3	★ <u>Last Train To San Fernando</u> / Rock-A-Billy Baby *(Columbia DB-3959)*
24 Aug 57	9	1	**JOHNNY DUNCAN & HIS BLUE GRASS BOYS**
			(Columbia SEG-7708) `EP`
			Freight Train Blues / Press On / Johnny's Blue Yodel / Out Of Business
5 Oct 57	4	3	★ <u>Blue Blue Heartache</u> / <u>Jig Along Home</u> *(Columbia DB-3996)*
23 Nov 57	8	1	★ <u>Footprints In The Snow</u> / <u>Get Along Home Cindy</u>
			(Columbia DB-4029)
22 Feb 58	12	2	**If You Love Me Baby** / Goodnight Irene *(Columbia DB-4074)*

Toni Dalli

15 Mar 58	**5**	1	**If You Love Me Baby** / Goodnight Irene *(Columbia DB-4074)* ***re-entry***
20 Feb 60	**5**	2	**Any Time** / Yellow Yellow Moon *(Columbia DB-4415)*
			Both sides by Johnny Duncan

See also Chris Barber's Jazz Band

TONY DUNNING & THE TREMOLOS   3

19-year-old teen-pop singer who recorded for the Palette label under the direction of Jack Heath and Cliff Adams. After three unsuccessful singles, he moved into songwriting and production.

| 19 Nov 60 | **15** | 2 | **Seventeen Tomorrow** / Be My Girl *(Palette PG-9006)* |
| 31 Dec 60 | **16** | 1 | **Seventeen Tomorrow** / Be My Girl *(Palette PG-9006)* ***re-entry*** |

JIMMY DURANTE   2

Popular New York comedian, singer and film star famous for his large nose and humorous songs.

| 30 Jul 55 | **21** | 2 | **I'm The Guy Who Found The Lost Chord** / |
| | | | Little Bit This, Little Bit That *(M.G.M. MGM-118)* |

SLIM DUSTY   6

Australia's King of Country Music, singer/songwriter/guitarist David Kirkpatrick, born in Nulla Nulla Creek, New South Wales in 1927.

20 Dec 58	**10**	2	★ **A Pub With No Beer** / Once When I Was Mustering
			(Columbia DB-4212)
17 Jan 59	**2**	2	★ **A Pub With No Beer** / Once When I Was Mustering
			(Columbia DB-4212) ***re-entry***
2 May 59	**9**	2	**The Answer To A Pub With No Beer** / Winter Winds
			(Columbia DB-4294)

DUTCH SWING COLLEGE BAND   3

Popular Dixieland revival band founded in the Netherlands in 1945 by clarinettist/saxophonist Peter Schilperoort.

22 Jan 55	**39**	1	**GEMS OF JAZZ NO. 1** *(Philips BBR-8018)* **LP**
			Boogietrap / Original Dixieland One-Step / Absent-Minded Blues / 1919 Rag /
			Buddy Bolden Blues / Freeze An' Melt / Mabel's Dream / Buddy's Habits
10 Sep 55	**12**	2	**When The Saints Go Marching In (Parts 1 & 2)** *(Philips PB-470)*
			Both sides by the Dutch Swing College Band with Neva Raphaello

VINCE EAGER   3

Larry Parnes-managed UK rock'n'roll singer born Roy Taylor.

3 Oct 59	**23**	1	**Makin' Love** / **Primrose Lane** *(Top Rank JAR-191)*
24 Oct 59	**7**	1	**Makin' Love** / **Primrose Lane** *(Top Rank JAR-191)* ***re-entry***
30 Jan 60	**9**	1	**El Paso** / Why *(Top Rank JAR-275)*

ROBERT EARL   35

Operatic balladeer born Monty Leigh in London in 1926. Sadly, his chart achievements failed to match those of his peers, David Whitfield and Malcolm Vaughan.

16 Oct 54	**4**	5	**My Son, My Son** / Far Away *(Philips PB-331)*
27 Nov 54	**32**	1	**My Son, My Son** / Far Away *(Philips PB-331)* ***re-entry***
25 Jun 55	**10**	1	**I Wonder** / My Loving Hands *(Philips PB-433)*
9 Jul 55	**10**	1	**I Wonder** / My Loving Hands *(Philips PB-433)* ***re-entry***
23 Jul 55	**15**	1	**Three Galleons** / Till The Last Rose Has Faded *(Philips PB-481)*
13 Aug 55	**15**	1	**Three Galleons** / Till The Last Rose Has Faded *(Philips PB-481)*
			1st re-entry
27 Aug 55	**10**	3	**Three Galleons** / Till The Last Rose Has Faded *(Philips PB-481)*
			2nd re-entry
1 Oct 55	**4**	3	**Three Galleons** / Till The Last Rose Has Faded *(Philips PB-481)*
			3rd re-entry

7 Jan 56	**20**	1	★ He / **With Your Love** *(Philips PB-517)*
10 Mar 56	**18**	1	★ **My September Love** / Now And Forever *(Philips PB-552)*
6 Oct 56	**6**	2	**More** / Your Home Can Be A Castle *(Philips PB-622)*
6 Oct 56	**18**	1	**Believe In Me** / If You Can Dream *(Philips PB-593)*
10 Nov 56	**2**	1	**More** / Your Home Can Be A Castle *(Philips PB-622)* *re-entry*
26 Jan 57	**7**	1	**I'm Free** / The Golden Key *(Philips PB-657)*
7 Sep 57	**9**	1	**Fascination** / Song Of The Valley *(Philips PB-730)*
7 Dec 57	**8**	2	**My Special Angel** / There's Only You *(Philips PB-767)*
25 Jan 58	**3**	1	**My Special Angel** / There's Only You *(Philips PB-767)* *re-entry*
29 Mar 58	**5**	2	★ **I May Never Pass This Way Again** / Someone *(Philips PB-805)*
5 Apr 58	**5**	1	★ **I May Never Pass This Way Again** / Someone *(Philips PB-805)* *re-entry*
18 Oct 58	**6**	1	★ **More Than Ever** / No One But You *(Philips PB-867)*
7 Feb 59	**3**	1	★ **The Wonderful Secret Of Love** / The Boulevard Of Broken Dreams *(Philips PB-891)*
10 Oct 59	**4**	1	**The Test Of Time** / **The Key** *(Philips PB-960)*
31 Oct 59	**16**	1	**The Test Of Time** / **The Key** *(Philips PB-960)* *re-entry*
27 Feb 60	**15**	1	**Oh, So Wunderbar** / I'm Rich *(Philips PB-986)*

EASY RIDERS   5

US folk trio guided by producer Mitch Miller, comprising singer/songwriter Terry Gilkyson, Frank Miller and Richard Dehr.

30 Mar 57	**2**	3	★ **Love Is A Golden Ring** *(Frankie Laine with the Easy Riders)* *(Philips PB-676)*
			Flip is 'There's Not A Moment To Spare' by Frankie Laine
30 Mar 57	**19**	1	**Marianne** / Goodbye Chiquita *(Philips PB-670)*
			Both sides as by Terry Gilkyson & The Easy Riders
15 Oct 60	**12**	1	**Young In Love** / Saturday's Child *(London HLR-9204)*

BILLY ECKSTINE   17

Jazz and pop singer born in Pittsburgh in 1914. Along with Nat 'King' Cole, he was one of the first black singers to achieve lasting success in the pop mainstream.

2 Oct 54	**25**	1	★ **No One But You** / I Let A Song Go Out Of My Heart *(M.G.M. MGM-763)*
6 Nov 54	**3**	1	★ **No One But You** / I Let A Song Go Out Of My Heart *(M.G.M. MGM-763)* *re-entry*
29 Jan 55	**43**	1	**Olay, Olay** / Beloved *(M.G.M. MGM-776)*
19 Feb 55	**10**	1	**Beloved** / Olay, Olay *(M.G.M. MGM-776)* *re-entry (flipped)*
9 Apr 55	**12**	4	**What More Is There To Say** / Prelude To A Kiss *(M.G.M. MGM-809)*
14 May 55	**20**	1	**What More Is There To Say** / Prelude To A Kiss *(M.G.M. MGM-809)* *re-entry*
30 Jul 55	**23**	2	**Love Me Or Leave Me** *(Billy Eckstine and the Pied Pipers)* / The Life Of The Party *(Billy Eckstine)* *(M.G.M. MGM-841)*
6 Oct 56	**18**	1	**DEDICATED TO YOU** *(M.G.M. MGM-EP-561)* **EP**
			Billy Eckstine and Sarah Vaughan
			Dedicated To You / You're All I Need / Ev'ryday / I Love You
14 Sep 57	**3**	2	★ **Passing Strangers** *(Sarah Vaughan and Billy Eckstine)* / The Door Is Open *(Billy Eckstine and Sarah Vaughan)* *(Mercury MT-164)*
15 Mar 58	**5**	1	**If I Can Help Somebody** / Boulevard Of Broken Dreams *(Mercury 7MT-191)*
17 Jan 59	**9**	1	★ **Gigi** / Trust In Me *(Mercury AMT-1018)*
7 Feb 59	**14**	1	★ **Gigi** / Trust In Me *(Mercury AMT-1018)* *re-entry*

DUANE EDDY   12

A native of Corning, New York, Duane Eddy was famed for his 'twangy' guitar sound and became most successful rock'n'roll instrumentalist of the '50s and early '60s.

| 16 Aug 58 | **1** | 3 | ★ **Rebel-Rouser** / Stalkin' *(London HL-8669)* |
| | | | *Both sides by Duane Eddy and His Twangy Guitar* |

8 Nov 58	2	2	**Ramrod** / **The Walker** (London HL-8723)
			Both sides by Duane Eddy, His 'Twangy' Guitar and the Rebels
29 Nov 58	9	1	**Ramrod** / **The Walker** (London HL-8723) *re-entry*
13 Dec 58	1	3	★ <u>**Cannonball**</u> / Mason Dixon Lion (London HL-8764)
			Both sides by Duane Eddy, His 'Twangy' Guitar and the Rebels
21 Mar 59	1	2	★ <u>**The Lonely One**</u> / Detour (London HLW-8821)
21 Jan 61	24	1	**Words Mean Nothing** / The Girl On Death Row (London HLW-9223)
			Both sides by Lee Hazlewood with Duane Eddy and His Orchestra

JIMMY EDWARDS (UK)

See Joy Nichols

JIMMY EDWARDS (USA)   1

Rockabilly singer born James Bullington in Senath, Missouri in 1925. His classic waxing was covered in the UK by Marty Wilde and Wee Willie Harris.

| 15 Mar 58 | 11 | 1 | **Love Bug Crawl** / Honey Lovin' (Mercury 7MT-193) |

TOMMY EDWARDS   10

Black American balladeer born in Richmond, Virginia. In 1958, he topped the charts on both sides of the Atlantic with 'It's All In The Game', but his follow-ups sold less well.

21 Mar 59	13	1	**Please Mr. Sun** / The Morning Side Of The Mountain
			(M.G.M. MGM-1006)
25 Apr 59	13	1	**Please Mr. Sun** / **The Morning Side Of The Mountain**
			(M.G.M. MGM-1006) *re-entry*
20 Jun 59	3	7	★ <u>**My Melancholy Baby**</u> / It's Only The Good Times (M.G.M. MGM-1020)
15 Oct 60	9	1	**Blue Heartaches** / It's Not The End Of Everything (M.G.M. MGM-1097)

DUKE ELLINGTON   22

Prominent black composer, pianist and jazz orchestra leader born Edward Kennedy Ellington in Washington, DC in 1899.

14 Aug 54	6	3	**Isle Of Capri** / Band Call (Capitol CL-14132)
			Both sides by Duke Ellington & His Famous Orchestra
11 Sep 54	15	1	**SKIN DEEP** (H.M.V. 7EG-8033) **EP**
			Duke Ellington & His Orchestra
			Skin Deep / Sophisticated Lady
25 Sep 54	13	3	**Satin Doll** / Bunny Hop Mambo (Capitol CL-14153)
			Both sides by Duke Ellington & His Famous Orchestra
2 Oct 54	13	1	**ELLINGTON '55** (Capitol LCT-6008) **LP**
			Duke Ellington & His Famous Orchestra
			Rockin' In Rhythm / Black And Tan Fantasy / Stompin' At The Savoy / In The Mood /
			One O'Clock Jump / Honeysuckle Rose / Happy Go Lucky Local / Flying Home
16 Oct 54	8	3	**ELLINGTON '55** (Capitol LCT-6008) **LP** *1st re-entry*
16 Oct 54	17	3	**MASTERPIECES** (Columbia 33SX-1022) **LP**
			Duke Ellington & His Orchestra
			Mood Indigo / Sophisticated Lady / The Tattooed Bride / Solitude
13 Nov 54	12	1	**ELLINGTON '55** (Capitol LCT-6008) **LP** *2nd re-entry*
13 Nov 54	14	3	**MASTERPIECES** (Columbia 33SX-1022) **LP** *re-entry*
27 Nov 54	19	1	**ELLINGTON '55** (Capitol LCT-6008) **LP** *3rd re-entry*
25 Dec 54	31	1	**ELLINGTON '55** (Capitol LCT-6008) **LP** *4th re-entry*
5 Feb 55	21	1	**ELLINGTON '55** (Capitol LCT-6008) **LP** *5th re-entry*
14 Apr 56	21	1	**SKIN DEEP** (H.M.V. 7EG-8033) **EP** *re-entry*

RAY ELLINGTON QUARTET   4

Drummer born Harry Pitts Brown Jr. in 1916 to a black American father and a Russian mother, and raised in London. He led a rocking jazz quartet that was a staple of the Goon shows in the '50s, and had a minor UK hit in 1962 with 'The Madison'.

| 2 Oct 54 | 35 | 1 | **Sky Blue Shirt And A Rainbow Tie** / My Mother's Eyes |
| | | | (Columbia DB-3500) |

13 Nov 54	**40**	1	**Sky Blue Shirt And A Rainbow Tie** / My Mother's Eyes
			(Columbia DB-3500) *1st re-entry*
4 Dec 54	**13**	1	**Sky Blue Shirt And A Rainbow Tie** / My Mother's Eyes
			(Columbia DB-3500) *2nd re-entry*
24 Nov 56	**5**	1	**The Green Door** / Giddy-Up-A Ding Dong (Columbia DB-3838)

PETER ELLIOTT   1

Smooth balladeer and former springboard diving champion and who failed to break into the charts despite regular exposure on the 'Oh Boy!' TV show.

| 16 Jul 60 | **11** | 1 | **Waiting For The Robert E. Lee** / Toot-Toot-Tootsie (Top Rank JAR-390) |

GEORGE ELRICK   4

Born in Aberdeen in 1903, George Elrick enjoyed a lengthy career as a bandleader and purveyor of comedy songs before changing direction in 1948 to become 'The Smiling Voice of Radio'. He is probably best remembered as the genial host of the popular BBC record request show 'Housewives' Choice' during the '50s and '60s.

11 Sep 54	**29**	1	**Gilly Gilly Ossenfeffer Katznellenbogen By The Sea** (George Elrick and the Lumberjacks) / Three Coins In The Fountain (Lumberjacks) (Decca F-10371)
25 Sep 54	**39**	1	**Gilly Gilly Ossenfeffer Katznellenbogen By The Sea** (George Elrick and the Lumberjacks) / Three Coins In The Fountain (Lumberjacks) (Decca F-10371) *1st re-entry*
9 Oct 54	**34**	1	**Gilly Gilly Ossenfeffer Katznellenbogen By The Sea** (George Elrick and the Lumberjacks) / Three Coins In The Fountain (Lumberjacks) (Decca F-10371) *2nd re-entry*
30 Oct 54	**35**	1	**Robert Wilson Medley [M]** / Robert Burns Medley **[M]** (Beltona BL-2595) *Robert Wilson Medley:* Westering Home – A Gordon For Me – The Gay Gordons / *Robert Burns Medley:* Ye Banks And Braes – My Love Is Like A Red, Red Rose – Comin' Thro The Rye

JACK EMBLOW

See Adriano

EMMETTONES   28

Studio folk ensemble from North of the Border consisting of Josh MacRae, Hamish Imlach and Bobby Campbell. 'Bold Robert Emmett', an Irish rebel song which they set to the tune of 'Streets Of Laredo' because they didn't care for the original, went to No. 1 in Ireland.

1 Oct 60	**1**	3	**Johnson's Motor Car** / Men Of The West (Beltona BL-2724)
1 Oct 60	**9**	1	**Bold Robert Emmett** / The Song Of The Fenian Brotherhood (Beltona BL-2722)
22 Oct 60	**3**	2	**Bold Robert Emmett** / The Song Of The Fenian Brotherhood (Beltona BL-2722) *1st re-entry*
12 Nov 60	**1**	3	**Bold Robert Emmett** / The Song Of The Fenian Brotherhood (Beltona BL-2722) *2nd re-entry*
26 Nov 60	**10**	2	**Father Murphy** / Erin Go Brah (Beltona BL-2723)
3 Dec 60	**11**	1	**A Scottish Soldier** / MacPherson's Rant (Beltona BL-2725)
10 Dec 60	**1**	7	**Bold Robert Emmett** / The Song Of The Fenian Brotherhood (Beltona BL-2722) *3rd re-entry*
17 Dec 60	**20**	1	**A Scottish Soldier** / MacPherson's Rant (Beltona BL-2725) *re-entry*
21 Jan 61	**1**	3	**Father Murphy** / Erin Go Brah (Beltona BL-2723) *1st re-entry*
11 Feb 61	**2**	1	**Johnson's Motor Car** / Men Of The West (Beltona BL-2724) *re-entry*
18 Feb 61	**1**	3	**Bold Robert Emmett** / The Song Of The Fenian Brotherhood (Beltona BL-2722) *4th re-entry*
18 Feb 61	**13**	1	**Father Murphy** / Erin Go Brah (Beltona BL-2723) *2nd re-entry*

See also Josh MacRae

PRESTON EPPS 9

Black bongo player from Oakland, California who briefly sparked a trend that became a lifelong career.

| 20 Jun 59 | **3** | 8 | **Bongo Rock** / Bongo Party *(Top Rank JAR-140)* |
| 16 Apr 60 | **8** | 1 | **Bongo Boogie** / Flamenco Bongo *(Top Rank JAR-345)* |

ALBERTO EREDE *(conductor)*

See Hilde Gueden

EUREKA BRASS BAND 1

Famous New Orleans brass band founded in 1920 by trumpeter Willie Wilson.

8 Jan 55	**46**	1	**NEW ORLEANS PARADE** *(Melodisc MLP 12-101)* **LP**
			George Lewis leading the Eureka Brass Band
			Sing On / West Lawn Dirge / Lady Be Good / Garlands Of Flowers

See also George Lewis

BARBARA EVANS 1

American teen-pop singer who recorded several unsuccessful singles between 1958 and 1962.

| 22 Aug 59 | **6** | 1 | **Souvenirs** / Pray For Me Mother *(R.C.A. RCA-1122)* |

MAUREEN EVANS 2

Pop singer from Cardiff, who scored six UK hits between 1960 and 1964. Her biggest was her 1962 cover of Nancy Sinatra's 'Like I Do', which made the Top Five.

| 16 Jan 60 | **5** | 1 | ★ **The Big Hurt** / I Can't Begin To Tell You *(Oriole CB-1533)* |
| 3 Dec 60 | **24** | 1 | **Till** / Why Don't You Believe Me *(Oriole CB-1581)* |

PAUL EVANS 7

Prolific singer/songwriter from New York, responsible for big hits like 'Roses Are Red', 'Seven Little Girls Sitting In The Back Seat' and 'When'.

7 Nov 59	**13**	3	★ **Seven Little Girls Sitting In The Back Seat** /
			Worshipping An Idol *(London HLL-8968)*
			Both sides by Paul Evans and the Curls
12 Mar 60	**13**	1	★ **Midnite Special** / Since I Met You, Baby *(London HLL-9045)*
10 Dec 60	**25**	1	**Hushabye Little Guitar** / Blind Boy *(London HLL-9239)*
21 Jan 61	**2**	2	**Hushabye Little Guitar** / Blind Boy *(London HLL-9239) re-entry*

EVERLY BROTHERS 8

Top harmony duo Don and Phil Everly racked up dozens of hits on both sides of the Atlantic between 1957 and 1968.

29 Jun 57	**1**	2	★ **Bye Bye, Love** / I Wonder If I Care As Much *(London HLA-8440)*
8 Mar 58	**2**	3	**This Little Girl Of Mine / Should We Tell Him** *(London HLA-8554)*
5 Apr 58	**15**	1	**This Little Girl Of Mine** / Should We Tell Him *(London HLA-8554)*
			re-entry
17 May 58	**4**	1	★ **All I Have To Do Is Dream** / **Claudette** *(London HLA-8618)*
6 Feb 60	**3**	1	★ **Let It Be Me** / Since You Broke My Heart *(London HLA-9039)*

FABIAN 8

Born Fabiano Forte in Philadelphia in 1941, Fabian was the archetypal manufactured teen idol with an untamed voice. 'Tiger' was his biggest hit stateside, but in the UK it was 'Hound Dog Man' that charted.

15 Aug 59	**8**	2	**Tiger** / Mighty Cold *(H.M.V. POP-643)*
30 Jan 60	**4**	2	★ **Hound Dog Man** / This Friendly World *(H.M.V. POP-695)*
5 Mar 60	**11**	1	★ **Hound Dog Man** / This Friendly World *(H.M.V. POP-695) re-entry*
26 Mar 60	**5**	1	**String Along** / About This Thing Called Love *(H.M.V. POP-724)*

16 Apr 60 **10** 1 **String Along** / About This Thing Called Love *(H.M.V. POP-724)*
re-entry
3 Sep 60 **12** 1 **Strollin' In The Springtime** / I'm Gonna Sit Right Down And
Write Myself A Letter *(H.M.V. POP-778)*

ADAM FAITH 2
Clean-cut fair-haired singer born Terence Nelhams-Wright. who in the early '60s rivalled Cliff Richard as Britain's No. 1 male vocalist. After his popularity faded, he became successful actor.

14 Nov 59 **3** 1 ★ **What Do You Want?** / From Now Until Forever *(Parlophone R-4591)*
12 Nov 60 **14** 1 ★ **ADAM** *(Parlophone PMC-1128)* LP
Wonderful Time / Diamond Ring / Summertime / Greenfinger / Piper Of Love /
A Girl Like You / Turn Me Loose / So Many Ways / Singin' In The Rain / Fare Thee
Well My Pretty Maid / I'm A Man / Hit The Road To Dreamland

PERCY FAITH & His Orchestra 3
Bandleader/composer celebrated for his lush orchestral arrangements of pop and rock hits. Although he was Canadian by birth, he later became an American citizen.

30 Apr 55 **28** 1 **Blue Mirage** / Under The Bridges Of Paris *(Philips PB-415)*
20 Feb 60 **1** 2 ★ **The Theme from 'A Summer Place'** / Go-Go-Po-Go *(Philips PB-989)*

ART FARMER 3
Trumpet- and flugelhorn-playing jazzman born in Council Bluffs, Iowa in 1928. He moved to Austria in the late '60s.

19 Jun 54 **6** 3 **CLIFFORD BROWN & ART FARMER
WITH THE SWEDISH ALL STARS (VOL. 2)** *(Esquire EP-3)* EP
Falling In Love With Love / Lover Come Back To Me

See also Swedish All Stars
Swedish-American All Stars

FAWKES–TURNER SEXTET 1
UK-based jazz outfit led by the English cartoonist Wally Fawkes (clarinet) and Canadian Bruce Turner (clarinet/sax).

29 Jan 55 **43** 1 **TAKIN' IT EASY (VOL. 1)** *(Decca DFE-6192)* EP
Fishmouth / Summertime / My Monday Date

JOHN FEENEY 1
Irish tenor born in Swinford, Co. Mayo in 1903. He emigrated to the USA in 1928 and became a major radio and recording star in the Irish-American community.

3 Sep 55 **26** 1 **The Soldier's Song** / Let Erin Remember *(Decca (Irish Series) F-12260)*

FENDERMEN 3
Powerhouse rock'n'roll guitar duo formed by University of Wisconsin-Madison students Paul Humphrey and Jim Sundquist. Unusually, they were both born on the same day: 26 November 1937.

9 Jul 60 **3** 1 ★ **Mule Skinner Blues** / Torture *(Top Rank JAR-395)*
30 Jul 60 **9** 1 ★ **Mule Skinner Blues** / Torture *(Top Rank JAR-395)* *re-entry*
22 Oct 60 **16** 1 **Don't You Just Know It** / Beach Party *(Top Rank JAR-513)*

JOHNNY FERGUSON 5
Deejay and country-pop singer born in Nashville, Tennessee in 1937. 'Angela Jones' was his only hit, but was outsold in the UK by Michael Cox's cover version.

12 Mar 60 **7** 1 ★ **Angela Jones** / Blue Serge And White Lace *(M.G.M. MGM-1059)*
4 Jun 60 **1** 1 ★ **Angela Jones** / Blue Serge And White Lace *(M.G.M. MGM-1059)*
1st re-entry
18 Jun 60 **1** 3 ★ **Angela Jones** / Blue Serge And White Lace *(M.G.M. MGM-1059)*
2nd re-entry

FERKO STRING BAND 5

Famous marching band from Philadelphia founded in 1923 by Joseph A. Ferko.

9 Jul 55	**26**	1	★ **Alabama Jubilee** / Sing A Little Melody *(London HLF-8140)*
23 Jul 55	**4**	3	★ **Alabama Jubilee** / Sing A Little Melody *(London HLF-8140) **re-entry***
19 Nov 55	**18**	1	**You Are My Sunshine** / Ma (She's Making Eyes At Me) *(London HLF-8183)*

FERRANTE & TEICHER 1

Arthur Ferrante and Louis Teicher were an American piano-playing duo who performed easy-listening arrangements of classical pieces, movie themes and show tunes. Although they performed together from 1930 until 1989, their chart popularity was highest during the '60s and early '70s.

6 Aug 60	**11**	1	★ **Theme from 'The Apartment'** / Lonely Room *(London HLT-9164)*

KATHLEEN FERRIER 6

Highly regarded English contralto who tragically died of cancer in 1953, aged just 41.

1 Jan 55	**19**	1	**A RECITAL OF BACH AND HANDEL ARIAS** *(Decca LXT-2757)* **LP**
			Kathleen Ferrier with the London Philharmonic Orchestra, cond. Sir Adrian Boult
			Bach: Qui Sedes *(Mass in B Minor)* / Grief For Sin *(St. Matthew Passion)* / All Is Fulfilled *(St. John Passion)* / Agnus Dei *(Mass In B Minor)* / Handel: Return O God Of Hosts *(Samson)* / O Thou That Tellest Glad Tidings *(Messiah)* / Father Of Heaven *(Judas Maccabaeus)* / He Was Despised *(Messiah)*
1 Jan 55	**26**	3	**What Is Life? (Che Faro?)** / Art Thou Troubled? *(Decca K-1466)*
22 Jan 55	**61**	1	**Blow The Wind Southerly** / Ma Bonny Lad – Keel Row **[M]** *(Decca F-9300)*
5 Feb 55	**14**	1	**What Is Life? (Che Faro?)** / Art Thou Troubled? *(Decca K-1466)* ***re-entry***

ERNIE FIELDS & His Orchestra 6

Black trombonist, pianist, bandleader and arranger born in Nacogdoches, Texas in 1904.

28 Nov 59	**3**	4	★ **In The Mood** / Christopher Columbus *(London HL-8985)*
			Both sides as by Ernie Field's Orchestra
23 Apr 60	**5**	1	★ **Chattanooga Choo Choo** / Workin' Out *(London HL-9100)*
26 Nov 60	**16**	1	**Raunchy** / My Prayer *(London HL-9227)*

GRACIE FIELDS 2

Actress, singer and comedienne born Grace Stansfield in Rochdale in 1898. A much-loved star of stage and screen, she made many memorable recordings including 'Sally', 'Wish Me Luck As You Wave Me Goodbye' and 'The Biggest Aspidistra in the World'.

7 Dec 57	**8**	2	**Mary's Boy Child** / Scarlet Ribbons *(Columbia DB-4047)*

FIESTAS 1

Black vocal quartet from Newark, New Jersey led by Tommy Bullock.

13 Jun 59	**14**	1	**So Fine** / Last Night I Dreamed *(London HL-8870)*

FIREBALLS 5

Instrumental group from Raton, New Mexico. They were conscripted by producer Norman Petty to overdub various Buddy Holly recordings after his death in February 1959.

21 Nov 59	**16**	2	**Torquay** / Cry Baby *(Top Rank JAR-218)*
30 Apr 60	**7**	1	**Foot-Patter** / Kissin' *(Top Rank JAR-354)*
24 Sep 60	**6**	2	**Vaquero** / Chief Whoopin-Koff *(Top Rank JAR-507)*

FIREFLIES 2

New York rock'n'roll guitar trio comprising Gerry Granahan, Vinnie Rogers and Lee Reynolds.

24 Oct 59	23	1	**You Were Mine** / Stella Got A Fella *(Top Rank JAR-198)*
12 Mar 60	9	1	**I Can't Say Goodbye** / What Did I Do Wrong *(London HLU-9057)*

See also Dicky Doo & The Don'ts
         Mandrake

FIREHOUSE FIVE + 2 1

New Orleans-style jazz band formed in 1949 by staff working at Walt Disney's animation studios in Hollywood.

29 Jan 55	43	1	**Runnin' Wild** / Lonesome Railroad Blues *(Good Time Jazz GV-2192)*

FIRESTONES 3

Pseudo-Latin dance music produced by veteran British jazz drummer George Fierstone.

26 Nov 60	10	2	**Party Cha (Parts 1 & 2) [M]** *(Decca F-11290)*
			Makin' Whoopee – Ida, Sweet As Apple Cider – Eternally – Last Night On The Back Porch / Isle Of Capri – If You Knew Susie – Little Serenade – C'est Si Bon
17 Dec 60	14	1	**Party Cha (Parts 1 & 2) [M]** *(Decca F-11290) re-entry*

EDDIE FISHER 56

Singer born born in Philadelphia in 1928. His strong, melodious tenor and good looks helped to make him one of the most popular balladeers of the '50s.

3 Jul 54	9	1	**A Girl! A Girl!** / I'm In The Mood For Love *(H.M.V. B-10688)*
7 Aug 54	1	12	**My Friend** / May I Sing To You *(H.M.V. B-10729)*
28 Aug 54	21	1	**How Do You Speak To An Angel** / My Arms, My Heart, My Love *(H.M.V. B-10737)*
18 Sep 54	2	6	★ <u>I Need You Now</u> / Heaven Was Never Like This *(H.M.V. B-10755)*
25 Sep 54	33	1	**How Do You Speak To An Angel** / My Arms, My Heart, My Love *(H.M.V. B-10737) 1st re-entry*
16 Oct 54	5	3	**How Do You Speak To An Angel / My Arms, My Heart, My Love** *(H.M.V. B-10737) 2nd re-entry*
6 Nov 54	4	5	**My Friend** / May I Sing To You *(H.M.V. B-10729) re-entry*
20 Nov 54	11	4	**Count Your Blessings Instead Of Sheep / White Christmas** *(H.M.V. B-10779)*
20 Nov 54	20	2	**How Do You Speak To An Angel** / My Arms, My Heart, My Love *(H.M.V. B-10737) 3rd re-entry*
18 Dec 54	39	3	**How Do You Speak To An Angel** / My Arms, My Heart, My Love *(H.M.V. B-10737) 4th re-entry*
1 Jan 55	19	2	**Count Your Blessings Instead Of Sheep / White Christmas** *(H.M.V. B-10779) re-entry*
19 Feb 55	36	1	★ <u>Wedding Bells</u> / A Man Chases A Girl *(H.M.V. B-10839)*
12 Mar 55	8	1	★ <u>Wedding Bells</u> / A Man Chases A Girl *(H.M.V. B-10839) re-entry*
2 Jul 55	28	1	**And This Is My Beloved** / Just One More Time *(H.M.V. B-10867)*
23 Jul 55	12	3	**And This Is My Beloved** / Just One More Time *(H.M.V. B-10867) re-entry*
17 Sep 55	12	1	**Don't Stay Away Too Long** / Take My Love *(H.M.V. B-10925)*
12 Nov 55	25	1	**Song Of The Dreamer** / I'm Just A Vagabond Lover *(H.M.V. POP-101)*
26 Nov 55	19	2	**Song Of The Dreamer** / I'm Just A Vagabond Lover *(H.M.V. POP-101) re-entry*
17 Dec 55	19	1	**Don't Stay Away Too Long** / Take My Love *(H.M.V. B-10925) 1st re-entry*
7 Jan 56	16	1	**Don't Stay Away Too Long** / Take My Love *(H.M.V. B-10925) 2nd re-entry*
3 Mar 56	22	1	**Dungaree Doll** / If It Hadn't Been For You *(H.M.V. POP-171)*
31 Mar 56	14	1	**Dungaree Doll** / If It Hadn't Been For You *(H.M.V. POP-171) re-entry*

| 9 Mar 57 | **13** | 1 | **BUNDLE OF JOY [OST]** *(H.M.V. 7EG-8207)* **EP** |

Worry About Tomorrow – Tomorrow *(Eddie Fisher)* / Some Day Soon *(Eddie Fisher)* / All About Love *(Eddie Fisher)* / Lullaby In Blue *(Eddie Fisher and Debbie Reynolds)* / I Never Felt This Way Before *(Eddie Fisher)*

| 16 Mar 57 | **9** | 1 | **Some Day Soon** / All About Love *(H.M.V. POP-296)* |

TONI FISHER   4

Singer from Los Angeles born Marion Nolan. 'The Big Hurt', written by her manager, Wayne Shanklin, is reputedly the first record ever to include phasing effects.

| 16 Jan 60 | **1** | 4 | ★ <u>**The Big Hurt**</u> / Memphis Belle *(Top Rank JAR-261)* |

ELLA FITZGERALD   42

Born in Newport News, Virginia in 1917, Ella Fitzgerald was the most influential and popular female jazz singer in the United States for over half a century.

| 19 Jun 54 | **18** | 1 | **ELLA SINGS GERSHWIN** *(Brunswick LA-8648)* **LP** |

Ella Fitzgerald with Ellis Larkin – piano
Someone To Watch Over Me / My One And Only / But Not For Me / Looking For A Boy / I've Got A Crush On You / How Long Has This Been Going On? / Maybe / Soon

14 May 55	**19**	3	**Lullaby Of Birdland** / Later *(Brunswick 05392)*
23 Jul 55	**25**	3	**Lullaby Of Birdland** / Later *(Brunswick 05392)* *re-entry*
8 Oct 55	**7**	4	**Pete Kelly's Blues** / Hard Hearted Hannah *(Brunswick 05473)*
12 Nov 55	**1**	9	**Pete Kelly's Blues** / **Hard Hearted Hannah** *(Brunswick 05473)* *re-entry*
14 Jan 56	**13**	1	**The Tender Trap** / My One And Only Love *(Brunswick 05514)*
26 May 56	**11**	1	**SWEET AND HOT** *(Brunswick LAT-8091)* **LP**

Thanks For The Memory / It Might As Well Be Spring / You'll Never Know / I Can't Get Started / Moanin' Low / Taking A Chance On Love / That Old Black Magic / Old Devil Moon / Lover, Come Back To Me / Between The Devil And The Deep Blue Sea / (If You Can't Sing It) You'll Have To Swing It

| 8 Dec 56 | **7** | 1 | **ELLA AND LOUIS** *(H.M.V. CLP-1098)* **LP** |

Ella Fitzgerald and Louis Armstrong
Can't We Be Friends / Isn't This A Lovely Day / Moonlight In Vermont / They Can't Take That Away From Me / Under The Blanket Of Blue / Tenderly / A Foggy Day / Stars Fell On Alabama / Cheek To Cheek / The Nearness Of You / April In Paris

5 Jan 57	**4**	1	**ELLA AND LOUIS** *(H.M.V. CLP-1098)* **LP** *re-entry*
14 Sep 57	**13**	1	**Manhattan** / Ev'ry Time We Say Goodbye *(H.M.V. POP-373)*
19 Oct 57	**5**	1	**Ev'ry Time We Say Goodbye** / **Manhattan** *(H.M.V. POP-373)* *1st re-entry (flipped)*
3 May 58	**6**	1	**ELLA SINGS 'PAL JOEY'** *(H.M.V. 7EG-8327)* **EP**

The Lady Is A Tramp / I Could Write A Book / Bewitched

17 May 58	**5**	1	★ <u>**The Swingin' Shepherd Blues**</u> *(Ella Fitzgerald and Her Shepherds)* / Midnight Sun *(H.M.V. POP-486)*
17 May 58	**8**	3	**Ev'ry Time We Say Goodbye** / Manhattan *(H.M.V. POP-373)* *2nd re-entry*
5 Jul 58	**2**	5	**St. Louis Blues** / Beale Street Blues *(H.M.V. POP-499)*
9 Aug 58	**12**	1	**Manhattan** / Ev'ry Time We Say Goodbye *(H.M.V. POP-373)* *3rd re-entry (flipped)*
23 Aug 58	**7**	1	**St. Louis Blues** / **Beale Street Blues** *(H.M.V. POP-499)* *re-entry*
22 Aug 59	**16**	1	**Ev'ry Time We Say Goodbye** / Manhattan *(H.M.V. POP-373)* *4th re-entry (flipped)*
3 Oct 59	**23**	1	★ <u>**But Not For Me**</u> / You Make Me Feel So Young *(H.M.V. POP-657)*
27 Feb 60	**11**	1	**Like Young** / Beat Me Daddy Eight To The Bar *(H.M.V. POP-701)*
1 Oct 60	**15**	1	★ <u>**How High The Moon (Parts 1 & 2)**</u> *(H.M.V. POP-782)*

FIVE CHESTERNUTS — 1

British rock'n'roll group led by drummer Pete Chester, son of comedian Charlie Chester.The line-up also included future Drifters/Shadows Hank Marvin and Bruce Welch.

26 Jul 58   **4** 1   **Teenage Love** / Jean Dorothy *(Columbia DB-4165)*

See also Pete Chester & The Consulates
           Cliff Richard & The Drifters
           Shadows

5 DeMARCO SISTERS — 12

Quintet of sisters from New York who were a show-business staple in the '40s and '50s, with regular radio, TV and movie appearances.

21 May 55   **1** 12   **Dreamboat** / Two Hearts, Two Kisses *(Brunswick 05425)*

FIVE SMITH BROTHERS — 1

Martin, Roy, Harold and Stan Smith from Newcastle Upon Tyne started performing as the Four Smith Brothers in 1932. When Martin died of a heart condition in 1936, he was replaced by another brother, Alf. In 1946, clarinettist Ronnie Culbertson was invited to join the group and they became the Five Smith Brothers. This was one of their last recordings.

11 Jun 55   **24** 1 ★ **I'm In Favour Of Friendship** / Don't Worry *(Decca F-10527)*

BUD FLANAGAN — 2

Born Chaim Weintrop in London in 1896, Bud Flanagan came to prominence in the years between the wars as one half of Flanagan & Allen, and as leader of the Crazy Gang. By the time this record was released, however, he was working as a solo act.

30 May 59   **11** 1   **Strollin'** / Home Is Where Your Heart Is *(Columbia DB-4265)*
2 Jul 60   **10** 1   **Strollin'** / Home Is Where Your Heart Is *(Columbia DB-4265)* *re-entry*

MICHAEL FLANDERS — 1

Actor, broadcaster, writer and humorist born in London in 1922. He is probably best remembered for his collaboration with pianist Donald Swann, with whom he wrote and performed comic songs

21 Feb 59   **4** 1 ★ **The Little Drummer Boy** *(Parlophone R-4528)*
                          Flip is 'The Youth Of The Heart' by Donald Swann

FLEE-RAKKERS — 7

British instrumental sextet led by Dutch saxophonist Peter Fleerakkers and produced by Joe Meek. Their name was later changed to the Flee-Rekkers.

18 Jun 60   **3** 4   **Chicka'roo** / Don't Pick On Me *(Triumph RGM-1009)*
                          Both sides by Ricky Wayne with the Fabulous Flee-Rakkers
24 Sep 60   **4** 2 ★ **Sunday Date** / Shiftless Sam *(Pye 7N.15288)*
25 Feb 61   **18** 1   **Blue Tango** / Bitter Rice *(Pye 7N.15326)*
                          Both sides as by the Flee-Rekkers

FLEETWOODS — 6

Soft harmony trio from Olympia, Washington comprising Barbara Ellis, Gretchen Christopher and Gary Troxel.

18 Apr 59   **14** 1 ★ **Come Softly To Me** / I Care So Much *(London HLU-8841)*
24 Oct 59   **4** 5   **Mr. Blue** / You Mean Everything To Me *(Top Rank JAR-202)*

WADE FLEMONS — 1

Smooth R&B singer born in Coffeyville, Kansas in 1942. He later helped to found the immensely successful '70s band Earth, Wind & Fire.

7 Nov 59   **20** 1   **Slow Motion** / Walkin' By The River *(Top Rank JAR-206)*

EDDIE FONTAINE   5

Singer/guitarist born Edward Reardon in Springfield, Massachusetts. Thanks to an appearance in 'The Girl Can't Help It' (1958), he enjoyed brief glory in the States with this rockabilly novelty, but found greater fame in the '60 and '70s as a TV actor.

1 Nov 58	**2**	2	**Nothin' Shakin'** / Don't Ya Know *(London HLM-8711)*
29 Nov 58	**7**	3	**Nothin' Shakin'** / Don't Ya Know *(London HLM-8711)* ***re-entry***

ARLENE FONTANA   3

New York singer who landed some London club bookings in 1959 thanks to the popularity of this teen-pop single – one of the first to appear on the new Pye International label. She later had a successful career on Broadway and as a nightclub performer.

28 Mar 59	**1**	3	**I'm In Love** / Easy *(Pye International 7N.25010)*

FONTANE SISTERS   13

Singing trio from New Milford, New Jersey who backed Perry Como on record and TV from 1949 to 1954, then switched to making pop covers of rock'n'roll hits.

2 Apr 55	**2**	3	**Hearts Of Stone** / Bless Your Heart *(London HL-8113)*
30 Apr 55	**13**	2	**Hearts Of Stone** / Bless Your Heart *(London HL-8113)* ***re-entry***
29 Oct 55	**1**	3	★ <u>Seventeen</u> / If I Could Be With You *(London HLD-8177)*
9 Mar 57	**2**	3	**The Banana Boat Song** / Lonesome Lover Blues *(London HLD-8378)*
1 Jun 57	**2**	2	**The Banana Boat Song** / Lonesome Lover Blues *(London HLD-8378)* ***re-entry***

BILL FORBES   3

Singer born in Colombo, Ceylon (now Sri Lanka) in 1938. After successfully auditioning for Jack Good's 'Oh Boy!', he was signed by Columbia but only managed one minor hit. In the mid-'60s, he sang vocals and played piano in a Huddersfield group called the Contrasts.

26 Dec 59	**3**	3	★ <u>Too Young</u> / It's Not The End Of The World *(Columbia DB-4386)*

CLINTON FORD   8

Versatile singer from Salford, born Ian Harrison. He recorded in a variety of styles, but is probably best remembered for humorous novelties like 'Fanlight Fanny' and 'The Old Bazaar In Cairo'. 'Mustapha' also bubbled under for Kemal Rachid and Staïffi et ses Mustafa's.

26 Sep 59	**6**	4	★ <u>Old Shep</u> / Nellie Dean Rock *(Oriole CB-1500)*
21 May 60	**7**	3	**Mustapha** / Two Brothers *(Oriole CB-1551)*
16 Jul 60	**9**	1	**Mustapha** / Two Brothers *(Oriole CB-1551)* ***re-entry***

EMILE FORD & THE CHECKMATES   5

Singer, multi-instrumentalist and pioneering sound engineer born Michael Emile Telford Miller in Castries, St. Lucia in 1937. He formed the Checkmates in 1959 with his half-brother, George Sweetnam-Ford, and found instant success with a revival of an old music hall tune.

17 Oct 59	**16**	2	★ <u>What Do You Want To Make Those Eyes At Me For?</u> / Don't Tell Me Your Troubles *(Pye Nixa 7N.15225)*
27 Aug 60	**5**	1	★ <u>Them There Eyes</u> / Question *(Pye 7N.15282)* Both sides as by Emile Ford
3 Dec 60	**11**	1	★ <u>Counting Teardrops</u> / White Christmas *(Pye 7N.15314)*
25 Feb 61	**6**	1	★ <u>What Am I Gonna Do</u> / A Kiss To Build A Dream On *(Pye 7N.15331)*

FRANKIE FORD   18

Piano-pounding New Orleans rock'n'roller born Vincent Francis Guzzo in Gretna, Louisiana in 1939. The energetic 'Sea Cruise' was a Top 20 smash in the States and came very close to breaking through in Britain.

25 Apr 59	**1**	5	**Sea Cruise** / Roberta *(London HL-8850)*
6 Jun 59	**4**	10	**Sea Cruise** / Roberta *(London HL-8850)* ***re-entry***
19 Nov 60	**3**	3	**You Talk Too Much** / If You've Got Troubles *(London HLP-9222)*

TENNESSEE ERNIE FORD 31

Born in Bristol, Tennessee in 1919, baritone singer Ernest Jennings Ford handled country, gospel and pop material with consummate ease, achieving stardom in the mid-'50s with crossover hits like 'Sixteen Tons' and 'The Ballad Of Davy Crockett'.

11 Sep 54	29	1	★ **River Of No Return** / Give Me Your Word *(Capitol CL-14005)*
25 Sep 54	22	2	★ **River Of No Return** / Give Me Your Word *(Capitol CL-14005)* **1st re-entry**
16 Oct 54	34	1	★ Give Me Your Word / **River Of No Return** *(Capitol CL-14005)* **2nd re-entry (flipped)**
23 Oct 54	18	1	**Somebody Bigger Than You And I** / Eins, Zwei, Drei *(Capitol CL-14178)*
6 Nov 54	33	1	★ Give Me Your Word / River Of No Return *(Capitol CL-14005)* **3rd re-entry**
27 Nov 54	58	2	★ Give Me Your Word / River Of No Return *(Capitol CL-14005)* **4th re-entry**
18 Dec 54	24	2	★ Give Me Your Word / River Of No Return *(Capitol CL-14005)* **5th re-entry**
8 Jan 55	4	2	★ Give Me Your Word / River Of No Return *(Capitol CL-14005)* **6th re-entry**
12 Mar 55	14	1	**Kiss Me Big** / Catfish Boogie *(Capitol CL-14006)*
4 Jun 55	13	1	**Losing You** / There Is Beauty In Everything *(Capitol CL-14273)*
18 Jun 55	9	1	**Losing You** / There Is Beauty In Everything *(Capitol CL-14273)* **1st re-entry**
16 Jul 55	18	1	**His Hands** / I'm A Pilgrim *(Capitol CL-14261)*
30 Jul 55	2	9	**His Hands** / I'm A Pilgrim *(Capitol CL-14261)* **re-entry**
13 Aug 55	8	1	**Losing You** / There Is Beauty In Everything *(Capitol CL-14273)* **2nd re-entry**
7 Jan 56	11	1	★ **The Ballad Of Davy Crockett** / Farewell *(Capitol CL-14506)*
21 Apr 56	17	1	**That's All** / Bright Lights And Blonde-Haired Women *(Capitol CL-14557)*
26 May 56	11	1	**That's All** / Bright Lights And Blonde-Haired Women *(Capitol CL-14557)* **re-entry**
13 Oct 56	5	1	**Who Will Shoe Your Pretty Little Foot** / Gaily The Troubadour *(Capitol CL-14616)*
30 Mar 57	17	1	**The Watermelon Song** / One Suit *(Capitol CL-14691)*

GEORGE FORMBY 4

Iconic actor, comedian, singer, songwriter and ukulele player born George Hoy Booth in Wigan, Lancashire in 1904. His grinning 'cheeky chappie' persona and 'Turned out nice again' catchphrase made him the favourite of millions. He died in 1961, aged just 56, following two heart attacks.

18 Jun 60	7	3	★ **Happy Go Lucky Me** / **Banjo Boy** *(Pye 7N.15269)*
16 Jul 60	11	1	★ **Happy Go Lucky Me** / **Banjo Boy** *(Pye 7N.15269)* **re-entry**

JANE FORREST 1

British singer who later also recorded for Woolworth's Embassy label.

10 Sep 55	13	1	**Malagueña** / Hard To Get *(Columbia DB-3652)*

BRUCE FORSYTH 2

Legendary British all-round entertainer whose career lasted an amazing 75 years. 'I'm in charge' was one of many catchphrases he used over the years (in this instance when trying to control participants in the 'Beat The Clock' game on ITV's 'Sunday Night at the London Palladium').

18 Apr 59	14	1	**I'M IN CHARGE** *(Parlophone GEP-8807)* **EP** I'm In Charge / My Little Budgie / I'm A Good Boy / Wave Your Little Handkerchief
6 Feb 60	7	1	**My Little Budgie** / I'm A Good Boy *(Parlophone R-4620)*

LANCE FORTUNE   4

Pop singer and classically trained pianist born Christopher Morris in Birkenhead in 1940.

| 23 Jan 60 | **7** | 1 | ★ | <u>**Be Mine**</u> / Action *(Pye 7N.15240)* |
| 16 Apr 60 | **1** | 3 | ★ | <u>**This Love I Have For You**</u> / All On My Own *(Pye 7N.15260)* |

FRANK FOSTER

See Paul Quinichette etc.

FOUR ACES   64

Top close harmony quartet from Chester, Pennsylvania.

3 Jul 54	**9**	5		**The Gang That Sang Heart Of My Heart** / Heaven Can Wait *(Brunswick 05256)*
21 Aug 54	**14**	2		**The Gang That Sang Heart Of My Heart** / Heaven Can Wait *(Brunswick 05256)* **re-entry**
4 Dec 54	**2**	5	★	<u>**Mister Sandman**</u> / I'll Be With You In Apple Blossom Time *(Brunswick 05355)*
29 Jan 55	**4**	3		**It's A Woman's World** / The Cuckoo Bird In The Pickle Tree *(Brunswick 05348)*
26 Mar 55	**8**	6		**There Goes My Heart** / Take Me In Your Arms *(Brunswick 05401)*
23 Apr 55	**9**	1		**It's A Woman's World** / The Cuckoo Bird In The Pickle Tree *(Brunswick 05348)* **re-entry**
23 Apr 55	**16**	2	★	<u>**Stranger In Paradise**</u> / You'll Always Be The One *(Brunswick 05418)*
14 May 55	**2**	1	★	<u>**Stranger In Paradise**</u> / You'll Always Be The One *(Brunswick 05418)* **re-entry**
21 May 55	**6**	8		**Melody Of Love** / There Is A Tavern In The Town *(Brunswick 05379)*
4 Jun 55	**5**	1		**There Goes My Heart** / **Take Me In Your Arms** *(Brunswick 05401)* **re-entry**
4 Jun 55	**8**	4		**Sluefoot** / I'm In The Mood For Love *(Brunswick 05429)*
16 Jul 55	**5**	6		**Sluefoot** / I'm In The Mood For Love *(Brunswick 05429)* **re-entry**
30 Jul 55	**8**	2		**Melody Of Love** / There Is A Tavern In The Town *(Brunswick 05379)* **re-entry**
29 Oct 55	**11**	1	★	<u>**Love Is A Many Splendored Thing**</u> / Shine On Harvest Moon *(Brunswick 05480)*
30 Jun 56	**3**	3		**The Gal With The Yaller Shoes** / Of This I'm Sure *(Brunswick 05566)*
8 Sep 56	**1**	6	★	<u>**A Woman In Love**</u> / I Only Know I Love You *(Brunswick 05589)*
6 Oct 56	**8**	1		**The Gal With The Yaller Shoes** / Of This I'm Sure *(Brunswick 05566)* **re-entry**
6 Apr 57	**7**	4		**Heart** / What A Difference A Day Made *(Brunswick 05651)*
4 Oct 58	**9**	2		**Hangin' Up A Horseshoe** / Two Arms, Two Lips, One Heart! *(Brunswick 05758)*
10 Jan 59	**1**	2	★	<u>**The World Outside**</u> / The Inn Of The Sixth Happiness *(Brunswick 05773)*

FOUR ESQUIRES   1

White vocal harmony quartet from Boston, Massachusetts.

| 25 Jan 58 | **3** | 1 | ★ | <u>**Love Me Forever**</u> / I Ain't Been Right Since You Left *(London HLO-8533)* |

FOUR GRADS   1

Mixed vocal group (one girl, three guys) from Canada who made their first recordings in the UK.

| 1 Dec 56 | **7** | 1 | | **The Night Is Young And You're So Beautiful** / Someone To Love *(Oriole CB-1334)* |

FOUR KNIGHTS   1

Smooth black vocal group from Charlotte, North Carolina.

| 9 Oct 54 | **29** | 1 | | **In The Chapel In The Moonlight** / Easy Street *(Capitol CL-14154)* |

FOUR LADS 27

Vocal harmony quartet from Toronto, Canada who also backed Frankie Laine and Johnnie Ray.

7 Aug 54	**14**	1	**Gilly Gilly Ossenfeffer Katzenellen Bogen By The Sea** / I Hear It Everywhere *(Philips PB-304)*
4 Sep 54	**17**	5	**Gilly Gilly Ossenfeffer Katzenellen Bogen By The Sea** / I Hear It Everywhere *(Philips PB-304)* *re-entry*
2 Oct 54	**1**	3	★ <u>Rain, Rain, Rain</u> *(Frankie Laine and the Four Lads) (Philips PB-311)* Flip is 'Your Heart – My Heart' by Frankie Laine
16 Oct 54	**21**	2	**Skokiaan** / Why Should I Love You? *(Philips PB-329)*
20 Nov 54	**42**	1	**Skokiaan** / Why Should I Love You? *(Philips PB-329)* *re-entry*
2 Jul 55	**14**	2	**I've Been Thinking** / Pledging My Love *(Philips PB-440)*
4 Feb 56	**11**	1	**Moments To Remember** / Dream On, My Love, Dream On *(Philips PB-520)*
3 Mar 56	**15**	1	**Moments To Remember** / Dream On, My Love, Dream On *(Philips PB-520)* *re-entry*
7 Apr 56	**1**	7	**No, Not Much** / I'll Never Know *(Philips PB-571)*
21 Apr 56	**3**	2	**I Heard The Angels Singing** *(Frankie Laine and the Four Lads) (Philips PB-585)* The flip, 'Hell Hath No Fury' by Frankie Laine, also bubbled under
25 Jun 60	**15**	1	**Goona Goona** / You're Nobody 'Til Somebody Loves You *(Philips PB-1020)*
20 Aug 60	**16**	1	**The Sheik Of Chicago** / Two Other People *(Philips PB-1051)*

FOUR PREPS 6

Versatile singing group formed by four students at Hollywood High who also did a neat line in parodies. Their biggest US hit was '26 Miles', but in the UK 'Big Man' came out on top.

26 Apr 58	**5**	1	**26 Miles (Santa Catalina)** / Fools Will Be Fools *(Capitol CL-14815)*
24 May 58	**1**	3	★ <u>Big Man</u> / Stop, Baby *(Capitol CL-14873)*
14 May 60	**2**	2	★ <u>Got A Girl</u> / Hear It From Me *(Capitol CL-15128)*

FOUR TOPHATTERS 1

Rockin' quartet named after the elegant Top Hat Club in Union City, New Jersey where they first performed in 1946.

10 Dec 55	**12**	1	**Forty-Five Men In A Telephone Booth** / Wild Rosie *(London HLA-8198)*

DON FOX 9

Singing tailor from London, whose attempt at stardom was sewn up in a couple of months.

19 Oct 57	**2**	3	**Be My Girl** / You'll Never Get To Heaven *(Decca F-10927)*
16 Nov 57	**2**	5	**Be My Girl** / You'll Never Get To Heaven *(Decca F-10927)* *re-entry*
23 Nov 57	**12**	1	**Party Time** / The Majesty Of Love *(Decca F-10955)*

FRANCHITO & His Orchestra 6

Obscure Latin music specalists who also recorded for Woolworth's budget label, Embassy. This may well have been a more famous UK outfit recording under a pseudonym – possibly Gordon Franks & His Orchestra, who also recorded for Embassy.

29 Nov 58	**7**	5	**Eso Es El Amor** / Enchiladas *(Oriole CB-1467)*
10 Jan 59	**6**	1	**Eso Es El Amor** / Enchiladas *(Oriole CB-1467)* *re-entry*

CONNIE FRANCIS 17

Singer born Concetta Franconero in Newark, New Jersey in 1938. She was one of the most popular and prolific female vocalists of the rock'n'roll era.

16 Mar 57	**9**	1	**My Sailor Boy** / Everyone Needs Someone *(M.G.M. MGM-932)*
22 Mar 58	**4**	2	★ <u>Who's Sorry Now</u> / You Were Only Fooling *(M.G.M. MGM-975)*
6 Sep 58	**1**	1	**My Sailor Boy** / Everyone Needs Someone *(M.G.M. MGM-932)* *re-entry*

6 Sep 58	9	1	**Eighteen** / Faded Orchid (M.G.M. MGM-962)
25 Oct 58	11	1	★ <u>**I'll Get By**</u> / <u>**Fallin'**</u> (M.G.M. MGM-993)
20 Dec 58	1	1	★ <u>**You Always Hurt The One You Love**</u> / In The Valley Of Love (M.G.M. MGM-998)
18 Apr 59	2	3	**If I Didn't Care** / Toward The End Of The Day (M.G.M. MGM-1012)
16 May 59	6	1	**If I Didn't Care** / Toward The End Of The Day (M.G.M. MGM-1012) **1st re-entry**
30 May 59	8	2	**If I Didn't Care** / Toward The End Of The Day (M.G.M. MGM-1012) **2nd re-entry**
13 Jun 59	1	3	★ <u>**Lipstick On Your Collar**</u> / Frankie (M.G.M. MGM-1018)
28 Nov 59	4	1	★ <u>**Among My Souvenirs**</u> / Do You Love Me Like You Kiss Me (M.G.M.)

JOHNNIE FRANCIS   3

English singer who later recorded for Embassy as Johnny Francis.

13 Nov 54	7	1	**I Still Believe** / **Madonna, Madonna** (Decca F-10380)
27 Nov 54	65	1	**I Still Believe** / **Madonna, Madonna** (Decca F-10380) **1st re-entry**
1 Jan 55	40	1	**I Still Believe** / **Madonna, Madonna** (Decca F-10380) **2nd re-entry**

JOHN FRASER   1

Theatre, film and TV actor and author born in Glasgow in 1931.

10 Aug 57	6	1	**Bye, Bye, Love** / Why Don't They Understand (Pye Nixa N.15098)

STAN FREBERG   11

Musical satirist from Pasadena, California who remorselessly parodied popular songs of the day. His partner in crime, Daws Butler, was also the voice of the Yogi Bear cartoon character.

6 Nov 54	1	2	★ <u>**Sh-Boom**</u> / C'est Si Bon (Capitol CL-14187)
21 Jan 56	7	1	★ <u>**The Yellow Rose Of Texas**</u> / Rock Around Stephen Foster (Capitol CL-14509)
19 May 56	9	1	**The Great Pretender** (Stan Freberg) / The Quest For Bridey Hammerschlaugen (Stan Freberg with June Foray) (Capitol CL-14571)
21 Jul 56	14	1	★ <u>**Rock Island Line**</u> / <u>**Heartbreak Hotel**</u> (Capitol CL-14608)
13 Apr 57	10	1	**Banana Boat (Day-O)** / Tele-Vee-Shun (Capitol CL-14712)
27 Apr 57	8	1	**Banana Boat (Day-O)** / Tele-Vee-Shun (Capitol CL-14712) **1st re-entry**
11 May 57	6	1	**Banana Boat (Day-O)** / Tele-Vee-Shun (Capitol CL-14712) **2nd re-entry**
9 Apr 60	3	2	★ <u>**The Old Payola Roll Blues**</u> / Sh-Boom (Capitol CL-15122) Both sides by Stan Freberg featuring Jesse White
10 Dec 60	25	1	**Green Chritma** / The Meaning Of Christmas (Capitol CL-14966)

FREDDY   1

Trading as 'Freddy Quinn' back home in Austria, Franz Eugen Helmut Manfred Niedl-Petz from Niederfladnitz was a huge star in Austria, Germany and Switzerland in the '50s and '60s.

30 Mar 57	4	1	**The Banana Boat Song** / Don't Forbid Me (Polydor BM-6063)

BOBBY FREEMAN   9

R&B singer from San Francisco best known for dance records, particularly his 1964 collaboration with Sly Stone, 'C'mon and Swim'.

5 Jul 58	4	2	**Do You Want To Dance** / Big Fat Woman (London HLJ-8644)
9 Aug 58	1	4	**Do You Want To Dance** / Big Fat Woman (London HLJ-8644) **re-entry**
7 Feb 59	14	1	**Shame On You Miss Johnson** / Need Your Love (London HLJ-8782)
23 Jan 60	8	1	**Sinbad** / Ebb Tide (London HLJ-9031)
3 Sep 60	14	1	**Shimmy Shimmy** / You Don't Understand Me (Parlophone R-4684)

ERNIE FREEMAN 11

Pianist, arranger and producer born in Cleveland, Ohio in 1922. He later became Frank Sinatra's musical director.

11 Jan 58	**1**	8	**Raunchy** / Puddin' *(London HLP-8523)*
5 Apr 58	**8**	1	**Dumplin's** / Beautiful Weekend *(London HLP-8558)*
6 Feb 60	**7**	1	**Big River** / Night Sounds *(London HLP-9041)*
14 May 60	**2**	1	**Beautiful Obsession** / Tenderfoot *(Warner Bros. WB-9)*
			Both sides as by Sir Chauncey & His Exciting Strings

JANE FROMAN 8

Despite chronic injuries sustained in a plane crash in 1943, Jane Froman became a successful actress and singer. The 1952 film 'With A Song In My Heart' was based on her life.

9 Apr 55	**17**	1	★ **I Wonder** / I'll Never Be The Same *(Capitol CL-14254)*
23 Apr 55	**26**	1	★ **I Wonder** / I'll Never Be The Same *(Capitol CL-14254)* **1st re-entry**
7 May 55	**5**	6	★ **I Wonder** / I'll Never Be The Same *(Capitol CL-14254)* **2nd re-entry**

JERRY FULLER 10

Singer/songwriter from Fort Worth, Texas. His biggest US hit was this rockin' treatment of 'Tennessee Waltz'. He later wrote songs for Ricky Nelson, the Union Gap and many others.

14 Nov 59	**1**	7	**Tennessee Waltz** / Charlene *(London HLH-8982)*
9 Jan 60	**4**	2	**Tennessee Waltz** / Charlene *(London HLH-8982)* **1st re-entry**
30 Jan 60	**1**	1	**Tennessee Waltz** / Charlene *(London HLH-8982)* **2nd re-entry**

WILHELM FURTWÄNGLER *(conductor)*

See Yehudi Menuhin

BILLY FURY 14

Rock'n'roll singer from Liverpool, born Ronald Wycherley. A protégé of impresario Larry Parnes, he managed to rack up 29 UK hits before a heart attack in 1983 claimed his life at the age of 42.

31 Jan 59	**8**	2	★ **Maybe Tomorrow** / Gonna Type A Letter *(Decca F-11102)*
21 Feb 59	**5**	1	★ **Maybe Tomorrow** / Gonna Type A Letter *(Decca F-11102)* **re-entry**
6 Jun 59	**2**	3	★ **Margo** / Don't Knock Upon My Door *(Decca F-11128)*
3 Oct 59	**16**	3	**Angel Face** / Time Has Come *(Decca F-11158)*
31 Oct 59	**21**	1	**Angel Face** / Time Has Come *(Decca F-11158)* **re-entry**
12 Dec 59	**12**	2	**My Christmas Prayer** / Last Kiss *(Decca F-11189)*
13 Feb 60	**3**	1	★ **Collette** / Baby How I Cried *(Decca F-11200)*
17 Sep 60	**20**	1	★ **Wondrous Place** / Alright, Goodbye *(Decca F-11267)*

GALAXIES 2

The Galaxies were Los Angeles musician Al Hazan plus two girls from his neighbourhood, whom he roped in to record the quirky 'Big Triangle'. The story of a boy in love with two girls, the recording features three intertwined vocals, each telling the story from their point of view.

8 Oct 60	**9**	1	**The Big Triangle** / Until The Next Time *(Capitol CL-15158)*
22 Oct 60	**12**	1	**The Big Triangle** / Until The Next Time *(Capitol CL-15158)* **re-entry**

BRIDIE GALLAGHER 34

Hugely popular singer from Creeslough, Co. Donegal who made Belfast her base for over half a century. She was particularly renowned for her moving rendition of 'The Boys From County Armagh'.

26 Jan 57	**1**	5	**A Mother's Love Is A Blessing** / I'll Remember You, Love, In My Prayers *(Beltona BE-2653)*
9 Mar 57	**8**	1	**A Mother's Love Is A Blessing** / I'll Remember You, Love, In My Prayers *(Beltona BE-2653)* **1st re-entry**
23 Mar 57	**3**	7	**A Mother's Love Is A Blessing** / I'll Remember You, Love, In My Prayers *(Beltona BE-2653)* **2nd re-entry**
18 May 57	**4**	1	**A Mother's Love Is A Blessing** / I'll Remember You, Love, In My Prayers *(Beltona BE-2653)* **3rd re-entry**

29 Jun 57	11	1	**Killarney And You** / The Boys From County Armagh
			(Beltona BE-2679)
13 Jul 57	2	2	**Killarney And You** / The Boys From County Armagh
			(Beltona BE-2679) ***1st re-entry***
22 Feb 58	4	2	**The Boys From County Armagh / Killarney And You**
			(Beltona BE-2679) ***2nd re-entry (flipped)***
26 Apr 58	14	1	**The Boys From County Armagh / Killarney And You**
			(Beltona BE-2679) ***3rd re-entry***
14 Jun 58	5	1	**Take This Message To My Mother / The Girl From Donegal**
			(Beltona BE-2696)
28 Jun 58	9	1	**At The Close Of An Irish Day** / Two Little Orphans *(Beltona BE-2697)*
28 Jun 58	14	2	**Take This Message To My Mother / The Girl From Donegal**
			(Beltona BE-2696) *re-entry*
2 Aug 58	8	1	**I'll Forgive But I'll Never Forget** / The Poor Orphan Boy
			(Beltona BE-2704)
16 Aug 58	16	1	**Hillside In Scotland** / Johnny Gray *(Beltona BE-2705)*
6 Sep 58	3	1	**The Boys From County Armagh / Killarney And You**
			(Beltona BE-2679) ***4th re-entry***
27 Sep 58	2	2	**The Boys From County Armagh / Killarney And You**
			(Beltona BE-2679) ***5th re-entry***
25 Oct 58	6	1	**The Boys From County Armagh / Killarney And You**
			(Beltona BE-2679) ***6th re-entry***
29 Nov 58	3	2	**Goodbye Johnny** / The Faithful Sailor Boy *(Beltona BE-2707)*
29 Nov 58	17	1	**The Boys From County Armagh / Killarney And You**
			(Beltona BE-2679) ***7th re-entry***
3 Dec 60	15	1	**The Boys From County Armagh** / Killarney And You
			(Beltona BE-2679) ***8th re-entry***

FRANK GALLUP   2

Radio and TV personality born in Boston, Massachusetts in 1900. He was the announcer and an occasional performer on Perry Como's TV shows from the mid-'50s to the mid-'60s.

| 2 Aug 58 | 6 | 2 | **Got A Match?** / I Beg Your Pardon *(H.M.V. POP-509)* |

PATRICK GALVIN with Al Jeffery   5

Cork-born playwright, poet and traditional folk singer accompanied by banjo player Al Jeffery.

22 Feb 58	8	2	**IRISH SONGS OF RESISTANCE (PART II)** *(Topic T-4)* `8" Mini-LP`
			The Bold Fenian Men / Clare's Dragoons / The Foggy Dew / Whack Fol De Diddle / The Smashing Of The Van / The Soldier's Song
15 Mar 58	15	1	**IRISH SONGS OF RESISTANCE (PART II)** *(Topic T-4)* `8" Mini-LP`
			1st re-entry
29 Mar 58	17	1	**IRISH SONGS OF RESISTANCE (PART II)** *(Topic T-4)* `8" Mini-LP`
			2nd re-entry
26 Apr 58	17	1	**IRISH SONGS OF RESISTANCE (PART II)** *(Topic T-4)* `8" Mini-LP`
			3rd re-entry

ALLAN GANLEY

See Jo Hunter etc.

JUDY GARLAND   23

The talented but troubled star of 'The Wizard of Oz', born Frances Ethel Gumm in Grand Rapids, Minnesota in 1922.

22 Jan 55	46	1	★	<u>**The Man That Got Away**</u> / Here's What I'm Here For *(Philips PB-366)*
29 Jan 55	3	6		**It's A New World** / Gotta Have Me Go With You *(Philips PB-394)*
12 Feb 55	24	1		**A STAR IS BORN [OST]** *(Philips BBL-7007)* `LP`
				Gotta Have Me Go With You / The Man That Got Away / Born In A Trunk / *Medley:* I'll Get By – You Took Advantage Of Me – Black Bottom – The Peanut Vendor – My Melancholy Baby – Swanee *(with Chorus)* / Here's What I'm Here For *(with Chorus)* / It's A New World / Someone At Last *(with Chorus)* / Lose That Long Face

12 Feb 55	26	2	★ **The Man That Got Away** / Here's What I'm Here For *(Philips PB-366)*
			1st re-entry
26 Mar 55	1	5	★ **The Man That Got Away** / Here's What I'm Here For *(Philips PB-366)*
			2nd re-entry
26 Mar 55	12	2	**It's A New World / Gotta Have Me Go With You** *(Philips PB-394)*
			re-entry
22 Apr 55	15	2	**A STAR IS BORN [OST]** *(Philips BBL-7007)* 🄻🄿 *re-entry*
21 May 55	20	1	★ **The Man That Got Away** / Here's What I'm Here For *(Philips PB-366)*
			3rd re-entry
5 May 56	7	2	**MISS SHOW BUSINESS** *(Capitol LCT-6103)* 🄻🄿

Medley: This Is The Time Of The Evening – While We're Young / Medley: You Made Me Love You (I Didn't Want To Do It) – For Me And My Gal – The Trolley Song / A Pretty Girl Milking Her Cow / Rock-A-Bye Your Baby With A Dixie Melody / Happiness Is A Thing Called Joe / Judy At The Palace Medley: Shine On Harvest Moon – Some Of These Days – My Man – I Don't Care / Carolina In The Morning / Danny Boy / After You've Gone / Over The Rainbow

26 May 56	9	1	**MISS SHOW BUSINESS** *(Capitol LCT-6103)* 🄻🄿 *re-entry*

See also Original Soundtrack (LES GIRLS / THE PIRATE)

ERROLL GARNER   1
Renowned jazz pianist and composer born in Pittsburgh, Pennsylvania in 1925.

7 Aug 54	18	1	**ERROLL GARNER** *(Columbia SEG-7510)* 🄴🄿

Sophisticated Lady / Poor Butterfly / Lover / Fine And Dandy

See also Gene Norman's 'Just Jazz'

SIR JONATHAN GASSER
See Paul Quinichette etc.

BILLY GAYE & THE GAYETONES   4
This obscure Scottish group's only release was the first single to be issued by the Edinburgh-based Waverley label and only just missed the charts.

28 May 60	2	4	**Oh, Honey Love Me** / I'll Never Say 'Never Again' Again
			(Waverley SLP-501)

GAYLORDS   2
Popular singing trio from Detroit formed in 1952 by Ronald Fredianelli, Burt Bonaldi and Don Rea. By the time this record was released, however, Fredianelli had embarked on a solo career as Ronnie Gaylord and had been replaced in the group by Billy Christ.

18 Dec 54	24	2	**Veni – Vidi – Vici** / A Kiss To Call My Own *(Mercury MB-3163)*

MEL GAYNOR   1
Featured vocalist with the Oscar Rabin Band, one of the most popular British bands of the '50s.

30 Apr 55	28	1	**How Important Can It Be?** / Just A Man *(Decca F-10497)*

GENE & EUNICE   6
Smooth West Coast duo Forest Gene Wilson and Eunice Levy were billed as 'The Sweethearts of Rhythm & Blues'. Their first US hit, 1955's 'Ko Ko Mo', was covered by everyone from Perry Como to Louis Armstrong.

18 May 57	11	1	**Move It Over, Baby** / This Is My Story *(Vogue V-9066)*
29 Jun 57	11	1	**Move It Over, Baby** / This Is My Story *(Vogue V-9066)* *1st re-entry*
13 Jul 57	12	1	**Move It Over, Baby / This Is My Story** *(Vogue V-9066)* *2nd re-entry*
27 Jul 57	9	1	**I Gotta Go Home** / Have You Changed Your Mind? *(Vogue V-9062)*
20 Dec 58	5	2	**The Vow** / Strange World *(Vogue Pop V-9126)*

JOHNNY GENTLE   1

Larry Parnes protégé from Liverpool who toured Scotland in 1960 with the Beatles (or 'Silver Beetles', as they were at the time) as his backing band.

22 Aug 59   **16**   1   **Milk From The Coconut** / I Like The Way *(Philips PB-945)*

GERALDO & His Orchestra   5

Top British bandleader born Gerald Walcan Bright in London in 1904.

31 Mar 56   **5**   4   **The Poor People Of Paris** / There Once Was A Beautiful
                                  (Oriole CB-1322)
5 May 56   **15**   1   **Rockin' Through Dixie** / Stranger Than Fiction *(Oriole CB-1323)*

STAN GETZ   2

Cool jazz saxophonist born Stanley Gayetsky in Philadelphia in 1927. In the early '60s, he became one of the leading figures of the bossa nova movement.

16 Oct 54   **34**   1   **STAN GETZ COLLATES** *(Esquire 32-011)* **LP**
                              There's A Small Hotel / I've Got You Under My Skin / What's New / Too Marvellous For Words / You Stepped Out Of A Dream / My Old Flame / Long Island Sound / Indian Summer / Marcia / Crazy Chords / Lady In Red / Wrap Your Troubles In Dreams
22 Oct 55   **25**   1   **THE ARTISTRY OF STAN GETZ** *(Columbia SEB-10001)* **EP**
                              These Foolish Things / How Deep Is The Ocean / Thanks For The Memory / Hymn To The Orient

GEORGIA GIBBS   24

Singer born Fredda Lipschitz in Worcester, Massachusetts. She began her solo recording career in 1950 as a big band vocalist, but is now chiefly remembered for covering R&B hits for the white market during the rock'n'roll era.

21 Aug 54   **19**   2   **Wait For Me Darling** / Whistle And I'll Dance *(Mercury MB-3130)*
30 Oct 54   **33**   2   **Wait For Me Darling** / Whistle And I'll Dance *(Mercury MB-3130)*
                              re-entry
6 Nov 54   **5**   6   **I Love Paris** / Under Paris Skies *(Mercury MB-3152)*
9 Apr 55   **8**   1   ★ **Tweedle Dee** / You're Wrong, All Wrong *(Mercury MB-3196)*
21 May 55   **9**   8   **Dance With Me Henry (Wallflower)** / Ballin' The Jack
                              (Mercury MB-3223)
23 Jul 55   **6**   3   **Dance With Me Henry (Wallflower)** / Ballin' The Jack
                              (Mercury MB-3223) *re-entry*
23 Jun 56   **6**   1   ★ **Kiss Me Another** / Rock Right *(Mercury MT-110)*
8 Nov 58   **4**   1   **The Hula Hoop Song** / Keep In Touch *(Columbia DB-4201)*

See also Various Artists (KISMET)

DON GIBSON   17

Prolific country singer/songwriter from Shelby, North Carolina. He specialised in songs of lost love and loneliness – though he didn't write his biggest UK hit, 'Sea Of Heartbreak' (1961).

19 Apr 58   **1**   1   **Oh, Lonesome Me** / I Can't Stop Lovin' You *(R.C.A. RCA-1056)*
31 May 58   **5**   4   **Oh, Lonesome Me** / I Can't Stop Lovin' You *(R.C.A. RCA-1056)*
                              re-entry
1 Nov 58   **6**   2   **Blue Blue Day** / Too Soon *(R.C.A. RCA-1073)*
10 Oct 59   **9**   1   **Don't Tell Me Your Troubles** / Heartbreak Avenue *(R.C.A. RCA-1150)*
31 Oct 59   **21**   1   **Don't Tell Me Your Troubles** / Heartbreak Avenue *(R.C.A. RCA-1150)*
                              1st re-entry
14 Nov 59   **20**   1   **Don't Tell Me Your Troubles** / Heartbreak Avenue *(R.C.A. RCA-1150)*
                              2nd re-entry
28 Nov 59   **10**   1   **Don't Tell Me Your Troubles** / Heartbreak Avenue *(R.C.A. RCA-1150)*
                              3rd re-entry
19 Dec 59   **9**   1   **I'm Movin' On** / Big Hearted Me *(R.C.A. RCA-1158)*
2 Apr 60   **3**   1   **Just One Time** / I May Never Get To Heaven *(R.C.A. RCA-1183)*
17 Sep 60   **12**   1   **Far Far Away** / A Legend In My Time *(R.C.A. RCA-1200)*
14 Jan 61   **4**   3   **Sweet Dreams** / The Same Street *(R.C.A. RCA-1217)*

JODY GIBSON & THE MULESKINNERS 4

Banjo and guitar player from New York, born Joseph Katzberg. He came pretty close to UK chart success with this bubbler, one of two singles he recorded while serving with the USAF in Britain.

30 Apr 60   **1**   4   **So You Think You've Got Troubles** / If You Don't Know
(Parlophone R-4645)

BENIAMINO GIGLI 1

Born in Recanati, Italy in 1890, Gigli was the most famous operatic tenor of his generation. He died in 1957.

1 Jan 55   **32**   1   **Silent Night, Holy Night** / Adeste Fideles (H.M.V. DA-1874)

TERRY GILKYSON & THE EASY RIDERS

See Easy Riders

JACKIE GLEASON 1

Brash comedian, actor and musician born in New York in 1916.

25 Dec 54   **31**   1   **MUSIC FOR LOVERS ONLY** (Capitol LC-6588) **LP**
Alone Together / My Funny Valentine / But Not For Me / Love (Your Spell Is
Everywhere) / I'm In The Mood For Love / Love Is Here To Stay / I Only Have
Eyes For You / Body And Soul

MARTY GOLD & His Orchestra 1

Composer, pianist and arranger born in New York in 1915. He cut his teeth with several 'sweet' bands of the '30s before turning to studio work.

22 Oct 60   **15**   1   **Never On Sunday** (R.C.A. RCA-1205)
Flip is 'Never On Sunday' by Ray Martin & His Orchestra

NAT GONELLA 1

Born in London in 1908, trumpeter, singer and bandleader Nat Gonella was a British jazz pioneer and one of its best-loved personalities. 'Georgia On My Mind' was his signature tune.

29 Oct 55   **35**   1   **Georgia On My Mind** / Moon Country (Decca F-6320)

BENNY GOODMAN 18

Famous jazz clarinettist and bandleader from Chicago known as the 'King of Swing'.

7 Aug 54   **4**   5   **CARNEGIE HALL JAZZ CONCERT** (Philips BBL-7001) **LP**
Jam Session: Honeysuckle Rose / *Trio:* Body And Soul / *Quartet:* Avalon / The Man
I Love / I Got Rhythm / Blue Skies / Loch Lomond / Blue Room / Swingtime In The
Rockies / Bei Mir Bist Du Schön / China Boy

22 Jan 55   **39**   1   **SESSION FOR SEXTET NO. 2** (Columbia 33SX-1035) **LP**
After You've Gone / Stardust / Benny's Bugle / On The Alamo / Shivers / Slipped
Disc / A Smo-o-o-oth One / AC-DC Current / Liza (All The Clouds'll Roll Away) /
As Long As I Live / Breakfast Feud / Gilly

22 Jan 55   **55**   1   **CARNEGIE HALL JAZZ CONCERT** (Philips BBL-7001) **LP**
1st re-entry

29 Jan 55   **3**   3   **B.G. JAZZ CONCERT NO. 2** (Philips BBE-12132) **EP**
Runnin' Wild (Benny Goodman Quartet) / My Gal Sal (Benny Goodman Quartet) /
Shine (Benny Goodman Quartet) / Body And Soul (Benny Goodman Trio)

5 Feb 55   **21**   1   **CARNEGIE HALL JAZZ CONCERT** (Philips BBL-7001) **LP**
2nd re-entry

5 Feb 55   **33**   1   **SESSION FOR SEXTET NO. 2** (Columbia 33SX-1035) **LP** *re-entry*

11 Feb 56   **6**   1   **Memories Of You** (Benny Goodman Trio with Rosemary Clooney) /
It's Bad For Me (Benny Goodman Sextet with Rosemary Clooney)
(Philips PB-547)

25 Feb 56   **2**   2   **Memories Of You** (Benny Goodman Trio with Rosemary Clooney) /
It's Bad For Me (Benny Goodman Sextet with Rosemary Clooney)
(Philips PB-547) **1st re-entry**

10 Mar 56	**6**	1	**CARNEGIE HALL JAZZ CONCERT** *(Philips BBL-7001)* **LP**
			3rd re-entry
10 Mar 56	**24**	1	**Don't Be That Way** / Down South Camp Meeting *(H.M.V. POP-166)*
			Both sides as by Benny Goodman & His Orchestra
31 Mar 56	**19**	1	**Memories Of You** *(Benny Goodman Trio with Rosemary Clooney)* /
			It's Bad For Me *(Benny Goodman Sextet with Rosemary Clooney)*
			(Philips PB-547) **2nd re-entry**

RON GOODWIN & His Concert Orchestra   6

Composer and arranger from Plymouth who became famed for his film scores.

23 Oct 54	**8**	1	**Cara Mia** / Three Coins In The Fountain *(Parlophone R-3889)*
23 Oct 54	**38**	1	**Theme from 'Modern Times'** / The Messenger Boy
			(Parlophone R-3890)
13 Nov 54	**44**	1	**On The Waterfront** / Midnight Blue *(Parlophone R-3923)*
10 Dec 55	**18**	1	**Summertime In Venice** / The Three Galleons *(Parlophone R-4041)*
28 Jul 56	**10**	1	**No Other Love** / The Headless Horsemen *(Parlophone R-4162)*
13 Aug 60	**17**	1	**The Girl From Corsica** / The Singing Piano *(Parlophone R-4649)*

GOONS   5

Madcap radio comedy ensemble comprising Spike Milligan, Peter Sellers and Harry Secombe – although this bubbler was actually by Milligan and Eric Sykes.

8 Dec 56	**3**	4	**My September Love** *(The Famous Eccles and Miss Freda Thing*
			with Mr. Reginald Owen & His Excruciating Orchestra) /
			You Gotta Go OWW! *(Count Jim Moriarty with Gravely Stephens*
			(Pharmacological Pianist) and the Massed Alberts)
			(Parlophone R-4251)
12 Jan 57	**2**	1	**My September Love** / You Gotta Go Oww! *(Parlophone R-4251)*
			re-entry

See also Harry Secombe
          Peter Sellers

DEXTER GORDON   1

Jazz saxophonist born in Los Angeles in 1923.

26 Jun 54	**17**	1	**GENE NORMAN PRESENTS THE CHASE**
			AND THE STEEPLECHASE *(Brunswick LA-8646)* **LP**
			Wardell Gray and Dexter Gordon
			The Chase / The Steeplechase

JOE GORDON FOLK FOUR   3

Popular Scottish folk group led by singer/guitarist Joe Gordon. They were regulars on radio and BBC TV's 'White Heather Club'.

2 May 59	**9**	1	**Barnyards O' Delgaty** / **Bonnie Wee Jeannie McColl**
			(H.M.V. POP-591)
30 Jul 60	**12**	1	**Barnyards O' Delgaty** / Bonnie Wee Jeannie McColl
			(H.M.V. POP-591) re-entry
30 Jul 60	**15**	1	**Twa Heids Are Better Than Yin** / The Bonnie Lass O' Fyvie
			(H.M.V. POP-678)

ROSCO GORDON   3

Influential R&B singer/pianist born in Memphis in 1928, whose habit of accenting the off-beat laid the foundations for Jamaican ska. He retired from music in 1962 to run a laundry.

30 Apr 60	**2**	3	**Goin' Home** / Just A Little Bit *(Top Rank JAR-332)*

EYDIE GORMÉ　　　　　　　　　　　　　　　　　　　　　　　　　2

Pop singer born Edith Gormezano in New York in 1928. She married pop balladeer Steve Lawrence in 1957 and sometimes performed with him as Steve & Eydie.

18 Jan 58	**7**	1	★ **Love Me Forever** / Until They Sail	*(H.M.V. POP-432)*
6 Sep 58	**3**	1	**You Need Hands** / The Gentleman Is A Dope	*(H.M.V. POP-493)*

See also Steve Lawrence

CHARLIE GRACIE　　　　　　　　　　　　　　　　　　　　　　　3

Rock'n'roll singer/guitarist born in Philadelphia in 1936.

13 Apr 57	**7**	1	★ **Butterfly** / Ninety-Nine Ways	*(Parlophone R-4290)*
8 Jun 57	**4**	1	★ **Fabulous** / Just Lookin'	*(Parlophone R-4313)*
12 Apr 58	**6**	1	**Crazy Girl** / Dressin' Up	*(London HLU-8596)*

BILLY GRAMMER　　　　　　　　　　　　　　　　　　　　　　　9

Country singer/songwriter and guitarist from Benton, Illinois who scored a Top Five hit in the States in 1958 with 'Gotta Travel On'. Although that record did nothing in the UK, the follow-up almost dented the British charts.

16 May 59	**1**	1	**Bonaparte's Retreat** / The Kissing Tree	*(Felsted AF-121)*
20 Jun 59	**5**	8	**Bonaparte's Retreat** / The Kissing Tree	*(Felsted AF-121)* *re-entry*

EARL GRANT　　　　　　　　　　　　　　　　　　　　　　　　1

Black organist/pianist and pop vocalist born in Idabel, Oklahoma. He died in a car crash in 1970, at the young age of 39.

5 Dec 58	**12**	1	**The End** / Hunky Dunky Doo	*(Brunswick 05762)*

GOGI GRANT　　　　　　　　　　　　　　　　　　　　　　　10

Myrtle Arinsberg from Philadelphia recorded as Audrey Brown and Audrey Grant before being rechristened 'Gogi Grant' by RCA's A&R supremo, Dave Kapp. 'Suddenly There's a Valley' was her first US hit.

24 Dec 55	**6**	4	**Suddenly There's A Valley** / Love Is	*(London HLB-8192)*
28 Jan 56	**5**	1	**Suddenly There's A Valley** / Love Is	*(London HLB-8192)* *re-entry*
9 Jun 56	**2**	3	★ **Wayward Wind** / No More Than Forever	*(London HLB-8282)*
4 Aug 56	**11**	1	**Who Are We** / We Believe In Love	*(London HLB-8257)*
25 Aug 56	**10**	1	**Who Are We** / We Believe In Love	*(London HLB-8257)* *re-entry*

NORMAN GRANZ　　　　　　　　　　　　　　　　　　　　　　4

Los Angeles impresario Norman Granz staged his first 'Jazz At The Philharmonic' concert in July 1944. Featuring the cream of the country's jazz talent, it was so successful that he began promoting JATP concert tours with a constantly varying line-up. They ran from 1945 until 1957, and live recordings were made of many of the shows. The album below was originally released in the USA as 'Norman Granz Jam Session #2' and features Ray Brown, Benny Carter, J.C. Heard, Johnny Hodges, Barney Kessel, Charlie Parker, Oscar Peterson, Flip Phillips and Ben Webster.

24 Sep 55	**23**	2	**JAM SESSION** *(Columbia 33CX-10008)* 🅛🅟
			What Is This Thing Called Love? / Funky Blues
15 Oct 55	**26**	1	**JAM SESSION** *(Columbia 33CX-10008)* 🅛🅟 *1st re-entry*
29 Oct 55	**26**	1	**JAM SESSION** *(Columbia 33CX-10008)* 🅛🅟 *2nd re-entry*

See also Norman Granz' Jazz At The Philharmonic

NORMAN GRANZ' JAZZ AT THE PHILHARMONIC 1

More live recordings from Norman Granz-promoted JATP concerts, this time featuring Irving Ashby, Buck Clayton, Billy Hadnott, Coleman Hawkins, Kenny Kersey, Charlie Parker, Buddy Rich, Willie Smith and Lester Young. The 12" LP below was compiled from two previously issued 10" LPs (Volumes 6 and 14). It was called 'New Volume 4' to differentiate it from the 10" 'Volume 4'.

3 Mar 56   **22**   1   **JAMMING WITH THE GREATS – NEW VOLUME 4**
                               (Columbia 33CX-10035) **LP**
                               J.A.T.P. Blues / Slow Drag / I Got Rhythm / I Surrender Dear

See also Norman Granz

JOHNNY (THE GASH) GRAY 2

Extrovert tenor saxophonist from Coventry, who played with George Shearing, Ambrose and Ted Heath before starting his own Band Of The Day.

12 Apr 58   **6**   1   **Tequila** / Big Guitar *(Fontana H-123)*
                               Both sides by Johnny (The Gash) Gray with Ken Jones & His Orchestra
24 May 58   **15**   1   **Tequila** / Big Guitar *(Fontana H-123)* ***re-entry***

WARDELL GRAY 3

Jazz tenor saxophonist born in Oklahoma City in 1921. He died in 1955, aged 34, apparently from a broken neck. His body was found dumped in the desert on the outskirts of Las Vegas.

26 Jun 54   **17**   1   **GENE NORMAN PRESENTS THE CHASE**
                               AND THE STEEPLECHASE *(Brunswick LA-8646)* **LP**
                               Wardell Gray and Dexter Gordon
                               The Chase / The Steeplechase
25 Sep 54   **31**   2   **The Man I Love** / One For Prez *(Vogue V-2262)*

See also Gene Norman's 'Just Jazz'

MILTON GRAYSON 3

Handsome black baritone Milton B. Grayson Jr. was a former member of Billy Ward's Dominoes, but failed to find success on either side of the Atlantic.

9 Apr 60   **5**   1   **Forget You** / The Puppet *(London HLU-9068)*
30 Apr 60   **9**   1   **Forget You** / The Puppet *(London HLU-9068)* ***1st re-entry***
14 May 60   **5**   1   **Forget You** / The Puppet *(London HLU-9068)* ***2nd re-entry***

BUDDY GRECO 3

Ultra-hip pop/jazz singer and pianist born Armando Greco in Philadelphia in 1926.

31 Aug 57   **3**   1   **With All My Heart** / Game Of Love *(London HLR-8452)*
                               Both sides by Buddy Greco and the B-G Skiffle Gang
14 Sep 57   **13**   1   **With All My Heart** / Game Of Love *(London HLR-8452)* ***re-entry***
2 Jul 60   **14**   1   ★ <u>**The Lady Is A Tramp**</u> / Like Young *(Fontana H-255)*

BENNY GREEN

See J.J. Johnson etc.
       Paul Quinichette etc.

PHILIP GREEN & His Orchestra 3

Popular British pianist/composer born in London in 1911. He was responsible for over 150 film scores from the mid-'40s onwards.

8 Jan 55   **37**   2   **Song Of The Barefoot Contessa** / Mexican Madness
                               (Parlophone R-3956)
26 Feb 55   **22**   1   **Song Of The Barefoot Contessa** / Mexican Madness
                               (Parlophone R-3956) ***re-entry***

See also Knightsbridge Strings

JO ANN GREER   10

Distinctive-voiced singer who was associated for many years with Les Brown & His Band of Renown. She also had a parallel career as an anonymous movie dubber singing famous stars' parts – in this case two of Rita Hayworth's songs from the 1953 musical 'Miss Sadie Thompson'.

19 Jun 54	2	9	**Sadie Thompson's Song** / The Heat Is On *(Mercury MB-3090)*
			Both sides as by Rita Hayworth
28 Aug 54	30	1	**Sadie Thompson's Song** / The Heat Is On *(Mercury MB-3090)*
			re-entry

IAIN GREGORY   2

Good-looking actor and singer from Eastcote, Middlesex produced by Joe Meek.

26 Nov 60	3	2	★ **Time Will Tell** / The Night You Told A Lie *(Pye 7N.15295)*
			Both sides as by Ian Gregory

KEN GRIFFIN   3

Organist born in Columbia, Missouri in 1909. 'You Can't Be True, Dear' was a massive US hit for him in 1948. Sadly, he never realised his full potential, as he died of a heart attack in 1956.

4 Dec 54	22	1	**In The Chapel In The Moonlight** / Our Favourite Waltz *(Philips PB-353)*
30 Jul 55	23	2	**The Cuckoo Waltz** / You Can't Be True, Dear *(Philips PB-471)*

GIGI GRYCE   11

Jazz saxophonist, flautist, clarinettist, bandleader and composer born George General Grice Jr. in Pensacola, Florida in 1925.

19 Jun 54	8	1	**Salute To The Bandbox (Parts 1 & 2)** *(Vogue V-2239)*
			Both sides by Gigi Gryce-Clifford Brown Sextet
3 Jul 54	3	5	**Salute To The Bandbox (Parts 1 & 2)** *(Vogue V-2239)*
			1st re-entry
14 Aug 54	4	3	**Salute To The Bandbox (Parts 1 & 2)** *(Vogue V-2239)*
			2nd re-entry
25 Dec 54	37	2	**Salute To The Bandbox (Parts 1 & 2)** *(Vogue V-2239)*
			3rd re-entry

HILDE GUEDEN
with the VIENNA PHILHARMONIC ORCHESTRA   1

Austrian soprano born Hilda Geiringer in Vienna in 1917. She was expecially renowned for her renditions of Mozart and Strauss arias.

27 Nov 54	32	1	**MOZART ARIAS** *(Decca LXT-5242)* 🅛🅟
			Don Giovanni: Batti, Batti, O Bel Masetto / Vedrai Carino (Orchestra cond. Josef Krips) / Die Zauberflöte: Ach, Ich Fühl's (Orchestra cond. Karl Bohn) / Le Nozze Di Figaro: Venite, Inginocchiatevi / Giunse Alfin il Momento... Deh Vieni, Non Tardar (Orchestra cond. Erich Kleiber) / Idomeneo: Se il Padre Perdei (Orchestra cond. Clemens Krauss) / Il Rè Pastore: L'Amerò, Sarò Costante / Exsultate, Jubilate – Motet (K.165) (Orchestra cond. Alberto Erede)

LARS GULLIN QUINTET   1

Influential Swedish jazz baritone saxophonist born in 1928. He worked with various visiting American musicians including Clifford Brown, James Moody, Zoot Sims, and most notably Lee Konitz. He died of a heart attack in 1973, aged just 48.

28 Aug 54	30	1	**LARS GULLIN QUINTET** *(Esquire EP-8)* 🅔🅟
			Bugs / Jump For Fan / Stocks And Bonds / I Fall In Love Too Easily

Ronnie Hilton

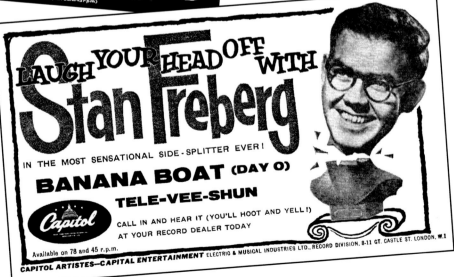

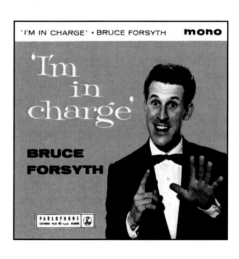

JIM GUNNER & THE ECHOES   6

Irish rock'n'roll instrumental outfit led by guitarist Jim Gunner (real name George Hesse) from Wexford. He later played with the popular Dave Glover Showband.

8 Oct 60	**11**	1	**Hoolee Jump** / Footloose *(Decca F-11276)*
22 Oct 60	**2**	2	**Hoolee Jump** / Footloose *(Decca F-11276)* ***1st re-entry***
12 Nov 60	**3**	3	**Hoolee Jump** / Footloose *(Decca F-11276)* ***2nd re-entry***

BILLY HADNOTT

See Norman Granz' Jazz At The Philharmonic

INGRID HAEBLER, PRO MUSICA SYMPHONY ORCHESTRA, VIENNA, *cond.* Heinrich Hollreiser   1

Esteemed Austrian classical pianist born in Vienna in 1926.

| 11 Sep 54 | **34** | 1 | **MOZART – CONCERTO FOR PIANO AND ORCHESTRA NO. 15 IN B FLAT MAJOR, K. 450 / NO. 18 IN B FLAT MAJOR, K. 456** *(Vox PL-8300)* 🆑 |
| | | | Concerto No. 15 In B Flat Major, K.450: Allegro / Andante / Allegro / Concerto No. 18 In B Flat, K 456: Allegro Vivace / Andante Un Poco Sostenuto / Allegro Vivace |

AL HAIG TRIO   2

Jazz pianist and bebop pioneer born in Newark, New Jersey in 1922.

6 Nov 54	**33**	1	**AL HAIG TRIO** *(Vogue LDE-092)* 🆑
			Just One Of Those Things / Yardbird Suite / Taboo / Mighty Like A Rose / S'Wonderful / Just You, Just Me / The Moon Is Yellow / 'Round About Midnight
27 Nov 54	**72**	1	**AL HAIG TRIO** *(Vogue LDE-092)* 🆑 ***re-entry***

DENNIS HALE   2

Singer born Dennis Hoare in Uckfield, East Sussex in 1922. He was featured vocalist in several bands including those of Oscar Rabin, Jack Parnell and Eric Winstone. He was killed in a car crash in 1960.

| 19 Nov 55 | **14** | 2 | **Tina Marie** / The Longest Walk *(Decca F-10623)* |

See also Jack Parnell & His Orchestra

BILL HALEY & HIS COMETS   91

One of the first white groups to play R&B, this hugely talented and versatile outfit broke rock'n'roll on both sides of the Atlantic.

23 Oct 54	**4**	11	★ <u>**Rock Around The Clock**</u> / Thirteen Women *(Brunswick 05317)*
27 Nov 54	**18**	3	★ <u>**Shake, Rattle And Roll**</u> / A.B.C. Boogie *(Brunswick 05338)*
22 Jan 55	**2**	5	**Dim, Dim The Lights** / Happy Baby *(Brunswick 05373)*
5 Mar 55	**10**	1	**Dim, Dim The Lights** / Happy Baby *(Brunswick 05373)* ***1st re-entry***
19 Mar 55	**8**	3	**Dim, Dim The Lights** / Happy Baby *(Brunswick 05373)* ***2nd re-entry***
26 Mar 55	**2**	1	★ <u>**Mambo Rock**</u> / Birth Of The Boogie *(Brunswick 05405)*
2 Apr 55	**12**	2	**Crazy Man, Crazy** / Whatcha Gonna Do *(London L-1190)*
30 Apr 55	**21**	1	**Dim, Dim The Lights** / Happy Baby *(Brunswick 05373)* ***3rd re-entry***
25 Jun 55	**1**	7	**Sundown Boogie** / Green Tree Boogie *(London HL-8142)*
30 Jul 55	**15**	4	★ <u>**Razzle Dazzle**</u> / Two Hound Dogs *(Brunswick 05453)*
27 Aug 55	**6**	1	**Farewell, So Long, Goodbye** / I'll Be True *(London HLF-8161)*
3 Sep 55	**26**	1	★ <u>**Razzle Dazzle**</u> / Two Hound Dogs *(Brunswick 05453)* ***1st re-entry***
17 Sep 55	**12**	1	★ <u>**Razzle Dazzle**</u> / Two Hound Dogs *(Brunswick 05453)* ***2nd re-entry***
19 Nov 55	**3**	4	**Ten Little Indians** / Rocking Chair On The Moon *(London HLF-8194)*
24 Dec 55	**12**	1	★ <u>**Rock-A-Beatin' Boogie**</u> / Burn That Candle *(Brunswick 05509)*
7 Jan 56	**5**	2	**Ten Little Indians** / Rocking Chair On The Moon *(London HLF-8194)* ***re-entry***
14 Jan 56	**8**	1	★ <u>**Razzle Dazzle**</u> / Two Hound Dogs *(Brunswick 05453)* ***3rd re-entry***
28 Jan 56	**2**	1	★ <u>**Razzle Dazzle**</u> / Two Hound Dogs *(Brunswick 05453)* ***4th re-entry***

| 11 Aug 56 | 4 | 2 | **LIVE IT UP (PART 1)** *(London RE-F-1049)* **EP** |

11 Aug 56	4	2	**LIVE IT UP (PART 1)** *(London RE-F-1049)* 🔲

11 Aug 56   **4**   2   **LIVE IT UP (PART 1)** *(London RE-F-1049)* 🔲
Live It Up / Real Rock Drive / Ten Little Indians / Chattanooga Choo Choo

1 Sep 56   **2**   1   **ROCK 'N ROLL** *(Brunswick OE-9214)* 🔲
Razzle Dazzle / Two Hound Dogs / Burn That Candle / Rock-A-Beatin' Boogie

1 Sep 56   **3**   2 ★ <u>**Razzle Dazzle**</u> / Two Hound Dogs *(Brunswick 05453)* **5th re-entry**

8 Sep 56   **1**   4   **ROCK AROUND THE CLOCK** *(Brunswick OE-9250)* 🔲
(We're Gonna) Rock Around The Clock / Mambo Rock / R-O-C-K / See You Later Alligator

6 Oct 56   **4**   1   **ROCK 'N ROLL** *(Brunswick OE-9214)* 🔲 *1st re-entry*

13 Oct 56   **7**   1   **ROCK AROUND THE CLOCK** *(Brunswick OE-9250)* 🔲
1st re-entry

13 Oct 56   **10**   1 ★ <u>**ROCK 'N ROLL STAGE SHOW**</u> *(Brunswick LAT-8139)* 🔲
Calling All Comets *(Saxophone [Tenor Solo]: Rudy Pompilli)* / Rockin' Through The Rye / A Rocking Little Tune *(Accordion [Solo]: Johnny Grande)* / Hide And Seek *(Vocal: Billy Williamson)* / Hey Then, There Now *(Vocal: The Three Comets)* / Goofin' Around *(Guitar [Solo]: Frank Beecher)* / Hook, Line And Sinker / Rudy's Rock *(Saxophone [Tenor Solo]: Rudy Pompilli)* / Choo Choo Ch'Boogie / Blue Comet Blues *(Guitar [Solo]: Frank Beecher)* / Hot Dog Buddy Buddy / Tonight's The Night *(Vocal: The Three Comets)*

3 Nov 56   **1**   4   **ROCK AROUND THE CLOCK** *(Brunswick OE-9250)* 🔲
2nd re-entry

17 Nov 56   **1**   1 ★ <u>**Rudy's Rock**</u> / Blue Comet Blues *(Brunswick 05616)*

24 Nov 56   **3**   1   **ROCK 'N ROLL** *(Brunswick OE-9214)* 🔲 *2nd re-entry*

5 Jan 57   **1**   1   **ROCK AROUND THE CLOCK** *(Brunswick OE-9250)* 🔲
3rd re-entry

19 Jan 57   **7**   1   **ROCK 'N ROLL** *(Brunswick OE-9214)* 🔲 *3rd re-entry*

26 Jan 57   **9**   1 ★ <u>**Rock The Joint**</u> / Yes Indeed! *(London HLF-8371)*

2 Feb 57   **12**   2   **ROCK AROUND THE CLOCK** *(Brunswick OE-9250)* 🔲
4th re-entry

9 Feb 57   **6**   2   **Hook, Line And Sinker** / Goofin' Around *(Brunswick 05641)*

13 Apr 57   **5**   4   **Forty Cups Of Coffee** / Choo Choo Ch'Boogie *(Brunswick 05658)*

13 Jul 57   **3**   4   **Billy Goat** / Rockin' Rollin' Rover *(Brunswick 05688)*

24 Aug 57   **11**   1   **Billy Goat** / Rockin' Rollin' Rover *(Brunswick 05688)*
1st re-entry

28 Sep 57   **3**   1   **Billy Goat** / Rockin' Rollin' Rover *(Brunswick 05688)*
2nd re-entry

12 Oct 57   **7**   1   **Forty Cups Of Coffee** / Choo Choo Ch'Boogie *(Brunswick 05658)*
re-entry

19 Oct 57   **8**   1   **Hook, Line And Sinker** / Goofin' Around *(Brunswick 05641)* *re-entry*

10 May 58   **3**   3   **Skinny Minnie** / How Many *(Brunswick 05742)*

29 Aug 59   **10**   1   **Shaky** / Caldonia *(Brunswick 05805)*

See also   Jodimars
           Kingsmen

ROBIN HALL & JIMMIE MacGREGOR   1

Popular Scottish folk duo featured on the BBC's 'Tonight' programme for fourteen years.

24 Sep 60   **11**   1   **Football Crazy** / Rosin The Beau *(Decca F-11266)*

HALLÉ ORCHESTRA, *cond.* Sir John Barbirolli   1

Orchestra founded in Manchester by Sir Charles Hallé in 1858.

9 Apr 55   **17**   1   **RIMSKY-KORSAKOV – CAPRICCIO ESPAGNOL /**
                               DEBUSSY – PRÉLUDE À L'APRÈS-MIDI D'UN FAUNE /
                               CHABRIER – ESPAÑA *(H.M.V. BLP-1058)* 🔲
Capriccio Espagnol, Op. 34: First Movement: Alborada / Second Movement: Variazioni / Third Movement: Alborada / Fourth Movement: Scena e Canto Gitano / Fifth Movement: Fandango Asturiano / Prélude à l'Après-Midi d'un Faune / España – Rhapsody

GEORGE HAMILTON IV   3

Teen idol from Winston-Salem, North Carolina. He later became a successful country artist.

8 Feb 58	6	1	★ **Why Don't They Understand** / Even Tho' *(H.M.V. POP-429)*
22 Feb 58	5	2	★ **Why Don't They Understand** / Even Tho' *(H.M.V. POP-429)*
			re-entry

ROY HAMILTON   1

Black balladeer born in Leesburg, Georgia in 1929, whose rendition of 'You'll Never Walk Alone' inspired Gerry & The Pacemakers' 1963 hit version.

| 9 Jul 55 | 11 | 1 | **Unchained Melody** / From Here To Eternity *(Philips PB-448)* |

RUSS HAMILTON   3

Singer born Ronald Hulme in Liverpool in 1932. The former Butlin's redcoat found immediate chart success with his first two releases, 'We Will Make Love' and 'Wedding Ring', but ultimately failed to stay the course.

18 May 57	1	1	★ **We Will Make Love** / Rainbow *(Oriole CB-1359)*
8 Feb 58	15	1	**My Mother's Eyes** / I Don't Know Why *(Oriole CB-1406)*
16 Aug 58	16	1	**Little One** / I Had A Dream *(Oriole CB-1404)*

LIONEL HAMPTON   7

Celebrated jazz vibraphonist, drummer, pianist and bandleader born in Louisville, Kentucky in 1908.

25 Dec 54	40	2	**VOLUME 3** *(Vogue LDE-063)* 🆚
			Lionel Hampton's Paris All Stars
			Real Crazy / I Only Have Eyes For You / Walking At The Trocadero / Real Crazy (Completely Crazy)
8 Jan 55	19	1	**GENE NORMAN PRESENTS 'JUST JAZZ' CONCERT** *(Brunswick LA-8531)* 🆚
			Lionel Hampton All Stars
			Stardust / The Man I Love
22 Jan 55	3	3	**APOLLO HALL CONCERT 1954** *(Philips BBL-7015)* 🆚
			Lionel Hampton & His Orchestra
			Introduction / How High The Moon / Stardust / Lover Man / Midnight Sun / Love Is Here To Stay / The Nearness Of You / Vibe Boogie / Flying Home
22 Jan 55	61	1	**GENE NORMAN PRESENTS 'JUST JAZZ' CONCERT** *(Brunswick LA-8531)* 🆚 *re-entry*

PAUL HANFORD   8

Singer from Hemel Hempstead. His cover version of Brian Hyland's US chart-topper was a hit all over Europe, Africa and the Far East, and even made No.1 in Mexico, but failed to break through in the UK.

| 16 Jul 60 | 3 | 8 | **Itsy Bitsy Teenie Weenie Yellow Polka Dot Bikini** / Why Have You Changed Your Mind *(Parlophone R-4680)* |

FRED HANNA BAND   12

Accordionist Fred Hanna from Portadown, Co. Armargh led a six-piece band featuring fiddle, piano, drums, bass and occasionally saxophone. At his second session for Beltona, in August 1957, he also recorded two medleys of Orange songs, which were released as by the 'Diamond Accordion Band' for the Protestant audience.

30 Jun 56	3	1	**Irish Marches No. 1 [M]** / Irish Waltz Medley No. 1 **[M]**
			(Beltona BE-2638)
			Irish Marches: Mountains Of Pomeroy – Kelly The Boy From Killann – Step Together – O Donnell Abu – The Boys Of Wexford / *Irish Waltz Medley:* The Wild Colonial Boy – Girl From Donegal – Hills Of Glenswilly – Banks Of My Own Lovely Lee
21 Jul 56	6	2	**Irish Waltz Medley No. 1 [M]** / Irish Marches No. 1 **[M]**
			(Beltona BE-2638) *1st re-entry (flipped)*

28 Jul 56	**13**	1	**Pride Of Erin No. 2 [M]** / Irish Military Two Step No. 1 **[M]**

(Beltona BE-2639)
Pride Of Erin: Teddy O'Neill – Star Of Donegal – Rose Of Tralee – Peggy O'Neill /
Irish Military Two Step: If You're Irish Come Into The Parlour – With My Shelelagh
Under My Arm – The Irish Washerwoman – The Burnt Potato – MacNamara's Band

11 Aug 56	**2**	1	**Irish Waltz Medley No. 1 [M]** / **Irish Marches No. 1 [M]**

(Beltona BE-2638) ***2nd re-entry***

18 Aug 56	**4**	2	**Pride Of Erin No. 2 [M]** / Irish Military Two Step No. 1 **[M]**

(Beltona BE-2639) ***re-entry***

1 Sep 56	**9**	1	**Irish Waltz Medley No. 1 [M]** / **Irish Marches No. 1 [M]**

(Beltona BE-2638) ***3rd re-entry***

5 Jul 58	**3**	1	**Irish Medley (Parts 1 & 2) [M]** *(Beltona BE-2694)*

Both sides as by the Diamond Accordion Band
The Sash – Derry's Walls – Green Grassy Slopes Of The Boyne / Boyne Water –
The Battle Of Garvagh – Protestant Boys – Dolly's Brae

16 Jul 60	**4**	3	**Irish Medley (Parts 1 & 2) [M]** *(Beltona BE-2694)* ***re-entry***

HAPPY WANDERERS   1

Jazz band who plied the streets of London's West End in the post-war years up to the early '60s.
Due to the strict vagrancy laws of the time, they had to keep moving while playing in order to
avoid arrest.

11 May 57	**3**	1	**JAZZ ON THE STREETS OF LONDON** *(Esquire 20-081)* **LP**

Happy Wanderer / South Rampart Street Parade / Birth Of The Blues / Don't Get
Around Much Anymore / High Society / Singing The Blues / That's A-Plenty / St. Louis
Blues / Don't Fence Me In / When The Saints Go Marching In / Happy Wanderer

HARMONICATS

See Jerry Murad's Harmonicats

JOE HARRIOTT

See Tony Kinsey Trio

MAX HARRIS with His Group   2

Bournemouth-born pianist, arranger and composer who scored a hit in 1960 with the theme to
Anthony Newley's quirky 'Gurney Slade' mini-series.

4 Mar 61	**9**	2	**Wheels** / Regency Ride *(Fontana H-296)*

RONNIE HARRIS   22

Former window cleaner from London who became a top British dance band singer of the early '50s.

21 Aug 54	**34**	1	★ <u>**The Story Of Tina**</u> / Guiding Star *(Columbia DB-3499)*

4 Sep 54	**3**	3	★ <u>**The Story Of Tina**</u> / Guiding Star *(Columbia DB-3499)* ***re-entry***

16 Oct 54	**5**	6	**I Love Paris** / I Still Believe *(Columbia DB-3529)*

6 Nov 54	**14**	1	**Hold My Hand** / No One Can Change Destiny *(Columbia DB-3520)*

11 Dec 54	**15**	1	**I Still Believe** / **I Love Paris** *(Columbia DB-3529)*

1st re-entry (flipped)

15 Jan 55	**42**	1	★ <u>**Don't Go To Strangers**</u> / Surprisingly *(Columbia DB-3555)*

Both sides by Ronnie Harris and the Coronets

19 Feb 55	**20**	1	**I Still Believe** / I Love Paris *(Columbia DB-3529)* ***2nd re-entry***

26 Feb 55	**6**	2	**Goin' Co'tin'** *(Ronnie Harris, Diana Decker, Ray Burns and Ruby Murray)* /

Spring, Spring, Spring *(Ruby Murray, Ray Burns, Diana Decker and*
Ronnie Harris) (Columbia DB-3567)

26 Mar 55	**33**	1	**I Still Believe** / I Love Paris *(Columbia DB-3529)* ***3rd re-entry***

23 Apr 55	**17**	1	**Stranger In Paradise** / **I Wonder** *(Columbia DB-3595)*

30 Apr 55	**16**	3	**Spring, Spring, Spring** *(Ruby Murray, Ray Burns, Diana Decker and*

Ronnie Harris) / **Goin' Co'tin'** *(Ronnie Harris, Diana Decker, Ray*
Burns and Ruby Murray) (Columbia DB-3567) ***re-entry (flipped)***

28 May 55	**30**	1	**I Wonder** / Stranger In Paradise *(Columbia DB-3595)*

re-entry (flipped)

THURSTON HARRIS   3
R&B vocalist from Indianapolis who sang lead with the Lamplighters before going solo. The Sharps, his backing group on these two numbers, evolved out of the Lamplighters.

21 Dec 57 **9** 2 **Little Bitty Pretty One** /
I Hope You Won't Hold It Against Me *(Vogue V-9092)*
Both sides by Thurston Harris and the Sharps
25 Jan 58 **9** 1 **Little Bitty Pretty One** /
I Hope You Won't Hold It Against Me *(Vogue V-9092)* *re-entry*

WEE WILLIE HARRIS   1
The wildest and most flamboyant of all British rock'n'rollers, born in London in 1933. He recorded this bubbler while working as resident pianist at the famous 2I's coffee house in Soho.

17 May 58 **21** 1 **Rockin' At The Two I's** / Back To School Again *(Decca F-10970)*

WYNONIE HARRIS   8
Powerful blues shouter born in Omaha, Nebraska in 1915. Although his risqué material was very popular with the black audience, his career was ultimately stifled by rock'n'roll.

16 Oct 54 **46** 1 **Bloodshot Eyes** / Lollipop Mama *(Vogue V-2127)*
Both sides by Wynonie 'Mr. Blues' Harris & His Orchestra
30 Oct 54 **6** 2 **Bloodshot Eyes** / Lollipop Mama *(Vogue V-2127)* *1st re-entry*
8 Jan 55 **37** 3 **Bloodshot Eyes** / Lollipop Mama *(Vogue V-2127)* *2nd re-entry*
22 Jan 55 **61** 1 **Loving Machine** / Luscious Woman *(Vogue V-2111)*
Both sides by Wynonie Harris with Todd Rhodes & His Orchestra
26 Mar 55 **33** 1 **Bloodshot Eyes** / Lollipop Mama *(Vogue V-2127)* *3rd re-entry*

WILBERT HARRISON   2
R&B singer, guitarist and pianist from Charlotte, North Carolina. He topped the US charts in 1959 with this jaunty interpretation of a Leiber & Stoller composition.

6 Jun 59 **4** 2 **Kansas City** / Listen My Darling *(Top Rank JAR-132)*

DERRY HART & THE HARTBEATS   1
Minor-league British rock'n'roll outfit from south London. Their lead singer sounded like a raucous Tommy Bruce.

23 May 59 **8** 1 **Nowhere In This World** / Come On Baby *(Decca F-11138)*

COLEMAN HAWKINS   2
The first great saxophonist of jazz, born in Saint Joseph, Missouri in 1904.

22 Jan 55 **50** 1 **THE HAWK TALKS** *(Brunswick OE-9166)* **EP**
Coleman Hawkins
Lost In A Fog / Carioca / Amber / Midnight Sun
5 Feb 55 **56** 1 **COLEMAN HAWKINS** *(Vogue EPV-1021)* **EP**
Coleman Hawkins & His Orchestra
It's Only A Paper Moon / I Surrender Dear / Bah-U-Bah / Sophisticated Lady

See also Norman Granz' Jazz At The Philharmonic

DALE HAWKINS   4
Wild rockabilly singer/guitarist from Goldmine, Louisiana. Cousin of Ronnie Hawkins (see below).

23 Nov 57 **11** 1 **Susie-Q** / Don't Treat Me That Way *(London HL-8482)*
25 Apr 59 **4** 1 **Yea-Yea** / Lonely Nights *(London HLM-8842)*
26 Dec 59 **7** 1 **Liza Jane** / Back To School Blues *(London HLM-9016)*
27 Feb 60 **6** 1 **Hot Dog** / **Our Turn** *(London HLM-9060)*

RONNIE HAWKINS & THE HAWKS

Rock'n'roll pioneer from Huntsville, Arkansas who moved to Toronto in the '60s and became a fixture on the Canadian music scene for half a century. Cousin of Dale Hawkins (see above).

10 Oct 59   **22** 1   **Mary Lou** / Need Your Lovin' *(Columbia DB-4345)*

JOHNNY HAWKSWORTH

See Jo Hunter etc.

RITA HAYWORTH

See Jo Ann Greer

LEE HAZLEWOOD

Singer, songwriter and record producer born in Manford, Oklahoma in 1929. He was best known for his work with Duane Eddy in the late '50s, and Nancy Sinatra in the '60s.

21 Jan 61   **24** 1   **Words Mean Nothing** / The Girl On Death Row *(London HLW-9223)*
                      Both sides by Lee Hazlewood with Duane Eddy and His Orchestra

J.C. HEARD

See Norman Granz

TED HEATH & HIS MUSIC   45

Born in London in 1902, trombonist Ted Heath led Britain's greatest post-war big band, whose appeal persisted long after the dance hall era – and Heath himself – had passed.

18 Sep 54   **26** 1   **Cuddle Me** *(Ted Heath & His Music featuring Dennis Lotis and the Johnston Brothers)* / Such A Night *(Dennis Lotis and the Johnston Brothers with Ted Heath & His Music) (Decca F-10287)*

25 Sep 54   **17** 3   **Cinnamon Sinner / They Were Doin' The Mambo** *(Decca F-10374)*
                      Both sides by Dennis Lotis and Ted Heath & His Music

9 Oct 54   **11** 2   **Cuddle Me** *(Ted Heath & His Music featuring Dennis Lotis and the Johnston Brothers)* / Such A Night *(Dennis Lotis and the Johnston Brothers with Ted Heath & His Music) (Decca F-10287)* **re-entry**

30 Oct 54   **6** 3   **Cinnamon Sinner / They Were Doin' The Mambo** *(Decca F-10374)* **re-entry**

13 Nov 54   **17** 1   **Skokiaan** / Bone Idle *(Decca F-10368)*

18 Dec 54   **39** 1   **Honey Love** / Manhattan Mambo *(Decca F-10392)*
                      Both sides by Dennis Lotis with Ted Heath & His Music

8 Jan 55   **11** 1   **Dig Deep** / Asia Minor *(Decca F-10425)*

22 Jan 55   **34** 1   **Dig Deep** / Asia Minor *(Decca F-10425)* **re-entry**

22 Jan 55   **61** 1   **Honey Love** / Manhattan Mambo *(Decca F-10392)* **re-entry**

5 Feb 55   **10** 3   **In The Mood (For Mambo)** / Peg O' My Heart – Mambo *(Decca F-10447)*

29 Oct 55   **5** 11   **Cloudburst / Malagueña** *(Decca F-10624)*

3 Mar 56   **8** 1   **The Rock And Roll Waltz** / Rock Around The Island *(Decca F-10701)*
                      Both sides by Ted Heath & His Music with Annette Klooger

31 Mar 56   **5** 1   **The Rock And Roll Waltz** / Rock Around The Island *(Decca F-10701)* **1st re-entry**

14 Apr 56   **12** 1   **The Rock And Roll Waltz** / Rock Around The Island *(Decca F-10701)* **2nd re-entry**

30 Jun 56   **14** 1   ★ **The Faithful Hussar** / Siboney *(Decca F-10746)*

29 Sep 56   **6** 1   **Canadian Sunset** / Oriental Holiday *(Decca F-10783)*

10 Nov 56   **8** 1   **Canadian Sunset** / Oriental Holiday *(Decca F-10783)* **re-entry**

10 Nov 56   **12** 1   **Autumn Concerto** / The Fool Of The Year *(Decca F-10777)*
                      Both sides by Ted Heath & His Music with Bobbie Britton

24 Nov 56   **4** 2   **Autumn Concerto** / The Fool Of The Year *(Decca F-10777)* **re-entry**

26 Jan 57   **9** 1   **Armen's Theme** / Baby Doll *(Decca F-10827)*

25 May 57   **4** 1   **Madagascar** / Jungle Drums *(Decca F-10856)*

5 Apr 58	8	1	★ **Tequila** / Little Serenade *(Decca F-11003)*
24 May 58	2	4	★ **Tom Hark** / Cha Cha Baby *(Decca F-11025)*
4 Jun 60	21	1	**Madison Time No. 1** *(Ted Heath & His Music with Paul Carpenter)* /

Madison Time No. 2 *(Ted Heath & His Music) (Decca F-11232)*

See also Dennis Lotis
Various Artists (Lord's Taverners Star Band Hit Parade)

BOBBY HELMS   5

Country singer born in Helmsburg, Indiana in 1933. Amazingly, his biggest US record, 'Jingle Bell Rock' – a Christmas hit in 1957, 1958, 1960, 1961 and 1962 – never charted in the UK.

23 Nov 57	5	1	★ **My Special Angel** / Standing At The End Of My World
			(Brunswick 05721)
8 Feb 58	10	1	★ **No Other Baby** / The Magic Song *(Brunswick 05730)*
5 Jul 58	8	1	★ **Jacqueline** / Living In The Shadow Of The Past *(Brunswick 05748)*
5 Jul 58	18	1	**Fraulein** / Heartsick Feeling *(Brunswick 05711)*
11 Oct 58	14	1	**Fraulein** / Heartsick Feeling *(Brunswick 05711)* ***re-entry***

JOE 'MR. PIANO' HENDERSON   31

Scottish pianist and composer, and occasional accompanist to Petula Clark (to whom he was also romantically attached for a time). Rumour has it that Henderson's 'friends' on the singalong medleys were Petula Clark, Alma Cogan and Stanley Black..

7 May 55	1	4	★ **Sing It With Joe (Parts 1 & 2) [M]** *(Polygon P-1167)*
			Margie – I'm Nobody's Sweetheart Now – Somebody Stole My Girl / Moonlight Bay – By The Light Of The Silvery Moon – Cuddle Up A Little Closer
28 May 55	6	1	**Crazy Otto Rag** *(Petula Clark, the Radio Revellers, Joe 'Mr. Piano' Henderson and Friends) (Polygon P-1169)*
			The flip, 'The Pendulum Song' by Petula Clark and the Radio Revellers, also bubbled under
11 Jun 55	11	2	**Crazy Otto Rag** *(Polygon P-1169)* ***re-entry***
			The flip, 'The Pendulum Song' by Petula Clark and the Radio Revellers, also bubbled under
30 Jul 55	1	5	★ **Sing It Again With Joe (Parts 1 & 2) [M]** *(Polygon P-1184)*
			Put Your Arms Around Me Honey – Ain't She Sweet – When You're Smiling / Shine On Harvest Moon – My Blue Heaven – Show Me The Way To Go Home
17 Dec 55	4	3	**Sing It With Joe (Scottish Medley) [M]** /
			Sing It With Joe (Irish Medley) [M] *(Pye Nixa N.15014)*
			Scottish Medley: Roamin' In The Gloamin' – Just A Wee Deoch An Doris – I Love A Lassie – Auld Lang Syne / *Irish Medley:* If You're Irish Come Into The Parlour – Mountains of Mourne – When Irish Eyes Are Smiling
17 Mar 56	13	1	**Theme from 'The Threepenny Opera'** / The Trouble With Harry
			(Pye Nixa N.15044)
31 Mar 56	1	3	**Theme from 'The Threepenny Opera'** / The Trouble With Harry
			(Pye Nixa N.15044) ***re-entry***
16 Jun 56	12	2	**Ask For Joe** / Heart Of Gold *(Pye Nixa N.15057)*
7 Jul 56	15	1	**Ask For Joe** / Heart Of Gold *(Pye Nixa N.15057)* ***re-entry***
3 Aug 57	5	1	**Forgotten Dreams** / **Coffee Bar Jive** *(Pye Nixa N.15099)*
17 Aug 57	7	1	**Forgotten Dreams** / **Coffee Bar Jive** *(Pye Nixa N.15099)* ***re-entry***
28 Jun 58	2	2	★ **Trudie** / Love Is The Sweetest Thing *(Pye Nixa 7N.15147)*
19 Jul 58	3	1	★ **Trudie** / Love Is The Sweetest Thing *(Pye Nixa 7N.15147)* ***re-entry***
21 Mar 59	13	1	**Mr. Piano Plays – Volume 1 (Parts 1 & 2) [M]** *(Pye Nixa 7N.15186)*
			I'll Be With You In Apple Blossom Time – My Happiness – All Of A Sudden My Heart Sings – Baby Face – Smoke Gets In Your Eyes – Does Your Chewing Gum Lose Its Flavour (On The Bedpost Overnight)?
21 Mar 59	13	1	**Chick** / Dream Of Olwen *(Pye Nixa 7N.15187)*
10 Oct 59	7	2	★ **Treble Chance** / Flirtation Waltz *(Pye Nixa 7N.15224)*

HERDMEN 1

In 1954, members of Woody Herman's orchestra, the Third Herd, toured Europe as 'The Third Herdmen' and recorded two LPs in France for Vogue. For some reason, however, the UK versions were credited only to 'The Herdmen'. The personnel consisted of Dick Collins (trumpet), Cy Touff (bass trumpet), Dick Hafer and Bill Perkins (tenor saxophone) and Red Kelly (bass), plus French musicians Henri Renaud (piano) and Jean-Louis Viale (drums).

7 Aug 54	6	1	**THE HERDMEN BLOW IN PARIS** *(Vogue LDE-058)* LP
			So What Could Be New / Gipsy / Potter's Luck (Pot Luck) / Thanks For You

See also Woody Herman

WOODY HERMAN & THE NEW THIRD HERD 1

Prominent jazz clarinettist, saxophonist, singer and bandleader born in Milwaukee in 1913.

29 Jan 55	24	1	**HERD FROM MARS (VOL. 1)** *(London REP-1001)* EP
			Beau Jazz / Men From Mars / Wooftie / Moten Stomp

See also Herdmen

AL HIBBLER 10

Blind baritone singer from Tyro, Mississippi who bridged the gap between R&B and pop.

30 Apr 55	1	2	★ **Unchained Melody** / Daybreak *(Brunswick 05420)*
24 Dec 55	4	5	**He** / Breeze *(Brunswick 05492)*
4 Feb 56	7	1	**He** / Breeze *(Brunswick 05492)* *re-entry*
10 Mar 56	20	2	**The Eleventh Hour Melody** / Let's Try Again *(Brunswick 05523)*

EDDIE HICKEY 1

British rock'n'roller with a decent voice who sadly didn't manage to break through This bubbler was the first and most successful of the three singles he recorded.

10 Oct 59	15	1	**Lady May** / Cap And Gown *(Decca F-11153)*

IRÈNE HILDA 10

Parisian star of the hit musical 'Can-Can', which opened at the London Coliseum in October 1954 and ran for 394 performances. These two tracks were lifted from the Original Cast album.

6 Nov 54	2	10	**I Love Paris** *(Irène Hilda)* / **C'est Magnifique** *(Irène Hilda and Edmund*
			Hockridge) (Parlophone R-3945)

HILLTOPPERS 14

Pop vocal quartet formed at Western Kentucky State College in 1952. The line-up included pianist Billy Vaughn, who went on to become a famous orchestra leader.

14 Jan 56	2	2	★ **Only You** / Until the Real Thing Comes Along *(London HLD-8221)*
2 Jun 56	13	1	**Do The Bop** / When You're Alone *(London HLD-8278)*
21 Jul 56	1	4	★ **Trying** / D-A-R-L-I-N' *(London HLD-8298)*
25 Aug 56	1	2	★ **Trying** / D-A-R-L-I-N' *(London HLD-8298)* *re-entry*
9 Mar 57	16	1	★ **Marianne** / You're Wasting Your Time *(London HLD-8381)*
23 Mar 57	7	2	★ **Marianne** / You're Wasting Your Time *(London HLD-8381)* *re-entry*
8 Feb 58	13	1	**The Joker** / Chicken, Chicken *(London HLD-8528)*
22 Feb 58	15	1	**The Joker** / Chicken, Chicken *(London HLD-8528)* *re-entry*

See also Billy Vaughn & His Orchestra

RONNIE HILTON 30

Romantic balladeer born Adrian Hill in Hull in 1926. He enjoyed considerable popularity in the '50s, but is now chiefly remembered for his 1965 novelty hit, 'A Windmill In Old Amsterdam'.

13 Nov 54	1	2	★ **I Still Believe** / **Veni – Vidi – Vici** *(H.M.V. B-10785)*
22 Jan 55	6	2	★ **A Blossom Fell** / Prize Of Gold *(H.M.V. B-10808)*
11 Jun 55	9	1	**My Loving Hands** / Just Say You Love Her *(H.M.V. B-10860)*

25 Jun 55	17	1		**My Loving Hands** / Just Say You Love Her *(H.M.V. B-10860)* **re-entry**
17 Sep 55	28	1	★	<u>**The Yellow Rose Of Texas**</u> / Have You Ever Been Lonely *(H.M.V. B-10924)*
1 Oct 55	7	2	★	<u>**The Yellow Rose Of Texas**</u> / Have You Ever Been Lonely *(H.M.V. B-10924)* **re-entry**
12 Nov 55	9	1		**Hey There!** / Overnight *(H.M.V. B-10930)*
21 Jan 56	4	1	★	<u>**Young And Foolish**</u> / Moments To Remember *(H.M.V. POP-154)*
4 Feb 56	1	1	★	<u>**Young And Foolish**</u> / Moments To Remember *(H.M.V. POP-154)* **re-entry**
30 Mar 57	4	1		**Heart** / Penny Serenade *(H.M.V. POP-318)*
30 Mar 57	19	1		**The Wisdom Of A Fool** / Amore *(H.M.V. POP-291)*
20 Apr 57	6	3		**Heart** / Penny Serenade *(H.M.V. POP-318)* **re-entry**
18 May 57	7	1	★	<u>**Around The World**</u> / I'd Give You The World *(H.M.V. POP-338)*
20 Jul 57	10	1	★	<u>**Wonderful! Wonderful!**</u> / The Miracle Of Love *(H.M.V. POP-364)*
12 Apr 58	9	1	★	<u>**I May Never Pass This Way Again**</u> / Love Walked In *(H.M.V. POP-468)*
24 May 58	1	4		**On The Street Where You Live** / I've Grown Accustomed To Her Face *(H.M.V. POP-479)*
5 Jul 58	14	1		**On The Street Where You Live** / I've Grown Accustomed To Her Face *(H.M.V. POP-479)* **1st re-entry**
2 Aug 58	14	1		**Her Hair Was Yellow** / Let Me Stay With You *(H.M.V. POP-497)*
31 Oct 59	6	1		**On The Street Where You Live** / I've Grown Accustomed To Her Face *(H.M.V. POP-479)* **2nd re-entry**
31 Oct 59	21	1		**Gigi** / Keep Your Kisses *(H.M.V. POP-560)*
5 Dec 59	5	2		**Happy Anniversary** / The Most Wonderful Thing In The World *(H.M.V. POP-684)*

EDMUND HOCKRIDGE   27

Canadian baritone singer and international cabaret artist who starred in several successful West End musicals during the early '50s including 'Carousel', 'Guys & Dolls' and 'Can-Can'.

6 Nov 54	2	10		**C'est Magnifique** *(Irène Hilda and Edmund Hockridge)* *(Parlophone R-3945)* *The flip, 'I Love Paris' by Irène Hilda, also bubbled under*
6 Nov 54	18	1		**My Friend** / When I Was A Little Boy *(Parlophone R-3884)*
23 Jul 55	19	1		**Stranger In Paradise** / It's Love *(Parlophone R-4011)*
26 Nov 55	34	1		**Hey There!** / A New Town Is A Blue Town *(H.M.V. POP-131)*
24 Dec 55	17	1		**Hey There!** / A New Town Is A Blue Town *(H.M.V. POP-131)* **re-entry**
28 Apr 56	2	2	★	<u>**No Other Love**</u> / This Same Heart *(Pye Nixa N.15048)*
28 Jul 56	14	2	★	<u>**By The Fountains Of Rome**</u> / I'll Need Your Love *(Pye Nixa N.15063)*
18 Aug 56	10	2	★	<u>**By The Fountains Of Rome**</u> / I'll Need Your Love *(Pye Nixa N.15063)* **re-entry**
15 Sep 56	1	1		**A Woman In Love** / Never Turn Back *(Pye Nixa N.15067)*
20 Oct 56	3	1		**A Woman In Love** / Never Turn Back *(Pye Nixa N.15067)* **re-entry**
15 Feb 58	8	1		**I'll Buy You A Star** / Love Letters *(Pye Nixa 7N.15117)*
5 Dec 58	1	1		**More Than Ever** / Some Enchanted Evening *(Pye Nixa 7N.15160)*
17 Jan 59	3	1		**Tonight** / Do I Love You? *(Pye Nixa 7N.15167)*
31 Jan 59	8	1		**Tonight** / Do I Love You? *(Pye Nixa 7N.15167)* **1st re-entry**
21 Feb 59	8	1		**Tonight** / Do I Love You? *(Pye Nixa 7N.15167)* **2nd re-entry**

JOHNNY HODGES

See Norman Granz

FRANK HOLDER   1

Vocalist and Latin percussionist from British Guiana who joined Johnny Dankworth's band in the '50s and went on to become a luminary of the London jazz scene.

| 9 Aug 58 | 12 | 1 | | **Nor The Moon By Night** / Bechuanaland *(Parlophone R-4459)* |

BILLIE HOLIDAY　　　　3

Extraordinary black jazz singer born Eleanora Fagan in Philadelphia in 1915. She led a troubled and turbulent existence, which ended in alcoholism and penury at the age of 44.

25 Sep 54　**35**　2　**THE BILLIE HOLIDAY AND TEDDY WILSON ORCHESTRAS**
(Columbia 33S-1034) **LP**
Why Was I Born / Body And Soul / Them There Eyes / Moanin' Low / Swing, Brother Swing / Billie's Blues / Some Other Spring / Falling In Love Again / These Foolish Things / I'll Get By

16 Oct 54　**26**　1　**THE BILLIE HOLIDAY AND TEDDY WILSON ORCHESTRAS**
(Columbia 33S-1034) **LP** *re-entry*

CHICO HOLIDAY　　　　1

Teen rocker from Waukesha, Wisconsin, born Ralph Vergolino. He later became a preacher. 'Young Ideas' was covered in the UK by Tommy Steele, whose version also bubbled under.

16 May 59　**3**　1　**Young Ideas** / Cuckoo Girl (R.C.A. RCA-1117)

MICHAEL HOLLIDAY　　　　17

Much-loved Crosby-style crooner born Norman Milne in Liverpool in 1924. His career was tragically cut short by a mental breakdown in 1961 followed by suicide two years later.

1 Oct 55　**4**　4　The Yellow Rose Of Texas / Stein Song (Columbia DB-3657)
21 Jan 56　**16**　1　Sixteen Tons / The Rose Tattoo (Columbia DB-3714)
24 Mar 56　**4**　1　★ Nothin' To Do / Perfume, Candy And Flowers (Columbia DB-3746)
26 May 56　**1**　3　★ Hot Diggity / The Gal With The Yaller Shoes (Columbia DB-3783)
29 Sep 56　**9**　1　★ Ten Thousand Miles / The Runaway Train (Columbia DB-3813)
2 Feb 57　**8**　2　Yaller Yaller Gold / I Saw Esau (Columbia DB-3871)
11 Jan 58　**6**　1　★ The Story Of My Life / Keep Your Heart (Columbia DB-4058)
10 May 58　**5**　1　★ Stairway Of Love / May I? (Columbia DB-4121)
12 Sep 59　**6**　1　My Heart Is An Open Book / Careless Hands (Columbia DB-4216)
12 Dec 59　**10**　1　★ Starry Eyed / The Steady Game (Columbia DB-4378)
26 Dec 59　**2**　2　★ Starry Eyed / The Steady Game (Columbia DB-4378) *re-entry*

HEINRICH HOLLREISER *(conductor)*
See Ingrid Haebler

BUDDY HOLLY　　　　13

Hugely influential rock'n'roll singer, songwriter and guitarist born in Lubbock, Texas in 1936. Some of his recordings appeared under his own name, while others were issued under the name of the group he led, the Crickets. He was killed in a plane crash on 3 February 1959, aged just 22.

30 Nov 57　**7**　1　★ Peggy Sue / Everyday (Vogue Coral Q-72293)
16 Aug 58　**2**　1　★ Early In The Morning / Now We're One (Coral Q-72333)
5 Dec 58　**2**　2　★ Heartbeat / Well... All Right (Coral Q-72346)
13 Jun 59　**1**　7　★ Midnight Shift / Rock Around With Ollie Vee (Brunswick 05800)
16 Apr 60　**10**　1　★ Heartbeat / Everyday (Coral Q-72392) *reissue*
15 Oct 60　**15**　1　★ Learning The Game / That Makes It Tough (Coral Q-72411)

See also Crickets

HOLLYWOOD FLAMES　　　　2

R&B vocal group from Los Angeles which included Earl Nelson (later of Bob & Earl) and Bobby Day.

22 Feb 58　**4**　1　Buzz, Buzz, Buzz / Crazy (London HL-8545)
15 Mar 58　**15**　1　Buzz, Buzz, Buzz / Crazy (London HL-8545) *re-entry*

See also Bobby Day

BILL HOLMAN OCTET 2

Jazz and pop saxophonist, composer and arranger born in Olive, California in 1927.

4 Dec 54 **12** 2 **KENTON PRESENTS JAZZ – BILL HOLMAN** *(Capitol KPL-101)* 🄻🄿
On The Town / Locomotion / Jughaid / Back To Minors / Sparkle / Tanglefoot / Song
Without Words / Awfully Busy

LEROY HOLMES & His Orchestra 6

Composer/arranger born Alvin Holmes in Pittsburgh, Pennsylvania in 1913.

16 Oct 54 **23** 2 **The High And The Mighty** *(Whistling by Fred Lowery) /*
Lisa (Vocal: Mary Mayo) (M.G.M. MGM-765)

27 Nov 54 **42** 2 **The High And The Mighty** *(Whistling by Fred Lowery) /*
Lisa (Vocal: Mary Mayo) (M.G.M. MGM-765) **1st re-entry**

8 Jan 55 **37** 1 **The High And The Mighty** *(Whistling by Fred Lowery) /*
Lisa (Vocal: Mary Mayo) (M.G.M. MGM-765) **2nd re-entry**

28 Nov 59 **10** 1 **Alice Blue Gown** / Sweet Leilani *(M.G.M. MGM-1044)*

HOMER & JETHRO 2

Guitarist Henry 'Homer' Haynes and mandolin player Kenneth 'Jethro' Burns specialised in country comedy and parodies of popular songs like the one below (a humorous reworking of Johnny Horton's 'Battle Of New Orleans'), which earned them a Grammy award.

10 Oct 59 **15** 2 **The Battle Of Kookamonga** / Waterloo *(R.C.A. RCA-1148)*

LYNN HOPE 1

Tenor saxophonist and sometime bandleader born in Birmingham, Alabama in 1926. His version of the Gershwin classic went down a storm in Jamaica, but less so in Britain.

25 Jan 58 **6** 1 **Blue Moon** / Blues For Anna Bacoa *(Vogue V-9081)*

LENA HORNE 13

Classy jazz and pop singer, and star of stage, screen and television born in New York in 1917.

16 Jul 55 **13** 1 **I Love To Love** / Love Me Or Leave Me *(H.M.V. B-10869)*
27 Aug 55 **6** 1 **I Love To Love** / Love Me Or Leave Me *(H.M.V. B-10869)*
1st re-entry

10 Sep 55 **16** 1 **I Love To Love** / Love Me Or Leave Me *(H.M.V. B-10869)*
2nd re-entry

15 Oct 55 **7** 6 **Love Me Or Leave Me** / I Love To Love *(H.M.V. B-10869)*
3rd re-entry (flipped)

6 Jun 59 **7** 2 **A New Fangled Tango** / Honeysuckle Rose *(R.C.A. RCA-1120)*
5 Dec 59 **3** 2 **A New Fangled Tango** / Honeysuckle Rose *(R.C.A. RCA-1120)*
re-entry

JOHNNY HORTON 5

Country singer/guitarist born in Los Angeles but raised in Texas. He was famed for his 'saga' songs – most notably 'The Battle Of New Orleans'. He died in a car crash in 1960, aged just 31.

5 Mar 60 **10** 1 **The Same Old Tale The Crow Told Me** / Sink The Bismarck!
(Philips PB-995)

19 Nov 60 **17** 1 ★ **North To Alaska** / The Mansion You Stole *(Philips PB-1062)*
10 Dec 60 **6** 3 ★ **North To Alaska** / The Mansion You Stole *(Philips PB-1062)* **re-entry**

ROBERT HORTON 1

Ruggedly handsome TV and film actor and singer born in Los Angeles in 1924. He starred in the TV western series, 'Wagon Train' (1957-62), so it was perhaps inevitable that he would record a cover of the theme. However, it was Jimmy O'Neill's original that was used in the show.

17 Sep 60 **20** 1 **Wagon Train** / Sail Ho! *(Pye 7N.15285)*

LES HOWARD 6

1940s/'50s band vocalist from Wigan, Lancashire, originally with Eric Winstone & His Orchestra. He later became director of the BBC Northern Dance Orchestra.

15 Oct 55	4	3	Blue Star / Three Galleons (H.M.V. B-10928)
26 Nov 55	14	2	Blue Star / Three Galleons (H.M.V. B-10928) *1st re-entry*
21 Jan 56	9	1	Three Galleons / Blue Star (H.M.V. B-10928) *2nd re-entry (flipped)*

DAVID HUGHES 4

Singer born Geoffrey Paddison in Birmingham in 1925. He dabbled in pop ballads before switching to opera in the early '60s.

13 Nov 54	51	1	Santo Natale / Not As A Stranger (Philips PB-350)
4 Dec 54	39	1	Santo Natale / Not As A Stranger (Philips PB-350) *re-entry*
26 Nov 55	19	1	Love Is A Many Splendoured Thing / Bella Notte (Philips PB-508)
5 Jan 57	4	1	Two Different Worlds / True Love (Philips PB-642)

See also Original London Cast (SUMMER SONG)

JO HUNTER, JIMMY DEUCHAR, KEITH CHRISTIE, DON RENDELL, JIMMY SKIDMORE, RONNIE ROSS, RALPH DOLLIMORE, DEREK SMITH, DILL JONES, JOHNNY HAWKSWORTH, SAMMY STOKES, ALLAN GANLEY and PHIL SEAMEN 1

The cream of Britain's jazz talent assembled for a one-off jam session.

| 27 Nov 54 | 59 | 1 | MUSIC IN THE MAKING (Vogue LDE-050) `LP` |
| | | | Ice Fall / Mountain Sunset / Where Or When / Best Keller / Presque Cubain – Almost Cuban |

TAB HUNTER 1

Handsome fair-haired pop singer and actor born Arthur Kelm in New York in 1931.

| 2 Feb 57 | 12 | 1 | ★ Young Love / Red Sails In The Sunset (London HLD-8380) |

HUNTERS 11

Dave Sampson's backing group. Like Cliff Richard's Drifters/Shadows, they were also an instrumental act in their own right.

14 May 60	13	1	★ Sweet Dreams / It's Lonesome (Columbia DB-4449)
			Both sides by Dave Sampson and the Hunters
10 Sep 60	9	2	If You Need Me / See You Around (Columbia DB-4502)
			Both sides by Dave Sampson and the Hunters
26 Nov 60	3	2	Teen Scene / Santa Monica Flyer (Fontana H-276)
17 Dec 60	8	1	Teen Scene / Santa Monica Flyer (Fontana H-276) *1st re-entry*
14 Jan 61	24	1	Teen Scene / Santa Monica Flyer (Fontana H-276) *2nd re-entry*
28 Jan 61	3	2	Teen Scene / Santa Monica Flyer (Fontana H-276) *3rd re-entry*
4 Mar 61	19	1	Teenage Love (Michael Cox and the Hunters) (H.M.V. POP-830)
			Flip is 'Linda' by Michael Cox and the Dave Lee Group
11 Mar 61	9	1	Why The Chicken (Dave Sampson and the Hunters)
			(Columbia DB-4597)
			Flip is '1999' by Dave Sampson

FERLIN HUSKY 23

Versatile country star from Cantwell, Missouri, who also had a comic alter ego named Simon Crum.

1 Jun 57	10	2	Gone / Missing Persons (Capitol CL-14702)
			Both sides by Ferlin Husky & His Hush Puppies
21 Jun 58	8	3	The Drunken Driver / Slow Down Brother (Capitol CL-14883)
			Both sides by Ferlin Husky & His Hush Puppies
26 Jul 58	9	1	The Drunken Driver / Slow Down Brother (Capitol CL-14883)
			1st re-entry
6 Sep 58	7	1	I Saw God / I Feel That Old Heartache Again (Capitol CL-14916)

6 Sep 58	**8**	1	**The Drunken Driver** / Slow Down Brother *(Capitol CL-14883)*	
			2nd re-entry	
25 Oct 58	**3**	1	**Terrific Together** / The Kingdom Of Love *(Capitol CL-14922)*	
25 Oct 58	**4**	1	**The Drunken Driver** / Slow Down Brother *(Capitol CL-14883)*	
			3rd re-entry	
22 Nov 58	**3**	1	**All Of The Time** / I Will *(Capitol CL-14954)*	
22 Nov 58	**3**	1	**I Saw God** / I Feel That Old Heartache Again *(Capitol CL-14916)*	
			re-entry	
29 Nov 58	**1**	2	**The Drunken Driver** / Slow Down Brother *(Capitol CL-14883)*	
			4th re-entry	
6 Jun 59	**16**	1	**Draggin' The River** / Sea Sand *(Capitol CL-15027)*	
31 Oct 59	**14**	1	**Morgan Poisoned The Water Hole** / I Fell Out Of Love With Love	
			Both sides as by Simon Crum (Capitol CL-15077)	
7 Jan 61	**13**	2	**Wings Of A Dove** / Next To Jimmy *(Capitol CL-15160)*	
28 Jan 61	**8**	2	**Wings Of A Dove** / Next To Jimmy *(Capitol CL-15160)* **1st re-entry**	
11 Feb 61	**4**	2	**Enormity In Motion** / Cuzz Yore So Sweet *(Capitol CL-15183)*	
			Both sides as by Simon Crum	
4 Mar 61	**19**	1	**Wings Of A Dove** / Next To Jimmy *(Capitol CL-15160)* **2nd re-entry**	

HUTTON SISTERS   1

Sisters Marion and Betty Thornburg from Battle Creek, Michigan, who reportedly changed their stage name to Hutton on the advice of a numerologist. Although they parted ways in 1940 (Marion became Glenn Miller's featured vocalist, while the effervescent Betty moved into films), they reunited in 1954 to record this bubbler.

16 Apr 55	**22**	1	**Ko Ko Mo** / Heart Throb *(Capitol CL-14250)*

DICK HYMAN TRIO   1

Jazz pianist, arranger and composer born in New York in 1927.

10 Mar 56	**24**	1	★ <u>**Theme from 'The Threepenny Opera'**</u> / Baubles, Bangles And Beads
			(M.G.M. MGM-890)

FRANK IFIELD   8

Coventry-born balladeer/yodeller raised in Australia, and the first British artist ever to have three consecutive No.1 hits in the UK.

30 Jan 60	**5**	1	★ <u>**Lucky Devil**</u> / Nobody Else But You *(Columbia DB-4399)*
4 Jun 60	**5**	1	**Happy-Go-Lucky Me** / Unchained Melody *(Columbia DB-4464)*
2 Jul 60	**14**	1	**Happy-Go-Lucky Me** / Unchained Melody *(Columbia DB-4464)*
			re-entry
17 Sep 60	**14**	1	★ <u>**Gotta Get A Date**</u> / No Love Tonight *(Columbia DB-4496)*
14 Jan 61	**6**	4	**That's The Way It Goes** / Phoebe Snow *(Columbia DB-4568)*

IMPALAS   10

Racially integrated doo-wop group from New York led by Joe 'Speedo' Frasier.

25 Apr 59	**8**	1	★ <u>**Sorry (I Ran All The Way Home)**</u> / Fool, Fool, Fool
			(M.G.M. MGM-1015)
9 May 59	**3**	1	★ <u>**Sorry (I Ran All The Way Home)**</u> / Fool, Fool, Fool
			(M.G.M. MGM-1015) **1st re-entry**
13 Jun 59	**6**	8	★ <u>**Sorry (I Ran All The Way Home)**</u> / Fool, Fool, Fool
			(M.G.M. MGM-1015) **2nd re-entry**

INADEQUATES   1

Studio teen vocal group created by Pasadena, California guitarist Bob Summers This was their only release.

22 Aug 59	**12**	1	**Audie** / Pretty Face *(Capitol CL-15051)*

See also Bob(by) Summers

INK SPOTS   1
Internationally famous black singing group from Indianapolis, active from 1934 until 1954.

23 Apr 55   **12**   1   ★ <u>**Melody Of Love**</u> / Am I Too Late *(Parlophone R-3977)*

JIMMY ISLE   1
Rockabilly singer from Memphis, Tennessee chiefly remembered for his classic Roulette waxing, 'Goin' Wild'. This bubbler was the first of three unsuccessful singles he cut for Sun.

4 Apr 59   **8**   1   **Diamond Ring** / I've Been Waitin' *(London HLS-8832)*

ISLEY BROTHERS   1
Exciting gospel-influenced trio from Cincinnati who provided Lulu with 'Shout' and the Beatles with 'Twist And Shout'. They were a constant presence in the American charts for over four decades.

7 Nov 59   **13**   1   **Shout (Parts 1 & 2)** *(R.C.A. RCA-1149)*

BURL IVES   5
Award-winning folk singer and actor born on a farm near Hunt City, Illinois in 1909.

28 Apr 56   **12**   1   **SONGS FOR AND ABOUT MEN (PART 1)** *(Brunswick OE-9200)* **EP**
    The Locktender's Lament / Ox Driver's Song / The Bold Soldier / The Young
    Married Man (Cod Liver Oil) / Sad Man's Song (Fare Thee Well, O Honey) /
    The Harlem Man

12 May 56   **6**   2   **SONGS FOR AND ABOUT MEN (PART 1)** *(Brunswick OE-9200)* **EP**
    re-entry

4 Aug 56   **4**   1   **SONGS FOR AND ABOUT MEN (PART 2)** *(Brunswick OE-9201)* **EP**
    The Western Settler / Waltzing Matilda / The Wild Rover / Frankie And Johnny /
    The Deceiver

25 Aug 56   **4**   1   **SONGS FOR AND ABOUT MEN (PART 3)** *(Brunswick OE-9202)* **EP**
    The Sailor's Return / When I Was Single / Prisoner's Song (Midnight Special) /
    John Henry

CHUBBY JACKSON'S ALL STARS   2
Jazz double-bassist and bandleader born Greig Jackson in New York in 1918.

6 Nov 54   **36**   2   **CHUBBY JACKSON'S ALL STARS** *(Esquire EP-201)* **EP**
    I May Be Wrong / So What / Leavin' Town / Sax Appeal

JIMMY JACKSON'S ROCK 'N' SKIFFLE   1
Singer/guitarist from Glasgow whose style was actually closer to Western swing than rock'n'roll or skiffle.

7 Sep 57   **3**   1   **I Shall Not Be Moved** / California Zephyr *(Columbia DB-3898)*

MAHALIA JACKSON   1
Internationally renowned 'Queen of Gospel', born in New Orleans in 1911.

1 Jan 55   **32**   1   **Silent Night, Holy Night** / I Gave Up *(Vogue V-306)*

MILT JACKSON MODERN JAZZ QUARTET   12
Leading jazz vibraphonist discovered by Dizzy Gillespie. He was born in Detroit in 1923.

28 Aug 54   **10**   3   **MILT JACKSON MODERN JAZZ QUARTET** *(Esquire EP-14)* **EP**
    The Queen's Fancy / Delaunay's Dilemma / Autumn In New York / But Not For Me

25 Sep 54   **8**   9   **MILT JACKSON MODERN JAZZ QUARTET** *(Esquire EP-14)* **EP**
    re-entry

WANDA JACKSON — 3

Legendary rockabilly and country singer, songwriter, pianist and guitarist from Maud, Oklahoma.

| 20 Aug 60 | 4 | 2 | ★ **Let's Have A Party** / Cool Love *(Capitol CL-15147)* |
| 14 Jan 61 | 2 | 1 | ★ **Mean, Mean Man** / Honey Bop *(Capitol CL-15176)* |

JACKSON BROTHERS — 1

Everlys-like duo who almost broke into the UK charts with their Leiber & Stioller-produced cover of Travis & Bob's US Top Ten hit.

| 16 May 59 | 3 | 1 | **Tell Him No** / Love Me *(London HLX-8845)* |

DICK JAMES — 14

Former band singer with Cyril Stapleton and original lead of the Stargazers born Leon Vapnick in London in 1920. He later became a successful music publisher (most notably for the Beatles).

15 Jan 55	33	1	**Veni – Vidi – Vici** / Your Heart, My Heart *(Parlophone R-3940)*
29 Oct 55	1	7	**Sing Song Time No. 1 (Parts 1 & 2) [M]** *(Parlophone R-4065)*
			Keep Your Sunny Side Up – When Irish Eyes Are Smiling – Don't Dilly Dally On The Way / I Belong To Glasgow – You Made Me Love You – I've Got A Lovely Bunch Of Cocoanuts
24 Dec 55	2	2	**Sing Song Time No. 1 (Parts 1 & 2) [M]** *(Parlophone R-4065)* **re-entry**
14 Jan 56	13	1	★ **Robin Hood** / **The Ballad Of Davy Crockett** *(Parlophone R-4117)*
12 May 56	2	1	**Summer Sing-Song (Parts 1 & 2) [M]** *(Parlophone R-4164)*
			I Do Like To Be Beside The Seaside – Cruising Down The River – You Are My Sunshine / The Chestnut Tree – Roamin' In The Gloamin' – Down At The Old Bull And Bush
20 Dec 58	3	2	**Daddy's Little Girl** / When You're Young *(Parlophone R-4498)*

HARRY JAMES & His Orchestra — 2

Influential trumpeter and bandleader born in Albany, Georgia in 1916. He married film star Betty Grable in 1943.

| 27 Nov 54 | 33 | 2 | **The High And The Mighty** / Three Coins In The Fountain *(Philips PB-326)* |

JONI JAMES — 9

Singer born Giovanna Babbo in Chicago in 1930. Her first hit, 'Why Don't You Believe Me' (1952), sold over a million copies.

9 Apr 55	17	2	**How Important Can It Be?** / This Is My Confession *(M.G.M. MGM-811)*
30 Apr 55	16	2	**How Important Can It Be?** / This Is My Confession *(M.G.M. MGM-811)* **1st re-entry**
21 May 55	26	1	**How Important Can It Be?** / This Is My Confession *(M.G.M. MGM-811)* **2nd re-entry**
4 Jun 55	18	3	**How Important Can It Be?** / This Is My Confession *(M.G.M. MGM-811)* **3rd re-entry**
24 Jan 59	5	1	★ **There Must Be A Way** / I'm Sorry For You, My Friend *(M.G.M. MGM-1002)*

SONNY JAMES — 6

Country singer/songwriter from Alabama born James Loden. He topped the US pop and country charts in 1957 with the first ever teenage country 'crossover' record, 'Young Love'.

27 Oct 56	5	2	★ **The Cat Came Back** / Hello Old Broken Heart *(Capitol CL-14635)*
24 Nov 56	2	1	★ **The Cat Came Back** / Hello Old Broken Heart *(Capitol CL-14635)* **re-entry**
2 Feb 57	16	1	★ **Young Love** / You're The Reason I'm In Love *(Capitol CL-14683)*
30 May 59	11	1	**Talk Of The School** / The Table *(Capitol CL-15022)*
			Both sides by Sonny James with the Eligibles
4 Jun 60	10	1	**Jenny Lou** / Passin' Through *(London HL-9132)*

JAN & ARNIE   1
Before Jan & Dean there was... Jan Berry and Arnie Ginsburg, who recorded three great rock'n'roll singles. The first and most successful of these was 'Jennie Lee', a song about a stripper.

9 Aug 58   **9**   1   **Jennie Lee** / Gotta Getta Date *(London HL-8653)*

AL JEFFERY
See Patrick Galvin

JIMMIE & THE NIGHT HOPPERS   1
These two storming rock'n'roll instrumentals recorded for the Hollywood-based Knight label (a subsidiary of Imperial) were an early studio-group production by Jimmie Haskell, who went on to forge a career as an arranger and composer.

28 Mar 59   **9**   1   **Night Hop** / Cruising *(London HLP-8830)*

JODIMARS   3
The Jodimars were formed in the summer of 1955 by three former members of Bill Haley's Comets: Joey Ambrose, Dick Richards and Marshall Lytle.

4 Feb 56   **9**   3   **Let's All Rock Together** / Well Now, Dig This *(Capitol CL-14518)*

See also Bill Haley & His Comets
          Kingsmen

LITTLE WILLIE JOHN   2
Soulful R&B singer born in Cullendale, Arkansas in 1937. He died in prison in 1968, aged just 30.

6 Oct 56   **11**   1   **Fever** / Letter From My Darling *(Parlophone R-4209)*
18 Feb 61   **19**   1   **Leave My Kitten Alone** / Let Nobody Love You *(Parlophone R-4571)*

JOHNNY & THE HURRICANES   7
Popular rock'n'roll instrumental group from Toledo, Ohio, led by saxophonist Johnny Paris.

15 Aug 59   **12**   2   **Crossfire** / Lazy *(London HL-8899)*
3 Oct 59   **6**   1   ★ **Red River Rock** / Buckeye *(London HL-8948)*
3 Oct 59   **10**   2   **Crossfire** / Lazy *(London HL-8899)* **re-entry**
19 Dec 59   **1**   1   ★ **Reveille Rock** / Time Bomb *(London HL-9017)*
24 Sep 60   **3**   1   ★ **Rocking Goose** / Revival *(London HL-9190)*

BRYAN JOHNSON   2
Singer, actor and younger brother of Teddy Johnson (see below), born in 1926. He represented the UK in the 1960 Eurovision Song Contest and came second with 'Looking High, High, High'.

27 Feb 60   **6**   2   ★ **Looking High, High, High** / Each Tomorrow *(Decca F-11213)*

BUNK JOHNSON   2
Influential jazz trumpeter born William Johnson in New Orleans in 1879. He was rediscovered in the late '30s and made his first recordings in 1942. He died in 1949.

16 Oct 54   **40**   1   **Ory's Creole Trombone** / The Girls Go Crazy
                         (Good Time Jazz GV-2212)
                         Both sides by Bunk Johnson & The Yerba Buena Jazz Band
10 Nov 56   **11**   1   **BUNK JOHNSON & HIS NEW ORLEANS BAND**
                         (Brunswick OE-9257) **EP**
                         Bunk Johnson & His New Orleans Band
                         Tishomingo Blues / You Always Hurt The One You Love / Alexander's Ragtime
                         Band / Maryland, My Maryland

J.J. JOHNSON, KAI WINDING, BENNY GREEN and WILLIE DENNIS 11

Ad hoc jazz ensemble assembled in Brooklyn, New York in 1953 by Charles Mingus and promoter Johnny Parros. The full line-up featured Mingus (bass), Art Taylor (drums), John Lewis (piano) and J.J. Johnson, Kai Winding, Benny Green and Willie Dennis (trombones).

19 Jun 54	2	3	**JAZZ WORKSHOP (VOL. 1)** *(Vogue/Debut LDE-066)* **LP**
			Move / Stardust / Yesterdays
7 Aug 54	10	1	**JAZZ WORKSHOP (VOL. 1)** *(Vogue/Debut LDE-066)* **LP** *1st re-entry*
23 Oct 54	6	7	**JAZZ WORKSHOP (VOL. 1)** *(Vogue/Debut LDE-066)* **LP** *2nd re-entry*

MARV JOHNSON 2

Popular R&B and soul singer born in Detroit in 1938. Discovered by Berry Gordy, he was the first artist to record for the Tamla label.

| 30 Jan 60 | 1 | 2 | ★ <u>**You Got What It Takes**</u> / Don't Leave Me *(London HLT-9013)* |

TEDDY JOHNSON 2

Born in Surbiton, Surrey in 1920, Teddy Johnson was the older brother of actor/singer Bryan Johnson (see above), and a successful solo singer and professional drummer. In 1955, he married Pearl Carr and formed a popular singing duo with her. They represented the UK in the 1959 Eurovision Song Contest and came second with 'Sing Little Birdie'.

| 16 Oct 54 | 34 | 1 | **C'est Magnifique** / Allez Vous En *(Columbia DB-3521)* |
| 20 Nov 54 | 34 | 1 | **C'est Magnifique** / Allez Vous En *(Columbia DB-3521)* *re-entry* |

JOHNSTON BROTHERS 77

Top male vocal harmony group led by Johnny Johnston (real name John Reine), who was also the driving force behind the Keynotes. The Johnston Brothers also did a lot of back-up work and advertising jingles.

14 Aug 54	10	7	★ <u>**Wait For Me, Darling**</u> (Joan Regan with the Johnston Brothers)
			(Decca F-10362)
			Flip is 'Two Kinds of Tears' by Joan Regan
28 Aug 54	24	1	**Sh-Boom** / Crazy 'bout Ya Baby *(Decca F-10364)*
4 Sep 54	5	7	**The Bandit** *(Decca F-10302)*
			Flip is 'A Dime And A Dollar' by the Keynotes
11 Sep 54	23	1	**Crazy 'bout Ya Baby** / Sh-Boom *(Decca F-10364)* *re-entry (flipped)*
18 Sep 54	26	1	**Cuddle Me** (Ted Heath & His Music featuring Dennis Lotis and the
			Johnston Brothers) / Such A Night (Dennis Lotis and the Johnston
			Brothers with Ted Heath & His Music) *(Decca F-10287)*
9 Oct 54	11	2	**Cuddle Me** (Ted Heath & His Music featuring Dennis Lotis and the
			Johnston Brothers) / Such A Night (Dennis Lotis and the Johnston
			Brothers with Ted Heath & His Music) *(Decca F-10287)* *re-entry*
16 Oct 54	20	1	★ <u>**Wait For Me, Darling**</u> (Joan Regan with the Johnston Brothers)
			(Decca F-10362) *1st re-entry*
30 Oct 54	35	1	★ <u>**Wait For Me, Darling**</u> (Joan Regan with the Johnston Brothers)
			(Decca F-10362) *2nd re-entry*
27 Nov 54	1	8	★ <u>**Happy Days And Lonely Nights**</u> / Tell Me, Tell Me *(Decca F-10389)*
			Both sides by Suzi Miller and the Johnston Brothers
27 Nov 54	50	1	**The Bandit** *(Decca F-10302)* *1st re-entry*
4 Dec 54	3	6	**Join In And Sing (Parts 1 & 2) [M]** *(Decca F-10414)*
			Somebody Stole My Gal – You Were Meant For Me – I Can't Give You Anything But
			Love / If You Knew Susie – Ain't She Sweet – Toot, Toot, Tootsie
11 Dec 54	18	1	**I Can't Tell A Waltz From A Tango** /
			For Better, For Worse *(Decca F-10404)*
			Both sides by Lorrae Desmond and the Johnston Brothers
11 Dec 54	35	1	**The Bandit** *(Decca F-10302)* *2nd re-entry*
12 Feb 55	3	9	**Majorca** / Heartbroken *(Decca F-10451)*
19 Feb 55	36	1	**Addio Amore** (Vera Lynn with the Johnston Brothers) *(Decca F-10463)*
			Flip is 'I Do' by Vera Lynn
19 Mar 55	24	2	**Addio Amore** / I Do *(Decca F-10463)* *1st re-entry*
23 Apr 55	9	1	**Addio Amore** / I Do *(Decca F-10463)* *2nd re-entry*

23 Apr 55	**26**	1	**The Right To Be Wrong** / Hot Potato Mambo *(Decca F-10490)*
14 May 55	**27**	1	**Chee Chee-oo Chee** / Hubble Bubble *(Decca F-10513)*
14 May 55	**27**	1	**Dance With Me Henry (Wallflower)**

(Suzi Miller and the Johnston Brothers) (Decca F-10512)
Flip is 'Butter Fingers' by Suzi Miller and the Marilyn Sisters

28 May 55	**8**	1	**Dance With Me Henry (Wallflower)**

(Suzi Miller and the Johnston Brothers) (Decca F-10512)
1st re-entry

4 Jun 55	**5**	3	**Chee Chee-oo Chee** / Hubble Bubble *(Decca F-10513)* **1st re-entry**
2 Jul 55	**26**	2	**Dance With Me Henry (Wallflower)**

(Suzi Miller and the Johnston Brothers) (Decca F-10512)
2nd re-entry

9 Jul 55	**12**	2	**Chee Chee-oo Chee** / Hubble Bubble *(Decca F-10513)* **2nd re-entry**
1 Oct 55	**23**	1	★ **Hernando's Hideaway** / Hey There *(Decca F-10608)*
12 Nov 55	**9**	1	★ **Join In And Sing Again (Parts 1 & 2) [M]** *(Decca F-10636)*

The Sheik Of Araby – Yes, Sir, That's My Baby – California Here I Come / Some Of
These Days – The Charleston – Margie

26 Nov 55	**25**	2	**Arrivederci Darling** / I'll Be Waiting *(Decca F-10635)*

Both sides by Lys Assia and the Johnston Brothers

18 Aug 56	**6**	1	**The Street Musician** / How Little We Know *(Decca F-10747)*
20 Oct 56	**3**	2	★ **In The Middle Of The House** *(Johnston Brothers and the Keynotes)* /

Stranded In The Jungle *(Johnston Brothers) (Decca F-10781)*

17 Nov 56	**10**	1	★ **Join In And Sing No. 3 (Parts 1 & 2) [M]** *(Decca F-10814)*

Coal Back Mammy – When You're Smiling – Alexander's Ragtime Band / Sweet
Sue, Just You – When You Wore A Tulip – If You Were The Only Girl In The World

24 Nov 56	**5**	1	★ **In The Middle Of The House** *(Johnston Brothers and the Keynotes)* /

Stranded In The Jungle *(Johnston Brothers) (Decca F-10781)*
re-entry

2 Feb 57	**3**	1	★ **Give Her My Love (When You Meet Her)** / A Rose And A Candy Bar

(Decca F-10828)

23 Mar 57	**15**	1	★ **Whatever Lola Wants** / Heart *(Decca F-10860)*
13 Apr 57	**7**	1	★ **Heart** / Whatever Lola Wants *(Decca F-10860)* **re-entry (flipped)**
21 Dec 57	**3**	3	**Join In And Sing No. 4 (Parts 1 & 2) [M]** *(Decca F-10962)*

*Both sides by the Johnston Brothers and the George Chisholm
Sour-Note Six*
Nobody's Sweetheart – I'm Looking Over A Four-Leaf Clover – Waiting For The
Robert E. Lee / Bye Bye Blackbird – After You've Gone – The Darktown Strutters'
Ball

See also Keynotes

JOHNSTONE'S SCOTTISH ACCORDION BAND   2

Dance band fronted by ace accordionist Jim Johnstone, born in Tranent, East Lothian in 1937.

12 Nov 60	**2**	2	**A Hundred Thousand Welcomes** / The Tartan *(Waverley SLP-507)*

*Both sides by Dennis Clancy with Johnstone's Scottish Accordion
Band*

AL JOLSON   3

*Dynamic singer and actor famous for appearing in blackface. He was born Asa Yoelson in
Seredžius, Lithuania in 1886 and moved to the USA with his family in 1894.*

14 Aug 54	**21**	1	**April Showers** / Rock-A-Bye Your Baby With A Dixie Melody

(Columbia DB-2613)

3 May 58	**3**	1	**AMONG MY SOUVENIRS (PART 1)** *(Brunswick OE-9363)* **EP**

Among My Souvenirs / Roses Of Picardy / Say It Isn't So / Little Pal

24 May 58	**7**	1	**AMONG MY SOUVENIRS (PART 1)** *(Brunswick OE-9363)* **EP**

re-entry

DAVY JONES 1

No, not the future Monkee, but a 21-year-old black singer from New York who moved to Britain in 1960. He performed with the Beatles in both Liverpool and Hamburg, but failed to achieve lasting success despite a strong start with 'Amapola'.

26 Mar 60   **2**   1   **Amapola** / Mighty Man *(Pye 7N.15254)*

DILL JONES

See Jo Hunter etc.

EDDIE JONES

See Paul Quinichette etc.

GEORGE JONES 4

Country singer/songwriter born in Saratoga, Texas in 1931. Although he became a huge C&W star in the '60s, these two bubblers date from his early 'rockabilly' phase.

25 Apr 59   **3**   1   **White Lightning** / Long Time To Forget *(Mercury AMT-1036)*
29 Aug 59   **2**   3   **Who Shot Sam** / Into My Arms Again *(Mercury AMT-1058)*

HANK JONES

See Paul Quinichette etc.

JIMMY JONES 3

Black singer with a trademark falsetto style, born in Birmingham, Alabama in 1937.

27 Feb 60   **1**   2   ★ **Handy Man** / The Search Is Over *(M.G.M. MGM-1051)*
12 Nov 60   **7**   1   ★ **Ready For Love** / For You *(M.G.M. MGM-1103)*

JOE JONES & His Orchestra 3

New Orleans singer, songwriter and arranger. He enjoyed a US Top Five hit with the catchy 'You Talk Too Much', then moved into production (most notably the Dixie Cups) and publishing.

19 Nov 60   **6**   1   **You Talk Too Much** / I Love You Still *(Columbia DB-4533)*
10 Dec 60   **15**   2   **You Talk Too Much** / I Love You Still *(Columbia DB-4533)* *re-entry*

SPIKE JONES & HIS CITY SLICKERS 2

Bandleader born Lindley Armstrong Jones in Long Beach, California in 1911. He specialised in zany reworkings of popular songs and had stacks of US hits in the '40s including 'Der Fuehrer's Face' and 'All I Want For Christmas Is My Two Front Teeth'.

20 Nov 54   **30**   1   **I Went To Your Wedding** / Lulu Had A Baby *(H.M.V. B-10482)*
 8 Jan 55   **52**   1   **Rudolph, The Red-Nosed Reindeer** / Yes! We Have No Bananas
                (H.M.V. B-9988)

DICK JORDAN 3

Teen-pop singer born Derrick Briscombe in Leeds in 1939. He enjoyed some chart success in 1960 with 'Little Christine' and a cover of Ray Charles's 'Hallelujah I Love Her So'.

28 May 60   **15**   2   ★ **Little Christine** / I'll Love You Forever *(Oriole CB-1548)*
28 Jan 61   **28**   1   **Angel On My Shoulder** / The Next Train Home *(Oriole CB-1591)*

JOY & DAVE 1

Originally from St. Helier, Jersey, brother/sister singing duo Dave and Joy Adams worked with producer Joe Meek. A talented songwriter and musican, Dave became one of Meek's chief collaborators and worked with him until his death in 1967.

19 Nov 60   **15**   1   **My Very Good Friend The Milkman** / Doopey Darling *(Decca F-11291)*

JULIAN   2

Good-looking Julian Lee from Camberley, Surrey was launched in 1959 as 'Julian – Britain's Fabian'. Finding himself dubbed 'Julian X' by the media, he changed his stage name to 'Julian Scott' a year later. The catchy 'Bo Diddley'-styled number, 'Sue Saturday', was his first recording.

19 Dec 59   **6**   2   **Sue Saturday** / Can't Wait *(Pye Nixa 7N.15236)*

JUMPIN' JACKS featuring Danny Lamego   1

Doo-wop outfit from New Jersey who recorded for Bruce, Andrea and ABC-Paramount (from whom this bubbler was leased). They eventually found chart success in 1961 as Danny Peppermint & The Jumping Jacks with a cover of Joey Dee's 'Peppermint Twist'.

22 Feb 58   **3**   1   **My Girl, My Girl** / Tried And Tested *(H.M.V. POP-440)*

ROSEMARY JUNE   2

American opera singer with a Bachelor of Music degree who switched to singing pop in 1954. Although she did not register any hits stateside, her version of 'I'll Be With You In Apple Blossom Time' made the UK Top 20 in 1959.

25 Apr 59   **5**   2   **With You Beside Me / I Used To Love You But It's All Over Now**
                          (Pye International 7N.25015)

ERIC JUPP & His Orchestra   1

Pianist, arranger, composer and bandleader born in Brighton in 1922. He became massively popular in Australia after emigrating there in the '60s.

13 Nov 54   **36**   1   **Skokiaan** / They Were Doin' The Mambo *(Columbia DB-3522)*

BERT KAEMPFERT & His Orchestra   5

German multi-instrumentalist, composer and orchestra leader born in Hamburg in 1923. His songwriting credits include 'Strangers In The Night' and 'Wooden Heart'.

31 Dec 60   **3**   3   **Wonderland By Night** / Dreaming The Blues *(Polydor NH-66639)*
28 Jan 61   **2**   2   **Wonderland By Night** / Dreaming The Blues *(Polydor NH-66639)*
                          re-entry

KALIN TWINS   7

Pop duo Hal and Herb Kalin will forever be remembered for their 1958 smash, 'When'. Sadly, despite some valiant efforts, they were never able to match its runaway success.

25 Oct 58   **1**   3   **Forget Me Not** / Dream Of Me *(Brunswick 05759)*
22 Nov 58   **10**   1   **Forget Me Not** / Dream Of Me *(Brunswick 05759)* ***re-entry***
28 Nov 59   **20**   1   **The Meaning Of The Blues** / Why Don't You Believe Me
                          (Brunswick 05814)
30 Jan 60   **9**   1   **The Meaning Of The Blues** / Why Don't You Believe Me
                          (Brunswick 05814) ***re-entry***
26 Nov 60   **12**   1   **Zing! Went The Strings Of My Heart** / No Money Can Buy
                          (Brunswick 05844)

KITTY KALLEN   4

Singer born in Philadelphia in 1921. She was a leading big band vocalist during the '40s, following which she enjoyed an equally successful solo career until 1965.

19 Jun 54   **1**   2   ★ <u>**Little Things Mean A Lot**</u> / I Don't Think You Love Me Anymore
                          (Brunswick 05287)
21 Aug 54   **24**   1   **In The Chapel In The Moonlight** / Are You Looking For A Sweetheart
                          (Brunswick 05261)
23 Oct 54   **49**   1   **In The Chapel In The Moonlight** / Are You Looking For A Sweetheart
                          (Brunswick 05261) ***re-entry***

AL KASHA   1
Brooklyn-born composer noted for his lengthy songwriting partnership with Joel Hirschhorn.

8 Oct 60	**11**	1	**Teardrops Are Falling** / No Matter Where You Are *(Coral Q-72410)*

MICKEY KATZ & His Orchestra   3
Yiddish mickey-taker born Meyer Myron Katz in Cleveland, Ohio in 1909.

19 May 56	**19**	1	**Duvid Crockett** / Keneh Hora *(Capitol CL-14579)*
2 Jun 56	**5**	1	**Duvid Crockett** / Keneh Hora *(Capitol CL-14579)* **1st re-entry**
14 Jul 56	**15**	1	**Duvid Crockett** / Keneh Hora *(Capitol CL-14579)* **2nd re-entry**

KATHIE KAY   62
Singer with a bubbly personality who was a 'Billy Cotton Band Show' favourite from 1949 until 1968. Although most people thought she was Scottish, on account of the fact that she lived and worked there for most of her career, she actually hailed from Gainsborough, Lincolnshire.

4 Feb 56	**7**	1	**Jimmy Unknown** / Dreams Can Tell A Lie *(H.M.V. POP-159)*
3 Mar 56	**12**	1	**Old Scotch Mother** / There Is Somebody Waiting For Me *(H.M.V. POP-167)*
17 Mar 56	**8**	3	**Old Scotch Mother** / There Is Somebody Waiting For Me *(H.M.V. POP-167)* **1st re-entry**
21 Apr 56	**17**	1	**Old Scotch Mother** / There Is Somebody Waiting For Me *(H.M.V. POP-167)* **2nd re-entry**
23 Jun 56	**21**	1	**Old Scotch Mother** / There Is Somebody Waiting For Me *(H.M.V. POP-167)* **3rd re-entry**
21 Jul 56	**14**	2	**Old Scotch Mother** / There Is Somebody Waiting For Me *(H.M.V. POP-167)* **4th re-entry**
8 Sep 56	**11**	1	**Old Scotch Mother** / There Is Somebody Waiting For Me *(H.M.V. POP-167)* **5th re-entry**
10 Nov 56	**8**	2	**A House With Love In It** / To Be Sure *(H.M.V. POP-265)*
1 Dec 56	**4**	1	**A House With Love In It** / To Be Sure *(H.M.V. POP-265)* **1st re-entry**
5 Jan 57	**4**	1	**Old Scotch Mother** / There Is Somebody Waiting For Me *(H.M.V. POP-167)* **6th re-entry**
13 Apr 57	**4**	1	**Every Day Is Mother's Day** / From The First Hello To The Last Goodbye *(H.M.V. POP-315)*
4 May 57	**4**	1	**Old Scotch Mother** / There Is Somebody Waiting For Me *(H.M.V. POP-167)* **7th re-entry**
18 May 57	**7**	3	**Old Scotch Mother** / There Is Somebody Waiting For Me *(H.M.V. POP-167)* **8th re-entry**
8 Jun 57	**10**	1	**Wind In The Willow** / We Will Make Love *(H.M.V. POP-352)*
22 Jun 57	**1**	12	**We Will Make Love** / **Wind In The Willow** *(H.M.V. POP-352)* **re-entry (flipped)**
14 Sep 57	**1**	2	**Tammy** / Away From You *(H.M.V. POP-385)*
19 Oct 57	**2**	1	**Tammy** / Away From You *(H.M.V. POP-385)* **1st re-entry**
2 Nov 57	**1**	3	**Tammy** / Away From You *(H.M.V. POP-385)* **2nd re-entry**
23 Nov 57	**1**	13	**Be Content** / **My Last Love** *(H.M.V. POP-410)*
3 May 58	**9**	1	**A House With Love In It** / To Be Sure *(H.M.V. POP-265)* **2nd re-entry**
24 May 58	**5**	2	**A House With Love In It** / To Be Sure *(H.M.V. POP-265)* **3rd re-entry**
14 Jun 58	**10**	1	**The Secret Of Happiness** / Summer Is A'Coming In *(H.M.V. POP-485)*
5 Jul 58	**23**	1	**Hillside In Scotland** / Tomorrow Is My Birthday *(H.M.V. POP-498)*
26 Jul 58	**2**	2	**Hillside In Scotland** / Tomorrow Is My Birthday *(H.M.V. POP-498)* **1st re-entry**
16 Aug 58	**8**	1	**Hillside In Scotland** / Tomorrow Is My Birthday *(H.M.V. POP-498)* **2nd re-entry**
25 Oct 58	**2**	1	**Old Scotch Mother** / There Is Somebody Waiting For Me *(H.M.V. POP-167)* **9th re-entry**
22 Nov 58	**8**	2	**Old Scotch Mother** / There Is Somebody Waiting For Me *(H.M.V. POP-167)* **10th re-entry**

DANNY KAYE 17

Much-loved singer, actor, dancer and comedian born David Daniel Kaminsky in New York in 1911.

3 Jul 54	6	5	**Knock On Wood** / All About You *(Brunswick 05296)*
14 Aug 54	21	1	**Knock On Wood** / All About You *(Brunswick 05296)* **1st re-entry**
28 Aug 54	30	1	**Knock On Wood** / All About You *(Brunswick 05296)* **2nd re-entry**
27 Nov 54	9	3	**White Christmas** / Snow *(Brunswick 05354)*
			Both sides by Bing Crosby, Danny Kaye, Peggy Lee and Trudy Stevens. (This was a re-recording of Bing's famous hit and was featured in the film, 'White Christmas'.)
25 Dec 54	37	1	**White Christmas** / Snow *(Brunswick 05354)* **1st re-entry**
8 Jan 55	12	2	**White Christmas** / Snow *(Brunswick 05354)* **2nd re-entry**
10 Mar 56	1	2	**Little Child (Daddy Dear)** / Laugh It Off Upsy Daisey *(Brunswick 05532)*
			Both sides by Danny Kaye and Dena Kaye
14 Apr 56	9	1	**Little Child (Daddy Dear)** / Laugh It Off Upsy Daisey *(Brunswick 05532)* **1st re-entry**
28 Apr 56	12	1	**Little Child (Daddy Dear)** / Laugh It Off Upsy Daisey *(Brunswick 05532)* **2nd re-entry**

See also Original Soundtrack (THE FIVE PENNIES)

DENA KAYE 4

Daughter of Danny Kaye, born in Fort Lauderdale, Florida in 1946.

10 Mar 56	1	2	**Little Child (Daddy Dear)** / Laugh It Off Upsy Daisey *(Brunswick 05532)*
			Both sides by Danny Kaye and Dena Kaye
14 Apr 56	9	1	**Little Child (Daddy Dear)** / Laugh It Off Upsy Daisey *(Brunswick 05532)* **1st re-entry**
28 Apr 56	12	1	**Little Child (Daddy Dear)** / Laugh It Off Upsy Daisey *(Brunswick 05532)* **2nd re-entry**

KAYE SISTERS 7

This glamorous British trio (Carol Lindsey, Sheila Jones and Shirley 'Shan' Palmer) were not real sisters at all, though they tried hard to look it. Carol Kaye later became an actress.

23 Nov 57	1	2	★ **Alone** / Shake Me I Rattle *(Philips PB-752)*
21 Dec 57	3	2	★ **Alone** / **Shake Me I Rattle** *(Philips PB-752)* **re-entry**
28 Jun 58	9	1	**Torero** / Stroll Me *(Philips PB-832)*
18 Apr 59	1	1	★ **Come Softly To Me** / Say Something Sweet To Your Sweetheart *(Philips PB-913)*
			Both sides by Frankie Vaughan and the Kaye Sisters
2 Jul 60	10	1	★ **Paper Roses** / If Only You'd Be Mine *(Philips PB-1024)*

MAURICE KEARY 1

Actor/balladeer billed as 'Erin's Ambassador of Song'. One of Ireland's top baritone/tenor singers, he starred in many musicals and also had his own shows on Radio Éireann and the BBC.

13 Nov 54	51	1	**Slievanamon** / The Ploughman *(Glenside W-126)*

HOWARD KEEL 24

Singer and star of stage, film and television born Harry Clifford Keel in Gillespie, Illinois in 1919. Most of his bubblers were from the 1954 box office smash, 'Seven Brides For Seven Brothers'.

18 Sep 54	23	1	**Rose Marie** *(M.G.M. MGM-750)*
			Flip is 'I'm A Mountie Who Never Got His Man' by Bert Lahr
22 Jan 55	14	4	**Sobbin' Women** (Howard Keel and Brothers) *(M.G.M. MGM-787)*
			Flip is 'June Bride' by Virginia Gibson and Girls
5 Mar 55	2	4	**Sobbin' Women** (Howard Keel and Brothers) *(M.G.M. MGM-787)* **1st re-entry**
5 Mar 55	13	1	**Bless Yore Beautiful Hide** *(M.G.M. MGM-785)*
			Flip is 'Wonderful, Wonderful Day' by Jane Powell

19 Mar 55	**27**	1	**When You're In Love** (*Jane Powell and Howard Keel*) / Spring, Spring, Spring (*Brothers* [with Howard Keel] & *Girls*) (*M.G.M. MGM-788*)
9 Apr 55	**17**	3	**Sobbin' Women** (*Howard Keel and Brothers*) (*M.G.M. MGM-787*) **2nd re-entry**
16 Apr 55	**4**	1	**When You're In Love** (*Jane Powell and Howard Keel*) / Spring, Spring, Spring (*Brothers* [with Howard Keel] & *Girls*) (*M.G.M. MGM-788*) **1st re-entry**
30 Apr 55	**2**	2	**When You're In Love** (*Jane Powell and Howard Keel*) / Spring, Spring, Spring (*Brothers* [with Howard Keel] & *Girls*) (*M.G.M. MGM-788*) **2nd re-entry**
30 Apr 55	**28**	1	**Bless Yore Beautiful Hide** (*Howard Keel*) (*M.G.M. MGM-785*) **re-entry** The flip, 'Wonderful, Wonderful Day' by Jane Powell, also bubbled under
7 May 55	**13**	1	**Sobbin' Women** (*Howard Keel and Brothers*) (*M.G.M. MGM-787*) **3rd re-entry**
21 May 55	**6**	2	**Sobbin' Women** (*Howard Keel and Brothers*) (*M.G.M. MGM-787*) **4th re-entry**
4 Jun 55	**13**	1	**When You're In Love** (*Jane Powell and Howard Keel*) / Spring, Spring, Spring (*Brothers* [with Howard Keel] & *Girls*) (*M.G.M. MGM-788*) **3rd re-entry**
2 Jul 55	**28**	1	**Sobbin' Women** (*Howard Keel and Brothers*) (*M.G.M. MGM-787*) **5th re-entry**

See also Original Soundtrack (SEVEN BRIDES FOR SEVEN BROTHERS)

NELSON KEENE 2

Larry Parnes protégé born Malcolm Holland in Farnborough, Hampshire in 1942. He went on to form the Guv'ners beat group with Bobby Shafto and Dickie Pride in 1963.

20 Aug 60	**14**	1	★ **Image Of A Girl** / Ocean Of Love (*H.M.V. POP-771*)
3 Dec 60	**26**	1	**Teenage Troubles** / Keep Loving Me (*H.M.V. POP-814*)

JERRY KELLER 3

Singer, songwriter and one hit wonder born in Fort Smith, Arkansas in 1937.

15 Aug 59	**4**	1	★ **Here Comes Summer** / Time Has A Way (*London HLR-8890*)
21 Nov 59	**21**	2	**If I Had A Girl** / Lovable (*London HLR-8980*)

GENE KELLY 3

Song-and-dance man who thrilled audiences with his stage and screen appearances in the '40s and '50s. This bubbler was from the Warner film 'Marjorie Morningstar' (1958).

26 Jul 58	**7**	1	**A Very Precious Love** (*R.C.A. RCA-1068*) Flip is 'Uncle Samson' by Ray Heindorf and Orchestra
9 Aug 58	**9**	2	**A Very Precious Love** (*R.C.A. RCA-1068*) **re-entry**

See also Original Soundtrack (LES GIRLS)

GRACE KELLY 1

Glamorous film star born in Philadelphia in 1929. In April 1956, she famously married Prince Rainier III of Monaco and retired from show business to concentrate on her new role.

17 Nov 56	**9**	1	★ **True Love** (*Bing Crosby and Grace Kelly*) (*Capitol CL-14645*) Flip is 'Well Did You Evah?' by Bing Crosby and Frank Sinatra

See also Original Soundtrack (HIGH SOCIETY)

KEITH KELLY 2

Singer/guitarist born Mike Pailthorpe in Selby, North Yorkshire in 1937. Originally with the John Barry Seven, he went solo in 1959 and scored hits with 'Tease Me' and 'Listen Little Girl'.

23 Jul 60	**2**	2	★ **Listen Little Girl** / Uh-Huh (*Parlophone R-4676*)

SALLY KELLY 3

The only female singer managed by Larry Parnes, Belfast-born Sally Kelly almost charted with this 'answer' to Jim Reeves' 1960 hit, 'He'll Have To Go'.

4 Jun 60	**7**	1	**He'll Have To Stay** / Honey That's Alright *(Decca F-11238)*
18 Jun 60	**2**	1	**He'll Have To Stay** / Honey That's Alright *(Decca F-11238)*
			1st re-entry
9 Jul 60	**14**	1	**He'll Have To Stay** / Honey That's Alright *(Decca F-11238)*
			2nd re-entry

NAT KENDRICK & THE SWANS 1

Godfather of Soul James Brown and his band moonlighting. Deejay Carlton 'King' Coleman provides the vocals.

30 Apr 60	**11**	1	**Mashed Potatoes (Parts 1 & 2)** *(Top Rank JAR-351)*

ENOCH KENT 28

Scottish singer Enoch Kent formed the Reivers folk group in 1958 with Josh MacRae, Moyna Flanagan and Rena Swankie. 'The Smashing Of The Van' relates to an incident following the Fenian Rising of 1867, when a police van transporting two of the leaders to jail was attacked in a bid to free them. Although the operation was a success, one police officer was killed in the melee, for which three of the attackers were later executed.

25 Jun 60	**1**	17	**The Smashing Of The Van** / Sean South Of Garryowen
			(Top Rank JAR-386)
12 Nov 60	**2**	10	**The Smashing Of The Van** / **Sean South Of Garryowen**
			(Top Rank JAR-386) **1st re-entry**
4 Mar 61	**1**	1	**The Smashing Of The Van** / Sean South Of Garryowen
			(Top Rank JAR-386) **2nd re-entry**

See also Reivers

STAN KENTON & His Orchestra 27

Innovative jazz pianist/bandleader born in Wichita, Kansas in 1911, whose experimental fusions with classical music, Latin and even C&W earned him praise and derision in equal measure. Featured musicians in the Kenton aggregation included Bob Cooper (sax), Bill Holman (sax), Frank Roselino (trombone), Bill Russo (trombone) and Claude Williamson (piano).

14 Aug 54	**6**	5	**NEW CONCEPTS OF ARTISTRY IN RHYTHM** *(Capitol LC-6595)* 🆛
			23°N – 82°W / Portait Of A Count / Improvisation / Invention For Guitar & Trumpet /
			My Lady / Young Blood / Frank Speaking
6 Nov 54	**30**	2	**How High The Moon** *(Vocal: June Christy)* / Balboa Bash
			(Capitol CL-13224)
27 Nov 54	**29**	2	**How High The Moon** *(Vocal: June Christy)* / Balboa Bash
			(Capitol CL-13224) **re-entry**
25 Dec 54	**18**	1	**KENTON SHOWCASE: THE MUSIC OF BILL RUSSO /**
			THE MUSIC OF BILL HOLMAN *(Capitol LCT-6009)* 🆛
			Music of Bill Russo: A Theme Of Four Values / A Study For Bass / Blues Before
			And After / Bacante / Thisbe / Egdon Heath / Sweets / Dusk / *Music of Bill Holman:*
			Bags / Hav-A-Havana / Solo For Buddy / The Opener / Fearless Finlay / Theme
			And Variations / In Lighter Vein / King Fish
22 Jan 55	**10**	3	**KENTON SHOWCASE: THE MUSIC OF BILL RUSSO /**
			THE MUSIC OF BILL HOLMAN *(Capitol LCT-6009)* 🆛 **re-entry**
17 Mar 56	**1**	2	**Portrait Of A Count** / **Invention For Guitar And Trumpet**
			(Capitol CL-14541)
24 Mar 56	**4**	4	**The Peanut Vendor** / Painted Rhythm *(Capitol CL-13016)*
24 Mar 56	**4**	1	**NEW CONCEPTS OF ARTISTRY IN RHYTHM** *(Capitol CL-6595)* 🆛
			re-entry
24 Mar 56	**11**	1	**Cherokee** / Limelight *(Capitol CL-14542)*
15 Sep 56	**14**	1	**STAN KENTON IN HI-FI** *(Capitol LCT-6109)* 🆛
			Artistry Jumps / Interlude / Intermission Riff / Minor Riff / Collaboration / Painted
			Rhythm / Southern Scandal / The Peanut Vendor / Eager Beaver / Concerto To End
			All Concertos / Artistry In Boogie / Lover / Unison Riff

Steve Lawrence

| 13 Oct 56 | 7 | 1 | **STAN KENTON IN HI-FI** *(Capitol LCT-6109)* **LP** *re-entry* |
| 17 Nov 56 | 3 | 1 | **CUBAN FIRE!** *(Capitol LCT-6118)* **LP** |

Fuego Cubano (Cuban Fire) / El Congo Valiente (Valiant Congo) / Recuerdos (Reminiscences) / Quien Sabe (Who Knows) / La Guera Baila (The Fair One Dances) / La Suerte De Los Tontos (Fortune Of Fools)

| 12 Apr 58 | 3 | 1 | **Tequila** / Cuban Mumble *(Capitol CL-14847)* |
| 27 Aug 60 | 16 | 2 | **My Love** / Steady *(Capitol CL-15144)* |

Both sides by Nat 'King' Cole and Stan Kenton (vocal)

See also Bob Cooper Sextet
Bill Holman Octet
Frank Rosolino Sextet
Claude Williamson Trio

KEN-TONES   1

British mixed vocal quartet comprising leader Ken Fowler, Vincent O'Hagan, Leslie Want and Celia Wright. As well as recording in their own right, they did back-up work for other artists.

| 2 Jun 56 | 17 | 1 | **In Port Afrique** / Get With It *(Parlophone R-4163)* |

KENNY KERSEY

See Norman Granz' Jazz At The Philharmonic

BARNEY KESSEL   9

Born in Muskogee, Oklahoma in 1923, Barney Kessel was arguably the best jazz guitarist of the twentieth century. He was also a member of the legendary 'Wrecking Crew', the pool of top Los Angeles studio musicians who supplied backings for many '60s and early '70s hits.

| 23 Oct 54 | 12 | 5 | **BARNEY KESSEL** *(Vogue LDE-085)* **LP** |

Tenderly / Just Squeeze Me / Bernardo / Vicky's Dream / Salute To Charlie Christian / What Is There To Say / Lullaby Of Birdland / I Let A Song Go Out Of My Heart

| 27 Nov 54 | 28 | 2 | **GENE NORMAN PRESENTS KAY STARR WITH BARNEY KESSEL** *(Vogue EPV-1014)* **EP** |

Them There Eyes / What Is This Thing Called Love / Ain't Misbehavin' / Good For Nothin' Joe

| 15 Jan 55 | 27 | 2 | **BARNEY KESSEL** *(Vogue LDE-085)* **LP** *re-entry* |

See also Norman Granz

KESTRELS   2

British singing group whose main claim to fame is teaching the Beatles to bow in unison. Members Roger Cook and Roger Greenaway later formed a successful singing partnership, David & Jonathan, and an even more successful songwriting partnership.

| 5 Dec 59 | 11 | 1 | **In The Chapel In The Moonlight** / There Comes A Time *(Pye Nixa 7N.15234)* |
| 26 Dec 59 | 16 | 1 | **In The Chapel In The Moonlight** / There Comes A Time *(Pye Nixa 7N.15234)* *re-entry* |

KEYNOTES   17

Ubiquitous British mixed vocal group formed in 1948 by Johnny Johnston. After going through several changes, the regular line-up finally became Johnston, Jean Campbell, Harry 'Miff' King, Eddie Lester and Frank Holmes. The Keynotes did a lot of studio back-up work, while the men in the group also doubled as the Johnston Brothers.

6 Nov 54	8	2	**This Ole House** *(Joan Regan with the Keynotes)* / Can This Be Love *(Joan Regan) (Decca F-10397)*
27 Nov 54	23	1	**This Ole House** / Can This Be Love *(Decca F-10397)* *re-entry*
11 Feb 56	7	1	**Dreams Can Tell A Lie** *(Dickie Valentine and the Keynotes) (Decca F-10667)*

Flip is 'Song Of The Trees' by Dickie Valentine

11 Feb 56	9	1	★ **Memories Are Made Of This** *(Dave King with the Keynotes)*
			(Decca F-10684)
			Flip is 'I've Changed My Mind A Thousand Times' by Dave King
31 Mar 56	9	1	**Scotland The Brave** / Lewis Bridal Song *(Decca F-10693)*
7 Apr 56	14	1	★ **You Can't Be True To Two** / A Little Bit Independent *(Decca F-10720)*
			Both sides by Dave King with the Keynotes
21 Apr 56	5	1	**Scotland The Brave** / Lewis Bridal Song *(Decca F-10693)*
			1st re-entry
5 May 56	4	4	**Scotland The Brave** / Lewis Bridal Song *(Decca F-10693)*
			2nd re-entry
4 Aug 56	11	1	**The Birds And The Bees** / Hotta Chocolotta *(Decca F-10741)*
			Both sides by Dave King with the Keynotes
1 Sep 56	12	1	**The Birds And The Bees** / Hotta Chocolotta *(Decca F-10741)* **re-entry**
20 Oct 56	3	2	★ **In The Middle Of The House** *(Johnston Brothers and the Keynotes)*
			(Decca F-10781)
			Flip is 'Stranded In The Jungle' by the Johnston Brothers
24 Nov 56	5	1	★ **In The Middle Of The House** *(Johnston Brothers and the Keynotes)*
			(Decca F-10781) **re-entry**

See also Jean Campbell
Johnston Brothers

JOHNNY KIDD & THE PIRATES — 2

Seminal British rock'n'roll group led by singer/songwriter Fred Heath aka 'Johnny Kidd'. They clocked up nine hits between 1959 and 1964, but disbanded following Kidd's death in 1966.

30 May 59	1	2	★ **Please Don't Touch** / Growl *(H.M.V. POP-615)*

NICKY KIDD — 6

Billed as 'the romantic voice of Scotland', Glaswegian vocal and piano stylist Nicky Kidd covered Nat 'King' Cole and Don Cherry with this bubbler.

19 May 56	5	6	**Too Young To Go Steady** / **Wild Cherry** *(Beltona BL-2645)*

BEN E. KING — 2

Former lead singer of the Drifters on hits like 'There Goes My Baby' and 'Save the Last Dance For Me' born Benjamin Earl Nelson in Henderson, North Carolina in 1938. In 1960, he kicked off an equally successful solo career with this classic coupling.

14 Jan 61	1	2	★ **First Taste Of Love** / Spanish Harlem *(London HLK-9258)*

See also Drifters

BERTIE KING

See Chris Barber's Jazz Band

DAVE KING — 15

Versatile singer, comedian and television personality from Twickenham born David Kingshott. He later became a successful character actor.

11 Feb 56	9	1	★ **Memories Are Made Of This** *(Dave King with the Keynotes)* /
			I've Changed My Mind A Thousand Times *(Dave King)*
			(Decca F-10684)
7 Apr 56	14	1	★ **You Can't Be True To Two** / A Little Bit Independent *(Decca F-10720)*
			Both sides by Dave King with the Keynotes
4 Aug 56	11	1	**The Birds And The Bees** / Hotta Chocolotta *(Decca F-10741)*
			Both sides by Dave King with the Keynotes
1 Sep 56	12	1	**The Birds And The Bees** / Hotta Chocolotta *(Decca F-10741)*
			re-entry
15 Dec 56	7	1	★ **Christmas And You** / You Make Nice *(Decca F-10791)*
30 Mar 57	19	1	**Love Is A Golden Ring** / If Your Heart Wants To Dance
			(Decca F-10865)

20 Apr 57	8	3	**Love Is A Golden Ring** / If Your Heart Wants To Dance (*Decca F-10865*) **re-entry**
24 Aug 57	8	1	**With All My Heart** / Red Shutters (*Decca F-10910*)
14 Sep 57	4	1	**With All My Heart** / Red Shutters (*Decca F-10910*) **re-entry**
23 Nov 57	8	1	**Chances Are** / Shake Me, I Rattle (*Decca F-10947*)
18 Jan 58	3	1	★ <u>**The Story Of My Life**</u> / I'll Buy You A Star (*Decca F-10973*)
28 Jun 58	17	2	**I Suddenly** / There's Only One Of You (*Decca F-11012*)

See also Various Artists (All Star Hit Parade)

KING BROTHERS   8

Real brothers from Essex, Denis (piano), Tony (bass) and Michael (guitar) King were regulars on TV in the '50s and early '60s, but ultimately proved too square to survive the rock'n'roll era.

18 May 57	7	1	**Marianne** / Little By Little (*Parlophone R-4288*)
9 Nov 57	1	3	★ <u>**Wake Up Little Susie**</u> / Winter Wonderland (*Parlophone R-4367*)
18 Jan 58	2	2	★ <u>**Put A Light In The Window**</u> / Miss Otis Regrets (*Parlophone R-4389*)
31 Dec 60	9	2	★ <u>**Doll House**</u> / Si Si Si (*Parlophone R-4715*)

See also Various Artists (Top Ten Special)

KINGSMEN   2

Bill Haley's Comets doing a spot of moonlighting.

| 15 Nov 58 | 3 | 2 | **Week-End** / Better Believe It (*London HLE-8735*) |

See also Bill Haley & His Comets
　　　　　Jodimars

KINGSTON TRIO   3

Immensely popular and influential folk group from Palo Alto, California, who exploded onto the music scene in 1958 with their rendition of the traditional song 'Tom Dooley' and never looked back.

25 Apr 59	15	1	**The Tijuana Jail** / Oh Cindy (*Capitol CL-15002*)
15 Aug 59	11	1	**M.T.A.** / All My Sorrows (*Capitol CL-15040*)
30 Jul 60	9	1	**Bad Man's Blunder** / The Escape Of Old John Webb (*Capitol CL-15138*)

DAVID KINNAIRD   31

Popular Scottish actor, singer and radio/TV personality.

11 Jun 60	2	7	**Mairi's Wedding / Northern Lights Of Aberdeen** (*Top Rank JAR-385*)
6 Aug 60	7	1	**Buttered Bannocks** / The Whistling Gypsy (*Top Rank JAR-414*)
13 Aug 60	3	3	**Mairi's Wedding / Northern Lights Of Aberdeen** (*Top Rank JAR-385*) **1st re-entry**
20 Aug 60	2	5	**Buttered Bannocks** / The Whistling Gypsy (*Top Rank JAR-414*) **re-entry**
1 Oct 60	20	1	**Mairi's Wedding / Northern Lights Of Aberdeen** (*Top Rank JAR-385*) **2nd re-entry**
19 Nov 60	8	1	**Mairi's Wedding / Northern Lights Of Aberdeen** (*Top Rank JAR-385*) **3rd re-entry**
26 Nov 60	25	1	**Auld Lang Syne** / A Guid New Year (*Pye 7N.15311*)
10 Dec 60	1	5	**Auld Lang Syne** / A Guid New Year (*Pye 7N.15311*) **re-entry**
7 Jan 61	8	5	**Northern Lights Of Old Aberdeen** / Mairi's Wedding (*Pye 7N.15317*) **reissue**
18 Feb 61	16	2	**Northern Lights Of Old Aberdeen** / Mairi's Wedding (*Pye 7N.15317*) **reissue, re-entry**

TONY KINSEY TRIO   6

Modern jazz trio led by drummer Tony Kinsey. After teaming up with Jamaican alto saxophonist Joe Harriott in 1954, they became a successful live attraction at London's Studio 51 club.

7 Aug 54	**14**	1	**'Deed I Do** / Zoot's Suite *(Esquire 10-368)*
			Tommy Whittle with the Tony Kinsey Trio
14 Aug 54	**26**	1	**Last Resort** / How Deep Is The Ocean *(Esquire 10-382)*
			Tony Kinsey Trio with Joe Harriott
4 Sep 54	**30**	1	**Best Behaviour** / Get Happy *(Esquire 10-392)*
			Tony Kinsey Trio with Joe Harriott
15 Jan 55	**20**	1	**Last Resort** / How Deep Is The Ocean *(Esquire 10-382)* **re-entry**
22 Jan 55	**34**	2	**TONY KINSEY TRIO WITH JOE HARRIOTT** *(Esquire EP-52)* 🎵**EP**
			Tony Kinsey Trio with Joe Harriott
			The Song Is You / It Don't Mean A Thing (If It Ain't Got That Swing)

KIRCHIN BAND   9

Innovative British band co-led by Ivor Kirchin and his drummer son, Basil. They were renowned for their boisterous playing style and varied repertoire which included jazz, standards and Latin American numbers.

22 Jan 55	**39**	1	**Minor Mambo** / Mother Goose Jumps *(Decca F-10434)*
5 Feb 55	**47**	1	**Mambo Macoco** / Tangerine *(Parlophone R-3958)*
12 Feb 55	**7**	3	**Minor Mambo** / Mother Goose Jumps *(Decca F-10434)* **re-entry**
19 Feb 55	**8**	2	**Lester Leaps The Mambo** / Lanigiro *(Parlophone R-3985)*
27 Aug 55	**9**	2	**Flying Hickory** / Comb And Paper Blues *(Vocal: Johnny Grant;*
			1st Comb and Paper: Norman Baron; 2nd Comb and Paper:
			Frank Donlan) (Parlophone R-4039)

EARTHA KITT   31

Born in South Carolina in 1927, this extravagant, multi-talented star of stage, screen and cabaret was famed for her feline sensuality and highly individual singing style.

7 Aug 54	**17**	2	**Let's Do It** / Santa Baby *(H.M.V. B-10728)*
11 Sep 54	**23**	1	**Santa Baby** / Let's Do It *(H.M.V. B-10728)* **1st re-entry (flipped)**
16 Oct 54	**40**	1	**I Want To Be Evil** / Annie Doesn't Live Here Anymore
			(H.M.V. B-10584)
23 Oct 54	**33**	1	★ <u>**Under The Bridges of Paris**</u> / Lovin' Spree *(H.M.V. B-10647)*
4 Dec 54	**22**	1	★ <u>**Under The Bridges of Paris**</u> / Lovin' Spree *(H.M.V. B-10647)*
			1st re-entry
8 Jan 55	**32**	2	**Monotonous** / African Lullaby *(H.M.V. B-10803)*
8 Jan 55	**32**	1	**Santa Baby** / Let's Do It *(H.M.V. B-10728)* **2nd re-entry**
5 Feb 55	**10**	5	**Monotonous** / African Lullaby *(H.M.V. B-10803)*
			1st re-entry
5 Feb 55	**47**	1	**Santa Baby** / Let's Do It *(H.M.V. B-10728)* **3rd re-entry**
12 Mar 55	**10**	3	★ <u>**Under The Bridges of Paris**</u> / Lovin' Spree *(H.M.V. B-10647)*
			2nd re-entry
14 May 55	**10**	1	**The Heel** / My Heart's Delight *(H.M.V. B-10854)*
9 Jul 55	**14**	3	**Santa Baby** / Let's Do It *(H.M.V. B-10728)* **4th re-entry**
16 Jul 55	**11**	1	**Freddy** / **Sweet And Gentle** *(H.M.V. B-10892)*
			Both sides by Eartha Kitt and Pérez Prado
19 Nov 55	**19**	3	**DOWN TO EARTHA** *(H.M.V. DLP-1087)* 🎵**LP**
			(If I Love Ya, Then I Need Ya, If I Need Ya) I Wantcha Around / Do You Remember /
			Looking For A Boy / I've Got That Lovin' Bug Itch / Oh John! / Strangers In The
			Starlight / The Day That The Circus Left Town / Après Moi / The Heel / Mambo de
			Paree / My Heart's Delight / Hey Jacque
14 Jul 56	**15**	1	**Honolulu Rock-A-Roll-A** / Je Cherche Un Homme
			(I Want A Man, A Man, A Man) *(H.M.V. POP-233)*
25 May 57	**10**	1	**Just An Old Fashioned Girl** / If I Can't Take It With Me When I Go
			(H.M.V. POP-309)
18 Jan 58	**7**	1	**Just An Old Fashioned Girl** / If I Can't Take It With Me When I Go
			(H.M.V. POP-309) **re-entry**
14 Jun 58	**14**	1	**African Lullaby** / **Monotonous** *(H.M.V. B-10803)*
			2nd re-entry (flipped)

24 Jan 59 **8** 1 **Just An Old Fashioned Girl** / If I Can't Take It With Me When I Go
(R.C.A. RCA-1087) **reissue**

See also Original Broadway Cast *(*NEW FACES)

ERICH KLEIBER *(conductor)*
See Concertgebouw Orchestra of Amsterdam
Hilde Gueden

ANNETTE KLOOGER   3
Australian big band vocalist who sang with Teddy Foster & His Orchestra in the early '50s, then teamed up with Ted Heath in 1956 for this novelty. She later had her own TV show Down Under.

3 Mar 56 **8** 1 **The Rock And Roll Waltz** / Rock Around The Island *(Decca F-10701)*
    Both sides by Ted Heath & His Music with Annette Klooger
31 Mar 56 **5** 1 **The Rock And Roll Waltz** / Rock Around The Island *(Decca F-10701)*
    1st re-entry
14 Apr 56 **12** 1 **The Rock And Roll Waltz** / Rock Around The Island *(Decca F-10701)*
    2nd re-entry

KNIGHTSBRIDGE CHORALE   1
Prolific sessioneers the Mike Sammes Singers recording under an alias.

7 Nov 59 **23** 1 **Eton Boating Song** / In A Shanty In Old Shanty Town
(Top Rank JAR-220)

See also Coronets

KNIGHTSBRIDGE STRINGS   5
Studio ensemble turning out easy-listening muzak. mostly arranged and conducted by Malcolm Lockyer and Reg Owen (although 'The Singer Not The Song' was directed by Philip Green).

5 Sep 59 **1** 3 **Cry** / The Windows Of Paris *(Top Rank JAR-170)*
20 Feb 60 **11** 1 **Ring Ding** / Walkin' Shoes *(Top Rank JAR-272)*
25 Feb 61 **18** 1 **The Singer Not The Song** / Anacleto's Theme *(Top Rank JAR-532)*

BUDDY KNOX   7
Rockabilly singer, songwriter and guitarist born in Happy, Texas in 1937. His debut release, 'Party Doll' topped the US charts in March 1957.

26 Oct 57 **4** 2 **Hula Love** / **Devil Woman** *(Columbia DB-4014)*
    Both sides by Buddy Knox with the Rhythm Orchids
29 Mar 58 **17** 1 **Swingin' Daddy** / Whenever I'm Lonely *(Columbia DB-4077)*
    Both sides by Buddy Knox with the Rhythm Orchids
26 Apr 58 **8** 1 **Hula Love** / Devil Woman *(Columbia DB-4014)* **re-entry**
16 May 59 **8** 1 **I Think I'm Gonna Kill Myself** / To Be With You *(Columbia DB-4302)*
28 Jan 61 **11** 2 **Lovey Dovey** / I Got You *(London HLG-9268)*

MOE KOFFMAN QUARTETTE   2
Jazz group led by Canadian flautist Morris Koffman, born in Toronto in 1928.

8 Mar 58 **1** 2 ★ **Swingin' Shepherd Blues** / Hambourg Bound *(London HLJ-8549)*
    Both sides as by the Moe Koffman Quartet

LEE KONITZ
See Gerry Mulligan Quartet

CLEMENS KRAUSS *(conductor)*
See Hilde Gueden

KREW KATS   1

Instrumental group formed from Marty Wilde's Wildcats. The line-up included drummer Brian Bennett (later of the Shadows) and lead guitarist and popular sessionman Big Jim Sullivan.

4 Mar 61   **13**   1   ★ <u>**Trambone**</u> / Peak Hour *(H.M.V. POP-840)*

JOSEF KRIPS *(conductor)*

See Hilde Gueden

GENE KRUPA & His Orchestra   2

Flamboyant big band and jazz drummer/bandleader born in Chicago in 1909.

22 Jan 55   **18**   2   **DRUMMIN' MAN** *(Columbia 33S-1051)* **LP**
Tuxedo Junction / Drum Boogie *(with Irene Daye and Ensemble)* / Knock Me A Kiss *(Vocal: Roy Eldridge)* / Leave Us Leap / Boogie Blues *(Vocal: Anita O'Day)* / That's What You Think *(Vocal: Anita O'Day)* / Let Me Off Uptown *(Vocal: Anita O'Day and Roy Eldridge)* / Drummin' Man *(Vocal: Irene Daye)*

CHARLIE KUNZ   8

Born in Allentown, Pennsylvania in 1896, Charlie Kunz came to Britain in 1922 as a pianist in a small dance band and stayed until his death in 1958. A popular soloist with a unique style, he was particularly celebrated for his medleys.

11 Dec 54   **4**   1   ★ <u>**Piano Medley No. 114 (Parts 1 & 2) [M]**</u> *(Decca F-10419)*
There Must Be A Reason – Hold My Hand – I'll Give My Heart To You / Little Things Mean A Lot – Make Her Mine – My Son, My Son

5 Feb 55   **34**   2   **Piano Medley No. 115 (Parts 1 & 2) [M]** *(Decca F-10441)*
My Friend – A Sky Blue Shirt And A Rainbow Tie – Sway / I Need You Now – No One But You – I Can't Tell A Waltz From A Tango

26 Mar 55   **8**   1   **Piano Medley No. 116 (Parts 1 & 2) [M]** *(Decca F-10481)*
Finger Of Suspicion – A Blossom Fell – Mister Sandman / Happy Days And Lonely Nights – Softly, Softly – The Naughty Lady of Shady Lane

9 Apr 55   **8**   1   **Piano Medley No. 116 (Parts 1 & 2) [M]** *(Decca F-10481) re-entry*
28 May 55   **30**   1   **Piano Medley No. 117 (Parts 1 & 2) [M]** *(Decca F-10528)*
Stranger In Paradise – Prize Of Gold – Cherry Pink And Apple Blossom White / If Anyone Finds This I Love You – Under The Bridges Of Paris – Open Up Your Heart And Let The Sunshine In

2 Jul 55   **14**   1   **Piano Medley No. 117 (Parts 1 & 2) [M]** *(Decca F-10528) re-entry*
24 Dec 55   **28**   1   **Christmas Medley (Parts 1 & 2) [M]** *(Decca F-10656)*
I Saw Mommy Kissing Santa Claus – Rudolph The Red-Nosed Reindeer – White Christmas / The Very First Christmas Of All – I'll Hang My Heart On A Christmas Tree – The Fairy On The Christmas Tree

FRANKIE LAINE   54

Powerful-voiced singer born Francesco LoVecchio in Chicago in 1913. One of the new breed of black-influenced white singers, he was one of the biggest hitmakers of the pre-rock'n'roll era.

10 Jul 54   **4**   5   ★ **Some Day** / <u>There Must Be A Reason</u> *(Philips PB-306)*
7 Aug 54   **1**   1   ★ <u>**My Friend**</u> / The Lord Don't Treat His Chillun That Way *(Philips PB-316)*
21 Aug 54   **1**   7   ★ <u>**There Must Be A Reason**</u> / Some Day *(Philips PB-306)*
       re-entry (flipped)
21 Aug 54   **34**   1   **After You've Gone** / A Hundred Years From To-day *(Philips PB-270)*
2 Oct 54   **1**   3   ★ <u>**Rain, Rain, Rain**</u> *(Frankie Laine and the Four Lads)* /
       Your Heart – My Heart *(Frankie Laine)* *(Philips PB-311)*
27 Nov 54   **59**   1   **THE VOICE OF YOUR CHOICE** *(Philips BBR-8014)* **LP**
Hey Joe / I Believe / Ramblin' Man / Your Cheatin' Heart / Answer Me (Mütterlein) / Te Amo / New Orleans / Blowing Wild (The Ballad Of Black Gold)

19 Feb 55   **1**   3   ★ <u>**In The Beginning**</u> / Old Shoes *(Philips PB-404)*
19 Mar 55   **16**   2   **High Society** / Back Where I Belong *(Philips PB-417)*
       Both sides by Jo Stafford and Frankie Laine

18 Jun 55	9	1	★	**Cool Water** / Bubbles *(Philips PB-465)*
				Both sides by Frankie Laine with the Mellomen
24 Sep 55	1	2	★	**Hummingbird** / My Little One *(Philips PB-498)*
24 Sep 55	23	1		**I'm Gonna Live 'Till I Die** *(Mercury MB-2959)*
				Flip is 'The Love Of A Gypsy' by Tony Fontane
19 Nov 55	9	1	★	**Hawk-Eye** / Your Love *(Philips PB-519)*
21 Apr 56	3	2	★	**Hell Hath No Fury** *(Frankie Laine)* / **I Heard The Angels Singing**
				(Frankie Laine and the Four Lads) (Philips PB-585)
9 Jun 56	4	3		**Moby Dick** / A Capital Ship *(Philips PB-587)*
7 Jul 56	15	1		**Moby Dick** / A Capital Ship *(Philips PB-587)* **1st re-entry**
14 Jul 56	13	1		**Ticky Ticky Tick** / Champion The Wonder Horse *(Philips PB-607)*
28 Jul 56	15	1		**Moby Dick** / A Capital Ship *(Philips PB-587)* **2nd re-entry**
25 Aug 56	12	2		**Ticky Ticky Tick** / **Champion The Wonder Horse** *(Philips PB-607)*
				1st re-entry
9 Feb 57	10	1		**Champion The Wonder Horse** / Ticky Ticky Tick *(Philips PB-607)*
				2nd re-entry (flipped)
9 Mar 57	16	1		**Champion The Wonder Horse** / Ticky Ticky Tick *(Philips PB-607)*
				3rd re-entry
30 Mar 57	2	3	★	**Love Is A Golden Ring** *(Frankie Laine with the Easy Riders)* /
				There's Not A Moment To Spare *(Frankie Laine) (Philips PB-676)*
25 May 57	6	1		**Without Him** / Lonely Man *(Philips PB-691)*
14 Sep 57	9	1		**Gunfight At The O.K. Corral** / The Thief *(Philips PB-709)*
14 Sep 57	11	1		**The 3.10 To Yuma** / You Know How It Is *(Philips PB-727)*
16 Nov 57	8	1		**Gunfight At The O.K. Corral** / The Thief *(Philips PB-709)*
				1st re-entry
7 Dec 57	11	2		**The Greater Sin** / East Is East *(Philips PB-760)*
25 Jan 58	9	1		**Gunfight At The O.K. Corral** / The Thief *(Philips PB-709)*
				2nd re-entry
5 Apr 58	15	1		**Gunfight At The O.K. Corral** / The Thief *(Philips PB-709)*
				3rd re-entry
10 May 58	13	1		**My Gal And A Prayer** / The Lonesome Road *(Philips PB-821)*
31 Oct 59	1	2	★	**Rawhide** / Journey's End *(Philips PB-965)*

LANA SISTERS   2

British singing trio formed in 1958, consisting of Lynne Abrams, Riss Long and Mary O'Brien (who later became Dusty Springfield).

28 Nov 59	20	1	**(Seven Little Girls) Sitting In The Back Seat** *(Lana Sisters with*
			Al Saxon) / Sitting On The Sidewalk *(Lana Sisters) (Fontana H-221)*
11 Jun 60	13	1	**Someone Loves You, Joe** / Tintarella di Luna *(Fontana H-252)*

DON LANG   10

Fast-singing trombonist from Halifax, West Yorkshire born Gordon Langhorn. He recorded the theme tune for the seminal '50s teen music show, '6.5 Special', on which he was also a regular.

22 Oct 55	3	2	★	**Cloudburst** / Seventeen *(H.M.V. POP-115)*
21 Jan 56	3	2		**I Want You To Be My Baby** / Four Brothers *(H.M.V. POP-150)*
2 Nov 57	4	1		**White Silver Sands** / Again 'n' Again 'n' Again *(H.M.V. POP-382)*
				Both sides by Don Lang & His Frantic Five
26 Apr 58	4	1		**Tequila** / Junior Hand Jive *(H.M.V. POP-465)*
				Both sides by Don Lang & His Frantic Five
17 May 58	19	1	★	**Witch Doctor** / Cool Baby Cool *(H.M.V. POP-488)*
				Both sides by Don Lang & His Frantic Five
23 Aug 58	3	1		**The Bird On My Head** / Hey Daddy *(H.M.V. POP-510)*
				Both sides by Don Lang & His Frantic Five
26 Sep 59	13	2		**A Hoot An' A Holler** / See You Friday *(H.M.V. POP-649)*
				Both sides by Don Lang & His Frantic Five

See also Cyril Stapleton & His Orchestra (Gordon Langhorn)

MARIO LANZA   40

Popular operatic tenor and film star born Alfredo Cocozza in Philadelphia in 1921. Plagued by depression, alcoholism and an assortment of medical problems, he died in 1959, aged just 38.

18 Sep 54	26	1	**Granada** / Lolita *(H.M.V. B-21310)*
30 Oct 54	35	1	★ **Serenade** / Drinking Song *(H.M.V. DA-2065)*
27 Nov 54	50	1	★ **Serenade** / Drinking Song *(H.M.V. DA-2065)* **1st re-entry**
1 Jan 55	1	5	★ **Serenade** / **Drinking Song** *(H.M.V. DA-2065)* **2nd re-entry**
8 Jan 55	1	6	★ **I'll Walk With God** / Beloved *(H.M.V. DA-2062)*
5 Feb 55	56	1	★ **SONGS FROM THE STUDENT PRINCE AND OTHER FAMOUS MELODIES** *(H.M.V. ALP-1186)* **LP**
			Orchestral Introduction / Serenade / Golden Days / Drinking Song / Summertime In Heidelberg *(with Elizabeth Doubleday)* / Beloved / Gaudeamus Igitur / Deep In My Heart, Dear *(with Elizabeth Doubleday)* / I'll Walk With God / Yours Is My Heart Alone / Romance / I'll See You Again / If I Loved You / I'll Be Seeing You / One Night Of Love
9 Apr 55	25	1	★ **SONGS FROM THE STUDENT PRINCE AND OTHER FAMOUS MELODIES** *(H.M.V. ALP-1186)* **LP** *re-entry*
7 May 55	13	1	**Summertime In Heidelberg** *(Mario Lanza and Elizabeth Doubleday)* / Gaudeamus Igitur *(Mario Lanza) (H.M.V. DA-2070)*
22 Oct 55	20	1	**ROMANCE IN SONG** *(H.M.V. 7EB-6025)* **EP**
			Someday I'll Find You / Day In – Day Out / Love Is The Sweetest Thing / Your Eyes Have Told Me So
18 Feb 56	1	1	**Valencia** / Besame Mucho *(H.M.V. DA-2083)*
3 Mar 56	22	1	**Valencia** / Besame Mucho *(H.M.V. DA-2083)* *re-entry*
21 Apr 56	13	1	★ **Serenade** / My Destiny *(H.M.V. DA-2085)* *reissue*
26 May 56	14	1	**Wanting You** / Some Day *(H.M.V. DA-2084)*
23 Jun 56	5	6	★ **Serenade** / My Destiny *(H.M.V. DA-2085)* *reissue, 1st re-entry*
11 Aug 56	1	5	★ **Serenade** / My Destiny *(H.M.V. DA-2085)* *reissue, 2nd re-entry*
22 Sep 56	10	1	**Earthbound** / This Land *(H.M.V. DA-2086)*
20 Oct 56	6	3	**Earthbound** / This Land *(H.M.V. DA-2086)* **1st re-entry**
24 Nov 56	14	1	**Earthbound** / This Land *(H.M.V. DA-2086)* **2nd re-entry**
23 Aug 58	5	1	**Seven Hills Of Rome** / Come Dance With Me *(R.C.A. RCA-1045)*
31 Oct 59	14	1	**Because** / Ave Maria *(R.C.A. RCA-1123)*

JULIUS LaROSA   5

Young Brooklyn-born singer who was controversially fired on live TV by variety show host Arthur Godfrey. Ironically, it harmed Godfrey's career more than it did LaRosa's.

26 Nov 55	1	3	★ **Suddenly There's A Valley** / Everytime That I Kiss Carrie *(London HLA-8193)*
19 May 56	19	1	**No Other Love** / Rosanne *(London HLA-8272)*
28 Jun 58	17	1	★ **Torero** / Milano *(R.C.A. RCA-1063)*

LARRY LAWRENCE & THE BAND OF GOLD   1

Thanks to Preston Epps (qv), bongos were the 'in' instrument of 1959, and jazz pianist/bandleader Larry Fotine was one of those who climbed aboard the bandwagon, masquerading as 'Larry Lawrence' on these recordings for the Van Nuys, California-based Balboa label.

21 Nov 59	13	1	**Bongo Boogie** / Goofin' Off *(Pye International 7N.25042)*

LEE LAWRENCE   4

Tenor from Salford, Lancashire born Leon Siroto. He was one of the most popular British male vocalists of the '50s, but died in 1961, aged just 40.

18 Sep 54	12	1	**The Story Of Tina** / For You My Love *(Decca F-10367)*
16 Oct 54	17	1	**The Story Of Tina** / For You My Love *(Decca F-10367)* *re-entry*
19 Nov 55	30	1	★ **Suddenly There's A Valley** / Mi Muchacha *(Columbia DB-3681)*
31 Mar 56	19	1	**Don't Tell Me Not To Love You** / Young And Foolish *(Columbia DB-3721)*

STEVE LAWRENCE   11

Pop singer and actor born Sidney Liebowitz in New York in 1935. He was married to singer Eydie Gormé and sometimes performed with her as Steve & Eydie.

11 May 57	**2**	3	**Party Doll** / Pum-Pa-Lum *(Vogue Coral Q-72243)*
8 Jun 57	**1**	4	**Party Doll** / Pum-Pa-Lum *(Vogue Coral Q-72243)* *re-entry*
16 May 59	**6**	1	**Only Love Me** / Loving Is A Way Of Living *(H.M.V. POP-604)*
30 May 59	**2**	1	**Only Love Me** / Loving Is A Way Of Living *(H.M.V. POP-604)* *re-entry*
20 Feb 60	**3**	1	**Pretty Blue Eyes** / You're Nearer *(H.M.V. POP-689)*
19 Mar 60	**5**	1	★ <u>**Footsteps**</u> / You Don't Know *(H.M.V. POP-726)*

See also Eydie Gormé

ENRICO LEANDROS & His Orchestra

See Werner Müller & His Orchestra

HENRY LECA & His Orchestra   5

French pianist and orchestra leader born in Vito, Corsica in 1914.

21 Aug 54	**6**	4	**The Bandit** / Music from the film 'O Cangaceiro' *(Philips PB-297)*
27 Nov 54	**28**	1	**The Bandit** / Music from the film 'O Cangaceiro' *(Philips PB-297)* *re-entry*

BRENDA LEE   6

Brenda Mae Tarpley from Atlanta, Georgia was blessed with a huge voice that belied her small stature, and went on to become the biggest-selling US female pop singer of the '60s.

27 Jul 57	**4**	1	**Love You 'Till I Die** / Dynamite *(Brunswick 05685)*
21 Mar 59	**7**	1	**Bill Bailey Won't You Please Come Home** / Hummin' The Blues Over You *(Brunswick 05780)*
20 Feb 60	**15**	1	★ <u>**Sweet Nuthin's**</u> / Weep No More My Baby *(Brunswick 05819)*
11 Jun 60	**14**	1	**Love You 'Till I Die** / Dynamite *(Brunswick 05685)* *re-entry*
25 Feb 61	**16**	2	★ <u>**Emotions**</u> / **I'm Learning About Love** *(Brunswick 05847)*

JOHNNIE LEE   4

Rock'n'roll singer from Leicester born Brian Shepherd. He learned to play the guitar while recovering from accidentally shooting himself in the foot. Sadly, chart success eluded him, but his third single, 'Cindy Lou', bubbled under strongly.

16 Jul 60	**4**	4	**Cindy Lou** / They're Wrong *(Fontana H-257)*

LAURA LEE   2

Classy singer born Isa McIntyre in Musselburgh, East Lothian in 1937. Despite rumours to the contrary, it has now been established that her cover of Marilyn Michaels' 'answer' to Ray Peterson's 'Tell Laura I Love Her' was produced by Johnny Keating, not Joe Meek.

29 Oct 60	**6**	2	**Tell Tommy I Miss Him** / I'm Sending Back Your Roses *(Triumph RGM-1030)*

PEGGY LEE   37

Influential singer, songwriter and actress born Norma Egstrom in Jamestown, North Dakota in 1920.

26 Jun 54	**15**	1	**BLACK COFFEE** *(Brunswick LA-8629)* **LP**
			Black Coffee / I've Got You Under My Skin / Easy Living / My Heart Belongs To Daddy / A Woman Alone With The Blues / I Didn't Know What Time It Was / When The World Was Young / Love Me Or Leave Me
7 Aug 54	**14**	3	**Johnny Guitar** / I Didn't Know What Time It Was *(Brunswick 05286)*
27 Nov 54	**9**	3	**White Christmas** / Snow *(Brunswick 05354)*
			Both sides by Bing Crosby, Danny Kaye, Peggy Lee and Trudy Stevens. (This was a re-recording of Bing's famous hit and was featured in the film, 'White Christmas'.)
25 Dec 54	**37**	1	**White Christmas** / Snow *(Brunswick 05354)* *1st re-entry*

8 Jan 55	12	2		White Christmas / Snow *(Brunswick 05354)* **2nd re-entry**
22 Jan 55	5	6		Let Me Go, Lover / Bouquet Of Blues *(Brunswick 05360)*
19 Mar 55	17	1		Apples, Peaches And Cherries / The Night Holds No Fear *(Brunswick 05221)*
5 Nov 55	6	4		He's A Tramp / The Siamese Cat Song *(Brunswick 05482)*
12 Nov 55	31	1		Sugar / What Can I Say After I Say I'm Sorry *(Brunswick 05471)*
10 Dec 55	18	1		He's A Tramp / The Siamese Cat Song *(Brunswick 05482)* **1st re-entry**
28 Jan 56	3	2		He's A Tramp / The Siamese Cat Song *(Brunswick 05482)* **2nd re-entry**
18 Feb 56	6	1		He's A Tramp / The Siamese Cat Song *(Brunswick 05482)* **3rd re-entry**
18 May 57	6	1	★	Mr. Wonderful / The Gypsy With Fire In His Shoes *(Brunswick 05671)*
7 Sep 57	9	1		SONGS FROM WALT DISNEY'S LADY AND THE TRAMP *(Brunswick LA-8731)* **LP** Bella Notte / Peace On Earth / Lady / What Is A Baby? / La La Lu / The Siamese Cat Song / He's A Tramp / Home Sweet Home / Bella Notte and Finale
2 Aug 58	1	2	★	Fever / You Don't Know *(Capitol CL-14902)*
13 Dec 58	5	1		Sweetheart / Light Of Love *(Capitol CL-14955)*
14 Feb 59	6	1		Alright, Okay, You Win / My Man *(Capitol CL-14984)*
16 Jan 60	2	2		You Deserve / Things Are Swingin' *(Capitol CL-15103)*
18 Feb 61	4	1	★	Till There Was You / Bucket Of Tears *(Capitol CL-15184)*
4 Mar 61	9	2	★	Till There Was You / Bucket Of Tears *(Capitol CL-15184)* **re-entry**

MICHEL LEGRAND & His Orchestra   1

French composer, arranger and jazz pianist born near Paris in 1932. He is especially renowned for haunting film scores like 'The Thomas Crown Affair' and 'The Umbrellas of Cherbourg'.

| 11 Jun 55 | 24 | 1 | I LOVE PARIS *(Philips BBL-7026)* **LP**
I Love Paris / Mademoiselle de Paris / Paris / Les Feuilles Mortes / Sous les Ponts
de Paris / La Seine / Paris In The Spring / Paris Canaille / April in Paris / À Paris /
La Vie en Rose / Sous le Ciel de Paris / Paris Je T'Aime / The Song from Moulin
Rouge / The Last Time I Saw Paris / I Love Paris |

TOM LEHRER   7

Singer/songwriter, pianist and cutting-edge satirist born in New York in 1928. He later lectured in mathematics at Harvard University.

| 20 Sep 58 | 1 | 7 | ★ | SONGS BY TOM LEHRER *(Decca LF-1311)* **LP**
The Dope Peddler / Be Prepared / The Wild West / I Wanna Go Back To Dixie /
Swanee / Fight Fiercely, Harvard / Lobachevsky / The Irish Ballad / The Hunting
Song / My Home Town / When You Are Old And Grey / I Hold Your Hand In Mine /
The Wiener Schnitzel Waltz |

LES CHAKACHAS   2

Studio outfit formed during the late '50s mambo and cha-cha-cha craze by Belgian percussionist Gaston Bogaert. 'Eso Es El Amor' (sung in Spanish) was a Belgian No. 1 in 1958.

| 28 Feb 59 | 3 | 2 | Eso Es El Amor / Ay! Mulata *(R.C.A. RCA-1097)* |

LES HOBEAUX   2

Six-man skiffle group led by singer/guitarist Les Bennetts. They took over from the Vipers as resident group at the 2I's coffee bar in 1957.

| 12 Oct 57 | 7 | 2 | Oh, Mary Don't You Weep / Toll The Bell Easy *(H.M.V. POP-377)* |

LORNE LESLEY   3

Cabaret singer from Tiger Bay, Cardiff born Irene Spetti. In 1968, she married antiques dealer David Dickinson (latterly of 'Bargain Hunt' and 'Real Deal' fame).

| 7 Jan 61 | 15 | 3 | We're Gonna Dance / Bloodshot Eyes *(Polydor NH-66956)* |

GEORGE LEWIS   12

Influential jazz clarinettist from New Orleans, born Joseph Louis François Zenon in 1900.

7 Aug 54	**8**	4	**Mama Don't Allow It** / Willie The Weeper *(Good Time Jazz GV-2253)*
			Both sides by George Lewis & His New Orleans Music
11 Sep 54	**34**	1	**Mama Don't Allow It** / Willie The Weeper *(Good Time Jazz GV-2253)*
			1st re-entry
23 Oct 54	**24**	2	**Mama Don't Allow It** / Willie The Weeper *(Good Time Jazz GV-2253)*
			2nd re-entry
8 Jan 55	**46**	1	**NEW ORLEANS PARADE** *(Melodisc MLP 12-101)* 🅛🅟
			George Lewis leading the Eureka Brass Band
			Sing On / West Lawn Dirge / Lady Be Good / Garlands Of Flowers
22 Jan 55	**61**	1	**Mama Don't Allow It** / Willie The Weeper *(Good Time Jazz GV-2253)*
			3rd re-entry
29 Jan 55	**21**	1	**GEORGE LEWIS & HIS NEW ORLEANS STOMPERS**
			(Vogue LAE-12005) 🅛🅟
			George Lewis & His New Orleans Stompers
			Climax Rag / Deep Bayou Blues / Milenberg Joys / Two Jim Blues / Fidgety Feet /
			Just A Closer Walk With Thee / Just A Little While Longer To Stay Here / Careless
			Love / Don't Go 'way Nobody / Dauphine Street Blues
5 Feb 55	**52**	1	**Fidgety Feet** / Dauphine Street Blues *(Vogue V-2054)*
			Both sides by George Lewis & His New Orleans Stompers
5 Feb 55	**56**	1	**Mama Don't Allow It** / Willie The Weeper *(Good Time Jazz GV-2253)*
			4th re-entry

JERRY LEWIS   7

The goofy half of the immensely successful Lewis & Martin comedy duo, born Joseph Levitch in Newark, New Jersey. Their partnership ended in July 1956, when Dean Martin decided to pursue a solo career as a singer.

25 Sep 54	**4**	4	**Ev'ry Street's A Boulevard In Old New York**
			(Dean Martin & Jerry Lewis) (Capitol CL-14150)
			The flip, 'How Do You Speak To An Angel?' by Dean Martin,
			bubbled under from 4 September and charted on 23 October.
28 Apr 56	**7**	2	**I Keep Her Picture Hanging Upside Down** / I Love A Murder Mystery
			(Capitol CL-14559)
22 Sep 56	**7**	1	**Pardners** *(Dean Martin & Jerry Lewis)* / Buckskin Beauty *(Jerry Lewis)*
			(Capitol CL-14626)

JERRY LEE LEWIS   18

Legendary piano-pounding rock'n'roll hellraiser from Ferriday, Louisiana known to all as 'The Killer'.

10 Aug 57	**10**	1	★ **Whole Lotta Shakin' Goin' On** / It'll Be Me *(London HLS-8457)*
7 Sep 57	**4**	3	★ **Whole Lotta Shakin' Goin' On** / It'll Be Me *(London HLS-8457)*
			re-entry
1 Mar 58	**4**	2	**You Win Again** / I'm Feelin' Sorry *(London HLS-8559)*
22 Mar 58	**10**	1	**You Win Again** / I'm Feelin' Sorry *(London HLS-8559)* *re-entry*
27 Sep 58	**4**	3	**Break-Up** / I'll Make It All Up To You *(London HLS-8700)*
17 Jan 59	**5**	1	★ **High School Confidential** / Fools Like Me *(London HLS-8780)*
18 Apr 59	**4**	1	★ **Lovin' Up A Storm** / Big Blon' Baby *(London HLS-8840)*
19 Sep 59	**5**	1	**Let's Talk About Us** / The Ballad Of Billy Joe *(London HLS-8941)*
10 Oct 59	**22**	1	**Let's Talk About Us** / The Ballad Of Billy Joe *(London HLS-8941)*
			re-entry
28 Nov 59	**18**	1	**Little Queenie** / I Could Never Be Ashamed *(London HLS-8993)*
19 Dec 59	**14**	1	**Little Queenie** / I Could Never Be Ashamed *(London HLS-8993)*
			re-entry
2 Apr 60	**2**	1	**I'll Sail My Ship Alone** / It Hurt Me So *(London HLS-9083)*
4 Jun 60	**3**	1	★ **Baby, Baby, Bye Bye** / Old Black Joe *(London HLS-9131)*

PATTI LEWIS   3

Canadian jazz singer who started her career in the UK. She also appeared in the 1956 'Goon Show' TV spin-offs 'The Idiot Weekly, Price 2d', 'A Show Called Fred' and 'Son Of Fred'.

27 Nov 54	**33**	2	**I Love Paris** / I Can't Tell A Waltz From A Tango *(Philips PB-367)*
18 Dec 54	**34**	1	**I Can't Tell A Waltz From A Tango** / I Love Paris *(Philips PB-367)*
			re-entry (flipped)

TINY LEWIS   2

Obscure rockabilly singer whose solitary recording was this raucous gem from the tiny Linda label in New York.

19 Dec 59	**4**	2	**Too Much Rockin'** / I Get Weak *(Parlophone R-4617)*

JOHN LEYTON   3

Good-looking actor from Frinton-on-Sea, Essex, whose ethereal 1961 UK chart-topper, 'Johnny Remember Me', remains an all-time classic.

20 Aug 60	**16**	1	**Tell Laura I Love Her** / Goodbye To Teenage Love
			(Top Rank JAR-426)
3 Sep 60	**16**	1	**Tell Laura I Love Her** / Goodbye To Teenage Love
			(Top Rank JAR-426) **re-entry**
12 Nov 60	**14**	1	**The Girl On The Floor Above** / Terry Brown's In Love With Mary Dee
			(H.M.V. POP-798)

LIBERACE   1

Flamboyant pianist born in West Allis, Wisconsin in 1919. At the height of his popularity in the '50s and '60s, he was the highest-paid entertainer in the world, and also had his own TV show, the theme for which was 'I'll Be Seeing You'.

17 Nov 56	**11**	1	**I'll Be Seeing You** / Faith Unlocks The Door *(Philips PB-625)*
			Both sides with George Liberace & His Orchestra

BEN LIGHT   2

Ragtime pianist born Benjamin Leight in New York in 1893.

17 Dec 55	**9**	2	**Bring Me A Bluebird** / You *(H.M.V. POP-147)*
			Both sides by Ben Light with the Mellowmen

TERRY LIGHTFOOT & HIS NEW ORLEANS JAZZMEN   1

Clarinettist/saxophonist born in Potters Bar, Middlesex in 1935. Along with Chris Barber, Acker Bilk and Kenny Ball, he was at the forefront of the British 'trad jazz' movement.

14 Jan 61	**29**	1	**The Old Pull 'n' Push** / Wimoweh *(Columbia DB-4567)*

KATHY LINDEN   10

Singer from New Jersey who sounded like – and was promoted as – a 14-year-old, but was actually a married woman in her twenties.

5 Apr 58	**15**	1	**Billy (I Always Dream Of Bill** / If I Could Hold You In My Arms
			(Felsted AF-102)
23 May 59	**2**	1	**Goodbye, Jimmy Goodbye** / Heartaches At Sweet Sixteen
			(Felsted AF-122)
20 Jun 59	**5**	8	**Goodbye, Jimmy Goodbye** / Heartaches At Sweet Sixteen
			(Felsted AF-122) **re-entry**

'BIG' TINY LITTLE   2

Pianist 'Big' Tiny Little (real name Dudley Little Jr.) was the son of diminutive Midwest bandleader Tiny Little. He acquired his nickname after joining ABC-TV's 'Lawrence Welk Show' as resident pianist in 1955.

13 Jul 57	**4**	2	**School Day** / That's The Only Way To Live *(Vogue Coral Q-72263)*

LITTLE RICHARD 17

Probably the most flamboyant of all the original rock'n'rollers, singer/pianist Richard Penniman from Macon, Georgia laid down some of the loudest and most energetic music of the era.

17 Nov 56	8	2	★ **Rip It Up** / Ready Teddy *(London HLO-8336)*
26 Jan 57	2	2	★ **Long Tall Sally** / **Tutti Frutti** *(London HLO-8366)*
9 Feb 57	5	3	**LITTLE RICHARD & HIS BAND (VOL. 1)** *(London REO-1071)* **EP**
			She's Got It / I'm Just A Lonely Guy / Heeby-Jeebies / Slippin' And Slidin'
23 Feb 57	2	2	★ **She's Got It** / **The Girl Can't Help It** *(London HLO-8382)*
16 Mar 57	13	1	**LITTLE RICHARD & HIS BAND (VOL. 1)** *(London REO-1071)* **EP**
			re-entry
7 Sep 57	5	1	★ **Jenny, Jenny** / Miss Ann *(London HLO-8470)*
28 Jun 58	1	2	★ **Ooh! My Soul** / **True, Fine Mama** *(London HLO-8647)*
20 Dec 58	4	2	★ **Baby Face** / I'll Never Let You Go *(London HLU-8770)*
28 Mar 59	6	1	★ **By The Light Of The Silvery Moon** / Early One Morning
			(London HLU-8831)
5 Mar 60	7	1	**I Got It** / Baby *(London HLU-9065)*

LITTLE TONY & HIS BROTHERS 2

Italian-born rock'n'roller Antonio Ciacchi and his brothers, Alberto and Enrico, enjoyed success in the UK and several other countries, as well as back home.

2 Jan 60	1	1	★ **Too Good** / Foxy Little Mamma *(Decca F-11190)*
2 Jul 60	10	1	**Kiss Me, Kiss Me** / Teddy Girl *(Decca F-21247)*

JIMMY LLOYD 1

Versatile balladeer born Lloyd James Boucher in Trinidad in 1929.

2 May 59	3	1	**I Kneel At Your Throne** / Sapphire *(Philips PB-909)*

KATHY LLOYD 1

Australian singer who worked with Ted Heath's orchestra and others while in UK.

26 Mar 55	24	1	**Unsuspecting Heart** / Our Future Has Only Begun *(Decca F-10464)*

HANK LOCKLIN 2

Country music singer/songwriter and long-standing member of the Grand Ole Opry born in McLellan, Florida in 1918.

30 Jul 60	4	2	★ **Please Help Me, I'm Falling** / My Old Home Town *(R.C.A. RCA-1188)*

LOLITA 2

Lolita was the stage name of Austrian singer Edith 'Ditta' Zuzer, born in Vienna in 1931. She had a massive international hit in 1960 with 'Seemann' – albeit not in the UK, where it was covered by both Petula Clark and Anne Shelton as 'Sailor'.

14 Jan 61	20	1	**Sailor** / La Luna *(Polydor NH-66818)*
11 Feb 61	12	1	**Sailor** / La Luna *(Polydor NH-66818)* **re-entry**

JULIE LONDON 1

Sultry American singer/actress born Gayle Peck in Santa Rosa, California in 1926. Her sensual voice is heard to good effect on this bubbler from the soundtrack of 'The Girl Can't Help It' (1956).

30 Mar 57	12	1	★ **Cry Me A River** / S'Wonderful *(London HLU-8240)*

LAURIE LONDON 3

Schoolboy singer born in London in 1944. Although he made many other recordings, he is chiefly remembered for his 1957 hit, 'He's Got The Whole World In His Hands'.

18 Jan 58	4	3	**She Sells Sea-Shells** / Handed Down *(Parlophone R-4388)*

LONDON PHILHARMONIC ORCHESTRA, *cond.* John Barbirolli — 1

Orchestra founded in 1932 by conductors Sir Thomas Beecham and Malcolm Sargent as a rival to the London Symphony and BBC Symphony Orchestras.

23 Oct 54   **8**   1   **TCHAIKOVSKY – BALLET SUITE: 'THE SWAN LAKE', OP. 20**
(H.M.V. C-2619/2620) `78x2`
❶ No.1: Scene / No.3: Dance Of The Little Swans / No.2: Waltz
❷ No.4: Scene *(Violin solo: Antonio Brosa)* / No.5: Hungarian Dance – Czardas

See also   Philharmonic Promenade Orchestra

LONDON PHILHARMONIC ORCHESTRA, *cond.* Sir Adrian Boult
See Kathleen Ferrier

LONDON PHILHARMONIC ORCHESTRA, *cond.* Antál Dorati — 1

Orchestra founded in 1932 by conductors Sir Thomas Beecham and Malcolm Sargent as a rival to the London Symphony and BBC Symphony Orchestras.

8 Jan 55   **37**   1   **TCHAIKOVSKY – SWAN LAKE – BALLET MUSIC**
(Columbia DX-869/870/871/872) `78x4`
❶ Act 1: Introduction / Act 2: Dance Of The Queen Of The Swans
❷ Act 1: Dance Of The Prince / Act 2: Dance Of The Queen Of The Swans /
Act 3: Waltz
❸ Act 2: Dance Of The Swans / Act 3: Spanish Dance / Act 3: Mazurka
❹ Act 4: Dance Of The Cygnets / Act 4: Finale

DENISE LOR — 2

Singer/actress born Denise Briault in Los Angeles in 1925. Although she charted in the USA with 'If I Give My Heart To You', Doris Day's version won out in the UK.

20 Nov 54   **10**   2   **If I Give My Heart To You** / Hallo Darling *(Parlophone R-3893)*

LORD MELODY — 1

Popular calypso artist born Fitzroy Alexander in San Fernando, Trinidad in 1926. His topical humour from the Caribbean doubtless struck a chord with many West Indian expats in the UK.

9 Aug 58   **11**   1   **The Devil** / No No No *(Melodisc 45/1440)*
Both sides by Lord Melody with the Four Lords

LORD ROCKINGHAM'S XI — 6

Resident band on ABC Television's teenage music show, 'Oh Boy!', led by Harry Robinson.

7 Jun 58   **13**   1   **Fried Onions** / The Squelch *(Decca F-11024)*
28 Jun 58   **4**   2   **Fried Onions** / The Squelch *(Decca F-11024)* **re-entry**
18 Oct 58   **1**   1   ★ **Hoots Mon** / Blue Train *(Decca F-11059)*
31 Jan 59   **8**   1   ★ **Wee Tom** / Lady Rockingham, I Presume? *(Decca F-11104)*
30 May 59   **1**   1   **Ra-Ra Rockingham** / Farewell To Rockingham *(Decca F-11139)*

JERRY LORDAN — 9

London-born singer who had three minor hits and a bubbler in 1960, but found much greater success as a songwriter for the Shadows and Jet Harris & Tony Meehan.

7 Nov 59   **6**   5   ★ **I'll Stay Single** / Can We Kiss *(Parlophone R-4588)*
20 Feb 60   **11**   1   ★ **Who Could Be Bluer?** / Do I Worry? *(Parlophone R-4627)*
21 May 60   **1**   2   ★ **Sing Like An Angel** / Ev'ry Time *(Parlophone R-4653)*
1 Oct 60   **12**   1   **Ring, Write Or Call** / I've Still Got You *(Parlophone R-4695)*

SOPHIA LOREN 1

Iconic Italian film star born Sofia Scicolone in Rome in 1934. She made her debut as a singer on this novelty comedy single conceived by record producer George Martin.

5 Nov 60 **10** 1 ★ **Goodness Gracious Me!** *(Peter Sellers and Sophia Loren)*
(*Parlophone R-4702*)
Flip is 'Grandpa's Grave by Peter Sellers

NASH LORRAINE 1

Malayan-born singer managed and produced by Bunny Lewis. This was his only record release.

5 Dec 59 **18** 1 **The Ways Of Love** / Belle From Barcelona *(Pye Nixa 7N.15235)*

DENNIS LOTIS 7

Sophisticated balladeer born in Johannesburg, South Africa in 1925. He was resident singer with Ted Heath's band from 1952 to 1955, and was voted 'Top UK Vocalist' in a Melody Maker poll in 1956. Even Frank Sinatra was a fan! Surprisingly, none of his records was a hit.

4 Feb 56 **11** 1 **C'est La Vie** / Por Favor *(Pye Nixa N.15017)*
3 Mar 56 **2** 1 **Por Favor** / C'est La Vie *(Pye Nixa N.15017)* **re-entry (flipped)**
24 Mar 56 **16** 1 **The Extra Day** / There's A Time And Place *(Pye Nixa N.15041)*
7 Apr 56 **19** 1 **The Extra Day** / There's A Time And Place *(Pye Nixa N.15041)*
re-entry
25 Jan 58 **6** 2 **Good Mornin' Life** / Valentina *(Columbia DB-4056)*
2 Apr 60 **4** 1 **Love Me A Little** / I Wish It Were You *(Columbia DB-4432)*

See also Ted Heath & His Music

LOUVIN BROTHERS 2

Outstanding C&W duo from Alabama, born Charlie and Ira Loudermilk. Tragically, Ira was killed in a car crash in 1961, aged just 41.

15 Mar 58 **11** 1 **TRAGIC SONGS OF LIFE** *(Capitol EAP1-769)* **EP**
Kentucky / I'll Be All Smiles Tonight / Katie Dear / My Brother's Will
29 Mar 58 **7** 1 **TRAGIC SONGS OF LIFE** *(Capitol EAP1-769)* **EP** *re-entry*

GEOFF LOVE & His Orchestra 4

Prolific arranger, composer and bandleader born in Todmorden, West Yorkshire in 1917.

15 Aug 59 **4** 2 ★ **The Honeymoon Song** / Proud Matador *(Columbia DB-4323)*
Both sides as by Manuel and the Music of the Mountains
14 Jan 61 **24** 1 **La Dolce Vita** / Venezia *(Columbia DB-4563)*
Both sides as by Manuel and the Music of the Mountains
28 Jan 61 **18** 1 **La Dolce Vita** / Venezia *(Columbia DB-4563)* *re-entry*

See also Billy's Banjo Band
Boy Scout Association

RONNIE LOVE 1

R&B singer who enjoyed a US crossover hit in 1961 with 'Chills And Fever'. Sadly, it failed to register in the UK charts, though Tom Jones covered it a couple of years later for his first single.

4 Feb 61 **12** 1 **Chills And Fever** / No Use Pledging My Love *(London HLD-9272)*

JOHNNY LUCK 1

15-year-old Brit whose one-off rock'n'roll outing was featured in the 1958 film, 'Violent Playground'.

14 Jun 58 **14** 1 **Play Rough** / Buzz, Buzz, Buzz *(Fontana H-110)*

ROBIN LUKE 1

While still at school, this young Californian living in Hawaii wrote a song dedicated to his five-year-old sister which became an unlikely global hit. He gave up the music business in 1965, studied for a Ph.D., and eventually became a university professor.

11 Oct 58   7   1   ★ **Susie Darlin'** / Living's Loving You *(London HLD-8676)*

LUMBERJACKS 3

Time has obscured the identities of the Lumberjacks, who don't appear to have made any other recordings. It is possible that they were the male members of the Stargazers, with whom George Elrick recorded other material in the summer of 1954.

11 Sep 54   **29**   1   **Gilly Gilly Ossenfeffer Katznellenbogen By The Sea** *(George Elrick and the Lumberjacks)* / Three Coins In The Fountain *(Lumberjacks)* *(Decca F-10371)*

25 Sep 54   **39**   1   **Gilly Gilly Ossenfeffer Katznellenbogen By The Sea** *(George Elrick and the Lumberjacks)* / Three Coins In The Fountain *(Lumberjacks)* *(Decca F-10371)* **1st re-entry**

9 Oct 54   **34**   1   **Gilly Gilly Ossenfeffer Katznellenbogen By The Sea** *(George Elrick and the Lumberjacks)* / Three Coins In The Fountain *(Lumberjacks)* *(Decca F-10371)* **2nd re-entry**

NELLIE LUTCHER 1

Jazz-inflected R&B pianist/singer born in Lake Charles, Louisiana in 1912.

27 Feb 60   **9**   1   **My Mother's Eyes** / The Heart Of A Clown *(Capitol CL-15106)*

ARTHUR LYMAN GROUP 6

Vibraphone and marimba player born in Hawaii in 1932. He played with exotica pioneer Martin Denny in the mid-'50s, then branched out on his own to become a leading exponent of the genre.

29 Aug 59   **5**   2   **Taboo** / Dahil Sayo *(Vogue Pop V-9153)*
19 Sep 59   **5**   4   **Taboo** / Dahil Sayo *(Vogue Pop V-9153)* **re-entry**

FRANKIE LYMON & THE TEENAGERS 17

Best-selling doo-wop group from New York whose focal point was the infectious soprano of boy singer Frankie Lymon.

16 Jun 56   **3**   2   ★ **Why Do Fools Fall In Love** / Please Be Mine *(Columbia DB-3772)*
                                    Both sides as the Teenagers featuring Frankie Lymon
4 Aug 56   **1**   1   **I Want You To Be My Girl** / I'm Not A Know It All *(Columbia DB-3797)*
                                    Both sides as the Teenagers featuring Frankie Lymon
18 Aug 56   **14**   2   **I Want You To Be My Girl** / I'm Not A Know It All *(Columbia DB-3797)*
                                    1st re-entry
22 Sep 56   **6**   1   **I Want You To Be My Girl** / I'm Not A Know It All *(Columbia DB-3797)*
                                    2nd re-entry
20 Oct 56   **6**   1   **I Promise To Remember** / Who Can Explain? *(Columbia DB-3819)*
9 Feb 57   **1**   7   ★ **Baby, Baby** / **I'm Not A Juvenile Delinquent** *(Columbia DB-3878)*
20 Apr 57   **7**   2   **Teenage Love** / Paper Castles *(Columbia DB-3910)*
14 Sep 57   **13**   1   ★ **Goody Goody** / Creation Of Love *(Columbia DB-3983)*

ALFRED LYNCH 1

London-born actor whose cheerful working-class charm made him a fixture of British war films and social dramas in the '60s and '70s.

31 Oct 59   **10**   1   **I'll Stay Single** / A Little Of What You Fancy *(Decca F-11171)*

JOE LYNCH 19

Much-loved Irish singer and actor born in Mallow, Co. Cork in 1925. He became very well known in the UK after starring in the ITV comedy series 'Never Mind The Quality, Feel The Width' (1968-72).

18 Sep 54   **29**   1   **Kevin Barry** / Let Me Carry Your Cross *(Glenside W-138)*
25 Sep 54   **37**   1   **Irish Soldier Boy** / Tipperary So Far Away *(Glenside W-108)*

30 Oct 54	**31**	1	**Irish Soldier Boy** / Tipperary So Far Away *(Glenside W-108)* ***re-entry***
10 Mar 56	**18**	1	**The Pride Of Tipperary** / Puff Puff To Ballyduff *(Decca (Irish Series) MU-15)*
24 Mar 56	**16**	1	**The Pride Of Tipperary** / Puff Puff To Ballyduff *(Decca (Irish Series) MU-15)* ***re-entry***
16 Jun 56	**8**	2	**The Old Bog Road** / The Irish Emigrant *(Beltona BE-2647)*
2 Feb 57	**4**	6	**Homes Of Donegal** / **Delaney's Donkey** *(Beltona BE-2672)*
23 Mar 57	**7**	5	**Homes Of Donegal** / **Delaney's Donkey** *(Beltona BE-2672)* ***re-entry***
22 Jan 61	**10**	1	**Irish Soldier Boy** / Tipperary So Far Away *(Glenside EPW-108)* ***reissue***

KENNY LYNCH   6

Versatile singer, songwriter, actor, dancer, ex-boxer and comedian born in London in 1939. He was the brother of jazz singer Maxine Daniels.

28 May 60	**7**	4	★ <u>Mountain Of Love</u> / Why Do You Treat Me This Way *(H.M.V. POP-751)*
1 Oct 60	**7**	2	**Slowcoach** / You Make Love So Well *(H.M.V. POP-786)*

VERA LYNN   58

Singer born Vera Welch in London in 1917. She enjoyed huge popularity throughout the war years as 'The Forces' Sweetheart' and became a national institution.

14 Aug 54	**4**	1	**My Friend** / There Must Be A Reason *(Decca F-10339)*
25 Sep 54	**39**	1	★ <u>My Son, My Son</u> / Our Heaven On Earth *(Decca F-10372)* Both sides by Vera Lynn and Frank Weir and His Saxophone
9 Oct 54	**10**	1	★ <u>My Son, My Son</u> / Our Heaven On Earth *(Decca F-10372)* ***re-entry***
16 Oct 54	**26**	1	**My Friend** / There Must Be A Reason *(Decca F-10339)* ***1st re-entry***
6 Nov 54	**18**	4	**My Friend** / **There Must Be A Reason** *(Decca F-10339)* ***2nd re-entry***
4 Dec 54	**5**	5	**Party Sing-Song (Parts 1 & 2) [M]** *(Decca F-10411)* Shine On Harvest Moon – Back In Your Own Backyard – For Me And My Girl / We All Have A Song In Our Heart – I'd Love To Live In Loveland With A Girl Like You – The Loveliest Night Of The Year
1 Jan 55	**36**	1	**There Must Be A Reason** / My Friend *(Decca F-10339)* ***3rd re-entry (flipped)***
19 Feb 55	**36**	1	**Addio Amore** (Vera Lynn with the Johnston Brothers) / I Do (Vera Lynn) *(Decca F-10463)*
19 Mar 55	**24**	2	**Addio Amore** / I Do *(Decca F-10463)* ***1st re-entry***
16 Apr 55	**19**	1	**Two Easter Sunday Sweethearts** / Du Bist Mein Liebchen *(Decca F-10253)*
23 Apr 55	**9**	1	**Addio Amore** / I Do *(Decca F-10463)* ***2nd re-entry***
18 Jun 55	**23**	3	**Doonaree** / Show Me The Way *(Decca F-10535)*
23 Jul 55	**19**	1	**Doonaree** / Show Me The Way *(Decca F-10535)* ***1st re-entry***
30 Jul 55	**2**	9	**Popular Medley No. 4 (Parts 1 & 2) [M]** *(Decca F-10561)* Both sides by Vera Lynn and the Clubmen Chee Chee-Oo Chee – Unchained Melody – Tomorrow / Dreamboat – I Wonder – Cherry Pink And Apple Blossom White
13 Aug 55	**12**	2	**Doonaree** / Show Me The Way *(Decca F-10535)* ***2nd re-entry***
20 Aug 55	**13**	3	**Ev'ry Day Of My Life** / My Lonely Lover *(Decca F-10566)*
8 Oct 55	**15**	3	**Popular Medley No. 4 (Parts 1 & 2) [M]** *(Decca F-10561)* ***re-entry***
22 Oct 55	**12**	1	**Unfaithful You** / With Your Love *(Decca F-10622)*
3 Dec 55	**37**	1	**Unfaithful You** / With Your Love *(Decca F-10622)* ***1st re-entry***
14 Jan 56	**7**	2	**With Your Love** / Unfaithful You *(Decca F-10622)* ***2nd re-entry (flipped)***
11 Feb 56	**1**	1	**With Your Love** / Unfaithful You *(Decca F-10622)* ***3rd re-entry***
3 Mar 56	**4**	1	**With Your Love** / Unfaithful You *(Decca F-10622)* ***4th re-entry***
21 Apr 56	**2**	2	★ <u>Who Are We</u> / I'll Be True To You *(Decca F-10715)*
28 Jul 56	**1**	5	**Walk Hand In Hand** / Come Back To Me *(Decca F-10737)*
8 Sep 56	**8**	1	**Walk Hand In Hand** / Come Back To Me *(Decca F-10737)* ***1st re-entry***
22 Sep 56	**10**	1	**Walk Hand In Hand** / Come Back To Me *(Decca F-10737)* ***2nd re-entry***
16 Feb 57	**10**	1	★ <u>The Faithful Hussar</u> / The One Beside You *(Decca F-10846)*

21 Feb 59	2	1	**Vera Sings Today's Pop Hits (Parts 1 & 2) [M]** *(Decca F-11106)*

The Day The Rains Came – I'll Remember Tonight – Love Makes The World Go 'round / To Know Him, Is To Love Him – Someday – Mandolins In The Moonlight

9 Mar 57	4	1	★ <u>**The Faithful Hussar**</u> / The One Beside You *(Decca F-10846)* ***re-entry***

See also Various Artists (MY FAIR LADY)

BARBARA LYON   4

Daughter of UK-based American actors Ben Lyon and Bebe Daniels, with whom she starred in the highly-popular BBC comedy radio show, 'Life With The Lyons' (1950-61). In 1955, she branched out as a singer, with some success.

11 Jun 55	17	2	★ <u>**Stowaway**</u> / The Pendulum Song *(Columbia DB-3619)*
24 Sep 55	16	2	**Hey There** / I Went To The Village *(Columbia DB-3649)*

HUMPHREY LYTTELTON & His Band   22

Jazz trumpeter/clarinettist, bandleader, cartoonist and radio personality. He was born in 1921 at Eton College, Berkshire, where his father – the second son of the 8th Viscount Cobham – was a housemaster.

27 Nov 54	28	1	**HUMPH AT THE CONWAY** *(Parlophone PMC-1012)* **LP**

Texas Moaner / Coal Black Shine / Last Smile Blues / Elephant Stomp Blues / Wally Plays The Blues / My Bucket's Got A Hole In It / I Double Dare You / That's The Blues Old Man / Feline Stomp / St. James Infirmary Blues / Memphis Shake / Mo Pas Lemmé Ças

18 Dec 54	19	4	**HUMPH AT THE CONWAY** *(Parlophone PMC-1012)* **LP** *1st re-entry*
22 Jan 55	10	2	**Ace In The Hole** / Coffee Grinder *(Parlophone R-3967)*
22 Jan 55	61	1	**Mezzy's Tune** / Jelly Bean Blues *(Parlophone R-3917)*
29 Jan 55	33	2	**HUMPH AT THE CONWAY** *(Parlophone PMC-1012)* **LP** *2nd re-entry*
12 Feb 55	13	1	**Ace In The Hole** / **Coffee Grinder** *(Parlophone R-3967)*

        1st re-entry

19 Feb 55	20	1	**Mezzy's Tune** / Jelly Bean Blues *(Parlophone R-3917)* ***re-entry***
5 Mar 55	9	1	**Coffee Grinder** / Ace In The Hole *(Parlophone R-3967)*

        2nd re-entry (flipped)

19 Mar 55	21	2	**Coffee Grinder** / **Ace In The Hole** *(Parlophone R-3967)*

        3rd re-entry

26 Mar 55	33	1	**DELVING BACK WITH HUMPH** *(Esquire 32-007)* **LP**

The Thin Red Line / Melancholy Blues / Cake Walkin' Babies / If You See Me Comin' / Panama / Working Man Blues / Fidgety Feet / Weary Blues / Ole Miss Rag / Vox Humana / Elizabeth / Blue For Waterloo / First Of Many / Blues For Two / High Society

7 May 55	28	1	**When The Saints Go Marching In** / Careless Love *(Tempo A-10)*
17 Sep 55	21	2	**P.T.Q. Rag** / Heat Wave *(Parlophone R-4060)*
14 Jan 56	20	1	**When The Saints Go Marching In** / Careless Love *(Tempo A-10)*

        re-entry

23 Mar 57	15	1	**Baby Doll** / Red Beans And Rice *(Parlophone R-4277)*
31 Aug 57	6	1	**Early Call (Bermondsey Bounce)** / Creole Serenade *(Parlophone R-4333)*

DAVID MacBETH   7

Singing Andrews Liver Salts salesman and former footballer born in Newcastle in 1935. He was discovered by Carroll Levis when he appeared on a talent show at the Sunderland Empire.

24 Oct 59	17	1	★ <u>**Mr. Blue**</u> / Here's A Heart *(Pye Nixa 7N.15231)*
22 Oct 60	16	1	**Pigtails In Paris** / Blue Blue Blue *(Pye 7N.15291)*
5 Nov 60	7	5	**Pigtails In Paris** / Blue Blue Blue *(Pye 7N.15291)* ***re-entry***

FATHER SYDNEY MacEWAN 4

Major Scottish singing star of the 1930s, '40s and '50s, born in Glasgow in 1909. He became a Catholic priest in 1944, but was permitted by his bishop to continue his singing career. He quit at the age of 50, because, as he put it, his voice had 'lost its bloom'.

18 Sep 54	9	1	**Scotland The Brave** / Killarney In The Spring *(Columbia DB-3120)*
9 Oct 54	29	2	**Scotland The Brave** / Killarney In The Spring *(Columbia DB-3120)*
			1st re-entry
27 Nov 54	32	1	**Scotland The Brave** / Killarney In The Spring *(Columbia DB-3120)*
			2nd re-entry

KEN MACKINTOSH & His Orchestra 6

Prodigious alto saxophonist from Liversedge, West Yorkshire, who led one of the top British dance bands of the post-war years. In 1954, he charted with 'The Creep', launching a dance craze in the process.

11 Jan 58	6	1	★	**Raunchy** / Mojo *(H.M.V. POP-426)*
8 Nov 58	8	3		**That Old Cha Cha Feeling** / Ulterior Motif *(H.M.V. POP-543)*
3 Oct 59	12	1		**Morgen** / Sleep Walk *(H.M.V. POP-656)*
24 Oct 59	13	1		**Morgen** / Sleep Walk *(H.M.V. POP-656)* *re-entry*

IAN MacLEISH 1

Scottish pianist. He co-authored a series of books with Jimmy Shand containing arrangements of tunes played by Shand's band.

| 6 Nov 54 | 33 | 1 | **The Star O' Robbie Burns** / Hail Caledonia *(Beltona BL-2607)* |

BOBBY MacLEOD & His Band

See Bobby McLeod & His Band

GORDON MacRAE 8

Actor and singer from East Orange, New Jersey fondly remembered for his appearances in 1950s film musicals like 'Oklahoma!' (1955) and 'Carousel' (1956).

30 Oct 54	13	1	**C'est Magnifique** / How Do You Speak To An Angel?
			(Capitol CL-14168)
13 Nov 54	9	3	**C'est Magnifique** / How Do You Speak To An Angel?
			(Capitol CL-14168) *re-entry*
30 Jun 56	9	2	**Who Are We** / There's A Lull In My Life *(Capitol CL-14576)*
4 Aug 56	14	1	**Who Are We** / There's A Lull In My Life *(Capitol CL-14576)* *re-entry*
22 Nov 58	10	1	**The Secret** / A Man Once Said *(Capitol CL-14920)*

See also Original Soundtrack (CAROUSEL)
Original Soundtrack (OKLAHOMA!)

JOSH MacRAE 12

Scottish folk singer born Iain MacRae. He formed the Reivers in 1958 with Enoch Kent, Moyna Flanagan and Rena Swankie, then sang briefly with the Emmettones before going solo in 1960.

20 Feb 60	11	1	★	**Talking Army Blues** / **Talking Guitar Blues** *(Top Rank JAR-290)*
5 Mar 60	1	2	★	**Talking Army Blues** / **Talking Guitar Blues** *(Top Rank JAR-290)*
				1st re-entry
4 Jun 60	1	3	★	**Talking Army Blues** / Talking Guitar Blues *(Top Rank JAR-290)*
				2nd re-entry
26 Nov 60	20	1		**Let Ramensky Go** / Sky High Joe *(Pye 7N.15307)*
10 Dec 60	5	1		**Let Ramensky Go** / Sky High Joe *(Pye 7N.15307)* *1st re-entry*
7 Jan 61	19	1		**WALKIN', TALKIN', SINGIN'** *(Pye NEP-24131)* 🅴🅿
				Talking Dust Bowl Blues / Old Blue / Arkansas Rambler / Rocky Mountain Belle
21 Jan 61	1	2	★	**Messing About On The River** / High Class Feeling *(Pye 7N.15319)*
21 Jan 61	24	1		**Let Ramensky Go** / Sky High Joe *(Pye 7N.15307)* *2nd re-entry*

See also Emmettones
Reivers

JOHNNY MADDOX with the Rhythmasters   4

Honky-tonk piano player born in Gallatin, Tennessee in 1927. His 'Crazy Otto Medley', consisting of pieces by the German pop and jazz pianist Fritz Schultz-Reichel aka Crazy Otto, became the first ragtime record to sell over a million copies and launched his career.

7 May 55	28	1	**Crazy Otto Medley [M]** / Humoresque *(London HL-8134)*
			Crazy Otto Medley: Ivory Rag – In Der Nacht Ist Der Mensch Nicht Gern Alleine – Das Machen Nur Die Beine Von Dolores – Was Macht Der Alte Seeman – Play A Simple Melody
10 Dec 55	18	1	**Do, Do, Do** / When You Wore A Tulip *(London HLU-8203)*
7 Jan 56	26	1	**Do, Do, Do** / When You Wore A Tulip *(London HLU-8203)* **re-entry**
25 Apr 59	15	1	**Old Fashioned Love** *(Johnny Maddox and the Rhythmasters)* / The Hurdy Gurdy Song *(Johnny Maddox and His Orchestra)* *(London HLD-8826)*

MAKADOPOULOS & HIS GREEK SERENADERS   1

This authentic-sounding interpretation of the famous film theme was actually recorded in Belgium for the Palette label by a group of session musicians under the direction of jazz pianist/arranger Willy Albimoor. (See also Milko Papayaki & His Orchestra.)

15 Oct 60	7	1	★ **<u>Never On Sunday</u>** / Yasou *(Palette PG-9005)*

MANDRAKE   2

Mandrake was New York session guitarist Vinnie Rogers recording under a pseudonym. Something of a pioneer, he played a specially adapted guitar on which he could produce a range of different effects and sounds. Sadly, he had a bad heart and died in 1965, aged just 23.

7 Jan 61	3	1	**Mandrake** / The Witch's Twist *(Philips PB-1093)*
21 Jan 61	20	1	**Mandrake** / The Witch's Twist *(Philips PB-1093)* **re-entry**

See also Fireflies

CARL MANN   1

Rockabilly singer/guitarist born in Huntingdon, Tennessee in 1942. His novel arrangement of Nat 'King' Cole's 'Mona Lisa' was a pop hit in 1959, as was the similar-sounding 'Pretend'.

13 Aug 60	13	1	**South Of The Border** / I'm Comin' Home *(London HLS-9170)*

LORIE MANN   3

Singer born Barbara Burke in London in 1931. She often appeared on radio and TV, including several episodes of 'Oh Boy!', and recorded with the Viscounts vocal group in the early '60s.

16 May 59	2	2	**A Penny A Kiss, A Penny A Hug** / Dream Lover *(Top Rank JAR-116)*
19 Dec 59	3	1	**So Many Ways** / I Wonder *(Top Rank JAR-237)*

SHELLY MANNE & HIS MEN   8

Versatile jazz drummer and composer born Sheldon Manne in New York in 1920.

26 Jun 54	7	1	**SHELLY MANNE & HIS MEN** *(Vogue LDE-072)* **LP**
			La Mucura / Mallets / You And The Night And The Music / Gazelle / Sweets / Afrodesia / You're My Thrill / Fugue
21 Aug 54	17	4	**SHELLY MANNE & HIS MEN** *(Vogue LDE-072)* **LP** **re-entry**
23 Oct 54	13	3	**THE WEST COAST SOUND** *(Contemporary/Vogue LAC-12138)* **LP**
			Grasshopper / La Mucura / Summer Night / Afrodesia / You And The Night And The Music / Gazelle / Sweets / Spring Is Here / Mallets / You're Getting To Be A Habit With Me / You're My Thrill / Fugue

See also Howard Rumsey's Lighthouse All Stars

BOB MANNING   1

Dick Haymes-influenced baritone singer born Manny Levin in Philadelphia in 1926.

7 Aug 54	11	1	**The Nearness Of You** / All I Desire *(Capitol CL-13958)*

MANTOVANI & His Orchestra   11

Annunzio Mantovani was born in Venice in 1905, and moved to England in 1912. He became one of the most successful orchestra leaders and recording artists in the history of popular music, and was especially famous for his cascading string arrangements.

8 Jan 55	9	5	★ **Lonely Ballerina** / **Lazy Gondolier** *(Decca F-10395)*
16 Apr 55	11	1	**Softly, Softly** *(Vocal: Kim Bennett)* / Longing *(Decca F-10468)*
1 Oct 55	11	1	**Brass Buttons** / Take My Love *(Decca F-10601)*
24 Dec 55	17	1	**Take My Love** / Brass Buttons *(Decca F-10601)* *re-entry (flipped)*
3 Mar 56	15	1	**Candlelight** / Begin The Beguine *(Decca F-10678)*
27 Jul 57	7	1	**Mandolin Serenade** / The Spring Song *(Decca F-10918)*
24 May 58	18	1	**I Could Have Danced All Night** / This Nearly Was Mine
			(Decca F-11017)

See also Various Artists (Lord's Taverners Star Band Hit Parade)

MANUEL AND THE MUSIC OF THE MOUNTAINS

See Geoff Love & His Orchestra

MARINO MARINI & His Quartet   9

Born in Seggiano, Tuscany in 1924, Marino Marini was a musical innovator who stamped his own character on material ranging from Neapolitan songs to US standards. More importantly, he helped to put Italian pop on the world map.

29 Mar 58	5	1	**The Pansy** / With All My Heart *(Durium DC-16629)*
19 Apr 58	1	3	**The Pansy** / With All My Heart *(Durium DC-16629)* *re-entry*
24 May 58	9	1	**MARINO MARINI & HIS HAPPY MUSIC (VOL. 1)**
			(Durium U-20007) **EP**
			Maruzzella / Aummo… Aummo / 'E Stele 'e Napule / Giuvanne Cu 'e Chitarra
7 Jun 58	5	1	**MARINO MARINI & HIS HAPPY MUSIC (VOL. 1)**
			(Durium U-20007) **EP** *re-entry*
30 Aug 58	4	1	★ **Come Prima** / **Volare** *(Durium DC-16632)*
13 Sep 58	3	1	★ **Come Prima** / **Volare** *(Durium DC-16632)* *re-entry*
25 Oct 58	11	1	**I Could Have Danced All Night** / Saunabad *(Durium DC-16634)*

GINO MARINUZZI *(conductor)*

See Chorus and Orchestra Sinfonica Dell'EIAR

STEVIE MARSH   2

Singer from Manchester born Eileen Taylor. She worked with the Sid Philips band for a number of years before embarking upon a solo career. This revival of a 1916 golden oldie was her only hit.

14 Nov 59	15	1	★ **If You Were The Only Boy In The World** / Leave Me Alone
			(Decca F-11181)
28 Nov 59	4	1	★ **If You Were The Only Boy In The World** / Leave Me Alone
			(Decca F-11181) *re-entry*

JACK MARSHALL, His Orchestra & Chorus   1

Guitarist and composer born in El Dorado, Kansas in 1921. He was one of US Capitol's top producers in the late '50s and early '60s, and also wrote the 'Munsters' TV theme.

| 5 Jul 58 | 23 | 1 | **Thunder Road Chase** / Finger Poppin' *(Capitol CL-14888)* |

LARRY MARSHALL   1

Genial Glaswegian host of STV's hugely popular sketch and song show, 'The One O'Clock Gang', from 1957 to the end of 1964.

| 14 Jan 61 | 9 | 1 | **The Ballad Of Rob Roy** / A Town Like Glasgow *(Parlophone R-4703)* |

Actor and singer born Dino Crocetti in Steubenville, Ohio in 1917. After ten years of playing the straight man in the immensely popular Lewis & Martin comedy duo, he walked out on his partner Jerry Lewis in July 1956 and successfully reinvented himself as a solo entertainer.

10 Jul 54	**1**	7	★ **Sway** / Pretty As A Picture *(Capitol CL-14138)*
14 Aug 54	**21**	1	**Hey Brother Pour The Wine** / I'd Cry Like A Baby *(Capitol CL-14123)*
4 Sep 54	**4**	4	★ **Sway** / Pretty As A Picture *(Capitol CL-14138)* *re-entry*
4 Sep 54	**21**	2	★ **How Do You Speak To An Angel?** *(Dean Martin)* / Ev'ry Street's A Boulevard In Old New York *(Dean Martin & Jerry Lewis)* *(Capitol CL-14150)*
25 Sep 54	**4**	4	★ **How Do You Speak To An Angel?** *(Dean Martin)* / **Ev'ry Street's A Boulevard In Old New York** *(Dean Martin & Jerry Lewis)* *(Capitol CL-14150)* *re-entry*
2 Oct 54	**25**	1	**Money Burns A Hole In My Pocket** / That's What I Like *(Capitol CL-14145)*
16 Oct 54	**1**	3	**The Peddler Man** / Try Again *(Capitol CL-14170)*
13 Nov 54	**20**	1	**The Peddler Man** / Try Again *(Capitol CL-14170)* *re-entry*
13 Nov 54	**26**	2	**Money Burns A Hole In My Pocket** / That's What I Like *(Capitol CL-14145)* *1st re-entry*
4 Dec 54	**51**	1	**Money Burns A Hole In My Pocket** / That's What I Like *(Capitol CL-14145)* *2nd re-entry*
22 Jan 55	**1**	2	★ **Mambo Italiano** / That's All I Want From You *(Capitol CL-14227)*
5 Feb 55	**37**	1	**One More Time** / If I Could Sing Like Bing *(Capitol CL-14180)*
5 Mar 55	**27**	1	**One More Time** / If I Could Sing Like Bing *(Capitol CL-14180)* *1st re-entry*
19 Mar 55	**5**	2	★ **Under The Bridges Of Paris** / What Could Be More Beautiful *(Capitol CL-14255)*
16 Apr 55	**16**	1	**One More Time** / If I Could Sing Like Bing *(Capitol CL-14180)* *2nd re-entry*
21 May 55	**8**	2	**Long, Long Ago** *(Nat 'King' Cole and Dean Martin)* / Open Up The Doghouse *(Dean Martin and Nat 'King' Cole)* *(Capitol CL-14215)*
11 Jun 55	**25**	2	**Open Up The Doghouse** *(Dean Martin and Nat 'King' Cole)* / Long, Long Ago *(Nat 'King' Cole and Dean Martin)* *(Capitol CL-14215)* *re-entry (flipped)*
5 Nov 55	**1**	12	**Relax-Ay-Voo** / Two Sleepy People *(Capitol CL-14356)* Both sides by Dean Martin and Line Renaud
25 Feb 56	**4**	4	★ **Innamorata** / You Look So Familiar *(Capitol CL-14507)*
21 Apr 56	**13**	1	★ **Innamorata** / You Look So Familiar *(Capitol CL-14507)* *re-entry*
16 Jun 56	**6**	3	**Watching The World Go By** / The Lady With The Big Umbrella *(Capitol CL-14586)*
14 Jul 56	**11**	2	**Watching The World Go By** / The Lady With The Big Umbrella *(Capitol CL-14586)* *1st re-entry*
4 Aug 56	**14**	1	**Watching The World Go By** / The Lady With The Big Umbrella *(Capitol CL-14586)* *2nd re-entry*
1 Sep 56	**12**	1	**Watching The World Go By** / The Lady With The Big Umbrella *(Capitol CL-14586)* *3rd re-entry*
22 Sep 56	**7**	1	**Pardners** *(Dean Martin & Jerry Lewis) (Capitol CL-14626)* Flip is 'Buckskin Beauty' by Jerry Lewis
23 Feb 57	**10**	1	★ **The Man Who Plays The Mandolino** / I Know I Can't Forget *(Capitol CL-14690)*
10 May 58	**2**	3	★ **Return To Me** / Forgetting You *(Capitol CL-14844)*
7 Jun 58	**2**	1	★ **Return To Me** / Forgetting You *(Capitol CL-14844)* *re-entry*
12 Sep 59	**5**	1	**Maybe** / I Ain't Gonna Lead This Life *(Capitol CL-15064)*
28 May 60	**15**	1	**Who Was That Lady?** / Love Me, My Love *(Capitol CL-15127)*
29 Oct 60	**13**	1	**Just In Time** / Humdinger *(Capitol CL-15155)*

RAY MARTIN & His Concert Orchestra 37

Composer and orchestra leader born Kurt Kohn in Vienna, Austria in 1918. He became one of the biggest names in British popular music during the '50s, and was a fixture on radio and TV.

15 Jan 55	15	1	**The Gentle Sex** / It's A Woman's World *(Columbia DB-3557)*
			Both sides by Ray Martin & His Concert Orchestra and Chorus
29 Jan 55	7	7	**It's A Woman's World** / The Gentle Sex *(Columbia DB-3557)*
			re-entry (flipped)
11 Jun 55	3	10	**The Elephants' Tango** / Blue Mirage *(Columbia DB-3631)*
24 Sep 55	3	7	**Hernando's Hideaway** / The Bavarian Wedding March *(Columbia DB-3658)*
19 Nov 55	3	8	**Hernando's Hideaway** / The Bavarian Wedding March *(Columbia DB-3658)* **1st re-entry**
21 Jan 56	9	1	**Hernando's Hideaway** / The Bavarian Wedding March *(Columbia DB-3658)* **2nd re-entry**
2 Jun 56	3	2	★ <u>**The Carousel Waltz**</u> / Port au Prince *(Columbia DB-3771)*
15 Sep 56	10	1	**Street Symphony** / Hello Young Lovers *(Columbia DB-3807)*

See also Original Soundtrack (IT'S GREAT TO BE YOUNG)

TONY MARTIN 15

Popular romantic balladeer and film star born Alvin Morris in Oakland, California in 1912.

23 Oct 54	3	10	**I Love Paris** / Boulevard Of Nightingales *(H.M.V. B-10771)*
9 Apr 55	1	2	★ <u>**Stranger In Paradise**</u> / Vera Cruz *(H.M.V. B-10849)*
9 Apr 55	17	1	**Melody Of Love** / You're Getting To Be A Habit With Me
			Both sides by Dinah Shore and Tony Martin (H.M.V. B-10831)
3 Sep 55	17	1	**Why, Oh Why?** *(Tony Martin, Vic Damone, Russ Tamblyn [actually Rex Dennis], Jane Powell, Debbie Reynolds and Ann Miller)* / Chiribiribee *(Kay Armen, Jane Powell, Tony Martin, Debbie Reynolds, Vic Damone and Russ Tamblyn [actually Rex Dennis])* *(M.G.M. MGM-837)*
7 Jul 56	11	1	★ <u>**Walk Hand In Hand**</u> / Flamenco Love *(H.M.V. POP-222)*

VINCE MARTIN 2

Folk singer/songwriter from New York, born Vincent Marcellino in 1937. He was initially teamed with the Tarriers by his record label, then formed a singing partnership with Fred Neil in the '60s.

1 Dec 56	2	2	★ <u>**Cindy, Oh Cindy**</u> / Only If You Praise The Lord *(London HLN-8340)*
			Both sides by Vince Martin with the Tarriers

MARTINAS & HIS MUSIC

See Martin Slavin

WINK MARTINDALE 2

Radio deejay and game show host born Winston Martindale in Jackson, Tennessee. His epic narration, 'Deck of Cards', charted in the UK in 1959, 1963 and 1973.

24 Oct 59	17	1	★ <u>**Deck Of Cards**</u> / Now You Know How It Feels *(London HLD-8962)*
21 Nov 59	4	1	★ <u>**Deck Of Cards**</u> / Now You Know How It Feels *(London HLD-8962)* **re-entry**

AL MARTINO 25

Italian American balladeer born Jasper Cini in Pennsylvania in 1927. In 1952, he had the distinction of being the first artist to have a UK No.1, with 'Here In My Heart'. In later years, he turned his hand to acting, memorably playing Johnny Fontane in the 'Godfather' movies.

18 Sep 54	1	2	★ <u>**The Story Of Tina**</u> / Destiny *(Capitol CL-14163)*
27 Nov 54	5	9	**I Still Believe** / When *(Capitol CL-14192)*
4 Dec 54	8	1	**No One But You** / Not As A Stranger *(Capitol CL-14202)*
18 Dec 54	30	1	**No One But You** / Not As A Stranger *(Capitol CL-14202)* **1st re-entry**
15 Jan 55	23	1	**No One But You** / Not As A Stranger *(Capitol CL-14202)* **2nd re-entry**

22 Jan 55	**55**	1	**Don't Go To Strangers** / Say It Again *(Capitol CL-14224)*
5 Feb 55	**56**	1	**Don't Go To Strangers** / Say It Again *(Capitol CL-14224)* ***1st re-entry***
19 Feb 55	**26**	2	**Don't Go To Strangers** / Say It Again *(Capitol CL-14224)* ***2nd re-entry***
12 Nov 55	**14**	4	**Small Talk** / Come Close To Me *(Capitol CL-14379)*
17 Mar 56	**10**	1	**Journey's End** / Sound Advice *(Capitol CL-14550)*
2 May 59	**11**	2	**I Can't Get You Out Of My Heart** / Two Hearts Are Better Than One *(Top Rank JAR-108)*

SPOKES MASHIYANE   3

Johannes Mashiyane was one of the leading pennywhistle players on the South African kwela scene from the '50s until the '70s. He acquired his nickname from the bicycle wheel spokes out of which he fashioned his first instrument.

| 7 Jun 58 | **7** | 1 | **The Boys Of Jo'burg** *(Spokes Mashiyane and France Pilane)* / **Jika Spokes** *(Spokes Mashiyane and Ben Nkosi) (Oriole CB-1441)* Both sides described as 'Kwela Penny Whistle Jive' |
| 28 Jun 58 | **6** | 2 | **The Boys Of Jo'burg** *(Spokes Mashiyane and France Pilane)* / **Jika Spokes** *(Spokes Mashiyane and Ben Nkosi) (Oriole CB-1441)* ***re-entry*** |

GLEN MASON   10

Versatile Scottish singer and actor born Tom Lennon in Stirling in 1930.

2 Jun 56	**1**	6	**Hot Diggity** / Baby Girl Of Mine *(Parlophone R-4176)*
21 Jul 56	**14**	2	**Hot Diggity** / Baby Girl Of Mine *(Parlophone R-4176)* ***re-entry***
26 Jul 58	**12**	1	**I May Never Pass This Way Again** / A Moment Ago *(Parlophone R-4415)*
29 Nov 58	**9**	1	**The End** / Fall In Love *(Parlophone R-4485)*

SAMMY MASTERS   1

Rockabilly singer/guitarist born Samuel T. Lawmaster in Sasakwa, Oklahoma in 1930.

| 4 Jun 60 | **7** | 1 | ★ **Rockin' Red Wing** / Lonely Weekend *(Warner Bros. WB-10)* |

VALERIE MASTERS   3

Singer and radio/TV presenter born in London in 1940. She sang with the Ray Ellington quartet from 1957 till 1959, and married their piano player, Dick Katz, in 1961.

| 25 Jun 60 | **15** | 1 | ★ **Banjo Boy** / Cow Cow Boogie *(Fontana H-253)* |
| 12 Nov 60 | **14** | 2 | **Sweeter As The Day Goes By** / Fools Fall In Love *(Fontana H-268)* |

MAT MATHEWS' QUINTET

See Carmen McRae

JOHNNY MATHIS   24

Smooth balladeer born in Gilmer, Texas in 1935. He became a household name after appearing on 'The Ed Sullivan Show' in June 1957 and has remained a star ever since.

22 Feb 58	**15**	1	**Wild Is The Wind** / No Love *(Fontana H-103)*
22 Mar 58	**8**	1	**Wild Is The Wind** / No Love *(Fontana H-103)* ***1st re-entry***
12 Apr 58	**9**	1	**Wild Is The Wind** / No Love *(Fontana H-103)* ***2nd re-entry***
7 Jun 58	**13**	1	**Chances Are** / The Twelfth Of Never *(Philips PB-749)*
21 Jun 58	**8**	1	**Wild Is The Wind** / No Love *(Fontana H-103)* ***3rd re-entry***
6 Sep 58	**6**	1	★ **A Certain Smile** / Let It Rain *(Fontana H-142)*
24 Jan 59	**4**	4	**Call Me** / Stairway To The Sea *(Fontana H-163)*
18 Apr 59	**12**	1	**You'd Be So Nice To Come Home To** / Let's Love *(Fontana H-186)*
9 May 59	**8**	1	**Let's Love** / You'd Be So Nice To Come Home To *(Fontana H-186)* ***1st re-entry (flipped)***
16 May 59	**11**	1	**THERE GOES MY HEART** *(Fontana TFE-17088)* **EP** I'm Glad There Is You / Street Of Dreams / There Goes My Heart / My One And Only Love

Dennis Lotis

JANE
MORGAN

featured in "Sunday Night at the London Palladium"
THE DAY THE RAINS CAME   HLR 8751

and her latest disc

If only I could live
my life again

b/w
TO LOVE AND BE LOVED

HLR 8810

45/78

LONDON RECORDS DIVISION OF THE DECCA RECORD COMPANY LT
DECCA HOUSE ALBERT EMBANKMENT LONDON S E 11

Their
biggest
HIT
yet!!!

FRANKIE LYMON
and the
Teenagers

sing

GOODY GOODY

with

Creation of Love DB3983 (45 & 78 r.p.m.)

COLUMBIA
records

(Regd. Trade Mark of Columbia Graphophone Co. Ltd.)

••• Visit
The Record Stand
at the Radio Show:
Earl's Court
August 28 to
September 7 •••

B.M.I. RECORDS LIMITED (Controlled by Electric & Musical Industries Ltd.)
8-11 Great Castle Street, London. W.1.

30 May 59	**4**	2	**Let's Love** / **You'd Be So Nice To Come Home To** *(Fontana H-186)*
			2nd re-entry
7 Nov 59	**1**	3	★ <u>**The Best Of Everything**</u> / Cherie *(Fontana H-218)*
18 Jun 60	**2**	5	★ <u>**Starbright**</u> / **All Is Well** *(Fontana H-254)*
1 Oct 60	**9**	1	★ <u>**My Love For You**</u> / Oh That Feeling *(Fontana H-267)*

BILLY MAY & His Orchestra   3

Pittsburgh-born trumpeter, composer and arranger for many famous singers including Nat 'King' Cole, Bing Crosby, Vic Damone, Ella Fitzgerald, Peggy Lee and Frank Sinatra.

25 Sep 54	**19**	1	**The Song Is You** / Anything Can Happen Mambo *(Capitol CL-14160)*
14 Apr 56	**5**	2	★ <u>**Main Title (from the film 'The Man With The Golden Arm')**</u> / Suzette
			(Capitol CL-14551)

JIMMY McCRACKLIN & His Band   4

West Coast-based R&B pianist and bandleader born in St. Louis, Missouri in 1921. He reputedly wrote 'The Walk' to demonstrate how easy it was to get a rock'n'roll hit simply by using a couple of banal phrases and a repetitive beat. He certainly proved his point in the US, where his record made the Top Ten, though the British audience proved more discerning.

| 19 Apr 58 | **5** | 2 | **The Walk** / I'm To Blame *(London HLM-8598)* |
| 17 May 58 | **11** | 2 | **The Walk** / I'm To Blame *(London HLM-8598)* *re-entry* |

CHAS McDEVITT SKIFFLE GROUP   4

Born in Eaglesham near Glasgow, guitarist Chas McDevitt was one of the leading lights of the skiffle movement. The infectious 'Freight Train', with folk singer Nancy Whiskey guesting on vocals, made the UK Top Five in 1957 and remains a classic of the genre.

9 Mar 57	**4**	1	★ <u>**Freight Train**</u> *(Chas McDevitt Skiffle Group featuring Nancy Whiskey)* /
			The Cotton Song *(Chas McDevitt Skiffle Group) (Oriole CB-1352)*
23 Mar 57	**10**	1	★ <u>**Freight Train**</u> *(Chas McDevitt Skiffle Group featuring Nancy Whiskey)* /
			The Cotton Song *(Chas McDevitt Skiffle Group) (Oriole CB-1352)*
			re-entry
1 Jun 57	**5**	1	★ <u>**Green Back Dollar**</u> *(Chas McDevitt Skiffle Group featuring Nancy*
			Whiskey) / I'm Satisfied *(Chas McDevitt Skiffle Group)*
			(Oriole CB-1371)
13 Jul 57	**10**	1	**It Takes A Worried Man (To Sing A Worried Song)** /
			House Of The Rising Sun *(Oriole CB-1357)*

See also Nancy Whiskey

CHARLIE McGEE   1

Irish balladeer and guitarist born in Londonderry in 1913. He was immensely popular all over the Emerald Isle in the '50s and '60s, and later moved to the USA.

| 23 Apr 55 | **23** | 1 | **Between You And Me** / Dacent Irish Boy *(Glenside W-183)* |

HOWARD McGHEE

See Gene Norman's 'Just Jazz'

BILL McGUFFIE & His Orchestra   2

Versatile piano player born in Carmyle near Glasgow in 1927. He was voted Britain's top pianist in 1953, 1954 and 1955, and played with dance bands and jazz ensembles, as well as composing film music.

| 20 Nov 54 | **42** | 2 | **On The Waterfront** / Smile *(Philips PB-356)* |

McGUIRE SISTERS   8

Classy singing trio comprising Christine, Dorothy and Phyllis McGuire from Middletown, Ohio.

5 Mar 55	**7**	4	★ <u>**Sincerely**</u> / <u>**No More**</u> *(Vogue Coral Q-72050)*
21 May 55	**26**	1	**Goodnight Sweetheart, Goodnight** / Heavenly Feeling
			(Vogue Coral Q-2003)

17 Dec 55	6	1	**He** / **Christmas Alphabet** *(Vogue Coral Q-72108)*
7 Apr 56	11	1	**Be Good To Me** / Missing *(Vogue Coral Q-72145)*
30 Mar 57	15	1	**Heart** / Sometimes I'm Happy *(Vogue Coral Q-72238)*

KENNETH McKELLAR   1

Operatically trained tenor born in Paisley, Renfrewshire in 1927 who switched to singing Scottish traditional songs with great success.

| 4 Aug 56 | 7 | 1 | **Scotland The Brave** / Loch Lomond *(Decca F-10537)* |

BOBBY McLEOD & His Band   18

Born in Tobermory, Isle of Mull in 1925, master accordionist Alasdair Robert Campbell MacLeod [sic] was one of Scottish dance music's most innovative and inspirational figures.

4 Jun 55	1	11	**Pride Of Erin Waltz [M]** / **Irish Military Two-Step [M]**
			(Philips Scottish Series YB-9500)
			Pride Of Erin Waltz: Terence's Farewell To Kathleen – Sweet Rosie O'Grady – Wild Colonial Boy – Oft In The Stilly Night / *Irish Military Two Step:* If You're Irish Come Into The Parlour – With Me Shilalegh Under Me Arm – McNamara's Band – Irish Washerwoman
13 Aug 55	23	1	**Highland Two-Step [M]** / Rory O'More **[M]**
			(Philips Scottish Series YB-9508)
			Highland Two-Step: Old Highland Air – The Quaker's Wife – The Campbells Are Coming – Lord Macdonald Of The Isles / *Rory O'More:* Original – Lanigan's Ball – Saddle The Pony
27 Aug 55	24	1	**Highland Two-Step [M]** / Rory O'More **[M]**
			(Philips Scottish Series YB-9508) **re-entry**
8 Oct 55	13	2	**Pride Of Erin Waltz [M]** / **Irish Military Two-Step [M]**
			(Philips Scottish Series YB-9500) **1st re-entry**
5 Nov 55	9	1	**Irish Military Two-Step [M]** / Pride Of Erin Waltz **[M]**
			(Philips Scottish Series YB-9500) **2nd re-entry (flipped)**
17 Dec 55	19	2	**Irish Military Two-Step [M]** / Pride Of Erin Waltz **[M]**
			(Philips Scottish Series YB-9500) **3rd re-entry**

CHARLIE McNAIR SKIFFLE GROUP   12

Not really a skiffle group at all, but an Edinburgh trad jazz outfit led by trumpeter Charlie McNair.

17 Nov 56	9	1	**Hiawatha** / Meadow Lane Stomp *(Beltona BL-2670)*
1 Dec 56	1	6	**Hiawatha** / **Meadow Lane Stomp** *(Beltona BL-2670)* **1st re-entry**
19 Jan 57	4	1	**Hiawatha** / Meadow Lane Stomp *(Beltona BL-2670)* **2nd re-entry**

See also Various Artists (SCOTS TRADITIONAL JAZZ CONCERT)

JOSEPH McNALLY   2

Popular old-school Irish tenor from Rathkeale, Co. Limerick.

12 May 56	13	1	**The March Hare** *(Joseph McNally with the George Mitchell Singers)*
			(Oriole CB-1325)
			Flip is 'I'm A Sentimental One' by Jean Campbell
30 Jun 56	14	1	**The March Hare** *(Joseph McNally with the George Mitchell Singers)*
			(Oriole CB-1325) **re-entry**

McNULTY FAMILY   2

Annie McNulty and her children Eileen and Peter were a very popular Irish American singing group. Ironically, despite being billed as 'The First Family of Irish Music', they never performed in the Emerald Isle.

2 Oct 54	31	1	**Back To Donegal** / I'm Sighing Tonight For Killarney And You
			(Decca (Irish Series) F-12089)
30 Oct 54	31	1	**Irish Soldier Boy** / When It's Teatime In The Meadows
			(Decca (Irish Series) F-12263)

CLYDE McPHATTER 9

R&B singer from Durham, North Carolina who made his name singing lead with Billy Ward's Dominoes and the Drifters before going solo. He died in 1972 after a long struggle with alcoholism, aged just 39.

28 Jul 56	**4**	1	★ **Treasure Of Love** / When You're Sincere *(London HLE-8293)*
11 Aug 56	**2**	2	★ **Treasure Of Love** / When You're Sincere *(London HLE-8293)* *re-entry*
11 Jan 58	**6**	1	**Rock And Cry** / You'll Be There *(London HLE-8525)*
31 Jan 59	**7**	1	**A Lover's Question** / I Can't Stand Up Alone *(London HLE-8755)*
9 Apr 60	**7**	2	**Think Me A Kiss** / When The Right Time Comes Along *(M.G.M. MGM-1061)*
30 Apr 60	**12**	1	**Think Me A Kiss** / When The Right Time Comes Along *(M.G.M. MGM-1061)* *re-entry*
17 Sep 60	**15**	1	**Ta Ta** / I Ain't Givin' Up Nothin' *(Mercury AMT-1108)*

See also Drifters
Billy Ward & The Dominoes

CARMEN McRAE with Mat Mathews' Quintet 1

Influential jazz singer, pianist and composer born in New York in 1922. Mat Mathews (real name Mathieu Schwarts) was a Dutch-born jazz accordionist based in New York.

1 Sep 56	**6**	1	**CARMEN McRAE (PART 1)** *(London American Jazz EZ-N-19016)* **EP**
			Easy To Love / If I'm Lucky (I'll Be The One) / Old Devil Moon / Tip Toe Gently

JOE MEDLIN 2

Former big band vocalist from Virginia and sometime member of the Ravens who only managed one minor solo hit. However, he went on to become Atlantic Records' top promoter in the '60s.

9 May 59	**7**	2	**I Kneel At Your Throne** / Out Of Sight Out Of Mind *(Mercury AMT-1032)*

MEGATRONS 1

New York studio outfit. 'Velvet Waters' features a memorable clarinet lead by jazzman Haywood Henry and was a medium-sized hit in the USA. The flip features Haywood on flute.

15 Aug 59	**6**	1	**Velvet Waters** / The Merry Piper *(Top Rank JAR-146)*

MELACHRINO ORCHESTRA 3

Born in London in 1909, George Melachrino led one of the finest British light orchestras in the years immediately following World War II. Although his fame also spread to North America, he failed to match Mantovani in terms of chart success.

23 Oct 54	**38**	1	**Smile** / Copenhagen Polka *(H.M.V. B-10738)*
29 Sep 56	**4**	2	★ **Autumn Concerto** / A Woman In Love *(H.M.V. B-10958)*

GEORGE MELLY 2

Liverpudlian writer, raconteur and jazz vocalist with an exuberant lifestyle and a natty dress sense.

19 Feb 55	**15**	2	**Frankie And Johnnie** / I'm Down In The Dumps *(Decca F-10457)*
			Both sides by George Melly with Alex Welsh & His Dixielanders

FELIX MENDELSSOHN & HIS HAWAIAAN SERENADERS 1

Bandleader born in London in 1911. Although he claimed to be a direct descendant of the great composer of the same name, this has now been disproved. His band and hula girl revue were extremely popular during the 1940s, but financial problems and ill health at the start of the '50s forced him into early retirement. He died of cancer in 1952, aged just 40.

23 Oct 54	**21**	1	**'Scotlandia' Medley (Parts 1 & 2) [M]** *(Columbia DB-2757)*
			I Belong To Glasgow – Annie Laurie – Wi' A Hundred Pipers – Auld Lang Syne / Roamin' In The Gloamin' – Comin' Thru The Rye – Bonny Mary Of Argyle – Loch Lomond

YEHUDI MENUHIN with the PHILHARMONIA ORCHESTRA, *cond.* Wilhelm Furtwängler   1

Classical violinist born in New York in 1916. He is widely regarded as one of the greatest violinists of the twentieth century.

27 Nov 54   **23** 1   **BEETHOVEN – VIOLIN CONCERTO IN D MAJOR, OP. 61**
              (H.M.V. ALP-1100) **LP**
              First Movement: Allegro Ma Non Troppo – Cadenza (by Kreisler) – Tempo I /
              Second Movement: Larghetto / Third Movement: Rondo (Allegro) – Cadenza (by
              Kreisler) – Tempo I

See also Philharmonia Orchestra

IAN MENZIES & HIS CLYDE VALLEY STOMPERS

See Clyde Valley Stompers

M.G.M. STUDIO ORCHESTRA, *cond.* Charles Wolcott   1

Born in Flint, Michigan in 1906, Charles Wolcott was MGM's general music director. He started out writing music for Walt Disney cartoons, eventually graduating to the top job in 1958. The two sides below are from the soundtrack of the crime drama 'Key Witness' (1960).

4 Feb 61   **6** 1   **Ruby Duby Du** / Leatherjacket Cowboy *(M.G.M. MGM-1115)*

MARILYN MICHAELS   3

Singer, actress and comedian born Marilyn Sternberg in New York in 1943. Her 'answer' to Ray Peterson's big US hit 'Tell Laura I Love Her' was covered in the UK by Laura Lee, whose version also bubbled under.

22 Oct 60   **5** 3   **Tell Tommy I Miss Him** / Everyone Was There But You
              (R.C.A. RCA-1208)

MIKI & GRIFF   3

Miki & Griff were husband-and-wife duo Barbara and Emyr Griffith, former members of the George Mitchell Minstrels who branched out into country music.

29 Aug 59   **5** 1   ★ **Hold Back Tomorrow** /
              Deedle-Dum-Doo-Die-Day *(Pye Nixa 7N.15213)*
              Both sides by Miki & Griff with the Lonnie Donegan Group
26 Sep 59   **1** 1   ★ **Hold Back Tomorrow** /
              Deedle-Dum-Doo-Die-Day *(Pye Nixa 7N.15213)* *re-entry*
27 Aug 60   **16** 1   **Someday You'll Call My Name** *(Miki & Griff with the Lonnie Donegan*
              Group) / Long Time To Forget *(Miki & Griff) (Pye 7N.15266)*

AMOS MILBURN   1

Husky-voiced jump blues singer/pianist from Houston, Texas, who eventually succumbed to the demon drink he sang about.

7 May 60   **7** 1   **Bad, Bad Whiskey** / One Scotch, One Bourbon, One Beer
              (Vogue Pop V-9163)
              Both side by Amos Milburn & His Aladdin Chickenshackers

PETER MILES   3

24-year-old English singer who won £100 and a recording contract with Columbia in ITV's nationwide 'Find The Singer' contest. Unfortunately, he was conscripted into the RAF shortly after, which effectively killed off his career.

3 May 58   **8** 3   **My Little Girl** / Goodnight, God Bless, Sleep Tight *(Columbia DB-4117)*

ANN MILLER   1

Singer, dancer and actress born Johnnie Collier in Chireno, Texas in 1923.

3 Sep 55	**17**	1	**Why, Oh Why?** *(Tony Martin, Vic Damone, Russ Tamblyn* [actually Rex Dennis], *Jane Powell, Debbie Reynolds and Ann Miller)* / Chiribiribee *(Kay Armen, Jane Powell, Tony Martin, Debbie Reynolds, Vic Damone and Russ Tamblyn* [actually Rex Dennis]*)* *(M.G.M. MGM-837)*

BETTY MILLER   3

'The Cockney Nightingale' Betty Miller sang with Sid Phillips' swing/jazz band for a couple of years, then went solo in 1955. She fared well during the rock'n'roll era thanks to her dynamic singing style, and later moved into cabaret and musicals.

26 Nov 55	**28**	1	**Georgia's Got A Moon** / The Next Train Out Of Town *(Pye Nixa N.15008)*
28 Jan 56	**10**	1	**Georgia's Got A Moon** / The Next Train Out Of Town *(Pye Nixa N.15008)* **re-entry**
9 May 59	**8**	1	**Pearly Gates / Old Time Religion** *(Top Rank JAR-115)*

CHUCK MILLER   6

Singer/pianist born in Wellington Kansas in 1924. In 1956, his cover of the Leroy Van Dyke novelty hit made No.59 in the Billboard Top 100, but both his bids for the UK charts were unsuccessful.

22 Jun 57	**11**	1	**The Auctioneer** / Me Head's In De Barrel *(Mercury MT-153)*
14 Feb 59	**3**	1	**The Auctioneer** / Baby Doll *(Mercury AMT-1026)* **reissue**
28 Feb 59	**2**	2	**The Auctioneer** / Baby Doll *(Mercury AMT-1026)* **1st re-entry**
4 Apr 59	**5**	2	**The Auctioneer** / Baby Doll *(Mercury AMT-1026)* **2nd re-entry**

GARY MILLER   8

Singer and actor from Blackpool, born Neville Williams. He had six hits in the UK, but a lack of original material ultimately let him down. He died of a heart attack in 1968, aged just 44.

13 Nov 54	**20**	1	**The High And The Mighty** / Hold My Hand *(Philips PB-335)*
4 Dec 54	**22**	1	**The High And The Mighty** / Hold My Hand *(Philips PB-335)* **re-entry**
15 Oct 55	**1**	1	★ <u>**The Yellow Rose Of Texas**</u> / The Man From Laramie *(Pye Nixa N.15004)*
7 Jan 56	**18**	1	★ <u>**Robin Hood**</u> / Ballad Of Davy Crockett *(Pye Nixa N.15020)*
13 Jul 57	**12**	1	★ <u>**Wonderful, Wonderful**</u> / Love Letters In The Sand *(Pye Nixa N.15094)*
26 Apr 58	**17**	1	**Lollipop** / Dancing With My Shadow *(Pye Nixa 7N.15136)*
17 May 58	**9**	1	**On The Street Where You Live** / That's For Me *(Pye Nixa 7N.15140)*
31 May 58	**3**	1	**On The Street Where You Live** / That's For Me *(Pye Nixa 7N.15140)* **re-entry**

GLENN MILLER & His Orchestra   7

Popular wartime bandleader born in Clarinda, Iowa in 1909. He disappeared in 1944 while his plane was crossing the English Channel – but his legend lived on.

19 Jun 54	**14**	1	**THE GLENN MILLER STORY [OST]** *(H.M.V. DLP-1024)* **LP** Moonlight Serenade / In The Mood / I Know Why / Tuxedo Junction / Pennsylvania 6-5000 / Chattanooga Choo-Choo / A String Of Pearls / At Last / American Patrol / Little Brown Jug
25 Sep 54	**39**	1	**Little Brown Jug** / Don't Sit Under The Apple Tree *(H.M.V. B-10662)*
29 Jan 55	**39**	1	**A String Of Pearls** / Blue Rain *(Vocal: Ray Eberle)* *(H.M.V. BD-5927)*
2 Apr 55	**18**	1	**THE GLENN MILLER STORY [OST]** *(H.M.V. DLP-1024)* **LP** **1st re-entry**
28 May 55	**36**	1	**THE GLENN MILLER STORY [OST]** *(H.M.V. DLP-1024)* **LP** **2nd re-entry**
20 Dec 58	**9**	2	**GLENN MILLER SPECIAL** *(H.M.V. 7EG-8204)* **EP** Slip Horn Jive / Glen Island Special / Sun Valley Jump / Boulder Buff

See also Modernaires

JIMMY MILLER & THE BARBECUES
See Station Skiffle Group

MITCH MILLER & His Orchestra and Chorus   3
A native of Rochester, New York, Mitch Miller was one of the most influential figures in American popular music during the '50s and early '60s. Although his relentlessly jolly arrangements and novelty material were not everyone's cup of tea, he became a best-selling artist, while at the same time doubling as A&R chief at Columbia Records.

24 Sep 55	3	2	★ **The Yellow Rose Of Texas** / Blackberry Winter *(Philips PB-505)*
14 Jan 56	13	1	**The Bonnie Blue Gal** / Bel Sante *(Philips PB-525)*

SUZI MILLER   12
Originally a band vocalist, Britain's Suzi Miller began her solo recording career in 1953 with 'My Heart Belongs To Only You'. After trying her hand at a few rock'n'roll covers in the mid-'50s, she relocated to West Germany with her pianist husband, Willy Solomons.

27 Nov 54	1	8	★ **Happy Days And Lonely Nights** / Tell Me, Tell Me *(Decca F-10389)*
			Both sides by Suzi Miller and the Johnston Brothers
14 May 55	27	1	**Dance With Me Henry (Wallflower)** *(Suzi Miller and the Johnston Brothers)* / Butter Fingers *(Suzi Miller and the Marilyn Sisters) (Decca F-10512)*
28 May 55	8	1	**Dance With Me Henry (Wallflower)** *(Suzi Miller and the Johnston Brothers)* / Butter Fingers *(Suzi Miller and the Marilyn Sisters) (Decca F-10512)* **1st re-entry**
2 Jul 55	26	2	**Dance With Me Henry (Wallflower)** *(Suzi Miller and the Johnston Brothers)* / Butter Fingers *(Suzi Miller and the Marilyn Sisters) (Decca F-10512)* **2nd re-entry**

FREDDIE MILLS   1
Actor, TV presenter, club owner and former world light-heavyweight boxing champion born in Bournemouth in 1919. In 1965, he was found shot dead in his car in highly suspicious circumstances. The coroner's verdict was suicide, though many alternative theories abounded.

30 Nov 57	12	1	**One For The Road (Parts 1 & 2) [M]** *(Parlophone R-4374)*
			Smile Darn Ya Smile – If You Knew Susie – California Here I Come – Knees Up Mother Brown / Two Lovely Black Eyes – She's A Lassie From Lancashire – Down At The Old Bull And Bush – I Belong To Glasgow

GARRY MILLS   3
Singer born in West Wickham, Kent in 1941. He was the nephew of jazz trumpeter Nat Gonella.

21 May 60	7	1	★ **Look For A Star** / Footsteps *(Top Rank JAR-336)*
2 Jul 60	3	1	★ **Look For A Star** / Footsteps *(Top Rank JAR-336)* **re-entry**
1 Oct 60	12	1	★ **Top Teen Baby** / Don't Cheat Me Again *(Top Rank JAR-500)*

JACKIE MILLS
See Gene Norman's 'Just Jazz'

MINNEAPOLIS SYMPHONY ORCHESTRA, *cond.* Antál Dorati   1
Orchestra founded in 1903 by the Bavarian-born conductor and composer Emil Oberhoffer. It was renamed the Minnesota Orchestra in 1968.

8 Jan 55	37	1	**TCHAIKOVSKY – THE NUTCRACKER, OP. 71**
			(Mercury Olympian Series MMA-11106/11107) **2-LP**
			❶ Overture / Act I – Tableau I: Decorating And Lighting The Christmas Tree / March / Dance Scene: Gallop And Dance Of The Parents / Scene: Presents For The Children / Scene: The Grandfather Dance / Scene: The Guests Depart – The Children Go To Bed – The Magic Spell Begins / Scene: The Nutcracker Battles The Army Of The Mouse King, He Wins And Is Transformed Into Prince Charming / Tableau II: Journey Through The Snow / Waltz Of The Snowflakes *(University of Minnesota Chamber Singers)*

❷ Act 2 – Scene: Arrival In Fairyland / Festival In Honour Of The Children And Prince Charming / Character Dances (Divertissement): Chocolate (Spanish Dance) / Coffee (Arabian Dance) / Tea (Chinese Dance) / Russian Dance (Trepak) / Dance Of The Toy Flutes / Dance Of The Clowns / Waltz Of The Flowers / Dances Of The Sugar-Plum Fairy And Prince Charming: Pas de Deux / Dance Of Prince Charming / Dance Of The Sugar-Plum Fairy / Coda / Waltz Finale and Apotheosis

MIRACLES 4

Led by William 'Smokey' Robinson, this aptly-named vocal group went on to enjoy superstardom in the '60s. The catchy 'Shop Around' was their first US hit, and almost broke through in the UK.

11 Feb 61   **5**   4   **Shop Around** / Who's Lovin' You *(London HL-9276)*

GUY MITCHELL 36

Popular singer from Detroit born Albert Cernik. Rechristened and groomed by Mitch Miller, he became an international recording star during the '50s, scoring sixteen hits in the UK between 1952 and 1959.

3 Jul 54	**15**	1	**Bob's Yer Uncle** / Got A Hole In My Sweater *(Philips PB-293)*
21 Aug 54	**34**	1	**Man And Woman** *(Rosemary Clooney and Guy Mitchell)* *(Philips PB-255)*
			Flip is 'Good Intentions' by Rosemary Clooney
16 Oct 54	**34**	1	**What Am I Doin' In Kansas City** / My Heaven And Earth *(Philips PB-330)*
8 Jan 55	**52**	1	**GUY MITCHELL** *(Columbia SEG-7513)* **EP**
			Pretty Little Black-Eyed Susie / She Wears Red Feathers / Feet Up / The Roving Kind
5 Feb 55	**47**	1	**Gee, But Ya Gotta Come Home** / I Met The Cutest Little Eyeful *(Philips PB-387)*
20 Aug 55	**1**	7	**Too Late / Let Us Be Sweethearts Over Again** *(Philips PB-487)*
10 Mar 56	**4**	2	**Ninety-Nine Years** / Perfume, Candy And Flowers *(Philips PB-556)*
7 Apr 56	**11**	2	**Ninety-Nine Years** / **Perfume, Candy And Flowers** *(Philips PB-556)* *re-entry*
19 May 56	**11**	2	**Green Grows The Grass** / Solo *(Philips PB-450)*
16 Jun 56	**13**	1	**Green Grows The Grass** / Solo *(Philips PB-450)* *re-entry*
1 Sep 56	**9**	2	**Give Me A Carriage With Eight White Horses** / I Used To Hate Ya *(Philips PB-610)*
17 Nov 56	**11**	1	**I'd Like To Say A Few Words About Texas** / Finders Keepers *(Philips PB-635)*
13 Jul 57	**1**	2	★ **Sweet Stuff** / **In The Middle Of A Dark, Dark Night** *(Philips PB-712)*
28 Jun 58	**14**	1	**Hangin' Around** / Honey Brown Eyes *(Philips PB-830)*
24 Oct 59	**1**	5	★ **Heartaches By The Number** / Two *(Philips PB-964)*
12 Mar 60	**9**	1	**The Same Old Me** / Build My Gallows High *(Philips PB-998)*
13 Aug 60	**8**	3	**Silver Moon Upon The Golden Sands** / My Shoes Keep Walking Back To You *(Philips PB-1050)*
1 Oct 60	**20**	1	**Silver Moon Upon The Golden Sands** / My Shoes Keep Walking Back To You *(Philips PB-1050)* *re-entry*
3 Dec 60	**9**	1	**One Way Street** / Sunshine Guitar *(Philips PB-1084)*

MODERNAIRES 12

Vocal group who performed with Glenn Miller & His Orchestra. After the bandleader's death in 1944, they recorded vocal versions of several of his instrumental hits including the one below.

11 Dec 54	**12**	7	**New Juke Box Saturday Night** / Bugle Call Rag *(Vogue Coral Q-2035)*
5 Feb 55	**15**	5	**New Juke Box Saturday Night** / Bugle Call Rag *(Vogue Coral Q-2035)* *re-entry*

See also Glenn Miller & His Orchestra

DOMENICO MODUGNO   2

Italian singer, songwriter and actor born in Polignano a Mare near Bari in 1928. His most famous recording was 'Nel blu dipinto di blu' (aka 'Volare'), winner of the 1958 San Remo Music Festival and third-placed in the Eurovision Song Contest that year.

7 Mar 59   **1** 1 ★ **Ciao Ciao Bambina** / Resta Cu'mme *(Oriole CB-1489)*
21 Mar 59 **1** 1 ★ **Ciao Ciao Bambina** / Resta Cu'mme *(Oriole CB-1489)* ***re-entry***

MONOGRAMS   2

King Brothers-style singing trio who had two releases on Parlophone, the first of which only just missed the charts.

7 Feb 59   **1** 2 **The Greatest Mistake Of My Life** / Juke Box Cha Cha
                (Parlophone R-4515)

MONOTONES   6

Black doo-wop sextet from Newark, New Jersey who recorded for Chess Records in Chicago.

31 May 58 **16** 1 **Book Of Love** / You Never Loved Me *(London HLM-8625)*
14 Jun 58   **2** 3 **Book Of Love** / You Never Loved Me *(London HLM-8625)*
                1st re-entry
12 Jul 58   **3** 2 **Book Of Love** / You Never Loved Me *(London HLM-8625)*
                2nd re-entry

MARILYN MONROE   2

Hollywood's most famous celebrity, the talented but tragic Norma Jeane Mortenson, who died in mysterious circumstances at the age 36 from an overdose of barbiturates.

6 Nov 54 **33** 1 **The River Of No Return** / I'm Gonna File My Claim *(H.M.V. B-10723)*
29 Aug 59 **10** 1 **I Wanna Be Loved By You** / I'm Thru' With Love *(London HLT-8862)*

VAUGHN MONROE   6

Popular singer, trumpeter and bandleader of the '40s and '50s born in Akron, Ohio in 1911. He had several chart-toppers in the USA including 'My Devotion', 'Ballerina' and 'Riders In The Sky'.

9 Oct 54 **15** 2 **They Were Doin' The Mambo** / Mister Sandman *(H.M.V. B-10751)*
30 Oct 54 **26** 1 **They Were Doin' The Mambo** / Mister Sandman *(H.M.V. B-10751)*
                1st re-entry
4 Dec 54 **58** 1 **They Were Doin' The Mambo** / Mister Sandman *(H.M.V. B-10751)*
                2nd re-entry
26 Nov 55 **14** 2 **Black Denim Trousers And Motorcycle Boots** / All By Myself
                (H.M.V. POP-122)

LOU MONTE   3

Singer born Louis Scaglione in New York in 1917. He is chiefly remembered for recording several Italian-themed novelties in the late '50s/early '60s, most notably 1962's 'Pepino The Italian Mouse'.

19 Apr 58 **13** 1 **Lazy Mary** / Angelique-O *(R.C.A. RCA-1048)*
17 May 58 **21** 1 **Lazy Mary** / Angelique-O *(R.C.A. RCA-1048)* ***re-entry***
26 Dec 59 **13** 1 **Santa Nicola** / All Because It's Christmas *(R.C.A. RCA-1161)*

CARLOS MONTOYA   1

Prominent Spanish flamenco guitarist born in Madrid in 1903.

27 Nov 54 **50** 1 **PLAYS IN A FIESTA FLAMENCA** *(Nixa SLPY-140)* **LP**
                Bulerias / Fandangos / Sevillanas / Alegrias / Saleares

JAMES MOODY SEXTET   1

Jazz saxophonist and flautist born in Savannah, Georgia in 1925. In 1948, he relocated to Europe for three years, during which time he recorded 'Moody's Mood For Love', the inspired improvisation on 'I'm In The Mood For Love' that was to become his enduring anthem.

11 Sep 54 **29** 1 **Lester Leaps In** / Indiana *(Esquire 10-386)*

ART MOONEY & His Orchestra 1

Singing bandleader from Lowell, Massachusetts. 'Honey Babe', from the film 'Battle Cry' (1955), was his fourth million-seller.

17 Sep 55   **19**   1   **Honey Babe** *(Vocal: Chorus)* / No Regrets *(Vocal: The Cloverleafs)*
(M.G.M. MGM-833)

SEAN MOONEY & TRIO 2

Popular baritone from Dublin.

21 Jul 56   **4**   2   **If We Only Had Old Ireland Over Here** / Are You There Moriarty
(H.M.V. POP-230)

MERRILL MOORE 10

Two-fisted country boogie pianist from Algona, Iowa highly rated by fans of the Jerry Lee Lewis school of playing.

11 Sep 54   **23**   1   **Bell Bottom Boogie** / The House Of Blue Lights *(Capitol CL-14057)*
18 Dec 54   **30**   2   **The House Of Blue Lights** / **Bell Bottom Boogie** *(Capitol CL-14057)*
1st re-entry (flipped)
8 Jan 55   **23**   2   **The House Of Blue Lights** / Bell Bottom Boogie *(Capitol CL-14057)*
2nd re-entry
5 Nov 55   **16**   1   **Five Foot Two, Eyes Of Blue** / Hard Top Race *(Capitol CL-14369)*
3 Dec 55   **10**   2   **Five Foot Two, Eyes Of Blue** / Hard Top Race *(Capitol CL-14369)*
1st re-entry
24 Dec 55   **24**   1   **Five Foot Two, Eyes Of Blue** / Hard Top Race *(Capitol CL-14369)*
2nd re-entry
21 Jan 56   **17**   1   **Five Foot Two, Eyes Of Blue** / Hard Top Race *(Capitol CL-14369)*
3rd re-entry

JANE MORGAN 14

Singer and actress born Florence Currier in Newton, Massachusetts in 1924. Unusually, she began her career in France after being offered a nightclub residency there in 1948, but returned to the States in 1954 and became a successful recording artist.

14 Sep 57   **13**   1   **Fascination** *(Jane Morgan with the Troubadours)* /
Why Don't They Leave Us Alone *(Jane Morgan) (London HLR-8468)*
14 Mar 59   **3**   2   ★ **If Only I Could Live My Life Again** / To Love And Be Loved
(London HLR-8810)
4 Apr 59   **2**   3   ★ **If Only I Could Live My Life Again** / To Love And Be Loved
(London HLR-8810) **1st re-entry**
2 May 59   **11**   2   ★ **If Only I Could Live My Life Again** / To Love And Be Loved
(London HLR-8810) **2nd re-entry**
29 Aug 59   **2**   4   **I Can't Begin To Tell You** / With Open Arms *(London HLR-8925)*
4 Jun 60   **16**   1   ★ **Romantica** / I Am A Heart *(London HLR-9120)*
26 Nov 60   **25**   1   **Lord And Master** / Where's The Boy *(London HLR-9210)*

JAYE P. MORGAN 2

Singer and actress born Mary Morgan in Mancos, Colorado in 1931. She was a frequent guest on mid-'50s TV variety shows and also a frequent US chart entrant.

21 Aug 54   **14**   2   **Just A Gigolo** / Wasted Tears *(London L-1212)*

KEN MORRIS 4

Pianist husband of British singer Joan Savage. He died of a brain tumour in 1968, aged just 46.

3 Oct 59   **9**   1   **Copper Knob** / Riviera *(H.M.V. POP-647)*
17 Oct 59   **3**   3   **Copper Knob** / Riviera *(H.M.V. POP-647)* **re-entry**

ELLA MAE MORSE 4

Versatile Texan singer from Mansfield, Texas who sang in a variety of styles including jazz, pop, country and R&B, yet somehow never achieved the star status she deserved.

| 22 Oct 55 | **7** | 2 | **Seventeen** / Piddly Patter Song *(Capitol CL-14362)* |
| 12 Nov 55 | **24** | 2 | **Seventeen** / Piddly Patter Song *(Capitol CL-14362)* ***re-entry*** |

BENNIE MOTEN & HIS KANSAS CITY ORCHESTRA 1

Influential jazz bandleader born in Kansas City, Missouri in 1894. He died in 1935 at the age of 40 following a failed tonsillectomy operation. His pianist, Count Basie, then set up his own orchestra, recruiting many of the great musicians in Moten's band.

| 4 Dec 54 | **17** | 1 | **KAY CEE JAZZ** *(H.M.V. DLP-1057)* **LP** |
| | | | South / Harmony Blues / She's No Trouble / Get Low Down Blues / Kansas City Shuffle / The New Tulsa Blues / Thick Lip Stomp / Pass Out Lightly / Ding-Dong Blues / Moten Stomp |

MUDLARKS 5

Singing siblings Jeff, Fred and Mary Mudd from Luton specialised in upbeat pop novelties like 'Lollipop' and 'Book Of Love', but were soon eclipsed by wilder rock'n'roll acts.

12 Apr 58	**6**	2	★ **Lollipop** / Young Dove's Calling *(Columbia DB-4099)*
31 May 58	**8**	1	★ **Book Of Love** / Yea, Yea *(Columbia DB-4133)*
29 Aug 59	**5**	1	**Waterloo** / Mary *(Columbia DB-4331)*
5 Mar 60	**12**	1	**Candy** / Never Marry A Fishmonger *(Columbia DB-4417)*

WERNER MÜLLER & His Orchestra 1

Well-known Berlin-born trombonist, composer and orchestra leader who occasionally recorded under pseudonyms like Ricardo Santos or Enrico Leandros.

| 21 Mar 59 | **10** | 1 | **Take Me Dreaming** / Tristesse Dance *(Oriole CB-1487)* |
| | | | *Both sides as by Enrico Leandros & His Orchestra* |

MOON MULLICAN 1

The king of hillbilly piano players, born Aubrey Mullican on a farm in Texas in 1909. He was a major influence on Jim Reeves, Hank Williams, Bill Haley and especially Jerry Lee Lewis.

| 18 Aug 56 | **9** | 1 | **Honolulu Rock-A-Roll-A** / Seven Nights To Rock *(Parlophone R-4195)* |
| | | | *Both sides by Moon Mullican with Boyd Bennett & His Rockets* |

See also Boyd Bennett & His Rockets

GERRY MULLIGAN QUARTET 39

Prominent baritone saxophonist of the cool jazz persuasion, born in New York in 1927.

7 Aug 54	**2**	3	**Swing House** / I May Be Wrong *(Vogue V-2258)*
7 Aug 54	**7**	1	**THE GERRY MULLIGAN QUARTET (VOL. 1)** *(Vogue EPV-1001)* **EP**
			I'm Beginning To See The Light / Love Me Or Leave Me / Tea For Two / Nearness Of You
21 Aug 54	**7**	1	**THE GERRY MULLIGAN QUARTET (VOL. 1)** *(Vogue EPV-1001)* **EP**
			1st re-entry
4 Sep 54	**6**	2	**THE GERRY MULLIGAN QUARTET (VOL. 4)** *(Vogue LDE-083)* **LP**
			I May Be Wrong / I'm Beginning To See The Light / The Nearness Of You / Tea For Two / Theme Song / Love Me Or Leave Me / Jeru / Darn That Dream / Swing House / Theme Song
4 Sep 54	**6**	2	**Jeru** / Love Me Or Leave Me *(Vogue V-2259)*
4 Sep 54	**7**	2	**GENE NORMAN PRESENTS THE GERRY MULLIGAN QUARTET** *(Vogue LDE-075)* **LP**
			Varsity Drag / Swing House / Love Me Or Leave Me / Half Nelson / Speak Low / Ladybird
25 Sep 54	**9**	3	**Love Me Or Leave Me** / Jeru *(Vogue V-2259)* ***re-entry (flipped)***
25 Sep 54	**19**	3	**Swing House** / I May Be Wrong *(Vogue V-2258)* ***re-entry***

25 Sep 54	**25**	1	THE GERRY MULLIGAN QUARTET (VOL. 2) *(Vogue EPV-1017)* **EP**

25 Sep 54   **25**   1   **THE GERRY MULLIGAN QUARTET (VOL. 2)** *(Vogue EPV-1017)* **EP**
Bernie's Tune / Walkin' Shoes / Nights At The Turntable / Lullaby Of The Leaves

2 Oct 54   **22**   2   **Darn That Dream** / **I'm Beginning To See The Light** *(Vogue V-2257)*

16 Oct 54   **26**   2   **The Nearness Of You** / **Tea For Two** *(Vogue V-2279)*

13 Nov 54   **20**   2   **THE GERRY MULLIGAN QUARTET (VOL. 1)** *(Vogue EPV-1001)* **EP**
2nd re-entry

11 Dec 54   **39**   1   **Bark For Barksdale** / Moonlight In Vermont *(Vogue V-2260)*

8 Jan 55   **26**   1   **THE GERRY MULLIGAN QUARTET (VOL. 2)** *(Vogue LDE-30)* **LP**
Carioca / Line For Lyons / My Funny Valentine / Bark For Barksdale / Turnstile /
The Lady Is A Tramp / Moonlight In Vermont / Limelight

15 Jan 55   **48**   1   **Lady Be Good** /
I Can't Believe That You're In Love With Me *(Vogue V-2305)*
Both sides by Gerry Mulligan Quartet with Lee Konitz

22 Jan 55   **28**   1   **Nights At The Turntable** / Frenesi *(Vogue V-2157)*

22 Jan 55   **31**   3   **Bark For Barksdale** / Moonlight In Vermont *(Vogue V-2260)* ***re-entry***

22 Jan 55   **50**   1   **THE GERRY MULLIGAN QUARTET (VOL. 2)** *(Vogue EPV-1017)* **EP**
re-entry

22 Jan 55   **55**   1   **Walkin' Shoes** / Lullaby Of The Leaves *(Vogue V-2225)*

5 Feb 55   **13**   2   **THE GERRY MULLIGAN QUARTET (VOL. 3)** *(Vogue EPV-1023)* **EP**
Gerry Mulligan Quartet with Lee Konitz
I Can't Believe That You're In Love With Me / Sextet / Lover Man / Lady Be Good

5 Feb 55   **14**   1   **Nights At The Turntable** / Frenesi *(Vogue V-2157)* ***re-entry***

5 Feb 55   **27**   1   **THE GERRY MULLIGAN QUARTET** *(Vogue EPV-1200)* **EP**
The Varsity Drag / Half Nelson / Speak Low / Ladybird

5 Mar 55   **27**   1   **Lady Be Good** / I Can't Believe That You're In Love With Me
(Vogue V-2305) ***re-entry***

26 Sep 59   **16**   1   **I Want To Live – Theme** / Black Nightgown *(London HLT-8901)*
Both sides by the Gerry Mulligan Combo

JERRY MURAD'S HARMONICATS   3

Harmonica trio led by Turkish-born Murad, who topped the US charts in 1947 with 'Peg O' My Heart' and remained popular throughout the '50s. This bubbler was their last US hit.

11 Feb 61   **6**   3   **Cherry Pink And Apple Blossom White** / Lonely Love
(Philips PB-1105)

BILLY MURE & His Orchestra   1

Pioneering electric guitarist born Sebastian Mure in New York in 1925. As well as recording in his own right, he worked as session musician and arranger for the likes of Della Reese and Bobby Freeman.

23 Apr 60   **2**   1   **Jambalaya** / Kaw-Liga *(Top Rank JAR-344)*

ALEX MURRAY   1

Singer born Alex Wharton in Scunthorpe in 1939. Originally one half of the Most Brothers duo, he went solo in 1959 when his partner, Mickie Most, decamped to South Africa in pursuit of a love interest. After briefly trying his hand at acting, he moved into A&R and record production.

27 Feb 60   **14**   1   **Teen Angel** / Paper Doll *(Decca F-11203)*

RUBY MURRAY   35

Colleen from Belfast who joined BBC TV's 'Quite Contrary' as resident singer in 1954 and became one of the biggest stars in the country. At one point during 1955 she had five singles in the UK Top 20 at the same time – an extraordinary achievement.

27 Nov 54   **2**   1   ★ **Heartbeat** / He's A Pal Of Mine *(Columbia DB-3542)*

26 Feb 55   **6**   2   **Goin' Co'tin'** *(Ronnie Harris, Diana Decker, Ray Burns and Ruby Murray)* /
Spring, Spring, Spring *(Ruby Murray, Ray Burns, Diana Decker and
Ronnie Harris) (Columbia DB-3567)*

30 Apr 55   **16**   3   **Spring, Spring, Spring** *(Ruby Murray, Ray Burns, Diana Decker and
Ronnie Harris)* / **Goin' Co'tin'** *(Ronnie Harris, Diana Decker, Ray
Burns and Ruby Murray) (Columbia DB-3567)* ***re-entry (flipped)***

14 May 55	2	3	★ **Evermore** / Bambino *(Columbia DB-3617)*
18 Jun 55	7	2	★ **Evermore** / Bambino *(Columbia DB-3617)* *re-entry*
17 Sep 55	4	4	★ **I'll Come When You Call** / It's The Irish In Me *(Columbia DB-3643)*
26 Nov 55	19	2	★ **The Very First Christmas Of All** / Slowly With Feeling *(Columbia DB-3680)*
24 Dec 55	28	1	**WHEN IRISH EYES ARE SMILING** *(Columbia 33S-1079)* 🅛🅟

When Irish Eyes Are Smiling / It's A Great Day For The Irish / The Mountains Of Mourne / If You're Irish Come Into The Parlour / Galway Bay / Too-Ra-Loo-Ra-Loo-Ral / Dear Old Donegal / How Can You Buy Killarney? / Phil The Fluter's Ball / Danny Boy

7 Apr 56	19	1	**I Know I'm Home** / Please Hold Me Tightly *(Columbia DB-3750)*
14 Apr 56	14	1	**Make Him Jealous** / For Now, For Ever *(Columbia DB-3718)*
14 Jul 56	3	2	★ **You Are My First Love** / Honestly, I Do *(Columbia DB-3770)*
18 Aug 56	2	1	★ **You Are My First Love** / Honestly, I Do *(Columbia DB-3770)* *re-entry*
15 Dec 56	5	3	**True Love** / Knock On Any Door *(Columbia DB-3849)*
27 Apr 57	8	2	**Heart** / From The First Hello – To The Last Goodbye *(Columbia DB-3911)*

Labels state 'All royalties due to Ruby Murray from this record will be paid to the Horder Centres for Arthritics.'

1 Jun 57	5	1	**Mr. Wonderful** / Pretty, Pretty *(Columbia DB-3933)*
15 Jun 57	5	1	**Mr. Wonderful** / Pretty, Pretty *(Columbia DB-3933)* *1st re-entry*
6 Jul 57	6	1	**Mr. Wonderful** / Pretty, Pretty *(Columbia DB-3933)* *2nd re-entry*
18 Oct 58	3	1	★ **Real Love** / Little One *(Columbia DB-4192)*
22 Nov 58	3	3	★ **Real Love** / Little One *(Columbia DB-4192)* *re-entry*

MYSTICS   1

Italian American soft harmony doo-wop quintet from Brooklyn, New York.

| 22 Aug 59 | 9 | 1 | **Hushabye** / Adam And Eve *(H.M.V. POP-646)* |

N.B.C. SYMPHONY ORCHESTRA, *cond.* Arturo Toscanini   1

Orchestra established in 1937 by David Sarnoff, chairman of RCA (the owners of NBC radio). It was specially created for the celebrated conductor Arturo Toscanini, who stayed in post for 17 years. Much to his distress, the orchestra was wound up following his retirement in April 1954.

| 27 Nov 54 | 65 | 1 | **BEETHOVEN – SYMPHONY NO. 5 IN C MINOR, OP. 67** *(H.M.V. DB-3822/3823/3824/3825)* 78x4 |

❶ First Movement: Allegro Con Brio (Part 1 and Conclusion)
❷ Second Movement: Andante Con Moto (Part 1 and Conclusion)
❸ Third Movement: Allegro (Part 1 and Conclusion) / 4th Movement: Allegro (Part 1)
❹ Fouth Movement: Allegro (Part 2 and Conclusion)

RICKY NELSON   35

Teen idol and actor born Eric Nelson in Teaneck, New Jersey in 1940. Thanks to regular exposure in his parents' TV sitcom, 'Ozzie & Harriet', he became a rock'n'roll star.

30 Nov 57	1	6	**Be-Bop Baby** / Have I Told You Lately That I Love You *(London HLP-8499)*
8 Feb 58	1	2	★ **Stood Up** / Waitin' In School *(London HLP-8542)*
19 Apr 58	5	1	**Believe What You Say** / My Bucket's Got A Hole In It *(London HLP-8594)*
10 May 58	1	4	**Believe What You Say** / My Bucket's Got A Hole In It *(London HLP-8594)* *re-entry*
9 Aug 58	1	2	★ **Poor Little Fool** / Don't Leave Me This Way *(London HLP-8670)*
1 Nov 58	4	1	★ **Someday** / **I Got A Feeling** *(London HLP-8732)*
6 Dec 58	8	1	**Lonesome Town** / My Babe *(London HLP-8738)*
20 Dec 58	5	2	**Lonesome Town** / My Babe *(London HLP-8738)* *1st re-entry*
10 Jan 59	6	1	**Lonesome Town** / My Babe *(London HLP-8738)* *2nd re-entry*
24 Jan 59	1	3	**Lonesome Town** / My Babe *(London HLP-8738)* *3rd re-entry*
21 Mar 59	7	1	★ **It's Late** / **Never Be Anyone Else But You** *(London HLP-8817)*
4 Apr 59	7	2	★ **It's Late** / **Never Be Anyone Else But You** *(London HLP-8817)* *re-entry*

9 Jan 60	1	1	★ **I Wanna Be Loved** / **Mighty Good** *(London HLP-9021)*
21 May 60	1	2	★ **Young Emotions** / Right By My Side *(London HLP-9121)*
11 Jun 60	8	1	★ **Young Emotions** / Right By My Side *(London HLP-9121)* *re-entry*
1 Oct 60	20	1	**Yes, Sir, That's My Baby** / I'm Not Afraid *(London HLP-9188)*
21 Jan 61	8	4	**Milk Cow Blues** / You Are The Only One *(London HLP-9260)*

SANDY NELSON   5

Sandy Nelson from Santa Monica, California built up a reputation as a West Coast session drummer before carving out a career for himself with a succession of drum-led instrumental hits.

24 Oct 59	13	1	★ **Teen Beat** / Big Jump *(Top Rank JAR-197)*
19 Dec 59	7	2	**Drum Party** / The Big Noise From Winnetka *(London HLP-9015)*
9 Jan 60	6	1	**Drum Party** / The Big Noise From Winnetka *(London HLP-9015)* **1st re-entry**
30 Jan 60	5	1	**Drum Party** / The Big Noise From Winnetka *(London HLP-9015)* **2nd re-entry**

NERVOUS NORVUS   2

Nervous Norvus was the alter ego of a 45-year-old jive-talking Californian truck driver named Jimmy Drake, whose ghoulish record about a succession of car crashes, 'Transfusion', shot into the US Top Ten in 1956. The similar-sounding but less gruesome 'Ape Call' was the follow-up.

| 23 Mar 57 | 12 | 2 | **Ape Call** / Wild Dog Of Kentucky *(London HLD-8338)* |

ANTHONY NEWLEY   8

One of Britain's most distinctive talents, actor, singer and songwriter Anthony Newley made a success of just about everything he touched. From humble beginnings in London's East End, he rose to become a top nightclub entertainer with sellout appearances in Las Vegas.

18 Apr 59	8	2	★ **IDLE ON PARADE [OST]** *(Decca DFE-6566)* **EP**
			I've Waited So Long / Idle Rock-A-Boogie / Idle On Parade / Sat'day Night Rock-A-Boogie
25 Apr 59	15	1	★ **I've Waited So Long** / Sat'day Night Rock-A-Boogie *(Decca F-11127)*
3 Oct 59	4	2	**Someone To Love** / It's All Over *(Decca F-11163)*
9 Jan 60	2	1	★ **Why** / Anything You Wanna Do *(Decca F-11194)*
9 Apr 60	7	1	**Someone To Love** / It's All Over *(Decca F-11163)* *re-entry*
11 Mar 61	8	1	★ **And The Heavens Cried** / Lonely Boy And Pretty Girl *(Decca F-11331)*

JOSEPH NEWMAN

See Paul Quinichette etc.

JOY NICHOLS   2

Australian singer, actress and comedienne who came to Britain in 1946. She became popular via her appearances on the BBC radio show 'Take It From Here', but moved to the USA in 1953 after marrying American show singer Wally Peterson.

15 Jan 55	20	1	**JOY NICHOLS** *(Parlophone GEP-8509)* **EP**
			The Little Red Monkey *(Joy Nichols, Dick Bentley and Jimmy Edwards)* / The Inchworm *(Joy Nichols)* / The Hippopotamus Song *(Joy Nichols)* / Froggie And The Catfish *(Joy Nichols)*
16 Jul 55	18	1	**Don't Worry** / I've Got A Feelin' You're Foolin' *(Mercury MB-3224)*

LENNIE NIEHAUS   1

West Coast jazz alto saxophonist and composer born in St. Louis, Missouri in 1929.

| 2 Jul 55 | 28 | 1 | **VOLUME 1: THE QUINTET** *(Vogue LDC-120)* **LP** |
| | | | I Remember You / Whose Blues / Prime Rib / Inside Out / You Stepped Out Of A Dream / I'll Take Romance / Day By Day / Bottoms Up |

NILSSON TWINS 1

Teenage twins Elsa and Eileen Nilsson from Wichita, Kansas were regulars on Spike Jones' live shows. They recorded a handful of singles, but failed to find chart success.

16 Mar 57 **18** 1 **Rain On My Window** / I Dance When I Walk *(Capitol CL-14698)*

NINA & FREDERIK 2

Danish/Dutch singing duo Nina Magdelene Møller-Hasselbalch and Frederik, Baron van Pallandt. They achieved international fame in the early '60s with their brand of easy-listening folk, calypso and pop songs.

15 Aug 59 **13** 1 ★ **Listen To The Ocean** / I Would Amor Her *(Columbia DB-4332)*
6 Aug 60 **11** 1 **Carnival** / My Home Town *(Columbia DB-4486)*

GENE NORMAN'S 'JUST JAZZ' 10

Inspired by the success of Norman Granz' 'Jazz At The Philharmonic' concerts (qv), Los Angeles-based deejay Gene Norman began promoting his own 'Just Jazz' concerts in 1947. As with Granz, these featured ad hoc ensembles of top jazz talent and were recorded. The line-up on 'One O'Clock Jump' and 'Three O'Clock Jump' includes Irving Ashby, Red Callender, Benny Carter, Vic Dickenson, Erroll Garner, Wardell Gray, Howard McGhee and Jackie Mills. 'Blue Lou' features Wardell Gray and Erroll Garner supported by Irving Ashby, Red Callender and Jackie Mills. 'Groovin' High' features Wardell Gray and Howard McGhee supported by Red Callender, Sonny Criss, Dodo Marmorosa and Jackie Mills.

4 Sep 54 **8** 2 **One O'Clock Jump** / Two O'Clock Jump *(Vogue V-2271)*
4 Sep 54 **16** 1 **Three O'Clock Jump** / Four O'Clock Jump *(Vogue V-2272)*
9 Oct 54 **18** 1 **One O'Clock Jump** / Two O'Clock Jump *(Vogue V-2271)*
    re-entry
20 Nov 54 **11** 2 **GENE NORMAN PRESENTS 'JUST JAZZ'** *(Vogue EPV-1002)* **EP**
    Blue Lou *(feat. Wardell Gray and Erroll Garner)* / Groovin' High *(feat. Wardell Gray and Howard McGhee)*
11 Dec 54 **19** 4 **GENE NORMAN PRESENTS 'JUST JAZZ'** *(Vogue EPV-1002)* **EP**
    re-entry

See also Wardell Gray and Dexter Gordon
    Lionel Hampton
    Gerry Mulligan Quartet
    Kay Starr with Barney Kessel
    Art Tatum
    Charlie Ventura Septet

MONTY NORMAN 3

London-born singer who found greater success as a composer – most famously with the iconic 'James Bond Theme'.

7 Jan 56 **6** 1 **The Shifting, Whispering Sands** / Bonnie Blue Gal *(H.M.V. POP-145)*
21 Jan 56 **22** 1 **The Shifting, Whispering Sands** / Bonnie Blue Gal *(H.M.V. POP-145)*
    re-entry
19 Jan 57 **5** 1 **The Garden Of Eden** / Priscilla *(H.M.V. POP-281)*

HUGH O'BRIAN 1

Rugged actor born Hugh Krampe in Rochester, New York in 1925. He came to prominence as the star of ABC-TV's western series 'The Life and Legend of Wyatt Earp' (1955-60).

24 Jan 59 **9** 1 **The Legend Of Wyatt Earp** / Down In The Meadow *(H.M.V. POP-539)*

DONALD O'CONNOR 1

Dancer, singer and actor born in Chicago in 1925. He appeared in many films, most notably 'Singin' In The Rain' (1952) and the 'Francis the Talking Mule' series (1950-56).

14 Aug 54 **26** 1 **Back In The Old Routine** / If There's Anybody Here *(Brunswick 05304)*
    Both sides by Bing Crosby and Donald O'Connor

MYLES O'CONNOR   3

Obscure Irish singer who recorded two singles for Beltona.

30 Jun 56	**6**	1	**Kevin Barry** / Ireland, Live On *(Beltona BE-2640)*
11 Aug 56	**9**	1	**Kevin Barry** / Ireland, Live On *(Beltona BE-2640)* ***1st re-entry***
9 Mar 57	**16**	1	**Kevin Barry** / Ireland, Live On *(Beltona BE-2640)* ***2nd re-entry***

JOHNNY OCTOBER   1

Teen idol born John Ottobre in Philadelphia in 1937.

24 Oct 59	**11**	1	**Growin' Prettier** / Young And In Love *(Capitol CL-15070)*

ANITA O'DAY   3

Superb jazz singer born Anita Belle Colton in Kansas City, Missouri in 1919. She worked with greats like Gene Krupa, Woody Herman, Stan Kenton and Count Basie, but also suffered career setbacks due to her long-standing heroin addiction.

17 Dec 60	**7**	3	**Tea For Two** / Sweet Georgia Brown *(H.M.V. POP-821)*

PATRICK O'HAGAN   12

Irish tenor born Charles Sherrard in Londonderry in 1924. His son is the Irish 1980 and 1987 Eurovision Song Contest winner Johnny Logan (Seán Sherrard).

6 Nov 54	**26**	2	**The Whistling Gypsy** / Cottage By The Sea *(Decca (Irish Series) F-18184)*
27 Nov 54	**22**	2	**The Whistling Gypsy** / Cottage By The Sea *(Decca (Irish Series) F-18184)* ***1st re-entry***
15 Jan 55	**15**	3	**The Wild Colonial Boy** / An Echo Of Ireland *(Decca F-9536)*
29 Jan 55	**24**	5	**The Whistling Gypsy** / Cottage By The Sea *(Decca (Irish Series) F-18184)* ***2nd re-entry***

OLYMPICS   2

Black doo-wop quintet from Los Angeles who specialised in upbeat R&B novelties and energetic dance numbers like the one below.

31 Dec 60	**9**	1	★ <u>**I Wish I Could Shimmy Like My Sister Kate**</u> / Workin' Hard *(Vogue Pop V-9174)*
14 Jan 61	**1**	1	★ <u>**I Wish I Could Shimmy Like My Sister Kate**</u> / Workin' Hard *(Vogue Pop V-9174)* ***re-entry***

JOHNNY O'NEILL   2

Country singer/guitarist from Austin, Texas. His 1959 recording of 'Wagon Train' was the second incarnation of the theme song used for the popular TV western series. Robert Horton, who played the part of scout Flint McCullough, also recorded a version (see entry).

25 Apr 59	**8**	1	**Wagon Train** / Somebody, Just Like You *(R.C.A. RCA-1114)*
23 May 59	**8**	1	**Wagon Train** / Somebody, Just Like You *(R.C.A. RCA-1114)* ***re-entry***

ROY ORBISON   2

Singer/songwriter from Vernon, Texas renowned for his plaintive ballads and emotional singing style. Sadly, he succumbed to a heart attack in 1988, aged just 52.

9 Jul 60	**9**	1	★ <u>**Only The Lonely**</u> / Here Comes That Song Again *(London HLU-9149)*
22 Oct 60	**16**	1	★ <u>**Blue Angel**</u> / Today's Teardrops *(London HLU-9207)*

ORCHESTRA DEI POMMERIGGI MUSICALI DI MILANO

See Fernando Corena

18 Dec 54 **31** 2 **COLE PORTER'S CAN-CAN** *(Capitol LCT-6010)* **LP**
Introduction – Maidens Typical Of France *(Laundresses)* / I'll Never Give Anything
Away *(Lilo and Laundresses)* / Quadrille *(Orchestra)* / C'Est Magnifique *(Lilo and
Peter Cookson)* / Come Along With Me *(Erik Rhodes and Hans Conreid)* / Live
And Let Live *(Lilo)* / I Am In Love *(Peter Cookson)* / If You Loved Me Truly *(Gwen
Verdon, Peter Cookson, Artists, Girls and Model)* / Montmart *(Ensemble, Peter
Cookson)* / Allez-Vous-En, Go Away *(Lilo)* / Never, Never Be An Artist *(Hans
Conreid, Artists and Model)* / It's All Right With Me *(Peter Cookson)* / Every Man
Is A Stupid Man *(Lilo)* / I Love Paris *(Lilo)* / Can-Can *(Lilo and Ensemble)*

2 Apr 55 **15** 1 **WONDERFUL TOWN** *(Brunswick LAT-8058)* **LP**
Christopher Street *(Warren Galjour and the Villagers Chorus)* / Ohio *(Rosalind
Russell and Edith Adams)* / One Hundred Easy Ways *(Rosalind Russell)* / What A
Waste *(George Gaynes, Warren Galjour and Albert Linville)* / A Little Bit Of Love
(Edith Adams) / Pass The Football *(Jordan Bentley)* / Conversation Piece *(Rosalind
Russell, Edith Adams, Cris Alexander, George Gaynes and Dort Clark)* / A Quiet
Girl *(George Gaynes)* / Conga! *(Rosalind Russell and the Cadets)* / My Darlin'
Eileen *(Edith Adams, Delbert Anderson and Police)* / Swing! *(Rosalind Russell and
the Villagers Chorus)* / It's Love *(Edith Adams, George Gaynes and the Villagers
Chorus)* / Ballet At The Village Vortex *(Orchestra)* / Wrong Note Rag *(Rosalind
Russell, Edith Adams and the Villagers Chorus)*

30 Apr 55 **2** 10 **KISMET** *(Philips BBL-7023)* **LP**
Overture *(Orchestra)* / Sands Of Time *(Richard Oneto)* / Rhymes Have I *(Alfred
Drake and Doretta Morrow)* / Fate *(Alfred Drake)* / Bazaar Of The Caravans
(Chorus) / Not Since Nineveh *(Joan Diener, Henry Calvin and Chorus)* / Baubles,
Bangles And Beads *(Doretta Morrow, Richard Oneto and Chorus)* / Stranger In
Paradise *(Doretta Morrow and Richard Kiley)* / He's In Love! *(Hal Hackett and
Chorus)* / Gesticulate *(Alfred Drake, Joan Diener, Henry Calvin and Chorus)* /
Night Of My Nights *(Richard Kiley and Chorus)* / Was I Wazir? *(Henry Calvin and
Chorus)* / Rahadlakum *(Alfred Drake, Joan Diener, Lucy Andonian and Chorus)* /
And This Is My Beloved *(Alfred Drake, Doretta Morrow, Richard Kiley and Henry
Calvin)* / The Olive Tree *(Alfred Drake)* / Zubbediya, Samaris' Dance *(Lucy
Andonian and Chorus)* / Finale – Sands Of Time *(Alfred Drake, Doretta Morrow,
Richard Kiley and Chorus)*

16 Jul 55 **12** 4 **KISMET** *(Philips BBL-7023)* **LP** *1st re-entry*

8 Oct 55 **8** 2 **THE PAJAMA GAME** *(Philips BBL-7050)* **LP**
Overture *(Orchestra)* / The Pajama Game *(Eddie Foy Jr.)* / Racing With The Clock
(Eddie Foy Jr. and Ensemble) / A New Town Is A Blue Town *(John Raitt)* / I'm Not At
All In Love *(Janis Paige and Girls)* / I'll Never Be Jealous Again *(Eddie Foy Jr. and
Reta Shaw)* / Hey There *(John Raitt)* / Her Is *(Stanley Prager and Carol Haney)* /
Once-A-Year Day *(John Raitt, Janis Paige and Ensemble)* / Small Talk *(John Raitt
and Janis Paige)* / There Once Was A Man *(John Raitt and Janis Paige)* / Steam
Heat *(Carol Haney, Buzz Miller and Peter Gennaro)* / Think Of The Time I Save
(Eddie Foy Jr. and Girls) / Hernando's Hideaway *(Carol Haney and Ensemble)* / 7½
cents *(Janis Paige, Stanley Prager and Ensemble)*

5 Nov 55 **24** 1 **THE PAJAMA GAME** *(Philips BBL-7050)* **LP** *1st re-entry*

19 Nov 55 **11** 8 **THE PAJAMA GAME** *(Philips BBL-7050)* **LP** *2nd re-entry*

7 Jan 56 **10** 2 **NEW FACES** *(H.M.V. 7EG-8134)* **EP**
Lucky Pierre *(Robert Clary, Virginia De Luce, Rosemary O'Reilly, Pat Hammerlee
and Bill Mullikin)* / I'm In Love With Miss Logan *(Virginia De Luce, Robert Clary with
Rosemary O'Reilly and Joe Lautner)* / Bal Petit Bal *(Robert Clary and Eartha Kitt)* /
Lizzie Borden *(Joe Lautner, Bill Mullikin, Paul Lynde, Pat Hammerlee and
Company)*

21 Jan 56   **13**   1   **THE PAJAMA GAME** *(Philips BBL-7050)* 🆑 *3rd re-entry*

19 May 56   **12**   1   **KISMET** *(Philips BBL-7023)* 🆑 *2nd re-entry*

23 Jun 56   **18**   1   **KISMET** *(Philips BBL-7023)* 🆑 *3rd re-entry*

29 Mar 58   **15**   1   **THE PAJAMA GAME** *(Philips BBL-7050)* 🆑 *4th re-entry*

9 Aug 58   **3**   2   **MY FAIR LADY (VOL. 1)** *(Philips BBE-12251)* 🆔
Overture *(Orchestra)* / Why Can't The English? *(Rex Harrison)* / Without You *(Julie Andrews)* / I've Grown Accustomed To Her Face *(Rex Harrison)*

ORIGINAL LONDON CAST

19 Jun 54   **7**   2   **WEDDING IN PARIS** *(Parlophone PMD-1011)* 🆑
A Wedding In Paris *(Susan Swinford)* / A Man Is A Man *(Evelyn Laye)* / Always Young *(Anton Walbrook)* / I Have Nothing To Declare *(Jeff Warren and Susan Swinford)* / It Only Took A Moment *(Jeff Warren and Susan Swinford)* / Strike Another Match *(Anton Walbrook)* / I Must Have Been Crazy *(Jeff Warren)* / In The Pink *(Evelyn Laye)*

1 Jan 55   **14**   1   **LOVE FROM JUDY** *(Columbia DX-1853/1854)* 78x2
❶ Introduction *(Chorus)* / Mardi Gras *(Chorus)* / I Never Dream When I'm Asleep *(Jean Carson)* / A Touch Of Voodoo *(Adelaide Hall and Chorus)* / Love From Judy *(Bill O'Connor)* / Daddy Long-Legs *(Jean Carson and Chorus)* / What Do I See In You? *(Johnny Brandon and Audrey Freeman)* / Here We Are *(June Whitfield and Chorus)*
❷ Go And Get Your Old Banjo *(Jean Carson and Chorus)* / Kind To Animals *(Adelaide Hall)* / I Ain't Gonna Marry *(Company)* / My True Love *(Bill O'Connor)* / Dum-Dum-Dum *(June Whitfield and Chorus)* / Love From Judy *(Jean Carson, Bill O'Connor and Full Company)*

5 Mar 55   **6**   1   **SALAD DAYS** *(Oriole MG-20004)* 🆑
The Things That Are Done By A Don *(Company)* / We Said We Wouldn't Look Back *(John Warner and Eleanor Drew)* / Find Yourself Something To Do *(Dorothy Reynolds)* / I Sit In The Sun *(Eleanor Drew)* / Oh Look At Me *(John Warner and Eleanor Drew)* / Hush-Hush *(James Cairncross)* / Out Of Breath *(Company)* / Cleopatra *(James Cairncross)* / It's Easier To Sing *(John Warner, Eleanor Drew and Michael Meacham)* / We're Looking For A Piano *(Company)* / The Time Of My Life *(Eleanor Drew)* / The Saucer Song *(James Cairncross, John Warner and Eleanor Drew)* / Reprise: We Said We Wouldn't Look Back *(John Warner and Eleanor Drew)* – It's Easy To Sing *(Company)* – I Sit In The Sun *(Company)* – We're Looking For A Piano *(Company)* – The Time Of My Life *(Company)* – Oh, Look At Me *(Company)*

16 Apr 55   **5**   2   **SALAD DAYS** *(Oriole MG-20004)* 🆑 *1st re-entry*

7 May 55   **4**   9   **SALAD DAYS** *(Oriole MG-20004)* 🆑 *2nd re-entry*

23 Jul 55   **19**   3   **SALAD DAYS** *(Oriole MG-20004)* 🆑 *3rd re-entry*

21 Apr 56   **13**   1   **SUMMER SONG** *(Philips BBL-7070)* 🆑
Overture *(Orchestra)* / I Loved My Love *(Chorus)* / Just Around The Corner *(Sally Ann Howes and Chorus)* / My Darling Karolka *(Sally Ann Howes)* / Once A Year Is Not Enough *(Bonita Primrose)* / Be She Dark, Be She Fair *(David Hughes and Chorus)* / Cotton Tail *(Edric Connor)* / No-One Told Me *(David Hughes)* / Sing Me A Song *(Chorus)* / Murphy's Pig *(Bonita Primrose and Chorus)* / Saturday Girl *(David Hughes, Sally Ann Howes and Chorus)* / One Boy Sends You A Rose *(Sally Ann Howes and Bonita Primrose)* / Dvorak's Letter Home *(Laurence Naismith)* / Deep Blue Evening *(Edric Connor and Chorus)* / Milli's Wedding *(Edric Connor, Van Atkins, Bonita Primrose and Chorus)* / Summer Song *(Sally Ann Howes and Chorus)* / Small Town Sweetheart *(David Hughes)* / New York '93 *(Chorus)* / I'll Be Remembering *(Sally Ann Howes and Chorus)* / Finale *(Sally Ann Howes and Chorus)*

2 Jun 56　**17**　1　**VOCAL GEMS FROM CAROUSEL** (Columbia SED-5536) **LP**
　　　　　　　　　　Sung by the cast of the Drury Lane Production accompanied by the Drury Lane
　　　　　　　　　　Theatre Orchestra conducted by Reginald Burston: June Is Bustin' Out All Over
　　　　　　　　　　(Marion Ross and Chorus) / Mr. Snow *(Margot Moser, Eric Mattison and Girls'*
　　　　　　　　　　Chorus) / When The Children Are Asleep *(Margot Moser and Eric Mattison)* / If I
　　　　　　　　　　Loved You *(Iva Withers and Stephen Douglass)* / A Real Nice Clambake *(Chorus*
　　　　　　　　　　Ensemble) / Blow High, Blow Low *(Morgan Davies and Male Chorus)* / What's
　　　　　　　　　　The Use Of Wondrin' *(Iva Withers and Girls' Chorus)* / My Little Girl *(Stephen*
　　　　　　　　　　Douglass) / You'll Never Walk Alone *(Marion Ross and Company)*

22 Aug 59　**1**　1　**THE MERMAID THEATRE PRESENTS**
　　　　　　　　　　'LOCK UP YOUR DAUGHTERS' (Decca LK-4320) **LP**
　　　　　　　　　　All's Well *(Robin Wentworth)* / A Proper Man *(Madeleine Newbury and Stephanie*
　　　　　　　　　　Voss) / It Must Be True *(Brendan Barry and John Sharp)* / Red Wine And A Wench
　　　　　　　　　　(Frederick Jaeger and Keith Marsh) / On The Side *(Richard Wordsworth)* / When
　　　　　　　　　　Does The Ravishing Begin *(Hy Hazell)* / Lovely Lover *(Stephanie Voss and Terence*
　　　　　　　　　　Cooper) / Lock Up Your Daughters *(Frederick Jaeger, Keith Marsh and Terence*
　　　　　　　　　　Cooper) / There's A Plot Afoot *(Company)* / Mister Jones *(Richard Wordsworth)* /
　　　　　　　　　　On A Sunny Sunday Morning *(Richard Wordsworth and Stephanie Voss)* / If I'd
　　　　　　　　　　Known You *(Keith Marsh)* / 'Tis Plain To See *(Frederick Jaeger, Stephanie Voss*
　　　　　　　　　　and Chorus) / Kind Fate *(Stephanie Voss, Terence Cooper and Chorus)* / I'll Be
　　　　　　　　　　There *(Hy Hazell and Company)* / Epilogue and Lock Up Your Daughters (Reprise)
　　　　　　　　　　(Stephanie Voss and Company)

ORIGINAL SOUNDTRACK

5 Mar 55　**5**　4　★　**SEVEN BRIDES FOR SEVEN BROTHERS (PART 1)** **EP**
　　　　　　　　　　(M.G.M. MGM-EP-513)
　　　　　　　　　　Bless Yore Beautiful Hide *(Howard Keel)* / Wonderful Wonderful Day *(Jane*
　　　　　　　　　　Powell) / Lament *(Bill Lee and Brothers)* / Goin' Co'tin' *(Jane Powell and Brothers)*

5 Mar 55　**20**　1　**YOUNG AT HEART** (Philips BBR-8040) **LP**
　　　　　　　　　　Till My Love Comes To Me *(Doris Day)* / Ready, Willing And Able *(Doris Day)* / Hold
　　　　　　　　　　Me In Your Arms *(Doris Day)* / You Can Take My Word For It Baby *(Frank Sinatra)* /
　　　　　　　　　　There's A Rising Moon *(Doris Day)* / One For My Baby (And One More For The
　　　　　　　　　　Road) *(Frank Sinatra)* / You My Love *(Doris Day)* / I'm Glad There Is You *(Frank*
　　　　　　　　　　Sinatra)

2 Apr 55　**2**　6　**CARMEN JONES** (H.M.V. CLP-1034) **LP**
　　　　　　　　　　Overture *(Orchestra)* / Opening Medley *(Chorus)* / Dat's Love (Habanera) *(Dorothy*
　　　　　　　　　　Dandridge, partially dubbed by Marilyn Horne) / You Talk Jus' Like My Maw *(LeVern*
　　　　　　　　　　Hutcherson and Olga James) / Dere's A Café On De Corner *(Marilyn Horne)* / Dis
　　　　　　　　　　Flower *(LeVern Hutcherson)* / Beat Out Dat Rhythm On A Drum *(Pearl Bailey)* /
　　　　　　　　　　Stan' Up An' Fight *(Marvin Hayes)* / Whizzin' Away Along De Track *(Marilyn Horne,*
　　　　　　　　　　Joseph E. Crawford, Bernice Peterson, Brock Peters and Pearl Bailey) / Card Song
　　　　　　　　　　(Marilyn Horne, Pearl Bailey and Chorus) / My Joe *(Olga James)* / Duet and Finale
　　　　　　　　　　(LeVern Hutcherson and Marilyn Horne)

23 Apr 55　**21**　2　★　**SEVEN BRIDES FOR SEVEN BROTHERS (PART 1)** **EP**
　　　　　　　　　　(M.G.M. MGM-EP-513) re-entry

28 May 55　**9**　2　**CARMEN JONES** (H.M.V. CLP-1034) **LP** *1st re-entry*

2 Jul 55　**14**　2　**CARMEN JONES** (H.M.V. CLP-1034) **LP** *2nd re-entry*

30 Jul 55　**23**　2　**CARMEN JONES** (H.M.V. CLP-1034) **LP** *3rd re-entry*

26 May 56　**2**　3　★　**CAROUSEL** (Capitol LCT-6105) **LP**
　　　　　　　　　　The Carousel Waltz *(Orchestra)* / You're A Queer One, Julie Jordan *(Shirley Jones*
　　　　　　　　　　and Barbara Ruick) / Mister Snow *(Barbara Ruick)* / If I Loved You *(Shirley Jones*
　　　　　　　　　　and Gordon MacRae) / June Is Bustin' Out All Over *(Claramae Turner, Barbara*

Ruick and Mixed Chorus) / Soliloquy (Gordon MacRae) / Blow High, Blow Low (Cameron Mitchell and Men's Chorus) / When The Children Are Asleep (Barbara Ruick and Robert Rounseville) / A Real Nice Clambake (Barbara Ruick, Claramae Turner, Robert Rounseville, Cameron Mitchell and Mixed Chorus) / Stonecutters Cut It On Stone (Cameron Mitchell and Mixed Chorus) / What's The Use Of Wondrin' (Shirley Jones and Girls' Chorus) / You'll Never Walk Alone (Claramae Turner) / If I Loved You (Reprise) (Gordon MacRae) / You'll Never Walk Alone (Finale) (Shirley Jones and Mixed Chorus)

30 Jun 56   **19**   1   **IT'S GREAT TO BE YOUNG** (Columbia SEG-7639) **EP**
Ray Martin & His Orchestra on all tracks, featured vocalists shown in brackets: It's Great To Be Young / You Are My First Love / Rhythm Is Our Business (Coronets) / Marching Strings / Original Dixieland One Step (John Mills)

15 Sep 56   **10**   1   ★ <u>**THE KING AND I**</u> (Capitol LCT-6108) **LP**
Overture (Orchestra) / I Whistle A Happy Tune (Marni Nixon, Rex Thompson and Chorus) / My Lord And Master (Leona Gordon) / Hello, Young Lovers (Marni Nixon) / The March Of The Siamese Children (Orchestra) / A Puzzlement (Yul Brynner) / Getting To Know You (Marni Nixon and Chorus) / We Kiss In A Shadow (Reuben Fuentes and Leona Gordon) / I Have Dreamed (Leona Gordon and Reuben Fuentes) / Shall I Tell You What I Think Of You? (Marni Nixon) / Something Wonderful (Terry Saunders) / Song Of The King (Yul Brynner and Marni Nixon) / Shall We Dance? (Marni Nixon and Yul Brynner) / Something Wonderful (Finale) (Orchestra and Chorus)

15 Sep 56   **14**   1   **OKLAHOMA! (PART 1)** (Capitol EAP1-595) **EP**
Overture (Orchestra) / Oh, What A Beautiful Mornin' (Gordon MacRae) / All Er Nothin' (Gloria Grahame and Gene Nelson) / Oklahoma (Gordon MacRae, Charlotte Greenwood, James Whitmore, Shirley Jones, Jay C. Flippen and Mixed Chorus)

24 Nov 56   **2**   3   ★ <u>**HIGH SOCIETY**</u> (Capitol LCT-6116) **LP**
High Society Overture (Orchestra) / High Society Calypso (Louis Armstrong & His Band) / Little One (Bing Crosby) / Who Wants To Be A Millionaire (Frank Sinatra and Celeste Holm) / True Love (Bing Crosby and Grace Kelly) / You're Sensational (Frank Sinatra) / I Love You, Samantha (Bing Crosby) / Now You Has Jazz (Bing Crosby and Louis Armstrong) / Well Did You Evah? (Bing Crosby and Frank Sinatra) / Mind If I Make Love To You (Frank Sinatra)

9 Feb 57   **15**   1   **THE KING AND I (PART 2)** (Capitol EAP2-740) **EP**
I Whistle A Happy Tune (Marni Nixon, Rex Thompson and Chorus) / Hello, Young Lovers (Marni Nixon) / Something Wonderful (Terry Saunders) / Song Of The King (Yul Brynner and Marni Nixon)

15 Mar 58   **15**   1   **LES GIRLS / THE PIRATE** (M.G.M. C-763) **LP**
Les Girls: Les Girls (Gene Kelly, Mitzi Gaynor, Kay Kendall and Taina Elg) / You're Just Too, Too! (Gene Kelly and Kay Kendall) / Ca C'est l'Amour (Taina Elg) / Ladies In Waiting (Mitzi Gaynor, Kay Kendall and Taina Elg) / Why Am I So Gone (About That Gal) (Gene Kelly) / The Pirate: Pirate Ballet (Lennie Hayton) / Be A Clown (Judy Garland and Gene Kelly) / Love Of My Life (Judy Garland) / You Can Do No Wrong (Judy Garland) / Nina (Gene Kelly) / Mac The Black (Judy Garland)

26 Apr 58   **17**   1   **APRIL LOVE** (London HA-D-2078) **LP**
Main Title (Lionel Newman) / Clover In The Meadow (Pat Boone) / Tugfire (Lionel Newman) / Give Me A Gentle Girl (Part 1) (Pat Boone) / First Meeting (Lionel Newman) / Give Me A Gentle Girl (Part 2) (Shirley Jones) / April Love (Pat Boone) / Tugfire's Escape (Lionel Newman) / April Love (Pat Boone and Shirley Jones) / The Sulky Race (Lionel Newman) / Do It Yourself (Pat Boone and Shirley Jones) / Lover's Quarrel (Lionel Newman) / Tugfire's Illness (Lionel Newman) / The Bentonville Fair (Pat Boone and Shirley Jones) / Finale (Pat Boone and Shirley Jones)

7 Nov 59 **23** 1 ★ **THE FIVE PENNIES** *(London HA-U-2189)* **LP**
Main Title *(Orchestra)* / The Five Pennies *(Danny Kaye)* / After You've Gone *(Louis Armstrong)* / Bill Bailey, Won't You Please Come Home *(Louis Armstrong)* / Indiana Radio Montage *(Danny Kaye)* / Indiana *(Danny Kaye)* / Good Night, Sleep Tight *(Louis Armstrong)* / Lullaby In Ragtime *(Danny Kaye and Eileen Wilson)* / Battle Hymn Of The Republic *(Red Nichols and Louis Armstrong)* / The Five Pennies Saints *(Louis Armstrong and Danny Kaye)* / College Montage: Washington And Lee Swing *(Orchestra)* – Runnin' Wild *(Orchestra)* – Follow The Leader *(Danny Kaye, Eileen Wilson and Harry Guardino)* / Good Night, Sleep Tight Medley *(Orchestra)* / Just The Blues *(Orchestra)* / Carnival Of Venice *(Danny Kaye)* / The Music Goes 'Round And 'Round *(Danny Kaye and Susan Gordon)* / Wail Of The Winds *(Orchestra)* / Jingle Bells *(Danny Kaye)* / The Five Pennies Finale *(Eileen Wilson)* and Battle Hymn Of The Republic Finale *(Red Nichols and Louis Armstrong)*

21 Nov 59 **19** 1 ★ **THE FIVE PENNIES** *(London HA-U-2189)* **LP** *re-entry*

See also Marlon Brando (GUYS AND DOLLS)
Doris Day (LOVE ME OR LEAVE ME)
Eddie Fisher (BUNDLE OF JOY)
Judy Garland (A STAR IS BORN)
Glenn Miller & His Orchestra (THE GLENN MILLER STORY)
Anthony Newley (IDLE ON PARADE)
Elvis Presley (KING CREOLE (VOL. 1) *and* KING CREOLE (VOL. 2))
Cliff Richard & The Drifters (SERIOUS CHARGE)
Shorty Rogers (THE WILD ONE)
Jean Simmons (GUYS AND DOLLS)
Frank Sinatra (YOUNG AT HEART)
Norman Wisdom (FOLLOW A STAR)

KID ORY'S CREOLE JAZZ BAND   16
Legendary New Orleans jazz trombonist and bandleader born Edward Ory on a plantation near LaPlace, Louisiana in 1886.

19 Jun 54 **7** 1 **KID ORY'S CREOLE JAZZ BAND** *(Tempo EXA-5)* **EP**
High Society / Ballin' The Jack / Dippermouth Blues / Savoy Blues
16 Oct 54 **11** 1 **KID ORY'S CREOLE JAZZ BAND** *(Tempo EXA-5)* **EP** *1st re-entry*
27 Nov 54 **23** 1 **Maryland, My Maryland** / Oh! Didn't He Ramble
(Good Time Jazz GV-2186)
22 Jan 55 **34** 1 **KID ORY'S CREOLE JAZZ BAND** *(Tempo EXA-5)* **EP** *2nd re-entry*
22 Jan 55 **39** 1 **12th Street Rag** / Savoy Blues *(Vogue V-2012)*
Both sides by Kid Ory & His Creole Jazz Band
5 Feb 55 **27** 1 **Maryland, My Maryland** / Oh! Didn't He Ramble
(Good Time Jazz GV-2186) *1st re-entry*
5 Feb 55 **33** 1 **Tiger Rag** / Eh Là-Bas! *(Vogue V-2011)*
Both sides by Kid Ory & His Creole Jazz Band
19 Feb 55 **36** 1 **Maryland, My Maryland** / Oh! Didn't He Ramble
(Good Time Jazz GV-2186) *2nd re-entry*
12 Mar 55 **18** 1 **Tiger Rag** / Eh Là-Bas! *(Vogue V-2011)* *1st re-entry*
9 Apr 55 **25** 1 **KID ORY'S CREOLE JAZZ BAND** *(Tempo EXA-5)* **EP** *3rd re-entry*
14 May 55 **33** 1 **KID ORY AND HIS CREOLE JAZZ BAND IN CONCERT**
(Good Time Jazz EPG-1006) **EP**
Kid Ory & His Creole Jazz Band
St. Louis Blues / Ory's Boogie / Blues For Jimmie Noone
13 Aug 55 **12** 1 **Tiger Rag** / Eh Là-Bas! *(Vogue V-2011)* *2nd re-entry*
3 Sep 55 **21** 1 **Tiger Rag** / Eh Là-Bas! *(Vogue V-2011)* *3rd re-entry*
17 Sep 55 **17** 1 **When The Saints Go Marching In** / Muskrat Ramble
(Good Time Jazz GV-2322)
17 Dec 55 **17** 1 **KID ORY'S CREOLE JAZZ BAND – 1953 (VOL. 1)**
(Good Time Jazz EPG-1217) **EP**
South Rampart Street Parade / The Girls Go Crazy About The Way I Walk /
St. James Infirmary / Bill Bailey, Won't You Please Come Home

2 Jun 56   **17**   1   **When The Saints Go Marching In** / Muskrat Ramble
(Good Time Jazz GV-2322) **re-entry**

JOHNNY OTIS SHOW   7

Singer, musician, bandleader, deejay, talent scout and impresario born John Veliotes in Vallejo, California in 1921. He recorded and toured extensively throughout the '50s, and discovered many R&B greats including Little Esther Phillips, Etta James, Jackie Wilson and Hank Ballard.

9 Nov 57   **5**   2   ★ **Ma (He's Making Eyes At Me)** /
                        Romance In The Dark *(Capitol CL-14794)*
                        Vocal on both sides by Marie Adams & The Three Tons of Joy
22 Mar 58   **6**   4   **All I Want Is Your Love** /
                        The Light Still Shines In My Window *(Capitol CL-14837)*
                        Vocal on both sides by Marie Adams
31 May 58   **16**   1   **The Johnny Otis Hand Jive** / Ring-A-Ling *(Capitol CL-14875)*
                        Vocal on both sides by Johnny Otis

REG OWEN & His Orchestra   1

Conductor, arranger and composer born George Owen Smith in London in 1911. He moved to Brussels in 1961 and thereafter worked all over the Continent.

21 Feb 59   **10**   1   ★ **Manhattan Spiritual** / Ritual Blues *(Pye International 7N.25009)*

PACKABEATS   3

British instrumental quartet produced by the legendary Joe Meek.

28 Jan 61   **3**   3   ★ **Gypsy Beat** / Big Man *(Parlophone R-4729)*

PATTI PAGE   26

Hugely popular singer born Clara Ann Fowler in Claremore, Oklahoma in 1927. Her records had a unique sound, due to her overdubbing her own backing vocals – a revolutionary technique at the time.

19 Jun 54   **8**   7   **Cross Over The Bridge** / My Restless Lover *(Mercury MB-3103)*
10 Jul 54   **12**   5   **Changing Partners** / Streets Of Laredo *(Mercury MB-3089)*
21 Aug 54   **31**   1   **Cross Over The Bridge** / My Restless Lover *(Mercury MB-3103)*
                        re-entry
13 Nov 54   **6**   10   **I Can't Tell A Waltz From A Tango** / The Mama Doll Song
                        (Mercury MB-3161)
22 Jan 55   **14**   2   **Let Me Go, Lover** / Hocus-Pocus *(Mercury MB-3182)*
19 Feb 55   **26**   1   **Let Me Go, Lover** / Hocus-Pocus *(Mercury MB-3182)* **re-entry**

MARTY PAICH DEK-TETTE

See Mel Tormé

MILKO PAPAYAKI & His Orchestra   1

Despite the heavy presence of bouzoukis, this was actually a French studio group who recorded this one-off for the Barclay subsidiary Bel-Air, rather than a bona fide Greek ensemble. (See also Makadopoulos & His Greek Serenaders.)

15 Oct 60   **9**   1   **Never On Sunday** / Hassapico Nostalgique *(H.M.V. POP-791)*

NORRIE PARAMOR & His Orchestra   20

Producer, arranger, composer, bandleader born in London 1914. He wrote or co-wrote many hits, and was also the brains behind several studio groups – most notably the Big Ben Banjo Band. He was also A&R man for Columbia, in which capacity he signed Cliff Richard, Frank Ifield, Helen Shapiro and other big names of the day.

13 Nov 54   **17**   4   **The High And The Mighty** / Rip Van Twinkle *(Columbia DB-3515)*
8 Jan 55   **42**   2   **The High And The Mighty** / Rip Van Twinkle *(Columbia DB-3515)*
                        re-entry

10 Mar 56	**10**	2	**The Threepenny Opera / The Poor People Of Paris**
			(Columbia DB-3745)
28 Apr 56	**4**	1	**The Threepenny Opera** / The Poor People Of Paris
			(Columbia DB-3745) *re-entry*
6 Oct 56	**1**	8	**Autumn Concerto** / Lullaby Of Birdland (Columbia DB-3815)
12 Jul 58	**5**	1	**I Could Have Danced All Night** / With A Little Bit Of Luck
			(Columbia DB-4119)
26 Jul 58	**11**	2	**I Could Have Danced All Night** / With A Little Bit Of Luck
			(Columbia DB-4119) *re-entry*

See also Big Ben Accordion Band
Big Ben Banjo Band

CHARLIE PARKER   4

Influential jazz saxophonist and composer born in Kansas City in 1920.

21 Aug 54	**21**	2	**Hot Blues** (Charlie Parker Quartet) /
			Bird Feathers (Charlie Parker Sextet) (Vogue V-2244)
30 Jul 55	**23**	2	**CHARLIE PARKER (VOL. 1)** (Vogue LDE-004) **LP**
			My Old Flame / Air Conditioning / Bird Feathers / Prezology / Out Of Nowhere /
			Hot Blues / Schnourphology / Bongo Beep

See also Norman Granz
Norman Granz' Jazz At The Philharmonic

JIMMY PARKINSON   4

Australian balladeer from Sydney who was already well established Down Under when he came to Britain in 1955. He scored three UK hits in 1956 ('The Great Pretender', 'Walk Hand In Hand' and 'The Middle of the House') before returning home the following year.

23 Jun 56	**12**	1	★ **Walk Hand In Hand** / Cry Baby (Columbia DB-3775)
7 Jul 56	**4**	1	★ **Walk Hand In Hand** / Cry Baby (Columbia DB-3775) *1st re-entry*
21 Jul 56	**7**	2	★ **Walk Hand In Hand** / Cry Baby (Columbia DB-3775) *2nd re-entry*

JACK PARNELL & His Orchestra   1

Highly-rated British bandleader/drummer from London. He was ATV's musical director from 1956 to 1981, and also composed the theme for 'The Muppet Show'. His uncle, Val Parnell, was general manager of the London Palladium.

| 2 Oct 54 | **13** | 1 | **The Bandit** (Vocal: Dennis Hale) / Annie's Blues (Vocal: Annie Ross) |
| | | | (Parlophone R-3870) |

BILL PARSONS & His Orchestra   4

It's a rather convoluted tale, but 'The All American Boy' was actually by Bobby Bare, not Bill Parsons. Apparently, Bare made a demo of the song so that Parsons could learn the vocal. Parsons then recorded it, but for some reason Bare's demo was released instead. Things got even trickier after it became a hit, as Parsons was unable to replicate Bare's voice on stage.

| 21 Feb 59 | **1** | 2 | ★ **The All American Boy** / Rubber Dolly (London HL-8798) |
| 21 Mar 59 | **2** | 2 | ★ **The All American Boy** / Rubber Dolly (London HL-8798) *re-entry* |

See also Bobby Bare

JOHNNY PATE QUINTET   2

Jazz bassist born in Chicago in 1923. He later worked as arranger and producer for various soul acts including the Impressions, Betty Everett and Peabo Bryson.

| 8 Mar 58 | **3** | 2 | **Swinging Shepherd Blues** / The Elder (Parlophone R-4404) |

OTTILIE PATTERSON

See Chris Barber's Jazz Band

LES PAUL & MARY FORD — 5

Solid-body electric guitar and multi-tracking pioneer born Lester Polfuss in Waukesha, Wisconsin in 1915. His singer/guitarist wife was born Iris Summers in El Monte, California in 1924. They enjoyed immense popularity throughout the '50s and early '60s.

20 Nov 54	**17**	1	**Mandolino** *(Les Paul)* / Whither Thou Goest *(Les Paul & Mary Ford)* *(Capitol CL-14185)*
1 Jan 55	**19**	2	**Mister Sandman** / That's What I Like *(Capitol CL-14212)*
22 Jan 55	**39**	1	**Mister Sandman** / That's What I Like *(Capitol CL-14212)* **1st re-entry**
12 Mar 55	**8**	1	**Mister Sandman** / That's What I Like *(Capitol CL-14212)* **2nd re-entry**

DONALD PEERS — 1

Enormously popular ballader and big band singer born in Ammanford, Carmarthenshire in 1908. Although he was rated Britain's No.1 vocalist of the '50s by Variety, chart success eluded him until 1969, when he had an unexpected hit with 'Please Don't Go'.

19 Dec 59	**6**	1	**Roses From Venice** / If There Are Stars In My Eyes *(Columbia DB-4369)*

PENGUINS — 1

Black vocal quartet from Los Angeles, whose 'Earth Angel' was one of the first rock'n'roll hits.

25 Jun 55	**11**	1	**Earth Angel** / Hey Senorita *(London HL-8114)*

ART PEPPER QUARTET — 1

Leading jazz alto saxophonist and clarinettist born in Gardena, California in 1925. Sadly, a long-standing addiction to heroin resulted in his career being interrupted by several prison sentences. He died of a stroke in 1982, aged 56.

26 Jun 54	**9**	1	**ART PEPPER QUARTET** *(Vogue LDE-067)* **LP**
			Brown Gold / Holiday Flight / These Foolish Things / Surf Ride / Tickle Toe / Everthing Happens To Me / Chili Pepper / Suzy The Poodle

CARL PERKINS — 4

Rockabilly singer/guitarist from Tiptonville, Tennessee renowned for his blue suede footwear.

12 May 56	**7**	1	★ <u>**Blue Suede Shoes**</u> / Honey Don't *(London HLU-8271)*
15 Mar 58	**9**	1	**Glad All Over** / Forever Yours *(London HLS-8527)*
26 Apr 58	**8**	1	**Glad All Over** / Forever Yours *(London HLS-8527)* **re-entry**
16 Jan 60	**14**	1	**I Don't See Me In Your Eyes Anymore** / One Ticket To Loneliness *(Philips PB-983)*

MAL PERRY — 1

Singer and songwriter born Malcolm Levy in Liverpool. He went to school with John Lennon and was one of the city's promising young talents before Beatlemania exploded.

21 Jun 58	**10**	1	**Make Me A Miracle** / That's When Your Heartaches Begin *(Fontana H-133)*

STEVE PERRY — 3

Young singer born in Guildford, Surrey in 1944. His cover of the Crests' 'Step By Step' was a minor hit, though his next four singles (all on Decca) went nowhere. Happily, he went on to enjoy some success as a ventriloquist and stage actor.

28 May 60	**2**	3	★ <u>**Step By Step**</u> / Because They're Young *(H.M.V. POP-745)*

OSCAR PETERSON — 5

Legendary Canadian jazz pianist and composer born in Montreal in 1925.

5 Feb 55	**56**	1	**OSCAR PETERSON PLAYS TENDERLY AND C JAM BLUES** *(H.M.V. 7EG-8635)* **EP**
			Oscar Peterson Trio
			Tenderly / C Jam Blues

19 Feb 55	**20**	1	Tenderly / Debut *(Columbia LB-150)*

Both sides by Oscar Peterson with Ray Brown, rhythm bass

19 Mar 55	**27**	2	Tenderly / Debut *(Columbia LB-150)*

re-entry

21 Jul 56	**8**	1	OSCAR PETERSON PLAYS RICHARD ROGERS

(Columbia 33CX-10028) 🔲
Oscar Peterson Trio
This Can't Be Love / It Might As Well Be Spring / Bewitched, Bothered And Bewildered / Johnny One Note / The Surrey With The Fringe / The Lady Is A Tramp / Blue Moon / Thou Swell / Isn't It Romantic / Manhattan / Lover

See also Norman Granz

RAY PETERSON   7
Ballad singer born in Denton, Texas in 1939. He later became a Baptist minister.

15 Aug 59	**2**	2	★ **The Wonder Of You** / I'm Gone *(R.C.A. RCA-1131)*
3 Sep 60	**2**	5	★ **Tell Laura I Love Her** / Wedding Day *(R.C.A. RCA-1195)*

OSCAR PETTIFORD SEXTET   2
Jazz double bassist, cellist and composer born in Okmulgee, Oklahoma in 1922.

6 Nov 54	**23**	2	OSCAR PETTIFORD SEXTET *(Vogue LDE-098)* 🔲

Burt's Pad / Marcel The Furrier / Ondine / Stardust / East Lag / Rhumblues

PHILHARMONIA ORCHESTRA, *cond.* Herbert von Karajan   1
London-based orchestra founded in 1945 by British classical impresario and record producer (and husband of German soprano Elisabeth Schwarzkopf) Walter Legge.

2 Apr 55	**18**	1	TCHAIKOVSKY – SYMPHONY NO. 4 IN F MINOR, OP. 36

(Columbia 33CX-1139) 🔲
First Movement: Andante Sostenuto – Moderato Con Anima / Second Movement: Andantino In Modo Di Canzona / Third Movement: Scherzo (Pizzicato Ostinato) / Fourth Movement: Finale (Allegro Con Fuoco)

See also Yehudi Menuhin

PHILHARMONIC PROMENADE ORCHESTRA, *cond.* Sir Adrian Boult   1
The London Philharmonic Orchestra recording under a pseudonym, due to contractual obligations.

18 Sep 54	**15**	1	GUSTAV HOLST – THE PLANETS, OP. 32 *(Nixa NLP-903)* 🔲

Mars, The Bringer Of War / Venus, The Bringer Of Peace / Mercury, The Winged Messenger / Jupiter, The Bringer Of Jollity / Saturn, The Bringer Of Old Age / Uranus, The Magician / Neptune, The Mystic

See also London Philharmonic Orchestra

FLIP PHILLIPS
See Norman Granz

PHIL PHILLIPS with the Twilights   5
Singer/songwriter born Philip Baptiste in Lake Charles, Louisiana in 1926. He was still working as a hotel bellhop when he hit No. 2 in the Billboard 'Hot 100' with his self-penned swamp-pop classic.

12 Sep 59	**7**	1	Sea Of Love / Juella *(Mercury AMT-1059)*
26 Sep 59	**3**	2	Sea Of Love / Juella *(Mercury AMT-1059)*

1st re-entry

17 Oct 59	**7**	2	Sea Of Love / Juella *(Mercury AMT-1059)*

2nd re-entry

Phil Phillips

HURRY! *(at the double!)* TO HEAR THIS NEW HIT OF HITS!

THE **NILSSON TWINS**

WITH *LES BAXTER'S ORCHESTRA*

AVAILABLE ON 78 AND 45 R.P.M.

'RAIN ON MY WINDOW'

AND 'I DANCE WHEN I WALK'

Capitol

CAPITOL ARTISTES—CAPITAL ENTERTAINMENT

Electric and Musical Industries Ltd., Record Division, 8-11 Great Castle St., London, W.1.

DANNY RIVERS

Manager — Bob Alexander

DECCA RECORDS

FREE FAN CLUB

President: Len Digby
304 Holloway Road, N.7

Northern Branch:
Carole Ward
24 Whitehouse Road
Walkley, Sheffield 6

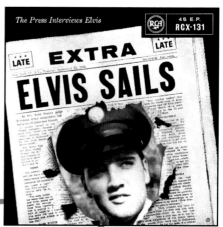

The Press Interviews Elvis

RCA 45 E.P. RCX-131

LATE EXTRA LATE

ELVIS SAILS

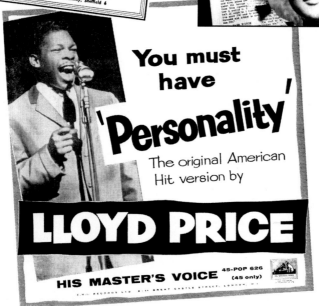

You must have 'Personality'

The original American Hit version by

LLOYD PRICE

HIS MASTER'S VOICE   45-POP 626 (45 only)

SID PHILLIPS BAND $\qquad$ 3

Clarinettist and pianist born Isador Simon in London in 1907. His top-notch jazz and swing band was Princess Margaret's favourite, and on several occasions in the '50s he played the annual Windsor Castle Christmas Ball at her request.

10 Dec 55	**12**	1	**Pete Kelly's Blues** / Hard Hearted Hannah *(H.M.V. POP-125)*
21 Jul 56	**12**	1	**Mamma Don't Allow** / Glad Rag Doll *(H.M.V. POP-226)*
1 Sep 56	**6**	1	**Mamma Don't Allow** / Glad Rag Doll *(H.M.V. POP-226)* ***re-entry***

ÉDITH PIAF $\qquad$ 5

Diminutive Édith Gassion was born in Paris in 1915 and lived a shambolic life full of tragedy and desperation that was reflected in her heartfelt singing. A cultural icon in her home country, she was arguably the greatest singer France has ever produced.

2 Apr 60	**1**	2	★	<u>**Milord**</u> / Je Sais Comment *(Columbia DC-754)*
7 May 60	**4**	1	★	<u>**Milord**</u> / Je Sais Comment *(Columbia DC-754)* ***re-entry***
11 Mar 61	**6**	1		**Non Je Ne Regrette Rien** / Les Amants d'Un Jour *(Columbia DB-4596)*

See also Various Artists (CABARET NIGHT IN PARIS)

WEBB PIERCE $\qquad$ 3

Hugely popular country star born in West Monroe, Louisiana in 1921.

25 Aug 56	**14**	1	**WEBB PIERCE (PART 1)** *(Brunswick OE-9253)* **EP**
			In The Jailhouse Now / More And More / Even Tho / Your Good-For-Nothing Heart
15 Sep 56	**10**	1	**WEBB PIERCE (PART 1)** *(Brunswick OE-9253)* **EP** ***re-entry***
13 Oct 56	**10**	1	**WEBB PIERCE (PART 3)** *(Brunswick OE-9255)* **EP**
			New Silver Bells / I'm Walking The Dog / I'll Go On Alone / I Don't Care

PILTDOWN MEN $\qquad$ 1

Studio group formed by Ed Cobb of the Four Preps and pianist/arranger Lincoln Mayorga. Curiously, their sax-heavy instrumental sound proved more popular in the UK than in the States.

3 Sep 60	**4**	1	★	<u>**McDonald's Cave**</u> / Brontosaurus Stomp *(Capitol CL-15149)*

PINKY & PERKY $\qquad$ 5

Puppet pigs created by Czechoslovakian immigrants Jan and Vlasta Dalibor. Britain's equivalent of the Chipmunks, they were a fixture on children's TV from 1957 until 1971.

17 Jan 59	**5**	1	**Tom Dooley** / The Velvet Glove (The Pinky & Perky Theme) *(Decca F-11095)*
7 Nov 59	**5**	2	**Party Sing-Song (Parts 1 & 2) [M]** *(Decca F-11174)*
			Side By Side – There's A Blue Ridge Round My Heart, Virginia – Pretty Baby / Carolina In The Morning – Broken Doll – For Me And My Gal
5 Dec 59	**10**	2	**Party Sing-Song (Parts 1 & 2) [M]** *(Decca F-11174)* ***re-entry***

GENE PITNEY $\qquad$ 2

Immensely successful singer/songwriter born in Hartford, Connecticut in 1940. He had 17 UK hits between 1961 and 1969, ten of which made the Top Ten.

4 Mar 61	**9**	2	★	<u>**Love My Life Away**</u> / I Laughed So Hard I Cried *(London HL-9270)*

PLATTERS $\qquad$ 33

Smooth black vocal group from Los Angeles who straddled the gap between Tin Pan Alley and rock'n'roll. They toured the UK in 1957, as a result of which they remained incredibly popular until the end of the decade.

18 Aug 56	**2**	3	★	<u>**Only You**</u> / <u>**The Great Pretender**</u> *(Mercury MT-117)*
10 Nov 56	**8**	1		**THE FABULOUS PLATTERS** *(Mercury MEP-9504)* **EP**
				The Magic Touch / Only You / The Great Pretender / My Prayer
1 Dec 56	**3**	1		**THE FABULOUS PLATTERS** *(Mercury MEP-9504)* **EP** ***1st re-entry***
5 Jan 57	**2**	2		**THE FABULOUS PLATTERS** *(Mercury MEP-9504)* **EP** ***2nd re-entry***
19 Jan 57	**3**	1	★	<u>**You'll Never Never Know**</u> / <u>**It Isn't Right**</u> *(Mercury MT-130)*

2 Feb 57	1	4	THE FABULOUS PLATTERS (Mercury MEP-9504) **EP** *3rd re-entry*
9 Mar 57	11	1	THE FABULOUS PLATTERS (Mercury MEP-9504) **EP** *4th re-entry*
23 Mar 57	9	3	THE FABULOUS PLATTERS (Mercury MEP-9504) **EP** *5th re-entry*
27 Apr 57	1	4	**On My Word Of Honor** / One In A Million (Mercury MT-143)
4 May 57	8	1	THE FABULOUS PLATTERS (Mercury MEP-9504) **EP** *6th re-entry*
21 Sep 57	4	1	**My Dream** / I Wanna (Mercury MT-156)
10 Jan 59	11	1	★ <u>**Smoke Gets In Your Eyes**</u> / No Matter What You Are (Mercury AMT-1016)
23 May 59	5	4	**Enchanted** / The Sound & The Fury (Mercury AMT-1039)
15 Aug 59	2	2	★ <u>**Remember When**</u> / Love Of A Lifetime (Mercury AMT-1053)
7 Nov 59	5	2	**My Blue Heaven** / Wish It Were Me (Mercury AMT-1066)
28 Nov 59	20	1	**My Blue Heaven** / Wish It Were Me (Mercury AMT-1066) *re-entry*
10 Sep 60	8	1	**Red Sails In The Sunset** / Sad River (Mercury AMT-1106)

PLAYMATES   6

Rock'n'roll trio from Waterbury, Connecticut. Because the BBC is not permitted to carry advertising, they had to re-record their big hit, 'Beep Beep', replacing the brand names 'Cadillac' and 'Nash Rambler' with 'limousine' and 'bubble car' in order to qualify for airplay in the UK.

9 Aug 58	6	1	**Don't Go Home** / Can't You Get It Through Your Head (Columbia DB-4151)
24 Jan 59	9	1	★ <u>**Beep Beep**</u> / Your Love (Columbia DB-4224)
14 Feb 59	5	2	★ <u>**Beep Beep**</u> / Your Love (Columbia DB-4224) *re-entry*
19 Sep 59	2	2	**What Is Love?** / I Am (Columbia DB-4338)

PONI-TAILS   5

Quite possibly the first-ever American 'teen' female trio not to be called 'Sisters', the Poni-Tails from Lyndhurst, Ohio are still fondly remembered for their classic teen-angst hit, 'Born Too Late'.

30 Aug 58	4	1	★ <u>**Born Too Late**</u> / Come On Joey Dance With Me (H.M.V. POP-516) Both sides as by the Pony-Tails
13 Sep 58	1	1	★ <u>**Born Too Late**</u> / Come On Joey Dance With Me (H.M.V. POP-516) Both sides as by the Pony-Tails *re-entry*
10 Jan 59	6	1	**Seven Minutes In Heaven** / Close Friends (H.M.V. POP-558)
28 Mar 59	4	1	★ <u>**Early To Bed**</u> / Father Time (H.M.V. POP-596)
22 Aug 59	9	1	**Moody** / Oom Pah Polka (H.M.V. POP-644)

BUD POWELL TRIO   8

Influential jazz pianist of the 'bop' persuasion born Earl Powell in New York in 1924.

19 Jun 54	9	1	**Indiana** / Everything Happens To Me (Vogue V-2240)
3 Jul 54	6	5	**Indiana** / Everything Happens To Me (Vogue V-2240) *re-entry*
5 Feb 55	42	1	THE AMAZING BUD POWELL TRIO (Vogue EPV-1030) **EP** My Heart Stood Still / Embraceable You / Woody'n You / You'd Be So Nice To Come Home To
19 Feb 55	20	1	THE AMAZING BUD POWELL TRIO (Vogue EPV-1030) **EP** *re-entry*

JANE POWELL   13

Singer, dancer and actress from Portland, Oregon, born Suzanne Burce. She starred in many movie musicals of the '40s and '50s, most famously 'Seven Brides For Seven Brothers' (1954).

19 Mar 55	27	1	**When You're In Love** (Jane Powell and Howard Keel) (M.G.M. MGM-788) The flip, 'Spring, Spring, Spring' by Brothers & Girls, also bubbled under [see Howard Keel]
16 Apr 55	4	1	**When You're In Love** (Jane Powell and Howard Keel) (M.G.M. MGM-788) *1st re-entry*
30 Apr 55	2	2	**When You're In Love** (Jane Powell and Howard Keel) (M.G.M. MGM-788) *2nd re-entry*
30 Apr 55	28	1	**Wonderful, Wonderful Day** (M.G.M. MGM-785) The flip, 'Bless Yore Beautiful Hide' by Howard Keel, also bubbled under

4 Jun 55	**13**	1	**When You're In Love** *(Jane Powell and Howard Keel)*

4 Jun 55   **13**   1   **When You're In Love** *(Jane Powell and Howard Keel)*
(M.G.M. MGM-788) **3rd re-entry**

3 Sep 55   **17**   1   **Why, Oh Why?** *(Tony Martin, Vic Damone, Russ Tamblyn [actually Rex Dennis], Jane Powell, Debbie Reynolds and Ann Miller) /* Chiribiribee *(Kay Armen, Jane Powell, Tony Martin, Debbie Reynolds, Vic Damone and Russ Tamblyn [actually Rex Dennis])* *(M.G.M. MGM-837)*

See also Original Soundtrack (SEVEN BRIDES FOR SEVEN BROTHERS)

DUFFY POWER   1

Singer born Raymond Howard in London in 1941. Although he failed to achieve commercial success as a rock'n'roller, he later became a respected blues performer.

13 Jun 59   **18**   1   **Dream Lover** / That's My Little Suzie *(Fontana H-194)*

PÉREZ PRADO & His Orchestra   7

Diminutive, hip-swinging bandleader born in Matanzas, Cuba in 1917. His unique blend of traditional mambo and North American jazz influences found great popularity in the US, becoming a national dance craze in the mid-'50s.

16 Oct 54   **34**   1   **The High And The Mighty** / Skokiaan *(H.M.V. B-10760)*

20 Nov 54   **34**   1   **The High And The Mighty** / Skokiaan *(H.M.V. B-10760)*

27 Nov 54   **14**   1   **MAMBOS** *(Seeco LDS-047)* **LP**
Mambo No. 5 / Habana / Mi Cazuelita / Saca la Mano / Electricidad / Hembra Mala / Actopan / Kandela

16 Jul 55   **11**   1   **Freddy** / **Sweet And Gentle** *(H.M.V. B-10892)*
Both sides by Eartha Kitt and Pérez Prado

5 Jul 58   **5**   3   ★ <u>**Patricia**</u> / Why Wait *(R.C.A. RCA-1067)*

ELVIS PRESLEY   28

The poor boy from Tupelo, Mississippi who grew up to be 'The King'.

5 May 56   **12**   1   ★ <u>**Heartbreak Hotel**</u> / I Was The One *(H.M.V. POP-182)*

14 Jul 56   **1**   1   ★ <u>**I Want You, I Need You, I Love You**</u> / My Baby Left Me *(H.M.V. POP-235)*

27 Oct 56   **5**   1   ★ <u>**ROCK 'N ROLL**</u> *(H.M.V. CLP-1093)* **LP**
Blue Suede Shoes / I Got A Sweetie (I Got A Woman) / I'm Counting On You / I'm Left, You're Right, She's Gone / That's All Right / Money Honey / Mystery Train / I'm Gonna Sit Right Down And Cry (Over You) / Tryin' To Get To You / One-Sided Love Affair / Lawdy Miss Clawdy / Shake, Rattle And Roll

10 Nov 56   **5**   1   ★ <u>**Blue Moon**</u> / <u>**I Don't Care If The Sun Don't Shine**</u> *(H.M.V. POP-272)*

12 Jan 57   **1**   4   **LOVE ME TENDER** *(H.M.V. 7EG-8199)* **EP**
Love Me Tender / Let Me / Poor Boy / We're Gonna Move

16 Feb 57   **3**   1   **LOVE ME TENDER** *(H.M.V. 7EG-8199)* **EP** *re-entry*

23 Feb 57   **1**   2   ★ <u>**Rip It Up**</u> / Baby Let's Play House *(H.M.V. POP-305)*

4 May 57   **4**   1   ★ <u>**Too Much**</u> / Playin' For Keeps *(H.M.V. POP-330)*
Both sides by Elvis Presley with the Jordanaires

22 Jun 57   **1**   1   ★ <u>**All Shook Up**</u> / That's When Your Heartaches Begin *(H.M.V. POP-359)*
Both sides by Elvis Presley with the Jordanaires

29 Jun 57   **11**   1   ★ <u>**PEACE IN THE VALLEY**</u> *(R.C.A. RCX-101)* **EP**
Elvis Presley with the Jordanaires
(There'll Be) Peace In The Valley (For Me) / It Is No Secret (What God Can Do) / I Believe / Take My Hand, Precious Lord

20 Jul 57   **10**   1   ★ <u>**PEACE IN THE VALLEY**</u> *(R.C.A. RCX-101)* **EP** *re-entry*

28 Sep 57   **1**   1   **GOOD ROCKIN' TONIGHT** *(H.M.V. 7EG-8256)* **EP**
Blue Moon Of Kentucky / Good Rockin' Tonight / Milk Cow Blues / Just Because

12 Oct 57   **3**   1   **ELVIS PRESLEY** *(R.C.A. RCX-104)* **EP**
Elvis Presley with the Jordaniares
I Need You So / Have I Told You Lately That I Love You / Blueberry Hill / Don't Leave Me Now

9 Nov 57   **10**   1   ★ <u>**Santa Bring My Baby Back**</u> / Santa Claus Is Back In Town *(R.C.A. RCA-1025)*

6 Sep 58	**1**	6	**KING CREOLE (VOL. 1) [OST]** *(R.C.A. RCX-117)* 🎵
			Elvis Presley with the Jordaniares
			King Creole / New Orleans / As Long As I Have You / Lover Doll
11 Oct 58	**7**	1	**KING CREOLE (VOL. 2) [OST]** *(R.C.A. RCX-118)* 🎵
			Elvis Presley with the Jordaniares
			Trouble / Young Dreams / Crawfish / Dixieland Rock
13 Dec 58	**7**	1	**ELVIS SAILS** *(R.C.A. RCX-131)* 🎵
			Press interview with Elvis Presley (at Brooklyn Army Terminal, September 22,
			1958) / Elvis Presley's newsreel interview / Pat Hernon interviews Elvis in the
			Library of the U.S.S. *Randall* at sailing
23 Jan 60	**8**	1	★ <u>**STRICTLY ELVIS**</u> *(R.C.A. RCX-175)* 🎵
			Old Shep / Any Place Is Paradise / Paralyzed / Is It So Strange
29 Oct 60	**2**	1	★ <u>**It's Now Or Never**</u> / Make Me Know It *(R.C.A. RCA-1207)*
			Both sides by Elvis Presley with the Jordaniares

JOHNNY PRESTON   6

Singer born John Preston Courville in Port Arthur, Texas. He had five UK hits in 1960, starting with the Big Bopper-penned 'Running Bear', which topped the charts on both sides of the Atlantic.

23 Jan 60	**2**	1	★ <u>**Running Bear**</u> / My Heart Knows *(Mercury AMT-1079)*
23 Jul 60	**13**	1	★ <u>**Feel So Fine**</u> / <u>**I'm Starting To Go Steady**</u> *(Mercury ATM-1104)*
12 Nov 60	**5**	4	★ <u>**Charming Billy**</u> / Up In The Air *(Mercury AMT-1114)*

MIKE PRESTON   5

Boxer-turned-singer born Jack Davies in London in 1938. He had four UK hits between 1959 and 1961, then emigrated to Australia, where he later also applied his talents to acting.

15 Nov 58	**8**	1	**My Lucky Love** / A House, A Car And A Wedding Ring
			(Decca F-11053)
17 Oct 59	**4**	1	★ <u>**Mr. Blue**</u> / Just Ask Your Heart *(Decca F-11167)*
30 Apr 60	**12**	1	**A Girl Like You** / Too Old *(Decca F-11222)*
13 Aug 60	**11**	1	★ <u>**I'd Do Anything**</u> / Where Is Love? *(Decca F-11255)*
12 Nov 60	**11**	1	★ <u>**Togetherness**</u> / Farewell My Love *(Decca F-11287)*

LLOYD PRICE   9

New Orleans-style R&B singer from Kenner, Louisiana. His hitmaking career stretched from 'Lawdy Miss Clawdy' in 1952 until the mid-70s.

22 Jun 57	**8**	2	**Just Because** / Why *(London HL-8438)*
17 Aug 57	**9**	1	**Just Because** / Why *(London HL-8438)* *re-entry*
7 Feb 59	**10**	1	★ <u>**Stagger Lee**</u> / You Need Love *(H.M.V. POP-580)*
2 May 59	**1**	1	★ <u>**Where Were You**</u> / Is It Really Love *(H.M.V. POP-598)*
6 Jun 59	**3**	1	★ <u>**Personality**</u> / Have You Ever Had The Blues *(H.M.V. POP-626)*
5 Sep 59	**12**	1	★ <u>**I'm Gonna Get Married**</u> / Three Little Pigs *(H.M.V. POP-650)*
28 Nov 59	**26**	1	**Come Into My Heart** / Wont'Cha Come Home *(H.M.V. POP-672)*
19 Mar 60	**5**	1	★ <u>**Lady Luck**</u> / Never Let Me Go *(H.M.V. POP-712)*

RIKKI PRICE   3

Shipyard worker from Sunderland who was discovered while singing in a local club. His first release, 'Tom Dooley', sold well enough for him to give up his day job.

| 5 Dec 58 | **12** | 1 | **Tom Dooley** / Cherry Blossom Lane *(Fontana H-162)* |
| 19 Dec 58 | **10** | 2 | **Tom Dooley** / Cherry Blossom Lane *(Fontana H-162)* *re-entry* |

LOUIS PRIMA with Sam Butera & The Witnesses   3

Exuberant scat-singing trumpeter from New Orleans who led a hot, swinging band for several decades and later voiced King Louis in Walt Disney's 'Jungle Book' movie (1967). He was married to singer Keely Smith from 1953 to 1961.

18 Jan 58	**6**	1	★ <u>**Buona Sera**</u> / Beep! Beep! *(Capitol CL-14821)*
8 Feb 58	**6**	1	★ <u>**Buona Sera**</u> / Beep! Beep! *(Capitol CL-14821)* *re-entry*
26 Apr 58	**17**	1	**5 Months, 2 Weeks, 2 Days** / Banana Split For My Baby
			(Capitol CL-14669)

PRO MUSICA SYMPHONY ORCHESTRA, VIENNA
See Ingrid Haebler

DANNY PURCHES   2
Gypsy busker born in Surrey in 1934 who was at one time romantically linked to singer Ruby Murray. He was discovered performing in Leicester Square by BBC producer Henry Caldwell, who arranged his first TV appearance.

| 16 Apr 55 | **22** | 1 | **A Rusty Old Halo** / Tomorrow *(Columbia DB-3604)* |
| 27 Aug 55 | **14** | 1 | **Mama** / Just One More Time *(Columbia DB-3626)* |

PAUL QUINICHETTE, BENNY GREEN, FRANK FOSTER, JOSEPH NEWMAN, HANK JONES, KENNY CLARKE, EDDIE JONES and SIR JONATHAN GASSER   12
The mid-'50s were a popular time for jazz jam sessions (see also Norman Granz and Gene Norman). This one was recorded in New York on 10 October 1953 by US Decca. 'Sir Jonathan Gasser' is a pseudonym for guitarist Johnny Smith, who was under contract to Roost at the time.

16 Oct 54	**17**	5	**JAZZ STUDIO 1** *(Brunswick LAT-8036)* **LP**
			Tenderly / Let's Split
11 Dec 54	**12**	4	**JAZZ STUDIO 1** *(Brunswick LAT-8036)* **LP** *1st re-entry*
22 Jan 55	**5**	3	**JAZZ STUDIO 1** *(Brunswick LAT-8036)* **LP** *2nd re-entry*

CARMEL QUINN   3
Singer and humorous storyteller born in Dublin in 1925. She moved to the USA in 1954 and became a star of theatre, film, radio and television.

| 10 Sep 55 | **22** | 1 | **Doonaree** / The Whistling Gypsy *(Philips PB-474)* |
| 5 May 56 | **11** | 2 | **Doonaree** / The Whistling Gypsy *(Philips PB-474)* *re-entry* |

QUINTET OF THE HOT CLUB OF FRANCE   1
Groundbreaking jazz string quintet founded in 1938 by guitarist Django Reinhardt and violinist Stephane Grappelly.

| 27 Nov 54 | **19** | 1 | **SWING FROM PARIS** *(London LB-810)* **LP** |
| | | | Swing From Paris / My Sweet / Improvisation / Sweet Georgia Brown / Three Little Words / Nocturne / Daphne / H.C.Q. Strut |

KEMAL RACHID ET SES OTTOMANS   3
Paris-based Algerian immigrant who covered Bob Azzam's big hit for Philips. Versions by Clinton Ford and Staïffi et ses Mustafa's also bubbled under.

| 7 May 60 | **9** | 1 | **Mustapha** / Loukoum *(Philips 370.280F (French))* |
| 6 Aug 60 | **9** | 2 | **Mustapha** / Loukoum *(Philips 370.280F (French))* *re-entry* |

RADIO REVELLERS   6
Long-lasting English male harmony quartet established in 1937.

3 Jul 54	**21**	1	★ <u>West Of Zanzibar</u> *(Anthony Steel with the Radio Revellers)* / Who Cares *(Radio Revellers)* *(Polygon P-1114)*
4 Sep 54	**24**	1	★ <u>West Of Zanzibar</u> *(Anthony Steel with the Radio Revellers)* / Who Cares *(Radio Revellers)* *(Polygon P-1114)* *re-entry*
19 Feb 55	**34**	1	**The Flame** *(Anthony Steel with the Radio Revellers)* / Under The Southern Cross *(Radio Revellers)* *(Polygon P-1154)*
28 May 55	**6**	1	**Crazy Otto Rag** *(Petula Clark, the Radio Revellers, Joe 'Mr. Piano' Henderson and Friends)* / **The Pendulum Song** *(Petula Clark and the Radio Revellers)* *(Polygon P-1169)*
11 Jun 55	**11**	2	**Crazy Otto Rag** / **The Pendulum Song** *(Polygon P-1169)* *re-entry*

JACKIE RAE 1

Singer/comedian born in Winnipeg in 1925. He came to Britain with the Canadian Air Force during World War II, then moved into TV work during the '50s, hosting his own variety show and game shows like 'Spot The Tune' (featuring Marion Ryan) and 'The Golden Shot'.

11 Jun 60	**12**	1	**Summer Place** / The Moon Got In My Eyes *(Fontana H-242)*

MARVIN RAINWATER 1

Rockabilly singer, guitarist and songwriter born in Wichita, Kansas in 1925. He was one quarter Cherokee, as a result of which his publicity shots often portrayed him in Native American costume.

27 Feb 58	**15**	1	★ <u>**Whole Lotta Woman**</u> / Baby, Don't Go *(M.G.M. MGM-974)*

DON RALKE

See Big Sound of Don Ralke

NEVA RAPHAELLO 2

UK-based jazz singer born in Sintra, Portugal in 1915.

10 Sep 55	**12**	2	**When The Saints Go Marching In (Parts 1 & 2)** *(Philips PB-470)*
			Both sides by the Dutch Swing College Band with Neva Raphaello

RENATO RASCEL 1

Italian actor, comedian, singer and composer of 'Arrivederci Roma', born Renato Ranucci in Turin in 1912. He represented Italy in the 1960 Eurovision Song Contest, coming eighth with 'Romantica'.

27 Aug 60	**16**	1	**Romantica** *(R.C.A. RCA-1177)*
			Flip is 'Libero' by Teddy Reno

JOHNNIE RAY 73

Influential singer of the immediate pre-rock'n'roll era born in Dallas, Oregon in 1927. His animated and emotional stage performances, during which he would often shed real tears, led to him, being dubbed 'The Prince of Wails'.

10 Jul 54	**1**	7	**Destiny** / Why Should I Be Sorry? *(Philips PB-301)*
7 Aug 54	**27**	1	**AT THE LONDON PALLADIUM** *(Philips BBR-8001)* **LP**
			Please Don't Talk About Me When I'm Gone / Glad Rag Doll / A Hundred Years From Today / Somebody Stole My Gal / With These Hands / Walkin' My Baby Back Home / As Time Goes By / Such A Night / The Little White Cloud That Cried / Cry / I'm Gonna Walk And Talk With My Lord
21 Aug 54	**18**	2	**AT THE LONDON PALLADIUM** *(Philips BBR-8001)* **LP** *1st re-entry*
4 Sep 54	**27**	1	**Destiny** / Why Should I Be Sorry *(Philips PB-301)* *1st re-entry*
25 Sep 54	**7**	7	**Destiny** / Why Should I Be Sorry *(Philips PB-301)* *2nd re-entry*
16 Oct 54	**38**	2	**Papa Loves Mambo** / The Only Girl I'll Ever Love *(Philips PB-346)*
6 Nov 54	**8**	10	**Papa Loves Mambo** / The Only Girl I'll Ever Love *(Philips PB-346)* *1st re-entry*
27 Nov 54	**72**	1	**Destiny** / Why Should I Be Sorry *(Philips PB-301)* *3rd re-entry*
8 Jan 55	**52**	1	**Destiny** / Why Should I Be Sorry *(Philips PB-301)* *4th re-entry*
29 Jan 55	**35**	1	**Papa Loves Mambo** / The Only Girl I'll Ever Love *(Philips PB-346)* *2nd re-entry*
5 Mar 55	**2**	1	★ <u>**If You Believe**</u> / Alexander's Ragtime Band *(Philips PB-379)*
23 Apr 55	**8**	4	★ <u>**Paths Of Paradise**</u> / Parade Of Broken Hearts *(Philips PB-441)*
14 May 55	**1**	5	**Flip, Flop And Fly** / Thine Eyes Are As The Eyes Of A Dove *(Philips PB-449)*
14 May 55	**15**	1	**AT THE LONDON PALLADIUM** *(Philips BBR-8001)* **LP** *2nd re-entry*
14 May 55	**20**	1	**Destiny** / Why Should I Be Sorry *(Philips PB-301)* *5th re-entry*
18 Jun 55	**2**	10	**Taking A Chance On Love** / My Love For You *(Philips PB-463)*
25 Jun 55	**7**	1	**Flip, Flop And Fly** / Thine Eyes Are As The Eyes Of A Dove *(Philips PB-449)* *1st re-entry*
9 Jul 55	**16**	1	**Flip, Flop And Fly** / Thine Eyes Are As The Eyes Of A Dove *(Philips PB-449)* *2nd re-entry*

1 Oct 55	2	1	★ **Hey There** / **Hernando's Hideaway** (*Philips PB-495*)
11 Feb 56	3	1	★ **Who's Sorry Now?** / A Heart Comes In Handy (*Philips PB-546*)
7 Jul 56	3	4	**Goodbye, Au Revoir, Adios** / Because I Love You (*Philips PB-596*)
13 Apr 57	12	1	**I Miss You So** / **So Long** (*Philips PB-683*)
11 May 57	2	1	**I Miss You So** / **So Long** (*Philips PB-683*) *re-entry*
11 Jan 58	4	1	**Pink Sweater Angel** / **Texas Tambourine** (*Philips PB-762*)
22 Feb 58	12	1	**Miss Me Just A Little** / Soliloquy Of A Fool (*Philips PB-785*)
19 Apr 58	15	1	**Strollin' Girl** / Plant A Little Seed (*Philips PB-808*)
19 Sep 59	5	1	★ **I'll Never Fall In Love Again** / **You're All That I Live For** (*Philips PB-952*)
24 Oct 59	17	1	★ **I'll Never Fall In Love Again** / You're All That I Live For (*Philips PB-952*) *1st re-entry*
14 Nov 59	6	3	★ **I'll Never Fall In Love Again** / You're All That I Live For (*Philips PB-952*) *2nd re-entry*

RAYS   3

Doo-wop quartet from Brooklyn, New York discovered by Bob Crewe and Frank Slay.

| 30 Nov 57 | 2 | 3 | **Silhouettes** / Daddy Cool (*London HLU-8505*) |

RALPH READER

See Boy Scout Association

JIM REEVES   8

C&W singer from Galloway, Texas. A hitmaker since 1953, he recast himself as a country crooner in the late '50s and achieved legendary status following a fatal plane crash in 1964.

19 Mar 60	2	1	★ **He'll Have To Go** / In A Mansion Stands My Love (*R.C.A. RCA-1168*)
7 Jan 61	8	4	**Am I Losing You** / I Missed Me (*R.C.A. RCA-1214*)
18 Feb 61	4	3	★ **Whispering Hope** / I'd Like To Be (*R.C.A. RCA-1223*)

JOAN REGAN   36

Glamorous singer born Siobhán Bethel in Romford, Essex in 1925. She achieved national fame in the '50s as resident vocalist on BBC TV's 'Quite Contrary' (1954), followed by four seasons of her own show, 'Be My Guest'.

26 Jun 54	11	1	**Jilted** / I'll Travel With You (*Decca F-10311*)
14 Aug 54	10	7	★ **Wait For Me, Darling** (*Joan Regan with the Johnston Brothers*) / Two Kinds of Tears (*Joan Regan*) (*Decca F-10362*)
18 Sep 54	5	2	★ **If I Give My Heart To You** / Faded Flowers (*Decca F-10373*)
16 Oct 54	20	1	★ **Wait For Me, Darling** (*Joan Regan with the Johnston Brothers*) / Two Kinds of Tears (*Joan Regan*) (*Decca F-10362*) *1st re-entry*
30 Oct 54	35	1	★ **Wait For Me, Darling** (*Joan Regan with the Johnston Brothers*) / Two Kinds of Tears (*Joan Regan*) (*Decca F-10362*) *2nd re-entry*
6 Nov 54	8	2	**This Ole House** (*Joan Regan with the Keynotes*) / Can This Be Love (*Joan Regan*) (*Decca F-10397*)
27 Nov 54	23	1	**This Ole House** / Can This Be Love (*Decca F-10397*) *re-entry*
5 Feb 55	1	7	★ **Prize Of Gold** / When You're In Love (*Decca F-10432*)
3 Dec 55	19	1	**The Rose And The Flame** / The Shepherd Boy (*Decca F-10598*)
7 Jan 56	20	1	★ **Croce di Oro** / Love And Marriage (*Decca F-10659*)
31 Mar 56	11	1	**Don't Take Me For Granted** / The Boy With The Magic Guitar (*Decca F-10710*)
9 Jun 56	14	1	**Honestly** (*Joan Regan*) / I'd Never Leave You Baby (*Joan Regan and the Johnston Brothers*) (*Decca F-10742*)
17 Jan 59	9	1	**Love Like Ours** / Take Me In Your Arms (*H.M.V. POP-555*)
28 Mar 59	10	1	★ **May You Always** / Have You Ever Been Lonely (*H.M.V. POP-593*)
11 Apr 59	1	3	★ **May You Always** / Have You Ever Been Lonely (*H.M.V. POP-593*) *re-entry*
5 Dec 59	1	3	★ **Happy Anniversary** / So Close To My Heart (*Pye Nixa 7N.15238*)
16 Jan 60	11	1	★ **Happy Anniversary** / So Close To My Heart (*Pye Nixa 7N.15238*) *re-entry*

23 Jul 60   **13**   1   ★ **Papa Loves Mama** *(Joan Regan with Rusty and Donna Regan)* /
                        When You Know Someone Loves You *(Joan Regan)*
                        (Pye 7N.15278)

See also Various Artists (All Star Hit Parade)

REIVERS   4
Scottish folk group formed in 1958 by Enoch Kent, Josh MacRae, Moyna Flanagan and Rena Swankie. 'The Wreck Of The John B.' is the same song as the Beach Boys' 'Sloop John B' (1966).

4 Jun 60   **21**   1   **The Wreck Of The John B.** / The Wee Magic Stane
                        (Top Rank JAR-244)
20 Aug 60   **13**   1   **The Wreck Of The John B. / The Wee Magic Stane**
                        (Top Rank JAR-244) **1st re-entry**
28 Jan 61   **8**   2   **The Wee Magic Stane** / The Wreck Of The John B.
                        (Top Rank JAR-244) **2nd re-entry (flipped)**

See also Enoch Kent
          Josh MacRae

LINE RENAUD   12
Popular French singer and actress born Jacqueline Enté in Nieppe in 1928. She recorded this bubbler in 1954 while visiting the USA to appear on several top TV shows.

5 Nov 55   **1**   12   **Relax-Ay-Voo** / Two Sleepy People *(Capitol CL-14356)*
                        Both sides by Dean Martin and Line Renaud

DON RENDELL
See Jo Hunter etc.

HENRI RENÉ & His Orchestra and Chorus   1
Orchestra leader, producer and arranger for stars like Perry Como, Eartha Kitt and Dinah Shore, born Harold Kirchstein in New York in 1906.

31 Oct 59   **7**   1   **Destiny** / La Shabla *(London HLP-8960)*

JOHNNY RESTIVO   3
Rock'n'roll singer born in New York in 1943. Paul Simon played guitar on his hit.

12 Sep 59   **4**   2   ★ **The Shape I'm In** / Ya Ya *(R.C.A. RCA-1143)*
3 Oct 59   **16**   1   ★ **The Shape I'm In** / Ya Ya *(R.C.A. RCA-1143)*
                        re-entry

LITTLE BOBBY REY & His Band   2
Saxophonist from Los Angeles who recorded a couple of rocked-up seasonal melodies for the Original Sound label in 1959. The following year, he was recruited by producer Gary Paxton for the Hollywood Argyles.

10 Dec 60   **3**   1   **Rockin' 'J' Bells** / Dance Of The New Year *(Top Rank JAR-525)*
31 Dec 60   **12**   1   **Rockin' 'J' Bells** / Dance Of The New Year *(Top Rank JAR-525)*
                        re-entry

DEBBIE REYNOLDS   5
Film actress, singer and dancer from El Paso, Texas, born Mary Frances Reynolds. She was Eddie Fisher's first wife (1955-59) and the mother of actress Carrie Fisher.

3 Sep 55   **17**   1   **Why, Oh Why?** *(Tony Martin, Vic Damone, Russ Tamblyn [actually
                        Rex Dennis], Jane Powell, Debbie Reynolds and Ann Miller)* /
                        Chiribiribee *(Kay Armen, Jane Powell, Tony Martin, Debbie
                        Reynolds, Vic Damone and Russ Tamblyn [actually Rex Dennis])*
                        (M.G.M. MGM-837)
25 Feb 56   **3**   2   **The Tender Trap** / Canoodlin' Rag *(M.G.M. MGM-881)*

4 Oct 58	9	1	**This Happy Feeling** / Hillside In Scotland *(Coral Q-72324)*
18 Oct 58	5	1	**This Happy Feeling** / Hillside In Scotland *(Coral Q-72324)*
			re-entry

See also Eddie Fisher (BUNDLE OF JOY)

BUDDY RICH

See Norman Granz' Jazz At The Philharmonic

CHARLIE RICH   3

Eclectic singer/pianist born in Colt, Arkansas in 1932. With the exception of 'Lonely Weekends' and 1965's 'Mohair Sam', chart success eluded him until he reinvented himself as a country balladeer in the 1970s.

30 Apr 60	2	1	**Lonely Weekends** / Everything I Do Is Wrong *(London HLU-9107)*
21 May 60	7	1	**Lonely Weekends** / Everything I Do Is Wrong *(London HLU-9107)*
			1st re-entry
4 Jun 60	10	1	**Lonely Weekends** / Everything I Do Is Wrong *(London HLU-9107)*
			2nd re-entry

CLIFF RICHARD & THE DRIFTERS   4

Britain's most successful rock'n'roll group. Cliff was born Harry Rodger Webb in Lucknow, India in 1940. The Drifters changed their name to the Shadows in 1959, after legal representations from the management of the similarly named American vocal group.

15 Nov 58	2	1	★ <u>**High Class Baby**</u> / My Feet Hit The Ground *(Columbia DB-4203)*
6 Jun 59	14	1	★ <u>**SERIOUS CHARGE**</u> **[OST]** *(Columbia SEG-7895)* **EP**
			Living Doll *(Cliff Richard & The Drifters)* / No Turning Back *(Cliff Richard & The Drifters)* / Mad About You *(Cliff Richard & The Drifters)* / Chinchilla *(Drifters)*
7 Nov 59	20	2	★ <u>**SERIOUS CHARGE**</u> **[OST]** *(Columbia SEG-7895)* **EP** *re-entry*

See also Five Chestnuts
           Shadows

NELSON RIDDLE & His Orchestra   6

Bandleader, arranger and composer from Oradell, New Jersey who provided orchestral backgrounds for major stars like Nat 'King' Cole, Ella Fitzgerald, Judy Garland, Peggy Lee, Dean Martin, Johnny Mathis and Frank Sinatra for over four decades.

| 21 Jan 56 | 10 | 2 | **In Old Lisbon** / Robin Hood *(Capitol CL-14510)* |
| 18 Feb 56 | 1 | 4 | **In Old Lisbon** / **Robin Hood** *(Capitol CL-14510)* *re-entry* |

JACKIE RIGGS   4

Male balladeer who recorded two singles for Philadelphia's Media label in 1956, then disappeared.

| 3 Mar 56 | 14 | 4 | ★ <u>**The Great Pretender**</u> / His Gold Will Melt *(London HLF-8244)* |

DANNY RIVERS   1

Rock'n'roll singer born in Liverpool in 1942. Despite being managed by Larry Parnes and produced by Joe Meek, he was destined to be a one-hit wonder.

| 7 Jan 61 | 15 | 1 | ★ <u>**Can't You Hear My Heart**</u> / I'm Waiting For Tomorrow *(Decca F-11294)* |

MARTY ROBBINS   16

Popular C&W balladeer born Martin Robinson in Glendale, Arizona in 1925. His recordings were mercilessly covered in the UK by Michael Holliday, Terry Dene and others.

29 Jun 57	1	1	**A White Sport Coat (And A Pink Carnation)** / Grown-Up Tears
			(Philips PB-696)
1 Feb 58	1	2	**The Story Of My Life** / Once-A-Week Date *(Fontana H-102)*
17 May 58	21	1	**Stairway Of Love** / Just Married *(Fontana H-128)*
21 Mar 59	10	1	**The Hanging Tree** / The Blues Country Style *(Fontana H-184)*

18 Apr 59	6	3	**The Hanging Tree** / The Blues Country Style *(Fontana H-184)*
			re-entry
5 Dec 59	18	1	★ **Cool Water** / <u>**Big Iron**</u> *(Fontana H-229)*
16 Jan 60	2	2	★ <u>**El Paso**</u> / Running Gun *(Fontana H-233)*
1 Oct 60	8	1	**Is There Any Chance** / I Told My Heart *(Fontana H-263)*
15 Oct 60	4	1	**Is There Any Chance** / I Told My Heart *(Fontana H-263)* *re-entry*
19 Nov 60	13	1	**Ballad Of The Alamo** / Five Brothers *(Fontana H-270)*
3 Dec 60	19	1	**Ballad Of The Alamo** / Five Brothers *(Fontana H-270)* *re-entry*
14 Jan 61	17	1	**MORE GUNFIGHTER BALLADS AND TRAIL SONGS**
			(Fontana TFL-5113) **LP**

San Angelo / Prairie Fire / Streets Of Laredo / Song Of The Bandit / I've Got No Use For Women / Five Brothers / Little Joe The Wrangler / Ride, Cowboy Ride / This Peaceful Sod / She Was Young And She Was Pretty / My Love

MEL ROBBINS   4

Singer/pianist born Hargus Melvin Robbins in Spring City, Tennessee. Later a much in-demand Nashville sessionman, he kicked off his recording career with this breathy rockabilly classic.

| 24 Oct 59 | 1 | 3 | **Save It** / To Know You *(London HLM-8966)* |
| 28 Nov 59 | 26 | 1 | **Save It** / To Know You *(London HLM-8966)* *re-entry* |

PAUL ROBESON   1

Famous black bass baritone singer, actor and civil rights activist born in Princeton, New Jersey in 1898. Banned from travelling abroad for most of the 1950s on account of his political views, he finally got his passport back in June 1958 and relocated to London, as is alluded to in the title of the EP below.

| 27 Sep 58 | 6 | 1 | **ROBESON'S HERE!** *(Topic TOP-32)* **EP** |

Going Home / Now Sleeps The Crimson Petal / Eriskay Love Lilt / My Curly Headed Baby

IVO ROBIĆ & THE SONG-MASTERS   2

Singer/songwriter born in Garešnica, Yugoslavia in 1923. 'Morgen', a collaboration with German tunesmith Bert Kaempfert, established him as an international artist.

| 24 Oct 59 | 4 | 2 | ★ <u>**Morgen**</u> / Ay Ay Ay Paloma *(Polydor NH-23923)* |

FLOYD ROBINSON   2

Country singer/songwriter born in Nashville in 1938. After a promising start, he failed to make much headway and eventually moved into session work. In the '70s, he produced a series of religious albums for children.

| 10 Oct 59 | 1 | 1 | ★ <u>**Makin' Love**</u> / My Girl *(R.C.A. RCA-1146)* |
| 9 Apr 60 | 6 | 1 | **I Believe In Love** / Tattletale *(R.C.A. RCA-1179)* |

ROCK-A-TEENS   4

Rockabilly sextet from Richmond, Virginia fronted by vocalist/guitarist Vic Mizelle.

| 14 Nov 59 | 1 | 4 | **Woo-Hoo** / Untrue *(Columbia DB-4361)* |

ROCKIN' R's   2

The Rockin' R's from Peoria, Illinois were guitarists Ron Volz and Ron Wernsman plus drummer Ted Minar. 'The Beat', a catchy instrumental shuffle, was their one and only US hit.

| 6 Jun 59 | 4 | 2 | **The Beat** / Crazy Baby *(London HL-8872)* |

ROCKIN' SAINTS   1

Rock'n'roll quintet from New Jersey which included saxophonist/vocalist Billy Crandall, formerly of the Royal Teens.

| 26 Nov 60 | 16 | 1 | **Cheat On Me, Baby** / Half And Half *(Brunswick 05843)* |

JIMMIE RODGERS   20

Pop-country singer/guitarist born in Camas, Washington in 1933. He enjoyed immense popularity in the late '50s and early '60s with folk-styled material like 'Honeycomb', 'Kisses Sweeter Than Wine' and 'English Country Garden'.

21 Sep 57	1	6	★ **Honey Comb** / Their Hearts Were Full Of Spring *(Columbia DB-3986)*
15 Mar 58	1	2	★ **Oh-Oh, I'm Falling In Love Again** / The Long Hot Summer *(Columbia DB-4078)*
7 Jun 58	10	1	★ **Secretly** / **Make Me A Miracle** *(Columbia DB-4130)*
28 Jun 58	2	3	★ **Secretly** / **Make Me A Miracle** *(Columbia DB-4130)* **1st re-entry**
26 Jul 58	12	1	★ **Secretly** / Make Me A Miracle *(Columbia DB-4130)* **2nd re-entry**
25 Oct 58	6	1	**Are You Really Mine** / The Wizard *(Columbia DB-4175)*
15 Nov 58	4	1	★ **Woman From Liberia** / Girl In The Wood *(Columbia DB-4206)*
29 Nov 58	5	2	★ **Woman From Liberia** / Girl In The Wood *(Columbia DB-4206)* **re-entry**
31 Jan 59	8	1	**Bimbombey** / You Understand Me *(Columbia DB-4235)*
25 Apr 59	4	1	**I'm Never Gonna Tell** / Because You're Young *(Columbia DB-4281)*
9 May 59	11	1	**I'm Never Gonna Tell** / Because You're Young *(Columbia DB-4281)* **re-entry**

SHORTY ROGERS   15

One of the leading figures in West Coast jazz, trumpeter/bandleader Milton Rajonsky was born in Great Barrington, Massachusetts in 1924.

23 Oct 54	11	4	**THE WILD ONE [OST]** *(H.M.V. 7EG-8044)* **EP**
			Shorty Rogers & His Orchestra
			Blues For Brando / Chino / The Wild One / Windswept
4 Dec 54	22	1	**THE WILD ONE [OST]** *(H.M.V. 7EG-8044)* **LP** *re-entry*
11 Dec 54	21	3	**COOL AND CRAZY** *(H.M.V. DLP-1030)* **LP**
			Shorty Rogers & His Orchestra featuring the Giants
			Coop De Graas / Infinity Promenade / Short Stop / Boar-Jibu / Contours / Tale Of An African Lobster / Chiquito Loco / Sweetheart Of Sigmund Freud
25 Dec 54	20	1	**SHORTY ROGERS AND HIS GIANTS** *(H.M.V. DLP-1058)* **LP**
			Shorty Rogers & His Giants
			Morpo / Bunny / Powder Puff / Mambo Del Crow / The Pesky Serpent / Diablo's Dance / Pirouette / Indian Club
7 Jul 56	6	1	**GIANTS OF MODERN JAZZ** *(H.M.V. 7EG-8174)* **EP**
			Shorty Rogers & His Giants
			The Goof And I / My Little Suede Shoes / Joycycle / The Lady Is A Tramp
4 Oct 58	3	2	**Cerveza** / Juicy *(R.C.A. RCA-1078)*
			Both sides as by Boots Brown & His Blockbusters
25 Oct 58	1	1	**Cerveza** / Juicy *(R.C.A. RCA-1078)* **1st re-entry**
8 Nov 58	10	2	**Cerveza** / Juicy *(R.C.A. RCA-1078)* **2nd re-entry**

See also Howard Rumsey's Lighthouse All Stars

JAN ROHDE   1

New York-born Norwegian Jan Rohde led a skiffle band in Bærum (just west of Oslo) in 1958. Like many others, they switched to rock'n'roll in the early '60s.

| 26 Nov 60 | 20 | 1 | **Come Back Baby** / So Shy *(Qualiton Offbeat PSP-7128)* |

CHAN ROMERO   4

Chicano rocker born Robert Lee Romero in Billings, Montana in 1941. His seminal 'Hippy Hippy Shake' fell just short of a chart placing in the UK, but fared better when revived by the Swinging Blue Jeans in 1964.

| 3 Oct 59 | 1 | 3 | **The Hippy Hippy Shake** / If I Had A Way *(Columbia DB-4341)* |
| 31 Oct 59 | 10 | 1 | **The Hippy Hippy Shake** / If I Had A Way *(Columbia DB-4341)* **re-entry** |

DON RONDO   2
Baritone singer born Donald Rondeau in Ware, Massachusetts in 1930.

| 21 Sep 57 | 4 | 1 | **White Silver Sands** / Stars Fell On Alabama *(London HLJ-8466)* |
| 5 Oct 57 | 4 | 1 | **White Silver Sands** / Stars Fell On Alabama *(London HLJ-8466)* **re-entry** |

EDMUNDO ROS & His Orchestra   6
Popular singing bandleader born Edmund Ross in Port of Spain, Trinidad in 1910. He was instrumental in introducing Latin American music to the British audience.

23 Apr 55	26	1	**Cherry Pink And Apple Blossom White** / **Olé Mambo** *(Decca F-10480)*
28 May 55	19	1	**Cherry Pink And Apple Blossom White** / Olé Mambo *(Decca F-10480)* **re-entry**
30 Jun 56	6	1	**Mister Cuckoo** / Don't Ringa Da Bell *(Decca F-10716)*
14 Jul 56	5	1	**Mister Cuckoo** / Don't Ringa Da Bell *(Decca F-10716)* **re-entry**

See also Various Artists (Lord's Taverners Star Band Hit Parade)

DAVID ROSE & His Orchestra   1
London-born American orchestra leader, arranger, pianist and composer. His best-known work is probably 'The Stripper'.

| 2 Jun 56 | 7 | 1 | **No Other Love** *(with Danny Welton on harmonica)* / Happiness Is A Thing Called Joe *(M.G.M. MGM-898)* |

JAN ROSOL   1
French folk singer/guitarist born in Le Havre in 1921. He based himself in Britain after the war and was a frequent presence on BBC radio in the late '40s and '50s.

| 11 Dec 54 | 43 | 1 | **I Love Paris** *(Jan Rosol and Gwen Campbell)* / C'est Magnifique *(Jan Rosol) (Polygon P-1136)* |

FRANK ROSOLINO SEXTET   1
Jazz trombonist born in Detroit in 1926.

| 11 Dec 54 | 21 | 1 | **KENTON PRESENTS JAZZ – FRANK ROSOLINO** *(Capitol KPL-104)* **LP** |

Ragamuffin / Embraceable You / I'm Gonna Sit Right Down And Write Myself A Letter / Besame Mucho (Kiss Me Much) / Linda / Frank 'n Earnest

RONNIE ROSS
See Jo Hunter etc.

SPENCER ROSS   1
'Spencer Ross' was a pseudonym for arranger Robert Mersey, who created this lush, string-laden instrumental for NBC-TV's 'The Philadelphia Story' in 1959. However, what made the record was the enchanting alto sax lead played by former Glenn Miller band member Jimmy Abato.

| 27 Feb 60 | 9 | 1 | **Tracy's Theme** / Thanksgiving Day Parade *(Philips PB-992)* |

STEVE ROSSI   1
Singer, actor and comedian born Joseph Tafarella in New York in 1932. In 1957, he formed the immensely successful comedy duo Allen & Rossi with Marty Allen.

| 15 Oct 60 | 14 | 1 | **Subito** / A Sweetheart's Prayer *(Philips PB-1061)* |

JEFF ROWENA GROUP   2

Resident band at the Mecca Tottenham Royal dance hall in North London from 1960 to 1964. They recorded a clutch of singles for Pye, Oriole and later CBS, but this instrumental was the closest they got to the charts.

11 Feb 61   **9**   2   **Peanut Vendor** / Bullfight *(Pye 7N.15328)*

ROYAL ROCKERS   1

Obscure rock'n'roll outfit who recorded this one-off instrumental disc for the Bee label of Reading, Pennsylvania.

2 Apr 60   **8**   1   **Jet II** / Swinging Mambo *(Top Rank JAR-329)*

ROYAL TEENS   3

Rock'n'roll band from Fort Lee, New Jersey who made No. 3 in the US charts with 'Short Shorts'. Piano player Bob Gaudio left in 1960 to join the Four Lovers, who later became the Four Seasons.

1 Mar 58   **11**   1   **Short Shorts** / Planet Rock *(H.M.V. POP-454)*
29 Mar 58   **8**   1   **Short Shorts** / Planet Rock *(H.M.V. POP-454)* **1st re-entry**
26 Apr 58   **17**   1   **Short Shorts** / Planet Rock *(H.M.V. POP-454)* **2nd re-entry**

ROYALTONES   1

Rock'n'roll instrumental outfit from Dearborn, Michigan who scored a US Top 20 hit with 'Poor Boy' in 1958. 'Flamingo Express' made the lower reaches of the Billboard 'Hot 100' at the start of 1961.

4 Mar 61   **11**   1   **Flamingo Express** / Tacos *(London HLU-9296)*

LITA ROZA   5

Singer born in Liverpool in 1926. She made her name as resident vocalist with the Ted Heath band and topped the UK charts in 1953 with '(How Much Is) That Doggie In The Window'.

17 Sep 55   **8**   2   **The Man In The Raincoat** / Today And Ev'ry Day *(Decca F-10541)*
1 Oct 55   **9**   1   ★ **Hey There** / Hernando's Hideaway *(Decca F-10611)*
9 Feb 57   **7**   2   **Hey! Jealous Lover** / Julie *(Decca F-10830)*

See also Various Artists (All Star Hit Parade)

HOWARD RUMSEY'S LIGHTHOUSE ALL STARS   13

Bass player and manager of the Lighthouse All-Stars (the resident band at his Lighthouse Café in Hermosa Beach, California) and a pivotal figure in the creation of the '50s West Coast 'cool jazz' movement. The rest of the line-up was Matt Bernhardt, Bob Cooper, Jimmy Giuffre, Shelly Manne, Frank Patchen, Shorty Rogers and Carlos Vidal.

27 Nov 54   **5**   13   **HOWARD RUMSEY'S LIGHTHOUSE ALL STARS (VOL. 1)**
  (Vogue EPV-1004) **EP**
  Out Of Somewhere / Big Girl / Swingshift / Viva Zapata

See also Bob Cooper Sextet
  Shelley Manne & His Men
  Shorty Rogers

JOHNNY RUSSELL   1

Folksy country singer/songwriter and comedian born in Moorhead, Mississippi in 1940.

4 Jun 60   **14**   1   **Lonesome Boy** / Baby Won't You Tell Me So *(M.G.M. MGM-1074)*

MARION RYAN   15

Glamorous singer from Leeds who joined the Ray Ellington Quartet in 1953 and became a regular on radio and TV. Her twin sons, Paul and Barry, became a successful singing duo in the '60s.

18 Aug 56   **8**   1   **Hot Diggity** / Why Do Fools Fall In Love *(Pye Nixa N.15058)*
8 Jun 57   **8**   1   **Mr. Wonderful** / Chantez Chantez *(Pye Nixa N-15091)*

2 Nov 57	**7**	3	**Ding Dong Rock-A-Billy Wedding** / **That's Happiness** *(Pye Nixa N.15105)*
21 Dec 57	**8**	2	**Ding Dong Rock-A-Billy Wedding** / **That's Happiness** *(Pye Nixa N.15105)* **1st re-entry**
11 Jan 58	**5**	1	**Ding Dong Rock-A-Billy Wedding** / **That's Happiness** *(Pye Nixa N.15105)* **2nd re-entry**
15 Mar 58	**5**	2	**Oh Oh, I'm Falling In Love Again** / **Always And Forever** *(Pye Nixa 7N.15130)*
19 Apr 58	**13**	1	**Oh Oh, I'm Falling In Love Again** / Always And Forever *(Pye Nixa 7N.15130)* **re-entry**
17 May 58	**15**	2	**Stairway Of Love** / I Need You *(Pye Nixa 7N.15138)*
17 Dec 60	**6**	2	★ <u>It's You That I Love</u> / Somebody *(Columbia DB-4550)*

BOBBY RYDELL   12

Clean-cut singer born Robert Ridarelli in Philadelphia. He was one of the teen idols who ruled the US charts in the late '50s and early '60s.

26 Sep 59	**5**	2	**Kissin' Time** / You'll Never Tame Me *(Top Rank JAR-181)*
17 Oct 59	**8**	1	**Kissin' Time** / You'll Never Tame Me *(Top Rank JAR-181)* **1st re-entry**
31 Oct 59	**6**	2	**Kissin' Time** / You'll Never Tame Me *(Top Rank JAR-181)* **2nd re-entry**
5 Mar 60	**2**	1	★ <u>Wild One</u> / Little Bitty Girl *(Columbia DB-4429)*
11 Jun 60	**4**	2	★ <u>Swingin' School</u> / Ding-A-Ling *(Columbia DB-4471)*
27 Aug 60	**5**	1	★ <u>Volare</u> / I'd Do It Again *(Columbia DB-4495)*
10 Dec 60	**5**	1	★ <u>Sway</u> / Groovy Tonight *(Columbia DB-4545)*
25 Feb 61	**3**	2	★ <u>Good Time Baby</u> / Cherie *(Columbia DB-4600)*

SAINTS JAZZ BAND   1

Hot 'trad jazz' septet formed in Manchester, Lancashire in 1942.

5 Feb 55	**13**	1	**When The Saints Go Marching In** / Savoy Blues *(Parlophone R-3544)*

SAMMY SALVO   4

Singer born Salvatore Anselmo in Birmingham, Alabama in 1933. His cover of the Crescendos' 'Oh Julie' was his only US hit.

8 Feb 58	**15**	1	**Oh Julie** / Say Yeah *(R.C.A. RCA-1032)*
22 Feb 58	**11**	1	**Oh Julie** / Say Yeah *(R.C.A. RCA-1032)* **1st re-entry**
8 Mar 58	**6**	1	**Oh Julie** / Say Yeah *(R.C.A. RCA-1032)* **2nd re-entry**
5 Apr 58	**12**	1	**Oh Julie** / Say Yeah *(R.C.A. RCA-1032)* **3rd re-entry**

DAVE SAMPSON   4

British rock'n'roll singer from Uttoxeter. 'Sweet Dreams' was his only hit. Like Cliff Richard's Shadows, his backing group were also an instrumental act in their own right.

14 May 60	**13**	1	★ <u>Sweet Dreams</u> / **It's Lonesome** *(Columbia DB-4449)* *Both sides by Dave Sampson and the Hunters*
10 Sep 60	**9**	2	**If You Need Me** / See You Around *(Columbia DB-4502)* *Both sides by Dave Sampson and the Hunters*
11 Mar 61	**9**	1	**Why The Chicken?** *(Dave Sampson and the Hunters)* / 1999 *(Dave Sampson)* *(Columbia DB-4597)*

See also Hunters

JODIE SANDS   4

Two-hit wonder born Eleanor DiSipio in Philadelphia. 'Someday' only managed to crawl to No. 95 in the Billboard 'Hot 100', but made the Top 20 in the UK.

10 Aug 57	**3**	3	**With All My Heart** / More Than Only Friends *(London HL-8456)* *Both sides as by Jodi Sands*
11 Oct 58	**1**	1	★ <u>Someday (You'll Want Me To Want You)</u> / Always In My Heart *(H.M.V. POP-533)*

TOMMY SANDS 11

Talented singer and actor from Chicago who recorded in a polished rockabilly style. He was married to Nancy Sinatra from 1960 to 1965.

16 Mar 57	7	1	**Teen-Age Crush** / Hep Dee Hootie *(Capitol CL-14695)*
30 Mar 57	10	1	**Teen-Age Crush** / Hep Dee Hootie *(Capitol CL-14695)* **re-entry**
19 Oct 57	5	1	**Let Me Be Loved** / Fantastically Foolish *(Capitol CL-14781)*
16 Nov 57	7	3	**Let Me Be Loved** / Fantastically Foolish *(Capitol CL-14781)* **1st re-entry**
21 Dec 57	11	2	**Let Me Be Loved** / Fantastically Foolish *(Capitol CL-14781)* **2nd re-entry**
22 Mar 58	6	1	**Sing Boy Sing** / Crazy 'cause I Love You *(Capitol CL-14834)*
5 Apr 58	12	1	**Sing Boy Sing** / Crazy 'cause I Love You *(Capitol CL-14834)* **1st re-entry**
17 May 58	21	1	**Sing Boy Sing** / Crazy 'cause I Love You *(Capitol CL-14834)* **2nd re-entry**

SANTO & JOHNNY 2

Brothers Santo and Johnny Farina from New York specialised in smooth steel guitar instrumentals. Their hypnotic debut release, 'Sleep Walk', topped the US charts in the summer of 1959.

| 26 Sep 59 | 14 | 2 | ★ <u>Sleep Walk</u> / All Night Diner *(Pye International 7N.25037)* |

SAUTER–FINEGAN ORCHESTRA 3

Highly innovative 1950s American swing jazz band masterminded by arrangers Eddie Sauter and Bill Finegan.

29 Jan 55	24	1	**Midnight Sleighride** / Eddie And The Witchdoctor *(H.M.V. B-10818)*
7 May 55	28	1	**Eddie And The Witchdoctor** / Midnight Sleighride *(H.M.V. B-10818)* **re-entry (flipped)**
17 Sep 55	19	1	**Honey Babe** / Joe's Tune *(H.M.V. B-10865)*

EDNA SAVAGE 11

Popular singer from Warrington, Lancashire, who sadly only managed one hit. She also had a brief but disastrous marriage to rock'n'roll singer Terry Dene.

28 May 55	24	1	**Evermore** / I'll Be There *(Parlophone R-4017)*
18 Jun 55	21	1	**Evermore** / I'll Be There *(Parlophone R-4017)* **1st re-entry**
30 Jul 55	3	2	**Evermore** / I'll Be There *(Parlophone R-4017)* **2nd re-entry**
20 Aug 55	19	2	**Stars Shine In Your Eyes** / A Star Is Born *(Parlophone R-4043)*
12 Nov 55	25	1	★ <u>Arrivederci Darling</u> / Bella Notte *(Parlophone R-4097)*
17 Dec 55	2	3	★ <u>Arrivederci Darling</u> / Bella Notte *(Parlophone R-4097)* **re-entry**
28 May 60	11	1	**All I Need** / Every Day *(Parlophone R-4648)*

JOAN SAVAGE 2

Blackpool-born singer/comedienne who was partnered on stage by her piano-playing husband, Ken Morris. After his death in 1968, she continued appearing in musicals and on the radio.

| 24 Aug 57 | 6 | 1 | **With All My Heart** / Love Letters In The Sand *(Columbia DB-3968)* |
| 7 Sep 57 | 5 | 1 | **With All My Heart** / Love Letters In The Sand *(Columbia DB-3968)* **re-entry** |

AL SAXON 5

Punchy pop singer from London whose real name was Allen Fowler. He later led a big band, briefly ran a record label (Phoenix) and recorded an album of Sinatra standards.

15 Aug 59	1	1	★ <u>Only Sixteen</u> / I'm All Right, Jack *(Fontana H-205)*
28 Nov 59	20	1	**(Seven Little Girls) Sitting In The Back Seat** *(Lana Sisters with Al Saxon) (Fontana H-221)* Flip is 'Sitting On The Sidewalk' by the Lana Sisters
3 Sep 60	15	1	**I've Heard That Song Before** / Someone Like You *(Fontana H-261)*
10 Dec 60	6	2	★ <u>Blue-Eyed Boy</u> / Don't Push Your Luck *(Fontana H-278)*

JACK SCOTT   17

Canadian rock'n'roll singer, guitarist and songwriter born Giovanni Scafone Jr. in Windsor, Ontario.

27 Sep 58	4	2	★ <u>My True Love</u> / Leroy *(London HLU-8626)*
4 Apr 59	2	1	**Goodbye Baby** / Save My Soul *(London HLL-8804)*
			Both sides by Jack Scott with the Chantones
2 May 59	6	1	**I Never Felt Like This** / Bella *(London HLL-8851)*
21 Nov 59	6	1	**There Comes A Time** / Baby Marie *(London HLL-8970)*
23 Jan 60	5	3	★ <u>What In The World's Come Over You</u> / Baby, Baby
			(Top Rank JAR-280)
20 Feb 60	1	2	★ <u>What In The World's Come Over You</u> / Baby, Baby
			(Top Rank JAR-280) **re-entry**
28 May 60	6	1	★ <u>Burning Bridges</u> / Oh Little One *(Top Rank JAR-375)*
20 Aug 60	15	1	**Cool Water** / It Only Happened Yesterday *(Top Rank JAR-419)*
3 Sep 60	5	1	**Cool Water** / It Only Happened Yesterday *(Top Rank JAR-419)*
			1st re-entry
17 Sep 60	8	1	**Cool Water** / It Only Happened Yesterday *(Top Rank JAR-419)*
			2nd re-entry
19 Nov 60	11	1	**Patsy** / Old Time Religion *(Top Rank JAR-524)*
3 Dec 60	19	1	**Old Time Religion** / Patsy *(Top Rank JAR-524)* **re-entry (flipped)**
11 Mar 61	3	1	**Found A Woman** / Is There Something On Your Mind
			(Top Rank JAR-547)

JUDY SCOTT   1

Pop singer from Durango, Colorado discovered by bandleader Ralph Flanagan. Although she went on to become a very successful Las Vegas act, 'With All My Heart' was her only US hit.

10 Aug 57	7	1	**With All My Heart** / The Game Of Love *(Brunswick 05687)*

RONNIE SCOTT ORCHESTRA   1

Influential tenor saxophonist and jazz club owner from London born Ronald Schatt.

5 Feb 55	42	1	**Perdido** / Cherokee *(Esquire 10-391)*

PHIL SEAMEN

See Jo Hunter etc.

HARRY SECOMBE   12

Stocky operatic tenor and comedian born in Swansea in 1921. Founder member of the Goons.

26 Nov 55	2	2	★ <u>On With The Motley</u> / Strange Harmony Of Contrasts *(Philips PB-523)*
3 Mar 56	12	1	**None Shall Sleep Tonight** / When The Stars Were Brightly Shining
			(Philips PB-550)
24 Mar 56	11	1	**None Shall Sleep Tonight** / When The Stars Were Brightly Shining
			(Philips PB-550) **re-entry**
28 Jul 56	4	1	**We'll Keep A Welcome** / The World Is Mine Tonight *(Philips PB-599)*
1 Sep 56	4	6	**We'll Keep A Welcome** / The World Is Mine Tonight *(Philips PB-599)*
			re-entry
16 Mar 57	13	1	**Come Back To Sorrento** / Catari, Catari *(Philips PB-658)*

See also Goons

NEIL SEDAKA   7

Classically trained pianist from New York who entered the Brill Building as a pop music composer and came out a pop star.

7 Feb 59	7	1	**No Vacancy** / The Diary *(R.C.A. RCA-1099)*
4 Apr 59	6	3	★ <u>I Go Ape</u> / Moon Of Gold *(R.C.A. RCA-1115)*
31 Oct 59	2	2	★ <u>Oh! Carol</u> / One Way Ticket *(R.C.A. RCA-1152)*
28 Jan 61	22	1	★ <u>Calendar Girl</u> / The Same Old Fool *(R.C.A. RCA-1220)*

PETER SELLERS 6

Talented actor, comedian and film star born Richard Henry Sellers in Southsea, Hampshire in 1925. Founder member of the Goons.

22 Nov 58	**1**	3	**I'm So Ashamed / A Drop Of The Hard Stuff** *(Parlophone R-4491)*
28 Nov 59	**4**	2	**My Old Dutch / Puttin' On The Smile** *(Parlophone R-4605)*
5 Nov 60	**10**	1	★ <u>**Goodness Gracious Me!**</u> *(Peter Sellers and Sophia Loren)* / Grandpa's Grave *(Peter Sellers) (Parlophone R-4702)*

See also Goons

DAVID SEVILLE 10

Singer, pianist, songwriter, actor and record producer born Rostom Bagdasarian in Fresno, California in 1919. He initially performed as 'Ross Bagdasarian', then adopted the stage name 'David Seville' and went on to invent the Chipmunks.

10 Mar 56	**1**	2	★ <u>**Trouble With Harry**</u> / A Little Beauty *(London HLU-8242)* *Both sides as by Alfi & Harry*
9 Feb 57	**7**	1	**Armen's Theme** / Carousel In Rome *(London HLU-8359)* *Both sides by David Seville & His Orchestra*
23 Feb 57	**3**	2	**Armen's Theme** / Carousel In Rome *(London HLU-8359)* ***1st re-entry***
11 May 57	**9**	1	**Armen's Theme** / Carousel In Rome *(London HLU-8359)* ***2nd re-entry***
17 May 58	**12**	1	★ <u>**Witch Doctor**</u> / Don't Whistle At Me Baby *(London HLU-8619)* *Both sides by David Seville & His Orchestra (Vocal: David Seville)*
10 Jan 59	**4**	1	**The Chipmunk Song** *(The Chipmunks with the Music of David Seville)* / Almost Good *(The Music of David Seville) (London HLU-8762)*
7 Feb 59	**14**	1	**The Chipmunk Song** / Almost Good *(London HLU-8762)* ***1st re-entry***
28 Feb 59	**4**	1	**The Chipmunk Song** / Almost Good *(London HLU-8762)* ***2nd re-entry***

See also Ross Bagdasarian *in* Various Artists (KISMET)

SHADOWS 1

The most successful British instrumental group of all time, as well as Cliff Richard's backing band until 1968 and at numerous reunions thereafter. Originally called the Drifters, they changed their name in the summer of 1959 after the management of the similarly-named American singing group threatened legal action.

16 Jul 60	**11**	1	★ <u>**Apache**</u> / Quatermasster's Stores *(Columbia DB-4484)*

See also Five Chesternuts
 Cliff Richard & The Drifters

JIMMY SHAND & His Band 60

A former miner from Auchtermuchty, Fife, accordionist Jimmy Shand was the doyen of Scottish country dance music. Frequently on TV, he sold millions of records during an amazing career spanning more than 70 years.

25 Sep 54	**25**	1	**An Irish Waltz [M]** / Teviot Brig **[M]** *(Parlophone F-3486)* *An Irish Waltz: The Gentle Maiden – Come Back to Erin / Teviot Brig: Intro – Teviot Brig – Kinloch Of Kinloch – The Hundred Pipers*
30 Oct 54	**17**	1	**Gay Gordons [M]** / The Queen Mary Waltz *(Parlophone F-3474)* *Gay Gordons: Hills Of Perth – Jim Baine – Miss Wilma McKay's Wedding March*
6 Nov 54	**18**	1	**An Irish Waltz [M]** / Teviot Brig **[M]** *(Parlophone F-3486)* ***1st re-entry***
6 Nov 54	**33**	2	**The Red House Reel [M]** / Gaelic Waltz Medley **[M]** *(Parlophone F-3464)* *The Red House Reel: Red House – The Persian Dance / Gaelic Waltz Medley: My Home – Tarry Lullaby – The Tockerlass – Praise Of Islay*
13 Nov 54	**23**	2	**The Northern Lights Of Aberdeen** / The Dashing White Sergeant *(H.M.V. B-10521)* *Both sides by Robert Wilson with Jimmy Shand & His Band*
13 Nov 54	**44**	1	★ <u>**Bluebell Polka**</u> / The Veleta *(Parlophone F-3436)*

| 13 Nov 54 | **44** | 1 | **The Gordon Waltz [M]** / The New Rigged Ship **[M]** |

(Parlophone F-3463)
The Gordon Waltz: O, My Jock McKay – A Gordon For Me – The Lass O' Lowrie /
The New Rigged Ship: The New Rigged Ship – The Stool Of Repentance – Off She
Goes

| 4 Dec 54 | **24** | 5 | **An Irish Waltz [M]** / **Teviot Brig [M]** *(Parlophone F-3486)* |

2nd re-entry

| 4 Dec 54 | **33** | 1 | **The Gordon Waltz [M]** / The New Rigged Ship **[M]** |

(Parlophone F-3463) **re-entry**

| 11 Dec 54 | **43** | 1 | ★ <u>Bluebell Polka</u> / The Veleta *(Parlophone F-3436)* **1st re-entry** |

| 25 Dec 54 | **37** | 1 | **SCOTTISH COUNTRY DANCES NO. 2** *(Parlophone PMD-1015)* 🆻 |

My Love She's But A Lassie Yet / Birks Of Invermay / St. Bernard Waltz / Teviot Brig /
De'il Amang The Tailors / Lord Hume's Reel / Primrose Polka / The Cumberland Reel

| 8 Jan 55 | **32** | 1 | ★ <u>Bluebell Polka</u> / The Veleta *(Parlophone F-3436)* **2nd re-entry** |

| 22 Jan 55 | **55** | 1 | **The Northern Lights Of Aberdeen** / The Dashing White Sergeant |

(H.M.V. B-10521) **1st re-entry**

| 5 Feb 55 | **30** | 2 | **The Northern Lights Of Aberdeen** / The Dashing White Sergeant |

(H.M.V. B-10521) **2nd re-entry**

| 5 Mar 55 | **10** | 1 | **The Northern Lights Of Aberdeen** / The Dashing White Sergeant |

(H.M.V. B-10521) **3rd re-entry**

| 23 Apr 55 | **3** | 6 | **Victory Waltz [M]** / Somebody – Barn Dance **[M]** *(Parlophone F-3500)* |

Victory Waltz: Nelly Kelly – Daisy Bell – I Belong To Glasgow – We Parted On
The Shore – When Irish Eyes Are Smiling

| 21 May 55 | **13** | 1 | **Royal Scots Polka** / La Rinka *(Parlophone F-3501)* |

| 2 Jul 55 | **23** | 2 | **Victory Waltz [M]** / Somebody – Barn Dance **[M]** *(Parlophone F-3500)* |

1st re-entry

| 23 Jul 55 | **25** | 1 | **Victory Waltz [M]** / Somebody – Barn Dance **[M]** *(Parlophone F-3500)* |

2nd re-entry

| 30 Jul 55 | **8** | 2 | **Gay Gordons [M]** / The Queen Mary Waltz *(Parlophone F-3474)* |

re-entry

| 13 Aug 55 | **10** | 2 | **Victory Waltz [M]** / Somebody – Barn Dance **[M]** *(Parlophone F-3500)* |

3rd re-entry

| 17 Sep 55 | **23** | 3 | **Victory Waltz [M]** / Somebody – Barn Dance **[M]** *(Parlophone F-3500)* |

4th re-entry

| 15 Oct 55 | **10** | 3 | **Victory Waltz [M]** / Somebody – Barn Dance **[M]** *(Parlophone F-3500)* |

5th re-entry

| 19 Nov 55 | **24** | 3 | **Victory Waltz [M]** / Somebody – Barn Dance **[M]** *(Parlophone F-3500)* |

6th re-entry

| 3 Dec 55 | **25** | 1 | **Peggy's Love [M]** / Donaree (Pride Of Erin Waltz) *(Parlophone F-3505)* |

Peggy's Love: Peggy's Love – Kirrie Kebbuck

| 10 Dec 55 | **6** | 1 | ★ <u>Bluebell Polka</u> / The Veleta *(Parlophone F-3436)* **3rd re-entry** |

| 24 Mar 56 | **3** | 2 | **Marching With Jimmy Shand [M]** / The New Scotland Strathspey **[M]** |

(Parlophone R-4151)
Marching With Jimmy Shand: Scotland The Brave – The Thistle Of Scotland –
We're No Awa Tae Bide Awa' / *The New Scotland Strathspey:* The New Scotland
Strathspey – Miss Drummond of Perth.

| 21 Apr 56 | **3** | 3 | **Marching With Jimmy Shand [M]** / The New Scotland Strathspey **[M]** |

(Parlophone R-4151) **1st re-entry**

| 19 May 56 | **4** | 3 | **Marching With Jimmy Shand [M]** / The New Scotland Strathspey **[M]** |

(Parlophone R-4151) **2nd re-entry**

| 28 Jul 56 | **13** | 1 | **Marching With Jimmy Shand [M]** / The New Scotland Strathspey **[M]** |

(Parlophone R-4151) **3rd re-entry**

| 11 Aug 56 | **10** | 1 | **Marching With Jimmy Shand [M]** / The New Scotland Strathspey **[M]** |

(Parlophone R-4151) **4th re-entry**

| 10 Nov 56 | **4** | 1 | **Marching With Jimmy Shand [M]** / The New Scotland Strathspey **[M]** |

(Parlophone R-4151) **5th re-entry**

| 17 Nov 56 | **4** | 1 | ★ <u>Sing With Jimmy Shand (Parts 1 & 2)</u> **[M]** *(Parlophone R-4242)* |

Both sides by Jimmy Shand *(accordion)* and the Balmoral Trio
Loch Lomond – I Belong To Glasgow – My Bonnie Lies Over The Ocean / Roamin'
In The Gloamin' – I Love A Lassie – Stop Your Tickling Jock – Just A Wee Deoch
And Doris

| 12 Jan 57 | **1** | 2 | **Marching With Jimmy Shand [M]** / The New Scotland Strathspey **[M]** |

(Parlophone R-4151) **6th re-entry**

1 Jan 58	**1**	1	**Sing In The New Year (Parts 1 & 2) [M]** *(Parlophone R-4382)*
			Scotland The Brave – Uist Tramping Song – We're No Awa' Tae Bide Awa' / A Guid New Year – Auld Lang Syne
10 Jan 59	**5**	1	**Memories O' Rabbie Burns (Parts 1 & 2) [M]** *(Parlophone R-4512)*
			Quickstep Medley: O Willie Brew'd A Peck O' Maut – Mary Morison – O' A' The Airts – There Was A Lad Was Born In Kyle / *Waltz Medley:* Whistle O'er The Lave O't – My Love Is Like A Red Red Rose – A Man's A Man For A' That – Ye Banks And Braes
7 Jan 61	**9**	1	**Sing In The New Year (Parts 1 & 2) [M]** *(Parlophone R-4382)*
			re-entry
11 Feb 61	**12**	2	**Sweetheart Waltz [M]** / Happy Hours – Polka *(Parlophone R-4373)*
			Sweetheart Waltz: She's A Lassie From Lancashire – Let Me Call You Sweetheart – In The Shade Of The Old Apple Tree

DICK SHANE · 1

Obscure British Pat Boone-styled singer who only made one record. His real name was Richard de las Casas and 'Don't Come Back Again' was his own composition.

| 4 Apr 59 | **10** | 1 | **Don't Come Back Again** / |
| | | | When Your Heart Is Only Seventeen Years Old *(Decca F-11122)* |

VALERIE SHANE · 4

Former singer with Ronnie Scott and the Kirchin Band born Valerie Kleiner. The second of her three singles bubbled under strongly, but sadly it's the closest she got to fortune and fame.

3 Jan 59	**1**	1	**Meet Me Tonight In Dreamland** / One Billion Seven Million Thirty-Three *(Philips PB-879)*
14 Feb 59	**2**	1	**Meet Me Tonight In Dreamland** / One Billion Seven Million Thirty-Three *(Philips PB-879)* ***1st re-entry***
4 Apr 59	**5**	2	**Meet Me Tonight In Dreamland** / One Billion Seven Million Thirty-Three *(Philips PB-879)* ***2nd re-entry***

HELEN SHAPIRO · 3

Pop and jazz singer born in London in 1946. She was first British female teen star of the 1960s.

| 25 Feb 61 | **7** | 3 | ★ <u>**Don't Treat Me Like A Child**</u> / When I'm With You *(Columbia DB-4589)* |

RAY SHARPE · 1

Black singer/guitarist from Fort Worth, Texas who was equally adept at R&B and rockabilly. The catchy 'Linda Lu', featuring Duane Eddy and Al Casey on guitars, was his only US hit.

| 24 Oct 59 | **20** | 1 | **Linda Lu** / Red Sails In The Sunset *(London HLW-8932)* |

SHARPS · 3

The Sharps evolved out of a Los Angeles doo-wop group called the Lamplighters, and by a twist of fate ended up backing their former lead singer on this 1957 US hit. They later became the Rivingtons and enjoyed further success with 'Papa-Oom-Mow-Mow' and 'The Bird's The Word'.

21 Dec 57	**9**	2	**Little Bitty Pretty One** /
			I Hope You Won't Hold It Against Me *(Vogue V-9092)*
			Both sides by Thurston Harris and the Sharps
25 Jan 58	**9**	1	**Little Bitty Pretty One** /
			I Hope You Won't Hold It Against Me *(Vogue V-9092)* ***re-entry***

ROLAND SHAW ORCHESTRA · 2

Orchestra leader, composer and arranger from Leicester who went on to specialise in spy movie theme albums in the '60s.

4 Dec 54	**51**	1	**The High And The Mighty** *(Whistling by Johnny Johnston)* /
			No One But You *(Vocal: Kim Bennett)* *(Decca F-10407)*
19 Feb 55	**17**	2	**Softly, Softly** *(Vocal: Kim Bennett)* / A Trumpeter's Lullaby *(Decca F-10449)*

GEORGE SHEARING QUINTET 8

Blind jazz pianist born in London in 1919. He emigrated to the USA in 1947, where he led an immensely popular jazz quintet until the '70s.

19 Jun 54	16	1	Spring Is Here / Easy To Love (M.G.M. MGM-741)
3 Jul 54	17	5	Spring Is Here / Easy To Love (M.G.M. MGM-741) *re-entry*
27 Nov 54	39	2	Body And Soul / The Lady Is A Tramp (M.G.M. MGM-638)

ANNE SHELTON 7

Born Patricia Sibley in London in 1928, Anne Shelton was one of the greatest British singing stars of the '40s and '50s, performing with legends like Glenn Miller and Bing Crosby.

18 Jun 55	25	1	I Remember Mama / What Have They Told You (H.M.V. B-10878)
17 Mar 56	13	1	★ Seven Days / The Great Pretender (Philips PB-567)
19 May 56	12	1	Too Young To Go Steady / The Madonna In Blue (Philips PB-437)
25 Aug 56	8	1	★ Lay Down Your Arms / Daydreams (Philips PB-616)
2 Feb 57	1	2	Give Her My Love (When You Meet Her) / A Man On The March (Philips PB-661)
1 Feb 58	2	1	Ha! Ha! Ha! / Until They Sail (Philips PB-779)

BILLY SHEPARD 3

Tenor born Herman Rombom in St. Louis. He recorded this single in Great Britain following the huge success of his London nightclub debut in the spring of 1954.

4 Sep 54	15	3	The Bandit / Oh Donna Clara (Columbia DB-3460)

PAULINE SHEPHERD 7

London-born singer who made her TV debut at the age of 16 on the BBC's 'Quite Contrary', then moved into film and TV acting. She had the first release on the Pye Nixa label.

29 Oct 55	32	1	Have You Ever Been Lonely / Don't Cry Little Donkey (Pye Nixa N.15000)
19 Nov 55	18	3	Have You Ever Been Lonely / Don't Cry Little Donkey (Pye Nixa N.15000) *re-entry*
31 Mar 56	14	1	Willie Can / No Not Much (Pye Nixa N.15043)
28 Apr 56	3	2	Willie Can / No Not Much (Pye Nixa N.15043) *re-entry*

SHEPHERD SISTERS 1

Quartet of real sisters (Martha, Gayle, Judith and MaryLou Shepherd) from Middletown, Ohio.

9 Nov 57	6	1	★ Alone / Congratulations To Someone (H.M.V. POP-411)

SHIRELLES 3

Quartet from Passaic, New Jersey, and the most popular of the early '60s US girl groups. 'Will You Love Me Tomorrow' was their biggest hit on both sides of the Atlantic.

31 May 58	8	1	I Met Him On A Sunday / I Want You To Be My Boyfriend (Brunswick 05746)
26 Nov 60	25	1	Tonight's The Night / The Dance Is Over (London HL-9233)
28 Jan 61	25	1	★ Will You Love Me Tomorrow / Boys (Top Rank JAR-540)

JOYCE SHOCK 1

Frankie Vaughan's sister-in-law, secretary and labelmate.

3 Oct 59	11	1	Cry, Baby, Cry / Dear Diary (Philips PB-957)

DINAH SHORE 1

American singing star, actress and TV personality born Frances Shore in Winchester, Tennessee in 1916.

9 Apr 55	17	1	Melody Of Love / You're Getting To Be A Habit With Me Both sides by Dinah Shore and Tony Martin (H.M.V. B-10831)

SILHOUETTES   4

Black gospel quartet from Philadelphia who turned to doo-wop to earn a living. Their catchy 'Get A Job' topped the pop charts in the USA, and almost broke through in Britain.

1 Mar 58	**7**	1	**Get A Job** / I Am Lonely *(Parlophone R-4407)*
15 Mar 58	**5**	3	**Get A Job** / I Am Lonely *(Parlophone R-4407)* **re-entry**

JEAN SIMMONS   4

Film actress and singer born in London in 1929. After making a name for herself in Britain, she married Stewart Granger in 1950 and moved to the USA, mainly appearing in Hollywood productions thereafter.

6 Oct 56	**2**	1	★ <u>GUYS AND DOLLS</u> [OST] *(Brunswick OE-9241)* **EP**

A Woman In Love *(Marlon Brando and Jean Simmons)* / I'll Know *(Marlon Brando and Jean Simmons)* / Luck Be A Lady *(Marlon Brando)* / If I Were A Bell *(Jean Simmons)*

SIMS–WHEELER VINTAGE JAZZ BAND   2

Trad jazz band formed by trumpeter Ken Sims (formerly with Acker Bilk) and clarinettist Ian Wheeler (ex Ken Colyer).

12 Nov 60	**6**	1	**Never On Sunday** / Ma Curly Headed Baby *(Polydor NH-66638)*
7 Jan 61	**24**	1	**Never On Sunday** / Ma Curly Headed Baby *(Polydor NH-66638)* **re-entry**

FRANK SINATRA   96

Outstanding singer born Francis Albert Sinatra in Hoboken, New Jersey in 1915.

19 Jun 54	**1**	1	★ <u>Young-At-Heart</u> / Take A Chance *(Capitol CL-14064)*
26 Jun 54	**11**	1	**SONGS FOR YOUNG LOVERS** *(Capitol LC-6654)* **LP**

My Funny Valentine / The Girl Next Door / A Foggy Day / Like Someone In Love / I Get A Kick Out Of You / Little Girl Blue / They Can't Take That Away From Me / Violets For Your Furs

3 Jul 54	**8**	1	**SONGS FOR YOUNG LOVERS** *(Capitol LC-6654)* **LP** **1st re-entry**
3 Jul 54	**9**	1	★ <u>Young-At-Heart</u> / Take A Chance *(Capitol CL-14064)* **re-entry**
10 Jul 54	**6**	1	★ <u>Three Coins In The Fountain</u> / I Could Have Told You *(Capitol CL-14120)*
14 Aug 54	**10**	3	**SONGS FOR YOUNG LOVERS** *(Capitol LC-6654)* **LP** **2nd re-entry**
13 Nov 54	**51**	1	**It Worries Me** / When I Stop Loving You *(Capitol CL-14188)*
20 Nov 54	**42**	1	**SING AND DANCE WITH FRANK SINATRA** *(Philips BBR-8003)* **LP**

Lover / It's Only A Paper Moon / My Blue Heaven / It All Depends On You / You Do Something To Me / Should I / The Continental (You Kiss While You're Dancing) / When You're Smiling (The Whole World Smiles)

27 Nov 54	**72**	1	**SONGS FOR YOUNG LOVERS** *(Capitol LC-6654)* **LP** **3rd re-entry**
11 Dec 54	**9**	4	**SWING EASY!** *(Capitol LC-6689)* **LP**

Just One Of Those Things / I'm Gonna Sit Right Down And Write Myself A Letter / Sunday / Wrap Your Troubles In Dreams / Taking A Chance On Love / Jeepers Creepers / Get Happy / All Of Me

25 Dec 54	**24**	1	**SONGS FOR YOUNG LOVERS** *(Capitol LC-6654)* **LP** **4th re-entry**
29 Jan 55	**43**	1	**The Gal That Got Away** / Someone To Watch Over Me *(Capitol CL-14221)*
5 Feb 55	**27**	1	**SWING EASY!** *(Capitol LC-6689)* **LP** **re-entry**
26 Feb 55	**3**	2	★ <u>You My Love</u> / **Just One Of Those Things** *(Capitol CL-14240)*
9 Apr 55	**1**	4	★ <u>You My Love</u> / **Just One Of Those Things** *(Capitol CL-14240)* **re-entry**
21 May 55	**12**	2	★ <u>Learnin' The Blues</u> / If I Had Three Wishes *(Capitol CL-14296)*
25 Jun 55	**18**	2	★ <u>Learnin' The Blues</u> / If I Had Three Wishes *(Capitol CL-14296)* **1st re-entry**
23 Jul 55	**1**	2	★ <u>Learnin' The Blues</u> / If I Had Three Wishes *(Capitol CL-14296)* **2nd re-entry**
13 Aug 55	**1**	3	★ <u>Not As A Stranger</u> / How Could You Do A Thing Like That To Me *(Capitol CL-14326)*

10 Sep 55	16	1	SESSION WITH SINATRA *(Capitol EAP1-629)* **EP**

Two Hearts, Two Kisses (Make One Love) / Don't Change Your Mind About Me / Learnin' The Blues / Why Should I Cry Over You

5 Nov 55	21	2	**My Funny Valentine** / **I Get A Kick Out Of You** *(Capitol CL-14352)*
26 Nov 55	14	2	**In The Wee Small Hours Of The Morning** / It Never Entered My Mind *(Capitol CL-14360)*
26 Nov 55	19	2	**Same Old Saturday Night** / Fairy Tale *(Capitol CL-14373)*
26 Nov 55	42	1	MOONLIGHT SINATRA *(H.M.V. 7EG-8128)* **EP**

Fools Rush In (Where Angels Fear To Tread) / The Lamplighter's Serenade / This Is The Beginning Of The End / Street Of Dreams

26 Nov 55	42	1	**My Funny Valentine** / **I Get A Kick Out Of You** *(Capitol CL-14352)* *re-entry*
7 Jan 56	2	1	★ <u>Love And Marriage</u> / Look To Your Heart *(Capitol CL-14503)*
28 Apr 56	12	1	**Flowers Mean Forgiveness** / You'll Get Yours *(Capitol CL-14564)*
16 Jun 56	12	2	**Five Hundred Guys** / How Little We Know *(Capitol CL-14584)*
30 Jun 56	14	1	**You'll Never Walk Alone** / If I Loved You *(Columbia DB-2705)*
14 Jul 56	10	1	**How Little We Know** / **Five Hundred Guys** *(Capitol CL-14584)* *1st re-entry (flipped)*
28 Jul 56	7	3	**How Little We Know** / Five Hundred Guys *(Capitol CL-14584)* *2nd re-entry*
28 Jul 56	15	1	**You'll Never Walk Alone** / If I Loved You *(Columbia DB-2705)* *1st re-entry*
18 Aug 56	10	1	**Johnny Concho Theme (Wait For Me)** / Hey! Jealous Lover *(Capitol CL-14607)*
1 Sep 56	4	1	**You'll Never Walk Alone** / If I Loved You *(Columbia DB-2705)* *2nd re-entry*
1 Sep 56	12	1	**How Little We Know** / Five Hundred Guys *(Capitol CL-14584)* *3rd re-entry*
15 Sep 56	4	1	**Our Town** / The Impatient Years *(Capitol CL-14620)*
15 Sep 56	14	1	YOUNG AT HEART [OST] *(Capitol EAP1-571)* **EP**

Young At Heart / Someone To Watch Over Me / Just One Of Those Things / You My Love

19 Jan 57	7	3	**Hey, Jealous Lover** / Johnny Concho Theme (Wait For Me) *(Capitol CL-14607)* *1st re-entry (flipped)*
2 Feb 57	9	1	**You're Sensational** / You Forgot All The Words *(Capitol CL-14646)*
23 Feb 57	10	1	**You're Sensational** / You Forgot All The Words *(Capitol CL-14646)* *1st re-entry*
2 Mar 57	8	3	**Hey, Jealous Lover** / Johnny Concho Theme (Wait For Me) *(Capitol CL-14607)* *2nd re-entry*
16 Mar 57	13	1	**Can I Steal A Little Love** / Your Love For Me *(Capitol CL-14696)*
16 Mar 57	18	1	**You're Sensational** / You Forgot All The Words *(Capitol CL-14646)* *2nd re-entry*
6 Apr 57	7	1	**Can I Steal A Little Love** / Your Love For Me *(Capitol CL-14696)* *1st re-entry*
6 Apr 57	15	1	**Hey, Jealous Lover** / Johnny Concho Theme (Wait For Me) *(Capitol CL-14607)* *3rd re-entry*
20 Apr 57	11	1	**Can I Steal A Little Love** / Your Love For Me *(Capitol CL-14696)* *2nd re-entry*
25 May 57	4	1	**Can I Steal A Little Love** / Your Love For Me *(Capitol CL-14696)* *3rd re-entry*
25 Jan 58	5	2	★ <u>Witchcraft</u> / Tell Her You Love Her *(Capitol CL-14819)*
17 May 58	1	5	**How Are Ya' Fixed For Love?** / **Nothing In Common** *(Capitol CL-14863)* *Both sides by Frank Sinatra and Keely Smith*
14 Jun 58	1	3	★ <u>SINATRA!</u> *(Capitol EAP1-1013)* **EP**

The Lady Is A Tramp / Witchcraft / Come Fly With Me / Tell Her You Love Her

14 Jun 58	8	1	★ <u>THIS IS SINATRA (VOL. 2)</u> *(Capitol LCT-6155)* **LP**

Hey! Jealous Lover / Everybody Loves Somebody / I Believe / Put Your Dreams Away (For Another Day) / Something Wonderful Happens In Summer / Half As Lovely (Twice As True) / So Long, My Love / It's The Same Old Dream / You're Cheatin' Yourself (If You're Cheatin' On Me) / You'll Always Be The One I Love / 'Johnny Concho' Theme (Wait For Me) / If You Are But A Dream / You Forgot All The Words / (How Little It Matters) How Little We Know / Time After Time / Crazy Love

28 Mar 59	16	1	★ <u>**French Foreign Legion**</u> / Time After Time *(Capitol CL-14997)*
22 Aug 59	16	1	★ <u>**High Hopes**</u> / All My Tomorrows *(Capitol CL-15052)*
28 Nov 59	6	3	**Talk To Me** / They Came To Cordura *(Capitol CL-15086)*
5 Mar 60	5	5	★ <u>**It's Nice To Go Trav'ling**</u> / Brazil *(Capitol CL-15116)*

See also Original Soundtrack (HIGH SOCIETY)
Original Soundtrack (YOUNG AT HEART)

SINFONICA DELL'EIAR

See Chorus and Orchestra Sinfonica dell'EIAR

THE SINGING DOGS   3

The brainchild of Danish recording engineer Carl Weismann, whose recordings of birdsong were frequently spoiled by barking dogs. He hit upon the idea of splicing together the barks of five different dogs to create tunes. The result was a million-selling international novelty hit.

| 29 Oct 55 | 7 | 3 | ★ <u>**Pat-A-Cake, Pat-A-Cake – Three Blind Mice – Jingle Bells**</u> **[M]** / |
| | | | Oh! Susanna *(Pye Nixa N.15009)* |

SIR CHAUNCEY & HIS EXCITING STRINGS

See Ernie Freeman & His Orchestra

JIMMY SKIDMORE

See Jo Hunter etc.

SKIP & FLIP   6

Singing duo comprising Clyde Battin and Gary S. Paxton. Paxton subsequently hooked up with producer Kim Fowley and formed the Hollywood Argyles.

| 22 Aug 59 | 5 | 1 | **It Was I** / Lunch Hour *(Top Rank JAR-156)* |
| 14 May 60 | 2 | 5 | **Cherry Pie** / Cryin' Over You *(Top Rank JAR-358)* |

JULIAN SLADE   8

Pianist and composer born in London in 1930. His biggest success was the musical 'Salad Days', which held the record as Britain's longest-running show for ten years.

27 Nov 54	19	1	**Music from 'Salad Days' (Parts 1 & 2) [M]** *(Parlophone R-3927)*
			We're Looking For A Piano – I Sit In The Sun – Oh! Look At Me / It's Easy To Sing –
			The Time Of My Life – We Said We Wouldn't Look Back – Oh! Look At Me
18 Dec 54	9	6	**Music from 'Salad Days' (Parts 1 & 2) [M]** *(Parlophone R-3927)*
			1st re-entry
12 Feb 55	18	1	**Music from 'Salad Days' (Parts 1 & 2) [M]** *(Parlophone R-3927)*
			2nd re-entry

MARTIN SLAVIN   3

London-born pianist/vibraphonist who was musical director for several British TV shows in the late '50s, and was also very active as a session musician and arranger. He later moved to Canada, and then Hollywood, where he composed, arranged and played film music.

5 Dec 58	1	2	★ <u>**Cha Cha Momma Brown**</u> / My Bonnie Lies Over The Ocean
			Both sides as by Martinas & His Music (Columbia DB-4223)
7 Jan 61	13	1	**Rock-A-Charleston** / The Charleston's Gonna Rock The Hop Tonight
			Both sides by Martin Slavin & His Gang (Oriole CB-1587)

BETTY SMITH'S SKIFFLE   2

Jazz singer, saxophonist and pianist born in Sileby, Leicestershire in 1929.

14 Sep 57	13	1	**There's A Blue Ridge Round My Heart Virginia** / Double Shuffle
			(Tempo A-162)
5 Oct 57	1	1	**There's A Blue Ridge Round My Heart Virginia** / Double Shuffle
			(Tempo A-162) **re-entry**

DEREK SMITH

See Jo Hunter etc.

EDDIE SMITH with the HORNETS   2

Obscure instrumental outfit who recorded for the Rel label in Westport, Connecticut. Smith was a native of Coats, North Carolina, but the provenance of the Hornets is unknown.

6 Feb 60	**2**	1	**Upturn** / Border Beat *(Top Rank JAR-285)*
20 Feb 60	**5**	1	**Upturn** / Border Beat *(Top Rank JAR-285)* **re-entry**

JOHNNY SMITH

See Paul Quinichette etc.

KEELY SMITH   5

Jazz and pop vocalist born Dorothy Keely in Norfolk, Virginia in 1928. She recorded some memorable duets with Louis Prima (to whom she was marrried from 1953 to 1961) and also Frank Sinatra.

17 May 58	**1**	5	**How Are Ya' Fixed For Love?** / **Nothing In Common**
			(Capitol CL-14863)
			Both sides by Frank Sinatra and Keely Smith

LOU SMITH   1

Country singer born in Joaquin, Texas in 1928. 'Cruel Love' was a Top Ten C&W hit for him in 1960.

10 Dec 60	**23**	1	**Cruel Love** / Close To My Heart *(Top Rank JAR-520)*

RAY SMITH   1

Rockabilly singer and pianist from Melber, Kentucky. He started out recording for Sam Phillips' Sun label in 1958, but had no hits until he recorded 'Rockin' Little Angel' for Judd, run by Phillips' brother. He committed suicide in 1979 at the age of 41.

20 Feb 60	**8**	1	**Rockin' Little Angel** / That's All Right *(London HL-9051)*

SOMETHIN' SMITH & THE REDHEADS   2

Lighthearted pop trio formed by three red-haired students at UCLA: Bob Robinson aka Somethin' Smith (vocals/guitar), Saul Striks (piano) and Major Short (violin).

18 Aug 56	**14**	1	**In A Shanty In Old Shanty Town** / Coal Dust On The Fiddle
			(Philips PB-609)
13 Oct 56	**10**	1	**In A Shanty In Old Shanty Town** / Coal Dust On The Fiddle
			(Philips PB-609) **re-entry**

WILLIE SMITH

See Norman Granz' Jazz At The Philharmonic

HANK SNOW   15

Country superstar born Clarence Eugene Snow in Brooklyn, Nova Scotia in 1914.

15 Mar 58	**2**	3	**COUNTRY GUITAR (VOL. 4)** *(R.C.A. RCX-116)* **EP**
			I'm Hurting All Over / Big Wheels / Nobody's Child / Why Do You Punish Me (For Loving You)
26 Apr 58	**8**	1	**COUNTRY GUITAR (VOL. 4)** *(R.C.A. RCX-116)* **EP** *1st re-entry*
31 May 58	**16**	1	**COUNTRY GUITAR (VOL. 4)** *(R.C.A. RCX-116)* **EP** *2nd re-entry*
6 Sep 58	**3**	1	**COUNTRY GUITAR (VOL. 4)** *(R.C.A. RCX-116)* **EP** *3rd re-entry*
27 Sep 58	**2**	2	**COUNTRY GUITAR (VOL. 4)** *(R.C.A. RCX-116)* **EP** *4th re-entry*
29 Nov 58	**15**	1	**COUNTRY GUITAR (VOL. 4)** *(R.C.A. RCX-116)* **EP** *5th re-entry*
17 Oct 59	**2**	6	**Old Shep** / The Last Ride *(R.C.A. RCA-1151)*

Edmundo Ros

JERI SOUTHERN   4

Classically trained jazz pianist/singer born Genevieve Hering in Royal, Nebraska in 1926.

25 May 57   **1**   4   ★ <u>**Fire Down Below**</u> / Smoke Gets In Your Eyes *(Brunswick 05665)*

SOUTHLANDERS   12

Jamaican/British vocal quartet. Originally formed in 1953 by Edric Connor and Vernon Nesbeth as the Caribbeans, they evolved into the Southlanders, comprising Nesbeth, Frank Mannah and brothers Allan and Harry Wilmot (father of singer/actor/comedian Gary Wilmot). Harry, who delivered the immortal 'I am a mole and I live in a hole' line, died in 1961.

12 Nov 55	**35**	1	**Ain't That A Shame** / Have You Ever Been Lonely (Parlophone R-4069)
25 Jan 58	**9**	1	**Peanuts** / I Never Dreamed *(Decca F-10958)*
8 Feb 58	**3**	1	★ <u>**Put A Light In The Window**</u> / Penny Loafers And Bobby Socks (Decca F-10982)
14 Jun 58	**16**	1	**Torero** / I Wanna Jive Tonight *(Decca F-11032)*
28 Jun 58	**3**	2	**Torero** / I Wanna Jive Tonight *(Decca F-11032) 1st re-entry*
26 Jul 58	**1**	2	**Torero** / I Wanna Jive Tonight *(Decca F-11032) 2nd re-entry*
16 Aug 58	**11**	1	**Torero** / I Wanna Jive Tonight *(Decca F-11032) 3rd re-entry*
22 Nov 58	**4**	3	**The Mole In A Hole** / Choo-Choo-Choo-Choo Cha-Cha-Cha (Decca F-11067)

MUGGSY SPANIER'S DIXIELAND BAND   1

Prominent white cornet player/bandleader of the hot jazz/Dixieland persuasion born Francis Spanier in Chicago in 1906.

3 Sep 55   **17**   1   **MUGGSY SPANIER'S DIXIELAND BAND** *(Tempo EXA-3)* **EP**
                        Bugle Call Rag / That's A Plenty / Muskrat Ramble / Tin Roof Blues

DOROTHY SQUIRES   2

Welsh singing star of the '40s and '50s born Edna May Squires in Pontyberem in 1915. She was married to actor Roger Moore from 1953 to 1961.

24 Dec 55   **4**   2   **When You Lose The One You Love** / In All The World
                        (Pye Nixa N.15010)

ROSEMARY SQUIRES   2

Britain's answer to Doris Day, born Joan Rosemary Yarrow in Bristol in 1928. A versatile singer who could handle both jazz and big band pop, she later became one of the top advertising jingle singers in Britain (that's her on the famous 'Hands that do dishes' Fairy Liquid commercial).

3 Mar 56   **22**   1   **Band Of Gold** / Where You Are *(Decca F-10685)*
22 Mar 58   **14**   1   **Happy Is The Bride** / Give Me The Simple Life *(H.M.V. POP-462)*

JO STAFFORD   13

Female singing star from Coalinga, California. Originally with the Stafford Sisters, then Tommy Dorsey's Pied Pipers, she went solo in 1944 and chalked up dozens of hits up to 1957.

18 Sep 54	**26**	1	**He Bought My Soul At Calvary** (Jo Stafford and the Lee Brothers) / It Is No Secret *(Jo Stafford and Quartette) (Columbia DB-2929)*
19 Mar 55	**16**	2	**High Society** / Back Where I Belong *(Philips PB-417)* *Both sides by Jo Stafford and Frankie Laine*
19 Nov 55	**24**	3	★ <u>**Suddenly There's A Valley**</u> / Nightwatch *(Philips PB-509)*
7 Jan 56	**20**	1	**Arrivederci Darling** / If You Want To Love (You Have To Cry) (Philips PB-527)
18 Feb 56	**5**	1	**Young And Foolish** / My Heart Goes A-Sailing *(Philips PB-538)*
10 Mar 56	**11**	1	**Young And Foolish** / My Heart Goes A-Sailing *(Philips PB-538)* *1st re-entry*
31 Mar 56	**4**	4	**Young And Foolish** / My Heart Goes A-Sailing *(Philips PB-538)* *2nd re-entry*

STAÏFFI ET SES MUSTAFA'S   3

French Algerian singer/songwriter Alberto Staïffi (real name Albert Darmon) got into the lower reaches of the UK charts with this cover of Bob Azzam's big hit. Versions by Clinton Ford and Kemal Rachid also bubbled under.

4 Jun 60	**18**	1	★ **Mustafa** / Zoubida *(Pye International 7N.25057)*
18 Jun 60	**9**	2	★ **Mustafa** / Zoubida *(Pye International 7N.25057)* **re-entry**

CYRIL STAPLETON & His Orchestra   17

Violinist/orchestra leader from Nottingham who became a household name after he was appointed conductor of the BBC Show Band in 1952. When it was abruptly wound up in 1957, he assembled his own orchestra and carried on.

3 Jul 54	**12**	5	**Lester Leaps In** / Midnight Sun *(Decca F-10313)*
7 May 55	**16**	3	★ **Elephant Tango** / Gabrielle *(Decca F-10488)*
10 Sep 55	**11**	2	★ **Blue Star** *(Vocal: Julie Dawn)* / Honey Babe *(Vocal: Gordon Langhorn)* *(Decca F-10559)*
17 Mar 56	**17**	1	★ **The Italian Theme** / Come Next Spring *(Decca F-10703)*
31 Mar 56	**19**	1	★ **The Italian Theme** / Come Next Spring *(Decca F-10703)* **re-entry**
26 May 56	**4**	1	★ **The Happy Whistler** *(Cyril Stapleton & His Orchestra featuring Desmond Lane, the Penny-Whistle Boy)* / Tiger Tango *(Cyril Stapleton & His Orchestra (Decca F-10735)*
24 Jan 59	**9**	1	**Nick Nack Paddy Wack** / The Inn Of The Sixth Happiness *(Vocal: Bill Elliott)* *(Decca F-11094)*
14 Feb 59	**4**	3	**Nick Nack Paddy Wack** / The Inn Of The Sixth Happiness *(Vocal: Bill Elliott)* *(Decca F-11094)* **re-entry**

See also Various Artists (MY FAIR LADY)

STARGAZERS   26

Britain's top vocal group of the '50s (four males and one female), formed in 1949 by Cliff Adams. They were frequently heard on the BBC and also backed many singers on recording sessions. Original members Dick James and Marie Benson went on to find success as solo artists.

20 Nov 54	**11**	2	**365 Kisses** / I Need You Now *(Decca F-10379)*
27 Nov 54	**7**	3	★ **The Finger Of Suspicion** *(Dickie Valentine with the Stargazers)* *(Decca F-10394)* Flip is 'Who's Afraid (Not I, Not I, Not I)' by Dickie Valentine
1 Jan 55	**19**	2	**365 Kisses** / I Need You Now *(Decca F-10379)* **re-entry**
15 Jan 55	**12**	7	★ **Somebody** / No More *(Decca F-10437)*
14 May 55	**3**	3	★ **The Crazy Otto Rag** / Hey Mr. Banjo *(Decca F-10523)*
3 Sep 55	**1**	1	★ **Close The Door** / I've Got Four Big Brothers *(Decca F-10594)*
29 Oct 55	**22**	2	★ **Twenty Tiny Fingers** / An Old Beer Bottle *(Decca F-10626)*
3 Mar 56	**2**	1	**Zambesi** / When The Swallows Say Goodbye *(Decca F-10696)*
7 Apr 56	**14**	1	**Zambesi** / When The Swallows Say Goodbye *(Decca F-10696)* **re-entry**
2 Jun 56	**10**	1	★ **Hot Diggity** / Rockin' And Rollin' *(Decca F-10731)*
6 Oct 56	**8**	2	**She Loves To Rock** / John Jacob Jingleheimer Smith *(Decca F-10775)*
27 Apr 57	**5**	1	**Mangos** / You Won't Be Around *(Decca F-10867)*

See also Adam Singers
           Cliff Adams Orchestra
           Marie Benson
           Dick James
           Various Artists (MY FAIR LADY)

KAY STARR   33

Jazz-influenced pop singer from Dougherty, Oklahoma born Katherine Starks. She sang with various bands including Glenn Miller's and Joe Venuti's before embarking on a very successful solo career in 1948. Even after the advent of rock'n'roll, she continued having hits until 1962.

18 Sep 54	1	4	★ **Am I A Toy Or Treasure** / **Fortune In Dreams** *(Capitol CL-14151)*
27 Nov 54	28	2	**GENE NORMAN PRESENTS**
			KAY STARR WITH BARNEY KESSEL *(Vogue EPV-1014)* **LP**
			Them There Eyes / What Is This Thing Called Love / Ain't Misbehavin' / Good For Nothin' Joe
12 Mar 55	2	7	**If Anyone Finds This, I Love You** / Turn Right *(H.M.V. B-10837)*
27 Aug 55	1	10	**Good And Lonesome** / Where, What Or When *(H.M.V. B-10895)*
12 Nov 55	35	1	**Good And Lonesome** / Where, What Or When *(H.M.V. B-10895)*
			re-entry
11 Feb 56	5	1	★ **Rock And Roll Waltz** / I've Changed My Mind A Thousand Times *(H.M.V. POP-168)*
14 Jul 56	2	4	**Second Fiddle** / Love Ain't Right *(H.M.V. POP-231)*
22 Jun 57	4	3	**Jamie Boy** / The Things I Never Had *(H.M.V. POP-357)*
23 Jan 60	12	1	**Riders In The Sky** / Night Train *(Capitol CL-15105)*

WILL STARR   10

Ace accordionist born William Starrs in the mining village of Croy, Stirlingshire in 1922.

12 Nov 55	9	4	**Savoy Scottish Medley** / Eightsome Reel **[M]** *(Parlophone R-4077)*
			Eightsome Reel: Mason's Apron – Speed The Plough – Mrs. MacLeod ('Savoy Scottish Medley' is one-step originally recorded by the Savoy Orpheans circa 1924 (Columbia 969). Arranged by Debroy Somers, it was not a medley of songs, but a mélange of Scottish tropes and gimmicks including quotes from dance tunes, bagpipe effects, bells, and similar.)
24 Dec 55	5	3	**Savoy Scottish Medley** / Eightsome Reel **[M]** *(Parlophone R-4077)*
			re-entry
24 Dec 55	17	3	**Tap-Wood Polka** / Liberton Pipe Band *(Parlophone R-4103)*

STATION SKIFFLE GROUP   2

In their day, the Station Skiffle Group were one of the hottest bands in London. Aspiring record producer Joe Meek recruited them to cut an audition disc for Columbia and renamed them 'Jimmy Miller & His Barbecues' after their lead singer and a sign he saw on a wall advertising a barbecue.

7 Sep 57	9	1	**Hugged My Honey** / Don't You Rock Me Daddy-O *(Esquire 10-503)*
19 Oct 57	8	1	**Sizzlin' Hot** / Free Wheelin' Baby *(Columbia DB-4006)*
			Both sides as by Jimmy Miller & The Barbecues

ANTHONY STEEL   3

Born in London, Cambridge educated and a former Grenadier Guards officer, Anthony Maitland Steel was an actor best known for his appearances in British war films of the '50s.

3 Jul 54	21	1	★ **West Of Zanzibar** *(Anthony Steel with the Radio Revellers)* *(Polygon P-1114)*
			Flip is 'Who Cares' by the Radio Revellers
4 Sep 54	24	1	★ **West Of Zanzibar** *(Anthony Steel with the Radio Revellers)* *(Polygon P-1114)* **re-entry**
19 Feb 55	34	1	**The Flame** *(Anthony Steel with the Radio Revellers)* *(Polygon P-1154)*
			Flip is 'Under The Southern Cross' by the Radio Revellers

TOMMY STEELE   49

Britain's first rock'n'roll star and teen idol, born Thomas Hicks in London in 1936.

20 Oct 56	3	1	★ **Rock With The Caveman** / Rock Around The Town *(Decca F-10795)*
			Both sides by Tommy Steele & The Steelmen
10 Nov 56	2	8	**Elevator Rock** / **Doomsday Rock** *(Decca F-10808)*
			Both sides by Tommy Steele & The Steelmen

8 Dec 56	1	1	★ **Singing The Blues** / Rebel Rock *(Decca F-10819)*
			Both sides by Tommy Steele & The Steelmen
16 Mar 57	13	2	**YOUNG LOVE** *(Decca DFE-6388)* **EP**
			Tommy Steele & The Steelmen
			Young Love / Doomsday Rock / Wedding Bells / Rock With The Caveman
1 Jun 57	9	1	★ **Shiralee** / Grandad's Rock *(Decca F-10896)*
			Both sides by Tommy Steele & The Steelmen
15 Jun 57	4	1	★ **Shiralee** / Grandad's Rock *(Decca F-10896)* **1st re-entry**
27 Jul 57	2	4	★ **Shiralee** / Grandad's Rock *(Decca F-10896)* **2nd re-entry**
10 Aug 57	4	1	★ **Water, Water** / **A Handful Of Songs** *(Decca F-10923)*
			Both sides by Tommy Steele & The Steelmen
31 Aug 57	3	1	**Elevator Rock** / Doomsday Rock *(Decca F-10808)* **re-entry**
26 Oct 57	2	3	★ **Hey You!** / **Plant A Kiss** *(Decca F-10941)*
			Both sides by Tommy Steele & The Steelmen
29 Mar 58	9	3	★ **Happy Guitar** *(Tommy Steele & The Steelmen)* /
			Princess *(Tommy Steele) (Decca F-10976)*
24 May 58	6	7	**It's All Happening** *(Tommy Steele)* / **What Do You Do** *(Tommy Steele and Tommy Steele) (Decca F-11026)*
5 Jul 58	12	1	★ **The Only Man On The Island** / I Puts The Lightie On *(Decca F-11041)*
			Both sides by Tommy Steele & The Steelmen
8 Nov 58	7	1	★ **Come On, Let's Go** / **Put A Ring On Her Finger** *(Decca F-11072)*
21 Mar 59	6	2	**Hiawatha** / The Trial *(Decca F-11117)*
25 Apr 59	8	1	**Hiawatha** / The Trial *(Decca F-11117)* **re-entry**
26 Sep 59	2	8	**You Were Mine** / Young Ideas *(Decca F-11162)*
21 Nov 59	16	1	★ **Little White Bull** / Singing Time *(Decca F-11177)*
			Picture sleeve states that 'Tommy Steele's royalties from this record will be donated by him to the Variety Club of Great Britain fund for a cancer research unit for children.'
18 Jun 60	3	1	★ **What A Mouth (What A North And South)** / Kookaburra
			(Decca F-11245)
17 Dec 60	16	1	★ **Must Be Santa** / Boys And Girls *(Decca F-11299)*

CONNIE STEVENS 1

Actress/singer born Concetta Ingoglia in New York in 1938. She appeared in many films and TV series from 1957 onwards, but became a household name after being cast as Cricket Blake in 'Hawaiian Eye' (1959-63). She was paired with fellow Warner Bros. artist Edd Byrnes (who starred in the '77 Sunset Strip' TV series as amateur sleuth Kookie) for this novelty single.

30 Apr 60	7	1	★ **Kookie Kookie (Lend Me Your Comb)**
			(Edward Byrnes and Connie Stevens) (Warner Bros. WB-5)
			Flip is 'You're The Top' by Edward Byrnes

DODIE STEVENS 3

Teenage singer/actress born Geraldine Pasquale in Chicago in 1946. She had several US chart successes in 1959 and 1960. 'Pink Shoe Laces', recorded when she was just 13, was also a minor hit in the UK.

| 11 Apr 59 | 2 | 2 | ★ **Pink Shoe Laces** / Coming Of Age *(London HLD-8834)* |
| 11 Feb 61 | 9 | 1 | **Yes, I'm Lonesome Tonight** / Too Young *(London HLD-9280)* |

KIRK STEVENS 11

Scottish singer and actor. He co-starred with Jon Pertwee in 'Pertwee's Progress' on BBC radio.

29 Jan 55	5	10	**Here's To The Gordons** / My Dearie, My Darling *(Parlophone R-3963)*
16 Apr 55	19	1	**Here's To The Gordons** / My Dearie, My Darling *(Parlophone R-3963)*
			re-entry

TERRI STEVENS 2

Singer born Rose Caruso in West Hartford, Connecticut. Shortly after her 18th birthday, she landed a gig at the legendary Copacabana nightclub in New York. Three years later, she was touring with the Desi Arnaz Band and appearing on top US TV shows.

14 May 55 **33** 1   **Unsuspecting Heart** / How Can I? *(Parlophone R-3983)*
25 Jun 55 **24** 1   **Unsuspecting Heart** / How Can I? *(Parlophone R-3983)* ***re-entry***

TRUDY STEVENS 6

In the movie 'White Christmas' (1954), actress Vera-Ellen's singing parts were voiced by Georgia Wood. On the soundtrack LP, however (from which both of the cuts below were taken), they were sung by Trudy Stevens, wife of bandleader Dick Stabile.

27 Nov 54 **9** 3   **White Christmas** / Snow *(Brunswick 05354)*
                     Both sides by Bing Crosby, Danny Kaye, Peggy Lee and Trudy Stevens. (This was a re-recording of Bing's famous hit and was featured in the film, 'White Christmas'.)
25 Dec 54 **37** 1   **White Christmas** / Snow *(Brunswick 05354)* ***1st re-entry***
 8 Jan 55 **12** 2   **White Christmas** / Snow *(Brunswick 05354)* ***2nd re-entry***

ANDY STEWART 12

Internationally famous Scottish singer, entertainer and TV star born in Glasgow in 1933.

 8 Oct 60   **1** 12 ★ **A Scottish Soldier** / The Muckin' O' Geordie's Byre
                     (Top Rank JAR-512)

GARY STITES 1

Guitarist/singer/songwriter born in Denver, Colorado in 1940. His biggest US hit was 'Lonely For You', but in Britain 'Starry-Eyed' was his strongest seller. Sadly for him, it lost out to a cover version by Michael Holliday, which went to the top of the UK charts in January 1960.

19 Dec 59 **17** 1   **Starry Eyed** / Without Your Love *(London HLL-9003)*

SAMMY STOKES

See Jo Hunter etc.

RHET STOLLER 2

Young guitarist born Barry Stoller in Camberwell, Surrey in 1945. 'Chariot', produced by Alex Wharton, is reputed to be the first British record to feature double-tracked guitar.

24 Sep 60 **9** 1   **Walk Don't Run** / All Rhet *(Decca F-11271)*
17 Dec 60 **8** 1 ★ **Chariot** / Night Theme *(Decca F-11302)*

MORRIS STOLOFF *(conductor)*

See Columbia Pictures Orchestra

GALE STORM 12

Actress/singer born Josephine Owaissa Cottle in Bloomington, Texas in 1922. She was discovered in 1954 by Randy Wood, president of Dot Records, and went on to score twelve US hits between 1955 and 1957.

28 Jan 56 **3** 2 ★ **I Hear You Knocking** / Never Leave Me *(London HLD-8222)*
 3 Mar 56 **1** 2 ★ **I Hear You Knocking** / Never Leave Me *(London HLD-8222)* ***re-entry***
30 Jun 56 **1** 6   **Why Do Fools Fall In Love** / I Walk Alone *(London HLD-8286)*
10 Aug 57 **7** 1   **Dark Moon** / A Little Too Late *(London HLD-8424)*
24 Aug 57 **9** 1   **Dark Moon** / A Little Too Late *(London HLD-8424)* ***re-entry***

ROBB STORME 7

Singer/guitarist from Luton, born Robert Scales. He recorded two very promising solo singles before teaming up with the Whispers for a further four, plus an EP.

5 Nov 60	10	1	**One Thousand Nine Hundred And When** / I Don't Need Your Love Anymore *(Decca F-11282)*
19 Nov 60	5	4	**One Thousand Nine Hundred And When** / I Don't Need Your Love Anymore *(Decca F-11282)* *re-entry*
21 Jan 61	4	2	**Music / Five Minutes More** *(Decca F-11313)*

WALLY STOTT ORCHESTRA 7

Highly respected British conductor, arranger and light music composer born in Leeds in 1924. In 1972, he underwent a sex-change operation and became Angela Morley.

27 Nov 54	32	2	**The Cat From Coos Bay** / The Night Ride *(Philips PB-351)*
1 Jan 55	7	4	**The Cat From Coos Bay** / The Night Ride *(Philips PB-351)* **1st re-entry**
5 Feb 55	52	1	**The Cat From Coos Bay** / The Night Ride *(Philips PB-351)* **2nd re-entry**

STRING-A-LONGS 2

Instrumental quintet from Plainview, Texas produced by Norman Petty, famous for his work with Buddy Holly and the Crickets.

| 11 Feb 61 | 5 | 2 | ★ **Wheels** / Am I Asking Too Much *(London HLU-9278)* |

BARRETT STRONG 1

Born in West Point, Mississippi in 1941, singer/songwriter Barrett Stong was a pivotal figure in Motown's formative years. It was his smash hit, 'Money', recorded for their Anna subsidiary, that provided the vital capital Berry Gordy needed to expand his fledgling operation.

| 9 Apr 60 | 3 | 1 | **Money (That's What I Want)** / Oh I Apologize *(London HLU-9088)* |

BOB(BY) SUMMERS 4

The younger brother of Mary Ford (Iris Summers), Bob Summers grew up under the influence of Les Paul and learned guitar at an early age. He became a prolific session musician, and famously produced, engineered and played all the instruments on Terry Stafford's 1964 hit, 'Suspicion'.

10 Oct 59	14	1	**Rattle Rhythm** / Excitement *(Capitol CL-15063)* Both sides by Bob Summers
28 May 60	9	1	**Little Brown Jug** / Twelfth Street Rag *(Capitol CL-15130)* Both sides by Bobby Summers
25 Jun 60	8	2	**Little Brown Jug** / Twelfth Street Rag *(Capitol CL-15130)* *re-entry*

See also Inadequates

SWE-DANES 1

Music/comendy/dance trio formed in 1958 by Swedish singer Alice Babs (real name Hildur Alice Nilsson), Danish jazz violinist Svend Asmussen, and Danish guitarist Ulrik Neumann.

| 11 Jun 60 | 3 | 1 | **Scandinavian Shuffle** / Hot Toddy *(Warner Bros. WB-7)* |

SWEDISH ALL STARS 3

Jazz ensemble comprising Åke Persson (trombone), Arne Domnérus (alto sax, clarinet), Lars Gullin (bari sax), Bengt Hallberg (piano), Gunnar Johnson (bass) and Jack Noren (drums).

| 19 Jun 54 | 6 | 3 | **CLIFFORD BROWN & ART FARMER WITH THE SWEDISH ALL STARS (VOL. 2)** *(Esquire EP-3)* **EP** Falling In Love With Love / Lover Come Back To Me |

See also Clifford Brown
Swedish-American All Stars

SWEDISH-AMERICAN ALL STARS   5

One-off jazz 'super-session' consisting of Art Farmer (trumpet), James Cleveland and Åke Persson (trombones), Arne Domnérus (alto sax, clarinet), Lars Gullin (bari sax), Bengt Hallberg (piano), Simon Brehm (bass) and Alan Dawson (drums).

10 Jul 54	**10**	4	**THE SWEDISH-AMERICAN ALL STARS** *(Esquire EP-5)* **EP**
			Pogo Stick / Liza (All The Clouds'll Roll Away)
14 Aug 54	**16**	1	**THE SWEDISH-AMERICAN ALL STARS** *(Esquire EP-5)* **EP** *re-entry*

See also Swedish All Stars

ERIC SYKES

See Goons

TOM TALL   3

Rockabilly singer born Tommie Lee Guthrie in Amarillo, Texas in 1937. 'Are You Mine', was his biggest US hit, reaching No. 2 on the C&W charts in 1955.

| 19 Nov 55 | **10** | 3 | **Are You Mine** / Boom Boom Boomerang *(London HL-8150)* |
| | | | *Both sides by Ginny Wright and Tom Tall* |

TANNER SISTERS   9

British close harmony duo Frances and Stella Tanner were radio and TV regulars in the '50s and were one of the support acts on Buddy Holly's 1958 UK tour. Stella went on to enjoy a long career as an actress.

3 Jul 54	**8**	6	**Friends And Neighbours** *(Max Bygraves and the Tanner Sisters)* /
			Chip Chopper Charlie *(Max Bygraves)* *(H.M.V. B-10703)*
21 Aug 54	**24**	2	**Friends And Neighbours** *(Max Bygraves and the Tanner Sisters)* /
			Chip Chopper Charlie *(Max Bygraves)* *(H.M.V. B-10703)*
			1st re-entry
2 Oct 54	**35**	1	**Friends And Neighbours** *(Max Bygraves and the Tanner Sisters)* /
			Chip Chopper Charlie *(Max Bygraves)* *(H.M.V. B-10703)*
			2nd re-entry

UGO TANSINI *(conductor)*

See Chorus and Orchestra Sinfonica Dell'EIAR

TARRIERS   3

Folk-pop trio from New York comprising Erik Darling, Alan Arkin and Bob Carey. Their two bubblers were both Top Ten hits in the US.

1 Dec 56	**2**	2	★ **Cindy, Oh Cindy** / Only If You Praise The Lord *(London HLN-8340)*
			Both sides by Vince Martin with the Tarriers
23 Feb 57	**3**	1	★ **The Banana Boat Song** / No Hidin' Place *(Columbia DB-3891)*

ART TATUM   1

Highly acclaimed blind jazz and stride pianist born in Toledo, Ohio in 1909.

11 Sep 54	**37**	1	**ART TATUM FROM GENE NORMAN'S 'JUST JAZZ'**
			(Vogue LDE-081) **LP**
			Yesterdays / Willow Weep For Me / Tatum Plays Pretty / I Know That You Know / Humoresque / Kerry Dance / Boogie Woogie / Someone To Watch Over Me / How High The Moon

AUSTIN TAYLOR   1

Produced and written by Bert Berns, 'Push Push' was recorded for the Laurie label in New York and became a minor US hit in November 1960. The unknown Austin Taylor was for some time rumoured to be soul singer Ted Taylor (real name Theodore Austin Taylor), but this has now been discounted.

| 1 Oct 60 | **15** | 1 | **Push Push** / A Heart That's True *(Top Rank JAR-511)* |

BILLY TAYLOR & His Rhythm   1

Distinguished jazz pianist and composer born in Greenville, North Carolina in 1921.

7 Aug 54   **23**   1   **PIANO PANORAMA** *(Felsted L-87001)* **LP**
                  Wrap Your Troubles In Dreams / What Is There To Say? / If I Had You / Thou
                  Swell / Willow Weep For Me / The Very Thought Of You / Somebody Loves Me /
                  Good Groove

NEVILLE TAYLOR   3

One of a handful of black rock'n'roll acts in Britain during the late '50s, Neville Taylor from British Guiana and his group, the Cutters, were a fixture on ITV's 'Oh Boy!' Sadly, they were unable to convert their popularity as live performers into record sales. Taylor also recorded for Woolworth's Embassy label as 'Hal Munro'.

26 Jul 58   **3**   2   **House Of Bamboo / Mercy, Mercy Percy** *(Parlophone R-4447)*
7 May 60   **9**   1   **Dance With A Dolly** / Free Passes *(Oriole CB-1546)*

TED TAYLOR FOUR   5

With their unusual clavoline lead, this instrumental combo was Britain's answer to Johnny & The Hurricanes. 'M.I.' (a misprint for 'M1') was originally called 'Left Hand Drive', but was retitled to capitalise on the publicity surrounding the opening of Britain's first motorway.

29 Nov 58   **9**   1   **Son Of Honky Tonk** / Farrago *(Oriole CB-1464)*
12 Nov 60   **14**   2   **M.I.** / You Are My Sunshine *(Oriole CB-1573)*
3 Dec 60   **15**   2   **M.I.** / You Are My Sunshine *(Oriole CB-1573)* *re-entry*

VINCE TAYLOR & HIS PLAYBOYS   3

Wild rock'n'roller born Brian Holden in Isleworth, Middlesex in 1939. Despite early great releases like 'Right Behind You Baby', 'Brand New Cadillac' and 'I'll Be Your Hero', it wasn't until he went to France in 1961 that he found the success that matched his talent.

27 Aug 60   **9**   2   ★   I'll Be Your Hero / Jet Black Machine *(Palette PG-9001)*
17 Sep 60   **4**   1   ★   I'll Be Your Hero / Jet Black Machine *(Palette PG-9001)* *re-entry*

TEEN BEATS   3

West Coast instrumental group who recorded several singles for Art Laboe's Original Sound label in Hollywood, California.

16 Apr 60   **1**   2   **The Slop Beat / Califf Boogie** *(Top Rank JAR-342)*
                  Both sides by the Teen Beats featuring Don Rivers & The Califfs
7 May 60   **9**   1   **The Slop Beat / Califf Boogie** *(Top Rank JAR-342)* *re-entry*

TEMPTATIONS   1

Not the Motown group, but a white doo-wop quartet from Flushing, New York managed by Artie Ripp and produced by George Goldner. They later became Neil Stevens & The Temptations.

11 Jun 60   **6**   1   **Barbara** / Someday *(Top Rank JAR-384)*

SONNY TERRY TRIO   3

Blind blues singer/harmonica player born Saunders Terrell in Greensboro, Georgia in 1911. From 1941 onwards, he frequently performed in a duo with singer/guitarist Brownie McGhee.

23 Jul 55   **19**   3   **Hootin' Blues** *(Parlophone R-3598)*
                  Flip is 'Bop! Goes The Weasel' by Tommy Reilly

INIA TE WIATA   2

The first internationally known Maori opera singer, born in Otaki, New Zealand in 1915. He became leading bass baritone at the Royal Opera House, Covent Garden in the early '50s, and soon after successfully branched out into radio plays, stage musicals, and TV and film acting.

9 Mar 57   **3**   2   **The Banana Boat Song** / Call Of The Sea *(H.M.V. POP-301)*

THIRD HERDMEN
See Herdmen
      Woody Herman

CARLOS THOMPSON   7
Argentinian actor born Juan Carlos Mundin-Schaffter in Buenos Aires in 1923. He moved to Europe in the '50s and appeared in a large number of German films, though in Britain he is mostly remembered for his role as Carlos Varela in the 1963 TV series, 'The Sentimental Agent'.

9 Oct 54	**18**	1	**By Candlelight** / The Peddler Man *(M.G.M. MGM-760)*
9 Oct 54	**34**	1	**No One But You** / Languida *(M.G.M. MGM-759)*
23 Oct 54	**5**	5	**No One But You** / Languida *(M.G.M. MGM-759)* ***re-entry***

HANK THOMPSON   14
Born in Waco, Texas in 1925, country singer Hank Thompson possessed a smooth baritone voice that perfectly complemented his light brand of Western swing. His 1952 C&W chart-topper, 'The Wild Side Of Life', is now a country music evergreen.

27 Nov 54	**42**	1	**Wake Up, Irene** / Honky-Tonk Girl *(Capitol CL-14161)*
			Both sides by Hank Thompson & His Brazos Valley Boys
29 Mar 58	**17**	1	**HANK** *(Capitol EAP1-826)* 🔲EP
			Hank Thompson & His Brazos Valley Boys
			Hang Your Head In Shame / Someone Can Steal You From Me / You'll Be The One / Don't Be That Way
22 Nov 58	**2**	3	**Squaws Along The Yukon** *(Hank Thompson & His Brazos Valley Boys)* / Gathering Flowers *(Hank Thompson & His Brazos Valley Boys with Merle Travis) (Capitol CL-14945)*
9 Jul 60	**14**	1	**The Wild Side Of Life** / Rub-A-Dub-Dub *(Capitol CL-13977)*
			Both sides by Hank Thompson & His Brazos Valley Boys
3 Sep 60	**9**	1	**The Wild Side Of Life** / Rub-A-Dub-Dub *(Capitol CL-13977)* ***re-entry***
8 Oct 60	**13**	1	**She's Just A Whole Lot Like You** /
			There My Future Goes *(Capitol CL-15156)*
14 Jan 61	**11**	2	**It Got To Be A Habit** / Will We Start It All Over Again *(Capitol CL-15177)*
4 Feb 61	**8**	2	**It Got To Be A Habit** / Will We Start It All Over Again *(Capitol CL-15177)* ***re-entry***
18 Feb 61	**10**	2	**SONGS FOR ROUNDERS** *(Capitol T-1246)* 🔲LP
			Three Times Seven / I'll Be A Bachelor Till I Die / Drunkard's Blues / Teach 'em How To Swim / Dry Bread / Cocaine Blues / Deep Elm / Bummin' Around / Little Blossom / Rovin' Gambler / Left My Gal In The Mountains / May I Sleep In Your Barn Tonight Mister?

TINY TOPSY   1
Tiny Topsy (born Otha Lee Moore in Chicago in 1930) was a stout, big-voiced female R&B singer who cut some memorable records including the original 'Just A Little Bit', later covered by Rosco Gordon. Sadly, she died of a brain haemorrhage in 1964, aged just 34.

1 Mar 58	**8**	1	**Come On, Come On, Come On** /
			Ring Around My Finger *(Parlophone R-4397)*
			Both sides by Tiny Topsy and the Charms

DIMITRI TIOMKIN & His Orchestra   3
Prolific film score composer and conductor born in Kremenchuk, Ukraine in 1894.

13 Nov 54	**40**	1	**Theme from 'The High And The Mighty'** /
			Theme from 'Dial "M" For Murder' *(Vogue Coral Q-2016)*
4 Dec 54	**43**	2	**Theme from 'The High And The Mighty'** /
			Theme from 'Dial "M" For Murder' *(Vogue Coral Q-2016)* ***re-entry***

ART & DOTTY TODD   1

American husband-and-wife singing duo formed in 1952. 'Chanson d'Amour' was a hit for them on both sides of the Atlantic and set them up for a long and successful career in Las Vegas.

24 May 58   **18**   1   ★ **Chanson d'Amour** / Along The Trail With You *(London HLB-8620)*

NICK TODD   2

Pat Boone's younger brother Cecil, born in Jacksonville, Florida in 1935.

1 Feb 58   **1**   2   ★ **At The Hop** / I Do *(London HLD-8537)*

SIDNEY TORCH & His Orchestra   9

Composer, arranger and one of the most popular and respected orchestra leaders in Britain, born Sidney Torchinsky in London in 1908.

20 Aug 55   **18**   2   **The Dam Busters** / Sweet Seventeen *(Parlophone R-4024)*
17 Sep 55   **18**   3   **The Dam Busters** / Sweet Seventeen *(Parlophone R-4024)*
                         1st re-entry
22 Oct 55   **25**   1   **The Dam Busters** / Sweet Seventeen *(Parlophone R-4024)*
                         2nd re-entry
5 Nov 55   **21**   1   **The Dam Busters** / Sweet Seventeen *(Parlophone R-4024)*
                         3rd re-entry
4 Feb 56   **7**   1   **Stranger Than Fiction** *(Bert Weedon with Sidney Torch & His Orch.)* /
                         China Boogie *(Sidney Torch & His Orchestra with Bert Weedon)*
                         (Parlophone R-4113)
8 Sep 56   **3**   1   **Reach For The Sky** / Bicycle Belles *(Parlophone R-4198)*

MEL TORMÉ   7

Jazz singer, drummer, composer, arranger and actor born in Chicago in 1925. A child prodigy, he first sang professionally at the age of four.

31 Mar 56   **5**   2   ★ **AT THE CRESCENDO** *(Vogue Coral LVA-9004)* 🆛
                         From This Moment On / That Old Black Magic / Get Out Of Town / Goody Goody /
                         Love Is Here To Stay / Blue Moon / Old Devil Moon / Get Happy / Mountain
                         Greenery / The County Fair / The Christmas Song (Merry Christmas To You) /
                         Jeepers Creepers / You're Driving Me Crazy / Bernie's Tune
21 Apr 56   **11**   1   ★ **Mountain Greenery** / Jeepers Creepers *(Vogue Coral Q-72150)*
4 Aug 56   **3**   1   ★ **MEL TORMÉ WITH THE MARTY PAICH 'DEK-TETTE'**
                         (London American Jazz LTZ-N-15009) 🆛
                         Lulu's Back In Town / When The Sun Comes Out / I Love To Watch The Moonlight /
                         Fascinating Rhythm / The Blues / The Carioca / The Lady Is A Tramp / I Like To
                         Recognise The Tune / Keepin' Myself For You / Lullaby of Birdland / When April
                         Comes Again / Sing For Your Supper
25 Aug 56   **10**   2   **Lulu's Back In Town** / The Lady Is A Tramp *(London HLN-8305)*
20 Oct 56   **10**   1   **Lulu's Back In Town** / The Lady Is A Tramp *(London HLN-8305)*
                         re-entry

MITCHELL TOROK   32

Hillbilly singer, guitarist and songwriter born in Houston, Texas in 1929. 'Caribbean' was a C&W No.1 in 1953, however British fans are more likely to remember him for the 1956 novelty, 'When Mexico Gave Up The Rhumba'.

30 Apr 55   **1**   15   ★ **Caribbean** / Weep Away *(London HL-8004)*
                         Both sides by Mitchell Torok with the Louisiana Hayride Band
18 Jun 55   **25**   1   **A Peasant's Guitar** / The World Keeps Turning Around
                         (Brunswick 05423)
20 Aug 55   **2**   7   ★ **Caribbean** / Weep Away *(London HL-8004)* ***1st re-entry***
15 Oct 55   **4**   7   ★ **Caribbean** / Weep Away *(London HL-8004)* ***2nd re-entry***
8 Sep 56   **7**   2   ★ **When Mexico Gave Up The Rhumba** /
                         I Wish I Was A Little Bit Younger *(Brunswick 05586)*

ARTURO TOSCANINI *(conductor)*
See N.B.C. Symphony Orchestra

TRADEWINDS 1
Rock'n'roll vocal group produced by New York producers Hugo & Luigi. Not to be confused with the Trade Winds on Red Bird, these were four high school lads from Newark, New Jersey.

26 Sep 59 **16** 1   **Furry Murray** / Crossroads *(R.C.A. RCA-1141)*

TRAVIS & BOB 2
Travis Prichett and Bob Weaver of Jackson, Alabama recorded their Everlys-styled classic,'Tell Him No', in a garage in Gulfport, Mississippi. It shot to No. 8 in the Billboard 'Hot 100' in 1959, and even made No. 2 in the Netherlands, but their later releases went nowhere.

9 May 59   **4** 1   **Tell Him No** / We're Too Young *(Pye International 7N.25018)*
6 Jun 59   **6** 1   **Tell Him No** / We're Too Young *(Pye International 7N.25018)* ***re-entry***

TRIO LOS PARAGUAYOS 3
South American group formed in Paraguay in 1945. They came to Europe in 1954 and quickly became firm favourites with British and Continental audiences.

30 May 59   **5** 1   **TRIO LOS PARAGUAYOS** *(Philips BBE-12176)* **EP**
                 Maria Dolores / Serenata / Malagueña / Pajaro Campana (Bell Bird)
22 Aug 59   **1** 1   **Bell Bird** / Misionera *(Philips PB-947)*
19 Sep 59 **12** 1   **Bell Bird** / Misionera *(Philips PB-947)* ***re-entry***

SAMMY TURNER 6
Smooth R&B singer born Samuel Black in Paterson, New Jersey in 1932. His rocked-up version of the standard 'Lavender Blue' was his biggest US hit, but just missed out in the UK.

22 Aug 59   **1** 4   **Lavender Blue** / Sweet Annie Laurie *(London HLX-8918)*
3 Oct 59 **21** 1   **Lavender Blue** / Sweet Annie Laurie *(London HLX-8918)* ***re-entry***
7 Nov 59   **4** 1   ★ <u>**Always**</u> / Symphony *(London HLX-8963)*

CONWAY TWITTY 10
Singer born Harold Lloyd Jenkins in Friars Point, Mississippi in 1933. He started out as a rock'n'roller, but later became a top country artist.

28 Nov 59   **2** 3   **Rosaleena** / Halfway To Heaven *(M.G.M. MGM-1047)*
27 Feb 60   **2** 3   **Lonely Blue Boy** / My One And Only You *(M.G.M. MGM-1056)*
30 Apr 60 **12** 1   **What Am I Living For** / The Hurt In My Heart *(M.G.M. MGM-1066)*
16 Jul 60   **9** 1   ★ <u>**Is A Blue Bird Blue**</u> / She's Mine *(M.G.M. MGM-1082)*
28 Jan 61   **8** 1   ★ <u>**C'est Si Bon**</u> / Don't You Dare Let Me Down *(M.G.M. MGM-1118)*
4 Feb 61 **16** 1   **The Flame** / Whole Lotta Shakin' Goin' On *(M.G.M. MGM-1108)*

THE TWO BILLS FROM BERMONDSEY 9
Bill Burnham (lead vocal, piano) and Bill 'Busty' French (second vocal) were a traditional Cockney pub duo, very much in the style later popularised by Chas & Dave. By day, Burnham was a delivery driver for the 'Star' newspaper, while French was a stoker in a brewery. Tommy Steele (who coincidentally also hailed from Bermondsey) had a hit in 1960 with his version of 'What A Mouth'.

1 Jan 55   **7** 9   **What A Mouth, What A Mouth** /
                 Cockney Capers [M] *(Parlophone R-3953)*
                 Cockney Capers: Any Old Iron – A Little Bit Off The Top – Boiled Beef And
                 Carrots – Down The Road – Liza Johnson – Knees Up Mother Brown

JERRY VALE 2
Singer from New York born Gennaro Vitaliano in 1932. He enjoyed a run of hits in the States from 1956 to 1966, but this bubbler was not one of them.

18 Jun 55 **17** 2   **And This Is My Beloved** / A Tear, A Kiss, A Smile *(Philips PB-462)*

RITCHIE VALENS 1

Revered Chicano rocker born Richard Valenzuela in Pacoima, Calfornia in 1941. Already an accomplished guitarist and performer in his mid-teens, he tragically perished in the same plane crash that killed the Big Bopper and Buddy Holly on 3 February 1959.

15 Aug 59	**8**	1	**That's My Little Suzie** / Bluebirds Over The Mountain *(London HL-8886)*

CATERINA VALENTE 12

Internationally renowned singer, dancer and actress born in Paris to Italian parents, both of whom were circus performers. She made her first recordings in West Germany in 1953.

30 Jul 55	**30**	2	**My Lonely Lover** / This Must Be Wrong *(Polydor BM-6001)*
24 Sep 55	**16**	1	**Malagueña** / Siboney *(Polydor BM-6006)*
8 Oct 55	**6**	5	**Malagueña** / Siboney *(Polydor BM-6006)* **1st re-entry**
19 Nov 55	**24**	1	**Malagueña** / Siboney *(Polydor BM-6006)* **2nd re-entry**
21 Jan 56	**22**	1	**Temptation** / Fiesta Cubana *(Polydor BM-6012)*
15 Oct 60	**15**	1	**Secret Love** / Malagueña *(Polydor NH-66816)*
17 Dec 60	**20**	1	**Amour** / Till *(Decca F-11306)*

BILLY VALENTINE 1

Smooth black singer/pianist born in Birmingham, Alabama in 1926. He briefly sang with Johnny Moore's Three Blazers (he was featured vocalist on their 1949 R&B hit, 'Walkin' Blues'), then formed his own group.

10 Sep 55	**16**	1	**It's A Sin** / Your Love Has Got Me (Reelin' And Rockin') *(Capitol CL-14320)*

DICKIE VALENTINE 28

Former child actor born Richard Bryce. He sang with the Ted Heath Band in the early '50s and went on to become one of the UK's top crooners. He died in a car crash in 1971, aged just 41.

21 Aug 54	**34**	1	★ **Endless** / I Could Have Told You *(Decca F-10346)*
25 Sep 54	**39**	1	★ **Endless** / I Could Have Told You *(Decca F-10346)* **1st re-entry**
9 Oct 54	**22**	1	★ **Endless** / I Could Have Told You *(Decca F-10346)* **2nd re-entry**
27 Nov 54	**7**	3	★ **The Finger Of Suspicion** (Dickie Valentine with the Stargazers) / Who's Afraid *(Dickie Valentine)* *(Decca F-10394)*
4 Dec 54	**3**	2	★ **Mister Sandman** / Runaround *(Decca F-10415)*
22 Jan 55	**4**	2	★ **A Blossom Fell** / I Want You All To Myself *(Decca F-10430)*
23 Apr 55	**26**	1	**HERE IS DICKIE VALENTINE** *(Decca LF-1211)* 🅛🅟

Dickie Valentine with the Skyrockets
For You / Mister Sandman / A Blossom Fell / Cleo And Meo / Finger Of Suspicion / I'm Singing A Song For The Old Folks / Pretty Baby / For Me And My Gal / The Clown Who Cried (Instrumental) / Tap Dancer (Part 1) (Instrumental) / Tap Dancer (Concluded) (Instrumental) / Knees Up, Mother Brown / Rock-A-Bye Your Baby With A Dixie Melody / Santa Lucia / Bye, Bye Blackbird / Broken Hearted

7 May 55	**5**	1	★ **I Wonder** / You Too Can Be A Dreamer *(Decca F-10493)*
21 May 55	**12**	2	★ **I Wonder** / You Too Can Be A Dreamer *(Decca F-10493)* **re-entry**
25 Jun 55	**12**	1	**Hello Mrs. Jones** / Lazy Gondolier *(Decca F-10517)*
27 Aug 55	**9**	1	**No Such Luck** / The Engagement Waltz *(Decca F-10549)*
3 Sep 55	**21**	1	**Lazy Gondolier** / **Hello Mrs. Jones** *(Decca F-10517)* **1st re-entry (flipped)**
17 Sep 55	**28**	1	**Lazy Gondolier** / **Hello Mrs. Jones** *(Decca F-10517)* **2nd re-entry**
1 Oct 55	**23**	1	**The Engagement Waltz** / No Such Luck *(Decca F-10549)* **re-entry (flipped)**
12 Nov 55	**14**	1	★ **Christmas Alphabet** / Where Are You Tonight? *(Decca F-10628)*
11 Feb 56	**7**	1	**Dreams Can Tell A Lie** (Dickie Valentine and the Keynotes) / Song Of The Trees *(Dickie Valentine)* *(Decca F-10667)*
21 Apr 56	**13**	1	**The Voice** / The Best Way To Hold A Girl *(Decca F-10714)*
12 Jan 57	**7**	1	**Rock'n'Roll Party (Parts 1 & 2) [M]** *(Decca F-10820)*

Christmas Rock'n'Roll – Mountain Greenery – A Woman In Love / When Mexico Gave Up The Rhumba – Just Walking In The Rain – Christmas Rock'n'Roll

27 Apr 57	10	1	**Chapel Of The Roses** / My Empty Arms *(Decca F-10874)*
25 May 57	10	1	**Chapel Of The Roses** / My Empty Arms *(Decca F-10874)* **re-entry**
7 Mar 59	1	1	★ <u>**Venus**</u> / Where? *(Pye Nixa 7N.15192)*
6 Jun 59	7	1	**A Teenager In Love** / My Favourite Song *(Pye Nixa 7N.15202)*
3 Oct 59	9	1	★ <u>**One More Sunrise**</u> / You Touch My Hand *(Pye Nixa 7N.15221)*

See also Various Artists (All Star Hit Parade)

DANNY VALENTINO   2

Teen idol from New York, born Vincent Pacimeo. He had a US hit in 1960 with the poppy 'Biology', but in Britain it was the rocking 'Stampede' that aroused most interest.

| 30 Jan 60 | 5 | 1 | **Stampede** / Music Man *(M.G.M. MGM-1049)* |
| 13 Feb 60 | 1 | 1 | **Stampede** / Music Man *(M.G.M. MGM-1049)* **re-entry** |

JUNE VALLI   1

Pop singer born June Foglia in New York in 1928. She was offered a record contract after winning on the 'Arthur Godfrey's Talent Scouts' TV show and had ten US hits between 1952 and 1960.

| 25 Sep 54 | 39 | 1 | **I Understand (Just How You Feel)** / Old Shoes And A Bag Of Rice *(H.M.V. B-10749)* |

VARIOUS ARTISTS

| 27 Nov 54 | 42 | 1 | **CABARET NIGHT IN PARIS** *(Columbia 33S-1008)* **LP** |

Sous les Toits de Paris *(Orchestre de Dance Alexander)* / La Mer *(Charles Trenet)* / Tout le Long des Rues *(Tino Rossi)* / Les Quais de la Seine *(Lucienne Delyle)* / Une Hirondelle *(Tino Rossi)* / La Seine *(Maurice Alexander)* / Retour à Paris *(Charles Trenet)* / La Vie en Rose *(Edith Piaf)* / Vous, Qui Passez Sans Me Voir *(Jean Sablon)* / J'Attendrai *(Tino Rossi)*

| 28 Apr 56 | 19 | 1 | **KISMET** *(Mercury EP1-3160)* **EP** |

Stranger In Paradise *(Vic Damone)* / Baubles, Bangles And Beads *(Georgia Gibbs)* / Not Since Nineveh *(Ross Bagdasarian)* / Zubbediya *(Ross Bagdasarian)*

| 23 Jun 56 | 1 | 1 | ★ <u>**All Star Hit Parade (Parts 1 & 2)**</u> [M] *(Decca F-10752)* |

Out Of Town *(Dickie Valentine)* – My September Love *(Joan Regan)* – Theme from 'The Threepenny Opera' *(Winifred Atwell)* / No Other Love *(Dave King)* – A Tear Fell *(Lita Roza)* – It's Almost Tomorrow *(David Whitfield)*

| 8 Dec 56 | 7 | 4 | **SCOTS TRADITIONAL JAZZ CONCERT** *(Beltona ABL-519)* **LP** |

Alan Mason's Jazzmen: That Da Da Strain / It Happened In Monterey / Milenberg Joys / *Charlie McNair New Orleans Jazz Group:* Oh, Didn't He Ramble / *Clyde Valley Stompers:* Très Moutarde / I Love A Lassie / When The Saints Go Marching In

| 12 Oct 57 | 2 | 3 | **Top Ten Special (Parts 1 & 2)** [M] *(Parlophone R-4356)* |

A Handful Of Songs *(King Brothers)* – All Shook Up *(Jim Dale)* – Last Train To San Fernando *(Vipers Skiffle Group)* / Putting On The Style *(Vipers Skiffle Group)* – Wanderin' Eyes *(Jim Dale)* – Build Your Love *(King Brothers)*

| 31 May 58 | 19 | 1 | **MY FAIR LADY** *(Decca DFE-6474)* **EP** |

Cyril Stapleton & His Orchestra on all tracks, featured vocalists shown in brackets: Wouldn't It Be Loverly *(Beverley Sisters)* / With A Little Bit Of Luck *(Stargazers)* / The Rain In Spain *(Vera Lynn and Pete Murray)* / On The Street Where You Live *(David Whitfield)* / Get Me To The Church On Time *(Jack Warner)* / I Could Have Danced All Night *(Diane Todd)*

| 9 Aug 58 | 4 | 2 | **Lord's Taverners Star Band Hit Parade (Parts 1 & 2)** [M] *(Decca F-11043)* |

Lollipop *(Ted Heath & His Music)* – Tulips from Amsterdam *(Mantovani & His Orchestra)* – Tom Hark *(Edmundo Ros & His Orchestra)* / Swingin' Shepherd Blues

(Edmundo Ros & His Orchestra) – I May Never Pass This Way Again (Mantovani & His Orchestra) – Who's Sorry Now (Ted Heath & His Music)

c 59   **5   1   A FESTIVAL OF EDINBURGH** *(Waverley LLP-1001)* 🔲 **LP**
Although the artists appearing on each side are listed, the sleeve does not indicate which artists performed which songs.
The Rowan Tree – Old Rustic Bridge – Patrol: A Highland Route March – Wiltshire – Scots Wha' Hae – Bannocks O' Bear Meal – Come Boat Me O'er *(City of Edinburgh Police Pipe Band, Pipe Major Ian McLeod, Massed Brass Bands of Carlton Main Frickley Colliery, Ransome & Marles, Grimethorpe Colliery Institute and Yorkshire Imperial Metals, conducted by G. Hespe; Organ of St. Cuthbert's Parish Church, organist W.O. Minay, Mus. Bach., F.R.C.O., A.R.C.M.; The Choir of Trinity Academy, conducted by Margaret Munro, A.R.C.M.; Massed Choir of Edinburgh Schoolchildren, conducted by J.B.R. Whitfield, Mus. Bach., F.R.C.O.) / A Gaelic Suite – The Keel Row – Hot Cross Buns – Lavender's Blue – Hickory Dickory Dock – Ce Moys de May – Margot Labourez les Vignes – Sonata from Bankolsongerlieser – The Deil Amang The Tailors – Marquis of Huntly – Scotland The Brave – We're No' Awa' Tae Bide Awa' – My Dream Angus – Martyrs (Eric Roberts String Orchestra, cond. Eric Roberts; Percussion Band of James Gillespie's High School for Girls, directed by Miss D.N. Nicoll; The Edinburgh University Singers, directed by Herrick Bunney; The Edinburgh Brass Ensemble, directed by C. Duncan; The massed Pipes and Drums, and massed Military Bands from the Edinburgh Military Tattoo (by permission of Edinburgh Corporation); The choir of Broughton Secondary School, conducted by Elizabeth Caldwell, Mus. Bach.)*

19 Dec 59   **3   2   A FESTIVAL OF EDINBURGH** *(Waverley LLP-1001)* 🔲 **LP** *re-entry*

17 Sep 60   **5   2   THE EDINBURGH MILITARY TATTOO** *(Waverley MLP-5001)* 🔲 **LP**
Unknown: Fanfare For A Dignified Occasion / Massed Pipes and Drums of the Lorne Scots, the Scots Guards, the Royal Scots, the Seaforth Highlanders, the Cameronians (Scottish Rifles), the Argyll & Seaforth Highlanders and the Queen's Own Cameron Highlanders: Queen Elizabeth The Queen Mother / Rhu Waternish / King George V's Army / Caber Feidh / Braes O' Tullymet / Bog-Allen / Lochanside / Loch Maree / Dancers and Instrumentalists of the Greek Royal Guard: Traditional Greek Warrior Dances / The Pipes and Drums, Bugle and Military Band of the Brigade of Gurkhas: Bugle March / Bonawe Highlanders / Scotland The Brave / Massed Pipes and Drums of the Lorne Scots, the Scots Guards, the Royal Scots, the Seaforth Highlanders, the Cameronians (Scottish Rifles), the Argyll & Seaforth Highlanders and the Queen's Own Cameron Highlanders + the Military Bands of the Royal Marines, the Royal Air Force Regiment, the Cameronians (Scottish Rifles) and the Queen's Own Cameron Highlanders: Within A Mile O' Edinburgh Town / Pibroch O' Donuil Dhu / General Salut – Garb Of Old Gaul / Sunset / The Last Post – Cavalry Last Post / Dream Angus / Scotland The Brave / We`re No Awa' To Bide Awa' / Bonnie Dundee

See also   Original Broadway Cast
Original London Cast
Original Soundtrack

FRANKIE VAUGHAN   62
Immensely popular singer/entertainer born Frank Abelson in Liverpool in 1928. Renowned for his his flamboyant high kicks and his trademark top hat and cane, he remained a hitmaker until 1968.

2 Oct 54	**2**	7	**Cinnamon Sinner / My Son, My Son** *(H.M.V. B-10766)*
13 Nov 54	**51**	1	★ <u>**Happy Days And Lonely Nights**</u> / Danger Signs *(H.M.V. B-10783)*
27 Nov 54	**32**	1	**Cinnamon Sinner / My Son, My Son** *(H.M.V. B-10766)* *re-entry*
11 Dec 54	**31**	1	★ <u>**Happy Days And Lonely Nights**</u> / Danger Signs *(H.M.V. B-10783)* **1st re-entry**
1 Jan 55	**8**	4	★ <u>**Happy Days And Lonely Nights**</u> / Danger Signs *(H.M.V. B-10783)* **2nd re-entry**
12 Mar 55	**17**	2	**Too Many Heartaches** / Unsuspecting Heart *(H.M.V. B-10845)*
26 Mar 55	**6**	4	★ <u>**Tweedlee-Dee / Give Me The Moonlight, Give Me The Girl**</u> *(Philips PB-423)*

7 May 55	28	1	Unsuspecting Heart / Too Many Heartaches *(H.M.V. B-10845)*
			1st re-entry (flipped)
18 Jun 55	25	2	Unsuspecting Heart / Too Many Heartaches *(H.M.V. B-10845)*
			2nd re-entry
24 Sep 55	23	1	That's How A Love Song Was Born / Wildfire *(Philips PB-438)*
22 Oct 55	17	2 ★	Seventeen / Meet Me On The Corner *(Philips PB-511)*
12 Nov 55	21	1 ★	Seventeen / Meet Me On The Corner *(Philips PB-511)* **1st re-entry**
26 Nov 55	19	1 ★	Seventeen / Meet Me On The Corner *(Philips PB-511)* **2nd re-entry**
21 Jan 56	17	1 ★	My Boy Flat Top / Stealin' *(Philips PB-544)*
31 Mar 56	3	2	This Is The Night / Rock Candy Baby *(Philips PB-559)*
27 Apr 57	23	1	Cold, Cold Shower / What's Behind That Strange Door
			(Philips PB-681)
24 Aug 57	1	4 ★	These Dangerous Years / Isn't This A Lovely Evening *(Philips PB-674)*
7 Sep 57	3	2	Cold, Cold Shower / What's Behind That Strange Door
			(Philips PB-681) **1st re-entry**
5 Oct 57	9	1	Cold, Cold Shower / What's Behind That Strange Door
			(Philips PB-681) **2nd re-entry**
19 Oct 57	8	1	Cold, Cold Shower / What's Behind That Strange Door
			(Philips PB-681) **3rd re-entry**
1 Mar 58	2	1 ★	We're Not Alone / Can't Get Along Without You *(Philips PB-793)*
3 May 58	9	1 ★	Kewpie Doll / So Many Women *(Philips PB-825)*
12 Jul 58	1	3 ★	Wonderful Things / Judy *(Philips PB-834)*
28 Mar 59	5	2	The Lady Is A Square / Honey Bunny Baby *(Philips PB-896)*
18 Apr 59	1	1 ★	Come Softly To Me /
			Say Something Sweet To Your Sweetheart *(Philips PB-913)*
			Both sides by Frankie Vaughan and the Kaye Sisters
18 Apr 59	7	1	The Lady Is A Square / Honey Bunny Baby *(Philips PB-896)* **re-entry**
6 Jun 59	3	7 ★	The Heart Of A Man / Sometime Somewhere *(Philips PB-930)*
12 Sep 59	2	1 ★	Walkin' Tall / I Ain't Gonna Lead This Life *(Philips PB-931)*
23 Jan 60	5	1 ★	What More Do You Want / The Very Very Young *(Philips PB-985)*
10 Sep 60	9	1 ★	Kookie Little Paradise / Mary Lou *(Philips PB-1054)*
4 Feb 61	8	3	The Day That It Happens To You / This World We Love In
			(Philips PB-1104)

MALCOLM VAUGHAN 21

Welsh balladeer born Malcolm Thomas in Abercynon in 1929. Originally a stage actor and then straight man in a comedy double act, he switched to singing in 1955 after being spotted by radio disc jockey Jack Jackson, who got him a contract with HMV.

25 Jun 55	12	1 ★	Ev'ry Day Of My Life / Mama *(H.M.V. B-10874)*
24 Dec 55	5	3 ★	With Your Love / Small Talk *(H.M.V. POP-130)*
21 Jan 56	4	1 ★	With Your Love / Small Talk *(H.M.V. POP-130)* **re-entry**
20 Oct 56	10	1 ★	St. Therese Of The Roses /
			Love Me As Though There Were No Tomorrow *(H.M.V. POP-250)*
9 Mar 57	16	1 ★	The World Is Mine / Now *(H.M.V. POP-303)*
23 Mar 57	1	3 ★	The World Is Mine / Now *(H.M.V. POP-303)* **re-entry**
13 Apr 57	4	3 ★	Chapel Of The Roses / Guardian Angel *(H.M.V. POP-325)*
7 Sep 57	9	1	What Is My Destiny / Oh! My Papa *(H.M.V. POP-381)*
23 Nov 57	5	2	What Is My Destiny / Oh! My Papa *(H.M.V. POP-381)* **re-entry**
15 Mar 58	11	1 ★	To Be Loved / My Loving Arms *(H.M.V. POP-459)*
23 Aug 58	4	1	Ev'ry Hour, Ev'ry Day Of My Life / Miss You *(H.M.V. POP-502)*
27 Sep 58	4	1	Ev'ry Hour, Ev'ry Day Of My Life / Miss You *(H.M.V. POP-502)*
			re-entry
11 Oct 58	2	1 ★	More Than Ever / A Night To Remember *(H.M.V. POP-538)*
20 Feb 60	8	1	Oh, So Wunderbar / For Everyone In Love *(H.M.V. POP-700)*

SARAH VAUGHAN 31

Jazz diva born in Newark, New Jersey in 1924. She cut her teeth singing with Earl Hines' and Billy Eckstine's bands in the mid-'40s, then signed with Mercury in 1953 and began recording more commercial material with considerable success.

| 26 Jun 54 | 2 | 8 | Shulie A Bop / Polka Dots And Moonbeams *(Mercury MB-3129)* |
| 22 Jan 55 | 15 | 3 | Make Yourself Comfortable / Old Devil Moon *(Mercury MB-3180)* |

26 Feb 55	12	1	**Make Yourself Comfortable** / Old Devil Moon *(Mercury MB-3180)*
			1st re-entry
5 Mar 55	12	2	**Make Yourself Comfortable** / Old Devil Moon *(Mercury MB-3180)*
			2nd re-entry
9 Apr 55	13	2	**How Important Can It Be?** / My Funny Valentine *(Mercury MB-3205)*
30 Apr 55	5	2	**How Important Can It Be?** / My Funny Valentine *(Mercury MB-3205)*
			re-entry
7 May 55	9	3	**And This Is My Beloved** / Waltzing Down The Aisle *(Mercury MB-3210)*
19 May 56	7	1	**SARAH VAUGHAN** *(Philips BBE-12036)* 🄴🄿
			Come Rain Or Come Shine / Nice Work If You Can Get It / The Nearness Of You /
			Ooh, What-Cha Doin' To Me
9 Jun 56	7	1	**SARAH VAUGHAN** *(Philips BBE-12036)* 🄴🄿 *re-entry*
6 Oct 56	18	1	**DEDICATED TO YOU** *(M.G.M. MGM-EP-561)* 🄴🄿
			Billy Eckstine and Sarah Vaughan
			Dedicated To You / You're All I Need / Ev'ryday / I Love You
9 Mar 57	4	1	**The Banana Boat Song** / I've Got A New Heartache *(Mercury MT-139)*
14 Sep 57	3	2	★ **Passing Strangers** *(Sarah Vaughan and Billy Eckstine)* /
			The Door Is Open *(Billy Eckstine and Sarah Vaughan)*
			(Mercury MT-164)
15 Mar 58	11	1	**My Darling, My Darling** / Bewitched *(Mercury 7MT-198)*
29 Aug 59	2	2	★ **Broken-Hearted Melody** / Misty *(Mercury AMT-1057)*
23 Jan 60	8	1	**Smooth Operator** *(Sarah Vaughan)* / Passing Strangers
			(Sarah Vaughan and Billy Eckstine) (Mercury AMT-1071)

BILLY VAUGHN & His Orchestra   14

Singer, self-taught multi-instrumentalist and orchestra leader born in Glasgow, Kentucky in 1919. He began his career as pianist/vocalist with the Hilltoppers, but left the group in 1954 to become musical director at Dot Records.

10 Dec 55	7	1	★ **The Shifting Whispering Sands (Parts 1 & 2)** *(London HLD-8205)*
10 Mar 56	2	2	★ **Theme from 'The Threepenny Opera'** / I'd Give A Million Tomorrows
			(London HLD-8238)
11 Jan 58	3	1	★ **Raunchy** / **Sail Along Silvery Moon** *(London HLD-8522)*
25 Jan 58	6	1	★ **Raunchy** / **Sail Along Silvery Moon** *(London HLD-8522)* **1st re-entry**
8 Feb 58	4	1	★ **Raunchy** / Sail Along Silvery Moon *(London HLD-8522)* **2nd re-entry**
3 Oct 59	3	8	**Morgen** / Sweet Leilani *(London HLD-8952)*

See also Hilltoppers

BOBBY VEE   1

One of the most durable teen idols of the early '60s, Bobby Vee was born Robert Thomas Velline in Fargo, North Dakota in 1943. He got his big break when he and his group, the Shadows, were booked as last-minute replacements for Buddy Holly for a show at Moorhead, Minnesota on the day of the infamous plane crash.

| 17 Sep 60 | 18 | 1 | **Devil Or Angel** / Since I Met You, Baby *(London HLG-9179)* |

CHARLIE VENTURA SEPTET   2

Jazz saxophonist/bandleader born Charles Venturo in Philadelphia in 1916.

25 Sep 54	15	1	**East Of Suez** / I'm Forever Blowing Bubbles *(Brunswick 05316)*
			Vocal both sides: Jackie Cain and Roy Kral
8 Jan 55	37	1	**GENE NORMAN PRESENTS 'JUST JAZZ'** *(Vogue LDE-107)* 🄻🄿
			Birdland / Flamingo / Body And Soul / Boptura / Dark Eyes / High On An Open Mike

VENTURES   3

Hugely influential instrumental group from Tacoma, Washington, founded in 1959 by guitarists Don Wilson and Bob Bogle.

13 Aug 60	5	1	★ **Walk Don't Run** / Home *(Top Rank JAR-417)*
19 Nov 60	4	1	★ **Perfidia** / No Trespassing *(London HLG-9232)*
4 Mar 61	2	1	★ **Ram-Bunk-Shush** / Lonely Heart *(London HLG-9292)*

VERDI and JIMMY SILVER & HIS MUSIC   1

In the late '50s and early '60s, Bertie Green's Astor Club in Berkeley Square was one of the top nightclubs in London, infamous both for its 'hostesses' and its clientele, which included everyone from royalty to gangsters. The post-cabaret sing-song, led here by compère Verdi Wright, was a much-loved tradition at the Astor.

31 Dec 60   **9**   1   **PARTY TIME AT THE ASTOR CLUB** *(Decca LK-4290)* **LP**
California, Here I Come – Bye, Bye, Blackbird – Enjoy Yourself – Give My Regards To Broadway – I'm Sitting On Top Of The World – I'm Looking Over A Four Leaf Clover – Bye, Bye Blackbird – Toot, Toot, Tootsie – California, Here I Come – Swanee – How Ya Gonna Keep 'em Down On The Farm – Margie – Don't Dilly-Dally On The Way – Hello, Hello, Who's Your Lady Friend – Who Were You With Last Night – It's A Long Way To Tipperary – Take Me Back To Dear Old Blighty – I've Got A Lovely Bunch Of Coconuts / Carolina In The Morning – Pretty Baby – Rock-A-Bye Your Baby With A Dixie Melody – You Made Me Love You – If You Were The Only Girl In The World – That Old Feeling – In A Shanty In Old Shanty Town – Dinah – Some Of These Days – The Gang That Sang 'Heart Of My Heart' – Lily Of Laguna – Oh, You Beautiful Doll – I Belong To Glasgow – When Irish Eyes Are Smiling

LARRY VERNE   2

Larry Vern Erickson from Minneapolis, Minnesota was working as a film stuntman when some songwriter friends persuaded him to supply the vocals for a demo. The demo was unexpectedly released by Era Records and 'Mr. Custer' went to the top of the US charts in 1960. Unfortunately for Mr. Verne, Charlie Drake's cover version came out on top in the UK.

22 Oct 60   **1**   2   **Mr. Custer** / Okeefenokee Two Step *(London HLN-9194)*

LYN VERNON   1

Former big band and jazz guitarist from Memphis who recorded a couple of rocking singles for the humorously named Cover Records, run by former Sun recording artist Buddy Blake Cunningham.

26 Mar 60   **7**   1   **Woodchoppers Ball** / Caravan *(Top Rank JAR-323)*

VIENNA PHILHARMONIC ORCHESTRA
See Hilde Gueden

GENE VINCENT   28

Influential rock'n'roll singer born Vincent Eugene Craddock in Norfolk, Virginia in 1935. Sadly, his reckless lifestyle and alcoholism led to his premature death in 1971, at the age of just 36.

14 Jul 56   **5**   1   ★ **Be-Bop-A-Lula** / Woman Love *(Capitol CL-14599)*
Both sides by Gene Vincent & His Blue Caps
22 Sep 56   **3**   3   ★ **Race With The Devil** / Gonna Back Up Baby *(Capitol CL-14628)*
Both sides by Gene Vincent & His Blue Caps
16 Mar 57   **7**   1   **Crazy Legs** / Important Words *(Capitol CL-14693)*
Both sides by Gene Vincent & His Blue Caps
22 Jun 57   **3**   2   **Five Days, Five Days** / B-I-Bickey-Bi, Bo-Bo-Go *(Capitol CL-14722)*
Both sides by Gene Vincent & His Blue Caps
15 Feb 58   **3**   3   **I Got A Baby** / **Walkin' Home From School** *(Capitol CL-14830)*
Both sides by Gene Vincent & His Blue Caps
17 May 58   **9**   2   **Baby Blue** / **True To You** *(Capitol CL-14868)*
Both sides by Gene Vincent & His Blue Caps
23 Aug 58   **1**   3   **Rocky Road Blues** / Yes I Love You, Baby *(Capitol CL-14908)*
Both sides by Gene Vincent & His Blue Caps
21 Feb 59   **7**   1   **Say Mama** / Be Bop Boogie Boy *(Capitol CL-14974)*
Both sides by Gene Vincent & His Blue Caps
28 Mar 59   **16**   1   **Over The Rainbow** / Who's Pushin' Your Swing *(Capitol CL-15000)*
Both sides by Gene Vincent & His Blue Caps
25 Apr 59   **15**   1   **Over The Rainbow** / Who's Pushin' Your Swing *(Capitol CL-15000)*
re-entry

13 Jun 59	18	1	**Summertime** *(Gene Vincent & The Blue Caps)* / Frankie And Johnny *(Gene Vincent & His Blue Caps)* *(Capitol CL-15035)*
22 Aug 59	12	1	**Summertime** *(Gene Vincent & The Blue Caps)* / Frankie And Johnny *(Gene Vincent & His Blue Caps)* *(Capitol CL-15035)* **1st re-entry**
19 Dec 59	2	3	★ **Wild Cat** / **Right Here On Earth** *(Capitol CL-15099)*
20 Feb 60	14	1	**Summertime** *(Gene Vincent & The Blue Caps)* / Frankie And Johnny *(Gene Vincent & His Blue Caps)* *(Capitol CL-15035)* **2nd re-entry**
5 Mar 60	7	1	★ **My Heart** / I've Got To Get You Yet *(Capitol CL-15115)*
30 Apr 60	16	1	**Summertime** *(Gene Vincent & The Blue Caps)* / Frankie And Johnny *(Gene Vincent & His Blue Caps)* *(Capitol CL-15035)* **3rd re-entry**
26 Nov 60	20	1	**Anna-Annabelle** / Ac-cent-tchu-ate The Positive *(Capitol CL-15169)*
4 Mar 61	19	1	**Mister Loneliness** / If You Want My Lovin' *(Capitol CL-15185)*

VIPERS SKIFFLE GROUP
20

Group formed in 1956 in London, initially as a trio of singers/guitarists. After adding a rhythm section, they were offered a residency at the famous 2I's coffee bar in Soho and became one of the UK's leading skiffle outfits. Singer/guitarist Wally Whyton went on to become a TV personality.

19 Jan 57	1	1	★ **Don't You Rock Me Daddy-O** / 10,000 Years Ago *(Parlophone R-4261)*
26 Jan 57	5	1	**Pick A Bale Of Cotton** / Ain't You Glad *(Parlophone R-4238)*
9 Mar 57	1	9	**Hey Liley, Liley Lo** / **Jim Dandy** *(Parlophone R-4286)*
16 Mar 57	3	1	★ **The Cumberland Gap** / Maggie May *(Parlophone R-4289)*
30 Mar 57	10	1	**Ain't You Glad** / Pick A Bale Of Cotton *(Parlophone R-4238)* **1st re-entry (flipped)**
25 May 57	6	1	★ **Streamline Train** / Railroad Steamboat *(Parlophone R-4308)*
8 Jun 57	4	1	**Ain't You Glad** / Pick A Bale Of Cotton *(Parlophone R-4238)* **2nd re-entry**
5 Oct 57	3	2	**Homing Bird** / Pay Me My Money Down *(Parlophone R-4351)*
16 Nov 57	10	1	**Homing Bird** / Pay Me My Money Down *(Parlophone R-4351)* **re-entry**
23 Nov 57	3	1	**Skiffle Party (Parts 1 & 2) [M]** *(Parlophone R-4371)* Comin' Round The Mountain – On Top Of Old Smokey – Rock Island Line / Wabash Cannonball – Gimme Crack Corn – Skip To My Lou.
19 Apr 58	9	1	**No Other Baby** / Baby Why? *(Parlophone R-4393)* Both sides as by the Vipers

See also Various Artists (Top Ten Special)

VISCOUNTS
2

British vocal trio formed by three members of Morton Fraser's Harmonica Gang: Don Paul, Ronnie Wells and Gordon Mills, who later managed Tom Jones and Engelbert Humperdinck.

| 6 Feb 60 | 9 | 1 | **Rockin' Little Angel** / That's All Right *(Pye 7N.15249)* |
| 4 Feb 61 | 16 | 1 | **Money (Is The Root Of All Evil)** / One Armed Bandit *(Pye 7N.15323)* |

THE VOICES
1

The line-up of this Scottish vocal group is lost in the mists of time, but their one and only recording serves to demonstrate that not all music on Beltona was traditional.

| 17 Nov 56 | 15 | 1 | **Rock 'n Roll Hit Parade (Parts 1 & 2) [M]** *(Beltona BL-2667)* Hound Dog – I Want You, I Need You, I Love You – Don't Be Cruel (To A Heart That's True) / Ka-Ding Dong – Fever – Race With The Devil |

HERBERT VON KARAJAN *(conductor)*
See Philharmonia Orchestra

STEPHANIE VOSS   1

Actress, singer and dancer born in London in 1936. She was leading lady in numerous British musical theatre productions, most notably the 1959 West End smash, 'Lock Up Your Daughters'.

3 Oct 59   **23**   1   **Lovely Lover** / Kind Fate *(Decca F-11165)*
                        Both sides by Stephanie Voss and Terence Cooper

See also Original London Cast (LOCK UP YOUR DAUGHTERS)

WAILERS   3

Tough rock'n'roll quintet from Tacoma, Washington. Their early singles were largely instrumental, in keeping with the fashions of the time, although 'Dirty Robber' featured a vocal.

31 Oct 59   **16**   2   **Tall Cool One** / Road-Runner *(London HL-8958)*
5 Dec 59   **11**   1   **Dirty Robber** / Mau-Mau *(London HL-8994)*

JERRY WALLACE   8

Smooth-voiced pop and country hitmaker from Guilford, Missouri. 'Primrose Lane', which made No. 8 in the Billboard 'Hot 100' in the summer of 1959, was his biggest US chart success.

17 Oct 59   **3**   2   **Primrose Lane** / By Your Side *(London HLH-8943)*
7 Nov 59   **10**   1   **Primrose Lane** / By Your Side *(London HLH-8943)* **re-entry**
14 May 60   **2**   4   ★ <u>**You're Singing Our Love Song To Somebody Else**</u> /
                         King Of The Mountain *(London HLH-9110)*
18 Jun 60   **6**   1   ★ <u>**You're Singing Our Love Song To Somebody Else**</u> /
                         King Of The Mountain *(London HLH-9110)* **re-entry**

FATS WALLER   1

Born in New York in 1904, portly Thomas Wright 'Fats' Waller was a jazz singer, pianist/organist and composer with an exuberant and humorous style that endeared him to his public. A club and radio star in the '30s and early '40s, he died of pneumonia in 1943.

28 May 60   **9**   1   **Dinah** / When Somebody Thinks You're Wonderful *(R.C.A. RCA-1189)*

GEORGE WALLINGTON TRIO   1

American jazz `bop' pianist and composer born Giacinto Figlia in Palermo, Sicily in 1924.

19 Jun 54   **21**   1   **NEW SOUNDS FROM EUROPE (VOL. 5: PARIS)** *(Vogue LDE-059)* **LP**
                         Fairyland / Woody'n You / Just One Of Those Things / Honeysuckle Rose / Star
                         Eyes / N.Y. / A Day In Paris / These Foolish Things

BILLY WARD & HIS DOMINOES   3

Black vocal group formed in New York by vocal coach/arranger Billy Ward and talent agent Rose Marks. They were very popular in the early '50s, and launched the careers of Clyde McPhatter and Jackie Wilson.

7 Sep 57   **8**   1   ★ <u>**Stardust**</u> / Lucinda *(London HLU-8465)*
                         Both sides as by Billy Ward & The Dominos
16 Nov 57   **10**   2   ★ <u>**Deep Purple**</u> / Do It Again *(London HLU-8502)*

See also Clyde McPhatter
          Jackie Wilson

ANNE WARREN   1

Twelve-year-old girl who duetted with Ruby Murray on her 1955 No. 4 hit, 'If Anyone Finds This, I Love You'. Sadly, her pairing with Tony Brent proved less successful.

23 Apr 55   **12**   1   **Open Up Your Heart** *(Tony Brent and Anne Warren)*
                         (Columbia DB-3579)
                         Flip is 'Hearts Of Stone' by Tony Brent and the Coronets

DINAH WASHINGTON 1

Hard-living R&B/jazz singer born Ruth Lee Jones in Tuscaloosa, Alabama in 1924. Although she was billed 'Queen of the Blues', from 1959 her material became more pop-orientated. She died in 1963 from an accidental overdose of sleeping pills, aged just 39.

9 Jul 60   **12**   1   **A Rockin' Good Way** *(Dinah Washington and Brook Benton)* /
                  I Believe *(Brook Benton and Dinah Washington)*
                  (Mercury AMT-1099)

RICKY WAYNE 4

Singer and professional bodybuilder born Learie Carasco in St. Lucia in 1938. Discovered and renamed by producer Joe Meek, he was teamed on record with Peter Fleerakkers' instrumental combo, the Fabulous Flee-Rakkers (later Flee-Rekkers) – almost a winning combination.

18 Jun 60   **3**   4   **Chicka'roo** / Don't Pick On Me *(Triumph RGM-1009)*
                  Both sides by Ricky Wayne with the Fabulous Flee-Rakkers

See also Flee-Rakkers

TERRY WAYNE 1

Underrated early rock'n'roller born in London in 1941. The first British artist to record Carl Perkins' songs, he stood in for Jerry Lee Lewis on his ill-fated 1958 UK tour. He subsequently emigrated to Sweden and became a civil servant.

9 Nov 57   **7**   1   **Matchbox** / Your True Love *(Columbia DB-4002)*

THOMAS WAYNE 3

Brother of Johnny Cash's bass player, Luther Perkins, born in Batesville, Mississippi in 1940. 'Tragedy' was his biggest US hit. Ironically, he also died in tragic circumstances – in a car crash in 1971.

23 May 59   **4**   1   **Tragedy** / Saturday Date *(London HLU-8846)*
6 Jun 59   **12**   2   **Tragedy** / Saturday Date *(London HLU-8846)* ***re-entry***

DON WEBB 1

A native of Lubbock, Texas, Don Webb was inspired by Buddy Holly to follow a musical career. He recorded this Holly-ish number at Norman Petty's studio in Clovis, New Mexico, but it failed to register on either side of the Atlantic.

27 Feb 60   **11**   1   **Little Ditty Baby** / I'll Be Back Home *(Coral Q-72385)*

JOAN WEBER 3

Singer born in Paulsboro, New Jersey in 1935. Weber was pregnant and working as a secretary at Columbia Records when she was asked to fill in for a singer who had failed to show up for a session. She did so under duress, had her baby and left the company. Despite the fact that her record topped the US charts, she never recorded again.

22 Jan 55   **27**   3   ★ **Let Me Go Lover** / Marionette *(Philips PB-389)*

BEN WEBSTER

See Norman Granz

BERT WEEDON 5

Guitarist and composer born in London in 1920. He was a major influence on British guitar players of the '50s and early '60s, thanks to a string of hits, regular TV appearances and his famous 'Play In A Day' manual.

4 Feb 56   **7**   1   **Stranger Than Fiction** *(Bert Weedon with Sidney Torch & His Orch.)* /
                  China Boogie *(Sidney Torch & His Orchestra with Bert Weedon)*
                  (Parlophone R-4113)
7 Nov 59   **2**   2   ★ **Nashville Boogie** / **King Size Guitar** *(Top Rank JAR-221)*
14 Nov 59   **11**   1   **Teenage Guitar** / Blue Guitar *(Top Rank JAR-136)*
28 Jan 61   **18**   1   ★ **Ginchy** / Yearning *(Top Rank JAR-537)*

FRANK WEIR & His Saxophone

Soprano saxophonist and orchestra leader born in London in 1911.

19 Jun 54	4	3	The Never-Never Land / The Little Shoemaker *(Decca F-10324)*
7 Aug 54	27	1	The Never-Never Land / The Little Shoemaker *(Decca F-10324)* **1st re-entry**
21 Aug 54	8	1	The Never-Never Land / The Little Shoemaker *(Decca F-10324)* **2nd re-entry**
11 Sep 54	37	1	The Happy Wanderer / From Your Lips *(Decca F-10271)*
18 Sep 54	15	1	The Never-Never Land / The Little Shoemaker *(Decca F-10324)* **3rd re-entry**
25 Sep 54	39	1	★ <u>My Son, My Son</u> / Our Heaven On Earth *(Decca F-10372)* *Both sides by Vera Lynn and Frank Weir and His Saxophone*
9 Oct 54	10	1	★ <u>My Son, My Son</u> / Our Heaven On Earth *(Decca F-10372)* **re-entry**
29 Jan 55	16	3	Theme from 'Journey Into Space' / Serenade To An Empty Room *(Decca F-10435)*
23 Jun 56	21	1	Mister Cuckoo / If You Ever Go To Paree *(Parlophone R-4157)*
23 Jul 60	7	2	★ <u>Caribbean Honeymoon</u> / Farewell My Love *(Oriole CB-1559)* *Both sides as by Frank Weir & His Orchestra*
20 Aug 60	3	2	★ <u>Caribbean Honeymoon</u> / Farewell My Love *(Oriole CB-1559)* **re-entry**

LAWRENCE WELK & His Orchestra

Accordionist, bandleader and TV impresario born in Strasburg, North Dakota in 1903.

4 Feb 61	1	2	★ <u>Calcutta</u> / Melodie d'Amour *(London HLD-9261)*

JOHNNY WELLS

Obscure crooner who recorded two singles for the tiny Astor label in Lodi, New Jersey. The gently swinging 'Lonely Moon' is now rated as a popcorn soul classic.

28 Nov 59	4	1	Lonely Moon / The One And Only One *(Columbia DB-4377)*

ALEX WELSH & HIS DIXIELANDERS

Singer, cornettist, trumpeter and bandleader born in Edinburgh in 1929. A stalwart of the UK jazz scene from the early '50s onwards, he had a minor hit with 'Tansy' in 1961.

19 Feb 55	15	2	Frankie And Johnnie / I'm Down In The Dumps *(Decca F-10457)* *Both sides by George Melly with Alex Welsh & His Dixielanders*

NANCY WHISKEY

Folk singer/guitarist born Anne Wilson in Glasgow in 1935. As well as being a performer in her own right, she was the lead voice on the Chas McDevitt Skiffle Group's two hits.

9 Mar 57	4	1	★ <u>Freight Train</u> *(Chas McDevitt Skiffle Group featuring Nancy Whiskey)* / *(Oriole CB-1352)* *Flip is 'The Cotton Song' by the Chas McDevitt Skiffle Group*
23 Mar 57	10	1	★ <u>Freight Train</u> *(Chas McDevitt Skiffle Group featuring Nancy Whiskey)* / *(Oriole CB-1352)* **re-entry**
1 Jun 57	5	1	★ <u>Green Back Dollar</u> *(Chas McDevitt Skiffle Group featuring Nancy Whiskey) (Oriole CB-1371)* *Flip is 'I'm Satisfied' by the Chas McDevitt Skiffle Group*
29 Mar 58	13	1	NANCY WHISKEY SINGS *(Topic 7T-10)* **7" Mini-LP** An Old Man Come 'A Courting / Bonnie Lad / The Bold Fenian Men / Poor Little Turtle Dove / Trooper And The Maid / The Farewell Song
26 Jul 58	1	4	I Know Where I'm Goin' / Hillside In Scotland *(Oriole CB-1452)*

DAVID WHITFIELD

Distinguished former Royal Navy serviceman born in Hull in 1925. With a vocal style closer to light opera than pop crooning, he was the UK's most popular tenor in the mid-'50s.

21 Aug 54	10	1	Smile / How, When Or Where *(Decca F-10355)*
4 Sep 54	5	2	Smile / How, When Or Where *(Decca F-10355)* **1st re-entry**

16 Oct 54	**11**	2	**Smile** / How, When Or Where *(Decca F-10355)* **2nd re-entry**
30 Oct 54	**35**	1	★ <u>Santo Natale</u> / Adeste Fideles *(Decca F-10399)*
6 Nov 54	**23**	1	**Smile** / How, When Or Where *(Decca F-10355)* **3rd re-entry**
11 Dec 54	**43**	1	**Smile** / How, When Or Where *(Decca F-10355)* **4th re-entry**
30 Apr 55	**3**	4	★ <u>Ev'rywhere</u> / **Mama** *(Decca F-10515)*
13 Aug 55	**4**	6	**The Lady** / Santa Rosa Lea Rose *(Decca F-10562)*
1 Oct 55	**1**	9	**I'll Never Stop Loving You** / **Lady Of Madrid** *(Decca F-10596)*
12 Nov 55	**14**	1	★ <u>When You Lose The One You Love</u> / Angelus *(Decca F-10627)*
24 Dec 55	**21**	1	**I'll Never Stop Loving You** / Lady Of Madrid *(Decca F-10596)* **1st re-entry**
14 Jan 56	**13**	1	**I'll Never Stop Loving You** / Lady Of Madrid *(Decca F-10596)* **2nd re-entry**
10 May 58	**7**	1	★ <u>On The Street Where You Live</u> / Afraid *(Decca F-11018)*
12 Jul 58	**5**	4	★ <u>The Right To Love</u> / That's When Your Heartaches Begin *(Decca F-11039)*
7 Feb 59	**3**	3	**Willingly** / William Tell *(Decca F-11101)*
14 Mar 59	**1**	1	**Willingly** / William Tell *(Decca F-11101)* **re-entry**
5 Sep 59	**12**	1	**A Million Stars** / Farewell My Love *(Decca F-11144)*

See also Various Artists (All Star Hit Parade)
Various Artists (MY FAIR LADY)

MARGARET WHITING   2

Born in Detroit in 1924, Margaret Whiting was America's best-selling female singer of the post-war years, and enjoyed a run of hits from 1946 to 1967. Her father, Richard Whiting, wrote many well-known songs including 'On The Good Ship Lollipop' and 'Hooray For Hollywood'.

18 Jun 55	**25**	1	**Stow-A-Way** / All I Want Is All There Is And Then Some *(Capitol CL-14307)*
9 Jul 55	**2**	1	**Stow-A-Way** / All I Want Is All There Is And Then Some *(Capitol CL-14307)* **re-entry**

SLIM WHITMAN   78

Popular country crooner/yodeller born Otis Dewey Whitman Jr. in Tampa, Florida in 1924.

28 Aug 54	**21**	1	★ <u>China Doll</u> / <u>Indian Love Call</u> *(London L-1149)*
18 Sep 54	**7**	2	★ <u>China Doll</u> / <u>Indian Love Call</u> *(London L-1149)* **1st re-entry**
8 Jan 55	**19**	1	★ <u>China Doll</u> / **Indian Love Call** *(London L-1149)* **2nd re-entry**
26 Mar 55	**24**	1	**Cattle Call** / When I Grow Too Old To Dream *(London HL-8125)*
4 Jun 55	**1**	6	★ <u>Rose Marie</u> / We Stood At The Altar *(London HL-8061)*
25 Jun 55	**22**	1	**When I Grow Too Old To Dream** / **Cattle Call** *(London HL-8125)* **1st re-entry (flipped)**
2 Jul 55	**23**	1	★ <u>Indian Love Call</u> / China Doll *(London L-1149)* **3rd re-entry (flipped)**
9 Jul 55	**19**	2	**Roll On Silvery Moon** / Haunted Hungry Heart *(London HL-8141)*
16 Jul 55	**1**	2	★ <u>Indian Love Call</u> / China Doll *(London L-1149)* **4th re-entry**
13 Aug 55	**2**	8	**Roll On Silvery Moon** / Haunted Hungry Heart *(London HL-8141)* **re-entry**
13 Aug 55	**5**	12	**Cattle Call** / When I Grow Too Old To Dream *(London HL-8125)* **2nd re-entry (flipped)**
13 Aug 55	**15**	1	**Danny Boy** / There's A Rainbow In Every Teardrop *(London L-1214)*
27 Aug 55	**9**	1	**Danny Boy** / There's A Rainbow In Every Teardrop *(London L-1214)* **1st re-entry**
3 Sep 55	**17**	2	**Bandera Waltz** / My Love Is Growing Stale *(London L-1191)*
10 Sep 55	**5**	2	**Danny Boy** / There's A Rainbow In Every Teardrop *(London L-1214)* **2nd re-entry**
17 Sep 55	**13**	3	**I'll Never Stop Loving You** / I'll Never Take You Back Again *(London HLU-8167)*
15 Oct 55	**19**	1	**Danny Boy** / There's A Rainbow In Every Teardrop *(London L-1214)* **3rd re-entry**
22 Oct 55	**15**	2	**I'll Never Stop Loving You** / **I'll Never Take You Back Again** *(London HLU-8167)* **re-entry**
12 Nov 55	**7**	6	**Song Of The Wild** / You Have My Heart *(London HLU-8196)*

3 Dec 55	**12**	2	**Cattle Call** / When I Grow Too Old To Dream *(London HL-8125)*
			3rd re-entry
14 Jan 56	**13**	1	**Song Of The Wild** / You Have My Heart *(London HLU-8196)*
			re-entry
18 Feb 56	**3**	1	★ <u>**Tumbling Tumbleweeds**</u> / Tell Me *(London HLU-8230)*
16 Jun 56	**9**	1	★ <u>**Serenade**</u> / I Talk To The Waves *(London HLU-8287)*
6 Oct 56	**18**	1	**Danny Boy** / There's A Rainbow In Every Teardrop *(London L-1214)*
			4th re-entry
27 Oct 56	**3**	2	**Whiffenpoof Song** / **Dear Mary** *(London HLU-8327)*
30 Mar 57	**4**	2	★ <u>**I'll Take You Home Again Kathleen**</u> / Careless Love
			(London HLP-8403)
11 May 57	**1**	7	**Gone** / An Amateur In Love *(London HLP-8420)*
26 Apr 58	**14**	1	**Unchain My Heart** / Hush-A-Bye *(London HLP-8518)*
3 May 58	**5**	3	**A Very Precious Love** / Careless Hands *(London HLP-8590)*
31 May 58	**13**	1	**A Very Precious Love** / Careless Hands *(London HLP-8590)*
			1st re-entry
28 Jun 58	**3**	1	**A Very Precious Love** / Careless Hands *(London HLP-8590)*
			2nd re-entry

TOMMY WHITTLE   1

Scottish jazz saxophonist born in Grangemouth in 1926. He was voted Britain's top tenor sax player in 1955 and 1956.

7 Aug 54	**14**	1	**'Deed I Do** / Zoot's Suite *(Esquire 10-368)*
			Tommy Whittle with the Tony Kinsey Trio

See also Tony Kinsey Trio

MARTY WILDE   11

Singer/guitarist born Reginald Smith in London in 1939. He was one of Britain's top rock'n'rollers in the late '50s, ranked alongside Cliff Richard and Tommy Steele.

26 Oct 57	**3**	2	**Honeycomb** / Wild Cat *(Philips PB-750)*
			Both sides by Marty Wilde & His Wildcats
30 Nov 57	**12**	1	**Honeycomb** / Wild Cat *(Philips PB-750)* **re-entry**
27 Sep 58	**8**	3	**My Lucky Love** / Misery's Child *(Philips PB-850)*
			Both sides by Marty Wilde & His Wildcats
19 Sep 59	**3**	1	★ <u>**Sea Of Love**</u> / Teenage Tears *(Philips PB-959)*
28 Nov 59	**4**	1	★ <u>**Bad Boy**</u> / It's Been Nice *(Philips PB-972)*
25 Jun 60	**5**	1	★ <u>**Angry**</u> / I Wanna Be Loved By You *(Philips PB-1037)*
9 Jul 60	**5**	1	★ <u>**Angry**</u> / I Wanna Be Loved By You *(Philips PB-1037)*
			re-entry
14 Jan 61	**17**	1	★ <u>**Rubber Ball**</u> / Like Makin' Love *(Philips PB-1101)*

See also Krew Kats

ANDY WILLIAMS   7

Pop vocalist supreme born Howard Andrew Williams in Wall Lake, Iowa in 1927. His hitmaking career started in 1955, when 'Canadian Sunset', reached No. 3 on the US charts. His fifth release, 'Butterfly', went to No. 1 on both sides of the Atlantic. The rest is history.

10 Nov 56	**12**	1	**Canadian Sunset** / High Upon A Mountain *(London HLA-8315)*
13 Apr 57	**3**	1	★ <u>**Butterfly**</u> / It Doesn't Take Very Long *(London HLA-8399)*
17 May 58	**5**	1	**Are You Sincere** / Be Mine Tonight *(London HLA-8587)*
25 Apr 59	**15**	1	**Hawaiian Wedding Song** / House Of Bamboo *(London HLA-8784)*
26 Dec 59	**11**	1	**Lonely Street** / Summer Love *(London HLA-8957)*
16 Jan 60	**9**	1	**Lonely Street** / Summer Love *(London HLA-8957)*
			re-entry
30 Apr 60	**12**	1	**Wake Me When It's Over** / We Have A Date *(London HLA-9099)*

BILLY WILLIAMS 6

Black singer born Wilfred Williams in Waco, Texas in 1910. He started out in 1930 as lead singer of the Charioteers gospel/pop group, then formed his own quartet in 1950. Sadly, he lost his voice in the '60s due to diabetes.

4 Dec 54	**24**	2	**Sh-Boom** / Whenever Wherever *(Vogue Coral Q-2012)*
			Both sides by the Billy Williams Quartet
11 Aug 56	**10**	1	**Cry Baby** / A Crazy Little Palace *(Vogue Coral Q-72149)*
			Both sides by the Billy Williams Quartet
20 Jul 57	**2**	2	★ <u>**I'm Gonna Sit Right Down And Write Myself A Letter**</u> /
			Date With The Blues *(Vogue Coral Q-72266)*
13 Aug 60	**14**	1	**I Cried For You** / The Lover Of All Lovers *(Coral Q-72402)*

CHARLES WILLIAMS & His Concert Orchestra 1

Light music and film score composer/conductor born Isaac Cozerbreit in London in 1893. He also wrote the signature tunes of several popular programmes of the day including 'Dick Barton, Special Agent', 'Jennings at School', 'BBC-TV Newsreel' and 'Friday Night is Music Night'.

9 Oct 54	**29**	1	**Tyrolean Tango** / La Mer *(Columbia DB-3471)*

HANK WILLIAMS 4

Legendary country singer/songwriter born Hiram King Williams in Mount Olive, Alabama in 1923. An alcoholic from the early '40s onwards, he later also became hooked on prescription drugs and died of an overdose in 1953, aged just 30.

28 Apr 56	**4**	1	**Your Cheatin' Heart** / A Teardrop On A Rose *(M.G.M. MGM-896)*
12 May 56	**7**	1	**Your Cheatin' Heart** / A Teardrop On A Rose *(M.G.M. MGM-896)*
			re-entry
22 Mar 58	**8**	1	**SONGS FOR A BROKEN HEART** *(M.G.M. MGM-EP-639)* **EP**
			Nobody's Lonesome For Me / You Win Again / Why Don't You Love Me / Take
			These Chains From My Heart
3 May 58	**11**	1	**SONGS FOR A BROKEN HEART** *(M.G.M. MGM-EP-639)* **EP** *re-entry*

LARRY WILLIAMS 8

Born in New Orleans in 1935, Larry Williams had a voice and piano style to rival Little Richard's, and he wrote and recorded some of rock'n'roll's all-time classics. However his wild lifestyle eventually caught up with him and he was found shot dead at home in 1980.

14 Sep 57	**1**	1	★ <u>**Short Fat Fannie**</u> / High School Dance *(London HLN-8472)*
26 Apr 58	**1**	4	**Dizzy Miss Lizzy** / Slow Down *(London HLU-8604)*
28 Jun 58	**17**	1	**Dizzy Miss Lizzy** / Slow Down *(London HLU-8604)* *re-entry*
2 May 59	**13**	1	**Bad Boy** / She Said 'Yeah' *(London HLU-8844)*
13 Jun 59	**6**	1	**Bad Boy** / She Said 'Yeah' *(London HLU-8844)* *re-entry*

MAURICE WILLIAMS & THE ZODIACS 1

Black vocal group from Lancaster, South Carolina, formerly known as the Gladiolas. Despite being only 1 minute 36 seconds long, the catchy 'Stay' charted for them on both sides of the Atlantic.

31 Dec 60	**2**	1	★ <u>**Stay**</u> / Do You Believe *(Top Rank JAR-526)*

ROGER WILLIAMS 2

Popular pianist born Louis Weertz in Omaha, Nebraska in 1924.

1 Nov 58	**4**	2	**Near You** / The Merry Widow Waltz *(London HLR-8690)*

CLAUDE WILLIAMSON TRIO 1

Jazz pianist born in Brattleboro, Vermont in 1926.

4 Dec 54	**46**	1	**KENTON PRESENTS JAZZ – CLAUDE WILLIAMSON**
			(Capitol KPL-103) **LP**
			Bouncing With Bud / Salute To Bud / Penny / Thou Swell / Obsession / Indiana /
			Over The Rainbow / Curtistan

Stephanie
Voss

CHUCK WILLIS   5

Successful R&B singer/songwriter born Harold Willis in Atlanta, Georgia in 1926. Ironically, he died of peritonitis in 1958, just after the release of 'What Am I Living For'.

29 Jun 57	5	1	**C.C. Rider** / Ease The Pain *(London HLE-8444)*
5 Jul 58	8	1	**What Am I Living For** / Hang Up My Rock And Roll Shoes *(London HLE-8635)*
5 Jul 58	23	1	**That Train Has Gone** / Love Me Cherry *(London HLE-8489)*
2 Aug 58	11	1	**What Am I Living For** / Hang Up My Rock And Roll Shoes *(London HLE-8635)* **1st re-entry**
16 Aug 58	8	1	**What Am I Living For** / Hang Up My Rock And Roll Shoes *(London HLE-8635)* **2nd re-entry**

WILLOWS   2

Pioneering R&B quintet formed in New York in 1950 as the Dovers. 'Church Bells May Ring' (on which Neil Sedaka played chimes) was their only US hit, but ranks as an all-time doo-wop classic.

| 18 Aug 56 | 8 | 2 | **Church Bells May Ring** / Baby Tell Me *(London HLL-8290)* |

JACKIE WILSON   7

Fabulous R&B singer and dynamic stage performer born in Detroit in 1934, who racked up 47 'Hot 100' entries between 1958 and 1975. A massive heart attack in 1975 left him in a persistent vegetative state from which he never recovered. He died in 1984, aged just 49.

2 Nov 57	5	2	★ <u>Reet Petite</u> / By The Light Of The Silvery Moon *(Vogue Coral Q-72290)*
9 May 59	3	3	**That's Why** / Love Is All *(Coral Q-72366)*
26 Dec 59	11	1	**Talk That Talk** / Only You, Only Me *(Coral Q-72384)*
12 Nov 60	5	1	★ <u>Alone At Last</u> / Am I The Man *(Coral Q-72412)*

See also Billy Ward & The Dominoes

ROBERT WILSON   13

Born in Cambuslang in 1907, Robert Wilson was an operatic tenor and a very popular figure on the Scottish music scene from the '30s until his premature death in 1964.

13 Nov 54	23	2	**The Northern Lights Of Aberdeen** / The Dashing White Sergeant *Both sides by Robert Wilson with Jimmy Shand & His Band* *(H.M.V. B-10521)*
20 Nov 54	23	1	**Here's To The Gordons** / My Scottish Homeland *(H.M.V. B-10780)*
27 Nov 54	32	1	**Scotland The Brave** / The Pride Of Donaghadee *(H.M.V. B-10401)*
15 Jan 55	37	2	**Here's To The Gordons** / My Scottish Homeland *(H.M.V. B-10780)* **re-entry**
22 Jan 55	55	1	**The Northern Lights Of Aberdeen** / The Dashing White Sergeant *(H.M.V. B-10521)* **1st re-entry**
5 Feb 55	30	2	**The Northern Lights Of Aberdeen** / The Dashing White Sergeant *(H.M.V. B-10521)* **2nd re-entry**
5 Mar 55	10	1	**The Northern Lights Of Aberdeen** / The Dashing White Sergeant *(H.M.V. B-10521)* **3rd re-entry**
1 Oct 55	18	1	**Doonaree** / The Black Watch *(H.M.V. B-10829)*
10 Mar 56	24	1	**My Bonnie Lassie** / A Cameron Lad *(H.M.V. B-10941)*
24 May 58	9	1	**The Hiking Song** / Always Together *(H.M.V. POP-362)*

TEDDY WILSON   3

Jazz pianist and bandleader born Theodore Wilson in Austin, Texas in 1912.

| 25 Sep 54 | 35 | 2 | **THE BILLIE HOLIDAY AND TEDDY WILSON ORCHESTRAS** *(Columbia 33S-1034)* **LP** Why Was I Born / Body And Soul / Them There Eyes / Moanin' Low / Swing, Brother Swing / Billie's Blues / Some Other Spring / Falling In Love Again / These Foolish Things / I'll Get By |
| 16 Oct 54 | 26 | 1 | **THE BILLIE HOLIDAY AND TEDDY WILSON ORCHESTRAS** *(Columbia 33S-1034)* **LP** *re-entry* |

KAI WINDING
See J.J. Johnson etc.

ERIC WINSTONE & His Orchestra   1
Born in London in 1913, Eric Winstone was a virtuoso piano-accordionist, composer and big band leader. He was frequently heard on the BBC's popular 'Music While You Work' radio show.

19 Mar 55   **17**   1   **Fanfare Boogie** / Slow Joe *(Polygon P-1153)*

LOIS WINTER   1
Classical soprano from New York who also sang backing vocals for everyone from Tony Bennett to Sister Rosetta Tharpe.

27 Aug 55   **24**   1   **The Breeze And I** / Malagueña *(Polygon P-1185)*

HUGO WINTERHALTER'S ORCHESTRA & CHORUS   8
Easy listening arranger and composer born in Wilkes-Barre, Pennsylvania in 1909.

8 Jan 55   **37**   2   **Song Of The Barefoot Contessa** / Land Of Dreams *(H.M.V. B-10791)*
29 Jan 55   **6**   5   **Song Of The Barefoot Contessa** / Land Of Dreams *(H.M.V. B-10791)*
                 1st re-entry
19 Mar 55   **27**   1   **Song Of The Barefoot Contessa** / Land Of Dreams *(H.M.V. B-10791)*
                 2nd re-entry

NORMAN WISDOM   4
Much-loved knockabout comedian, singer and film star born in London in 1915.

5 Nov 55   **26**   1   **Beware** / Dream For Sale *(Columbia DB-3654)*
9 Mar 57   **11**   1   ★ **The Wisdom Of A Fool** / Happy Ending *(Columbia DB-3903)*
30 Apr 60   **16**   1   **Follow A Star** / Give Me A Night In June *(Top Rank JAR-246)*
14 May 60   **13**   1   **FOLLOW A STAR [OST]** *(Top Rank JKP-2052)* **EP**
                 Follow A Star / Give Me A Night In June / I Love You / The Bath Song

CHARLES WOLCOTT
See M.G.M. Studio Orchestra

SHEB WOOLEY   1
Prolific actor and country singer born Shelby Wooley in Erick, Oklahoma in 1921. His self-penned novelty single topped the Billboard 'Hot 100' in the summer of 1958.

14 Jun 58   **10**   1   ★ **The Purple People Eater** / Recipe For Love *(M.G.M. MGM-981)*

LINK WRAY & HIS RAY MEN   3
Cult guitarist born Fred Lincoln Wray Jr. in Dunn, North Carolina in 1929. Packed with power chords, distortion and feedback, his moody debut single, 'Rumble', was nothing short of revolutionary and paved the way for several generations of hard rockers.

31 May 58   **8**   1   **Rumble** / The Swag *(London HLA-8623)*
28 Jun 58   **17**   2   **Rumble** / The Swag *(London HLA-8623)* **re-entry**

DALE WRIGHT   1
Rock'n'roll singer and radio deejay born Harlan Dale Riffe in Middletown, Ohio in 1939. He had a couple of US hits in 1958 with 'She's Neat' and 'Please Don't Do It', but 'That's Show Biz' was the only recording to create any interest in the UK.

13 Jun 59   **16**   1   **That's Show Biz** / That's My Gal *(Pye International 7N.25022)*
                 Both sides by Dale Wright with the Wright Guys

GINNY WRIGHT 3

Country singer born in Twin City, Georgia in 1936. She had a No. 3 C&W hit in 1954 with Jim Reeves called 'I Love You', and her 1955 duet with Tom Tall, 'Are You Mine', went one higher, but she withdrew from the music business soon after to raise a family.

19 Nov 55	**10**	3	**Are You Mine** / Boom Boom Boomerang *(London HL-8150)*
			Both sides by Ginny Wright and Tom Tall

MARK WYNTER 6

British balladeer born Terence Lewis in Woking, Surrey in 1943. He enjoyed a string of hits between 1960 and 1964, after which he turned his attention to acting.

13 Aug 60	**5**	2	★ <u>**Image Of A Girl**</u> / Glory Of Love *(Decca F-11263)*
22 Oct 60	**2**	3	★ <u>**Kickin' Up The Leaves**</u> / That's What I Thought *(Decca F-11279)*
25 Feb 61	**2**	1	★ <u>**Dream Girl**</u> / Two Little Girls *(Decca F-11323)*

RUSTY YORK 1

Born in Harlan, Kentucky in 1935, Charles Edward 'Rusty' York started out as a hillbilly singer/ guitarist, but switched to rockabilly in 1957. Although these two rocking sides with Bonnie Lou were commercially unsuccessful, he did score a minor US hit the following year with 'Sugaree'.

5 Apr 58	**8**	1	**La Dee Dah** / Let The School Bell Ring Ding-A-Ling
			Both sides by Bonnie Lou and Rusty York (Parlophone R-4409)

See also Bonnie Lou

YORKSHIRE JAZZ BAND 1

Popular and long-lasting trad jazz band led by tuba player Bob Barclay, who also ran the Studio 20 jazz club in Leeds.

22 Jan 55	**46**	1	**Muskrat Ramble** / Big Chief Battle Axe *(Tempo A-17)*

FARON YOUNG 17

Top country singer, guitarist and songwriter born in Shreveport, Louisiana in 1932. Between 1953 and 1989, he racked up no fewer than 89 hits on the Billboard C&W chart.

24 Sep 55	**21**	1	**Live Fast, Love Hard, Die Young** / Forgive Me, Dear
			(Capitol CL-14336)
22 Oct 55	**25**	3	**Live Fast, Love Hard, Die Young** / Forgive Me, Dear
			(Capitol CL-14336) **re-entry**
9 Jun 56	**12**	3	**If You Ain't Lovin' (You Ain't Livin')** / All Right *(Capitol CL-14574)*
16 Nov 57	**6**	1	**SWEETHEARTS OR STRANGERS (PART 1)** *(Capitol EAP1-778)* 🅴🅿
			Sweethearts Or Strangers / Your Cheatin' Heart / Shame On You / I Can't Tell My Heart
15 Mar 58	**2**	2	**SWEETHEARTS OR STRANGERS (PART 3)** *(Capitol EAP3-778)* 🅴🅿
			I'm A Poor Boy / I Can't Help It / You Are My Sunshine / That's What It's Like To Be Lonesome
4 Oct 58	**7**	1	**I Hate Myself / That's The Way I Feel** *(Capitol CL-14930)*
10 Oct 59	**22**	1	**I Hear You Talkin'** / Country Girl *(Capitol CL-15050)*
8 Oct 60	**5**	1	**There's Not Any Like You Left** / Is She All You Thought She'd Be *(Capitol CL-15151)*
10 Dec 60	**9**	2	**Forget The Past** / A World So Full Of Love *(Capitol CL-15173)*
7 Jan 61	**24**	1	**Forget The Past** / A World So Full Of Love *(Capitol CL-15173)* **1st re-entry**
21 Jan 61	**20**	1	**Forget The Past** / A World So Full Of Love *(Capitol CL-15173)* **2nd re-entry**

JIMMY YOUNG 13

Balladeer born Leslie Ronald Young in Cinderford, Gloucestershire in 1921. He changed career direction in the '60s and became a popular radio presenter.

28 Aug 54	**27**	1	**Little Things Mean A Lot** / Here *(Decca F-10317)*
18 Sep 54	**7**	1	**Little Things Mean A Lot** / Here *(Decca F-10317)* **1st re-entry**

23 Oct 54	**12**	1	**Little Things Mean A Lot** / Here *(Decca F-10317)* **2nd re-entry**
20 Nov 54	**42**	1	**Moonlight In Mayo** / Darling, They're Playing Our Song *(Decca F-10343)*
18 Dec 54	**34**	3	**I Understand Just How You Feel** / The High And The Mighty *(Decca F-10370)*
30 Apr 55	**21**	1	★ <u>**Unchained Melody**</u> / Help Me Forget *(Decca F-10502)*
3 Mar 56	**4**	1	★ <u>**Chain Gang**</u> / Capri In May *(Decca F-10694)*
22 Sep 56	**4**	1	★ <u>**More**</u> / I'm Gonna Steal You Away *(Decca F-10774)*
9 Feb 57	**5**	2	**My Faith, My Hope, My Love** / Lovin' Baby *(Decca F-10842)*
27 Apr 57	**6**	1	★ <u>**Round And Round**</u> / Walkin' After Midnight *(Decca F-10875)*

LESTER YOUNG — 3

Jazz tenor saxophonist/clarinettist born in Woodville, Mississippi in 1909. Renowned for his relaxed, cool tone and sophisticated harmonies, he first came to prominence in the late 1930s while playing in Count Basie's orchestra.

| 6 Nov 54 | **35** | 2 | **COUNT BASIE / LESTER YOUNG** *(Oriole/Mercury MG-25015)* **LP**
 Count Basie & His Kansas City Seven: Lester Leaps Again / After Theatre Jump / Destination K.C. / *Lester Young Quartet:* I Never Knew / Just You, Just Me / Afternoon Of A Basie-ite / Sometimes I'm Happy |
| 18 Dec 54 | **34** | 1 | **COUNT BASIE / LESTER YOUNG** *(Oriole/Mercury MG-25015)* **LP**
 re-entry |

See Norman Granz' Jazz At The Philharmonic

ROY YOUNG — 1

Rock'n'roll singer/pianist from London. In the early '60s, he led the house band at the famous Star-Club in Hamburg, then formed the Roy Young Band in the early '70s. His hard-rocking style was once described as a mixture of Little Richard, Ray Charles and Joe Cocker.

| 17 Oct 59 | **8** | 1 | **Hey Little Girl** / Just Ask Your Heart *(Fontana H-215)* |

VICKI YOUNG — 3

Pop singer/songwriter born Wanda Stegall in Vinson, Oklahoma in 1925. During the rock'n'roll era, she covered R&B hits of the day for the white market, much like Georgia Gibbs did for Mercury.

| 18 Dec 54 | **16** | 3 | **Honey Love** / Riot In Cell Block Number Nine *(Capitol CL-14144)* |

VICTOR YOUNG & HIS SINGING STRINGS — 8

Internationally renowned violinist, arranger, composer, songwriter, conductor and record producer born in Chicago in 1900.

| 2 Oct 54 | **15** | 3 | **The High And The Mighty** / The Song from 'The Caine Mutiny' *(Brunswick 05320)* |
| 6 Nov 54 | **2** | 5 | **The High And The Mighty** / The Song from 'The Caine Mutiny' *(Brunswick 05320)* **re-entry** |

ZACHARIAS & HIS MAGIC VIOLINS — 1

Orchestra led by virtuoso violinist Helmut Zacharias, born in Berlin in 1920.

| 14 Jan 61 | **24** | 1 | **Never On Sunday** / Theme from 'The Apartment' *(Polydor NH-66635)* |

JOHN ZACHERLE — 1

Born in Philadelphia in 1918, actor John Zacherle found his niche as a TV horror movie show host and made a career out of it. He scored a US Top Ten hit in 1958 with this horror-rock novelty, and might have done far better in the UK had the BBC not banned it from airplay.

| 10 May 58 | **9** | 1 | **Dinner With Drac (Part 1)** / Dinner With Drac (Conclusion) *(London HLU-8599)* |

TOMMY ZANG   1

Singer who began his career in the mid-'50s as lead vocalist with the Airmen of Note, the USAF's official dance orchestra and successor to the Glenn Miller Army Air Force Band. He subsequently recorded for a variety of labels between 1958 and 1963 without much success, but this popped-up version of the Hank Williams classic licensed from Hickory came good for him in the UK.

28 Jan 61   **22**   1   ★ **<u>Hey Good Lookin'</u>** / With Love *(Polydor NH-66957)*

ZÉ DO NORTE   4

Pseudonym of Brazilian singer/composer Alfredo Ricardo do Nascimento, who contributed both of these haunting tunes to the soundtrack of the 1953 cult film 'O Cangaceiro' (The Bandit).

28 Aug 54   **6**   4   **Lua Bonita** *(Zé do Norte) (H.M.V. JO-377)*
                        The flip, 'Mulher Rendeira' by Coro Mixto, also bubbled under

ZULU RHYTHM BOYS   1

This South African ensemble created something of a stir with their sole UK release, but it would be another eighteen months before kwela music achieved mass acceptance in Britain via 'Tom Hark' by Elias & His Zag-Zag Jive Flutes.

13 Oct 56   **7**   1   **Fanagalo** / Believe Me *(Decca F-10784)*

GARY MILLER

Dir. Keith Devon
Bernard Delfont
Agency
Whitehall 9901.

BERNARD BRESSLAW

Direction: ERIC L'EPINE SMITH
7 Vigo Street, London, W.1

THE FABULOUS FLEE REKKERS

Direction:
Denny Boyce Entertainments
411 Oxford Street, W.1
Tel. MAYfair 5312/3
Personal Manager: Bob Alexander
RIChmond 3873

KATHIE KAY

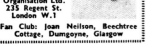

Agent:
Sydney Grace
The Grade
Organisation Ltd.
235 Regent St.
London W.1
Fan Club: Joan Neilson, Beechtree
Cottage, Dumgoyne, Glasgow

JOAN REGAN

Direction :
Keith Devon,
Bernard Delfont
Ltd.
Joan Regan Sup-
porters Club, 73
Longlands Rd.,
Sidcup

RUSS CONWAY

Direction:
NOEL GAY
ARTISTS
24 Denmark St.,
W.C.2

TEMple Bar
3941/5

ALMA COGAN

c/o
Sydney Grace,
235 Regent St.,
W.
Tel.: REG 5821

JOE LYNCH

Films, Television, Radio
Personal Rep: May Bleazard
REGent 0928

BRIDIE GALLAGHER

THE GIRL FROM DONEGAL

Bridie Gallagher
Promotions Ltd.
7 Bedford St.
Belfast
Phone 31508

PATRICK O'HAGAN

Dir.: The Grade Organisation Ltd.,
REGent 5821

RICKY WAYNE

THE SENSATIONAL BEAT SINGER

Triumph Recording Artiste and D.J.

Fan Club: Tony Pickett, 81 Peak Hill,
London S.E.26

Direction:
Denny Boyce Entertainments
411 Oxford Street, W.1
Tel: MAYfair 5312/3

Bubbling Under Facts and Figures

Artists with the most *Bubbling Under* records			

Total	Hit	Non-hit	
32	12	20	Frank Sinatra
27	12	15	Alma Cogan
26	8	18	Nat 'King' Cole
21	13	8	Fats Domino
21	10	11	Frankie Laine
21	8	13	Bill Haley & His Comets
			Johnston Brothers
21	–	21	Johnny Cash
20	13	7	Frankie Vaughan
19	11	8	Max Bygraves
18	7	11	Doris Day
			Dean Martin
17	11	6	Elvis Presley
17	1	16	Chris Barber's Jazz Band
16	11	5	Tommy Steele
16	8	8	Dickie Valentine
16	3	13	Ted Heath & His Music
16	2	14	Guy Mitchell
16	–	16	Gerry Mulligan Quartet
15	9	6	Robert Earl
15	7	8	Ronnie Hilton
15	5	10	Lonnie Donegan
			Johnnie Ray
			Slim Whitman
15	2	13	Jimmy Shand & His Band
14	11	3	Pat Boone
14	6	8	Winifred Atwell
14	4	10	Gene Vincent
14	3	11	Peggy Lee
13	7	6	Joan Regan
13	6	7	Ruby Murray
13	5	8	Four Aces
13	4	9	Vera Lynn
13	3	10	Ella Fitzgerald
12	7	5	Russ Conway
12	6	6	Bing Crosby
12	5	7	Sammy Davis Jr.
12	4	8	Mario Lanza
12	2	10	Eddie Fisher
11	6	5	Ricky Nelson
11	4	7	Joe 'Mr. Piano' Henderson

Total	Hit	Non-hit	
11	2	9	Louis Armstrong
			Sarah Vaughan
11	–	11	Earl Bostic & His Orchestra
			Tony Brent
10	7	3	Malcolm Vaughan
10	6	4	Perry Como
			Michael Holliday
			Stargazers
10	5	5	Petula Clark
			David Whitfield
10	4	6	Platters
10	2	8	Rosemary Clooney
			Edmund Hockridge
10	–	10	Stan Kenton & His Orchestra
9	7	2	Little Richard
9	4	5	Eddie Calvert
			Dave King
			Jerry Lee Lewis
			Johnny Mathis
9	2	7	Beverley Sisters
			Tennessee Ernie Ford
			Marty Robbins
9	1	8	Four Lads
			Eartha Kitt
9	–	9	Ferlin Husky
			Kathie Kay
8	6	2	Shirley Bassey
			Craig Douglas
8	5	3	Connie Francis
8	4	4	Jimmy Young
8	3	5	Chuck Berry
			Billy Eckstine
			Vipers Skiffle Group
8	2	6	Kay Starr
8	–	8	Humphrey Lyttelton & His Band
			Faron Young
7	5	2	Frankie Avalon
			Lloyd Price
7	4	3	Stan Freberg
			Jimmie Rodgers
7	3	4	Brook Benton
			Teresa Brewer
			Coronets
			Keynotes
7	2	5	Big Ben Banjo Band
			Don Lang
7	1	6	Al Martino
7	–	7	Bridie Gallagher
			Kid Ory's Creole Jazz Band
			Hank Thompson
6	5	1	Paul Anka
			Bobby Rydell
6	4	2	Coasters
			Billy Fury
			Cyril Stapleton & His Orchestra
			Marty Wilde
6	3	3	Harry Belafonte
			Johnny Duncan & The Blue Grass Boys
			Frankie Lymon & The Teenagers
			Gary Miller

Total	Hit	Non-hit	
6	2	4	Champs
			Georgia Gibbs
			Ronnie Harris
			Anne Shelton
			Conway Twitty
			Frank Weir & His Saxophone
6	1	5	Les Baxter & His Orchestra and Chorus
			Eve Boswell
			Ronnie Carroll
			Mantovani & His Orchestra
			Marion Ryan
			Andy Williams
6	–	6	Ron Goodwin & His Concert Orchestra
			Robert Wilson
5	5	–	Buddy Holly
5	4	1	Eddie Cochran
			Anthony Newley
5	3	2	Mr. Acker Bilk's Paramount Jazz Band
			Drifters
			Duane Eddy
			Hilltoppers
			Mike Preston
5	2	3	John Barry
			Tony Bennett
			Terry Dene
			Jane Morgan
5	1	4	Browns
			Frank Chacksfield & His Orchestra
			Clyde Valley Stompers
			Don Cornell
			Judy Garland
			Hunters
			Dick James
			Charlie Kunz
			Ray Martin & His Concert Orchestra
			Tony Martin
			McGuire Sisters
			Clyde McPhatter
			Southlanders
			Jo Stafford
5	–	5	Dave Brubeck
			Ken Colyer's Jazzmen
			Duke Ellington
			Benny Goodman
			Joe Lynch
			Shorty Rogers
			Caterina Valente

Artists with most weeks on the *Bubbling Under* chart

96	Frank Sinatra		27	Four Lads
91	Bill Haley & His Comets			Edmund Hockridge
90	Alma Cogan			Stan Kenton & His Orchestra
78	Nat 'King' Cole		26	Patti Page
	Slim Whitman			Stargazers
77	Johnston Brothers		25	Rosemary Clooney
73	Johnnie Ray			Al Martino
70	Dean Martin		24	Brook Brothers
69	Doris Day			Petula Clark
65	Max Bygraves			Georgia Gibbs
64	Four Aces			Howard Keel
62	Kathie Kay			Johnny Mathis
	Frankie Vaughan		23	Judy Garland
60	Jimmy Shand & His Band			Ferlin Husky
58	Vera Lynn		22	Duke Ellington
56	Eddie Fisher			Ronnie Harris
54	Frankie Laine			Humphrey Lyttelton & His Band
51	Fats Domino		21	Malcolm Vaughan
49	Tommy Steele		20	Ray Burns
46	Tony Brent			Eddie Calvert
	Clyde Valley Stompers			Norrie Paramor & His Orchestra
	Sammy Davis Jr.			Jimmie Rodgers
45	Ted Heath & His Music			Vipers Skiffle Group
42	Johnny Cash		19	Earl Bostic & His Orchestra
	Ella Fitzgerald			Joe Lynch
40	Mario Lanza		18	Tony Bennett
	David Whitfield			Craig Douglas
39	Gerry Mulligan Quartet			Frankie Ford
38	Chris Barber's Jazz Band			Benny Goodman
	Lonnie Donegan			Jerry Lee Lewis
37	Louis Armstrong			Bobby MacLeod & His Band
	Peggy Lee		17	Johnny Carson
	Ray Martin & His Concert Orchestra			Coasters
36	Big Ben Banjo Band			Eddie Cochran
	Guy Mitchell			Russ Conway
	Joan Regan			Billy Eckstine
35	Robert Earl			Connie Francis
	Ruby Murray			Don Gibson
	Ricky Nelson			Michael Holliday
34	Bridie Gallagher			Danny Kaye
33	Bing Crosby			Keynotes
	Platters			Little Richard
	Kay Starr			Frankie Lymon & The Teenagers
32	Perry Como			Jack Scott
	Mitchell Torok			Cyril Stapleton & His Orchestra
31	Winifred Atwell			Frank Weir & His Saxophone
	Coronets			Faron Young
	Tennessee Ernie Ford		16	Chuck Berry
	Joe 'Mr. Piano' Henderson			Crew-Cuts
	David Kinnaird			Kid Ory's Creole Jazz Band
	Eartha Kitt			Marty Robbins
	Sarah Vaughan		15	Shirley Bassey
30	Les Baxter & His Orchestra and Chorus			Beverley Sisters
	Pat Boone			Frank Chacksfield & His Orchestra
	Ronnie Hilton			Crazy Otto
29	Eric Delaney & His Band			Dave King
28	Emmettones			Tony Martin
	Enoch Kent			Shorty Rogers
	Elvis Presley			Marion Ryan
	Dickie Valentine			Hank Snow
	Gene Vincent			

29   Mitchell Torok - **Caribbean** *(London HL-8004)*
28   Enoch Kent - **The Smashing Of The Van / Sean South Of Garryowen** *(Top Rank JAR-386)*
22   Clyde Valley Stompers - **Milenberg Joys / Bill Bailey, Won't You Please Come Home**
        (Decca Jazz F-10897)
21   Sammy Davis Jr - **Because Of You (Parts 1 & 2)** *(Brunswick 05326)*
20   Jimmy Shand - **Victory Waltz [M]** *(Parlophone F-3500)*
18   Johnnie Ray - **Destiny** *(Philips PB-301)*
17   Eddie Fisher - **My Friend** *(H.M.V. B-10729)*
        Kathie Kay - **Old Scotch Mother** *(H.M.V. POP-167)*
16   Emmettones - **Bold Robert Emmett** *(Beltona BL-2722)*
        Howard Keel and Brothers - **Sobbin' Women** *(M.G.M. MGM-787)*
        Bobby MacLeod & His Band - **Pride Of Erin Waltz [M] / Irish Military Two-Step [M]**
        (Philips Scottish Series YB-9500)
        Ray Martin & His Concert Orch. - **Hernando's Hideaway** *(Columbia DB-3658)*
        OBC - **KISMET** *(Philips BBL-7023)* **LP**
        Slim Whitman - **When I Grow Too Old To Dream / Cattle Call** *(London HL-8125)*
15   Brook Brothers - **Say The Word / Everything But Love** *(Pye 7N.15298)*
        Frankie Ford - **Sea Cruise** *(London HL-8850)*
        OLC - **SALAD DAYS** *(Oriole MG-20004)* **LP**
14   Tony Brent - **Sway / Three Coins In The Fountain** *(Columbia DB-3496)*
        Bridie Gallagher - **A Mother's Love Is A Blessing** *(Beltona BE-2653)*
13   Tony Bennett - **Close Your Eyes** *(Philips PB-445)*
        Crazy Otto - **Glad Rag Doll / Smiles** *(Polydor BM-6003)*
        Doris Day - **The Blue Bells Of Broadway / I Speak To The Stars** *(Philips PB-295)*
        Eric Delaney & His Band - **Oranges And Lemons / Delaney's Delight** *(Mercury MB-3143)*
        Ella Fitzgerald - **Pete Kelly's Blues / Hard Hearted Hannah** *(Brunswick 05473)*
        Kathie Kay - **Be Content / My Last Love** *(H.M.V. POP-410)*
        Kathie Kay - **Wind In The Willow / We Will Make Love** *(H.M.V. POP-352)*
        OBC - **THE PAJAMA GAME** *(Philips BBL-7050)* **LP**
        Platters - **THE FABULOUS PLATTERS** *(Mercury MEP-9504)* **EP**
        Johnnie Ray - **Papa Loves Mambo** *(Philips PB-346)*
        Howard Rumsey's Lighthouse All Stars -
            HOWARD RUMSEY'S LIGHTHOUSE ALL STARS (VOL. 1) *(Vogue EPV-1004)* **EP**
        Jimmy Shand & His Band - **Marching With Jimmy Shand [M]** *(Parlophone R-4151)*
12   Les Baxter & His Orch. - **The High And The Mighty** *(Capitol CL-14147)*
        Big Ben Banjo Band with the Coronets - **The Crazy Otto Rag / Hey Mr. Banjo**
        (Columbia DB-3620)
        Central Band of the Royal Air Force - **The Dam Busters – March** *(H.M.V. B-10877)*
        Concert Orchestra, *cond.* Eric Coates - **The Dam Busters March** *(Pye Nixa N.15003)*
        5 DeMarco Sisters - **Dreamboat** *(Brunswick 05425)*
        Bridie Gallagher - **The Boys From County Armagh / Killarney And You** *(Beltona BE-2679)*
        Bill Haley & His Comets - **ROCK AROUND THE CLOCK** *(Brunswick OE-9250)* **EP**
        Milt Jackson Modern Jazz Quartet -
            MILT JACKSON MODERN JAZZ QUARTET *(Esquire EP-14)* **EP**
        David Kinnaird - **Mairi's Wedding / Northern Lights Of Aberdeen** *(Top Rank JAR-385)*
        Frankie Laine - **There Must Be A Reason / Some Day** *(Philips PB-306)*
        Mario Lanza - **Serenade** *(H.M.V. DA-2085)* [1956 reissue]
        Vera Lynn - **Popular Medley No. 4 [M]** *(Decca F-10561)*
        Dean Martin and Line Renaud - **Relax-Ay-Voo** *(Capitol CL-14356)*
        Modernaires - **New Juke Box Saturday Night** *(Vogue Coral Q-2035)*
        OST - **CARMEN JONES** *(H.M.V. CLP-1034)* **LP**
        Paul Quinichette, Benny Green, Frank Foster, Joseph Newman,
        Hank Jones, Kenny Clarke, Eddie Jones and Sir Jonathan Gasser -
            JAZZ STUDIO 1 *(Brunswick LAT-8036)* **LP**
        Andy Stewart - **A Scottish Soldier** *(Top Rank JAR-512)*
11   Cathy Carr - **Ivory Tower** *(London HLH-8274)*
        Johnny Carson - **The Train Of Love** *(Fontana H-259)*
        Tennessee Ernie Ford - **River Of No Return / Give Me Your Word** *(Capitol CL-14005)*
        Georgia Gibbs - **Dance With Me Henry (Wallflower)** *(Mercury MB-3223)*
        Gigi Gryce–Clifford Brown Sextet - **Salute To The Bandbox (Parts 1 & 2)** *(Vogue V-2239)*

Bill Haley & His Comets - **Rock Around The Clock** (*Brunswick 05317*)
Ted Heath & His Music - **Malagueña / Cloudburst** (*Decca F-10624*)
J.J. Johnson, Kai Winding, Benny Green and Willie Dennis -
    JAZZ WORKSHOP (VOL. 1) (*Vogue/Debut LDE-066*) **LP**
Joe Lynch - **Homes of Donegal / Delaney's Donkey** (*Beltona BE-2672*)
Dean Martin - **Sway** (*Capitol CL-14138*)
Kay Starr - **Good And Lonesome** (*H.M.V. B-10895*)
Kirk Stevens - **Here's To The Gordons** (*Parlophone R-3963*)
David Whitfield - **I'll Never Stop Loving You / Lady Of Madrid** (*Decca F-10596*)
10   Johnny Angel - **You're Thrilling** (*Parlophone R-4679*)
Elmer Bernstein & Orch. - **Clark Street (Parts 1 & 2)** (*Brunswick 05544*)
Alma Cogan - **Don't Ring-a Da Bell / Bluebell** (*H.M.V. POP-189*)
Alma Cogan - **Love And Marriage** (*H.M.V. POP-163*)
Nat 'King' Cole - **Unbelievable / Hajji Baba** (*Capitol CL-14155*)
Billy Daniels - **Smile / Mom-e-le** (*Mercury MB-3142*)
Danny Davis - **You're My Only Girl / Love Me** (*Parlophone R-4657*)
Eric Delaney & His Band - **Roamin' In The Gloamin' / Ting-A-Ling** (*Mercury MB-3213*)
Eddie Fisher - **How Do You Speak To An Angel / My Arms, My Heart, My Love**
    (*H.M.V. B-10737*)
Tennessee Ernie Ford - **His Hands / I'm A Pilgrim** (*Capitol CL-14261*)
Four Aces - **Melody Of Love** (*Brunswick 05379*)
Jerry Fuller - **Tennessee Waltz** (*London HLH-8982*)
Bill Haley & His Comets - **Dim, Dim The Lights** (*Brunswick 05373*)
Bill Haley & His Comets - **Razzle Dazzle / Two Hound Dogs** (*Brunswick 05453*)
Rita Hayworth [actually Jo Ann Greer] - **Sadie Thompson's Song** (*Mercury MB-3090*)
Irène Hilda - **I Love Paris** / Irène Hilda and Edmund Hockridge - **C'est Magnifique**
    (*Parlophone R-3945*)
Ray Martin & His Concert Orch. - **The Elephants' Tango** (*Columbia DB-3631*)
Tony Martin - **I Love Paris** (*H.M.V. B-10771*)
Ian Menzies & His Clyde Valley Stompers - **The Fish Man** (*Pye 7NJ-2031*)
Patti Page - **I Can't Tell A Waltz From A Tango / Mama Doll Song** (*Mercury MB-3161*)
Johnnie Ray - **Taking A Chance On Love** (*Philips PB-463*)
Slim Whitman - **Roll On Silvery Moon** (*London HL-8141*)
9   Bing Crosby and Louis Armstrong - **Now You Has Jazz** (*Capitol CL-14643*)
Max Bygraves and the Tanner Sisters - **Friends And Neighbours** (*H.M.V. B-10703*)
Johnny Cash - **Ballad Of A Teenage Queen** (*London HLS-8586*)
Alma Cogan - **Chee-Chee-Oo-Chee / Tika Tika Tok** (*H.M.V. B-10862*)
Nat 'King' Cole - **Papa Loves Mambo / Teach Me Tonight** (*Capitol CL-14207*)
Billy Cotton & His Band - **Yellow Rose Of Texas** (*Decca F-10602*)
Four Aces - **Sluefoot** (*Brunswick 05429*)
Judy Garland - **The Man That Got Away** (*Philips PB-366*)
Billy Grammer - **Bonaparte's Retreat** (*Felsted AF-121*)
Ronnie Harris - **I Still Believe / I Love Paris** (*Columbia DB-3529*)
Lena Horne - **I Love To Love / Love Me Or Leave Me** (*H.M.V. B-10869*)
Dick James - **Sing Song Time No. 1 [M]** (*Parlophone R-4065*)
Johnston Brothers - **The Bandit** (*Decca F-10302*)
Johnston Brothers - **Majorca** (*Decca F-10451*)
George Lewis & His New Orleans Music - **Mama Don't Allow It**
    (*Good Time Jazz GV-2253*)
Kathy Linden - **Goodbye Jimmy, Goodbye** (*Felsted AF-122*)
Al Martino - **I Still Believe** (*Capitol CL-14192*)
Patrick O'Hagan - **The Whistling Gypsy** (*Decca (Irish Series) F-18184*)
Joan Regan with the Johnston Brothers - **Wait For Me Darling** (*Decca F-10362*)
Hank Snow - **COUNTRY GUITAR (VOL. 4)** (*R.C.A. RCX-116*) **EP**
Tommy Steele & The Steelmen - **Elevator Rock / Doomsday Rock** (*Decca F-10808*)
The Two Bills from Bermondsey - **What A Mouth, What A Mouth / Cockney Capers [M]**
    (*Parlophone R-3953*)
Vipers Skiffle Group - **Hey Liley, Liley Lo / Jim Dandy** (*Parlophone R-4286*)
8   Louis Armstrong - **Basin Street Blues (Parts 1 & 2)** (*Brunswick 05303*)
Les Baxter & His Orch. - **I Love Paris** (*Capitol CL-14166*)
Big Ben Banjo Band - **Let's Get Together No. 2 [M]** (*Columbia DB-3554*)
Tony Brent - **With Your Love** (*Columbia DB-3675*)

Norman Brooks - **A Sky-Blue Shirt And A Rainbow Tie** *(London L-1228)*
Ray Burns - **Blue Star** *(Columbia DB-3670)*
Max Bygraves - **Mister Sandman / Do You Love Old Santa Claus** *(H.M.V. B-10821)*
Max Bygraves - **Tomorrow** *(H.M.V. B-10842)*
Freddy Cannon - **Tallahassee Lassie** *(Top Rank JAR-135)*
Clyde Valley Stompers - **Pearly Gates / Old Time Religion** *(Beltona BL-2650)*
Coasters - **Along Came Jones** *(London HLE-8882)*
Nat 'King' Cole - **There Goes My Heart / I Am In Love** *(Capitol CL-14172)*
Bob Cooper Sextet - **KENTON PRESENTS JAZZ – BOB COOPER** *(Capitol KPL-102)* **LP**
Cowboy Copas - **Alabam** *(Melodisc 45/1566)*
Johnny Desmond - **The Yellow Rose Of Texas** *(Vogue Coral Q-72099)*
Robert Earl - **Three Galleons** *(Philips PB-481)*
Duke Ellington - **ELLINGTON '55** *(Capitol LCT-6008)* **LP**
Preston Epps - **Bongo Rock** *(Top Rank JAR-140)*
Don Fox - **Be My Girl** *(Decca F-10927)*
Ernie Freeman - **Raunchy** *(London HLP-8523)*
Jane Froman - **I Wonder** *(Capitol CL-14254)*
Judy Garland - **It's A New World / Gotta Have Me Go With You** *(Philips PB-394)*
Benny Goodman - **CARNEGIE HALL JAZZ CONCERT** *(Philips BBL-7001)* **LP**
Paul Hanford - **Itsy Bitsy Teenie Weenie Yellow Polka Dot Bikini** *(Parlophone R-4680)*
Ferlin Husky - **The Drunken Driver** *(Capitol CL-14883)*
Joni James - **How Important Can It Be?** *(M.G.M. MGM-811)*
Eartha Kitt - **Santa Baby / Let's Do It** *(H.M.V. B-10728)*
Eartha Kitt - **African Lullaby / Monotonous** *(H.M.V. B-10803)*
Peggy Lee - **He's A Tramp** *(Brunswick 05482)*
Ray Martin & His Concert Orch. - **The Gentle Sex / It's A Woman's World**
    (Columbia DB-3557)
Glen Mason - **Hot Diggity** *(Parlophone R-4176)*
Charlie McNair Skiffle Group - **Hiawatha Rag / Meadow Lane Stomp** *(Beltona BL-2670)*
Suzi Miller and the Johnston Brothers - **Happy Days And Lonely Nights** *(Decca F-10389)*
Patti Page - **Cross Over The Bridge / My Restless Lover** *(Mercury MB-3103)*
Norrie Paramor & His Orch. - **Autumn Concerto** *(Columbia DB-3815)*
Frank Sinatra - **Johnny Concho Theme (Wait For Me) / Hey, Jealous Lover**
    (Capitol CL-14607)
Tommy Steele - **You Were Mine** *(Decca F-11162)*
Frankie Vaughan - **Cinnamon Sinner / My Son, My Son** *(H.M.V. B-10766)*
Sarah Vaughan - **Shulie A Bop** *(Mercury MB-3129)*
Billy Vaughn & His Orch. - **Morgen** *(London HLD-8952)*
Hugo Winterhalter's Orchestra & Chorus - **Song Of The Barefoot Contessa**
    (H.M.V. B-10791)
Victor Young & His Singing Strings - **The High And The Mighty** *(Brunswick 05320)*
7   Aquatones - **You** *(London HLO-8631)*
Les Baxter & His Orch. - **Poor John** *(Capitol CL-14533)*
Boyd Bennett & His Rockets - **Seventeen** *(Parlophone R-4063)*
Big Ben Banjo Band - **Alabama Jubilee** *(Columbia DB-3641)*
Earl Bostic & His Orch. - **Flamingo** *(Vogue V-2145)*
Nappy Brown - **Don't Be Angry** *(London HL-8145)*
Max Bygraves - **Seventeen Tons / Try Another Cherry Tree** *(H.M.V. POP-208)*
Eddie Calvert - **My Son, My Son** *(Columbia DB-3507)*
Frank Chacksfield & His Orch. - **Smile** *(Decca F-10354)*
Rosemary Clooney - **Go On By** *(Philips PB-499)*
Nat 'King' Cole - **Hold My Hand / If I Give My Heart To You** *(Capitol CL-14203)*
Nat 'King' Cole - **Looking Back** *(Capitol CL-14882)*
Jerry Colonna - **Ebb Tide / The Velvet Glove** *(Brunswick 05243)*
Perry Como - **Ko Ko Mo / You'll Always Be My Lifetime Sweetheart** *(H.M.V. B-10841)*
Crew-Cuts - **Two Hearts, Two Kisses / Unchained Melody** *(Mercury MB-3222)*
Doris Day - **Jimmy Unknown** *(Philips PB-542)*
Doris Day - **Two Hearts, Two Kisses** *(Philips PB-451)*
De Castro Sisters - **Teach Me Tonight** *(London HL-8104)*
Deep River Boys - **Rock Around The Clock** *(H.M.V. POP-113)*
Craig Douglas - **Where's The Girl / My Hour Of Love** *(Top Rank JAR-515)*
Tommy Edwards - **My Melancholy Baby** *(M.G.M. MGM-1020)*

Ella Fitzgerald - **Ev'ry Time We Say Goodbye / Manhattan** *(H.M.V. POP-373)*
Four Aces - **The Gang That Sang Heart Of My Heart** *(Brunswick 05256)*
Four Aces - **There Goes My Heart / Take Me In Your Arms** *(Brunswick 05401)*
Four Lads - **No, Not Much** *(Philips PB-571)*
Bill Haley & His Comets - **Sundown Boogie / Green Tree Boogie** *(London HL-8142)*
Wynonie Harris - **Bloodshot Eyes** *(Vogue V-2127)*
Buddy Holly - **Midnight Shift** *(Brunswick 05800)*
Danny Kaye - **Knock On Wood** *(Brunswick 05296)*
Barney Kessel - **BARNEY KESSEL** *(Vogue LDE-085)* **LP**
David Kinnaird - **Northern Lights Of Old Aberdeen** *(Pye 7N.15317)*
Mario Lanza - **Serenade / Drinking Song** *(H.M.V. DA-2065)*
Steve Lawrence - **Party Doll** *(Vogue Coral Q-72243)*
Tom Lehrer - **SONGS BY TOM LEHRER** *(Decca LF-1311)* **LP**
Frankie Lymon & The Teenagers - **Baby Baby / I'm Not A Juvenile Delinquent**
    (Columbia DB-3878)
Vera Lynn - **My Friend / There Must Be A Reason** *(Decca F-10339)*
Vera Lynn - **Walk Hand In Hand** *(Decca F-10737)*
Humphrey Lyttelton & His Band - **HUMPH AT THE CONWAY** *(Parlophone PMC-1012)* **LP**
Dean Martin - **Watching The World Go By** *(Capitol CL-14586)*
Guy Mitchell - **Too Late / Let Us Be Sweethearts Over Again** *(Philips PB-487)*
Jane Morgan - **If Only I Could Live My Life Again** *(London HLR-8810)*
Ricky Nelson - **Lonesome Town** *(London HLP-8738)*
Johnnie Ray - **Flip, Flop And Fly** *(Philips PB-449)*
Joan Regan - **Prize Of Gold / When You're In Love** *(Decca F-10432)*
Harry Secombe - **We'll Keep A Welcome** *(Philips PB-599)*
Jimmy Shand & His Band - **An Irish Waltz [M] / Teviot Brig [M]** *(Parlophone F-3486)*
Frank Sinatra - **How Little We Know / Five Hundred Guys** *(Capitol CL-14584)*
Frank Sinatra - **SONGS FOR YOUNG LOVERS** *(Capitol LC-6654)* **LP**
Julian Slade - **Music from 'Salad Days' [M]** *(Parlophone R-3927)*
Stargazers - **Somebody / No More** *(Decca F-10437)*
Kay Starr - **If Anyone Finds This, I Love You** *(H.M.V. B-10837)*
Will Starr - **Savoy Scottish Medley** *(Parlophone R-4077)*
Tommy Steele - **It's All Happening / What Do You Do** *(Decca F-11026)*
Wally Stott Orchestra - **The Cat From Coos Bay** *(Philips PB-351)*
Sidney Torch & His Orch. - **The Dam Busters** *(Parlophone R-4024)*
Caterina Valente - **Malagueña** *(Polydor BM-6006)*
Frankie Vaughan - **The Heart Of A Man** *(Philips PB-930)*
David Whitfield - **Smile** *(Decca F-10355)*
Slim Whitman - **China Doll / Indian Love Call** *(London L-1149)*
Slim Whitman - **Gone** *(London HLP-8420)*
Slim Whitman - **Song Of The Wild** *(London HLU-8196)*
6 Richard Allen - **Doctor In Love** *(Parlophone R-4673)*
Paul Anka - **Crazy Love / Let The Bells Keep Ringing** *(Columbia DB-4110)*
Chris Barber / Lonnie Donegan - **NEW ORLEANS JOYS** *(Decca LF-1198)* **LP**
Chris Barber's Jazz Band - **White Christmas / On A Christmas Day** *(Columbia DC-672)*
Pat Boone - **A Fool's Hall Of Fame** *(London HLD-8974)*
Tony Brent - **When I Leave The World Behind** *(Columbia DB-3428)*
Teresa Brewer - **Nora Malone / When I Leave The World Behind** *(Vogue Coral Q-72224)*
Petula Clark - **Memories Are Made Of This / Band Of Gold** *(Pye Nixa N.15040)*
Alma Cogan - **Little Things Mean A Lot** *(H.M.V. B-10717)*
Alma Cogan - **Make Love To Me** *(H.M.V. B-10677)*
Alma Cogan - **Softly, Softly / Paper Kisses** *(H.M.V. B-10828)*
Alma Cogan - **Tweedle-Dee** *(H.M.V. B-10848)*
Perry Como - **Round And Round / My House Is Your House** *(H.M.V. POP-328)*
Perry Como - **Tina Marie** *(H.M.V. POP-103)*
Edric Connor - **Manchester United Calypso** *(Oriole CB-1362)*
Crew-Cuts - **Sh-Boom** *(Mercury MB-3140)*
Bing Crosby, Danny Kaye, Peggy Lee and Trudy Stevens - **White Christmas**
    (Brunswick 05354)
Xavier Cugat & His Orch. - **Cherry Pink And Apple Blossom White** *(Philips PB-413)*
Sammy Davis Jr. - **In A Persian Market / Man With The Golden Arm** *(Brunswick 05518)*
Doris Day - **Ooh Bang Jiggilly Jang / Ol' Saint Nicholas** *(Philips PB-532)*

Doris Day - **Ready, Willing And Able / You My Love** *(Philips PB-402)*
Ken Dodd - **Dream That I Love You** *(Decca F-11293)*
Fats Domino - **Blue Monday** *(London HLP-8377)*
Lonnie Donegan - **Diggin' My Potatoes / Bury My Body** *(Decca Jazz FJ-10695)*
Robert Earl - **My Son, My Son** *(Philips PB-331)*
Duke Ellington - **MASTERPIECES** *(Columbia 33SX-1022)* 🆔LP
Emmettones - **Father Murphy** *(Beltona BL-2723)*
Eddie Fisher - **Count Your Blessings Instead Of Sheep / White Christmas**
    (H.M.V. B-10779)
Eddie Fisher - **I Need You Now / Heaven Was Never Like This** *(H.M.V. B-10755)*
Ella Fitzgerald - **Lullaby Of Birdland** *(Brunswick 05392)*
Ella Fitzgerald - **St. Louis Blues / Beale Street Blues** *(H.M.V. POP-499)*
Four Aces - **A Woman In Love** *(Brunswick 05589)*
Four Lads - **Gilly Gilly Ossenfeffer Katzenellen Bogen By The Sea** *(Philips PB-304)*
Franchito & His Orch. - **Eso Es El Amor** *(Oriole CB-1467)*
Connie Francis - **If I Didn't Care** *(M.G.M. MGM-1012)*
Bobby Freeman - **Do You Want To Dance** *(London HLJ-8644)*
Georgia Gibbs - **I Love Paris** *(Mercury MB-3152)*
Jim Gunner & The Echoes - **Hoolee Jump** *(Decca F-11276)*
Bill Haley & His Comets - **Billy Goat** *(Brunswick 05688)*
Bill Haley & His Comets - **Ten Little Indians** *(London HLF-8194)*
Ted Heath & His Music - **Cinnamon Sinner / They Were Doin' The Mambo**
    (Decca F-10374)
Al Hibbler - **He** *(Brunswick 05492)*
Hilltoppers - **Trying / D-A-R-L-I-N'** *(London HLD-8298)*
Ronnie Hilton - **On The Street Where You Live** *(H.M.V. POP-479)*
Les Howard - **Blue Star / Three Galleons** *(H.M.V. B-10928)*
Hunters - **Teen Scene** *(Fontana H-276)*
Johnston Brothers - **Chee Chee-oo Chee** *(Decca F-10513)*
Johnston Brothers - **Join In And Sing [M]** *(Decca F-10414)*
Kathie Kay - **A House With Love In It** *(H.M.V. POP-265)*
Kathie Kay - **Tammy** *(H.M.V. POP-385)*
Stan Kenton & His Orch. -
    NEW CONCEPTS OF ARTISTRY IN RHYTHM *(Capitol LC-6595)* 🆔LP
Keynotes - **Scotland The Brave** *(Decca F-10693)*
Nicky Kidd - **Too Young To Go Steady / Wild Cherry** *(Beltona BL-2645)*
David Kinnaird - **Auld Lang Syne** *(Pye 7N.15311)*
David Kinnaird - **Buttered Bannocks** *(Top Rank JAR-414)*
Mario Lanza - **I'll Walk With God** *(H.M.V. DA-2062)*
Peggy Lee - **Let Me Go, Lover** *(Brunswick 05360)*
Arthur Lyman Group - **Taboo** *(Vogue Pop V-9153)*
Vera Lynn - **Doonaree** *(Decca F-10535)*
Vera Lynn - **With Your Love / Unfaithful You** *(Decca F-10622)*
Humphrey Lyttelton & His Band - **Ace In The Hole / Coffee Grinder** *(Parlophone R-3967)*
David MacBeth - **Pigtails In Paris** *(Pye 7N.15291)*
Josh MacRae - **Talking Army Blues / Talking Guitar Blues** *(Top Rank JAR-290)*
Dean Martin - **How Do You Speak To An Angel?** / Dean Martin & Jerry Lewis -
    Ev'ry Street's A Boulevard In Old New York *(Capitol CL-14150)*
Monotones - **Book Of Love** *(London HLM-8625)*
Gerry Mulligan Quartet - **Swing House / I May Be Wrong** *(Vogue V-2258)*
Ricky Nelson - **Be-Bop Baby** *(London HLP-8499)*
Gene Norman's 'Just Jazz' - **GENE NORMAN PRESENTS 'JUST JAZZ'**
    (Vogue EPV-1002) 🆔EP
OST - **SEVEN BRIDES FOR SEVEN BROTHERS (PART 1)** *(M.G.M. MGM-EP-513)* 🆔EP
Norrie Paramor & His Orch. - **The High And The Mighty** *(Columbia DB-3515)*
Bud Powell Trio - **Indiana** *(Vogue V-2240)*
Elvis Presley - **KING CREOLE (VOL. 1) [OST]** *(R.C.A. RCX-117)* 🆔EP
Nelson Riddle & His Orch. - **In Old Lisbon / Robin Hood** *(Capitol CL-14510)*
Jimmie Rodgers - **Honey Comb** *(Columbia DB-3986)*
Marion Ryan - **Ding Dong Rock-A-Billy Wedding / That's Happiness** *(Pye Nixa N.15105)*
Tommy Sands - **Let Me Be Loved** *(Capitol CL-14781)*
George Shearing Quintet - **Spring Is Here** *(M.G.M. MGM-741)*

Frank Sinatra - **Learnin' The Blues** *(Capitol CL-14296)*
Frank Sinatra - **You My Love / Just One Of Those Things** *(Capitol CL-14240)*
Hank Snow - **Old Shep** *(R.C.A. RCA-1151)*
Southlanders - **Torero** *(Decca F-11032)*
Jo Stafford - **Young And Foolish** *(Philips PB-538)*
Tommy Steele & The Steelmen - **Shiralee** *(Decca F-10896)*
Gale Storm - **Why Do Fools Fall In Love** *(London HLD-8286)*
Carlos Thompson - **No One But You** *(M.G.M. MGM-759)*
Sarah Vaughan - **Make Yourself Comfortable** *(Mercury MB-3180)*
Frank Weir & His Saxophone - **The Never-Never Land / The Little Shoemaker**
    (Decca F-10324)
David Whitfield - **The Lady** *(Decca F-10562)*
Slim Whitman - **Danny Boy** *(London L-1214)*
Slim Whitman - **Rose Marie** *(London HL-8061)*
Robert Wilson with Jimmy Shand & His Band - **The Northern Lights Of Aberdeen**
    (H.M.V. B-10521)
5   Louis Armstrong - **Theme from 'The Threepenny Opera'** *(Philips PB-574)*
Eddy Arnold - **Before This Day Ends / Just Out Of Reach** *(R.C.A. RCA-1212)*
Winifred Atwell - **The Charleston / Dill Pickles** *(Philips PB-266)*
U.S. Bonds - **New Orleans** *(Top Rank JAR-527)*
Issy Bonn - **Mom-e-le / My Friend** *(Columbia DB-3504)*
Eve Boswell - **Cookie / It's Almost Tomorrow** *(Parlophone R-4143)*
Tony Brent - **How Important Can It Be?** *(Columbia DB-3610)*
Tony Brent - **The Magic Tango** *(Columbia DB-3514)*
Boots Brown & His Blockbusters [Shorty Rogers] - **Cerveza** *(R.C.A. RCA-1078)*
Johnny Burnette - **Dreamin'** *(London HLG-9172)*
Ray Burns with the Coronets - **That's How A Love Song Was Born** *(Columbia DB-3640)*
Max Bygraves - **The Pendulum Song** *(H.M.V. B-10876)*
Jeff Chandler - **I Should Care** *(Brunswick 05264)*
Chubby Checker - **The Hucklebuck / Whole Lotta Shakin' Goin' On** *(Columbia DB-4541)*
Petula Clark - **Smile / Somebody** *(Polygon P-1128)*
Eddie Cochran - **20 Flight Rock** *(London HLU-8386)*
Eddie Cochran - **C'mon Everybody** *(London HLU-8792)*
Nat 'King' Cole - **You Are My First Love** *(Capitol CL-14688)*
Ken Colyer's Jazzmen - **BACK TO THE DELTA** *(Decca LF-1196)* **LP**
Perry Como - **Papa Loves Mambo** *(H.M.V. B-10776)*
Don Cornell - **No Man Is An Island** *(Vogue Coral Q-72058)*
Coronets - **Lizzie Borden** *(Columbia DB-3728)*
Coronets - **Twenty Tiny Fingers / Meet Me On The Corner** *(Columbia DB-3671)*
Bing Crosby - **Count Your Blessings Instead Of Sheep** *(Brunswick 05339)*
Sammy Davis Jr. - **Something's Gotta Give / Love Me Or Leave Me** *(Brunswick 05428)*
Doris Day - **A Very Precious Love / Teacher's Pet** *(Philips PB-799)*
Doris Day - **Let It Ring** *(Philips PB-560)*
Eric Delaney & His Band - **Truckin'** *(Mercury MB-3168)*
Jimmy Deuchar Quartet / Victor Feldman -
    THE JIMMY DEUCHAR QUARTET WITH VICTOR FELDMAN *(Esquire EP-53)* **EP**
Diamonds - **The Stroll** *(Mercury 7MT-195)*
Diamonds - **Walking Along** *(Mercury AMT-1004)*
Fats Domino - **I Want To Walk You Home / I'm Gonna Be A Wheel Some Day**
    (London HLP-8942)
Fats Domino - **Whole Lotta Loving** *(London HLP-8759)*
Billy Eckstine - **What More Is There To Say** *(M.G.M. MGM-809)*
Johnny Ferguson - **Angela Jones** *(M.G.M. MGM-1059)*
Fleetwoods - **Mr. Blue** *(Top Rank JAR-202)*
Eddie Fontaine - **Nothin' Shakin'** *(London HLM-8711)*
Fontane Sisters - **The Banana Boat Song** *(London HLD-8378)*
Fontane Sisters - **Hearts Of Stone** *(London HL-8113)*
Four Aces - **Mister Sandman** *(Brunswick 05355)*
Patrick Galvin with Al Jeffery - **IRISH SONGS OF RESISTANCE (PART II)**
    (Topic T-4) **8" Mini-LP**
Don Gibson - **Oh, Lonesome Me** *(R.C.A. RCA-1056)*
Goons - **My September Love** *(Parlophone R-4251)*

Gogi Grant - **Suddenly There's A Valley** *(London HLB-8192)*
Bill Haley & His Comets - **Forty Cups Of Coffee** *(Brunswick 05658)*
Fred Hanna Band - **Irish Waltz Medley No. 1 [M] / Irish Marches No. 1 [M]** *(Beltona BE-2638)*
Joe 'Mr. Piano' Henderson - **Sing It Again With Joe [M]** *(Polygon P-1184)*
Leroy Holmes & His Orch. - **The High And The Mighty** *(M.G.M. MGM-765)*
Ferlin Husky - **Wings Of A Dove** *(Capitol CL-15160)*
Bert Kaempfert & His Orch. - **Wonderland By Night** *(Polydor NH-66639)*
Eartha Kitt - **Under The Bridges Of Paris** *(H.M.V. B-10647)*
Frankie Laine - **Moby Dick** *(Philips PB-587)*
Frankie Laine - **Ticky Ticky Tick / Champion The Wonder Horse** *(Philips PB-607)*
Mario Lanza - **Earthbound** *(H.M.V. DA-2086)*
Henry Leca & His Orch. - **The Bandit** *(Philips PB-297)*
Jerry Lordan - **I'll Stay Single** *(Parlophone R-4588)*
Vera Lynn - **Party Sing-Song [M]** *(Decca F-10411)*
Shelly Manne & His Men - **SHELLY MANNE & HIS MEN** *(Vogue LDE-072)* LP
Mantovani & His Orch. - **Lonely Ballerina / Lazy Gondolier** *(Decca F-10395)*
Dean Martin - **Innamorata** *(Capitol CL-14507)*
Johnny Mathis - **Starbright / All Is Well** *(Fontana H-254)*
Chuck Miller - **The Auctioneer** *(Mercury AMT-1026)* [1959 reissue]
Guy Mitchell - **Heartaches By The Number** *(Philips PB-964)*
Merrill Moore - **The House Of Blue Lights / Bell Bottom Boogie** *(Capitol CL-14057)*
Merrill Moore - **Five Foot Two, Eyes Of Blue** *(Capitol CL-14369)*
Gerry Mulligan Quartet - **Jeru / Love Me Or Leave Me** *(Vogue V-2259)*
Ruby Murray - **Evermore** *(Columbia DB-3617)*
Ruby Murray, Ray Burns, Diana Decker and Ronnie Harris - **Spring, Spring, Spring** / Ronnie Harris, Diana Decker, Ray Burns and Ruby Murray - **Goin' Co'tin'** *(Columbia DB-3567)*
Ricky Nelson - **Believe What You Say / My Bucket's Got A Hole In It** *(London HLP-8594)*
Patti Page - **Changing Partners** *(Mercury MB-3089)*
Ray Peterson - **Tell Laura I Love Her** *(R.C.A. RCA-1195)*
Phil Phillips with the Twilights - **Sea Of Love** *(Mercury AMT-1059)*
Jane Powell and Howard Keel - **When You're In Love** / Brothers & Girls - **Spring, Spring, Spring** *(M.G.M. MGM-788)*
Elvis Presley - **LOVE ME TENDER** *(H.M.V. 7EG-8199)* EP
Johnnie Ray - **I'll Never Fall In Love Again / You're All That I Live For** *(Philips PB-952)*
Jimmie Rodgers - **Secretly / Make Me A Miracle** *(Columbia DB-4130)*
Shorty Rogers & His Orch. - **THE WILD ONE [OST]** *(H.M.V. 7EG-8044)* EP
Bobby Rydell - **Kissin' Time** *(Top Rank JAR-181)*
Jack Scott - **What In The World's Come Over You** *(Top Rank JAR-280)*
Frank Sinatra - **It's Nice To Go Trav'ling / Brazil** *(Capitol CL-15116)*
Frank Sinatra - **SWING EASY!** *(Capitol LC-6689)* LP
Frank Sinatra and Keely Smith - **How Are Ya' Fixed For Love? / Nothing In Common** *(Capitol CL-14863)*
Skip & Flip - **Cherry Pie** *(Top Rank JAR-358)*
Cyril Stapleton & His Orch. - **Lester Leaps In** *(Decca F-10313)*
Robb Storme - **One Thousand Nine Hundred And When** *(Decca F-11282)*
Swedish-American All Stars - **THE SWEDISH-AMERICAN ALL STARS** *(Esquire EP-5)* EP
Sammy Turner - **Lavender Blue** *(London HLX-8918)*
Frankie Vaughan - **Cold, Cold Shower** *(Philips PB-681)*
Frankie Vaughan - **Too Many Heartaches / Unsuspecting Heart** *(H.M.V. B-10845)*
Jerry Wallace - **You're Singing Our Love Song To Somebody Else** *(London HLH-9110)*
Slim Whitman - **A Very Precious Love** *(London HLP-8590)*
Slim Whitman - **I'll Never Stop Loving You / I'll Never Take You Back Again** *(London HLU-8167)*
Larry Williams - **Dizzy Miss Lizzy / Slow Down** *(London HLU-8604)*

Non-hit records with most weeks at No.1

11   Enoch Kent - **The Smashing Of The Van / Sean South Of Garryowen** *(Top Rank JAR-386)*
7   Kathie Kay - **Wind In The Willow / We Will Make Love** *(H.M.V. POP-352)*
6   Emmettones - **Bold Robert Emmett** *(Beltona BL-2722)*
5   Big Ben Banjo Band - **Let's Get Together No. 2 [M]** *(Columbia DB-3554)*
    Johnny Cash - **Ballad Of A Teenage Queen** *(London HLS-8586)*
    Kathie Kay - **Be Content / My Last Love** *(H.M.V. POP-410)*
4   Louis Armstrong - **Basin Street Blues (Parts 1 & 2)** *(Brunswick 05303)*
    Bill Haley & His Comets - **ROCK AROUND THE CLOCK** *(Brunswick OE-9250)* **EP**
    Norrie Paramor & His Orchestra - **Autumn Concerto** *(Columbia DB-3815)*
3   Beverley Sisters - **Come Home To My Arms** *(Decca F-10813)*
    Max Bygraves - **That Dear Old Gentleman** *(H.M.V. POP-262)*
    Clyde Valley Stompers - **Milenberg Joys / Bill Bailey, Won't You Please Come Home**
        (Decca Jazz F-10897)
    Fats Domino - **Whole Lotta Loving** *(London HLP-8759)*
    5 DeMarco Sisters - **Dreamboat** *(Brunswick 05425)*
    Four Lads - **No, Not Much** *(Philips PB-571)*
    Kathie Kay - **Tammy** *(H.M.V. POP-385)*
    Guy Mitchell - **Too Late / Let Us Be Sweethearts Over Again** *(Philips PB-487)*
    Elvis Presley - **KING CREOLE (VOL. 1) [OST]** *(R.C.A. RCX-117)* **EP**
2   Brook Brothers - **Say The Word / Everything But Love** *(Pye 7N.15298)*
    Eddie Fisher - **My Friend** *(H.M.V. B-10729)*
    Frankie Ford - **Sea Cruise** *(London HL-8850)*
    Jerry Fuller - **Tennessee Waltz** *(London HLH-8982)*
    Joe 'Mr. Piano' Henderson - **Theme from 'The Threepenny Opera'** *(Pye Nixa N.15044)*
    Ferlin Husky - **The Drunken Driver** *(Capitol CL-14883)*
    David Kinnaird - **Auld Lang Syne** *(Pye 7N.15311)*
    Platters - **On My Word Of Honor / One In A Million** *(Mercury MT-143)*
    Johnnie Ray - **Flip, Flop And Fly** *(Philips PB-449)*
    Nelson Riddle & His Orch. - **In Old Lisbon / Robin Hood** *(Capitol CL-14510)*
    Kay Starr - **Good And Lonesome** *(H.M.V. B-10895)*
    Gale Storm - **Why Do Fools Fall In Love** *(London HLD-8286)*
    Slim Whitman - **Gone** *(London HLP-8420)*
1   Winifred Atwell - **Raunchy** *(Decca F-10987)*
    Winifred Atwell - **Vendetta** *(Philips PB-332)*
    Chris Barber's Jazz Band -
        CHRIS BARBER PLAYS SPIRITUALS *(Columbia SEG-7568)* **EP**
    Shirley Bassey - **Crazy Rhythm / Love For Sale** *(Philips PB-917)*
    Chuck Berry - **Too Pooped To Pop / Let It Rock** *(London HLM-9069)*
    Billy & Lillie - **La Dee Dah** *(London HLU-8564)*
    Owen Bradley Quintet - **Big Guitar** *(Brunswick 05736)*
    Tony Brent - **With Your Love** *(Columbia DB-3675)*
    Boots Brown & His Blockbusters [Shorty Rogers] - **Cerveza** *(R.C.A. RCA-1078)*
    Johnny Cash - **Seasons Of My Heart / Smiling Bill McCall** *(Philips PB-1017)*
    Sanford Clark - **Son-Of-A-Gun** *(London HLW-9026)*
    Clyde Valley Stompers - **Keep Right On To The End Of The Road** *(Beltona BL-2648)*
    Alma Cogan - **Don't Ring-a Da Bell / Bluebell** *(H.M.V. POP-189)*
    Alma Cogan - **Love And Marriage** *(H.M.V. POP-163)*
    Alma Cogan - **Mama Teach Me To Dance** *(H.M.V. POP-239)*
    Nat 'King' Cole - **Angel Smile** *(Capitol CL-14820)*
    Nat 'King' Cole - **Looking Back** *(Capitol CL-14882)*
    Perry Como - **Round And Round / My House Is Your House** *(H.M.V. POP-328)*
    Perry Como - **SO SMOOTH** *(H.M.V. 7EG-8171)* **EP**
    Concert Orchestra, *cond.* Eric Coates - **The Dam Busters March** *(Pye Nixa N.15003)*
    Russ Conway- **'My Fair Lady' Pops [M]** *(Columbia DB-4191)*
    Don Cornell - **No Man Is An Island** *(Vogue Coral Q-72058)*
    Dave 'Baby' Cortez - **The Happy Organ** *(London HLU-8852)*
    Crazy Otto - **Glad Rag Doll / Smiles** *(Polydor BM-6003)*
    Doris Day - **Jimmy Unknown** *(Philips PB-542)*
    Deep River Boys - **Rock Around The Clock** *(H.M.V. POP-113)*
    Bo Diddley - **Road Runner** *(London HLM-9112)*

Lonnie Donegan - **Beneath The Willow / Leave My Woman Alone** *(Pye 7N.15330)*
Lonnie Donegan - **LONNIE DONEGAN HIT PARADE** *(Pye Nixa NEP-24031)* **EP**
Lonnie Donegan - **RELAX WITH LONNIE** *(Pye Nixa NEP-24107)* **EP**
Emmettones - **Father Murphy** *(Beltona BL-2723)*
Emmettones - **Johnson's Motor Car** *(Beltona BL-2724)*
Ella Fitzgerald - **Pete Kelly's Blues / Hard Hearted Hannah** *(Brunswick 05473)*
Arlene Fontana - **I'm In Love** *(Pye International 7N.25010)*
Connie Francis - **My Sailor Boy** *(M.G.M. MGM-932)*
Bobby Freeman - **Do You Want To Dance** *(London HLJ-8644)*
Ernie Freeman - **Raunchy** *(London HLP-8523)*
Bridie Gallagher - **A Mother's Love Is A Blessing** *(Beltona BE-2653)*
Don Gibson - **Oh, Lonesome Me** *(R.C.A. RCA-1056)*
Jody Gibson - **So You Think You've Got Troubles** *(Parlophone R-4645)*
Billy Grammer - **Bonaparte's Retreat** *(Felsted AF-121)*
Bill Haley & His Comets - **Sundown Boogie / Green Tree Boogie** *(London HL-8142)*
Ronnie Hilton - **On The Street Where You Live** *(H.M.V. POP-479)*
Edmund Hockridge - **A Woman In Love** *(Pye Nixa N.15067)*
Edmund Hockridge - **More Than Ever** *(Pye Nixa 7N.15160)*
Dick James - **Sing Song Time No. 1 [M]** *(Parlophone R-4065)*
Kalin Twins - **Forget Me Not** *(Brunswick 05759)*
Danny Kaye and Dena Kaye - **Little Child (Daddy Dear)** *(Brunswick 05532)*
Stan Kenton & His Orch. - **Portrait Of A Count / Invention For Guitar And Trumpet**
    (Capitol CL-14541)
Knightsbridge Strings - **Cry** *(Top Rank JAR-170)*
Mario Lanza - **Valencia** *(H.M.V. DA-2083)*
Steve Lawrence - **Party Doll** *(Vogue Coral Q-72243)*
Lord Rockingham's XI - **Ra-Ra Rockingham** *(Decca F-11139)*
Frankie Lymon & The Teenagers - **I Want You To Be My Girl** *(Columbia DB-3797)*
Vera Lynn - **Walk Hand In Hand** *(Decca F-10737)*
Vera Lynn - **With Your Love / Unfaithful You** *(Decca F-10622)*
Bobby MacLeod & His Band - **Pride Of Erin Waltz [M] / Irish Military Two-Step [M]**
    (Philips Scottish Series YB-9500)
Marino Marini & His Quartet - **The Pansy** *(Durium DC-16629)*
Dean Martin - **The Peddler Man** *(Capitol CL-14170)*
Dean Martin and Line Renaud - **Relax-Ay-Voo** / Two Sleepy People *(Capitol CL-14356)*
Glen Mason - **Hot Diggity** *(Parlophone R-4176)*
Charlie McNair Skiffle Group - **Hiawatha Rag / Meadow Lane Stomp** *(Beltona BL-2670)*
Monograms - **The Greatest Mistake Of My Life** *(Parlophone R-4515)*
Ricky Nelson - **Be-Bop Baby** *(London HLP-8499)*
Ricky Nelson - **Believe What You Say / My Bucket's Got A Hole In It** *(London HLP-8594)*
Ricky Nelson - **Lonesome Town** *(London HLP-8738)*
OLC - **THE MERMAID THEATRE PRESENTS 'LOCK UP YOUR DAUGHTERS'**
    (Decca LK-4320) **LP**
Platters - **THE FABULOUS PLATTERS** *(Mercury MEP-9504)* **EP**
Elvis Presley - **GOOD ROCKIN' TONIGHT** *(H.M.V. 7EG-8256)* **EP**
Elvis Presley - **LOVE ME TENDER** *(H.M.V. 7EG-8199)* **EP**
Johnnie Ray - **Destiny** *(Philips PB-301)*
Marty Robbins - **A White Sport Coat (And A Pink Carnation)** *(Philips PB-696)*
Marty Robbins - **The Story Of My Life** *(Fontana H-102)*
Mel Robbins - **Save It** *(London HLM-8966)*
Rock-A-Teens - **Woo-Hoo** *(Columbia DB-4361)*
Chan Romero - **The Hippy Hippy Shake** *(Columbia DB-4341)*
Peter Sellers - **I'm So Ashamed / A Drop Of The Hard Stuff** *(Parlophone R-4491)*
Jimmy Shand & His Band - **Marching With Jimmy Shand [M]** *(Parlophone R-4151)*
Jimmy Shand & His Band - **Sing In The New Year [M]** *(Parlophone R-4382)*
Valerie Shane - **Meet Me Tonight In Dreamland** *(Philips PB-879)*
Anne Shelton - **Give Her My Love (When You Meet Her) / A Man On The March**
    (Philips PB-661)
Frank Sinatra and Keely Smith - **How Are Ya' Fixed For Love? / Nothing In Common**
    (Capitol CL-14863)
Betty Smith's Skiffle - **There's A Blue Ridge Round My Heart Virginia** *(Tempo A-162)*
Southlanders - **Torero** *(Decca F-11032)*

Teen Beats - **Slop Beat / Califf Boogie** *(Top Rank JAR-342)*
Trio Los Paraguayos - **Bell Bird** *(Philips PB-947)*
Sammy Turner - **Lavender Blue** *(London HLX-8918)*
Danny Valentino - **Stampede** *(M.G.M. MGM-1049)*
Larry Verne - **Mr. Custer** *(London HLN-9194)*
Gene Vincent & His Blue Caps - **Rocky Road Blues** *(Capitol CL-14908)*
Vipers Skiffle Group - **Hey Liley, Liley Lo / Jim Dandy** *(Parlophone R-4286)*
Nancy Whiskey - **I Know Where I'm Goin' / Hillside In Scotland** *(Oriole CB-1452)*
David Whitfield - **I'll Never Stop Loving You / Lady Of Madrid** *(Decca F-10596)*
David Whitfield - **Willingly** *(Decca F-11101)*
Larry Williams - **Dizzy Miss Lizzy / Slow Down** *(London HLU-8604)*

Bubblers with most re-entries

10   Kathie Kay - **Old Scotch Mother** *(H.M.V. POP-167)*
8   Bridie Gallagher - **The Boys From County Armagh / Killarney And You** *(Beltona BE-2679)*
7   Eric Delaney & His Band - **Oranges And Lemons / Delaney's Delight** *(Mercury MB-3143)*
6   Tennessee Ernie Ford - **River Of No Return / Give Me Your Word** *(Capitol CL-14005)*
    Platters - **THE FABULOUS PLATTERS** *(Mercury MEP-9504)* **EP**
    Jimmy Shand - **Victory Waltz [M]** *(Parlophone F-3500)*
5   Bing Crosby and Louis Armstrong - **Now You Has Jazz** *(Capitol CL-14643)*
    Clyde Valley Stompers - **Milenberg Joys / Bill Bailey, Won't You Please Come Home**
       (Decca Jazz F-10897)
    Sammy Davis Jr. - **Because Of You (Parts 1 & 2)** *(Brunswick 05326)*
    Duke Ellington - **ELLINGTON '55** *(Capitol LCT-6008)* **LP**
    Bill Haley & His Comets - **Razzle Dazzle / Two Hound Dogs** *(Brunswick 05453)*
    Howard Keel and Brothers - **Sobbin' Women** *(M.G.M. MGM-787)*
    David Kinnaird - **Mairi's Wedding / Northern Lights Of Aberdeen** *(Top Rank JAR-385)*
    Johnnie Ray - **Destiny** *(Philips PB-301)*
    Jimmy Shand & His Band - **Marching With Jimmy Shand [M]** *(Parlophone R-4151)*
    Hank Snow - **COUNTRY GUITAR (VOL. 4)** *(R.C.A. RCX-116)* **EP**
4   Earl Bostic & His Orch. - **Flamingo** *(Vogue V-2145)*
    Eddie Cochran - **20 Flight Rock** *(London HLU-8386)*
    Nat 'King' Cole - **Papa Loves Mambo / Teach Me Tonight** *(Capitol CL-14207)*
    Billy Cotton & His Band - **Yellow Rose Of Texas** *(Decca F-10602)*
    Doris Day - **The Blue Bells Of Broadway / I Speak To The Stars** *(Philips PB-295)*
    Emmettones - **Bold Robert Emmett** *(Beltona BL-2722)*
    Eddie Fisher - **How Do You Speak To An Angel / My Arms, My Heart, My Love**
       (H.M.V. B-10737)
    Ella Fitzgerald - **Ev'ry Time We Say Goodbye / Manhattan** *(H.M.V. POP-373)*
    Bill Haley & His Comets - **ROCK AROUND THE CLOCK** *(Brunswick OE-9250)* **EP**
    Ferlin Husky - **The Drunken Driver** *(Capitol CL-14883)*
    Eartha Kitt - **Santa Baby / Let's Do It** *(H.M.V. B-10728)*
    George Lewis & His New Orleans Music - **Mama Don't Allow It** *(Good Time Jazz GV-2253)*
    Vera Lynn - **With Your Love / Unfaithful You** *(Decca F-10622)*
    OBC - **THE PAJAMA GAME** *(Philips BBL-7050)* **LP**
    Frank Sinatra - **SONGS FOR YOUNG LOVERS** *(Capitol LC-6654)* **LP**
    David Whitfield - **Smile** *(Decca F-10355)*
    Slim Whitman - **China Doll / Indian Love Call** *(London L-1149)*
    Slim Whitman - **Danny Boy** *(London L-1214)*

The Weekly *Bubbling Under* Charts

OBC = Original Broadway Cast
OLC = Original London Cast
OST = Original Soundtrack

JUNE 1954

19		26
1	Frank Sinatra - **Young-At-Heart** *(Capitol CL-14064)*	
2	Concertgebouw Orchestra of Amsterdam, *cond.* Erich Kleiber - **BEETHOVEN – SYMPHONY NO. 5** *(Decca LXT-2851)* 🆔	2
2	J.J. Johnson, Kai Winding, Benny Green and Willie Dennis - **JAZZ WORKSHOP (VOL. 1)** *(Vogue/Debut LDE-066)* 🆔	19
4	Nat 'King' Cole - **SINGS FOR TWO IN LOVE** *(Capitol LC-6627)* 🆔	
4	Rita Hayworth - **Sadie Thompson's Song** *(Mercury MB-3090)*	19
4	Frank Weir & His Saxophone - **The Never-Never Land** *(Decca F-10324)*	4
7	Kid Ory's Creole Jazz Band - **KID ORY'S CREOLE JAZZ BAND** *(Tempo EXA-5)* 🆔	
8	Gigi Gryce–Clifford Brown Sextet - **Salute To The Bandbox** *(Vogue V-2239)*	
9	Bud Powell Trio - **Indiana** *(Vogue V-2240)*	
10	Louis Armstrong - **Basin Street Blues** *(Brunswick 05303)*	16
10	Eddie Calvert - **Midnight** *(Columbia DB-3444)*	
10	Kitty Kallen - **Little Things Mean A Lot** *(Brunswick 05287)*	1
10	Patti Page - **Cross Over The Bridge** *(Mercury MB-3103)*	11
14	Doris Day - **The Blue Bells Of Broadway / I Speak To The Stars** *(Philips PB-295)*	11
14	Glenn Miller & His Orch. - **THE GLENN MILLER STORY [OST]** *(H.M.V. DLP-1024)* 🆔	
16	OLC - **WEDDING IN PARIS** *(Parlophone PMD-1011)* 🆔	7
16	George Shearing Quintet - **Spring Is Here** *(M.G.M. MGM-741)*	
18	Alma Cogan - **Make Love To Me** *(H.M.V. B-10677)*	
18	Ella Fitzgerald - **ELLA SINGS GERSHWIN** *(Brunswick LA-8648)* 🆔	
20	Clifford Brown / Art Farmer / Swedish All Stars - **CLIFFORD BROWN & ART FARMER WITH THE SWEDISH ALL STARS (VOL. 2)** *(Esquire EP-3)* 🆔	6
21	Nat 'King' Cole - **Sleeping Beauty** *(Capitol CL-14126)*	
21	George Wallington Trio - **NEW SOUNDS FROM EUROPE (VOL. 5: PARIS)** *(Vogue LDE-059)* 🆔	
	Sarah Vaughan - **Shulie A Bop** *(Mercury MB-3129)*	2
	Chet Baker Quartet - **Winter Wonderland** *(Vogue V-2232)*	4
	Shelly Manne & His Men - **SHELLY MANNE & HIS MEN** *(Vogue LDE-072)* 🆔	7
	Art Pepper Quartet - **ART PEPPER QUARTET** *(Vogue LDE-067)* 🆔	9
	Winifred Atwell - **The Story Of Three Loves** *(Philips PB-234)*	9
	Joan Regan - **Jilted** *(Decca F-10311)*	11
	Frank Sinatra - **SONGS FOR YOUNG LOVERS** *(Capitol LC-6654)* 🆔	11
	Peggy Lee - **BLACK COFFEE** *(Brunswick LA-8629)* 🆔 †*See note on next page*	15
	Winifred Atwell - **The Charleston** *(Philips PB-266)*	17
	Wardell Gray and Dexter Gordon - **GENE NORMAN PRESENTS THE CHASE AND THE STEEPLECHASE** *(Brunswick LA-8646)* 🆔	17
	Billy Daniels - **It's A Good Day** *(Mercury MB-3127)*	19

3		10	17	24	31
★	Kitty Kallen - **Little Things Mean A Lot** *(Brunswick 05287)*				
1	Alma Cogan - **Little Things Mean A Lot** *(H.M.V. B-10717)*	3	3	3	3
2	Rita Hayworth - **Sadie Thompson's Song** *(Mercury MB-3090)*	2	2	2	2
3	Gigi Gryce–Clifford Brown Sextet - **Salute To The Bandbox** *(Vogue V-2239)*	8	7	7	7
4	Louis Armstrong - **Basin Street Blues** *(Brunswick 05303)*	1	1	1	1
4	Sarah Vaughan - **Shulie A Bop** *(Mercury MB-3129)*	4	4	4	4
6	Danny Kaye - **Knock On Wood** *(Brunswick 05296)*	20	19	18	18
6	Bud Powell Trio - **Indiana** *(Vogue V-2240)*	6	6	6	6
8	Frank Sinatra - **SONGS FOR YOUNG LOVERS** *(Capitol LC-6654)* **LP**				
9	Clifford Brown / Art Farmer / Swedish All Stars - **CLIFFORD BROWN & ART FARMER WITH THE SWEDISH ALL STARS (VOL. 2)** *(Esquire EP-3)* **EP**				
9	Bing Crosby - **Young At Heart / Oh Baby Mine I Get So Lonely** *(Brunswick 05277)*				
9	Eddie Fisher - **A Girl! A Girl!** *(H.M.V. B-10688)*				
9	Four Aces - **The Gang That Sang Heart Of My Heart** *(Brunswick 05256)*	17	16	15	15
9	Frank Sinatra - **Young-At-Heart** *(Capitol CL-14064)*	★			
14	Max Bygraves and the Tanner Sisters - **Friends And Neighbours** *(H.M.V. B-10703)*	9	8	8	8
15	J.J. Johnson, Kai Winding, Benny Green and Willie Dennis - **JAZZ WORKSHOP (VOL. 1)** *(Vogue/Debut LDE-066)* **LP**				
15	Guy Mitchell - **Bob's Yer Uncle** *(Philips PB-293)*				
17	Winifred Atwell - **The Story Of Three Loves** *(Philips PB-234)*	11	10	★	
17	George Shearing Quintet - **Spring Is Here** *(M.G.M. MGM-741)*	20	19	18	18
17	Frank Weir & His Saxophone - **The Never-Never Land / The Little Shoemaker** *(Decca F-10324)*				
20	Cyril Stapleton & His Orch. - **Lester Leaps In** *(Decca F-10313)*	14	13	12	12
21	Jimmy Deuchar Quartet with Victor Feldman - **THE JIMMY DEUCHAR QUARTET WITH VICTOR FELDMAN** *(Esquire EP-53)* **EP**	17	16	15	15
21	Patti Page - **Cross Over The Bridge / My Restless Lover** *(Mercury MB-3103)*	9	8	8	8
21	Anthony Steel with the Radio Revellers - **West Of Zanzibar** *(Polygon P-1114)*				
	Frankie Laine - **Some Day** *(Philips PB-306)*	4	4	4	4
	Frank Sinatra - **Three Coins In The Fountain** *(Capitol CL-14120)*	6	★		
	Johnnie Ray - **Destiny** *(Philips PB-301)*	11	10	10	10
	Swedish-American All Stars - **THE SWEDISH-AMERICAN ALL STARS** *(Esquire EP-5)* **EP**	11	10	10	10
	Dean Martin - **Sway** *(Capitol CL-14138)*	14	13	12	12
	Patti Page - **Changing Partners** *(Mercury MB-3089)*	14	13	12	12
	Doris Day - **The Blue Bells Of Broadway / I Speak To The Stars** *(Philips PB-295)*	17	16	15	15
	Alma Cogan - **Make Love To Me** *(H.M.V. B-10677)*	22	21	20	20
	Jerry Colonna - **Ebb Tide** *(Brunswick 05243)*	22	21	20	20
	Hélène Cordet - **Ki Ri** *(Planet E-1011)*	22	21	20	20
	Betty Driver - **I Know You're Mine** *(Planet E-1012)*	25	24	23	23

Record Mirror was not published on 17, 24 and 31 July, so for these three weeks the positions of 10 July have been repeated, except for those records which charted.

---

† *Note re Peggy Lee's* **BLACK COFFEE** *LP on previous page:* This 10" LP bubbled under for one week. It eventually charted in October 1961 after being reissued in 12" format, with additional tracks, on Decca's Ace of Hearts budget label.

AUGUST 1954

7		14	21	28
1	Frankie Laine - **My Friend** (Philips PB-316)	★		
2	Eddie Fisher - **My Friend** (H.M.V. B-10729)	10	3	1
2	Johnnie Ray - **Destiny** (Philips PB-301)	1	14	
4	Doris Day - **The Blue Bells Of Broadway / I Speak To The Stars** (Philips PB-295)			
4	Benny Goodman - **CARNEGIE HALL JAZZ CONCERT** (Philips BBL-7001) 🆑	17	34	10
6	Herdmen - **THE HERDMEN BLOW IN PARIS** (Vogue LDE-058) 🆑			
7	Winifred Atwell - **The Charleston** (Philips PB-266)	8		
7	Gerry Mulligan Quartet - **THE GERRY MULLIGAN QUARTET (VOL. 1)** (Vogue EPV-1001) 🇪🇵		7	
9	Gerry Mulligan Quartet - **Swing House** (Vogue V-2258)	2	5	
10	J.J. Johnson, Kai Winding, Benny Green and Willie Dennis - **JAZZ WORKSHOP (VOL. 1)** (Vogue/Debut LDE-066) 🆑			
11	George Lewis & His New Orleans Music - **Mama Don't Allow It** (Good Time Jazz GV-2253)	8	19	16
11	Bob Manning - **The Nearness Of You** (Capitol CL-13958)			
11	Dean Martin - **Sway** (Capitol CL-14138)	26	1	
14	Four Lads - **Gilly Gilly Ossenfeffer Katzenellen Bogen By The Sea** (Philips PB-304)			
14	Peggy Lee - **Johnny Guitar** (Brunswick 05286)	17	31	
14	Sarah Vaughan - **Shulie A Bop** (Mercury MB-3129)	26		
14	Tommy Whittle with the Tony Kinsey Trio - **'Deed I Do** (Esquire 10-368)			
18	Tony Brent - **Sway / Three Coins In The Fountain** (Columbia DB-3496)	3	2	13
18	Max Bygraves and the Tanner Sisters - **Friends And Neighbours** (H.M.V. B-10703)		24	30
18	Erroll Garner - **ERROLL GARNER** (Columbia SEG-7510) 🇪🇵			
18	Rita Hayworth - **Sadie Thompson's Song** (Mercury MB-3090)	21		30
18	Patti Page - **Changing Partners** (Mercury MB-3089)			
23	Eddie Calvert - **Midnight** (Columbia DB-3444)			
23	Alma Cogan - **Make Love To Me** (H.M.V. B-10677)			
23	Eartha Kitt - **Let's Do It** (H.M.V. B-10728)	17		
23	Billy Taylor & His Rhythm - **PIANO PANORAMA** (Felsted L-87001) 🆑			
27	Earl Bostic & His Orch. - **Jungle Drums** (Parlophone R-3881)			
27	Doris Day - **Kiss Me Again, Stranger** (Philips PB-264)			
27	Doris Day - **The Black Hills Of Dakota** (Philips PB-287)	10	34	★
27	Frankie Laine - **Some Day** (Philips PB-306)		19	30
27	Johnnie Ray - **AT THE LONDON PALLADIUM** (Philips BBR-8001) 🆑		24	18
27	Frank Weir & His Saxophone - **The Never-Never Land** (Decca F-10324)		8	
	Gigi Gryce–Clifford Brown Sextet - **Salute To The Bandbox** (Vogue V-2239)	4	8	5
	Vera Lynn - **My Friend** (Decca F-10339)	4		
	Duke Ellington - **Isle Of Capri** (Capitol CL-14132)	6	14	13
	Stan Kenton & His Orch. - **NEW CONCEPTS OF ARTISTRY IN RHYTHM** (Capitol LC-6595) 🆑	7	10	6
	Max Bygraves - **Gilly Gilly Ossenfeffer Katzenellen Bogen By The Sea** (H.M.V. B-10734)	10	10	4
	Jeff Chandler - **I Should Care** (Brunswick 05264)	10		16
	Billy Daniels - **Smile** (Mercury MB-3142)	10	14	6
	Frank Sinatra - **SONGS FOR YOUNG LOVERS** (Capitol LC-6654) 🆑	10	13	10
	Swedish-American All Stars - **THE SWEDISH-AMERICAN ALL STARS** (Esquire EP-5) 🇪🇵	16		
	Joan Regan with the Johnston Brothers - **Wait For Me Darling** (Decca F-10362)	17	19	10
	Louis Armstrong - **Basin Street Blues** (Brunswick 05303)	21		
	Al Jolson - **April Showers** (Columbia DB-2613)	21		
	Danny Kaye - **Knock On Wood** (Brunswick 05296)	21		30
	Dean Martin - **Hey Brother Pour The Wine** (Capitol CL-14123)	21		
	Bing Crosby and Donald O'Connor - **Back In The Old Routine** (Brunswick 05304)	26		
	Diana Decker - **Kitty In The Basket / Never Never Land** (Columbia DB-3489)	26		
	Tony Kinsey Trio with Joe Harriott - **Last Resort** (Esquire 10-382)	26		
	Crew-Cuts - **Sh-Boom** (Mercury MB-3140)		3	3

4		11	18	25
1	Nat 'King' Cole - **Smile / Make Her Mine** (Capitol CL-14149)	★		
2	Winifred Atwell - **Dixieland** (Philips PB-300)	2		
3	Ronnie Harris - **The Story Of Tina** (Columbia DB-3499)	8	6	★
4	Eddie Fisher - **My Friend** (H.M.V. B-10729)	7	12	2
5	David Whitfield - **Smile** (Decca F-10355)	37		
6	Gerry Mulligan Quartet - **THE GERRY MULLIGAN QUARTET (VOL. 4)** (Vogue LDE-083) 🅛🅟	14		
7	Crew-Cuts - **Sh-Boom** (Mercury MB-3140)	5	20	19
7	Gerry Mulligan Quartet - **GENE NORMAN PRESENTS THE GERRY MULLIGAN QUARTET** (Vogue LDE-075) 🅛🅟	11		
7	Coro Mixto - **Mulher Rendeira** / Zé do Norte - **Lua Bonita** (H.M.V. JO-377)	29	20	
10	Jeff Chandler - **I Should Care** (Brunswick 05264)	17		30
10	Alma Cogan - **The Little Shoemaker** (H.M.V. B-10698)			
10	Milt Jackson Modern Jazz Quartet - **MILT JACKSON MODERN JAZZ QUARTET** (Esquire EP-14) 🅔🅟	10		11
10	Henry Leca & His Orch. - **The Bandit** (Philips PB-297)	11		
14	Dean Martin - **Sway** (Capitol CL-14138)	4	4	6
14	Gene Norman's 'Just Jazz' - **One O'Clock Jump** (Vogue V-2271)	8		
16	Gene Norman's 'Just Jazz' - **Three O'Clock Jump** (Vogue V-2272)			
17	Four Lads - **Gilly Gilly Ossenfeffer Katzenellen Bogen By The Sea** (Philips PB-304)	23	29	25
17	Johnston Brothers - **The Bandit** (Decca F-10302)	17	29	7
19	Frankie Laine - **There Must Be A Reason / Some Day** (Philips PB-306)	1	20	19
19	Gerry Mulligan Quartet - **Jeru / Love Me Or Leave Me** (Vogue V-2259)	6		9
21	Max Bygraves - **Gilly Gilly Ossenfeffer Katzenellen Bogen By The Sea** (H.M.V. B-10734)	★		
21	Shelly Manne & His Men - **SHELLY MANNE & HIS MEN** (Vogue LDE-072) 🅛🅟	17		
21	Dean Martin - **How Do You Speak To An Angel?** (Capitol CL-14150)	29		33
24	Tony Brent - **Sway / Three Coins In The Fountain** (Columbia DB-3496)	3	3	7
24	Benny Goodman - **CARNEGIE HALL JAZZ CONCERT** (Philips BBL-7001) 🅛🅟			
24	Anthony Steel with the Radio Revellers - **West Of Zanzibar** (Polygon P-1114)	★		
27	Stan Kenton & His Orch. - **NEW CONCEPTS OF ARTISTRY IN RHYTHM** (Capitol LC-6595) 🅛🅟	23		
27	Johnnie Ray - **Destiny** (Philips PB-301)			15
27	Billy Shepard - **The Bandit** (Columbia DB-3460)	37	15	
30	Winifred Atwell - **The Charleston / Dill Pickles** (Philips PB-266)	37		
30	Tony Kinsey Trio with Joe Harriott - **Best Behaviour** (Esquire 10-392)			
30	Joan Regan with the Johnston Brothers - **Wait For Me Darling** (Decca F-10362)	23	29	19
	Billy Daniels - **Smile / Mom-e-le** (Mercury MB-3142)	11	4	15
	Duke Ellington - **SKIN DEEP** (H.M.V. 7EG-8033) 🅔🅟	15		
	Earl Bostic & His Orch. - **Flamingo** (Vogue V-2145)	16		
	Tony Brent - **The Magic Tango** (Columbia DB-3514)	20	9	13
	Dave Brubeck Trio - **Singing In The Rain / Perfidia** (Vogue V-2264)	20		33
	Frank Chacksfield & His Orch. - **Smile** (Decca F-10354)	20	15	12
	Johnston Brothers - **Crazy 'bout Ya Baby** (Decca F-10364)	23		
	Eartha Kitt - **Santa Baby** (H.M.V. B-10728)	23		
	Merrill Moore - **Bell Bottom Boogie** (Capitol CL-14057)	23		
	George Elrick and the Lumberjacks - **Gilly Gilly Ossenfeffer Katzenellenbogen By The Sea** (Decca F-10371)	29		39
	Tennessee Ernie Ford - **River Of No Return** (Capitol CL-14005)	29		39
	James Moody Sextet - **Lester Leaps In** (Esquire 10-386)	29		
	Earl Bostic & His Orch. - **Blue Skies / Mambolino** (Parlophone R-3892)	34		30
	Ingrid Haebler - **MOZART – CONCERTO FOR PIANO AND ORCHESTRA NO. 15 / NO. 18** (Vox PL-8300) 🅛🅟	34		
	George Lewis & His New Orleans Music - **Mama Don't Allow It** (Good Time Jazz GV-2253)	34		
	Art Tatum - **ART TATUM FROM GENE NORMAN'S 'JUST JAZZ'** (Vogue LDE-081) 🅛🅟	37		

	11	18	25
Frank Weir & His Saxophone - **The Happy Wanderer** (Decca F-10271)	37		
Al Martino - **The Story Of Tina** (Capitol CL-14163)		1	1
Kay Starr - **Am I A Toy Or A Treasure / Fortune In Dreams** (Capitol CL-14151)		2	3
Slim Whitman - **China Doll** (London L-1149)		7	15
Jimmy Young - **Little Things Mean A Lot** (Decca F-10317)		7	
Father Sydney MacEwan - **Scotland The Brave** (Columbia DB-3120)		9	
Joan Regan - **If I Give My Heart To You** (Decca F-10373)		9	5
Les Baxter & His Orch. - **The High And The Mighty** (Capitol CL-14147)		12	25
Lee Lawrence - **The Story Of Tina** (Decca F-10367)		12	
Doris Day - **The Blue Bells Of Broadway / I Speak To The Stars** (Philips PB-295)		15	
Philharmonic Promenade Orchestra, cond. Sir Adrian Boult - **GUSTAV HOLST – THE PLANETS** (Nixa NLP-903) **LP**		15	
Frank Weir & His Saxophone - **The Never-Never Land / The Little Shoemaker** (Decca F-10324)		15	
Doris Day - **If I Give My Heart To You** (Philips PB-325)		23	4
Eddie Fisher - **I Need You Now / Heaven Was Never Like This** (H.M.V. B-10755)		23	19
Howard Keel - **Rose Marie** (M.G.M. MGM-750)		23	
Ted Heath & His Music - **Cuddle Me** (Decca F-10287)		26	
Mario Lanza - **Granada** (H.M.V. B-21310)		26	
Jo Stafford - **He Bought My Soul At Calvary** (Columbia DB-2929)		26	
Norman Brooks - **A Sky-Blue Shirt And A Rainbow Tie** (London L-1228)		29	39
Marie Bryant - **Tomato** (Lyragon J-701)		29	39
Joe Lynch - **Kevin Barry** (Glenside W-138)		29	
Billie Anthony - **This Ole House** (Columbia DB-3519)			9
Duke Ellington - **Satin Doll** (Capitol CL-14153)			13
Charlie Ventura Septet - **East Of Suez** (Brunswick 05316)			15
Billy May & His Orch. - **The Song Is You** (Capitol CL-14160)			19
Gerry Mulligan Quartet - **Swing House / I May Be Wrong** (Vogue V-2258)			19
Concertgebouw Orchestra of Amsterdam, cond. Erich Kleiber - **BEETHOVEN – SYMPHONY NO. 5** (Decca LXT-2851) **LP**			25
Gerry Mulligan Quartet - **THE GERRY MULLIGAN QUARTET (VOL. 2)** (Vogue EPV-1017) **EP**			25
Jimmy Shand & His Band - **An Irish Waltz [M]** (Parlophone F-3486)			25
Ted Heath & His Music - **Cinnamon Sinner** (Decca F-10374)			30
Issy Bonn - **Mom-e-le / My Friend** (Columbia DB-3504)			33
Eddie Fisher - **How Do You Speak To An Angel** (H.M.V. B-10737)			33
Wardell Gray - **The Man I Love** (Vogue V-2262)			37
Joe Lynch - **Irish Soldier Boy** (Glenside W-108)			37
Eddie Calvert - **Faraway** (Columbia DB-3462)			39
Billie Holiday / Teddy Wilson - **THE BILLIE HOLIDAY AND TEDDY WILSON ORCHESTRAS** (Columbia 33S-1034) **LP**			39
Vera Lynn and Frank Weir - **My Son, My Son** (Decca F-10372)			39
Glenn Miller & His Orch. - **Little Brown Jug** (H.M.V. B-10662)			39
Dickie Valentine - **Endless** (Decca F-10346)			39
June Valli - **I Understand (Just How You Feel)** (H.M.V. B-10749)			39

David Whitfield

Duke Ellington

Billie Anthony

Mario Lanza

2		9	16	23	30
★	Crew-Cuts - **Sh-Boom** (Mercury MB-3140)				
★	Doris Day - **If I Give My Heart To You** (Philips PB-325)				
★	Dean Martin - **Sway** (Capitol CL-14138)				
★	Al Martino - **The Story Of Tina** (Capitol CL-14163)				
★	Joan Regan - **If I Give My Heart To You** (Decca F-10373)				
1	Billie Anthony - **This Ole House** (Columbia DB-3519)	2	★		
1	Kay Starr - **Am I A Toy Or A Treasure / Fortune In Dreams** (Capitol CL-14151)	1	★		
3	Eddie Fisher - **My Friend** (H.M.V. B-10729)	4	1	4	
4	Frankie Laine - **There Must Be A Reason / Some Day** (Philips PB-306)	★			
5	Johnston Brothers - **The Bandit** (Decca F-10302)	18	40		
6	Dean Martin - **How Do You Speak To An Angel?** / Dean Martin & Jerry Lewis - **Ev'ry Street's A Boulevard In Old New York** (Capitol CL-14150)	6	4	★	
7	Tony Brent - **Sway / Three Coins In The Fountain** (Columbia DB-3496)	5	8	26	13
8	Tony Brent - **The Magic Tango** (Columbia DB-3514)	24			
8	Frankie Laine and the Four Lads - **Rain, Rain, Rain** (Philips PB-311)	3	1	★	
10	Eddie Fisher - **I Need You Now** (H.M.V. B-10755)	7	20	2	★
11	Rosemary Clooney - **This Ole House** (Philips PB-336)	★			
11	Milt Jackson Modern Jazz Quartet - **MILT JACKSON MODERN JAZZ QUARTET** (Esquire EP-14) 🅔🅟	12	15	26	21
13	Duke Ellington - **ELLINGTON '55** (Capitol LCT-6008) 🅛🅟		23	8	9
13	Jack Parnell & His Orch. - **The Bandit** (Parlophone R-3870)				
15	Les Baxter & His Orch. - **The High And The Mighty** (Capitol CL-14147)	24	23	21	
15	Beverley Sisters - **Val De Ri, Val De Ra** (Philips PB-239)				
15	Duke Ellington - **Satin Doll** (Capitol CL-14153)	14			
18	Billy Daniels - **Smile / Mom-e-le** (Mercury MB-3142)	34	11	38	
18	Gerry Mulligan Quartet - **Love Me Or Leave Me / Jeru** (Vogue V-2259)	13			
20	Ted Heath & His Music - **Cinnamon Sinner / They Were Doin' The Mambo** (Decca F-10374)	17			6
20	Gerry Mulligan Quartet - **Swing House / I May Be Wrong** (Vogue V-2258)	22			
22	Tennessee Ernie Ford - **Give Me Your Word / River Of No Return** (Capitol CL-14005)		34		
22	Gerry Mulligan Quartet - **Darn That Dream / I'm Beginning To See The Light** (Vogue V-2257)	24			
22	Johnnie Ray - **Destiny** (Philips PB-301)	18	7	18	26
25	Eric Delaney & His Band - **Oranges And Lemons** (Mercury MB-3143)		49		
25	Billy Eckstine - **No One But You** (M.G.M. MGM-763)				
25	Four Lads - **Gilly Gilly Ossenfeffer Katzenellen Bogen By The Sea** (Philips PB-304)				
25	Dean Martin - **Money Burns A Hole In My Pocket** (Capitol CL-14145)				
29	Dave Brubeck Trio - **Perfidia / Singing In The Rain** (Vogue V-2264)	15			
29	Frankie Vaughan - **Cinnamon Sinner / My Son, My Son** (H.M.V. B-10766)	8	29	30	2
31	Micky Andrews with the Jackie Brown Quintet and the Coronets - **I Can't Believe That You're In Love With Me** (Columbia DB-3517)				
31	Norman Brooks - **A Sky-Blue Shirt And A Rainbow Tie** (London L-1228)	9	8	5	11
31	Wardell Gray - **The Man I Love** (Vogue V-2262)				
31	McNulty Family - **Back To Donegal** (Decca (Irish Series) F-12089)				
35	Winifred Atwell - **Vendetta** (Philips PB-332)			1	2
35	Max Bygraves and the Tanner Sisters - **Friends And Neighbours** (H.M.V. B-10703)				
35	Eddie Calvert - **My Son, My Son** (Columbia DB-3507)	24	3	2	26
35	Ray Ellington Quartet - **Sky-Blue Shirt And A Rainbow Tie** (Columbia DB-3500)				
35	Billie Holiday / Teddy Wilson - **THE BILLIE HOLIDAY AND TEDDY WILSON ORCHESTRAS** (Columbia 33S-1034) 🅛🅟		26		
35	Victor Young & His Singing Strings - **The High And The Mighty** (Brunswick 05320)	15	34		
	Vera Lynn and Frank Weir - **My Son, My Son** (Decca F-10372)	10	★		

	9	16	23	30
Ted Heath & His Music - **Cuddle Me** (Decca F-10287)	11	40		
Gene Norman's 'Just Jazz' - **One O'Clock Jump** (Vogue V-2271)	18			
Carlos Thompson - **By Candlelight** (M.G.M. MGM-760)	18			
Dickie Valentine - **Endless** (Decca F-10346)	22			
Doris Day - **I Speak To The Stars** / **The Blue Bells Of Broadway** (Philips PB-295)	24	46	12	17
Earl Bostic & His Orch. - **Offshore** (Parlophone R-3818)	29			
Four Knights - **In The Chapel In The Moonlight** (Capitol CL-14154)	29			
Father Sydney MacEwan - **Scotland The Brave** (Columbia DB-3120)	29	29		
Paul Quinichette, Benny Green, Frank Foster, Joseph Newman, Hank Jones, Kenny Clarke, Eddie Jones and Sir Jonathan Gasser - **JAZZ STUDIO 1** (Brunswick LAT-8036) 🔲	29	17	25	35
Charles Williams & His Concert Orch. - **Tyrolean Tango** (Columbia DB-3471)	29			
Frank Chacksfield & His Orch. - **Smile** (Decca F-10354)	34	4	38	
Petula Clark - **Smile** (Polygon P-1128)	34	11	38	
George Elrick and the Lumberjacks - **Gilly Gilly Ossenfeffer Katznellenbogen By The Sea** (Decca F-10371)	34			
Vaughn Monroe - **They Were Doin' The Mambo** (H.M.V. B-10751)	34	15		26
Carlos Thompson - **No One But You** (M.G.M. MGM-759)	34		12	21
Dean Martin - **The Peddler Man** (Capitol CL-14170)		6	26	1
Eddie Fisher - **How Do You Speak To An Angel** / **My Arms, My Heart, My Love** (H.M.V. B-10737)		10	5	9
Kid Ory's Creole Jazz Band - **KID ORY'S CREOLE JAZZ BAND** (Tempo EXA-5) 🔲		11		
David Whitfield - **Smile** (Decca F-10355)		11	38	
Ronnie Harris - **I Love Paris** (Columbia DB-3529)		17	30	13
Lee Lawrence - **The Story Of Tina** (Decca F-10367)		17		
Duke Ellington - **MASTERPIECES** (Columbia 33SX-1022) 🔲		20	21	17
Joan Regan with the Johnston Brothers - **Wait For Me Darling** (Decca F-10362)		20		35
Leroy Holmes & His Orch. - **The High And The Mighty** (M.G.M. MGM-765)		23	38	
Vera Lynn - **My Friend** (Decca F-10339)		26		
Gerry Mulligan Quartet - **The Nearness Of You** / **Tea For Two** (Vogue V-2279)		26	33	
Louis Armstrong - **PERIOD – 1926** (Columbia 33SX-1029) 🔲		29		
Jim Cameron & His Band - **Grand March [M]** (Beltona BL-2596)		29	33	
Robert Earl - **My Son, My Son** (Philips PB-331)		29	8	4
Stan Getz - **STAN GETZ COLLATES** (Esquire 32-011) 🔲		34		
Teddy Johnson - **C'est Magnifique** (Columbia DB-3521)		34		
Guy Mitchell - **What Am I Doin' In Kansas City** (Philips PB-330)		34		
Pérez Prado & His Orch. - **The High And The Mighty** (H.M.V. B-10760)		34		
Louis Armstrong - **The Whiffenpoof Song** (Brunswick 05235)		40		

	9	16	23	30
Bunk Johnson & The Yerba Buena Jazz Band - **Ory's Creole Trombone** (*Good Time Jazz GV-2212*)	40			
Eartha Kitt - **I Want To Be Evil** (*H.M.V. B-10584*)	40			
Johnnie Ray - **Papa Loves Mambo** (*Philips PB-346*)	40	38		
Les Baxter & His Orch. - **I Love Paris** (*Capitol CL-14166*)	46	38	24	
Four Lads - **Skokiaan** (*Philips PB-329*)	46	21		
Wynonie Harris - **Bloodshot Eyes** (*Vogue V-2127*)	46		31	
Jerry Colonna - **Ebb Tide / The Velvet Glove** (*Brunswick 05243*)		5	31	
Ron Goodwin & His Concert Orch. - **Cara Mia** (*Parlophone R-3889*)		8		
London Philharmonic Orchestra, *cond.* John Barbirolli - **TCHAIKOVSKY – BALLET SUITE: 'THE SWAN LAKE'** (*H.M.V. C-2619/2620*) 78x2		8		
Issy Bonn - **My Friend** (*Columbia DB-3504*)		12		
Nat 'King' Cole - **There Goes My Heart / I Am In Love** (*Capitol CL-14172*)		12	7	
Barney Kessel - **BARNEY KESSEL** (*Vogue LDE-085*) LP		12	13	
Jimmy Young - **Little Things Mean A Lot** (*Decca F-10317*)		12		
Tennessee Ernie Ford - **Somebody Bigger Than You And I** (*Capitol CL-14178*)		18		
J.J. Johnson, Kai Winding, Benny Green and Willie Dennis - **JAZZ WORKSHOP (VOL. 1)** (*Vogue/Debut LDE-066*) LP		18	7	
Felix Mendelssohn & His Hawaiian Serenaders - **'Scotlandia' Medley [M]** (*Columbia DB-2757*)		21		
Tony Martin - **I Love Paris** (*H.M.V. B-10771*)		26	5	
Shorty Rogers & His Orch. - **THE WILD ONE [OST]** (*H.M.V. 7EG-8044*) EP		30	11	
Bill Haley & His Comets - **Rock Around The Clock** (*Brunswick 05317*)		33	21	
Eartha Kitt - **Under The Bridges Of Paris** (*H.M.V. B-10647*)		33		
George Lewis & His New Orleans Music - **Mama Don't Allow It** (*Good Time Jazz GV-2253*)		33	24	
Louis Armstrong - **Skokiaan** (*Brunswick 05332*)		38	17	
Perry Como - **Papa Loves Mambo** (*H.M.V. B-10776*)		38		
Ron Goodwin & His Concert Orch. - **Theme from 'Modern Times'** (*Parlophone R-3890*)		38		
Melachrino Orchestra - **Smile** (*H.M.V. B-10738*)		38		
Chorus & Orchestra Sinfonica dell'EIAR - **Nabucco (Act 3)** (*Parlophone Odeon BSP-3001*)		49		
Kitty Kallen - **In The Chapel In The Moonlight** (*Brunswick 05261*)		49		
Shelly Manne & His Men - **THE WEST COAST SOUND** (*Contemporary/Vogue LAC-12138*) LP		49	26	
Gordon MacRae - **C'est Magnifique** (*Capitol CL-14168*)			13	
Jimmy Shand & His Band - **Gay Gordons [M]** (*Parlophone F-3474*)			17	
Billy Daniels - **Bye Bye Blackbird** (*Mercury MB-3144*)			26	
Joe Lynch - **Irish Soldier Boy** (*Glenside W-108*)			31	
McNulty Family - **Irish Soldier Boy** (*Decca (Irish Series) F-12263*)			31	
George Elrick - **Robert Wilson Medley [M]** (*Beltona BL-2595*)			35	
Georgia Gibbs - **Wait For Me Darling** (*Mercury MB-3130*)			35	
Mario Lanza - **Serenade** (*H.M.V. DA-2065*)			35	
David Whitfield - **Santo Natale** (*Decca F-10399*)			35	

Johnnie Ray

Winifred Atwell

Jerry Colonna

Louis Armstrong

6		13	20	27
★	Joan Regan with the Johnston Brothers - **Wait For Me Darling** (Decca F-10362)			
★	Dickie Valentine - **Endless** (Decca F-10346)			
1	Stan Freberg - **Sh-Boom** (Capitol CL-14187)	1	★	
2	Irène Hilda - **I Love Paris** / Irène Hilda and Edmund Hockridge - **C'est Magnifique** (Parlophone R-3945)	2	2	11
3	Billy Eckstine - **No One But You** (M.G.M. MGM-763)	★		
4	Eddie Fisher - **My Friend** (H.M.V. B-10729)	11	11	42
5	Carlos Thompson - **No One But You** (M.G.M. MGM-759)	6	42	
6	Wynonie Harris - **Bloodshot Eyes** (Vogue V-2127)			
6	J.J. Johnson, Kai Winding, Benny Green and Willie Dennis - **JAZZ WORKSHOP (VOL. 1)** (Vogue/Debut LDE-066) **LP**	20	17	65
8	Norman Brooks - **A Sky-Blue Shirt And A Rainbow Tie** (London L-1228)	★		
8	Robert Earl - **My Son, My Son** (Philips PB-331)	14		32
8	Ronnie Harris - **I Love Paris** (Columbia DB-3529)	7	5	
8	Milt Jackson Modern Jazz Quartet - **MILT JACKSON MODERN JAZZ QUARTET** (Esquire EP-14) **EP**	30	28	
8	Joan Regan with the Keynotes - **This Ole House** (Decca F-10397)	12		23
13	Shelly Manne & His Men - **THE WEST COAST SOUND** (Contemporary/Vogue LAC-12138) **LP**			
14	Bill Haley & His Comets - **Rock Around The Clock** (Brunswick 05317)	4	5	5
14	Ronnie Harris - **Hold My Hand** (Columbia DB-3520)			
14	Shorty Rogers & His Orch. - **THE WILD ONE [OST]** (H.M.V. 7EG-8044) **EP**	44		
14	Frankie Vaughan - **Cinnamon Sinner** / **My Son, My Son** (H.M.V. B-10766)	5		32
18	Ted Heath & His Music - **Cinnamon Sinner** / **They Were Doin' The Mambo** (Decca F-10374)	44		
18	Edmund Hockridge - **My Friend** (Parlophone R-3884)			
18	Barney Kessel - **BARNEY KESSEL** (Vogue LDE-085) **LP**	40	30	
18	Vera Lynn - **My Friend** / **There Must Be A Reason** (Decca F-10339)	30	30	72
18	Jimmy Shand & His Band - **An Irish Waltz [M]** (Parlophone F-3486)			
23	Tony Brent - **Tell Me, Tell Me** / **Nicolette** (Columbia DB-3532)	36		
23	Tony Martin - **I Love Paris** (H.M.V. B-10771)	7	3	5
23	Oscar Pettiford Sextet - **OSCAR PETTIFORD SEXTET** (Vogue LDE-098) **LP**	26		
23	David Whitfield - **Smile** (Decca F-10355)			
27	Louis Armstrong - **Skokiaan** (Brunswick 05332)		42	
27	Winifred Atwell - **Vendetta** (Philips PB-332)			
27	Issy Bonn - **My Friend** (Columbia DB-3504)	20		
27	Bonnie Lou - **Wait For Me, Darling** (Parlophone R-3895)			72
27	Patrick O'Hagan - **The Whistling Gypsy** (Decca (Irish Series) F-18184)	26		32
27	Paul Quinichette, Benny Green, Frank Foster, Joseph Newman, Hank Jones, Kenny Clarke, Eddie Jones and Sir Jonathan Gasser - **JAZZ STUDIO 1** (Brunswick LAT-8036) **LP**			
33	Les Baxter & His Orch. - **I Love Paris** (Capitol CL-14166)	44	30	
33	Tennessee Ernie Ford - **Give Me Your Word** (Capitol CL-14005)			59
33	Georgia Gibbs - **Wait For Me Darling** (Mercury MB-3130)			
33	Georgia Gibbs - **I Love Paris** (Mercury MB-3152)	14	23	5
33	Al Haig Trio - **AL HAIG TRIO** (Vogue LDE-092) **LP**			72
33	Ian MacLeish - **The Star O' Robbie Burns** (Beltona BL-2607)			
33	Marilyn Monroe - **The River Of No Return** (H.M.V. B-10723)			
33	Jimmy Shand & His Band - **Red House Reel [M]** (Parlophone F-3464)	36		
41	Earl Bostic & His Orch. - **Mambostic** (Parlophone R-3932)			
41	Nat 'King' Cole - **There Goes My Heart** (Capitol CL-14172)	30	34	50
41	Chubby Jackson's All Stars - **CHUBBY JACKSON'S ALL STARS** (Esquire EP-201) **EP**	36		
44	Count Basie & His Kansas City Seven / Lester Young Quartet - **COUNT BASIE / LESTER YOUNG** (Oriole/Mercury MG-25015) **LP**	35		
44	Tony Brent - **Sway** (Columbia DB-3496)			
44	Stan Kenton & His Orch. - **How High The Moon** (Capitol CL-13224)	30		42
44	Johnnie Ray - **Destiny** (Philips PB-301)			72

	13	20	27
44 Johnnie Ray - **Papa Loves Mambo** (*Philips PB-346*)	26	8	50
44 Victor Young & His Singing Strings - **The High And The Mighty** (*Brunswick 05320*)	2	5	5
David Whitfield - **Santo Natale** (*Decca F-10399*)	★		
Johnnie Francis - **I Still Believe / Madonna, Madonna** (*Decca F-10380*)	7		65
Eddie Calvert - **My Son, My Son** (*Columbia DB-3507*)	10		28
Duke Ellington - **ELLINGTON '55** (*Capitol LCT-6008*) 🅛🅟	12		19
Duke Ellington - **MASTERPIECES** (*Columbia 33SX-1022*) 🅛🅟	14	23	50
Les Baxter & His Orch. - **The High And The Mighty** (*Capitol CL-14147*)	17	34	5
Chris Barber's Jazz Band - **White Christmas / On A Christmas Day** (*Columbia DC-672*)	17	9	14
Ted Heath & His Music - **Skokiaan** (*Decca F-10368*)	17		
Perry Como - **Papa Loves Mambo** (*H.M.V. B-10776*)	20	11	32
Ronnie Hilton - **I Still Believe / Veni – Vidi – Vici** (*H.M.V. B-10785*)	20	1	★
Dean Martin - **The Peddler Man** (*Capitol CL-14170*)	20		
Gary Miller - **The High And The Mighty** (*Philips PB-335*)	20		
Dean Martin - **Money Burns A Hole In My Pocket** (*Capitol CL-14145*)	26	34	
Norrie Paramor & His Orch. - **The High And The Mighty** (*Columbia DB-3515*)	30	17	59
Eric Jupp & His Orch. - **Skokiaan** (*Columbia DB-3522*)	36		
Ray Ellington Quartet - **Sky-Blue Shirt And A Rainbow Tie** (*Columbia DB-3500*)	40		
Dimitri Tiomkin & His Orch. - **Theme from 'The High And The Mighty'** (*Vogue Coral Q-2016*)	40		
Robert Wilson with Jimmy Shand & His Band - **The Northern Lights Of Aberdeen** (*H.M.V. B-10521*)	40	23	
Ron Goodwin & His Concert Orch. - **On The Waterfront** (*Parlophone R-3923*)	44		
Gordon MacRae - **C'est Magnifique** (*Capitol CL-14168*)	44	9	42
Jimmy Shand & His Band - **Bluebell Polka** (*Parlophone F-3436*)	44		
Jimmy Shand & His Band - **The Gordon Waltz [M]** (*Parlophone F-3463*)	44		
David Hughes - **Santo Natale** (*Philips PB-350*)	51		
Maurice Keary - **Slievanamon** (*Glenside W-126*)	51		
Gerry Mulligan Quartet - **THE GERRY MULLIGAN QUARTET (VOL. 1)** (*Vogue EPV-1001*) 🅔🅟	51	20	
Patti Page - **I Can't Tell A Waltz From A Tango / Mama Doll Song** (*Mercury MB-3161*)	51	20	19
Frank Sinatra - **It Worries Me** (*Capitol CL-14188*)	51		
Frankie Vaughan - **Happy Days And Lonely Nights** (*H.M.V. B-10783*)	51		
Big Ben Banjo Band - **Let's Get Together No. 1 [M]** (*Columbia DB-3549*)		4	1
Eddie Fisher - **Count Your Blessings Instead Of Sheep / White Christmas** (*H.M.V. B-10779*)		11	59
Gene Norman's 'Just Jazz' - **GENE NORMAN PRESENTS 'JUST JAZZ'** (*Vogue EPV-1002*) 🅔🅟		11	32
Louis Armstrong - **1927** (*Columbia 33S-1041*) 🅛🅟		15	23
Denise Lor - **If I Give My Heart To You** (*Parlophone R-3893*)		15	10
Les Paul - **Mandolino** (*Capitol CL-14185*)		17	
Eddie Fisher - **How Do You Speak To An Angel** (*H.M.V. B-10737*)		20	65
Jerry Colonna - **Sweet Adeline** (*Brunswick 05125*)		23	
Robert Wilson - **Here's To The Gordons** (*H.M.V. B-10780*)		23	
Bing Crosby - **Count Your Blessings Instead Of Sheep** (*Brunswick 05339*)		28	14
Spike Jones & His City Slickers - **I Went To Your Wedding** (*H.M.V. B-10482*)		30	
Dave Brubeck Quartet - **DAVE BRUBECK QUARTET** (*Vogue EPV-1063*) 🅔🅟		34	
Eric Delaney & His Band - **Oranges And Lemons** (*Mercury MB-3143*)		34	
Johnny Desmond - **The High And The Mighty** (*Vogue Coral Q-2019*)		34	
Teddy Johnson - **C'est Magnifique** (*Columbia DB-3521*)		34	
Pérez Prado & His Orch. - **The High And The Mighty** (*H.M.V. B-10760*)		34	
Four Lads - **Skokiaan** (*Philips PB-329*)		42	
Bill McGuffie & His Orch. - **On The Waterfront** (*Philips PB-356*)		42	65
Frank Sinatra - **SING AND DANCE WITH FRANK SINATRA** (*Philips BBR-8003*) 🅛🅟		42	
Stargazers - **365 Kisses** (*Decca F-10379*)		42	11
Jimmy Young - **Moonlight In Mayo** (*Decca F-10343*)		42	
Ruby Murray - **Heartbeat** (*Columbia DB-3542*)			2
Nat 'King' Cole - **Hold My Hand / If I Give My Heart To You** (*Capitol CL-14203*)			3

DECEMBER 1954

4		11	18	25
★	Alma Cogan - **I Can't Tell A Waltz From A Tango** (*H.M.V. B-10786*)			
★	Ruby Murray - **Heartbeat** (*Columbia DB-3542*)			
1	Big Ben Banjo Band - **Let's Get Together No. 2 [M]** (*Columbia DB-3554*)	1	1	1
2	Big Ben Banjo Band - **Let's Get Together No. 1 [M]** (*Columbia DB-3549*)	★		
3	Irène Hilda - **I Love Paris** / Irène Hilda and Edmund Hockridge - **C'est Magnifique** (*Parlophone R-3945*)	12	15	16
4	Nat 'King' Cole - **Hold My Hand** / **If I Give My Heart To You** (*Capitol CL-14203*)	5	12	24
5	Max Bygraves - **Mister Sandman** / **Do You Love Old Santa Claus** (*H.M.V. B-10821*)	2	3	4
6	Bill Haley & His Comets - **Rock Around The Clock** (*Brunswick 05317*)	43	4	5
7	Al Martino - **I Still Believe** (*Capitol CL-14192*)	6	5	8
8	Perry Como - **Papa Loves Mambo** (*H.M.V. B-10776*)	★		
8	Al Martino - **No One But You** (*Capitol CL-14202*)		30	
10	Chris Barber's Jazz Band - **White Christmas** / **On A Christmas Day** (*Columbia DC-672*)	9	10	
10	Beverley Sisters - **The Mama Doll Song** (*Philips PB-370*)			
10	Bob Cooper Sextet - **KENTON PRESENTS JAZZ – BOB COOPER** (*Capitol KPL-102*) LP	15	22	
13	Ray Ellington Quartet - **Sky-Blue Shirt And A Rainbow Tie** (*Columbia DB-3500*)			
13	Bill Holman Octet - **KENTON PRESENTS JAZZ – BILL HOLMAN** (*Capitol KPL-101*) LP	12		
13	Vera Lynn - **Party Sing-Song [M]** (*Decca F-10411*)	21	8	5
13	Johnnie Ray - **Papa Loves Mambo** (*Philips PB-346*)	24	13	18
17	Les Baxter & His Orch. - **I Love Paris** (*Capitol CL-14166*)			
17	Johnston Brothers - **Join In And Sing [M]** (*Decca F-10414*)	24	8	3
17	Suzi Miller and the Johnston Brothers - **Happy Days And Lonely Nights** (*Decca F-10389*)	15	7	7
17	Bennie Moten & His Kansas City Orch. - **KAY CEE JAZZ** (*H.M.V. DLP-1057*) LP			
17	Patti Page - **I Can't Tell A Waltz From A Tango** / **Mama Doll Song** (*Mercury MB-3161*)	11	6	11
22	Bing Crosby, Danny Kaye, Peggy Lee and Trudy Stevens - **White Christmas** (*Brunswick 05354*)	9		37
22	Ken Griffin - **In The Chapel In The Moonlight** (*Philips PB-353*)			
22	Eartha Kitt - **Under The Bridges Of Paris** (*H.M.V. B-10647*)			
22	Gary Miller - **The High And The Mighty** (*Philips PB-335*)			
22	Patrick O'Hagan - **The Whistling Gypsy** (*Decca (Irish Series) F-18184*)			
22	Shorty Rogers & His Orch. - **THE WILD ONE [OST]** (*H.M.V. 7EG-8044*) EP			
22	Dickie Valentine with the Stargazers - **The Finger Of Suspicion** / Dickie Valentine - **Who's Afraid** (*Decca F-10394*)	7	★	
29	Eddie Fisher - **Count Your Blessings Instead Of Sheep** / **White Christmas** (*H.M.V. B-10779*)	24		
29	Stan Kenton & His Orch. - **How High The Moon** (*Capitol CL-13224*)			
29	Tony Martin - **I Love Paris** (*H.M.V. B-10771*)	39	24	31
29	Howard Rumsey's Lighthouse All Stars - **HOWARD RUMSEY'S LIGHTHOUSE ALL STARS (VOL. 1)** (*Vogue EPV-1004*) EP	18	18	14
33	Eddie Fisher - **My Friend** (*H.M.V. B-10729*)			
33	Harry James & His Orch. - **The High And The Mighty** (*Philips PB-326*)			
33	Patti Lewis - **I Can't Tell A Waltz From A Tango** (*Philips PB-367*)		34	
33	Jimmy Shand & His Band - **The Gordon Waltz [M]** (*Parlophone F-3463*)			
33	Jimmy Shand & His Band - **An Irish Waltz [M]** / **Teviot Brig [M]** (*Parlophone F-3486*)	43	24	24
33	Kay Starr with Barney Kessel - **GENE NORMAN PRESENTS KAY STARR WITH BARNEY KESSEL** (*Vogue EPV-1014*) EP			
39	Jimmy Boyd - **Rudolph The Red-Nosed Reindeer** (*Philips PB-358*)	39		
39	Bing Crosby - **Count Your Blessings Instead Of Sheep** (*Brunswick 05339*)		39	43
39	Georgia Gibbs - **I Love Paris** (*Mercury MB-3152*)	24		
39	David Hughes - **Santo Natale** (*Philips PB-350*)			
39	George Shearing Quintet - **Body And Soul** (*M.G.M. MGM-638*)			

4	<<< DECEMBER 1954 >>>	11	18	25
39	Dickie Valentine - **Mister Sandman** (Decca F-10415)	3	★	
39	Billy Williams Quartet - **Sh-Boom** (Vogue Coral Q-2012)	24		
46	Nat 'King' Cole - **There Goes My Heart / I Am In Love** (Capitol CL-14172)		24	
46	Bill Haley & His Comets - **Shake, Rattle And Roll** (Brunswick 05338)	18	★	
46	Leroy Holmes & His Orch. - **The High And The Mighty** (M.G.M. MGM-765)			
46	Dimitri Tiomkin & His Orch. - **Theme from 'The High And The Mighty'** (Vogue Coral Q-2016)	43		
46	Claude Williamson Trio - **KENTON PRESENTS JAZZ – CLAUDE WILLIAMSON** (Capitol KPL-103) **LP**			
51	Dave Brubeck Trio - **DAVE BRUBECK TRIO** (Vogue LDE-090) **LP**			
51	Four Aces - **Mister Sandman** (Brunswick 05355)	8	2	2
51	Dean Martin - **Money Burns A Hole In My Pocket** (Capitol CL-14145)			
51	Norrie Paramor & His Orch. - **The High And The Mighty** (Columbia DB-3515)			
51	Roland Shaw Orchestra - **The High And The Mighty** (Decca F-10407)			
51	Wally Stott Orchestra - **The Cat From Coos Bay** (Philips PB-351)			
51	Victor Young & His Singing Strings - **The High And The Mighty** (Brunswick 05320)			
58	Bonnie Lou - **Wait For Me, Darling** (Parlophone R-3895)			
58	Tennessee Ernie Ford - **Give Me Your Word** (Capitol CL-14005)		24	24
58	J.J. Johnson, Kai Winding, Benny Green and Willie Dennis - **JAZZ WORKSHOP (VOL. 1)** (Vogue/Debut LDE-066) **LP**			
58	Vaughn Monroe - **They Were Doin' The Mambo** (H.M.V. B-10751)			
	Charlie Kunz - **Piano Medley No. 114 [M]** (Decca F-10419)	4	★	
	Modernaires - **New Juke Box Saturday Night** (Vogue Coral Q-2035)	12	22	21
	Ronnie Harris - **I Still Believe / I Love Paris** (Columbia DB-3529)	15		
	Lorrae Desmond and the Johnston Brothers - **I Can't Tell A Waltz From A Tango** (Decca F-10404)	18		
	Nat 'King' Cole - **Papa Loves Mambo / Teach Me Tonight** (Capitol CL-14207)	21	15	14
	Frank Rosolino Sextet - **KENTON PRESENTS JAZZ – FRANK ROSOLINO** (Capitol KPL-104) **LP**	21		
	Frank Sinatra - **SWING EASY!** (Capitol LC-6689) **LP** †	24	20	9
	Chris Barber / Lonnie Donegan - **NEW ORLEANS JOYS** (Decca LF-1198) **LP**	30	15	11
	Earl Bostic & His Orch. - **Memories** (Parlophone R-3782)	31		
	Earl Bostic & His Orch. - **These Foolish Things** (Parlophone R-3932)	31		
	Ken Colyer's Jazzmen - **BACK TO THE DELTA** (Decca LF-1196) **LP**	31	30	37
	Frankie Vaughan - **Happy Days And Lonely Nights** (H.M.V. B-10783)	31		
	Les Baxter & His Orch. - **The High And The Mighty** (Capitol CL-14147)	35	30	31
	Sammy Davis Jr. - **Because Of You** (Brunswick 05326)	35		
	Johnston Brothers - **The Bandit** (Decca F-10302)	35		

---

† This 10" LP bubbled under for five weeks in December, January and February. It eventually charted in October 1960 after being reissued in 12" format, with additional tracks.

	11	18	25
Shorty Rogers & His Orchestra featuring the Giants - **COOL AND CRAZY** (H.M.V. DLP-1030)	35	39	21
Gerry Mulligan Quartet - **Bark For Barksdale** (Vogue V-2260)	39		
Paul Quinichette, Benny Green, Frank Foster, Joseph Newman, Hank Jones, Kenny Clarke, Eddie Jones and Sir Jonathan Gasser - **JAZZ STUDIO 1** (Brunswick LAT-8036)	39	14	13
Bonnie Lou - **Two Step – Side Step** (Parlophone R-3931)	43		
Gene Norman's 'Just Jazz' - **GENE NORMAN PRESENTS 'JUST JAZZ'** (Vogue EPV-1002)	43	19	21
Jan Rosol and Gwen Campbell - **I Love Paris** (Polygon P-1136)	43		
Jimmy Shand & His Band - **Bluebell Polka** (Parlophone F-3436)	43		
David Whitfield - **Smile** (Decca F-10355)	43		
Julian Slade - **Music from 'Salad Days' [M]** (Parlophone R-3927)		11	10
Vicki Young - **Honey Love** (Capitol CL-14144)		20	16
Gaylords - **Veni – Vidi – Vici** (Mercury MB-3163)		24	24
Humphrey Lyttelton & His Band - **HUMPH AT THE CONWAY** (Parlophone PMC-1012)		24	24
Merrill Moore - **The House Of Blue Lights** / Bell Bottom Boogie (Capitol CL-14057)		30	31
Count Basie & His Kansas City Seven / Lester Young Quartet **COUNT BASIE / LESTER YOUNG** (Oriole/Mercury MG-25015)		34	
Earl Bostic & His Orch. - **Flamingo** (Vogue V-2145)		34	
Nat 'King' Cole - **Unbelievable** / **Hajji Baba** (Capitol CL-14155)		34	37
OBC - **COLE PORTER'S CAN-CAN** (Capitol LCT-6010)		34	31
Jimmy Young - **I Understand Just How You Feel** (Decca F-10370)		34	37
Eddie Fisher - **How Do You Speak To An Angel** (H.M.V. B-10737)		39	43
Ted Heath & His Music - **Honey Love** (Decca F-10392)		39	
Stan Kenton & His Orch. - **KENTON SHOWCASE: THE MUSIC OF BILL RUSSO / THE MUSIC OF BILL HOLMAN** (Capitol LCT-6009)			18
Shorty Rogers & His Giants - **SHORTY ROGERS AND HIS GIANTS** (H.M.V. DLP-1058)			20
De Castro Sisters - **Teach Me Tonight** (London HL-8104)			24
Frank Sinatra - **SONGS FOR YOUNG LOVERS** (Capitol LC-6654)			24
Duke Ellington - **ELLINGTON '55** (Capitol LCT-6008)			31
Jackie Gleason - **MUSIC FOR LOVERS ONLY** (Capitol LC-6588)			31
Gigi Gryce–Clifford Brown Sextet - **Salute To The Bandbox** (Vogue V-2239)			37
Jimmy Shand & His Band - **SCOTTISH COUNTRY DANCES NO. 2** (Parlophone PMD-1015)			37
Earl Bostic & His Orch. - **EARL BOSTIC, HIS ALTO SAX AND HIS ORCHESTRA** (Vogue LDE-100)			43
Lionel Hampton's Paris All Stars - **VOLUME 3** (Vogue LDE-063)			43

1		8	15	22	29
1	Big Ben Banjo Band - **Let's Get Together No. 2 [M]** (Columbia DB-3554)	6	10		
2	Four Aces - **Mister Sandman** (Brunswick 05355)	★			
3	Max Bygraves - **Mister Sandman** (H.M.V. B-10821)	1	4	★	
4	Suzi Miller and the Johnston Brothers - **Happy Days And Lonely Nights** (Decca F-10389)	2	1	★	
5	Johnston Brothers - **Join In And Sing [M]** (Decca F-10414)	19			
6	Mario Lanza - **Serenade / Drinking Song** (H.M.V. DA-2065)	3	2	2	1
7	Bill Haley & His Comets - **Rock Around The Clock** (Brunswick 05317)	★			
8	Vera Lynn - **Party Sing-Song [M]** (Decca F-10411)				
9	Julian Slade - **Music from 'Salad Days' [M]** (Parlophone R-3927)	13	12	50	
10	Al Martino - **I Still Believe** (Capitol CL-14192)	8	8	28	
11	Patti Page - **I Can't Tell A Waltz From A Tango / Mama Doll Song** (Mercury MB-3161)	7	33		
12	Paul Quinichette, Benny Green, Frank Foster, Joseph Newman, Hank Jones, Kenny Clarke, Eddie Jones and Sir Jonathan Gasser - **JAZZ STUDIO 1** (Brunswick LAT-8036) LP			16	13
13	Howard Rumsey's Lighthouse All Stars - **HOWARD RUMSEY'S LIGHTHOUSE ALL STARS (VOL. 1)** (Vogue EPV-1004) EP	5	6	14	21
14	OLC - **LOVE FROM JUDY** (Columbia DX-1853/1854) 78x2				
14	Frank Sinatra - **SWING EASY!** (Capitol LC-6689) LP †				
16	Chris Barber's Jazz Band - **Merrydown Rag** (Decca F-10417)				
16	Bob Cooper Sextet - **KENTON PRESENTS JAZZ – BOB COOPER** (Capitol KPL-102) LP	46		39	11
16	Modernaires - **New Juke Box Saturday Night** (Vogue Coral Q-2035)	37	33	22	
19	Chris Barber / Lonnie Donegan - **NEW ORLEANS JOYS** (Decca LF-1198) LP	32		22	
19	Kathleen Ferrier - **A RECITAL OF BACH AND HANDEL ARIAS** (Decca LXT-2757) LP				
19	Stargazers - **365 Kisses / I Need You Now** (Decca F-10379)	19			
19	Vicki Young - **Honey Love** (Capitol CL-14144)				
23	Gene Norman's 'Just Jazz' - **GENE NORMAN PRESENTS 'JUST JAZZ'** (Vogue EPV-1002) EP				
23	Johnnie Ray - **Papa Loves Mambo** (Philips PB-346)	26			35
23	Wally Stott Orchestra - **The Cat From Coos Bay** (Philips PB-351)	13	7	34	
26	Nat 'King' Cole - **Hold My Hand / If I Give My Heart To You** (Capitol CL-14203)	46			
26	De Castro Sisters - **Teach Me Tonight** (London HL-8104)	13	37	46	35
26	Kathleen Ferrier - **What Is Life? (Che Faro?)** (Decca K-1466)	26	42		
26	Humphrey Lyttelton & His Band - **HUMPH AT THE CONWAY** (Parlophone PMC-1012) LP	19			43
26	Les Paul & Mary Ford - **Mister Sandman** (Capitol CL-14212)	19		39	
26	Frankie Vaughan - **Happy Days And Lonely Nights** (H.M.V. B-10783)	46	8	8	★
32	Beniamino Gigli - **Silent Night, Holy Night** (H.M.V. DA-1874)				
32	Irène Hilda - **I Love Paris** / Irène Hilda and Edmund Hockridge - **C'est Magnifique** (Parlophone R-3945)	37			
32	Mahalia Jackson - **Silent Night, Holy Night** (Vogue V-306)				
32	The Two Bills from Bermondsey - **What A Mouth, What A Mouth / Cockney Capers [M]** (Parlophone R-3953)	52	23	28	15
36	Eddie Fisher - **Count Your Blessings Instead Of Sheep / White Christmas** (H.M.V. B-10779)	19			
36	Gigi Gryce–Clifford Brown Sextet - **Salute To The Bandbox** (Vogue V-2239)				
36	Vera Lynn - **There Must Be A Reason** (Decca F-10339)				
36	Jimmy Young - **I Understand Just How You Feel** (Decca F-10370)				
40	Nat 'King' Cole - **Unbelievable / Hajji Baba** (Capitol CL-14155)	11	15	4	10
40	Eddie Fisher - **How Do You Speak To An Angel** (H.M.V. B-10737)				
40	Johnnie Francis - **I Still Believe / Madonna, Madonna** (Decca F-10380)				

† This 10" LP bubbled under for five weeks in December, January and February. It eventually charted in October 1960 after being reissued in 12" format, with additional tracks.

1	<<< JANUARY 1955 >>>	8	15	22	29
	Hugo Winterhalter's Orchestra & Chorus - **Song Of The Barefoot Contessa** (H.M.V. B-10791)	46	37		39
	Eric Delaney & His Band - **Oranges And Lemons / Delaney's Delight** (Mercury MB-3143)	52		12	43
	Spike Jones & His City Slickers - **Rudolph, The Red-Nosed Reindeer** (H.M.V. B-9988)	52			
	Guy Mitchell - **GUY MITCHELL** (Columbia SEG-7513) EP	52			
	Norrie Paramor & His Orch. - **The High And The Mighty** (Columbia DB-3515)	52	42		
	Johnnie Ray - **Destiny** (Philips PB-301)	52			
	Ames Brothers - **The Naughty Lady Of Shady Lane** (H.M.V. B-10800)		10	12	5
	Nat 'King' Cole - **Papa Loves Mambo / Teach Me Tonight** (Capitol CL-14207)		12	16	18
	Ray Burns - **Mobile** (Columbia DB-3563)		15	3	★
	Ken Colyer's Jazzmen - **BACK TO THE DELTA** (Decca LF-1196) LP		15	28	
	Ray Martin & His Concert Orch. - **The Gentle Sex / It's A Woman's World** (Columbia DB-3557)		15		28
	Patrick O'Hagan - **Wild Colonial Boy** (Decca F-9536)		15	22	43
	Tony Kinsey Trio with Joe Harriott - **Last Resort** (Esquire 10-382)		20		
	Joy Nichols - **JOY NICHOLS** (Parlophone GEP-8509) EP		20		
	Les Baxter & His Orch. - **I Love Paris** (Capitol CL-14166)		23		
	Al Martino - **No One But You** (Capitol CL-14202)		23		
	Jerry Allen - **S'posin'** (Decca F-10428)		27		
	Archie Bleyer & His Orch. - **The Naughty Lady Of Shady Lane** (London HL-8111)		27	28	
	Petula Clark - **Majorca** (Polygon P-1146)		27	61	21
	Barney Kessel - **BARNEY KESSEL** (Vogue LDE-085) LP		27	55	
	Stargazers - **Somebody / No More** (Decca F-10437)		27	18	39
	Dick James - **Veni – Vidi – Vici** (Parlophone R-3940)		33		
	Robert Wilson - **Here's To The Gordons** (H.M.V. B-10780)		37	55	
	Dave Brubeck Quartet - **DAVE BRUBECK QUARTET** (Vogue EPV-1063) EP		42		
	Ronnie Harris and the Coronets - **Don't Go To Strangers** (Columbia DB-3555)		42	★	
	Teresa Brewer - **Let, Me Go Lover** (Vogue Coral Q-72043)		48	★	
	Marie Bryant - **Tomato** (Lyragon J-701)		48		
	Gerry Mulligan Quartet with Lee Konitz - **Lady Be Good** (Vogue V-2305)		48		
	Dean Martin - **Mambo Italiano** (Capitol CL-14227)			1	2
	Dickie Valentine - **A Blossom Fell** (Decca F-10430)			4	8
	Ronnie Hilton - **A Blossom Fell** (H.M.V. B-10808)			6	6
	Peggy Lee - **Let Me Go, Lover** (Brunswick 05360)			7	39
	Humphrey Lyttelton & His Band - **Ace In The Hole** (Parlophone R-3967)			10	28
	Patti Page - **Let Me Go, Lover** (Mercury MB-3182)			14	31
	Chris Barber's Jazz Band - **CHRIS BARBER PLAYS SPIRITUALS** (Columbia SEG-7568) EP			18	24

Entry	1	8	15	22	29
Bill Haley & His Comets - **Dim, Dim The Lights** (Brunswick 05373)				18	4
Dave Brubeck Quartet - **DAVE BRUBECK QUARTET (VOL . 2)** (Vogue LDE-104) [LP]				22	
Sarah Vaughan - **Make Yourself Comfortable** (Mercury MB-3180)				22	15
Stan Kenton & His Orch. - **KENTON SHOWCASE: THE MUSIC OF BILL RUSSO / THE MUSIC OF BILL HOLMAN** (Capitol LCT-6009) [LP]				28	15
Gerry Mulligan Quartet - **Nights At The Turntable** (Vogue V-2157)				28	
Lionel Hampton & His Orch. - **APOLLO HALL CONCERT 1954** (Philips BBL-7015) [LP]				34	11
Tony Kinsey Trio with Joe Harriott - **TONY KINSEY TRIO WITH JOE HARRIOTT** (Esquire EP-52) [EP]				34	35
Kid Ory's Creole Jazz Band - **KID ORY'S CREOLE JAZZ BAND** (Tempo EXA-5) [EP]				34	
Dutch Swing College Band - **GEMS OF JAZZ NO. 1** (Philips BBR-8018) [LP]				39	
Benny Goodman - **SESSION FOR SEXTET NO. 2** (Columbia 33SX-1035) [LP]				39	
Howard Keel and Brothers - **Sobbin' Women** (M.G.M. MGM-787)				39	24
Kirchin Band - **Minor Mambo** (Decca F-10434)				39	
Kid Ory & His Creole Jazz Band - **12th Street Rag** (Vogue V-2012)				39	
Judy Garland - **The Man That Got Away** (Philips PB-366)				46	
Gene Krupa & His Orch. - **DRUMMIN' MAN** (Columbia 33S-1051) [LP]				46	18
Yorkshire Jazz Band - **Muskrat Ramble** (Tempo A-17)				46	
Doris Day - **The Blue Bells Of Broadway / I Speak To The Stars** (Philips PB-295)				50	
Coleman Hawkins - **THE HAWK TALKS** (Brunswick OE-9166) [EP]				50	
Gerry Mulligan Quartet - **Bark For Barksdale** (Vogue V-2260)				50	31
Gerry Mulligan Quartet - **THE GERRY MULLIGAN QUARTET (VOL. 2)** (Vogue EPV-1017)				50	
Benny Goodman - **CARNEGIE HALL JAZZ CONCERT** (Philips BBL-7001) [LP]				55	
Al Martino - **Don't Go To Strangers** (Capitol CL-14224)				55	
Gerry Mulligan Quartet - **Walkin' Shoes** (Vogue V-2225)				55	
Robert Wilson with Jimmy Shand & His Band - **The Northern Lights Of Aberdeen** (H.M.V. B-10521)				55	
Kathleen Ferrier - **Blow The Wind Southerly** (Decca F-9300)				61	
Wynonie Harris - **Loving Machine** (Vogue V-2111)				61	
Ted Heath & His Music - **Honey Love** (Decca F-10392)				61	
George Lewis & His New Orleans Music - **Mama Don't Allow It** (Good Time Jazz GV-2253)				61	
Humphrey Lyttelton & His Band - **Mezzy's Tune** (Parlophone R-3917)				61	
Joan Weber - **Let Me Go Lover** (Philips PB-389)				61	31
Four Aces - **It's A Woman's World** (Brunswick 05348)					7
Benny Goodman - **B.G. JAZZ CONCERT NO. 2** (Philips BBE-12132) [EP]					13
Frank Weir & His Saxophone - **Theme from 'Journey Into Space'** (Decca F-10435)					18
George Lewis & His New Orleans Stompers - **GEORGE LEWIS & HIS NEW ORLEANS STOMPERS** (Vogue LAE-12005) [LP]					21
Sauter–Finegan Orchestra - **Midnight Sleighride** (H.M.V. B-10818)					24
Woody Herman & The New Third Herd - **HERD FROM MARS (VOL. 1)** (London REP-1001) [EP]					24
Judy Garland - **It's A New World** (Philips PB-394)					28
Tony Brent - **It's A Woman's World** (Columbia DB-3556)					31
Kirk Stevens - **Here's To The Gordons** (Parlophone R-3963)					35
Glenn Miller & His Orch. - **A String Of Pearls** (H.M.V. BD-5927)					39
Billy Eckstine - **Olay, Olay / Beloved** (M.G.M. MGM-776)					43
Fawkes–Turner Sextet - **TAKIN' IT EASY (VOL. 1)** (Decca DFE-6192) [EP]					43
Firehouse Five + 2 - **Runnin' Wild** (Good Time Jazz GV-2192)					43
Patrick O'Hagan - **The Whistling Gypsy** (Decca (Irish Series) F-18184)					43
Frank Sinatra - **The Gal That Got Away** (Capitol CL-14221)					43

5		12	19	26
★	Ames Brothers - **The Naughty Lady Of Shady Lane** (H.M.V. B-10800)			
★	Ronnie Hilton - **A Blossom Fell** (H.M.V. B-10808)			
★	Mario Lanza - **Serenade** / **Drinking Song** (H.M.V. DA-2065)			
★	Dean Martin - **Mambo Italiano** (Capitol CL-14227)			
★	Dickie Valentine - **A Blossom Fell** (Decca F-10430)			
1	Mario Lanza - **I'll Walk With God** (H.M.V. DA-2062)	3	★	
2	Bill Haley & His Comets - **Dim, Dim The Lights** (Brunswick 05373)	2	5	
3	Benny Goodman - **B.G. JAZZ CONCERT NO. 2** (Philips BBE-12132) [EP]	30		
3	Lionel Hampton & His Orch. - **APOLLO HALL CONCERT 1954** (Philips BBL-7015) [LP]			
5	De Castro Sisters - **Teach Me Tonight** (London HL-8104)	★		
5	Peggy Lee - **Let Me Go, Lover** (Brunswick 05360)	18	24	17
5	Paul Quinichette, Benny Green, Frank Foster, Joseph Newman, Hank Jones, Kenny Clarke, Eddie Jones and Sir Jonathan Gasser - **JAZZ STUDIO 1** (Brunswick LAT-8036) [LP]			
8	Four Aces - **It's A Woman's World** (Brunswick 05348)	4		
9	Nat 'King' Cole - **Unbelievable** / **Hajji Baba** (Capitol CL-14155)			
10	Bob Cooper Sextet - **KENTON PRESENTS JAZZ – BOB COOPER** (Capitol KPL-102) [LP]			
10	Ted Heath & His Music - **In The Mood (For Mambo)** (Decca F-10447)	24	29	
10	Stan Kenton & His Orch. - **KENTON SHOWCASE: THE MUSIC OF BILL RUSSO / THE MUSIC OF BILL HOLMAN** (Capitol LCT-6009) [LP]			
13	Saints Jazz Band - **When The Saints Go Marching In** (Parlophone R-3544)			
14	Kathleen Ferrier - **What Is Life? (Che Faro?)** (Decca K-1466)			
14	Howard Keel and Brothers - **Sobbin' Women** (M.G.M. MGM-787)	21		
14	Gerry Mulligan Quartet - **Nights At The Turntable** (Vogue V-2157)			
17	Nat 'King' Cole - **A Blossom Fell** (Capitol CL-14235)		3	★
17	Mantovani & His Orch. - **Lonely Ballerina** / **Lazy Gondolier** (Decca F-10395)	★		
17	Howard Rumsey's Lighthouse All Stars - **HOWARD RUMSEY'S LIGHTHOUSE ALL STARS (VOL. 1)** (Vogue EPV-1004) [EP]	16	36	
17	The Two Bills from Bermondsey - **What A Mouth, What A Mouth** / **Cockney Capers** [M] (Parlophone R-3953)	7	10	8
21	Earl Bostic & His Orch. - **Flamingo** (Vogue V-2145)			
21	Duke Ellington - **ELLINGTON '55** (Capitol LCT-6008) [LP]			
21	Benny Goodman - **CARNEGIE HALL JAZZ CONCERT** (Philips BBL-7001) [LP]			
21	Ray Martin & His Concert Orch. - **It's A Woman's World** / **The Gentle Sex** (Columbia DB-3557)	7	15	10
21	Gerry Mulligan Quartet with Lee Konitz - **THE GERRY MULLIGAN QUARTET (VOL. 3)** (Vogue EPV-1023) [EP]	13		
21	Frank Weir & His Saxophone - **Theme from 'Journey Into Space'** (Decca F-10435)	16		
27	Don Cornell - **S'posin'** (Vogue Coral Q-2037)	7	10	
27	Eartha Kitt - **Monotonous** (H.M.V. B-10803)	21	29	22
27	Gerry Mulligan Quartet - **THE GERRY MULLIGAN QUARTET** (Vogue EPV-1200) [EP]			
27	Kid Ory's Creole Jazz Band - **Maryland, My Maryland** (Good Time Jazz GV-2186)		36	
27	Frank Sinatra - **SWING EASY!** (Capitol LC-6689) [LP] †			
27	Joan Weber - **Let Me Go Lover** (Philips PB-389)	★		
33	Benny Goodman - **SESSION FOR SEXTET NO. 2** (Columbia 33SX-1035) [LP]			
33	Humphrey Lyttelton & His Band - **HUMPH AT THE CONWAY** (Parlophone PMC-1012) [LP]			
33	Kid Ory & His Creole Jazz Band - **Tiger Rag** (Vogue V-2011)			
33	Robert Wilson with Jimmy Shand & His Band - **The Northern Lights Of Aberdeen** (H.M.V. B-10521)	30		

† This 10" LP bubbled under for five weeks in December, January and February. It eventually charted in October 1960 after being reissued in 12" format, with additional tracks.

5	<<< FEBRUARY 1955 >>>	12	19	26
37	Les Brown & His Band of Renown - **CONCERT AT THE LONDON PALLADIUM (VOL. 2)** *(Vogue Coral LVA-9002)* 🄻🄿			
37	Deep River Boys - **Shake, Rattle And Roll** *(H.M.V. B-10790)*			
37	Judy Garland - **It's A New World** *(Philips PB-394)*	21	15	3
37	Dean Martin - **One More Time** *(Capitol CL-14180)*			
37	Gerry Mulligan Quartet - **Bark For Barksdale** *(Vogue V-2260)*			
42	Eric Delaney & His Band - **Oranges And Lemons / Delaney's Delight** *(Mercury MB-3143)*	11	8	26
42	Modernaires - **New Juke Box Saturday Night** *(Vogue Coral Q-2035)*	24	29	22
42	Bud Powell Trio - **THE AMAZING BUD POWELL TRIO** *(Vogue EPV-1030)* 🄴🄿		20	
42	Ronnie Scott Orchestra - **Perdido** *(Esquire 10-391)*			
42	Sarah Vaughan - **Make Yourself Comfortable** *(Mercury MB-3180)*			12
47	Kirchin Band - **Mambo Macoco** *(Parlophone R-3958)*			
47	Eartha Kitt - **Santa Baby** *(H.M.V. B-10728)*			
47	Guy Mitchell - **Gee, But Ya Gotta Come Home** *(Philips PB-387)*			
47	Kirk Stevens - **Here's To The Gordons** *(Parlophone R-3963)*	5	9	10
47	Hugo Winterhalter's Orchestra & Chorus - **Song Of The Barefoot Contessa** *(H.M.V. B-10791)*	13	6	21
52	Charlie Kunz - **Piano Medley No. 115 [M]** *(Decca F-10441)*	34		
52	George Lewis & His New Orleans Stompers - **Fidgety Feet** *(Vogue V-2054)*			
52	Stargazers - **Somebody / No More** *(Decca F-10437)*	24	34	12
52	Wally Stott Orchestra - **The Cat From Coos Bay** *(Philips PB-351)*			
56	Eric Delaney & His Band - **Truckin'** *(Mercury MB-3168)*			
56	Coleman Hawkins & His Orch. - **COLEMAN HAWKINS** *(Vogue EPV-1021)* 🄴🄿			
56	Mario Lanza - **SONGS FROM THE STUDENT PRINCE AND OTHER FAMOUS MELODIES** *(H.M.V. ALP-1186)* 🄻🄿			
56	George Lewis & His New Orleans Music - **Mama Don't Allow It** *(Good Time Jazz GV-2253)*			
56	Al Martino - **Don't Go To Strangers** *(Capitol CL-14224)*		36	26
56	Patrick O'Hagan - **The Whistling Gypsy** *(Decca (Irish Series) F-18184)*	30	24	26
56	Oscar Peterson Trio - **OSCAR PETERSON PLAYS TENDERLY AND C JAM BLUES** *(H.M.V. 7EG-8635)* 🄴🄿			
56	Joan Regan - **Prize Of Gold / When You're In Love** *(Decca F-10432)*	18	28	12
	Alma Cogan - **The Naughty Lady Of Shady Lane / Mambo Italiano** *(H.M.V. B-10832)*	1	★	
	Chris Barber's Jazz Band - **CHRIS BARBER PLAYS SPIRITUALS** *(Columbia SEG-7568)* 🄴🄿	5	1	
	Kirchin Band - **Minor Mambo** *(Decca F-10434)*	7	36	17
	Boy Scout Association - **Boy Scout** *(Philips PB-151)*	11		
	Humphrey Lyttelton & His Band - **Ace In The Hole / Coffee Grinder** *(Parlophone R-3967)*	13		

5 **<<< FEBRUARY 1955 >>>**	**12**	**19**	**26**
Julian Slade - **Music from 'Salad Days' [M]** *(Parlophone R-3927)*	18		
Petula Clark - **Majorca** *(Polygon P-1146)*	24	★	
Judy Garland - **A STAR IS BORN [OST]** *(Philips BBL-7007)* **LP**	24		
Johnston Brothers - **Majorca** *(Decca F-10451)*	24	10	6
Nat 'King' Cole - **Teach Me Tonight** *(Capitol CL-14207)*	30		
Judy Garland - **The Man That Got Away** *(Philips PB-366)*	34	26	
Frankie Laine - **In The Beginning** *(Philips PB-404)*		1	1
Alma Cogan - **Softly, Softly / Paper Kisses** *(H.M.V. B-10828)*		4	6
Johnny Brandon - **Tomorrow** *(Polygon P-1131)*		6	5
Archie Bleyer & His Orch. - **The Naughty Lady Of Shady Lane** *(London HL-8111)*		10	12
Billy Eckstine - **Beloved** *(M.G.M. MGM-776)*		10	
Chet Baker Quartet - **CHET BAKER QUARTET** *(Vogue EPV-1007)* **EP**		15	
Beverley Sisters - **The Naughty Lady Of Shady Lane** *(Philips PB-395)*		15	
George Melly with Alex Welsh & His Dixielanders - **Frankie And Johnny** *(Decca F-10457)*		15	22
Ronnie Harris - **I Still Believe** *(Columbia DB-3529)*		20	
Humphrey Lyttelton & His Band - **Mezzy's Tune** *(Parlophone R-3917)*		20	
Oscar Peterson with Ray Brown - **Tenderly** *(Columbia LB-150)*		20	
Patti Page - **Let Me Go, Lover** *(Mercury MB-3182)*		26	
Doris Day - **Ready, Willing And Able / You My Love** *(Philips PB-402)*		29	2
Roland Shaw Orchestra - **Softly, Softly** *(Decca F-10449)*		29	17
Anthony Steel with the Radio Revellers - **The Flame** *(Polygon P-1154)*		34	
Jeff Chandler - **Always** *(Brunswick 05380)*		36	
Eddie Fisher - **Wedding Bells / A Man Chases A Girl** *(H.M.V. B-10839)*		36	
Kirchin Band - **Lester Leaps The Mambo / Lanigiro** *(Parlophone R-3985)*		36	8
Vera Lynn with the Johnston Brothers - **Addio Amore** *(Decca F-10463)*		36	
Frank Sinatra - **You My Love / Just One Of Those Things** *(Capitol CL-14240)*			3
Ronnie Harris, Diana Decker, Ray Burns and Ruby Murray - **Goin' Co'tin'** *(Columbia DB-3567)*			12
Winifred Atwell - **The Black Mask Waltz / Song Of The Sea** *(Decca F-10448)*			17
Philip Green & His Orch. - **Song Of The Barefoot Contessa** *(Parlophone R-3956)*			22

5		12	19	26
★	Stargazers - **Somebody / No More** (Decca F-10437)			
1	Frankie Laine - **In The Beginning** (Philips PB-404)	★		
2	Johnnie Ray - **If You Believe** (Philips PB-379)	★		
3	Johnny Brandon - **Tomorrow** (Polygon P-1131)	★		
4	Joan Regan - **Prize Of Gold / When You're In Love** (Decca F-10432)	1	2	★
5	OST - **SEVEN BRIDES FOR SEVEN BROTHERS (PART 1)** (M.G.M. MGM-EP-513) **EP**	5	9	8
6	Ronnie Harris, Diana Decker, Ray Burns and Ruby Murray - **Goin' Co'tin'** (Columbia DB-3567)			
6	OLC - **SALAD DAYS** (Oriole MG-20004) **LP**			
6	Kirk Stevens - **Here's To The Gordons** (Parlophone R-3963)	7	11	29
9	Humphrey Lyttelton & His Band - **Coffee Grinder / Ace In The Hole** (Parlophone R-3967)		27	21
10	Bill Haley & His Comets - **Dim, Dim The Lights** (Brunswick 05373)		8	23
10	Eartha Kitt - **Monotonous** (H.M.V. B-10803)			
10	Robert Wilson with Jimmy Shand & His Band - **The Northern Lights Of Aberdeen** (H.M.V. B-10521)			
13	Johnston Brothers - **Majorca** (Decca F-10451)	3	15	17
13	Howard Keel - **Bless Yore Beautiful Hide** (M.G.M. MGM-785)			
15	Nat 'King' Cole - **Hajji Baba** (Capitol CL-14155)	18		
15	Nat 'King' Cole - **Teach Me Tonight** (Capitol CL-14207)			
15	Modernaires - **New Juke Box Saturday Night** (Vogue Coral Q-2035)			
18	Petula Clark - **Somebody** (Polygon P-1128)		16	
18	Howard Keel and Brothers - **Sobbin' Women** (M.G.M. MGM-787)	2	2	14
20	Max Bygraves - **Tomorrow** (H.M.V. B-10842)	14	21	11
20	Alma Cogan - **Softly, Softly / Paper Kisses** (H.M.V. B-10828)	18	9	10
20	Judy Garland - **It's A New World / Gotta Have Me Go With You** (Philips PB-394)		12	13
20	Ray Martin & His Concert Orch. - **It's A Woman's World / The Gentle Sex** (Columbia DB-3557)	12		
20	Frank Sinatra - **YOUNG AT HEART [OST]** (Philips BBR-8040) **LP**			
20	Frank Sinatra - **You My Love / Just One Of Those Things** (Capitol CL-14240)			
20	Sarah Vaughan - **Make Yourself Comfortable** (Mercury MB-3180)	12		
27	Dean Martin - **One More Time** (Capitol CL-14180)			
27	McGuire Sisters - **Sincerely / No More** (Vogue Coral Q-72050)	14	7	24
27	Gerry Mulligan Quartet with Lee Konitz - **Lady Be Good** (Vogue V-2305)			
	Kay Starr - **If Anyone Finds This, I Love You** (H.M.V. B-10837)	4	4	5
	Doris Day - **Ready, Willing And Able / You My Love** (Philips PB-402)	6	12	4
	Eddie Fisher - **Wedding Bells / A Man Chases A Girl** (H.M.V. B-10839)	8	★	
	Les Paul & Mary Ford - **Mister Sandman** (Capitol CL-14212)	8		

5	**<<< MARCH 1955 >>>**	**12**	**19**	**26**

	12	19	26
Don Cornell - **No Man Is An Island** (*Vogue Coral Q-72058*)	10	1	15
Eartha Kitt - **Under The Bridges Of Paris** (*H.M.V. B-10647*)	10	14	21
Eric Delaney & His Band - **Oranges And Lemons** (*Mercury MB-3143*)	14		
Tennessee Ernie Ford - **Kiss Me Big** (*Capitol CL-14006*)	14		
Kid Ory & His Creole Jazz Band - **Tiger Rag** (*Vogue V-2011*)	18		
Frankie Vaughan - **Too Many Heartaches** (*H.M.V. B-10845*)	18	17	
Eddie Calvert - **Cherry Pink (And Apple Blossom White)** (*Columbia DB-3581*)		4	1
Perry Como - **Ko Ko Mo** (*H.M.V. B-10841*)		6	3
Peggy Lee - **Apples, Peaches And Cherries** (*Brunswick 05221*)		17	
Jo Stafford and Frankie Laine - **High Society** (*Philips PB-417*)		17	17
Eric Winstone & His Orch. - **Fanfare Boogie** (*Polygon P-1153*)		17	
Winifred Atwell - **Song Of The Sea** (*Decca F-10448*)		21	33
Big Ben Banjo Band - **There's No Business Like Show Business [M]** (*Columbia DB-3584*)		21	
Tony Brent - **When I Leave The World Behind** (*Columbia DB-3428*)		24	24
Vera Lynn with the Johnston Brothers - **Addio Amore** (*Decca F-10463*)		24	29
Dean Martin - **Under The Bridges Of Paris** (*Capitol CL-14255*)		24	5
Oscar Peterson with Ray Brown - **Tenderly** (*Columbia LB-150*)		27	29
Jane Powell and Howard Keel - **When You're In Love** (*M.G.M. MGM-788*)		27	
Hugo Winterhalter's Orchestra & Chorus - **Song Of The Barefoot Contessa** (*H.M.V. B-10791*)		27	
Bill Haley & His Comets - **Mambo Rock** (*Brunswick 05405*)			2
Judy Garland - **The Man That Got Away** (*Philips PB-366*)			7
Charlie Kunz - **Piano Medley No. 116 [M]** (*Decca F-10481*)			8
Four Aces - **There Goes My Heart** (*Brunswick 05401*)			11
Ottilie Patterson with Chris Barber's Jazz Band - **Reckless Blues** (*Decca Jazz F-10472*)			15
Crew-Cuts - **Earth Angel** / **Ko Ko Mo** (*Mercury MB-3202*)			17
Frankie Vaughan - **Tweedle-Dee** / **Give Me The Moonlight, Give Me The Girl** (*Philips PB-423*)			17
Billie Anthony - **Tweedle Dee** (*Columbia DB-3592*)			24
Kathy Lloyd - **Unsuspecting Heart** (*Decca F-10464*)			24
Slim Whitman - **Cattle Call** (*London HL-8125*)			24
Sammy Davis Jr. - **The Birth Of The Blues** (*Brunswick 05383*)			29
Ronnie Harris - **I Still Believe** (*Columbia DB-3529*)			33
Wynonie Harris - **Bloodshot Eyes** (*Vogue V-2127*)			33
Humphrey Lyttelton & His Band - **DELVING BACK WITH HUMPH** (*Esquire 32-007*) **LP**			33

2		9	16	23	30
★	Bill Haley & His Comets - **Mambo Rock** (Brunswick 05405)				
★	Eartha Kitt - **Under The Bridges Of Paris** (H.M.V. B-10647)				
★	Dean Martin - **Under The Bridges Of Paris** (Capitol CL-14255)				
★	McGuire Sisters - **Sincerely / No More** (Vogue Coral Q-72050)				
1	Eddie Calvert - **Cherry Pink (And Apple Blossom White)** (Columbia DB-3581)	★			
2	Kay Starr - **If Anyone Finds This, I Love You** (H.M.V. B-10837)	17	2	12	
3	Perry Como - **Ko Ko Mo** (H.M.V. B-10841)	3	3		10
4	Judy Garland - **The Man That Got Away** (Philips PB-366)	4	5	1	
5	Crew-Cuts - **Earth Angel / Ko Ko Mo** (Mercury MB-3202)	1	★		
6	Frankie Vaughan - **Tweedlee-Dee / Give Me The Moonlight, Give Me The Girl** (Philips PB-423)	8	13	★	
7	Doris Day - **Ready, Willing And Able / You My Love** (Philips PB-402)	★			
8	Chris Barber's Jazz Band - **Bobby Shafto** (Decca Jazz F-10492)			7	
9	Fontane Sisters - **Hearts Of Stone** (London HL-8113)	2	8		16
9	Four Aces - **There Goes My Heart** (Brunswick 05401)	12	8	17	28
9	Bill Haley & His Comets - **Dim, Dim The Lights** (Brunswick 05373)				21
9	Kirk Stevens - **Here's To The Gordons** (Parlophone R-3963)		19		
13	Ottilie Patterson with Chris Barber's Jazz Band - **Reckless Blues** (Decca Jazz F-10472)				
13	Bill Haley & His Comets - **Crazy Man, Crazy** (London L-1190)	12			
15	Nat 'King' Cole - **Papa Loves Mambo** (Capitol CL-14207)				
15	Judy Garland - **A STAR IS BORN [OST]** (Philips BBL-7007) LP	25			
15	OBC - **WONDERFUL TOWN** (Brunswick LAT-8058) LP				
18	Don Cornell - **No Man Is An Island** (Vogue Coral Q-72058)	17			
18	Sammy Davis Jr. - **Six Bridges To Cross** (Brunswick 05389)	25			
18	Glenn Miller & His Orch. - **THE GLENN MILLER STORY [OST]** (H.M.V. DLP-1024) LP				
18	OST - **CARMEN JONES** (H.M.V. CLP-1034) LP	8	11	4	11
18	Philharmonia Orchestra, *cond.* Herbert von Karajan - **TCHAIKOVSKY – SYMPHONY NO. 4** (Columbia 33CX-1139) LP				
23	Tony Brent - **When I Leave The World Behind** (Columbia DB-3428)				
23	Johnston Brothers - **Majorca** (Decca F-10451)	12			
	Xavier Cugat & His Orch. - **Cherry Pink And Apple Blossom White** (Philips PB-413)	4			21
	Tony Bennett - **Stranger In Paradise** (Philips PB-420)	6	★		
	Tony Martin - **Stranger In Paradise** (H.M.V. B-10849)	7	1	★	
	Georgia Gibbs - **Tweedle Dee** (Mercury MB-3196)	8	★		
	Charlie Kunz - **Piano Medley No. 116 [M]** (Decca F-10481)	8			
	Bonnie Lou - **A Rusty Old Halo** (Parlophone R-4012)	12			
	Frank Sinatra - **You My Love / Just One Of Those Things** (Capitol CL-14240)	12	16	2	1
	Max Bygraves - **Tomorrow** (H.M.V. B-10842)	17	7		20
	Billy Eckstine - **What More Is There To Say** (M.G.M. MGM-809)	17	13	12	14
	Jane Froman - **I Wonder** (Capitol CL-14254)	17	26		
	Hallé Orchestra, *cond.* Sir John Barbirolli - **RIMSKY-KORSAKOV – CAPRICCIO ESPAGNOL** (H.M.V. BLP-1058) LP	17			
	Joni James - **How Important Can It Be?** (M.G.M. MGM-811)	17	22		16
	Dinah Shore and Tony Martin - **Melody Of Love** (H.M.V. B-10831)	17			
	Mario Lanza - **SONGS FROM THE STUDENT PRINCE AND OTHER FAMOUS MELODIES** (H.M.V. ALP-1186) LP	25			
	Kid Ory's Creole Jazz Band - **KID ORY'S CREOLE JAZZ BAND** (Tempo EXA-5) EP	25			
	Sarah Vaughan - **How Important Can It Be?** (Mercury MB-3205)	25	13		5
	Eric Delaney & His Band - **Roamin' In The Gloamin' / Ting-A-Ling** (Mercury MB-3213)	30	22	17	21
	Frank Chacksfield & His Orch. - **Blue Mirage** (Decca F-10467)	30			

Artist / Title	9	16	23	30
Howard Keel and Brothers - **Sobbin' Women** (M.G.M. MGM-787)	30	22	17	
Jane Powell and Howard Keel - **When You're In Love** /		4		2
Brothers & Girls - **Spring, Spring, Spring** (M.G.M. MGM-788)				
Bing Crosby - **Stranger In Paradise** (Brunswick 05410)		6	5	★
Nat 'King' Cole - **The Sand And The Sea** (Capitol CL-14251)		10	12	5
Mantovani & His Orch. - **Softly, Softly** (Decca F-10468)		11		
Dean Martin - **One More Time** (Capitol CL-14180)		16		
Don Cornell - **Stranger In Paradise** (Vogue Coral Q-72073)		18	★	
Vera Lynn - **Two Easter Sunday Sweethearts** (Decca F-10253)		19		
OLC - **SALAD DAYS** (Oriole MG-20004) 🄻🄿		19	5	
Eric Delaney & His Band - **Oranges And Lemons / Delaney's Delight** (Mercury MB-3143)		22		
Hutton Sisters - **Ko Ko Mo** (Capitol CL-14250)		22		
Danny Purches - **A Rusty Old Halo** (Columbia DB-3604)		22		
Jimmy Shand & His Band - **Victory Waltz [M]** (Parlophone F-3500)			3	5
Charms - **Hearts Of Stone** (Parlophone R-3988)			7	
Rosemary Clooney - **Where Will The Dimple Be?** (Philips PB-428)			9	9
Four Aces - **It's A Woman's World** (Brunswick 05348)			9	
Vera Lynn with the Johnston Brothers - **Addio Amore** (Decca F-10463)			9	
Tony Brent and Anne Warren - **Open Up Your Heart** (Columbia DB-3579)			12	
Ink Spots - **Melody Of Love** (Parlophone R-3977)			12	★
Ronnie Harris - **Stranger In Paradise / I Wonder** (Columbia DB-3595)			17	
Johnnie Ray - **Paths Of Paradise** (Philips PB-441)			17	13
Gail and Rosemary Clooney - **Open Up Your Heart** (Philips PB-409)			23	
Four Aces - **Stranger In Paradise** (Brunswick 05418)			23	16
Charlie McGee - **Between You And Me** (Glenside W-183)			23	
Alma Cogan - **Tweedle-Dee** (H.M.V. B-10848)			26	3
Marie Benson - **Our Old Pi-anna** (Philips PB-431)			26	28
Johnston Brothers - **The Right To Be Wrong** (Decca F-10490)			26	
OST - **SEVEN BRIDES FOR SEVEN BROTHERS (PART 1)** (M.G.M. MGM-EP-513) 🄴🄿			26	21
Edmundo Ros & His Orch. - **Cherry Pink And Apple Blossom White / Olé Mambo** (Decca F-10480)			26	
Dickie Valentine - **HERE IS DICKIE VALENTINE** (Decca LF-1211) 🄻🄿			26	
Al Hibbler - **Unchained Melody** (Brunswick 05420)				3
Eddie Calvert - **Stranger In Paradise** (Columbia DB-3594)				5
Tony Brent - **How Important Can It Be?** (Columbia DB-3610)				11
OBC - **KISMET** (Philips BBL-7023) 🄻🄿				14
Earl Bostic & His Orch. - **Deep Purple** (Parlophone R-3838)				16
Jerry Colonna - **Let Me Go, Lover** (Parlophone R-4007)				21
Mitchell Torok - **Caribbean** (London HL-8004)				21
Jimmy Young - **Unchained Melody** (Decca F-10502)				21
Cowboy Church Sunday School - **Open Up Your Heart** (Brunswick 05371)				28
Percy Faith & His Orch. - **Blue Mirage** (Philips PB-415)				28
Mel Gaynor - **How Important Can It Be?** (Decca F-10497)				28
Howard Keel - **Bless Yore Beautiful Hide** / Jane Powell - **Wonderful, Wonderful Day** (M.G.M. MGM-785)				28
Ruby Murray, Ray Burns, Diana Decker and Ronnie Harris - **Spring, Spring, Spring** / Ronnie Harris, Diana Decker, Ray Burns and Ruby Murray - **Goin' Co'tin'** (Columbia DB-3567)				28
David Whitfield - **Ev'rywhere / Mama** (Decca F-10515)				28

7		14	21	28
★	Frank Sinatra - **You My Love / Just One Of Those Things** (Capitol CL-14240)			
★	Jimmy Young - **Unchained Melody** (Decca F-10502)			
1	Al Hibbler - **Unchained Melody** (Brunswick 05420)	★		
2	OST - **CARMEN JONES** (H.M.V. CLP-1034) **LP**			24
3	David Whitfield - **Ev'rywhere / Mama** (Decca F-10515)	10	6	★
4	Jimmy Shand & His Band - **Victory Waltz [M]** (Parlophone F-3500)	8	9	24
5	Tony Brent - **How Important Can It Be?** (Columbia DB-3610)	10	26	12
5	Eddie Calvert - **Stranger In Paradise** (Columbia DB-3594)	★		
5	Dickie Valentine - **I Wonder** (Decca F-10493)		17	12
8	OBC - **KISMET** (Philips BBL-7023) **LP**	3	2	8
9	Les Baxter & His Orch. - **Unchained Melody / The Medic Theme** (Capitol CL-14257)	★		
10	OLC - **SALAD DAYS** (Oriole MG-20004) **LP**	5	4	12
10	Jane Powell and Howard Keel - **When You're In Love** / Brothers & Girls - **Spring, Spring, Spring** (M.G.M. MGM-788)			
12	Johnnie Ray - **Paths Of Paradise** (Philips PB-441)	8	★	
13	Fontane Sisters - **Hearts Of Stone** (London HL-8113)			
13	Howard Keel and Brothers - **Sobbin' Women** (M.G.M. MGM-787)		13	6
13	Mario Lanza and Elizabeth Doubleday - **Summertime In Heidelberg** (H.M.V. DA-2070)			
16	Earl Bostic & His Orch. - **Melody Of Love** (Parlophone R-4003)			
16	Alma Cogan - **Tweedle-Dee** (H.M.V. B-10848)	18		36
16	Alma Cogan - **Chee-Chee-Oo-Chee / Tika Tika Tok** (H.M.V. B-10862)	20	15	19
16	Doris Day - **Hold Me In Your Arms** (Philips PB-401)			
16	Ruby Murray, Ray Burns, Diana Decker and Ronnie Harris - **Spring, Spring, Spring** / Ronnie Harris, Diana Decker, Ray Burns and Ruby Murray - **Goin' Co'tin'** (Columbia DB-3567)	30		
16	Cyril Stapleton & His Orch. - **Elephant Tango** (Decca F-10488)	30	20	★
16	Mitchell Torok - **Caribbean** (London HL-8004)	20	20	24
16	Sarah Vaughan - **How Important Can It Be?** (Mercury MB-3205)			
24	Eric Delaney & His Band - **Roamin' In The Gloamin' / Ting-A-Ling** (Mercury MB-3213)	30	26	30
24	Joni James - **How Important Can It Be?** (M.G.M. MGM-811)		26	
26	Jane Froman - **I Wonder** (Capitol CL-14254)	5	9	36
26	Joe 'Mr. Piano' Henderson - **Sing It With Joe [M]** (Polygon P-1167)	10	6	1
28	Jerry Colonna - **Let Me Go Lover** (Parlophone R-4007)			12
28	Humphrey Lyttelton & His Band - **When The Saints Go Marching In** (Tempo A-10)			

	14	21	28
28 Johnny Maddox - **Crazy Otto Medley [M]** (London HL-8134)			
28 Sauter–Finegan Orchestra - **Eddie And The Witchdoctor** (H.M.V. B-10818)			
28 Frankie Vaughan - **Unsuspecting Heart** (H.M.V. B-10845)			
28 Sarah Vaughan - **And This Is My Beloved** (Mercury MB-3210)	15	9	
Johnnie Ray - **Flip, Flop And Fly** (Philips PB-449)	1	1	4
Four Aces - **Stranger In Paradise** (Brunswick 05418)	2	★	
Stargazers - **The Crazy Otto Rag** (Decca F-10523)	3	9	2
Xavier Cugat & His Orch. - **Cherry Pink And Apple Blossom White** (Philips PB-413)	5	26	30
Rosemary Clooney - **Where Will The Dimple Be?** (Philips PB-428)	10	★	
Eartha Kitt - **The Heel** (H.M.V. B-10854)	10		
Big Ben Banjo Band with the Coronets - **The Crazy Otto Rag** (Columbia DB-3620)	15	5	3
Johnnie Ray - **AT THE LONDON PALLADIUM** (Philips BBR-8001) 🅛🅟	15		
Ruby Murray - **Evermore** (Columbia DB-3617)	18	2	19
Marie Benson - **Our Old Pi-anna** (Philips PB-431)	20		
Alma Cogan - **Dreamboat** (H.M.V. B-10872)	20	17	★
Billy Eckstine - **What More Is There To Say** (M.G.M. MGM-809)	20		
Ella Fitzgerald - **Lullaby Of Birdland** (Brunswick 05392)	20	20	19
Johnnie Ray - **Destiny** (Philips PB-301)	20		
Sammy Davis Jr. - **Because Of You** (Brunswick 05326)	27	26	30
Johnston Brothers - **Chee Chee-oo Chee** (Decca F-10513)	27		
Suzi Miller and the Johnston Brothers - **Dance With Me Henry (Wallflower)** (Decca F-10512)	27		8
Kid Ory & His Creole Jazz Band - **KID ORY AND HIS CREOLE JAZZ BAND IN CONCERT** (Good Time Jazz EPG-1006) 🅔🅟	33		
Terri Stevens - **Unsuspecting Heart** (Parlophone R-3983)	33		
Lorrae Desmond - **Where Will The Dimple Be** (Decca F-10510)		6	19
Jimmy Shand & His Band - **Royal Scots Polka** (Parlophone F-3501)		13	
5 DeMarco Sisters - **Dreamboat** (Brunswick 05425)		15	8
Tony Bennett - **Close Your Eyes** (Philips PB-445)		17	
Four Aces - **Melody Of Love** (Brunswick 05379)		20	30
Judy Garland - **The Man That Got Away** (Philips PB-366)		20	
Dean Martin and Nat 'King' Cole - **Long, Long Ago** (Capitol CL-14215)		20	8
Max Bygraves - **Tomorrow** (H.M.V. B-10842)		26	
Georgia Gibbs - **Dance With Me Henry (Wallflower)** (Mercury MB-3223)		26	24
McGuire Sisters - **Goodnight Sweetheart, Goodnight** (Vogue Coral Q-2003)		26	
Frank Sinatra - **Learnin' The Blues** (Capitol CL-14296)		26	12
Crew Cuts - **Two Hearts, Two Kisses** (Mercury MB-3222)			5
Petula Clark - **Crazy Otto Rag / The Pendulum Song** (Polygon P-1169)			6
Chris Barber's Jazz Band - **The Martinque / Bobby Shafto** (Decca Jazz F-10492)			12
Cowboy Church Sunday School - **Open Up Your Heart** (Brunswick 05371)			12
Edmundo Ros & His Orch. - **Cherry Pink And Apple Blossom White** (Decca F-10480)			19
Doris Day - **Two Hearts, Two Kisses** (Philips PB-451)			24
Edna Savage - **Evermore** (Parlophone R-4017)			24
Ronnie Harris - **I Wonder** (Columbia DB-3595)			30
Charlie Kunz - **Piano Medley No. 117 [M]** (Decca F-10528)			30
Max Bygraves - **The Pendulum Song** (H.M.V. B-10876)			36
Glenn Miller & His Orch. - **THE GLENN MILLER STORY [OST]** (H.M.V. DLP-1024) 🅛🅟			36

4		11	18	25
★	Joe 'Mr. Piano' Henderson - **Sing It With Joe [M]** *(Polygon P-1167)*			
★	Stargazers - **The Crazy Otto Rag** *(Decca F-10523)*			
★	Dickie Valentine - **I Wonder** *(Decca F-10493)*			
1	5 DeMarco Sisters - **Dreamboat** *(Brunswick 05425)*	1	1	2
2	Big Ben Banjo Band with the Coronets - **The Crazy Otto Rag** *(Columbia DB-3620)*	17	14	7
3	OBC - **KISMET** *(Philips BBL-7023)* 🅛🅟	24	25	17
3	Slim Whitman - **Rose Marie** *(London HL-8061)*	2	3	1
5	Alma Cogan - **Chee-Chee-Oo-Chee / Tika Tika Tok** *(H.M.V. B-10862)*	24	17	22
5	Four Aces - **There Goes My Heart / Take Me In Your Arms** *(Brunswick 05401)*			
5	OLC - **SALAD DAYS** *(Oriole MG-20004)* 🅛🅟	9	14	24
5	Mitchell Torok - **Caribbean** *(London HL-8004)*	7	11	17
9	Four Aces - **Melody Of Love** *(Brunswick 05379)*	9	21	12
9	Georgia Gibbs - **Dance With Me Henry (Wallflower)** *(Mercury MB-3223)*	13	11	17
9	Bobby MacLeod & His Band - **Pride Of Erin Waltz [M]** *(Philips Scottish Series YB-9500)*	3	6	4
9	OST - **CARMEN JONES** *(H.M.V. CLP-1034)* 🅛🅟			
13	Xavier Cugat & His Orch. - **Cherry Pink And Apple Blossom White** *(Philips PB-413)*			
13	Vic Damone - **Hello Mrs. Jones** *(Mercury MB-3219)*			
13	Tennessee Ernie Ford - **Losing You** *(Capitol CL-14273)*		9	
13	Jane Powell and Howard Keel - **When You're In Love** / Brothers & Girls - **Spring, Spring, Spring** *(M.G.M. MGM-788)*			
13	Johnnie Ray - **Flip, Flop And Fly** *(Philips PB-449)*	9		7
18	Doris Day - **Two Hearts, Two Kisses** *(Philips PB-451)*			6
18	Four Aces - **Sluefoot** *(Brunswick 05429)*	8	17	30
18	Jane Froman - **I Wonder** *(Capitol CL-14254)*	24	★	
18	Joni James - **How Important Can It Be?** *(M.G.M. MGM-811)*	31	25	
18	Johnston Brothers - **Chee Chee-oo Chee** *(Decca F-10513)*	17	5	
	Judy Garland - **The Man That Got Away** *(Philips PB-366)*	★		
	Ray Martin & His Concert Orch. - **The Elephants' Tango** *(Columbia DB-3631)*	4	3	5
	Crew-Cuts - **Two Hearts, Two Kisses / Unchained Melody** *(Mercury MB-3222)*	5	6	
	Sammy Davis Jr. - **Because Of You** *(Brunswick 05326)*	5		17
	Ronnie Hilton - **My Loving Hands** *(H.M.V. B-10860)*	9		17
	Tony Brent - **When I Leave The World Behind** *(Columbia DB-3428)*	13	25	
	Petula Clark - **Crazy Otto Rag / The Pendulum Song** *(Polygon P-1169)*	13	11	
	Perry Como - **You'll Always Be My Lifetime Sweetheart** *(H.M.V. B-10841)*	13		
	Barbara Lyon - **Stowaway** *(Columbia DB-3619)*	17	17	★
	Marie Benson - **Our Old Pi-anna** *(Philips PB-431)*	20		
	Jean Campbell - **Dance With Me Henry (The Wallflower)** *(Parlophone R-4026)*	20		

2		9	16	23	30
★	Johnny Brandon - **Don't Worry** *(Polygon P-1163)*				
★	Ruby Murray - **Evermore** *(Columbia DB-3617)*				
★	Malcolm Vaughan - **Ev'ry Day Of My Life** *(H.M.V. B-10874)*				
1	Bill Haley & His Comets - **Sundown Boogie / Green Tree Boogie** *(London HL-8142)*	7	5	8	15
2	Slim Whitman - **Rose Marie** *(London HL-8061)*	1	★		
3	5 DeMarco Sisters - **Dreamboat** *(Brunswick 05425)*	14	5	3	9
4	Bobby MacLeod & His Band - **Pride Of Erin Waltz [M]** / **Irish Military Two-Step [M]** *(Philips Scottish Series YB-9500)*	5	5	10	2
5	Sammy Davis Jr. - **Something's Gotta Give / Love Me Or Leave Me** *(Brunswick 05428)*	6	2	2	★
6	Four Aces - **Melody Of Love** *(Brunswick 05379)*	16			9
7	Big Ben Banjo Band with the Coronets - **The Crazy Otto Rag / Hey Mr. Banjo** *(Columbia DB-3620)*	11			
7	Johnnie Ray - **Taking A Chance On Love** *(Philips PB-463)*	4	4	7	9
9	Crew-Cuts - **Two Hearts, Two Kisses / Unchained Melody** *(Mercury MB-3222)*	9	18		
9	Georgia Gibbs - **Dance With Me Henry (Wallflower)** *(Mercury MB-3223)*	11		15	7
9	Ray Martin & His Concert Orch. - **The Elephants' Tango** *(Columbia DB-3631)*	16	5	8	7
12	Tony Bennett - **Close Your Eyes** *(Philips PB-445)*	24		19	24
13	Tony Brent - **When I Leave The World Behind** *(Columbia DB-3428)*				
14	Eddie Calvert - **John And Julie** *(Columbia DB-3624)*				★
14	Four Lads - **I've Been Thinking** *(Philips PB-440)*	14			
14	Charlie Kunz - **Piano Medley No. 117 [M]** *(Decca F-10528)*				
14	OST - **CARMEN JONES** *(H.M.V. CLP-1034)* 🆲	26			24
18	Alma Cogan - **Chee-Chee-Oo-Chee / Tika Tika Tok** *(H.M.V. B-10862)*				
18	Doris Day - **Two Hearts, Two Kisses** *(Philips PB-451)*	19			17
18	Frank Sinatra - **Learnin' The Blues** *(Capitol CL-14296)*			4	1
21	OBC - **KISMET** *(Philips BBL-7023)* 🆲		23	12	17
21	Mitchell Torok - **Caribbean** *(London HL-8004)*	2	1	6	31
23	Billie Anthony - **Something's Gotta Give / Boom Boom Boomerang** *(Columbia DB-3627)*				
23	Vera Lynn - **Doonaree** *(Decca F-10535)*			19	
23	OLC - **SALAD DAYS** *(Oriole MG-20004)* 🆲			19	22
23	Jimmy Shand & His Band - **Victory Waltz [M]** *(Parlophone F-3500)*	24		25	
23	Slim Whitman - **Indian Love Call / China Doll** *(London L-1149)*		3	1	★
28	Eddie Fisher - **And This Is My Beloved / Just One More Time** *(H.M.V. B-10867)*			12	17
28	Howard Keel and Brothers - **Sobbin' Women** *(M.G.M. MGM-787)*				
28	Suzi Miller and the Johnston Brothers - **Dance With Me Henry (Wallflower)** *(Decca F-10512)*	26			
28	Lennie Niehaus - **VOLUME 1: THE QUINTET** *(Vogue LDC-120)* 🆲				
	Margaret Whiting - **Stow-A-Way** *(Capitol CL-14307)*	2			
	Sammy Davis Jr. - **Because Of You** *(Brunswick 05326)*	8	5	15	15
	Robert Earl - **I Wonder** *(Philips PB-433)*	10			
	Roy Hamilton - **Unchained Melody** *(Philips PB-448)*	11			
	Johnnie Ray - **Flip, Flop And Fly** *(Philips PB-449)*	16			
	Jerry Colonna - **Ebb Tide** *(Brunswick 05243)*	19			

2 <<< JULY 1955 >>>

	9	**16**	**23**	**30**
Johnston Brothers - **Chee Chee-oo Chee** (Decca F-10513)	19	12		
Eartha Kitt - **Santa Baby** (H.M.V. B-10728)	19	14	25	
Slim Whitman - **Roll On Silvery Moon** (London HL-8141)	19	23		
Ray Burns with the Coronets - **That's How A Love Song Was Born** (Columbia DB-3640)	26	14	12	4
Max Bygraves - **The Pendulum Song** (H.M.V. B-10876)	26			
Ferko String Band - **Alabama Jubilee** (London HLF-8140)	26		4	17
Four Aces - **Sluefoot** (Brunswick 05429)		5	10	9
Eartha Kitt and Pérez Prado - **Freddy / Sweet And Gentle** (H.M.V. B-10892)		11		
Lena Horne - **I Love To Love** (H.M.V. B-10869)		13		
Ray Anthony & His Orch. - **Sluefoot** (Capitol CL-14306)		14		24
Tony Brent - **Mirror, Mirror / Love And Kisses** (Columbia DB-3638)		14	15	
Nat 'King' Cole - **I'd Rather Have The Blues** (Capitol CL-14317)		18		
Reginald Dixon - **Dancing At The Tower No. 16 [M]** (Columbia FB-3744)		18		
Tennessee Ernie Ford - **His Hands / I'm A Pilgrim** (Capitol CL-14261)		18		9
Joy Nichols - **Don't Worry** (Mercury MB-3224)		18		
Five Smith Brothers - **I'm In Favour Of Friendship** (Decca F-10527)			★	
Robert Earl - **Three Galleons** (Philips PB-481)			15	
Central Band of the Royal Air Force - **The Dam Busters – March** (H.M.V. B-10877)			19	31
Edmund Hockridge - **Stranger In Paradise** (Parlophone R-4011)			19	
Sonny Terry Trio - **Hootin' Blues** (Parlophone R-3598)			19	24
Earl Bostic & His Orch. - **Night And Day** (Parlophone R-4028)			25	
Ella Fitzgerald - **Lullaby Of Birdland** (Brunswick 05392)			25	31
Joe 'Mr. Piano' Henderson - **Sing It Again With Joe [M]** (Polygon P-1184)				2
Vera Lynn - **Popular Medley No. 4 [M]** (Decca F-10561)				4
Edna Savage - **Evermore** (Parlophone R-4017)				4
Jimmy Shand & His Band - **Gay Gordons [M]** (Parlophone F-3474)				9
Toni Arden - **Beware** (H.M.V. B-10893)				17
Jimmy Durante - **I'm The Guy Who Found The Lost Chord** (M.G.M. MGM-118)				22
Billy Eckstine - **Love Me Or Leave Me** (M.G.M. MGM-841)				24
Ken Griffin - **The Cuckoo Waltz** (Philips PB-471)				24
Charlie Parker - **CHARLIE PARKER (VOL. 1)** (Vogue LDE-004) **LP**				24
Bill Haley & His Comets - **Razzle Dazzle** (Brunswick 05453)				31
Caterina Valente - **My Lonely Lover** (Polydor BM-6001)				31

6		13	20	27
★	Frank Sinatra - **Learnin' The Blues** (Capitol CL-14296)			
1	Joe 'Mr. Piano' Henderson - **Sing It Again With Joe [M]** (Polygon P-1184)	23	5	22
1	Bobby MacLeod & His Band - **Pride Of Erin Waltz [M]** /	8		
	Irish Military Two-Step [M] (Philips Scottish Series YB-9500)			
3	Ray Burns with the Coronets - **That's How A Love Song Was Born**			★
	(Columbia DB-3640)			
3	Vera Lynn - **Popular Medley No. 4 [M]** (Decca F-10561)	3	3	2
3	Edna Savage - **Evermore** (Parlophone R-4017)			
6	Georgia Gibbs - **Dance With Me Henry (Wallflower)** (Mercury MB-3223)			
6	Ray Martin & His Concert Orch. - **The Elephants' Tango** (Columbia DB-3631)	6		
8	5 DeMarco Sisters - **Dreamboat** (Brunswick 05425)			
8	Tennessee Ernie Ford - **His Hands** / **I'm A Pilgrim** (Capitol CL-14261)	6	2	14
8	Four Aces - **Melody Of Love** (Brunswick 05379)			
8	Four Aces - **Sluefoot** (Brunswick 05429)	19	9	
8	Johnnie Ray - **Taking A Chance On Love** (Philips PB-463)	4	16	
8	Jimmy Shand & His Band - **Gay Gordons [M]** (Parlophone F-3474)			
14	Sammy Davis Jr. - **Because Of You** (Brunswick 05326)	12	14	9
14	Bill Haley & His Comets - **Sundown Boogie** / **Green Tree Boogie**			
	(London HL-8142)			
16	Toni Arden - **Beware** (H.M.V. B-10893)			
16	Doris Day - **Two Hearts, Two Kisses** (Philips PB-451)			
16	Ferko String Band - **Alabama Jubilee** (London HLF-8140)	★		
16	Eddie Fisher - **And This Is My Beloved** / **Just One More Time** (H.M.V. B-10867)			
16	OBC - **KISMET** (Philips BBL-7023) 🔲			
21	Jimmy Durante - **I'm The Guy Who Found The Lost Chord** (M.G.M. MGM-118)			
21	OLC - **SALAD DAYS** (Oriole MG-20004) 🔲			
23	Ray Anthony & His Orch. - **Sluefoot** (Capitol CL-14306)	19		
23	Tony Bennett - **Close Your Eyes** (Philips PB-445)	19	19	6
23	Billy Eckstine - **Love Me Or Leave Me** (M.G.M. MGM-841)			
23	Ken Griffin - **The Cuckoo Waltz** (Philips PB-471)			
23	OST - **CARMEN JONES** (H.M.V. CLP-1034) 🔲			
23	Charlie Parker - **CHARLIE PARKER (VOL. 1)** (Vogue LDE-004) 🔲			
23	Sonny Terry Trio - **Hootin' Blues** (Parlophone R-3598)			
30	Central Band of the Royal Air Force - **The Dam Busters – March** (H.M.V. B-10877)		9	14
30	Ella Fitzgerald - **Lullaby Of Birdland** (Brunswick 05392)			
30	Mitchell Torok - **Caribbean** (London HL-8004)		9	4
30	Bill Haley & His Comets - **Razzle Dazzle** / **Two Hound Dogs** (Brunswick 05453)	15	24	
30	Caterina Valente - **My Lonely Lover** (Polydor BM-6001)			
	Frank Sinatra - **Not As A Stranger** (Capitol CL-14326)	1	9	14

6	<<< AUGUST 1955 >>>	13	20	27
Big Ben Banjo Band - **Alabama Jubilee** (Columbia DB-3641)		2	9	24
Slim Whitman - **Roll On Silvery Moon** (London HL-8141)		4	4	2
Tennessee Ernie Ford - **Losing You** (Capitol CL-14273)		8		
Jimmy Shand & His Band - **Victory Waltz [M]** (Parlophone F-3500)		10	16	
Slim Whitman - **Cattle Call** (London HL-8125)		10	5	9
Vera Lynn - **Doonaree** (Decca F-10535)		12	19	
Kid Ory & His Creole Jazz Band - **Tiger Rag** (Vogue V-2011)		12		
Big Ben Banjo Band with the Coronets - **The Crazy Otto Rag** (Columbia DB-3620)		15	5	
Robert Earl - **Three Galleons** (Philips PB-481)		15		18
Slim Whitman - **Danny Boy** (London L-1214)		15		9
Nat 'King' Cole - **My One Sin** (Capitol CL-14327)		19	8	★
Bobby MacLeod & His Band - **Highland Two-Step [M]** (Philips Scottish Series YB-9508)		23		24
David Whitfield - **The Lady** (Decca F-10562)		23	19	4
Guy Mitchell - **Too Late** (Philips PB-487)			1	1
Eric Delaney & His Band - **Oranges And Lemons** (Mercury MB-3143)			14	
Sidney Torch & His Orch. - **The Dam Busters** (Parlophone R-4024)			18	18
Alma Cogan - **Where Will The Dimple Be** (H.M.V. B-10887)			19	
Edna Savage - **Stars Shine In Your Eyes** (Parlophone R-4043)			19	24
Vera Lynn - **Ev'ry Day Of My Life** (Decca F-10566)			24	22
Bill Haley & His Comets - **Farewell, So Long, Goodbye** (London HLF-8161)				6
Lena Horne - **I Love To Love** / **Love Me Or Leave Me** (H.M.V. B-10869)				6
Kirchin Band - **Flying Hickory** (Parlophone R-4039)				9
Dickie Valentine - **No Such Luck** (Decca F-10549)				9
Danny Purches - **Mama** (Columbia DB-3626)				14
Alan Dale - **Sweet And Gentle** (Vogue Coral Q-72089)				18
Kay Starr - **Good And Lonesome** (H.M.V. B-10895)				18
Alma Cogan - **The Banjo's Back In Town** (H.M.V. B-10917)				24
Doris Day - **You Made Me Love You** (Philips PB-489)				24
Lois Winter - **The Breeze And I** (Polygon P-1185)				24

3		10	17	24
★	Joe 'Mr. Piano' Henderson - **Sing It Again With Joe [M]** (*Polygon P-1184*)			
★	Frank Sinatra - **Not As A Stranger** (*Capitol CL-14326*)			
1	Stargazers - **Close The Door** (*Decca F-10594*)	★		
2	Mitchell Torok - **Caribbean** (*London HL-8004*)	2	6	2
3	Tennessee Ernie Ford - **His Hands** / **I'm A Pilgrim** (*Capitol CL-14261*)	8	6	23
3	Guy Mitchell - **Too Late** / **Let Us Be Sweethearts Over Again** (*Philips PB-487*)	1	2	16
5	Crew-Cuts - **Unchained Melody** (*Mercury MB-3222*)			
6	Vera Lynn - **Popular Medley No. 4 [M]** (*Decca F-10561*)	8	6	6
6	David Whitfield - **The Lady** (*Decca F-10562*)	15	17	
8	Ken Colyer's Jazzmen - **Red Wing** (*Decca Jazz F-10565*)		23	11
8	Slim Whitman - **Cattle Call** (*London HL-8125*)	13	23	12
10	Big Ben Banjo Band - **Alabama Jubilee** (*Columbia DB-3641*)	22		
10	Central Band of the Royal Air Force - **The Dam Busters – March** (*H.M.V. B-10877*)	22	6	3
10	Robert Earl - **Three Galleons** (*Philips PB-481*)	10		
13	Alma Cogan - **The Banjo's Back In Town** (*H.M.V. B-10917*)		19	★
13	Doris Day - **Love Me Or Leave Me** (*Philips PB-479*)	★		
13	Vera Lynn - **Ev'ry Day Of My Life** (*Decca F-10566*)			
13	Slim Whitman - **Roll On Silvery Moon** (*London HL-8141*)	5	4	5
17	Kirchin Band - **Flying Hickory** (*Parlophone R-4039*)			
17	Tony Martin, Vic Damone, Russ Tamblyn, Jane Powell, Debbie Reynolds and Ann Miller - **Why, Oh Why?** (*M.G.M. MGM-837*)			
17	Muggsy Spanier's Dixieland Band - **MUGGSY SPANIER'S DIXIELAND BAND** (*Tempo EXA-3*) **EP**			
17	Slim Whitman - **Bandera Waltz** (*London L-1191*)	22		
21	Big Ben Banjo Band with the Coronets - **The Crazy Otto Rag** (*Columbia DB-3620*)			
21	Sammy Davis Jr. - **Because Of You** (*Brunswick 05326*)	11	3	10
21	Kid Ory & His Creole Jazz Band - **Tiger Rag** (*Vogue V-2011*)			
21	Kay Starr - **Good And Lonesome** (*H.M.V. B-10895*)	4	1	4
21	Dickie Valentine - **Lazy Gondolier** / **Hello Mrs. Jones** (*Decca F-10517*)		28	
26	Tony Bennett - **Close Your Eyes** (*Philips PB-445*)	5	★	
26	Alma Cogan - **Give A Fool A Chance** (*H.M.V. B-10896*)			
26	Sammy Davis Jr. - **That Old Black Magic** / **Give A Fool A Chance** (*Brunswick 05450*)	2	5	1
26	John Feeney - **The Soldier's Song** (*Decca (Irish Series) F-12260*)			
26	Bill Haley & His Comets - **Razzle Dazzle** (*Brunswick 05453*)		12	
	Slim Whitman - **Danny Boy** (*London L-1214*)	5	12	
	Doris Day - **LOVE ME OR LEAVE ME [OST]** (*Philips BBL-7047*) **LP**	12		
	Jane Forrest - **Malagueña** (*Columbia DB-3652*)	13		

3   **<<< SEPTEMBER 1955 >>>**   **10 17 24**

	10	17	24
Bowhill Colliery & District Pipe Band - **Selection Of Marches [M]** (Parlophone F-3400)	16		
Doris Day - **You Made Me Love You** (Philips PB-489)	16		
Dutch Swing College Band with Neva Raphaello - **When The Saints Go Marching In** (Philips PB-470)	16	12	
Lena Horne - **I Love To Love / Love Me Or Leave Me** (H.M.V. B-10869)	16		
Frank Sinatra - **SESSION WITH SINATRA** (Capitol EAP1-629) **EP**	16		
Billy Valentine - **It's A Sin** (Capitol CL-14320)	16		
Chordettes - **Humming Bird** (London HLA-8169)	22		7
Ken Colyer's Jazzmen - **The Entertainer / If You Ever Cease To Love** (Decca Jazz F-10519)	22		23
Carmel Quinn - **Doonaree** (Philips PB-474)	22		
Cyril Stapleton & His Orch. - **Blue Star** (Decca F-10559)	22	11	★
Charlie Applewhite - **Blue Star** (Brunswick 05416)		10	★
Eddie Fisher - **Don't Stay Away Too Long** (H.M.V. B-10925)		12	
Ruby Murray - **I'll Come When You Call** (Columbia DB-3643)		12	8
Kid Ory's Creole Jazz Band - **When The Saints Go Marching In / Muskrat Ramble** (Good Time Jazz GV-2322)		17	
Art Mooney & His Orch. - **Honey Babe** (M.G.M. MGM-833)		19	
Sauter–Finegan Orchestra - **Honey Babe** (H.M.V. B-10865)		19	
Slim Whitman - **I'll Never Stop Loving You** (London HLU-8167)		19	13
Humphrey Lyttelton & His Band - **P.T.Q. Rag** (Parlophone R-4060)		23	21
Lita Roza - **The Man In The Raincoat** (Decca F-10541)		23	8
Sidney Torch & His Orch. - **The Dam Busters** (Parlophone R-4024)		23	23
Ronnie Hilton - **The Yellow Rose Of Texas** (H.M.V. B-10924)		28	
Jimmy Shand & His Band - **Victory Waltz [M]** (Parlophone F-3500)		28	23
Billy Cotton & His Band - **Yellow Rose Of Texas** (Decca F-10602)			13
Ray Martin & His Concert Orch. - **Hernando's Hideaway** (Columbia DB-3658)			13
Frankie Laine - **Hummingbird** (Philips PB-498)			16
Barbara Lyon - **Hey There** (Columbia DB-3649)			16
Mitch Miller & His Orch. - **The Yellow Rose Of Texas** (Philips PB-505)			16
Caterina Valente - **Malagueña** (Polydor BM-6006)			16
Faron Young - **Live Fast, Love Hard, Die Young** (Capitol CL-14336)			21
Pat Boone - **Ain't That A Shame** (London HLD-8172)			23
Sammy Davis Jr. - **Hey There** (Brunswick 05469)			23
Norman Granz - **JAM SESSION** (Columbia 33CX-10008) **LP**			23
Frankie Laine - **I'm Gonna Live 'Till I Die** (Mercury MB-2959)			23
Frankie Vaughan - **That's How A Love Song Was Born** (Philips PB-438)			23

1		8	15	22	29
★	Sammy Davis Jr. - **That Old Black Magic** (Brunswick 05450)				
1	Frankie Laine - **Hummingbird** (Philips PB-498)	★			
2	Johnnie Ray - **Hey There / Hernando's Hideaway** (Philips PB-495)	★			
3	Mitch Miller & His Orch. - **The Yellow Rose Of Texas** (Philips PB-505)	★			
4	Robert Earl - **Three Galleons** (Philips PB-481)	15	7		
5	Ruby Murray - **I'll Come When You Call** (Columbia DB-3643)	4	★		
6	Central Band of the Royal Air Force - **The Dam Busters – March** (H.M.V. B-10877)	1	5	★	
7	Ronnie Hilton - **The Yellow Rose Of Texas** (H.M.V. B-10924)	15	★		
8	Doris Day - **I'll Never Stop Loving You** (Philips PB-497)		4	★	
9	Sammy Davis Jr. - **Because Of You** (Brunswick 05326)	15		17	
9	Lita Roza - **Hey There** (Decca F-10611)		★		
11	Mantovani & His Orch. - **Brass Buttons** (Decca F-10601)				
12	Archie Bleyer & His Orch. - **Hernando's Hideaway** (London HLA-8176)	7	9		
13	Mitchell Torok - **Caribbean** (London HL-8004)		17	12	4
14	Michael Holliday - **The Yellow Rose Of Texas** (Columbia DB-3657)	4	11	6	
14	Slim Whitman - **Cattle Call** (London HL-8125)	9	21	3	22
16	Kay Starr - **Good And Lonesome** (H.M.V. B-10895)	9	6	1	9
16	David Whitfield - **I'll Never Stop Loving You / Lady Of Madrid** (Decca F-10596)	20	2	25	1
18	Ray Martin & His Concert Orch. - **Hernando's Hideaway** (Columbia DB-3658)	3	13	7	11
18	Sidney Torch & His Orch. - **The Dam Busters** (Parlophone R-4024)		25		
18	Slim Whitman - **Roll On Silvery Moon** (London HL-8141)				
18	Slim Whitman - **I'll Never Stop Loving You / I'll Never Take You Back Again** (London HLU-8167)			20	15
18	Robert Wilson - **Doonaree** (H.M.V. B-10829)				
23	Bowhill Colliery & District Pipe Band - **Selection Of Marches [M]** (Parlophone F-3400)				
23	Johnston Brothers - **Hernando's Hideaway / Hey There** (Decca F-10608) ★				
23	Barbara Lyon - **Hey There** (Columbia DB-3649)				
23	Guy Mitchell - **Too Late** (Philips PB-487)				
28	Dickie Valentine - **The Engagement Waltz** (Decca F-10549)				
29	Jimmy Shand & His Band - **Victory Waltz [M]** (Parlophone F-3500)		22	10	26
29	Norman Granz - **JAM SESSION** (Columbia 33CX-10008) **LP**		26		26
	Sammy Davis Jr. - **Hey There** (Brunswick 05469)	★			
	Ray Burns - **Blue Star** (Columbia DB-3670)	2	11	12	15
	Caterina Valente - **Malagueña** (Polydor BM-6006)	6	22	12	15
	OBC - **THE PAJAMA GAME** (Philips BBL-7050) **LP**	8	13		
	Johnny Desmond - **The Yellow Rose Of Texas** (Vogue Coral Q-72099)	9	9	4	13
	Billy Cotton & His Band - **Yellow Rose Of Texas** (Decca F-10602)	12	2		15
	Doris Day - **You Made Me Love You** (Philips PB-489)	12			
	Ella Fitzgerald - **Pete Kelly's Blues** (Brunswick 05473)	12	13	11	7
	Vera Lynn - **Popular Medley No. 4 [M]** (Decca F-10561)	15	22	25	
	Bobby MacLeod & His Band - **Pride Of Erin Waltz [M]** / **Irish Military Two-Step [M]** (Philips Scottish Series YB-9500)	15	13		
	Crazy Otto - **Glad Rag Doll** (Polydor BM-6003)	21	19	1	4
	Beverley Sisters - **Humming Bird** (Decca F-10603)	22			
	Big Ben Banjo Band - **Alabama Jubilee** (Columbia DB-3641)	22			37
	Rosemary Clooney - **Go On By** (Philips PB-499)	22	25	25	26
	Gary Miller - **The Yellow Rose Of Texas** (Pye Nixa N.15004)		1	★	
	Les Howard - **Blue Star** (H.M.V. B-10928)		7	4	10
	Lena Horne - **I Love To Love / Love Me Or Leave Me** (H.M.V. B-10869)		17	7	22
	Slim Whitman - **Danny Boy** (London L-1214)		19		
	Chris Barber's Jazz Band - **Precious Lord, Lead Me On / Tiger Rag** (Tempo A-116)		26		
	Johnny Brandon - **Anyone Can Be A Millionaire** (Polygon P-1174)		26		
	Ella Mae Morse - **Seventeen** (Capitol CL-14362)			7	26
	Lonnie Donegan - **BACKSTAIRS SESSION** (Jazz Today JTE-107) **EP**			12	32

3 <<< OCTOBER 1955 >>>   8 15 22 29

	8	15	22	29
Vera Lynn - **Unfaithful You** (Decca F-10622)	12			
Nappy Brown - **Don't Be Angry** (London HL-8145)		17	37	
Frankie Vaughan - **Seventeen** (Philips PB-511)		17	22	
Johnny Brandon - **Home** (Polygon P-1187)		20		
Concert Orchestra, *cond.* Eric Coates - **The Dam Busters March** (Pye Nixa N.15003)		20	15	
Don Lang - **Cloudburst** (H.M.V. POP-115)		20	3	
Mario Lanza - **ROMANCE IN SONG** (H.M.V. 7EB-6025) **EP**		20		
Les Baxter & His Orch. - **Wake The Town And Tell The People** (Capitol CL-14344)		25		
Coronets - **Twenty Tiny Fingers / Meet Me On The Corner** (Columbia DB-3671)		25	37	
Stan Getz - **THE ARTISTRY OF STAN GETZ** (Columbia SEB-10001) **EP**		25		
Faron Young - **Live Fast, Love Hard, Die Young** (Capitol CL-14336)		25	37	
Dick James - **Sing Song Time No. 1 [M]** (Parlophone R-4065)			2	
Boyd Bennett & His Rockets - **Seventeen** (Parlophone R-4063)			4	
Max Bygraves - **Meet Me On The Corner** (H.M.V. POP-116)			7	
Four Aces - **Love Is A Many Splendored Thing** (Brunswick 05480)			11	
Fontane Sisters - **Seventeen** (London HLD-8177)			13	
Billy Cotton & His Band - **The Dam Busters March** (Decca F-10630)			15	
The Singing Dogs - **Pat-A-Cake, Pat-A-Cake – Three Blind Mice – Jingle Bells [M]** (Pye Nixa N.15009)			15	
Stargazers - **Twenty Tiny Fingers** (Decca F-10626)				22
Alma Cogan - **Hernando's Hideaway** (H.M.V. B-10929)				26
Nat 'King' Cole - **Love Is A Many Splendored Thing** (Capitol CL-14364)				26
Ted Heath & His Music - **Cloudburst** (Decca F-10624)				32
Pauline Shepherd - **Have You Ever Been Lonely** (Pye Nixa N.15000)				32
Don Cornell - **Love Is A Many Splendoured Thing** (Vogue Coral Q-72104)				35
Nat Gonella - **Georgia On My Mind** (Decca F-6320)				35
Pat Boone - **Ain't That A Shame** (London HLD-8172)				37
Perry Como - **Tina Marie** (H.M.V. POP-103)				37

NOVEMBER 1955

5		12	19	26
★	Nat 'King' Cole - **Love Is A Many Splendored Thing** (*Capitol CL-14364*)			
★	Billy Cotton & His Band - **The Dam Busters March** (*Decca F-10630*)			
★	Four Aces - **Love Is A Many Splendored Thing** (*Brunswick 05480*)			
★	Don Lang - **Cloudburst** (*H.M.V. POP-115*)			
1	Dick James - **Sing Song Time No. 1 [M]** (*Parlophone R-4065*)	2	2	11
2	Ray Burns - **Blue Star** (*Columbia DB-3670*)	4	6	28
3	Pat Boone - **Ain't That A Shame** (*London HLD-8172*)	★		
4	Coronets - **Twenty Tiny Fingers / Meet Me On The Corner** (*Columbia DB-3671*)	6	34	★
4	David Whitfield - **I'll Never Stop Loving You / Lady Of Madrid** (*Decca F-10596*)	12	30	7
6	Caterina Valente - **Malagueña** (*Polydor BM-6006*)		24	
7	Lena Horne - **I Love To Love / Love Me Or Leave Me** (*H.M.V. B-10869*)	31	7	
7	The Singing Dogs - **Pat-A-Cake, Pat-A-Cake – Three Blind Mice – Jingle Bells [M]** (*Pye Nixa N.15009*)	14	★	
9	Max Bygraves - **Meet Me On The Corner** (*H.M.V. POP-116*)	★		
9	Ray Martin & His Concert Orch. - **Hernando's Hideaway** (*Columbia DB-3658*)		7	7
9	Bobby MacLeod & His Band - **Irish Military Two-Step [M]** (*Philips Scottish Series YB-9500*)			
12	Beverley Sisters - **Humming Bird** (*Decca F-10603*)			
12	Alma Cogan - **Hernando's Hideaway** (*H.M.V. B-10929*)			
12	Crazy Otto - **Glad Rag Doll** (*Polydor BM-6003*)	14	9	17
12	Fontane Sisters - **Seventeen** (*London HLD-8177*)	1	★	
16	Boyd Bennett & His Rockets - **Seventeen** (*Parlophone R-4063*)	14	4	2
16	Nappy Brown - **Don't Be Angry** (*London HL-8145*)	31	12	7
16	Merrill Moore - **Five Foot Two, Eyes Of Blue** (*Capitol CL-14369*)			
16	Mitchell Torok - **Caribbean** (*London HL-8004*)	23	24	5
20	Concert Orchestra, *cond.* Eric Coates - **The Dam Busters March** (*Pye Nixa N.15003*)	14	2	
21	Ted Heath & His Music - **Malagueña / Cloudburst** (*Decca F-10624*)	9	5	42
21	Frank Sinatra - **My Funny Valentine / I Get A Kick Out Of You** (*Capitol CL-14352*)	35		42
21	Sidney Torch & His Orch. - **The Dam Busters** (*Parlophone R-4024*)			
24	Dean Martin and Line Renaud - **Relax-Ay-Voo** (*Capitol CL-14356*)	25	34	15
24	OBC - **THE PAJAMA GAME** (*Philips BBL-7050*) 🎵		18	34
26	Eve Boswell - **Blue Star** (*Parlophone R-4082*)	23	★	
26	Peggy Lee - **He's A Tramp** (*Brunswick 05482*)	6	18	11
26	Stargazers - **Twenty Tiny Fingers** (*Decca F-10626*)	★		
26	Norman Wisdom - **Beware** (*Columbia DB-3654*)			
26	Faron Young - **Live Fast, Love Hard, Die Young** (*Capitol CL-14336*)			
	Ella Fitzgerald - **Pete Kelly's Blues / Hard Hearted Hannah** (*Brunswick 05473*)	2	34	6
	Big Ben Banjo Band - **Let's Get Together Again [M]** (*Columbia DB-3676*)	4	9	3
	Johnny Desmond - **The Yellow Rose Of Texas** (*Vogue Coral Q-72099*)	6	12	42
	Ronnie Hilton - **Hey There!** (*H.M.V. B-10930*)	9		
	Johnston Brothers - **Join In And Sing Again [M]** (*Decca F-10636*)	9	★	
	Will Starr - **Savoy Scottish Medley** (*Parlophone R-4077*)	9	34	34
	Billy Cotton & His Band - **Yellow Rose Of Texas** (*Decca F-10602*)	12	34	28
	Al Martino - **Small Talk** (*Capitol CL-14379*)	14	30	17
	Dickie Valentine - **Christmas Alphabet** (*Decca F-10628*)	14	★	
	David Whitfield - **When You Lose The One You Love** (*Decca F-10627*)	14	★	
	Deep River Boys - **Rock Around The Clock** (*H.M.V. POP-113*)	21	14	1
	Frankie Vaughan - **Seventeen** (*Philips PB-511*)	21		19
	Rosemary Clooney - **Go On By** (*Philips PB-499*)	25	18	
	Eddie Fisher - **Song Of The Dreamer** (*H.M.V. POP-101*)	25		28
	Ella Mae Morse - **Seventeen** (*Capitol CL-14362*)	25	24	
	Edna Savage - **Arrivederci Darling** (*Parlophone R-4097*)	25		
	Slim Whitman - **Song Of The Wild** (*London HLU-8196*)	25	34	7
	Ken Colyer's Jazzmen - **Take This Hammer** (*Decca Jazz F-10631*)	31		
	Peggy Lee - **Sugar** (*Brunswick 05471*)	31		
	Southlanders - **Ain't That A Shame** (*Parlophone R-4069*)	35		
	Kay Starr - **Good And Lonesome** (*H.M.V. B-10895*)	35		

	12	19	26
Petula Clark - **Suddenly There's A Valley** (Pye Nixa N.15013)		1	★
Frankie Laine - **Hawk-Eye** (Philips PB-519)		9	★
Rossano Brazzi - **Summertime In Venice** (H.M.V. B-10920)		14	
Perry Como - **Tina Marie** (H.M.V. POP-103)		14	13
Dennis Hale - **Tina Marie** (Decca F-10623)		14	34
Ferko String Band - **You Are My Sunshine** (London HLF-8183)		18	
Bill Haley & His Comets - **Ten Little Indians** (London HLF-8194)		18	3
Pauline Shepherd - **Have You Ever Been Lonely** (Pye Nixa N.15000)		18	42
Jimmy Shand & His Band - **Victory Waltz [M]** (Parlophone F-3500)		24	28
Jo Stafford - **Suddenly There's A Valley** (Philips PB-509)		24	34
Ginny Wright and Tom Tall - **Are You Mine** (London HL-8150)		24	42
Eartha Kitt - **DOWN TO EARTHA** (H.M.V. DLP-1087) LP		30	19
Lee Lawrence - **Suddenly There's A Valley** (Columbia DB-3681)		30	★
Ray Anthony & His Orch. - **Hernando's Hideaway** (Capitol CL-14354)			13
Harry Secombe - **On With The Motley** (Philips PB-523)			15
Marie Benson - **Twenty Tiny Fingers** (Philips PB-512)			19
Lonnie Donegan - **Rock Island Line** (Decca Jazz F-10647)			19
Les Howard - **Blue Star** (H.M.V. B-10928)			19
David Hughes - **Love Is A Many Splendoured Thing** (Philips PB-508)			19
Julius LaRosa - **Suddenly There's A Valley** (London HLA-8193)			19
Ruby Murray - **The Very First Christmas Of All** (Columbia DB-3680)			19
Frank Sinatra - **In The Wee Small Hours Of The Morning** (Capitol CL-14360)			19
Alma Cogan - **Never Do A Tango With An Eskimo** (H.M.V. POP-129)			28
Betty Miller - **Georgia's Got A Moon** (Pye Nixa N.15008)			28
Lys Assia and the Johnston Brothers - **Arrivederci Darling** (Decca F-10635)			34
Edmund Hockridge - **Hey There!** (H.M.V. POP-131)			34
Vaughn Monroe - **Black Denim Trousers And Motorcycle Boots** (H.M.V. POP-122)			34
Frank Sinatra - **Same Old Saturday Night** (Capitol CL-14373)			34
Frank Sinatra - **MOONLIGHT SINATRA** (H.M.V. 7EG-8128) EP			42

3		10	17	24	31
★	Mitchell Torok - **Caribbean** (London HL-8004)				
★	Frankie Vaughan - **Seventeen** (Philips PB-511)				
1	Julius LaRosa - **Suddenly There's A Valley** (London HLA-8193)	1	★		
2	Deep River Boys - **Rock Around The Clock** (H.M.V. POP-113)	5		4	11
2	Ella Fitzgerald - **Pete Kelly's Blues** / **Hard Hearted Hannah** (Brunswick 05473)	1	13	24	3
2	Harry Secombe - **On With The Motley** (Philips PB-523)	★			
5	Big Ben Banjo Band - **Let's Get Together Again [M]** (Columbia DB-3676)	★			
6	Boyd Bennett & His Rockets - **Seventeen** (Parlophone R-4063)		12	★	
7	Bill Haley & His Comets - **Ten Little Indians** (London HLF-8194)	18			
8	Marie Benson - **Twenty Tiny Fingers** (Philips PB-512)				
8	Nappy Brown - **Don't Be Angry** (London HL-8145)				
10	Dick James - **Sing Song Time No. 1 [M]** (Parlophone R-4065)	8		2	8
10	Dean Martin and Line Renaud - **Relax-Ay-Voo** (Capitol CL-14356)	1	6	12	18
10	Merrill Moore - **Five Foot Two, Eyes Of Blue** (Capitol CL-14369)	10		24	
10	Ginny Wright and Tom Tall - **Are You Mine** (London HL-8150)				
14	Les Howard - **Blue Star** (H.M.V. B-10928)				
14	Ray Martin & His Concert Orch. - **Hernando's Hideaway** (Columbia DB-3658)	8	4	4	3
14	Vaughn Monroe - **Black Denim Trousers And Motorcycle Boots** (H.M.V. POP-122)				
14	Frank Sinatra - **In The Wee Small Hours Of The Morning** (Capitol CL-14360)				
18	Perry Como - **Tina Marie** (H.M.V. POP-103)	1	1	★	
19	Bowhill Colliery & District Pipe Band - **Selection Of Marches [M]** (Parlophone F-3400)				
19	Eddie Fisher - **Song Of The Dreamer** (H.M.V. POP-101)				
19	Ruby Murray - **The Very First Christmas Of All** (Columbia DB-3680)	★			
19	OBC - **THE PAJAMA GAME** (Philips BBL-7050) 🄻🄿	11	13	21	21
19	Joan Regan - **The Rose And The Flame** (Decca F-10598)				
19	Frank Sinatra - **Same Old Saturday Night** (Capitol CL-14373)				
25	Lys Assia and the Johnston Brothers - **Arrivederci Darling** (Decca F-10635)				
25	Johnny Desmond - **The Yellow Rose Of Texas** (Vogue Coral Q-72099)				
25	Eartha Kitt - **DOWN TO EARTHA** (H.M.V. DLP-1087) 🄻🄿				
25	Jimmy Shand & His Band - **Peggy's Love [M]** (Parlophone F-3505)				
29	Alma Cogan - **Hernando's Hideaway** (H.M.V. B-10929)				
29	Concert Orchestra, cond. Eric Coates - **The Dam Busters March** (Pye Nixa N.15003)		1	4	15
29	Will Starr - **Savoy Scottish Medley** (Parlophone R-4077)			12	5
32	Al Martino - **Small Talk** (Capitol CL-14379)				
32	Jimmy Shand & His Band - **Victory Waltz [M]** (Parlophone F-3500)				
32	Pauline Shepherd - **Have You Ever Been Lonely** (Pye Nixa N.15000)				
32	Jo Stafford - **Suddenly There's A Valley** (Philips PB-509)	★			
32	Slim Whitman - **Song Of The Wild** (London HLU-8196)	12	13		
37	Ted Heath & His Music - **Malagueña** / **Cloudburst** (Decca F-10624)	18	17	17	9
37	Vera Lynn - **Unfaithful You** (Decca F-10622)				
37	Slim Whitman - **Cattle Call** (London HL-8125)	12			
	Jimmy Shand & His Band - **Bluebell Polka** (Parlophone F-3436)	6	★		
	Billy Vaughn & His Orch. - **The Shifting Whispering Sands** (London HLD-8205)	7	★		
	Coronets - **Make It A Party [M]** (Columbia DB-3678)	12		26	
	Four Tophatters - **Forty-Five Men In A Telephone Booth** (London HLA-8198)	12			
	Sid Phillips Band - **Pete Kelly's Blues** (H.M.V. POP-125)	12			
	Alma Cogan - **Never Do A Tango With An Eskimo** / **Twenty Tiny Fingers** (H.M.V. POP-125)	17	6	★	
	Doris Day - **Ooh Bang Jiggilly Jang** / **Ol' Saint Nicholas** (Philips PB-532)	18			14
	Ron Goodwin & His Concert Orch. - **Summertime In Venice** (Parlophone R-4041)	18			
	Peggy Lee - **He's A Tramp** (Brunswick 05482)	18			
	Johnny Maddox - **Do, Do, Do** (London HLU-8203)	18			
	Lonnie Donegan - **Rock Island Line** (Decca Jazz F-10647)		1	1	1

291

3	<<< DECEMBER 1955 >>>	10	17	24	31
Joe 'Mr. Piano' Henderson - **Sing It With Joe (Scottish Medley) [M]** / **Sing It With Joe (Irish Medley) [M]** *(Pye Nixa N.15014)*	4	9	16	
McGuire Sisters - **He** / **Christmas Alphabet** *(Vogue Coral Q-72108)*	6			
Crazy Otto - **Glad Rag Doll** *(Polydor BM-6003)*	9	3	9	
Ben Light - **Bring Me A Bluebird** *(H.M.V. POP-147)*	9	12		
Edna Savage - **Arrivederci Darling** *(Parlophone R-4097)*	9	9	2	
751st U.S.A.F. Band - **St. Louis Blues March** *(H.M.V. B-10937)*	13			
Kid Ory's Creole Jazz Band - **KID ORY'S CREOLE JAZZ BAND – 1953 (VOL. 1)** *(Good Time Jazz EPG-1217)* **EP**	17			
Billy's Banjo Band - **Join In The Chorus [M]** *(H.M.V. POP-139)*	19			
Eddie Fisher - **Don't Stay Away Too Long** *(H.M.V. B-10925)*	19			
Bobby MacLeod & His Band - **Irish Military Two-Step [M]** *(Philips Scottish Series YB-9500)*	19	26		
Don Cornell - **Love Is A Many Splendoured Thing** *(Vogue Coral Q-72104)*		4	11	
Dorothy Squires - **When You Lose The One You Love** *(Pye Nixa N.15010)*		4	11	
Rosemary Clooney - **C-H-R-I-S-T-M-A-S** *(Philips PB-530)*		9	16	
Bill Haley & His Comets - **Rock-A-Beatin' Boogie** *(Brunswick 05509)*		12	★	
Malcolm Vaughan - **With Your Love** *(H.M.V. POP-130)*		12	5	
Edmund Hockridge - **Hey There!** *(H.M.V. POP-131)*		17		
Mantovani & His Orch. - **Take My Love** *(Decca F-10601)*		17		
Will Starr - **Tap-Wood Polka** *(Parlophone R-4103)*		17	20	
Gogi Grant - **Suddenly There's A Valley** *(London HLB-8192)*		21	7	
David Whitfield - **I'll Never Stop Loving You** *(Decca F-10596)*		21		
Al Hibbler - **He** *(Brunswick 05492)*			28	22
Charlie Kunz - **Christmas Medley [M]** *(Decca F-10656)*			28	
Ruby Murray - **WHEN IRISH EYES ARE SMILING** *(Columbia 33S-1079)* **LP**			28	
Billy Cotton & His Band - **Yellow Rose Of Texas** *(Decca F-10602)*				18

Eartha Kitt

Eddie Fisher

Nappy Brown

Rosemary Clooney

JANUARY 1956

7		14	21	28
★	Lonnie Donegan - **Rock Island Line** (Decca Jazz F-10647)			
★	Edna Savage - **Arrivederci Darling** (Parlophone R-4097)			
1	Eamonn Andrews - **The Shifting Whispering Sands** (Parlophone R-4106)	1	★	
2	Doris Day - **Ooh Bang Jiggilly Jang** (Philips PB-532)	3	4	7
2	Ella Fitzgerald - **Pete Kelly's Blues** / **Hard Hearted Hannah** (Brunswick 05473)			
2	Frank Sinatra - **Love And Marriage** (Capitol CL-14503)	★		
5	Billy Cotton & His Band - **Yellow Rose Of Texas** (Decca F-10602)			
6	751st U.S.A.F. Band - **St. Louis Blues March** (H.M.V. B-10937)	20		
6	Alma Cogan - **Love And Marriage** (H.M.V. POP-163)	6	1	
6	Gogi Grant - **Suddenly There's A Valley** (London HLB-8192)	9		5
6	Monty Norman - **The Shifting, Whispering Sands** (H.M.V. POP-145)		22	
10	OBC - **NEW FACES** (H.M.V. 7EG-8134) **EP**	13		
11	Johnny Desmond - **Sixteen Tons** (Vogue Coral Q-72115)	2		
11	Tennessee Ernie Ford - **The Ballad Of Davy Crockett** (Capitol CL-14506)	★		
11	Ted Heath & His Music - **Malagueña** / **Cloudburst** (Decca F-10596)			
11	Will Starr - **Savoy Scottish Medley** (Parlophone R-4077)			
11	Malcolm Vaughan - **With Your Love** (H.M.V. POP-130)		4	★
16	Eddie Fisher - **Don't Stay Away Too Long** (H.M.V. B-10925)			
16	Ray Martin & His Concert Orch. - **Hernando's Hideaway** (Columbia DB-3658)	9		
18	Gary Miller - **Robin Hood** / **Ballad of Davy Crockett** (Pye Nixa N.15020)	★		
18	OBC - **THE PAJAMA GAME** (Philips BBL-7050) **LP**	13		
20	Robert Earl - **He** / **With Your Love** (Philips PB-517)			
20	Bill Haley & His Comets - **Ten Little Indians** (London HLF-8194)	5		
20	Dean Martin and Line Renaud - **Relax-Ay-Voo** (Capitol CL-14356)	11	17	
20	Joan Regan - **Croce di Oro** / **Love And Marriage** (Decca F-10659)	★		
20	Jo Stafford - **Arrivederci Darling** (Philips PB-527)			
20	Will Starr - **Tap-Wood Polka** (Parlophone R-4103)			
26	Concert Orchestra, *cond.* Eric Coates - **The Dam Busters March** (Pye Nixa N.15003)	13		
26	Johnny Maddox - **Do, Do, Do** (London HLU-8203)			
28	Eddie Calvert - **The Holy City** (Columbia DB-3674)	20		
28	Al Hibbler - **He** (Brunswick 05492)	4	13	
	Crazy Otto - **Glad Rag Doll** / **Smiles** (Polydor BM-6003)	6	17	
	Bill Haley & His Comets - **Razzle Dazzle** (Brunswick 05453)	8		2
	Tony Brent - **With Your Love** (Columbia DB-3675)	9	13	1
	Sammy Davis Jr. - **Back Track** (Brunswick 05478)	11		
	Ella Fitzgerald - **The Tender Trap** (Brunswick 05514)	13		
	Dick James - **Robin Hood** / **The Ballad Of Davy Crockett** (Parlophone R-4117)	13	★	
	Mitch Miller & His Orch. - **The Bonnie Blue Gal** (Philips PB-525)	13		

293

FEBRUARY 1956

4		11	18	25
★	Dream Weavers - **It's Almost Tomorrow** (Brunswick 05515)			
★	Frankie Vaughan - **My Boy Flat Top** (Philips PB-544)			
1	Ronnie Hilton - **Young And Foolish** (H.M.V. POP-154)	★		
2	Alma Cogan - **Love And Marriage** (H.M.V. POP-163)	3	6	
3	Tony Brent - **With Your Love** (Columbia DB-3675)			
3	Peggy Lee - **He's A Tramp** (Brunswick 05482)		6	
3	Gale Storm - **I Hear You Knocking** (London HLD-8222)			
6	Rosemary Clooney - **Go On By** (Philips PB-499)			
7	Doris Day - **Jimmy Unknown** (Philips PB-542)	7	3	
7	Al Hibbler - **He** (Brunswick 05492)			
7	Kathie Kay - **Jimmy Unknown** (H.M.V. POP-159)			
7	Bert Weedon with Sidney Torch & His Orch. - **Stranger Than Fiction** (Parlophone R-4113)			
11	Four Lads - **Moments To Remember** (Philips PB-520)			
11	Jodimars - **Let's All Rock Together** (Capitol CL-14518)	9	9	
11	Dennis Lotis - **C'est La Vie** (Pye Nixa N.15017)			
	Vera Lynn - **With Your Love** (Decca F-10622)	1		
	Sammy Davis Jr. - **Back Track** (Brunswick 05478)	2		
	Johnnie Ray - **Who's Sorry Now?** (Philips PB-546)	3	★	
	Kay Starr - **Rock And Roll Waltz** (H.M.V. POP-168)	5	★	
	Benny Goodman Trio with Rosemary Clooney - **Memories Of You** (Philips PB-547)	6		2
	Dickie Valentine and the Keynotes - **Dreams Can Tell A Lie** (Decca F-10667)	7		
	Dave King with the Keynotes - **Memories Are Made Of This** (Decca F-10684)	9	★	
	Max Bygraves - **The Ballad Of Davy Crockett** (H.M.V. POP-153)		★	
	Mario Lanza - **Valencia** (H.M.V. DA-2083)		1	
	Nelson Riddle & His Orch. - **In Old Lisbon** (Capitol CL-14510)		2	1
	Slim Whitman - **Tumbling Tumbleweeds** (London HLU-8230)		3	
	Jo Stafford - **Young And Foolish** (Philips PB-538)		5	
	Coronets - **Lizzie Borden** (Columbia DB-3728)		8	4
	Steve Allen - **What Is A Wife?** (Vogue Coral Q-72126)		9	
	Robert Earl - **With Your Love** (Philips PB-517)			★
	Debbie Reynolds - **The Tender Trap** (M.G.M. MGM-881)			3
	Dean Martin - **Innamorata** (Capitol CL-14507)			4

3		10	17	24	31
★	Slim Whitman - **Tumbling Tumbleweeds** (London HLU-8230)				
1	Doris Day - **Jimmy Unknown** (Philips PB-542)	9	13		
2	Dennis Lotis - **Por Favor** (Pye Nixa N.15017)				
2	Stargazers - **Zambesi** (Decca F-10696)				
4	Benny Goodman Trio with Rosemary Clooney - **Memories Of You** (Philips PB-547)				19
4	Vera Lynn - **With Your Love** (Decca F-10622)				
4	Nelson Riddle & His Orch. - **In Old Lisbon / Robin Hood** (Capitol CL-14510)	1			
4	Jimmy Young - **Chain Gang** (Decca F-10694)	★			
8	Tony Brent - **With Your Love** (Columbia DB-3675)	6	8		11
8	Alma Cogan - **Love And Marriage** (H.M.V. POP-163)	4	4	8	
8	Ted Heath & His Music with Annette Klooger - **Rock And Roll Waltz** (Decca F-10701)				5
8	Debbie Reynolds - **The Tender Trap** (M.G.M. MGM-881)				
12	Kathie Kay - **Old Scotch Mother** (H.M.V. POP-167)		8	8	14
12	Dean Martin - **Innamorata** (Capitol CL-14507)	4	4		
12	Harry Secombe - **None Shall Sleep Tonight** (Philips PB-550)			11	
15	Four Lads - **Moments To Remember** (Philips PB-520)				
15	Mantovani & His Orch. - **Candlelight** (Decca F-10678)				
17	Petula Clark - **Memories Are Made Of This / Band Of Gold** (Pye Nixa N.15040)	18			9
17	Lonnie Donegan - **Diggin' My Potatoes / Bury My Body** (Decca Jazz FJ-10695)	18	20		
17	Jackie Riggs - **The Great Pretender** (London HLF-8244)	18		14	19
20	Billy Cotton & His Band - **Robin Hood** (Decca F-10682)	13	20		
20	Gale Storm - **I Hear You Knocking** (London HLD-8222)	1	★		
22	Sammy Davis Jr. - **In A Persian Market** (Brunswick 05518)	13		1	2
22	Eddie Fisher - **Dungaree Doll** (H.M.V. POP-171)				14
22	Norman Granz' Jazz At The Philharmonic - **JAMMING WITH THE GREATS – NEW VOLUME 4** (Columbia 33CX-10035) 🔲				
22	Mario Lanza - **Valencia** (H.M.V. DA-2083)				
22	Rosemary Squires - **Band Of Gold** (Decca F-10685)				
	Danny Kaye and Dena Kaye - **Little Child (Daddy Dear)** (Brunswick 05532)	1	7		
	Louis Armstrong - **Theme from 'The Threepenny Opera'** (Philips PB-574)	6	13	7	5
	Benny Goodman - **CARNEGIE HALL JAZZ CONCERT** (Philips BBL-7001) 🔲	6			
	Les Baxter & His Orch. - **Poor John** (Capitol CL-14533)	9	17	8	
	Dickie Bennett - **Dungaree Doll** (Decca F-10697)	11			
	Jo Stafford - **Young And Foolish** (Philips PB-538)	11			5
	Alfi & Harry - **Trouble With Harry** (London HLU-8242)	13	1	★	
	Coronets - **Lizzie Borden** (Columbia DB-3728)	13	17		8
	Billy Vaughn & His Orch. - **Theme from 'The Threepenny Opera'** (London HLD-8238)	13	2	★	
	Frank Chacksfield & His Orch. - **Love Is A Many Splendoured Thing** (Decca F-10639)	18			
	Robert Earl - **My September Love** (Philips PB-552)	18	★		
	Joe Lynch - **The Pride Of Tipperary** (Decca (Irish Series) MU-15)	18		16	
	Max Bygraves - **Nothin' To Do** (H.M.V. POP-185)	24			
	Ronnie Carroll - **Last Love** (Philips PB-553)	24			
	Benny Goodman - **Don't Be That Way** (H.M.V. POP-166)	24			
	Al Hibbler - **The Eleventh Hour Melody** (Brunswick 05523)	24	20		
	Dick Hyman Trio - **Theme from 'The Threepenny Opera'** (M.G.M. MGM-890)	24	★		
	Guy Mitchell - **Ninety-Nine Years** (Philips PB-556)	24	4		
	Norrie Paramor & His Orch. - **The Threepenny Opera / The Poor People Of Paris** (Columbia DB-3745)	24	10		
	Robert Wilson - **My Bonnie Lassie** (H.M.V. B-10941)	24			
	Alma Cogan - **Willie Can / Lizzie Borden** (H.M.V. POP-187)		3	3	★
	Stan Kenton & His Orch. - **Portrait Of A Count / Invention For Guitar And Trumpet** (Capitol CL-14541)		10	1	

7		14	21	28
★	Cyril Stapleton & His Orch. - **The Italian Theme** (Decca F-10703)			
1	Joe 'Mr. Piano' Henderson - **Theme from 'The Threepenny Opera'** (Pye Nixa N.15044)	4		
2	Louis Armstrong - **Theme from 'The Threepenny Opera'** (Philips PB-574)	★		
3	Bing Crosby - **In A Little Spanish Town** (Brunswick 05543)	★		
4	Jo Stafford - **Young And Foolish** (Philips PB-538)	4	5	
5	Les Baxter & His Orch. - **Poor John** (Capitol CL-14533)	2		12
5	Elmer Bernstein & Orch. - **Clark Street** (Brunswick 05544)	14		4
5	Eve Boswell - **Cookie** / **It's Almost Tomorrow** (Parlophone R-4143)	14		
5	Four Lads - **No, Not Much** (Philips PB-571)	6	1	1
5	Geraldo & His Orch. - **The Poor People Of Paris** (Oriole CB-1322)	12	8	
5	Stan Kenton & His Orch. - **The Peanut Vendor** (Capitol CL-13016)	6		
11	Petula Clark - **Memories Are Made Of This** / **Band Of Gold** (Pye Nixa N.15040)		9	11
11	McGuire Sisters - **Be Good To Me** (Vogue Coral Q-72145)			
11	Guy Mitchell - **Ninety-Nine Years** / **Perfume, Candy And Flowers** (Philips PB-556)	21		
14	Pat Boone - **I'll Be Home** / **Tutti Frutti** (London HLD-8253)	2	★	
14	Rose Brennan - **Band Of Gold** (H.M.V. POP-180)			
14	Sammy Davis Jr. - **In A Persian Market** / **Man With The Golden Arm** (Brunswick 05518)	1	★	
14	Dave King with the Keynotes - **You Can't Be True To Two** (Decca F-10720)	★		
14	Stargazers - **Zambesi** (Decca F-10696)			
19	Beverley Sisters - **Willie Can** (Decca F-10705)	★		
19	Dennis Lotis - **The Extra Day** (Pye Nixa N.15041)			
19	Ruby Murray - **I Know I'm Home** (Columbia DB-3750)			
19	Frankie Vaughan - **This Is The Night** / **Rock Candy Baby** (Philips PB-559)			
	Jackie Riggs - **The Great Pretender** (London HLF-8244)	★		
	Perry Como - **Juke Box Baby** (H.M.V. POP-191)	6	★	
	Paddy Carney - **An Irish Mother's Prayer** (Decca (Irish Series) MU-12)	9		
	Danny Kaye and Dena Kaye - **Little Child (Daddy Dear)** (Brunswick 05532)	9		12
	Ted Heath & His Music with Annette Klooger - **Rock And Roll Waltz** (Decca F-10701)	12		
	Doris Day - **Jimmy Unknown** (Philips PB-542)	14		
	Lonnie Donegan - **Diggin' My Potatoes** (Decca Jazz FJ-10695)	14		
	Lonnie Donegan - **Lost John** / **Stewball** (Pye Nixa N.15036)	14	★	
	Billy May & His Orch. - **Main Title (from the film 'The Man With The Golden Arm')** (Capitol CL-14551)	14	5	★
	Ruby Murray - **Make Him Jealous** (Columbia DB-3718)	14		
	Alma Cogan - **Don't Ring-a Da Bell** (H.M.V. POP-189)	21		12
	Duke Ellington - **SKIN DEEP** (H.M.V. 7EG-8033) **EP**	21		

MAY 1956

5		12	19	26
★	Frankie Laine - **Hell Hath No Fury** (Philips PB-585)			
1	Winifred Atwell - **Port-au-Prince** (Decca F-10727)	1	★	
2	Four Lads - **No, Not Much** (Philips PB-571)	4	1	
3	Pauline Shepherd - **Willie Can / No Not Much** (Pye Nixa N.15043)			
4	Keynotes - **Scotland The Brave** (Decca F-10693)	13	12	14
5	Edmund Hockridge - **No Other Love** (Pye Nixa N.15048)	★		
6	Les Baxter & His Orch. - **Poor John** (Capitol CL-14533)			
7	Jill Day - **A Tear Fell** (H.M.V. POP-199)			
7	Lonnie Donegan - **BACKSTAIRS SESSION** (Pye Nixa NJE-1014) EP			
7	Judy Garland - **MISS SHOW BUSINESS** (Capitol LCT-6103) LP	7		9
10	Paddy Carney - **An Irish Mother's Prayer** (Decca (Irish Series) MU-12)			
10	Alma Cogan - **Don't Ring-a Da Bell / Bluebell** (H.M.V. POP-189)	13		1
12	Max Bygraves - **Out Of Town** (H.M.V. POP-164)	2	3	★
12	Elvis Presley - **Heartbreak Hotel** (H.M.V. POP-182)	★		
12	Jimmy Shand & His Band - **Marching With Jimmy Shand [M]** (Parlophone R-4151)		4	5
15	Eve Boswell - **Cookie** (Parlophone R-4143)	7		
15	Doris Day - **Let It Ring** (Philips PB-560)	13		
15	Geraldo & His Orch. - **Rockin' Through Dixie** (Oriole CB-1323)			
15	Jerry Lewis - **I Keep Her Picture Hanging Upside Down** (Capitol CL-14559)			
15	Carmel Quinn - **Doonaree** (Philips PB-474)	11		
	Dick James - **Summer Sing-Song [M]** (Parlophone R-4164)	2		
	Elmer Bernstein & Orch. - **Clark Street** (Brunswick 05544)	4	7	2
	Burl Ives - **SONGS FOR AND ABOUT MEN (PART 1)** (Brunswick OE-9200) EP	6	19	
	Carl Perkins - **Blue Suede Shoes** (London HLU-8271)	7	★	
	Hank Williams - **Your Cheatin' Heart** (M.G.M. MGM-896)	7		
	Billy Daniels - **That Old Black Magic** (Oriole CB-1095)	12		
	Joseph McNally - **The March Hare** (Oriole CB-1325)	13		
	Cathy Carr - **Ivory Tower** (London HLH-8274)		2	5
	Don Cherry - **Wild Cherry** (Philips PB-581)		5	
	Mel Tormé - **AT THE CRESCENDO** (Vogue Coral LVA-9004) LP		5	
	Sarah Vaughan - **SARAH VAUGHAN** (Philips BBE-12036) EP		7	
	Louis Armstrong - **TAKE IT SATCH!** (Philips BBE-12035) EP		9	2
	Concert Orchestra, cond Eric Coates - **The Dam Busters March** (Pye Nixa N.15003)		9	
	Stan Freberg - **The Great Pretender** (Capitol CL-14571)		9	
	Ray Bloch & His Orch. - **Donkey Tango** (Vogue Coral Q-72131)		12	
	Columbia Pictures Orchestra - **Moonglow and Theme from 'Picnic'** (Brunswick 05553)		12	
	OBC - **KISMET** (Philips BBL-7023) LP		12	
	Anne Shelton - **Too Young To Go Steady** (Philips PB-437)		12	
	Teddy Buckner - **When The Saints Go Marching In** (Vogue V-2375)		17	
	Max Bygraves - **Seventeen Tons** (H.M.V. POP-208)		17	5
	Mickey Katz & His Orch. - **Duvid Crockett** (Capitol CL-14579)		19	
	Nicky Kidd - **Too Young To Go Steady** (Beltona BL-2645)		19	14
	Julius LaRosa - **No Other Love** (London HLA-8272)		19	
	Guy Mitchell - **Green Grows The Grass** (Philips PB-450)		19	11
	Cyril Stapleton & His Orch. - **The Happy Whistler** (Decca F-10735)			4
	OST - **CAROUSEL** (Capitol LCT-6105) LP			5
	Michael Holliday - **Hot Diggity** (Columbia DB-3783)			9
	Ella Fitzgerald - **SWEET AND HOT** (Brunswick LAT-8091) LP			11
	Tennessee Ernie Ford - **That's All** (Capitol CL-14557)			11
	Boyd Bennett & His Rockets - **Blue Suede Shoes** (Parlophone R-4167)			14
	Mario Lanza - **Wanting You** (H.M.V. DA-2084)			14

JUNE 1956

2		9	16	23	30
★	Columbia Pictures Orchestra - **Moonglow** *and* **Theme from 'Picnic'** *(Brunswick 05553)*				
★	Cyril Stapleton & His Orch. - **The Happy Whistler** *(Decca F-10735)*				
1	Louis Armstrong - **TAKE IT SATCH!** *(Philips BBE-12035)* EP	★			
2	Alma Cogan - **Don't Ring-a Da Bell** / **Bluebell** *(H.M.V. POP-189)*	7	2	10	17
2	OST - **CAROUSEL** *(Capitol LCT-6105)* LP	2	★		
4	Elmer Bernstein & Orch. - **Clark Street** *(Brunswick 05544)*	6	9		
5	Mickey Katz & His Orch. - **Duvid Crockett** *(Capitol CL-14579)*				
6	Michael Holliday - **Hot Diggity** / **The Gal With The Yaller Shoes** *(Columbia DB-3783)*	1	★		
7	Glen Mason - **Hot Diggity** *(Parlophone R-4176)*	4	1	4	3
7	David Rose & His Orch. - **No Other Love** *(M.G.M. MGM-898)*				
9	Boyd Bennett & His Rockets - **Blue Suede Shoes** *(Parlophone R-4167)*				
10	Lonnie Donegan - **BACKSTAIRS SESSION** *(Pye Nixa NJE-1014)* EP				5
10	Nicky Kidd - **Too Young To Go Steady** / **Wild Cherry** *(Beltona BL-2645)*	7	5	18	
10	Stargazers - **Hot Diggity** *(Decca F-10731)*	★			
13	Hilltoppers - **Do The Bop** *(London HLD-8278)*				
14	Max Bygraves - **Seventeen Tons** / **Try Another Cherry Tree** *(H.M.V. POP-208)*	5	3	12	12
14	Eric Delaney & His Band - **Cockles And Mussels** *(Pye Nixa N.15046)*				
14	Lonnie Donegan - **Diggin' My Potatoes** *(Decca Jazz FJ-10695)*				
17	Chris Barber's Jazz Band - **The World Is Waiting For The Sunrise** *(Decca Jazz FJ-10724)*				
17	Cathy Carr - **Ivory Tower** *(London HLH-8274)*	14	9		6
17	Ken-Tones - **In Port Afrique** *(Parlophone R-4163)*				
17	Ray Martin & His Concert Orch. - **The Carousel Waltz** *(Columbia DB-3771)*	3	★		
17	OLC - **VOCAL GEMS FROM CAROUSEL** *(Columbia SED-5536)* LP				
17	Kid Ory's Creole Jazz Band - **When The Saints Go Marching In** *(Good Time Jazz GV-2322)*				
17	Jimmy Shand & His Band - **Marching With Jimmy Shand [M]** *(Parlophone R-4151)*				
	Vera Lynn - **Who Are We** *(Decca F-10715)*	★			
	Sarah Vaughan - **SARAH VAUGHAN** *(Philips BBE-12036)* EP	7			
	Max Bygraves - **Nothin' To Do** *(H.M.V. POP-185)*	10			
	Doris Day - **Let It Ring** *(Philips PB-560)*	10			
	Gogi Grant - **Wayward Wind** *(London HLB-8282)*	12	5	2	★
	Faron Young - **If You Ain't Lovin' (You Ain't Livin')** *(Capitol CL-14574)*	12	13	12	
	Frankie Laine - **Moby Dick** *(Philips PB-587)*	14	9	4	
	Joan Regan - **Honestly** *(Decca F-10742)*	14			

Sarah Vaughan — Come rain or come shine / Nice work if you can get it / The nearness of you / Ooh, what-cha doin' to me — PHILIPS Extended Play 45

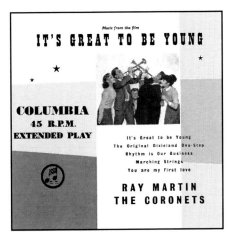

Music from the film
IT'S GREAT TO BE YOUNG
COLUMBIA 45 R.P.M. EXTENDED PLAY
It's Great to be Young / The Original Dixieland One-Step / Rhythm Is Our Business / Marching Strings / You are my first love
RAY MARTIN / THE CORONETS

2 <<< JUNE 1956 >>>	9	16	23	30
Frankie Lymon & The Teenagers - **Why Do Fools Fall In Love** (Columbia DB-3772)		4	3	★
Dean Martin - **Watching The World Go By** (Capitol CL-14586)		7	6	10
Joe Lynch - **The Old Bog Road** (Beltona BE-2647)		8	10	
Slim Whitman - **Serenade** (London HLU-8287)		9	★	
Doris Day - **Whatever Will Be, Will Be** (Philips PB-586)		13	12	★
Joe 'Mr. Piano' Henderson - **Ask for Joe** (Pye Nixa N.15057)		13	12	
Guy Mitchell - **Green Grows The Grass** (Philips PB-450)		13		
Frank Sinatra - **Five Hundred Guys** (Capitol CL-14584)		13	12	
Various Artists - **All Star Hit Parade** (Decca F-10752)			1	★
Georgia Gibbs - **Kiss Me Another** (Mercury MT-110)			6	
Acker Bilk - **Where The River Shannon Flows** (Tempo A-134)			8	
Alma Cogan - **The Birds And The Bees** (H.M.V. POP-223)			8	
Jimmy Parkinson - **Walk Hand In Hand** (Columbia DB-3775)			12	
Fats Domino - **My Blue Heaven** (London HLU-8280)			18	
OBC - **KISMET** (Philips BBL-7023) 🇱🇵			18	
Pat Boone - **Long Tall Sally** (London HLD-8291)			21	
Kathie Kay - **Old Scotch Mother** (H.M.V. POP-167)			21	
Mario Lanza - **Serenade** (H.M.V. DA-2085)			21	6
Frank Weir & His Saxophone - **Mister Cuckoo** (Parlophone R-4157)			21	
Lonnie Donegan - **SKIFFLE SESSION** (Pye Nixa NJE-1017) 🇪🇵				1
Gale Storm - **Why Do Fools Fall In Love** (London HLD-8286)				2
Fred Hanna Band - **Irish Marches No. 1 [M]** (Beltona BE-2638)				3
Myles O'Connor - **Kevin Barry** (Beltona BE-2640)				6
Edmundo Ros & His Orch. - **Mister Cuckoo** (Decca F-10716)				6
Ken Colyer's Skiffle Group - **Mule Skinner** (Decca Jazz F-10751)				10
Gordon MacRae - **Who Are We** (Capitol CL-14576)				12
Ted Heath & His Music - **The Faithful Hussar** (Decca F-10746)				14
Joseph McNally - **The March Hare** (Oriole CB-1325)				14
Frank Sinatra - **You'll Never Walk Alone** (Columbia DB-2705)				14
Four Aces - **The Gal With The Yaller Shoes** (Brunswick 05566)				17
Chris Barber's Jazz Band - **CHRIS BARBER PLAYS (VOL. 2)** (Pye Nixa NJT-502) 🇱🇵				19
OST - **IT'S GREAT TO BE YOUNG** (Columbia SEG-7639) 🇪🇵				19

7		14	21	28
★	Lonnie Donegan - **SKIFFLE SESSION** (Pye Nixa NJE-1017) 🔲			
★	Ted Heath & His Music - **The Faithful Hussar** (Decca F-10746)			
1	Gale Storm - **Why Do Fools Fall In Love** (London HLD-8286)	15	4	3
2	Cathy Carr - **Ivory Tower** (London HLH-8274)			
3	Four Aces - **The Gal With The Yaller Shoes** (Brunswick 05566)	9		
4	Jimmy Parkinson - **Walk Hand In Hand** (Columbia DB-3775)		14	7
5	Pat Boone - **Long Tall Sally** (London HLD-8291)	10	1	★
6	Alma Cogan - **Why Do Fools Fall In Love?** / **The Birds And The Bees** (H.M.V. POP-223)	★		
6	Mario Lanza - **Serenade** (H.M.V. DA-2085)	5	13	13
6	Shorty Rogers & His Giants - **GIANTS OF MODERN JAZZ** (H.M.V. 7EG-8174) 🔲			
9	Fats Domino - **I'm In Love Again** (London HLU-8280)	15	1	★
9	Gordon MacRae - **Who Are We** (Capitol CL-14576)			
11	Eve Boswell - **Down By The Sugar Cane** (Parlophone R-4181)			
11	Tony Martin - **Walk Hand In Hand** (H.M.V. POP-222)	★		
11	Glen Mason - **Hot Diggity** (Parlophone R-4176)		14	15
11	Johnnie Ray - **Goodbye, Au Revoir, Adios** (Philips PB-596)	3	6	15
15	Ray Bloch & His Orch. - **The Carousel Waltz** (Vogue Coral Q-72165)			
15	Lonnie Donegan - **Diggin' My Potatoes** (Decca Jazz FJ-10695)			
15	Joe 'Mr. Piano' Henderson - **Ask for Joe** (Pye Nixa N.15057)			
15	Frankie Laine - **Moby Dick** (Philips PB-587)			15
19	Teresa Brewer - **A Sweet Old Fashioned Girl** (Vogue Coral Q-72172)	★		
	Georgia Gibbs - **Kiss Me Another** (Mercury MT-110)	★		
	Perry Como - **SO SMOOTH** (H.M.V. 7EG-8171) 🔲	1	3	9
	Elvis Presley - **I Want You, I Need You, I Love You** (H.M.V. POP-235)	1	★	
	Ruby Murray - **You Are My First Love** / **Honestly, I Do** (Columbia DB-3770)	3	10	
	Edmundo Ros & His Orch. - **Mister Cuckoo** (Decca F-10716)	5		
	Kay Starr - **Second Fiddle** (H.M.V. POP-231)	5	14	2
	Gene Vincent & His Blue Caps - **Be-Bop-A-Lula** (Capitol CL-14599)	5	★	
	Frank Sinatra - **How Little We Know** / **Five Hundred Guys** (Capitol CL-14584)	10		10
	Dean Martin - **Watching The World Go By** (Capitol CL-14586)	12	11	
	Paddy Carney - **They Can't Change The Name Of Ireland** (Decca (Irish Series) MU-12)	13		
	Frankie Laine - **Ticky Ticky Tick** (Philips PB-607)	13		
	Winifred Atwell - **The Left Bank** (Decca F-10762)	15	★	
	Elmer Bernstein & Orch. - **Clark Street** (Brunswick 05544)	15		
	Buck Clayton - **JUMPIN' AT THE WOODSIDE** (Philips BBL-7087) 🔲	15		
	Mickey Katz & His Orch. - **Duvid Crockett** (Capitol CL-14579)	15		
	Eartha Kitt - **Honolulu Rock-A-Roll-A** (H.M.V. POP-233)	15		
	Sean Mooney & Trio - **If We Only Had Old Ireland Over Here** (H.M.V. POP-230)		5	4
	Fred Hanna Band - **Irish Waltz Medley No. 1 [M]** / **Irish Marches No. 1 [M]** (Beltona BE-2638)		6	7
	Hilltoppers - **Trying** (London HLD-8298)		8	1
	Oscar Peterson Trio - **OSCAR PETERSON PLAYS RICHARD ROGERS** (Columbia 33CX-10028) 🔲		8	
	Sid Phillips Band - **Mamma Don't Allow** (H.M.V. POP-226)		12	
	Stan Freberg - **Rock Island Line** / **Heartbreak Hotel** (Capitol CL-14608)		14	★
	Kathie Kay - **Old Scotch Mother** (H.M.V. POP-167)		14	15
	Mel Tormé - **AT THE CRESCENDO** (Vogue Coral LVA-9004) 🔲			★
	Clyde McPhatter - **Treasure Of Love** (London HLE-8293)			4
	Harry Secombe - **We'll Keep A Welcome** (Philips PB-599)			4
	Ron Goodwin & His Concert Orch. - **No Other Love** (Parlophone R-4162)			10
	Fred Hanna Band - **Pride Of Erin No. 2 [M]** (Beltona BE-2639)			13
	Jimmy Shand & His Band - **Marching With Jimmy Shand [M]** (Parlophone R-4151)			13
	Edmund Hockridge - **By The Fountains Of Rome** (Pye Nixa N.15063)			15
	Vera Lynn - **Walk Hand In Hand** (Decca F-10737)			15
	Frank Sinatra - **You'll Never Walk Alone** (Columbia DB-2705)			15

4		11	18	25
★	Jimmy Parkinson - **Walk Hand In Hand** (Columbia DB-3775)			
1	Frankie Lymon & The Teenagers - **I Want You To Be My Girl** (Columbia DB-3797)		14	14
1	Gale Storm - **Why Do Fools Fall In Love** (London HLD-8286)			
3	Mel Tormé - **MEL TORMÉ WITH THE MARTY PAICH 'DEK-TETTE'** (London American Jazz LTZ-N-15009) 🄻🄿		★	
4	Cathy Carr - **Ivory Tower** (London HLH-8274)	7	14	
4	Frank Chacksfield & His Orch. - **The Donkey Cart** (Decca F-10743)	3	5	13
4	Burl Ives - **SONGS FOR AND ABOUT MEN (PART 2)** (Brunswick OE-9201) 🄴🄿			
7	Hilltoppers - **Trying** / **D-A-R-L-I-N'** (London HLD-8298)	10		1
7	Kenneth McKellar - **Scotland The Brave** (Decca F-10537)			
7	Frank Sinatra - **How Little We Know** (Capitol CL-14584)	7		
7	Kay Starr - **Second Fiddle** (H.M.V. POP-231)			
11	Gogi Grant - **Who Are We** (London HLB-8257)			10
11	Dave King with the Keynotes - **The Birds And The Bees** (Decca F-10741)			
11	Vera Lynn - **Walk Hand In Hand** (Decca F-10737)	1	2	4
14	Edmund Hockridge - **By The Fountains Of Rome** (Pye Nixa N.15063)		10	10
14	Gordon MacRae - **Who Are We** (Capitol CL-14576)			
14	Dean Martin - **Watching The World Go By** (Capitol CL-14586)			
	Mario Lanza - **SONGS FROM THE STUDENT PRINCE AND OTHER FAMOUS MELODIES** (H.M.V. ALP-1186) 🄻🄿	★		
	Fred Hanna Band - **Irish Waltz Medley No. 1 [M]** (Beltona BE-2638)	2		
	Bill Haley & His Comets - **LIVE IT UP (PART 1)** (London RE-F-1049) 🄴🄿	4	14	
	Mario Lanza - **Serenade** (H.M.V. DA-2085)	4	1	2
	Clyde McPhatter - **Treasure Of Love** (London HLE-8293)	4	2	★
	Myles O'Connor - **Kevin Barry** (Beltona BE-2640)	9		
	Jimmy Shand & His Band - **Marching With Jimmy Shand [M]** (Parlophone R-4151)	10		
	Billy Williams Quartet - **Cry Baby** (Vogue Coral Q-72149)	10		
	Ruby Murray - **You Are My First Love** / **Honestly, I Do** (Columbia DB-3770)		2	★
	Chordettes - **Born To Be With You** (London HLA-8302)		6	★
	Johnston Brothers - **The Street Musician** (Decca F-10747)		6	
	Marion Ryan - **Hot Diggity** (Pye Nixa N.15058)		8	
	Moon Mullican with Boyd Bennett & His Rockets - **Honolulu Rock-A-Roll-A** (Parlophone R-4195)		9	
	Sammy Davis Jr. - **Adelaide** (Brunswick 05583)		10	
	Frank Sinatra - **Johnny Concho Theme (Wait For Me)** (Capitol CL-14607)		10	
	Willows - **Church Bells May Ring** (London HLL-8290)		10	8
	Fred Hanna Band - **Pride Of Erin No. 2 [M]** (Beltona BE-2639)		14	4
	Platters - **Only You** / **The Great Pretender** (Mercury MT-117)		14	2
	Somethin' Smith & The Redheads - **In A Shanty In Old Shanty Town** (Philips PB-609)		14	
	Anne Shelton - **Lay Down Your Arms** (Philips PB-616)			8
	Carmen Cavallaro - **To Love Again** (Brunswick 05576)			4
	Burl Ives - **SONGS FOR AND ABOUT MEN (PART 3)** (Brunswick OE-9202) 🄴🄿			4
	Mel Tormé - **Lulu's Back In Town** (London HLN-8305)			10
	Frankie Laine - **Ticky Ticky Tick** / **Champion The Wonder Horse** (Philips PB-607)			14
	Webb Pierce - **WEBB PIERCE (PART 1)** (Brunswick OE-9253) 🄴🄿			14

1		8	15	22	29
★	Frank Chacksfield & His Orch. - **The Donkey Cart** (Decca F-10743)				
★	Edmund Hockridge - **By The Fountains Of Rome** (Pye Nixa N.15063)				
★	Anne Shelton - **Lay Down Your Arms** (Philips PB-616)				
1	Hilltoppers - **Trying / D-A-R-L-I-N'** (London HLD-8298)			★	
2	Bill Haley & His Comets - **ROCK 'N ROLL** (Brunswick OE-9214) **EP**				
2	Platters - **Only You / The Great Pretender** (Mercury MT-117)	★			
4	Harry Secombe - **We'll Keep A Welcome** (Philips PB-599)	11	10	10	6
4	Frank Sinatra - **You'll Never Walk Alone** (Columbia DB-2705)				
6	Carmen McRae - **CARMEN McRAE (PART 1)** (London American Jazz EZ-N-19016) **EP**				
6	Sid Phillips Band - **Mamma Don't Allow** (H.M.V. POP-226)				
8	Clyde Valley Stompers - **Keep Right On To The End Of The Road** (Beltona BL-2648)	1	7	7	
9	Bill Haley & His Comets - **Razzle Dazzle** (Brunswick 05453)	3	★		
9	Fred Hanna Band - **Irish Waltz Medley No. 1 [M] / Irish Marches No. 1 [M]** (Beltona BE-2638)				
9	Guy Mitchell - **Give Me A Carriage With Eight White Horses** (Philips PB-610)	10			
12	Cathy Carr - **Ivory Tower** (London HLH-8274)				
12	Dave King with the Keynotes - **The Birds And The Bees** (Decca F-10741)				
12	Frankie Laine - **Ticky Ticky Tick / Champion The Wonder Horse** (Philips PB-607)				
12	Mario Lanza - **Serenade** (H.M.V. DA-2085)	3	★		
12	Dean Martin - **Watching The World Go By** (Capitol CL-14586)				
12	Frank Sinatra - **How Little We Know** (Capitol CL-14584)				
12	Mel Tormé - **Lulu's Back In Town** (London HLN-8305)				
	Clyde Valley Stompers - **Old Rustic Bridge By The Mill** (Beltona BL-2649)	2	4		
	Bill Haley & His Comets - **ROCK AROUND THE CLOCK** (Brunswick OE-9250) **EP**	3	4	1	1
	Sidney Torch & His Orch. - **Reach For The Sky** (Parlophone R-4198)	3			
	Four Aces - **A Woman In Love** (Brunswick 05589)	7	7	4	3
	Vera Lynn - **Walk Hand In Hand** (Decca F-10737)	8	10		
	Mitchell Torok - **When Mexico Gave Up The Rhumba** (Brunswick 05586)	8	7	★	
	Kathie Kay - **Old Scotch Mother** (H.M.V. POP-167)	11			
	Edmund Hockridge - **A Woman In Love** (Pye Nixa N.15067)		1		
	Clyde Valley Stompers - **Pearly Gates** (Beltona BL-2650)		2	2	2
	Carmen Cavallaro - **To Love Again** (Brunswick 05576)		3		
	Frank Sinatra - **Our Town** (Capitol CL-14620)		4		
	Ray Martin & His Concert Orch. - **Street Symphony** (Columbia DB-3807)		10		
	OST - **THE KING AND I** (Capitol LCT-6108) **LP**		10	★	
	Webb Pierce - **WEBB PIERCE (PART 1)** (Brunswick OE-9253) **EP**		10		
	Chris Barber's Jazz Band - **Whistlin' Rufus** (Pye Nixa NJ-2011)		14	10	
	Stan Kenton & His Orch. - **STAN KENTON IN HI-FI** (Capitol LCT-6109) **LP**		14		
	OST - **OKLAHOMA! (PART 1)** (Capitol EAP1-595) **EP**		14		
	Frank Sinatra - **YOUNG AT HEART [OST]** (Capitol EAP1-571) **EP**		14		
	Gene Vincent & His Blue Caps - **Race With The Devil** (Capitol CL-14628)			3	8
	Jimmy Young - **More** (Decca F-10774)			4	★
	Frankie Lymon & The Teenagers - **I Want You To Be My Girl** (Columbia DB-3797)			6	
	Eve Boswell - **Come Back My Love** (Parlophone R-4189)			7	
	Dean Martin & Jerry Lewis - **Pardners** (Capitol CL-14626)			7	
	Pat Boone - **Rich In Love** (London HLD-8316)			10	
	Mario Lanza - **Earthbound** (H.M.V. DA-2086)			10	
	Fats Domino - **When My Dream Boat Comes Home** (London HLU-8309)				4
	Melachrino Orchestra - **Autumn Concerto** (H.M.V. B-10958)				4
	Ted Heath & His Music - **Canadian Sunset** (Decca F-10783)				6
	Frank Chacksfield Tunesmiths - **Fanagalo** (Decca F-10786)				9
	Michael Holliday - **Ten Thousand Miles** (Columbia DB-3813)				9

6		13	20	27
★	Michael Holliday - **Ten Thousand Miles** (Columbia DB-3813)			
1	Four Aces - **A Woman In Love** (Brunswick 05589)	2	★	
2	Marlon Brando / Jean Simmons - **GUYS AND DOLLS [OST]** (Brunswick OE-9241) EP	★		
2	Clyde Valley Stompers - **Pearly Gates** (Beltona BL-2650)	2		
4	Bill Haley & His Comets - **ROCK 'N ROLL** (Brunswick OE-9214) EP			
5	Fats Domino - **When My Dream Boat Comes Home** (London HLU-8309)			
6	Frank Chacksfield Tunesmiths - **Fanagalo** (Decca F-10786)			
6	Melachrino Orchestra - **Autumn Concerto** (H.M.V. B-10958)	★		
8	Four Aces - **The Gal With The Yaller Shoes** (Brunswick 05566)			
8	Harry Secombe - **We'll Keep A Welcome** (Philips PB-599)			
8	Stargazers - **She Loves To Rock** (Decca F-10775)	10		
11	Robert Earl - **More** (Philips PB-622)	6		
11	Little Willie John - **Fever** (Parlophone R-4209)			
11	Norrie Paramor & His Orch. - **Autumn Concerto** (Columbia DB-3815)	10	1	1
14	Pat Boone - **Rich In Love** (London HLD-8316)			
15	Chris Barber's Jazz Band - **Whistlin' Rufus** (Pye Nixa NJ-2011)			
15	Chris Barber's Jazz Band with Bertie King - **JAZZ AT THE ROYAL FESTIVAL HALL** (Decca Jazz DFE-6238) EP			
15	Gene Vincent & His Blue Caps - **Race With The Devil** (Capitol CL-14628)	★		
18	Winifred Atwell - **Bumble Boogie** (Decca F-10785)			
18	Robert Earl - **Believe In Me** (Philips PB-593)			
18	Billy Eckstine and Sarah Vaughan - **DEDICATED TO YOU** (M.G.M. MGM-EP-561) EP			
18	Slim Whitman - **Danny Boy** (London L-1214)			
	Alma Cogan - **Mama Teach Me To Dance** (H.M.V. POP-239)	1	6	
	Tony Crombie & His Rockets - **Teach You To Rock** (Columbia DB-3822)	4	★	
	Tennessee Ernie Ford - **Who Will Shoe Your Pretty Little Foot** (Capitol CL-14616)	5		
	Bill Haley & His Comets - **ROCK AROUND THE CLOCK** (Brunswick OE-9250) EP	7		
	Stan Kenton & His Orch. - **STAN KENTON IN HI-FI** (Capitol LCT-6109) LP	7		
	Zulu Rhythm Boys - **Fanagalo** (Decca F-10784)	7		
	Bill Haley & His Comets - **ROCK 'N ROLL STAGE SHOW** (Brunswick LAT-8139) LP	10	★	
	Webb Pierce - **WEBB PIERCE (PART 3)** (Brunswick OE-9255) EP	10		
	Somethin' Smith & The Redheads - **In A Shanty In Old Shanty Town** (Philips PB-609)	10		
	Noël Coward - **AT LAS VEGAS** (Philips BBL-7108) LP		2	
	Edmund Hockridge - **A Woman In Love** (Pye Nixa N.15067)		3	
	Johnston Brothers and the Keynotes - **In The Middle Of The House** (Decca F-10781)		3	3
	Tommy Steele & The Steelmen - **Rock With The Caveman** (Decca F-10795)		3	★
	Frankie Lymon & The Teenagers - **I Promise To Remember** (Columbia DB-3819)		6	
	Beverley Sisters - **Born To Be With You** (Decca F-10770)		8	
	Mario Lanza - **Earthbound** (H.M.V. DA-2086)		8	8
	Winifred Atwell - **Make It A Party [M]** (Decca F-10796)		10	★
	Tony Bennett - **Happiness Street** (Philips PB-628)		10	
	Nat 'King' Cole - **My Dream Sonata** (Capitol CL-14632)		10	
	Mel Tormé - **Lulu's Back In Town** (London HLN-8305)		10	
	Malcolm Vaughan - **St. Therese Of The Roses** (H.M.V. POP-250)		10	★
	Big Ben Accordion Band - **Rock'n'Roll No. 1 [M]** (Columbia DB-3835)			2
	Ronnie Carroll - **It Only Hurts For A Little While** (Philips PB-623)			4
	Elvis Presley - **ROCK 'N ROLL** (H.M.V. CLP-1093) LP			5
	Deep River Boys - **That's Right** (H.M.V. POP-263)			6
	Sonny James - **The Cat Came Back** (Capitol CL-14635)			6
	Alma Cogan - **In The Middle Of The House** (H.M.V. POP-261)			8
	Slim Whitman - **The Whiffenpoof Song** (London HLU-8327)			8

3		10	17	24
★	Alma Cogan - **In The Middle Of The House** (H.M.V. POP-261)			
★	Elvis Presley - **ROCK 'N ROLL** (H.M.V. CLP-1093) 🅛🅟			
1	Norrie Paramor & His Orch. - **Autumn Concerto** (Columbia DB-3815)	1	5	10
2	Big Ben Accordion Band - **Rock'n'Roll No. 1 [M]** (Columbia DB-3835)		5	
3	Bill Haley & His Comets - **ROCK AROUND THE CLOCK** (Brunswick OE-9250) 🅔🅟	5	5	1
3	Slim Whitman - **The Whiffenpoof Song** / **Dear Mary** (London HLU-8327)			
5	Sonny James - **The Cat Came Back** (Capitol CL-14635)			2
6	Mario Lanza - **Earthbound** (H.M.V. DA-2086)			14
	Robert Earl - **More** (Philips PB-622)	2		
	Deep River Boys - **That's Right** (H.M.V. POP-263)	3	15	
	Jimmy Shand & His Band - **Marching With Jimmy Shand [M]** (Parlophone R-4151)	4		
	Elvis Presley - **Blue Moon** / **I Don't Care If The Sun Don't Shine** (H.M.V. POP-272)	5	★	
	Tommy Steele & The Steelmen - **Elevator Rock** / **Doomsday Rock** (Decca F-10808)	5	2	4
	Ted Heath & His Music - **Canadian Sunset** (Decca F-10783)	8		
	Kathie Kay - **A House With Love In It** (H.M.V. POP-265)	8	11	
	Platters - **THE FABULOUS PLATTERS** (Mercury MEP-9504) 🅔🅟	8		
	Bunk Johnson & His New Orleans Band - **BUNK JOHNSON & HIS NEW ORLEANS BAND** (Brunswick OE-9257) 🅔🅟	11		
	Ted Heath & His Music - **Autumn Concerto** (Decca F-10777)	12		10
	Andy Williams - **Canadian Sunset** (London HLA-8315)	12		
	Bill Haley & His Comets - **Rudy's Rock** (Brunswick 05616)		1	★
	Stan Kenton & His Orch. - **CUBAN FIRE!** (Capitol LCT-6118) 🅛🅟		3	
	Jimmy Shand and the Balmoral Trio - **Sing With Jimmy Shand [M]** (Parlophone R-4242)		4	
	Little Richard - **Rip It Up** (London HLO-8336)		8	14
	Bing Crosby and Grace Kelly - **True Love** (Capitol CL-14645)		9	★
	Charlie McNair Skiffle Group - **Hiawatha Rag** (Beltona BL-2670)		9	
	Arthur Baird Skiffle Group - **Union Maid** (Beltona BL-2669)		11	
	Liberace - **I'll Be Seeing You** (Philips PB-625)		11	
	Guy Mitchell - **I'd Like To Say A Few Words About Texas** (Philips PB-635)		11	
	Carmen Cavallaro - **Autumn Concerto** (Brunswick 05609)		15	
	Voices - **Rock 'n Roll Hit Parade [M]** (Beltona BL-2667)		15	
	Bill Haley & His Comets - **ROCK 'N ROLL** (Brunswick OE-9214) 🅔🅟			3
	Sammy Davis Jr. - **Frankie And Johnny** (Brunswick 05611)			5
	Ray Ellington Quartet - **The Green Door** (Columbia DB-3838)			5
	Johnston Brothers and the Keynotes - **In The Middle Of The House** (Decca F-10781)			5
	Fats Domino - **Blueberry Hill** (London HLU-8330)			8
	Bing Crosby and Louis Armstrong - **Now You Has Jazz** (Capitol CL-14643)			9
	Johnston Brothers - **Join In And Sing No. 3 [M]** (Decca F-10814)			10
	OST - **HIGH SOCIETY** (Capitol LCT-6116) 🅛🅟			10

1		8	15	22	29
★	Fats Domino - **Blueberry Hill** *(London HLU-8330)*				
★	Sonny James - **The Cat Came Back** *(Capitol CL-14635)*				
★	Johnston Brothers and the Keynotes - **In The Middle Of The House** *(Decca F-10781)*				
★	Jimmy Shand and the Balmoral Trio - **Sing With Jimmy Shand [M]** *(Parlophone R-4242)*				
1	Charlie McNair Skiffle Group - **Hiawatha Rag / Meadow Lane Stomp** *(Beltona BL-2670)*	2	3	3	3
2	OST - **HIGH SOCIETY** *(Capitol LCT-6116)* **LP**	5	★		
3	Platters - **THE FABULOUS PLATTERS** *(Mercury MEP-9504)* **EP**				
4	Ted Heath & His Music - **Autumn Concerto** *(Decca F-10777)*				
4	Kathie Kay - **A House With Love In It** *(H.M.V. POP-265)*				
4	Tommy Steele & The Steelmen - **Elevator Rock / Doomsday Rock** *(Decca F-10808)*	5	7	7	7
7	Four Grads - **The Night Is Young And You're So Beautiful** *(Oriole CB-1334)*				
7	Vince Martin with the Tarriers - **Cindy, Oh Cindy** *(London HLN-8340)*	2	★		
	Deep River Boys - **That's Right** *(H.M.V. POP-263)*	★			
	Johnston Brothers - **Join In And Sing No. 3 [M]** *(Decca F-10814)*	★			
	Tommy Steele & The Steelmen - **Singing The Blues** *(Decca F-10819)*	1	★		
	Art Baxter & His Rock'n'Roll Sinners - **Rock And Roll Rag** *(Philips PB-652)*	4			
	Bing Crosby and Louis Armstrong - **Now You Has Jazz** *(Capitol CL-14643)*	7	5	5	5
	Ella Fitzgerald and Louis Armstrong - **ELLA AND LOUIS** *(H.M.V. CLP-1098)* **LP**	7			
	Goons - **My September Love** *(Parlophone R-4251)*	7	3	3	3
	Various Artists - **SCOTS TRADITIONAL JAZZ CONCERT** *(Beltona ABL-519)* **LP**	10	7	7	7
	Little Richard - **Rip It Up** *(London HLO-8336)*		★		
	Beverley Sisters - **Come Home To My Arms** *(Decca F-10813)*		1	1	1
	Max Bygraves - **That Dear Old Gentleman** *(H.M.V. POP-262)*		1	1	1
	Ruby Murray - **True Love** *(Columbia DB-3849)*		5	5	5
	Carmen Cavallaro - **Autumn Concerto** *(Brunswick 05609)*		7	7	7
	Dave King - **Christmas And You** *(Decca F-10791)*		7	★	

There were no new bubblers in the week of 22 December. *Record Mirror* was not published on 29 December, so the previous week's positions have been repeated.

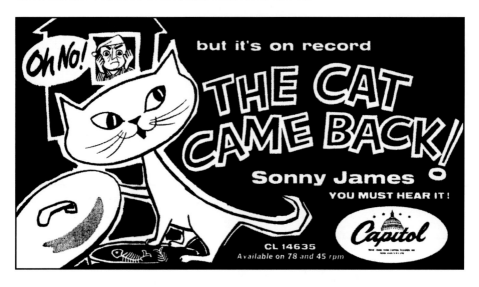

	5	12	19	26
Bill Haley & His Comets - **ROCK AROUND THE CLOCK** (Brunswick OE-9250) **EP**	1			
Platters - **THE FABULOUS PLATTERS** (Mercury MEP-9504) **EP**	2	2		
Charlie McNair - **Hiawatha Rag** (Beltona BL-2670)	3		4	
Ella Fitzgerald and Louis Armstrong - **ELLA AND LOUIS** (H.M.V. CLP-1098) **LP**	4			
David Hughes - **Two Different Worlds** (Philips PB-642)	4			
Kathie Kay - **Old Scotch Mother** (H.M.V. POP-167)	4			
Jimmy Shand & His Band - **Marching With Jimmy Shand [M]** (Parlophone R-4151)		1	7	
Bing Crosby and Louis Armstrong - **Now You Has Jazz** (Capitol CL-14643)		2		3
Bill Doggett Combo - **Honky Tonk** (Parlophone R-4231)		2		
Goons - **My September Love** (Parlophone R-4251)		2		
Alma Cogan - **You, Me And Us** (H.M.V. POP-284)		6	★	
Clyde Valley Stompers - **Pearly Gates** / **Old Time Religion** (Beltona BL-2650)		7		9
Fats Domino - **Ain't That A Shame** (London HLU-8173)		7	5	★
Fats Domino - **Honey Chile** (London HLU-8356)		7		
Elvis Presley - **LOVE ME TENDER** (H.M.V. 7EG-8199) **EP**		7	2	5
Dickie Valentine - **Rock'n'Roll Party [M]** (Decca F-10820)		7		
Vipers Skiffle Group - **Don't You Rock Me Daddy-O** (Parlophone R-4261)			1	★
Platters - **You'll Never Never Know** / **It Isn't Right** (Mercury MT-130)			3	★
Monty Norman - **The Garden Of Eden** (H.M.V. POP-281)			5	
Lynne Allison - **Mama From The Train** (Columbia DB-3867)			7	
Nat 'King' Cole - **To The Ends Of The Earth** (Capitol CL-14661)			7	
Bill Haley & His Comets - **ROCK 'N ROLL** (Brunswick OE-9214) **EP**			7	
Frank Sinatra - **Hey, Jealous Lover** (Capitol CL-14607)			7	7
Bridie Gallagher - **A Mother's Love Is A Blessing** (Beltona BE-2653)				1
Little Richard - **Long Tall Sally** / **Tutti Frutti** (London HLO-8366)				2
Bob Cort Skiffle Group - **Don't You Rock Me Daddy-O** (Decca Jazz FJ-10831)				3
Vipers Skiffle Group - **Pick A Bale Of Cotton** (Parlophone R-4238)				5
Robert Earl - **I'm Free** (Philips PB-657)				7
Doris Day - **Julie** (Philips PB-634)				9
Bill Haley & His Comets - **Rock The Joint** (London HLF-8371)				9
Ted Heath & His Music - **Armen's Theme** (Decca F-10827)				9

2		9	16	23
★	Fats Domino - **Honey Chile** (London HLU-8356)			
★	Bill Haley & His Comets - **Rock The Joint** (London HLF-8371)			
1	Lonnie Donegan - **LONNIE DONEGAN HIT PARADE** (Pye Nixa NEP-24031) **EP**	7		
1	Elvis Presley - **LOVE ME TENDER** (H.M.V. 7EG-8199) **EP**		3	
3	Johnston Brothers - **Give Her My Love (When You Meet Her)** (Decca F-10828)	★		
3	Little Richard - **Long Tall Sally / Tutti Frutti** (London HLO-8366)	★		
5	Doris Day - **Julie** (Philips PB-634)			
5	Bridie Gallagher - **A Mother's Love Is A Blessing** (Beltona BE-2653)	11	10	8
5	Platters - **THE FABULOUS PLATTERS** (Mercury MEP-9504) **EP**	2	1	6
8	Michael Holliday - **Yaller Yaller Gold** (Columbia DB-3871)	12		
9	Joe Lynch - **Homes Of Donegal** (Beltona BE-2672)	5	4	5
9	Anne Shelton - **Give Her My Love (When You Meet Her) / A Man On The March** (Philips PB-661)	1		
9	Frank Sinatra - **You're Sensational** (Capitol CL-14646)			10
12	Chris Barber's Skiffle Group - **THE CHRIS BARBER SKIFFLE GROUP** (Pye Nixa NJE-1025) **EP**		9	
12	Jill Day - **I Dreamed / Give Her My Love When You Meet Her** (H.M.V. POP-288)			
12	Tab Hunter - **Young Love** (London HLD-8380)		★	
12	Frank Sinatra - **Hey, Jealous Lover** (Capitol CL-14607)			
16	Lynne Allison - **Mama From The Train** (Columbia DB-3867)			
16	Chris Barber's Jazz Band - **CHRIS BARBER PLAYS (VOL. 3)** (Pye Nixa NJT-505) **LP**			
16	Bill Haley & His Comets - **ROCK AROUND THE CLOCK** (Brunswick OE-9250) **EP**	12		
16	Sonny James - **Young Love** (Capitol CL-14683)	★		
	Fats Domino - **Blue Monday** (London HLP-8377)	2	7	
	Frankie Lymon & The Teenagers - **Baby Baby / I'm Not A Juvenile Delinquent** (Columbia DB-3878)	2	2	1
	Jimmy Young - **My Faith, My Hope, My Love** (Decca F-10842)	5	7	
	Lita Roza - **Hey! Jealous Lover** (Decca F-10830)	7	10	
	David Seville & His Orch. - **Armen's Theme** (London HLU-8359)	7		10
	Frankie Laine - **Champion The Wonder Horse** (Philips PB-607)	10		
	Little Richard - **LITTLE RICHARD & HIS BAND (VOL. 1)** (London REO-1071) **EP**	12	5	7
	Bill Haley & His Comets - **Hook, Line And Sinker** (Brunswick 05641)	15	6	
	OST - **THE KING AND I (PART 2)** (Capitol EAP2-740) **EP**	15		
	Teresa Brewer - **When I Leave The World Behind** (Vogue Coral Q-72224)		7	
	Vera Lynn - **The Faithful Hussar** (Decca F-10846)		10	
	Elvis Presley - **Rip It Up** (H.M.V. POP-305)			2
	Little Richard - **She's Got It / The Girl Can't Help It** (London HLO-8382)			3
	Tarriers - **The Banana Boat Song** (Columbia DB-3891)			3
	Billie Anthony - **I Dreamed** (Columbia DB-3874)			8
	Dean Martin - **The Man Who Plays The Mandolino** (Capitol CL-14690)			10

Jimmy Young

Michael Holliday

Lita Roza

Fats Domino

2		9	16	23	30
★	Tarriers - **The Banana Boat Song** (Columbia DB-3891)				
1	Elvis Presley - **Rip It Up** (H.M.V. POP-305)	★			
2	Little Richard - **She's Got It** / **The Girl Can't Help It** (London HLO-8382)	★			
3	Fats Domino - **Blue Monday** (London HLP-8377)	1	1	4	★
3	Frankie Lymon & The Teenagers - **Baby Baby** / **I'm Not A Juvenile Delinquent** (Columbia DB-3878)	8	18	2	★
3	David Seville & His Orch. - **Armen's Theme** (London HLU-8359)				
6	Nat 'King' Cole - **You Are My First Love** (Capitol CL-14688)	8	3	4	7
7	Joe Lynch - **Homes of Donegal** / **Delaney's Donkey** (Beltona BE-2672)	13		10	12
8	Frank Sinatra - **Hey, Jealous Lover** (Capitol CL-14607)	16	9		
	Jill Day - **I Dreamed** / **Give Her My Love When You Meet Her** (H.M.V. POP-288)	★			
	Ronnie Carroll - **The Wisdom Of A Fool** / **Without Love** (Philips PB-667)	2	6	3	★
	Fontane Sisters - **The Banana Boat Song** (London HLD-8378)	2	2	8	
	Beverley Sisters - **Greensleeves** (Decca F-10853)	4			
	Vera Lynn - **The Faithful Hussar** (Decca F-10846)	4	★		
	Chas McDevitt Skiffle Group feat. Nancy Whiskey - **Freight Train** (Oriole CB-1352)	4		10	★
	Sarah Vaughan - **The Banana Boat Song** (Mercury MT-139)	4			
	Bridie Gallagher - **A Mother's Love Is A Blessing** (Beltona BE-2653)	8		8	3
	Platters - **THE FABULOUS PLATTERS** (Mercury MEP-9504) **EP**	11		15	17
	Norman Wisdom - **The Wisdom Of A Fool** (Columbia DB-3903)	11	★		
	Eddie Fisher - **BUNDLE OF JOY [OST]** (H.M.V. 7EG-8207) **EP**	13			
	Inia Te Wiata - **The Banana Boat Song** (H.M.V. POP-301)	13	3		
	Hilltoppers - **Marianne** (London HLD-8381)	16		7	15
	Frankie Laine - **Champion The Wonder Horse** (Philips PB-607)	16			
	Myles O'Connor - **Kevin Barry** (Beltona BE-2640)	16			
	Malcolm Vaughan - **The World Is Mine** (H.M.V. POP-303)	16		10	1
	Vipers Skiffle Group - **Hey Liley, Liley Lo** / **Jim Dandy** (Parlophone R-4286)	21	12	1	2
	Vipers Skiffle Group - **The Cumberland Gap** (Parlophone R-4289)		3	★	
	Tommy Sands - **Teen-Age Crush** (Capitol CL-14695)		7		10
	Gene Vincent & His Blue Caps - **Crazy Legs** (Capitol CL-14693)		7		
	Eddie Fisher - **Some Day Soon** (H.M.V. POP-296)		9		
	Connie Francis - **My Sailor Boy** (M.G.M. MGM-932)		9		
	Rose Brennan - **Without Love** (H.M.V. POP-302)		13		
	Little Richard - **LITTLE RICHARD & HIS BAND (VOL. 1)** (London REO-1071) **EP**		13		
	Harry Secombe - **Come Back To Sorrento** (Philips PB-658)		13		
	Frank Sinatra - **Can I Steal A Little Love** (Capitol CL-14696)		13		

'TENNESSEE' ERNIE FORD
(this time with Calypso beat)
'The Watermelon Song'
and
'ONE SUIT'
Both records available on 78 and 45 r.p.m.

Capitol

DEAN MARTIN
'The man who plays the Mandolino'
with 'I know I can't forget'

2 <<< MARCH 1957 >>>	9	16	23	30
Tommy Steele & The Steelmen - **YOUNG LOVE** *(Decca DFE-6388)* 🇪🇵	13	13		
Bob Cort Skiffle Group - **It Takes A Worried Man To Sing A Worried Blues** *(Decca Jazz FJ-10831)*	18			
Nilsson Twins - **Rain On My Window** *(Capitol CL-14698)*	18			
Frank Sinatra - **You're Sensational** *(Capitol CL-14646)*	18			
Dean Martin - **The Man Who Plays The Mandolino** *(Capitol CL-14690)*			★	
Max Bygraves - **Heart** *(Decca F-10862)*			4	4
Teresa Brewer - **Nora Malone** *(Vogue Coral Q-72224)*			13	
Alma Cogan - **Whatever Lola Wants** *(H.M.V. POP-317)*			15	★
Johnston Brothers - **Whatever Lola Wants** *(Decca F-10860)*			15	
Humphrey Lyttelton & His Band - **Baby Doll** *(Parlophone R-4277)*			15	
Nervous Norvus - **Ape Call** *(London HLD-8338)*			15	12
Freddy - **The Banana Boat Song** *(Polydor BM-6063)*				4
Ronnie Hilton - **Heart** *(H.M.V. POP-318)*				4
Dickie Bishop & The Sidekicks - **Cumberland Gap** *(Decca F-10869)*				7
Slim Whitman - **I'll Take You Home Again Kathleen** *(London HLP-8403)*				7
Vipers Skiffle Group - **Ain't You Glad** *(Parlophone R-4238)*				10
Julie London - **Cry Me A River** *(London HLU-8240)*				12
McGuire Sisters - **Heart** *(Vogue Coral Q-72238)*				15
Tennessee Ernie Ford - **The Watermelon Song** *(Capitol CL-14691)*				17
Terry Gilkyson & The Easy Riders - **Marianne** *(Philips PB-670)*				19
Ronnie Hilton - **The Wisdom Of A Fool** *(H.M.V. POP-291)*				19
Dave King - **Love Is A Golden Ring** *(Decca F-10865)*				19
Frankie Laine with the Easy Riders - **Love Is A Golden Ring** *(Philips PB-676)*				19

Teresa Brewer

Slim Whitman

McGuire Sisters

Little Richard

6	Artist - Title	13	20	27
★	Max Bygraves - **Heart** (Decca F-10862)			
★	Hilltoppers - **Marianne** (London HLD-8381)			
★	Julie London - **Cry Me A River** (London HLU-8240)			
1	Edric Connor - **Manchester United Calypso** (Oriole CB-1362)	1	1	15
2	Malcolm Vaughan - **The World Is Mine** (H.M.V. POP-303)	★		
2	Vipers Skiffle Group - **Hey Liley, Liley Lo / Jim Dandy** (Parlophone R-4286)	7	12	10
4	Bridie Gallagher - **A Mother's Love Is A Blessing** (Beltona BE-2653)	4	4	6
4	Slim Whitman - **I'll Take You Home Again Kathleen** (London HLP-8403)	★		
6	Teresa Brewer - **Nora Malone** (Vogue Coral Q-72224)	20		1
7	Joe Lynch - **Homes of Donegal / Delaney's Donkey** (Beltona BE-2672)	12	7	
7	Frank Sinatra - **Can I Steal A Little Love** (Capitol CL-14696)		11	
9	Eddie Cochran - **20 Flight Rock** (London HLU-8386)			12
9	Four Aces - **Heart** (Brunswick 05651)	17	7	8
9	Frankie Laine with the Easy Riders - **Love Is A Golden Ring** (Philips PB-676)	2	★	
9	Platters - **THE FABULOUS PLATTERS** (Mercury MEP-9504) **EP**			
13	Harry Belafonte - **CALYPSO** (H.M.V. 7EG-8211) **EP**			
13	Nappy Brown - **Little By Little** (London HLC-8384)	17		
15	Dickie Bishop & The Sidekicks - **Cumberland Gap** (Decca F-10869)			
15	Pat Boone - **Why Baby Why** (London HLD-8404)	4	3	★
15	Frank Sinatra - **Hey, Jealous Lover** (Capitol CL-14607)			
	Andy Williams - **Butterfly** (London HLA-8399)	3	★	
	Kathie Kay - **Every Day Is Mother's Day** (H.M.V. POP-315)	4		
	Charlie Gracie - **Butterfly** (Parlophone R-4290)	7	★	
	Johnston Brothers - **Heart** (Decca F-10860)	7	★	
	Stan Freberg - **Banana Boat (Day-O)** (Capitol CL-14712)	10		8
	Fats Domino - **I'm Walkin' / I'm In The Mood For Love** (London HLP-8407)	11	★	
	Johnnie Ray - **I Miss You So / So Long** (Philips PB-683)	12		
	Malcolm Vaughan - **Chapel Of The Roses** (H.M.V. POP-325)	12	10	4
	Nat 'King' Cole - **NIGHT LIGHTS** (Capitol EAP1-801) **EP**	15		
	Bill Haley & His Comets - **Forty Cups Of Coffee** (Brunswick 05658)	15	5	18
	Teresa Brewer - **I'm Drowning My Sorrows** (Vogue Coral Q-72239)	17		
	Perry Como - **Round And Round / My House Is Your House** (H.M.V. POP-328)		2	1
	Ronnie Hilton - **Heart** (H.M.V. POP-318)		6	23
	Frankie Lymon & The Teenagers - **Teenage Love** (Columbia DB-3910)		7	18
	Dave King - **Love Is A Golden Ring** (Decca F-10865)		12	15
	Platters - **On My Word Of Honor / One In A Million** (Mercury MT-143)			3
	Stargazers - **Mangos** (Decca F-10867)			5
	Jimmy Young - **Round And Round / Walkin' After Midnight** (Decca F-10875)			6
	Dickie Valentine - **Chapel Of The Roses** (Decca F-10874)			10
	2.19 Skiffle Group - **Freight Train Blues** (Esquire 10-497)			12
	Andrews Sisters - **Rum And Coca-Cola** (Capitol CL-14705)			14
	Ruby Murray - **Heart** (Columbia DB-3911)			15
	Enid Blyton - **Noddy Is Naughty** (H.M.V. BD-1299)			18
	Johnny Burnette Trio - **Lonesome Train** (Vogue Coral Q-72277)			18
	Paddy Carney - **They Can't Change The Name Of Ireland** (Decca (Irish Series) MU-12)			18
	Frankie Vaughan - **Cold, Cold Shower** (Philips PB-681)			23

4		11	18	25
★	Jimmy Young - **Round And Round / Walkin' After Midnight** (Decca F-10875)			
1	Platters - **On My Word Of Honor / One In A Million** (Mercury MT-143)	1	3	
2	Perry Como - **Round And Round / My House Is Your House** (H.M.V. POP-328)	11	4	
3	Bridie Gallagher - **A Mother's Love Is A Blessing** (Beltona BE-2653)		4	
4	Kathie Kay - **Old Scotch Mother** (H.M.V. POP-167)		7	10
4	Elvis Presley - **Too Much** (H.M.V. POP-330)	★		
6	Edric Connor - **Manchester United Calypso** (Oriole CB-1362)	4		
6	Vipers Skiffle Group - **Hey Liley, Liley Lo / Jim Dandy** (Parlophone R-4286)			
8	Teresa Brewer - **Nora Malone** (Vogue Coral Q-72224)	★		
8	Bill Haley & His Comets - **Forty Cups Of Coffee** (Brunswick 05658)			
8	Ronnie Hilton - **Heart** (H.M.V. POP-318)			
8	Dave King - **Love Is A Golden Ring** (Decca F-10865)			
8	Ruby Murray - **Heart** (Columbia DB-3911)			
8	Platters - **THE FABULOUS PLATTERS** (Mercury MEP-9504) `EP`			
	Malcolm Vaughan - **Chapel Of The Roses** (H.M.V. POP-325)	★		
	Johnnie Ray - **I Miss You So / So Long** (Philips PB-683)	2		
	Happy Wanderers - **JAZZ ON THE STREETS OF LONDON** (Esquire 20-081) `LP`	3		
	2.19 Skiffle Group - **Freight Train Blues** (Esquire 10-497)	4		
	Stan Freberg - **Banana Boat (Day-O)** (Capitol CL-14712)	6		
	Steve Lawrence - **Party Doll** (Vogue Coral Q-72243)	6	7	2
	Slim Whitman - **Gone** (London HLP-8420)	6	2	1
	Dell-Vikings - **Come Go With Me** (London HLD-8405)	9	11	
	David Seville & His Orch. - **Armen's Theme** (London HLU-8359)	9		
	Russ Hamilton - **We Will Make Love** (Oriole CB-1359)		1	★
	Peggy Lee - **Mr. Wonderful** (Brunswick 05671)		6	★
	Ronnie Hilton - **Around The World** (H.M.V. POP-338)		7	★
	King Brothers - **Marianne** (Parlophone R-4288)		7	
	Bing Crosby - **Around The World** (Brunswick 05674)		11	★
	Gene & Eunice - **Move It Over, Baby** (Vogue V-9066)		11	
	Sammy Davis Jr. - **Too Close For Comfort** (Brunswick 05668)			3
	Ted Heath & His Music - **Madagascar** (Decca F-10856)			4
	Frank Sinatra - **Can I Steal A Little Love** (Capitol CL-14696)			4
	Frankie Laine - **Without Him** (Philips PB-691)			6
	Jeri Southern - **Fire Down Below** (Brunswick 05665)			6
	Vipers Skiffle Group - **Streamline Train** (Parlophone R-4308)			6
	Terry Dene - **A White Sport Coat (And A Pink Carnation)** (Decca F-10895)			9
	Eartha Kitt - **Just An Old Fashioned Girl** (H.M.V. POP-309)			10
	Dickie Valentine - **Chapel Of The Roses** (Decca F-10874)			10

1		8	15	22	29
★	Vipers Skiffle Group - **Streamline Train** (Parlophone R-4308)				
1	Jeri Southern - **Fire Down Below** (Brunswick 05665)	6	3	★	
2	Perry Como - **The Girl With The Golden Braids** (R.C.A. RCA-1001)				
2	Fontane Sisters - **The Banana Boat Song** (London HLD-8378)	8			
4	Chuck Berry - **School Day** (Columbia DB-3951)	7	6	★	
5	Clyde Valley Stompers - **Milenberg Joys** /	3		2	1
	Bill Bailey, Won't You Please Come Home (Decca Jazz F-10897)				
5	Bob Cort Skiffle - **Six-Five Special** (Decca F-10892)				
5	Chas McDevitt Skiffle Group feat. Nancy Whiskey - **Green Back Dollar**		★		
	(Oriole CB-1371)				
5	Ruby Murray - **Mr. Wonderful** (Columbia DB-3933)		5		
9	Tommy Steele & The Steelmen - **Shiralee** (Decca F-10896)		4		
10	Perry Como - **Round And Round / My House Is Your House**				
	(H.M.V. POP-328)				
10	Ferlin Husky - **Gone** (Capitol CL-14702)	10			
10	Kathie Kay - **Old Scotch Mother** (H.M.V. POP-167)				
10	Slim Whitman - **Gone** (London HLP-8420)	6	1	3	
	Terry Dene - **A White Sport Coat (And A Pink Carnation)** (Decca F-10895)	★			
	Harry Belafonte - **Island In The Sun** (R.C.A. RCA-1007)	1	★		
	Steve Lawrence - **Party Doll** (Vogue Coral Q-72243)	2	1	11	5
	Charlie Gracie - **Fabulous** (Parlophone R-4313)	4	★		
	Vipers Skiffle Group - **Ain't You Glad** (Parlophone R-4238)	4			
	Marion Ryan - **Mr. Wonderful** (Pye Nixa N-15091)	8			
	Eddie Cochran - **20 Flight Rock** (London HLU-8386)	10		8	
	Kathie Kay - **Wind In The Willow / We Will Make Love** (H.M.V. POP-352)	10		5	5
	Elvis Presley - **All Shook Up** (H.M.V. POP-359)			1	★
	Gene Vincent & His Blue Caps - **Five Days, Five Days** (Capitol CL-14722)			3	8
	Dell-Vikings - **Come Go With Me** (London HLD-8405)			5	8
	Kay Starr - **Jamie Boy** (H.M.V. POP-357)			7	4
	Ronnie Carroll - **Around The World** (Philips PB-695)			8	
	Lloyd Price - **Just Because** (London HL-8438)			8	11
	Chuck Miller - **The Auctioneer** (Mercury MT-153)			11	
	Marty Robbins - **A White Sport Coat (And A Pink Carnation)**				1
	(Philips PB-696)				
	Everly Brothers - **Bye Bye, Love** (London HLA-8440)				3
	Chuck Willis - **C.C. Rider** (London HLE-8444)				5
	Nat 'King' Cole - **It's All In The Game** (Capitol CL-14733)				8
	Harry Belafonte - **Mama Looka Boo Boo** (H.M.V. POP-339)				11
	Bridie Gallagher - **Killarney And You** (Beltona BE-2679)				11
	Gene & Eunice - **Move It Over, Baby** (Vogue V-9066)				11
	Elvis Presley - **PEACE IN THE VALLEY** (R.C.A. RCX-101) **EP** †				11

Charlie Gracie

Fontane Sisters

Terry Dene

Eddie Cochran

† This EP eventually charted in September 1961.

6		13	20	27
★	Nat 'King' Cole - **When Rock And Roll Came To Trinidad** (Capitol CL-14733) [†]			
1	Everly Brothers - **Bye Bye, Love** (London HLA-8440)	★		
2	Clyde Valley Stompers - **Milenberg Joys** /	9	7	4
	Bill Bailey, Won't You Please Come Home (Decca Jazz F-10897)			
2	Kathie Kay - **Wind In The Willow** / **We Will Make Love** (H.M.V. POP-352)	4	1	1
4	Bob Cort Skiffle - **School Day** (Decca F-10905)			
5	Ronnie Carroll - **Around The World** (Philips PB-695)	10		
6	Fats Domino - **Valley Of Tears** (London HLP-8449)	2	★	
6	Johnny Duncan & The Blue Grass Boys - **Last Train To San Fernando**	5	2	★
	(Columbia DB-3959)			
6	Ruby Murray - **Mr. Wonderful** (Columbia DB-3933)			
9	Kay Starr - **Jamie Boy** (H.M.V. POP-357)			
	Guy Mitchell - **Sweet Stuff** / **In The Middle Of A Dark, Dark Night**	1	6	★
	(Philips PB-712)			
	Eve Boswell - **Sugar Candy** (Parlophone R-4328)	2		
	Bridie Gallagher - **Killarney And You** (Beltona BE-2679)	5	2	
	'Big' Tiny Little - **School Day** (Vogue Coral Q-72263)	5	4	
	Eve Boswell - **Chantez, Chantez** (Parlophone R-4299)	8		
	Chas McDevitt Skiffle Group - **It Takes A Worried Man (To Sing A Worried Song)**	10		
	(Oriole CB-1357)			
	Gene & Eunice - **Move It Over Baby** / **This Is My Story** (Vogue V-9066)	12		
	Bill Haley & His Comets - **Billy Goat** (Brunswick 05688)	12	5	4
	Gary Miller - **Wonderful, Wonderful** (Pye Nixa N.15094)	12	★	
	Petula Clark - **With All My Heart** (Pye Nixa N.15096)		7	★
	Billy Williams - **I'm Gonna Sit Right Down And Write Myself A Letter**		9	2
	(Vogue Coral Q-72266)			
	Jim Dale - **Piccadilly Line** (Parlophone R-4329)		10	
	Ronnie Hilton - **Wonderful! Wonderful!** (H.M.V. POP-364)		10	
	Elvis Presley - **PEACE IN THE VALLEY** (R.C.A. RCX-101) **EP** [‡]		10	
	Russ Conway - **Soho Fair** (Columbia DB-3971)			3
	Brenda Lee - **Love You 'Till I Die** (Brunswick 05685)			4
	Mantovani & Hs Orch. - **Mandolin Serenade** (Decca F-10918)			7
	Tommy Steele & The Steelmen - **Shiralee** (Decca F-10896)			7
	Gene & Eunice - **I Gotta Go Home** (Vogue V-9062)			9
	Harry Belafonte - **Scarlet Ribbons** (H.M.V. POP-360)			10

[†] Flip of 'It's All In The Game'.
[‡] This EP eventually charted in September 1961.

3	Artist - Title	10	17	24	31
★	Ronnie Hilton - **Wonderful! Wonderful!** (H.M.V. POP-364)				
★	Billy Williams - **I'm Gonna Sit Right Down And Write Myself A Letter** (Vogue Coral Q-72266)				
1	Kathie Kay - **We Will Make Love / Wind In The Willow** (H.M.V. POP-352)	1	1	1	1
2	Tommy Steele & The Steelmen - **Shiralee** (Decca F-10896)	4	5		★
3	Bill Haley & His Comets - **Billy Goat** (Brunswick 05688)			11	
4	Clyde Valley Stompers - **Milenberg Joys /** **Bill Bailey, Won't You Please Come Home** (Decca Jazz F-10897)	2	2	1	1
5	Joe 'Mr. Piano' Henderson - **Forgotten Dreams / Coffee Bar Jive** (Pye Nixa N.15099)		7		
	Jodie Sands - **With All My Heart** (London HL-8456)	3	5	3	
	Tommy Steele & The Steelmen - **Water, Water / A Handful Of Songs** (Decca F-10923)	4	★		
	John Fraser - **Bye, Bye, Love** (Pye Nixa N.15098)	6			
	Judy Scott - **With All My Heart** (Brunswick 05687)	7			
	Gale Storm - **Dark Moon** (London HLD-8424)	7		9	
	Eddie Cochran - **20 Flight Rock** (London HLU-8386)	9			
	Jerry Lee Lewis - **Whole Lotta Shakin' Goin' On** (London HLS-8457)	10			
	Coasters - **Searchin'** (London HLE-8450)		3	5	5
	Shirley Bassey - **Fire Down Below / You, You Romeo** (Philips PB-723)		4	★	
	Tony Bennett - **One For My Baby** (Philips PB-710)		8		
	Lloyd Price - **Just Because** (London HL-8438)		9		
	Lorrae Desmond - **Kansas City Special** (Parlophone R-4320)			3	
	Tony Bennett - **In The Middle Of An Island / I Am** (Philips PB-724)			6	8
	Joan Savage - **With All My Heart** (Columbia DB-3968)			6	
	Dave King - **With All My Heart** (Decca F-10910)			8	
	Johnny Duncan & The Blue Grass Boys - **JOHNNY DUNCAN & HIS BLUE GRASS BOYS** (Columbia SEG-7708) EP			9	
	Frankie Vaughan - **These Dangerous Years** (Philips PB-674)			11	6
	Buddy Greco - **With All My Heart** (London HLR-8452)				3
	Tommy Steele & The Steelmen - **Elevator Rock** (Decca F-10808)				3
	Humphrey Lyttelton & His Band - **Early Call (Bermondsey Bounce)** (Parlophone R-4333)				6

7		14	21	28
★	Harry Belafonte - **Scarlet Ribbons** (H.M.V. POP-360)			
1	Frankie Vaughan - **These Dangerous Years** (Philips PB-674)	3	★	
2	Clyde Valley Stompers - **Milenberg Joys** / **Bill Bailey, Won't You Please Come Home** (Decca Jazz F-10897)	4	2	
3	Jimmy Jackson's Rock 'n' Skiffle - **I Shall Not Be Moved** (Columbia DB-3898)			
3	Frankie Vaughan - **Cold, Cold Shower** (Philips PB-681)	13		
5	Kathie Kay - **We Will Make Love** / **Wind In The Willow** (H.M.V. POP-352)			
5	Little Richard - **Jenny Jenny** (London HLO-8470)	★		
5	Joan Savage - **With All My Heart** (Columbia DB-3968)			
8	Billy Ward & The Dominos - **Stardust** (London HLU-8465)	★		
9	Murray Campbell - **Mandolin Serenade** (Philips PB-718)			
9	Dell-Vikings - **Whispering Bells** (London HLD-8464)	4		
9	Robert Earl - **Fascination** (Philips PB-730)			
9	Peggy Lee - **SONGS FROM WALT DISNEY'S LADY AND THE TRAMP** (Brunswick LA-8731) 🅛🅟			
9	Jerry Lee Lewis - **Whole Lotta Shakin' Goin' On** (London HLS-8457)	10	4	★
9	Station Skiffle Group - **Hugged My Honey** (Esquire 10-503)			
9	Malcolm Vaughan - **What Is My Destiny** (H.M.V. POP-381)			
	Larry Williams - **Short Fat Fannie** (London HLN-8472)	1	★	
	Kathie Kay - **Tammy** (H.M.V. POP-385)	2	1	
	Coasters - **Searchin'** (London HLE-8450)	4		★
	Nat 'King' Cole - **My Personal Possession** / **Send For Me** (Capitol CL-14765)	4		
	Dave King - **With All My Heart** (Decca F-10910)	4		
	Frankie Laine - **Gunfight At The O.K. Corral** (Philips PB-709)	9		
	Lorrae Desmond - **Kansas City Special** (Parlophone R-4320)	11		
	Frankie Laine - **The 3.10 To Yuma** (Philips PB-727)	11		
	Ella Fitzgerald - **Manhattan** (H.M.V. POP-373)	13		
	Buddy Greco - **With All My Heart** (London HLR-8452)	13		
	Frankie Lymon & The Teenagers - **Goody Goody** (Columbia DB-3983)	13	★	
	Jane Morgan - **Fascination** (London HLR-8468)	13		
	Betty Smith's Skiffle - **There's A Blue Ridge Round My Heart Virginia** (Tempo A-162)	13		
	Sarah Vaughan and Billy Eckstine - **Passing Strangers** (Mercury MT-164)	13	3	★
	Fats Domino - **When I See You** / **What Will I Tell My Heart** (London HLP-8471)		4	3
	Platters - **My Dream** (Mercury MT-156)		4	
	Don Rondo - **White Silver Sands** (London HLJ-8466)		4	
	Tony Brent - **Deep Within Me** (Columbia DB-3987)		8	
	Jimmie Rodgers - **Honey Comb** (Columbia DB-3986)		9	2
	Pat Boone - **Remember You're Mine** / **There's A Goldmine In The Sky** (London HLD-8479)		10	★
	Crickets - **That'll Be The Day** (Vogue Coral Q-72279)		10	★
	Elvis Presley - **GOOD ROCKIN' TONIGHT** (H.M.V. 7EG-8256) 🅔🅟			1
	Bill Haley & His Comets - **Billy Goat** (Brunswick 05688)			3
	Bing Crosby and Louis Armstrong - **Now You Has Jazz** (Capitol CL-14643)			5

Jerry Lee Lewis

Larry Williams

The Crickets

Peggy Lee

OCTOBER 1957

5		12	19	26
1	Betty Smith's Skiffle - **There's A Blue Ridge Round My Heart Virginia** *(Tempo A-162)*			
2	Jimmie Rodgers - **Honey Comb** *(Columbia DB-3986)*	1	1	1
3	Nat 'King' Cole - **My Personal Possession / Send For Me** *(Capitol CL-14765)*	7	★	
4	Dell-Vikings - **Whispering Bells** *(London HLD-8464)*			
4	Johnny Duncan & The Blue Grass Boys - **Blue Blue Heartache / Jig Along Home** *(Columbia DB-3996)*	6	4	★
4	Don Rondo - **White Silver Sands** *(London HLJ-8466)*			
4	Vipers Skiffle Group - **Homing Bird** *(Parlophone R-4351)*	3		
8	Fats Domino - **When I See You / What Will I Tell My Heart** *(London HLP-8471)*			
9	Frankie Vaughan - **Cold, Cold Shower** *(Philips PB-681)*		8	
	Various Artists - **Top Ten Special** *(Parlophone R-4356)*	2	3	2
	Elvis Presley - **ELVIS PRESLEY** *(R.C.A. RCX-104)* **EP**	3		
	Ames Brothers - **Tammy** *(R.C.A. RCA-1015)*	5		
	Bing Crosby and Louis Armstrong - **Now You Has Jazz** *(Capitol CL-14643)*	7		
	Bill Haley & His Comets - **Forty Cups Of Coffee** *(Brunswick 05658)*	7		
	Les Hobeaux - **Oh, Mary Don't You Weep** *(H.M.V. POP-377)*	7	8	
	Kathie Kay - **Tammy** *(H.M.V. POP-385)*		2	
	Terry Dene - **Teenage Dream** *(Decca F-10938)*		5	
	Ella Fitzgerald - **Ev'ry Time We Say Goodbye / Manhattan** *(H.M.V. POP-373)*		5	
	Tommy Sands - **Let Me Be Loved** *(Capitol CL-14781)*		5	
	Don Fox - **Be My Girl** *(Decca F-10927)*		8	5
	Bill Haley & His Comets - **Hook, Line And Sinker** *(Brunswick 05641)*		8	
	Jimmy Miller & The Barbecues - **Sizzlin' Hot** *(Columbia DB-4006)*		8	
	Tommy Steele & The Steelmen - **Hey You!** *(Decca F-10941)*			2
	Buddy Knox - **Hula Love / Devil Woman** *(Columbia DB-4014)*			4
	Marty Wilde & His Wildcats - **Honeycomb** *(Philips PB-750)*			6

2		9	16	23	30
★	Jimmie Rodgers - **Honey Comb** (Columbia DB-3986)				
1	Kathie Kay - **Tammy** (H.M.V. POP-385)	1	3		
2	Don Fox - **Be My Girl** (Decca F-10927)		3	2	4
3	Marty Wilde & His Wildcats - **Honeycomb** (Philips PB-750)				12
4	Terry Dene - **Teenage Dream** (Decca F-10938)				
4	Don Lang & His Frantic Five - **White Silver Sands** (H.M.V. POP-382)				
4	Tommy Steele & The Steelmen - **Hey You! / Plant A Kiss** (Decca F-10941)	3	★		
7	Buddy Knox - **Hula Love / Devil Woman** (Columbia DB-4014)				
7	Marion Ryan - **Ding Dong Rock-A-Billy Wedding / That's Happiness** (Pye Nixa N.15105)	10	10		
9	Russ Conway - **The Red Cat** (Columbia DB-3999)	7	6		
9	Jackie Wilson - **Reet Petite** (Vogue Coral Q-72290)	5	★		
	Clyde Valley Stompers - **Milenberg Joys** (Decca Jazz F-10897)	2	2		
	King Brothers - **Wake Up Little Susie** (Parlophone R-4367)	4	1	1	
	Shepherd Sisters - **Alone** (H.M.V. POP-411)	6	★		
	Bobbettes - **Mr. Lee** (London HLE-8477)	7	8	12	
	Terry Wayne - **Matchbox** (Columbia DB-4002)	7			
	Clyde Valley Stompers - **Pearly Gates** (Beltona BL-2650)	10			
	Johnny Otis Show - **Ma (He's Making Eyes At Me)** (Capitol CL-14794)	10	5	★	
	Elvis Presley - **Santa Bring My Baby Back** (R.C.A. RCA-1025)	10	★		
	Faron Young - **SWEETHEARTS OR STRANGERS (PART 1)** (Capitol EAP1-778) EP		6		
	Frankie Laine - **Gunfight At The O.K. Corral** (Philips PB-709)		8		
	Shirley Bassey - **Puh-leeze! Mister Brown** (Philips PB-757)		10		5
	Bing Crosby - **MERRY CHRISTMAS (VOL. 1)** (Brunswick OE-9069) EP		10		
	Vic Damone - **An Affair To Remember** (Philips PB-745)		10		12
	Tommy Sands - **Let Me Be Loved** (Capitol CL-14781)		10	12	7
	Vipers Skiffle Group - **Homing Bird** (Parlophone R-4351)		10		
	Billy Ward & His Dominoes - **Deep Purple** (London HLU-8502)		10	12	★
	Vipers Skiffle Group - **Skiffle Party [M]** (Parlophone R-4371)		3		
	Kaye Sisters - **Alone** (Philips PB-752)		4		1
	Brother Sisters - **Alone** (Mercury MT-186)		5		
	Bobby Helms - **My Special Angel** (Brunswick 05721)		5		★
	Malcolm Vaughan - **What Is My Destiny** (H.M.V. POP-381)		5		10
	Sam Cooke - **You Send Me** (London HLU-8506)		8		
	Johnny Duncan & The Blue Grass Boys - **Footprints In The Snow / Get Along Home Cindy** (Columbia DB-4029)		8		★
	Dave King - **Chances Are** (Decca F-10947)		8		
	Dale Hawkins - **Susie-Q** (London HL-8482)		11		
	Ames Brothers - **Melodie d'Amour** (R.C.A. RCA-1021)		12		
	Don Fox - **Party Time** (Decca F-10955)		12		
	Kathie Kay - **Be Content / My Last Love** (H.M.V. POP-410)		12		5
	Ricky Nelson - **Be-Bop Baby** (London HLP-8499)				1
	Rays - **Silhouettes** (London HLU-8505)				3
	Eric Delaney & His Band - **Truckin'** (Mercury MB-3168)				7
	Buddy Holly - **Peggy Sue** (Vogue Coral Q-72293)				7
	Pat Boone - **April Love** (London HLD-8512)				10
	Winifred Atwell - **Let's Have A Ball [M]** (Decca F-10956)				12
	Freddie Mills - **One For The Road [M]** (Parlophone R-4374)				12

7		14	21	28
★	Winifred Atwell - **Let's Have A Ball [M]** *(Decca F-10956)*			
★	Pat Boone - **April Love** *(London HLD-8512)*			
★	Vic Damone - **An Affair To Remember** *(Philips PB-745)*			
★	Buddy Holly - **Peggy Sue** *(Vogue Coral Q-72293)*			
★	King Brothers - **Wake Up Little Susie** *(Parlophone R-4367)*			
1	Kathie Kay - **Be Content / My Last Love** *(H.M.V. POP-410)*	1	2	2
2	Rays - **Silhouettes** *(London HLU-8505)*	2		
3	Brother Sisters - **Alone** *(Mercury MT-186)*	3		
3	Jim Dale - **Crazy Dream / Just Born** *(Parlophone R-4376)*	3	1	1
5	Ricky Nelson - **Be-Bop Baby** *(London HLP-8499)*	5	4	4
6	Bing Crosby - **Man On Fire** *(Capitol CL-14761)*	6		
7	Don Fox - **Be My Girl** *(Decca F-10927)*	7		
8	Russ Conway - **Piano Pops No. 1 [M]** *(Columbia DB-4015)*	8		
8	Robert Earl - **My Special Angel** *(Philips PB-767)*	8		
8	Gracie Fields - **Mary's Boy Child** *(Columbia DB-4047)*	8		
11	Frankie Laine - **The Greater Sin** *(Philips PB-760)*	11		
	Kaye Sisters - **Alone / Shake Me I Rattle** *(Philips PB-752)*		3	3
	Fats Domino - **Wait And See** *(London HLP-8519)*		5	5
	Frank D'Rone - **My Special Angel** *(Mercury MT-183)*		6	6
	Johnston Brothers - **Join In And Sing No. 4 [M]** *(Decca F-10962)*		6	6
	Marion Ryan - **Ding Dong Rock-A-Billy Wedding / That's Happiness** *(Pye Nixa N.15105)*		8	8
	Clyde Valley Stompers - **Milenberg Joys** *(Decca Jazz F-10897)*		9	9
	Thurston Harris and the Sharps - **Little Bitty Pretty One** *(Vogue V-9092)*		9	9
	Tommy Sands - **Let Me Be Loved** *(Capitol CL-14781)*		11	11

Dealers' returns were not published on 14 or 28 December, so for these weeks the positions of the preceding week have been repeated, except for those records which charted.

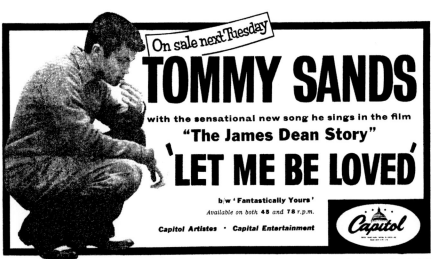

4			11	18	25
★	Jim Dale - **Crazy Dream** / **Just Born** (*Parlophone R-4376*)				
★	Kaye Sisters - **Alone** / **Shake Me I Rattle** (*Philips PB-752*)				
1	Jimmy Shand & His Band - **Sing In The New Year [M]** (*Parlophone R-4382*)				
2	Kathie Kay - **Be Content** (*H.M.V. POP-410*)		1	1	1
3	Johnston Brothers - **Join In And Sing No. 4 [M]** (*Decca F-10962*)				
4	Sam Cooke - **You Send Me** (*London HLU-8506*)		2	★	
4	Ricky Nelson - **Be-Bop Baby** (*London HLP-8499*)				
	Billy Vaughn & His Orch. - **Raunchy** / **Sail Along Silvery Moon** (*London HLD-8522*)		3		6
	Johnnie Ray - **Pink Sweater Angel** / **Texas Tambourine** (*Philips PB-762*)		4		
	Marion Ryan - **Ding Dong Rock-A-Billy Wedding** (*Pye Nixa N.15105*)		5		
	Danny & The Juniors - **At The Hop** (*H.M.V. POP-436*)		6	★	
	Delta Skiffle Group - **K.C. Moan** (*Esquire 10-507*)		6		
	Ernie Freeman - **Raunchy** (*London HLP-8523*)		6	2	9
	Michael Holliday - **The Story Of My Life** (*Columbia DB-4058*)		6	★	
	Ken Mackintosh & His Orch. - **Raunchy** (*H.M.V. POP-426*)		6		
	Clyde McPhatter - **Rock And Cry** (*London HLE-8525*)		6		
	Dave King - **The Story Of My Life** (*Decca F-10973*)			3	★
	Laurie London - **She Sells Sea Shells** (*Parlophone R-4388*)			4	9
	King Brothers - **Put A Light In The Window** (*Parlophone R-4389*)			5	2
	Louis Prima - **Buona Sera** (*Capitol CL-14821*)			6	
	Clyde Valley Stompers - **Milenberg Joys** (*Decca Jazz F-10897*)			7	
	Eydie Gormé - **Love Me Forever** (*H.M.V. POP-432*)			7	★
	Eartha Kitt - **Just An Old Fashioned Girl** (*H.M.V. POP-309*)			7	
	Robert Earl - **My Special Angel** (*Philips PB-767*)				3
	Four Esquires - **Love Me Forever** (*London HLO-8533*)				3
	Frank Sinatra - **Witchcraft** (*Capitol CL-14819*)				5
	Lynn Hope - **Blue Moon** (*Vogue V-9081*)				6
	Dennis Lotis - **Good Mornin' Life** (*Columbia DB-4056*)				6
	Thurston Harris and the Sharps - **Little Bitty Pretty One** (*Vogue V-9092*)				9
	Frankie Laine - **Gunfight At The O.K. Corral** (*Philips PB-709*)				9
	Southlanders - **Peanuts** (*Decca F-10958*)				9

Laurie London
HANDED DOWN
She sells sea-shells
PARLOPHONE R4388
Regd. Trade Mark of The Parlophone Co. Ltd.

Marion Ryan
That's Happiness
Ding Dong Rock-a-Billy Wedding
Nixa N 15105

1		8	15	22
★	Four Esquires - **Love Me Forever** (London HLO-8533)			
★	King Brothers - **Put A Light In The Window** (Parlophone R-4389)			
1	Marty Robbins - **The Story Of My Life** (Fontana H-102)	6		
2	Kathie Kay - **Be Content** (H.M.V. POP-410)	5	4	
2	Anne Shelton - **Ha! Ha! Ha!** (Philips PB-779)			
2	Nick Todd - **At The Hop** (London HLD-8537)	1	★	
5	Ernie Freeman - **Raunchy** (London HLP-8523)	2	1	6
6	Diamonds - **The Stroll** (Mercury 7MT-195)	14	7	4
7	Laurie London - **She Sells Sea Shells** (Parlophone R-4388)			
7	Dennis Lotis - **Good Mornin' Life** (Columbia DB-4056)			
7	Frank Sinatra - **Witchcraft** (Capitol CL-14819)	★		
	Ken Mackintosh & His Orch. - **Raunchy** (H.M.V. POP-426)	★		
	Southlanders - **Put A Light In The Window** (Decca F-10982)	3	★	
	Billy Vaughn & His Orch. - **Raunchy** (London HLD-8522)	4	★	
	George Hamilton IV - **Why Don't They Understand** (H.M.V. POP-429)	6		6
	Louis Prima - **Buona Sera** (Capitol CL-14821)	6		★
	Chuck Berry - **Rock And Roll Music** (London HLM-8531)	9	4	6
	Winifred Atwell - **Raunchy** (Decca F-10987)	10		
	Margaret Barry - **If You Ever Go To Ireland** (Topic TRC-99)	10		
	Bobby Helms - **No Other Baby** (Brunswick 05730)	10	★	
	Hilltoppers - **The Joker** (London HLD-8528)	13		15
	Clyde Valley Stompers - **Milenberg Joys** (Decca Jazz F-10897)	15		
	Russ Hamilton - **My Mother's Eyes** (Oriole CB-1406)	15		
	Ricky Nelson - **Stood Up** (London HLP-8542)	15	1	★
	Sammy Salvo - **Oh Julie** (R.C.A. RCA-1032)	15		11
	Nat 'King' Cole - **Angel Smile** (Capitol CL-14820)		1	
	Gene Vincent & His Blue Caps - **I Got A Baby** / **Walkin' Home From School** (Capitol CL-14830)		4	6
	Edmund Hockridge - **I'll Buy You A Star** (Pye Nixa 7N.15117)		8	
	Fats Domino - **Wait And See** (London HLP-8519)		9	
	Petula Clark - **Baby Lover** (Pye Nixa 7N.15126)			1
	Jim Dale - **Sugartime** / **Don't Let Go** (Parlophone R-4402)			1
	Jumpin' Jacks - **My Girl, My Girl** (H.M.V. POP-440)			3
	Hollywood Flames - **Buzz, Buzz, Buzz** (London HL-8545)			4
	Bridie Gallagher - **The Boys From County Armagh** / **Killarney And You** (Beltona BE-2679)			6
	Dave Brubeck Quartet - **JAZZ AT THE BLACKHAWK** (Vogue LAE-12094) `LP`			12
	Johnny Duncan & The Blue Grass Boys - **If You Love Me Baby** (Columbia DB-4074)			12
	Johnnie Ray - **Miss Me Just A Little** (Philips PB-785)			12
	Patrick Galvin with Al Jeffery - **IRISH SONGS OF RESISTANCE (PART II)** (Topic T-4) `8" Mini-LP`			15
	Johnny Mathis - **Wild Is The Wind** (Fontana H-103)			15
	Marvin Rainwater - **Whole Lotta Woman** (M.G.M. MGM-974)			15

Chuck Berry

Russ Hamilton

Petula Clark

The Southlanders

1		8	15	22	29
★	Petula Clark - **Baby Lover** *(Pye Nixa 7N.15126)*				
★	Edric Connor - **Manchester United Calypso** *(Oriole CB-1362)*				
★	Marvin Rainwater - **Whole Lotta Woman** *(M.G.M. MGM-974)*				
1	Jim Dale - **Sugartime / Don't Let Go** *(Parlophone R-4402)*	★			
2	Frankie Vaughan - **We're Not Alone / Can't Get Along Without You** *(Philips PB-793)*	★			
3	Gene Vincent & His Blue Caps - **I Got A Baby / Walkin' Home From School** *(Capitol CL-14830)*				
4	Bridie Gallagher - **The Boys From County Armagh / Killarney And You** *(Beltona BE-2679)*				
5	Ernie Freeman - **Raunchy** *(London HLP-8523)*				
5	George Hamilton IV - **Why Don't They Understand** *(H.M.V. POP-429)*	★			
7	Silhouettes - **Get A Job** *(Parlophone R-4407)*		5	5	5
8	Chuck Berry - **Rock And Roll Music** *(London HLM-8531)*				
8	Patrick Galvin with Al Jeffery - **IRISH SONGS OF RESISTANCE (PART II)** *(Topic T-4)* 8" Mini-LP		15		17
8	Tiny Topsy and the Charms - **Come On, Come On, Come On** *(Parlophone R-4397)*				
11	Diamonds - **The Stroll** *(Mercury 7MT-195)*				
11	Johnny Duncan & The Blue Grass Boys - **If You Love Me Baby** *(Columbia DB-4074)*		5		
11	Jerry Lee Lewis - **You Win Again** *(London HLS-8559)*	4		10	
11	Royal Teens - **Short Shorts** *(H.M.V. POP-454)*				8
	Winifred Atwell - **Raunchy** *(Decca F-10987)*	1			
	Crickets - **Maybe Baby** *(Coral Q-72307)*	1	★		
	Moe Koffman Quartet - **Swingin' Shepherd Blues** *(London HLJ-8549)*	1	1	★	
	Johnny Pate Quintet - **Swinging Shepherd Blues** *(Parlophone R-4404)*	5	3		
	Sammy Salvo - **Oh Julie** *(R.C.A. RCA-1032)*	6			
	Everly Brothers - **This Little Girl Of Mine / Should We Tell Him** *(London HLA-8554)*	7	9	2	
	Faron Young - **SWEETHEARTS OR STRANGERS (PART 3)** *(Capitol EAP3-778)* EP		2	10	
	Jimmie Rodgers - **Oh-Oh, I'm Falling In Love Again** *(Columbia DB-4078)*		4	1	★
	Billy Eckstine - **If I Can Help Somebody** *(Mercury 7MT-191)*		5		
	Marion Ryan - **Oh Oh, I'm Falling In Love Again / Always And Forever** *(Pye Nixa 7N.15130)*		5	7	
	Carl Perkins - **Glad All Over** *(London HLS-8527)*		9		
	Jimmy Edwards - **Love Bug Crawl** *(Mercury 7MT-193)*		11		
	Louvin Brothers - **TRAGIC SONGS OF LIFE** *(Capitol EAP1-769)* EP		11		7

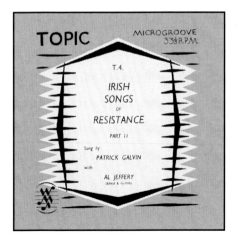

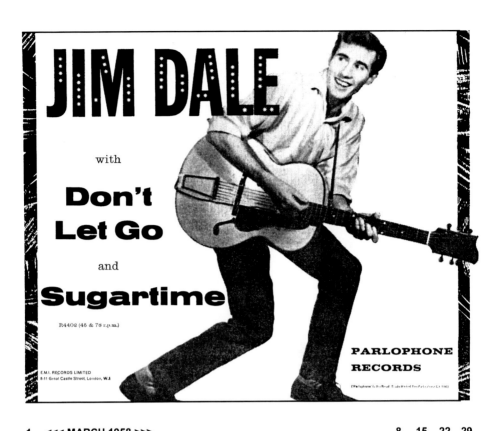

1 <<< MARCH 1958 >>>	8	15	22	29
Malcolm Vaughan - **To Be Loved** (H.M.V. POP-459)	11	★		
Sarah Vaughan - **My Darling, My Darling** (Mercury 7MT-198)	11			
Hollywood Flames - **Buzz, Buzz, Buzz** (London HL-8545)	15			
OST - **LES GIRLS / THE PIRATE** (M.G.M. C-763) **LP**	15			
Hank Snow - **COUNTRY GUITAR (VOL. 4)** (R.C.A. RCX-116) **EP**	15	14	2	
Fats Domino - **The Big Beat** (London HLP-8575)		3	★	
Pat Boone - **A Wonderful Time Up There** (London HLD-8574)		4	1	
Tommy Sands - **Sing Boy Sing** (Capitol CL-14834)		6		
Johnny Mathis - **Wild Is The Wind** (Fontana H-103)		8		
Hank Williams - **SONGS FOR A BROKEN HEART** (M.G.M. MGM-EP-639) **EP**		8		
Connie Francis - **Who's Sorry Now** (M.G.M. MGM-975)		10	4	
Johnny Otis Show - **All I Want Is Your Love** (Capitol CL-14837)		10	11	
Johnny Cash - **Give My Love To Rose / Home Of The Blues** (London HLS-8514)		14		
Rosemary Squires - **Happy Is The Bride** (H.M.V. POP-462)		14		
Champs - **Tequila** (London HLU-8580)			3	
Marino Marini & His Quartet - **The Pansy** (Durium DC-16629)			5	
Billy & Lillie - **La Dee Dah** (London HLU-8564)			8	
Russ Conway - **Piano Pops No. 3 [M]** (Columbia DB-4097)			8	
Robert Earl - **I May Never Pass This Way Again** (Philips PB-805)			11	
Owen Bradley Quintet - **Big Guitar** (Brunswick 05736)			13	
Nancy Whiskey - **NANCY WHISKEY SINGS** (Topic 7T-10) **7" Mini-LP**			13	
OBC - **THE PAJAMA GAME** (Philips BBL-7050) **LP**			15	
Tommy Steele & The Steelmen - **Happy Guitar / Princess** (Decca F-10976)			15	
Buddy Knox - **Swingin' Daddy** (Columbia DB-4077)			17	
Hank Thompson & His Brazos Valley Boys - **HANK** (Capitol EAP1-826) **EP**			17	

APRIL 1958

5		12	19	26
★	Pat Boone - **A Wonderful Time Up There** / **It's Too Soon To Know** (London HLD-8574)			
★	Champs - **Tequila** (London HLU-8580)			
★	Connie Francis - **Who's Sorry Now** (M.G.M. MGM-975)			
1	Chuck Berry - **Sweet Little Sixteen** (London HLM-8585)	2	★	
1	Billy & Lillie - **La Dee Dah** (London HLU-8564)			
1	Owen Bradley Quintet - **Big Guitar** (Brunswick 05736)			
1	Johnny Cash - **Ballad Of A Teenage Queen** (London HLS-8586)		1	1
5	Robert Earl - **I May Never Pass This Way Again** (Philips PB-805)		5	★
6	Tommy Collins - **Think It Over, Boys** (Capitol CL-14838)			
6	Johnny Otis Show - **All I Want Is Your Love** / **The Light Still Shines In My Window** (Capitol CL-14837)	9		
8	Bonnie Lou and Rusty York - **La Dee Dah** (Parlophone R-4409)			
8	Floyd Cramer - **Flip, Flop And Bop** (R.C.A. RCA-1050)	4		
8	Ernie Freeman - **Dumplin's** (London HLP-8558)			
8	Ted Heath & His Music - **Tequila** (Decca F-11003)	★		
12	Chordettes - **Lollipop** (London HLA-8584)	1	★	
12	Sammy Salvo - **Oh Julie** (R.C.A. RCA-1032)			
12	Tommy Sands - **Sing Boy Sing** (Capitol CL-14834)			
15	Bing Crosby - **Man On Fire** (Capitol CL-14761)			
15	Toni Dalli - **If You Loved Me** / **Just Say I Love Her** (Columbia DB-4096)			8
15	Danny & The Juniors - **Rock And Roll Is Here To Stay** (H.M.V. POP-467)	4	9	
15	Everly Brothers - **This Little Girl Of Mine** (London HLA-8554)			
15	Frankie Laine - **Gunfight At The O.K. Corral** (Philips PB-709)			
15	Kathy Linden - **Billy** (Felsted AF-102)			
15	Tommy Steele & The Steelmen - **Happy Guitar** / **Princess** (Decca F-10976)	9	★	
	Stan Kenton & His Orch. - **Tequila** (Capitol CL-14847)	3		
	Charlie Gracie - **Crazy Girl** (London HLU-8596)	6		
	Johnny (The Gash) Gray - **Tequila** (Fontana H-123)	6		
	Mudlarks - **Lollipop** (Columbia DB-4099)	6	9	★
	Ronnie Hilton - **I May Never Pass This Way Again** (H.M.V. POP-468)	9	★	
	Johnny Mathis - **Wild Is The Wind** (Fontana H-103)	9		
	Don Gibson - **Oh, Lonesome Me** (R.C.A. RCA-1056)		1	
	Marino Marini & His Quartet - **The Pansy** (Durium DC-16629)		1	17
	John Barry Seven - **Big Guitar** (Parlophone R-4418)		4	
	Dicky Doo & The Don'ts - **Click Clack** (London HLU-8589)		5	12
	Jimmy McCracklin & His Band - **The Walk** (London HLM-8598)		5	17
	Ricky Nelson - **Believe What You Say** (London HLP-8594)		5	
	Paul Anka - **Crazy Love** / **Let The Bells Keep Ringing** (Columbia DB-4110)		9	17

3		10	17	24	31
★	Max Bygraves - **Tulips From Amsterdam / You Need Hands** *(Decca F-11004)*				
1	Johnny Cash - **Ballad Of A Teenage Queen** *(London HLS-8586)*	2	1		12
2	Paul Anka - **Crazy Love / Let The Bells Keep Ringing** *(Columbia DB-4110)*	3	3	15	★
3	Al Jolson - **AMONG MY SOUVENIRS (PART 1)** *(Brunswick OE-9363)* **EP**			7	
4	Frankie Avalon - **Dede Dinah** *(H.M.V. POP-453)*		5	★	
4	Doris Day - **A Very Precious Love / Teacher's Pet** *(Philips PB-799)*			6	3
6	Ella Fitzgerald - **ELLA SINGS 'PAL JOEY'** *(H.M.V. 7EG-8327)* **EP**				
6	Larry Williams - **Dizzy Miss Lizzy / Slow Down** *(London HLU-8604)*	1	12		
8	Toni Dalli - **If You Loved Me / Just Say I Love Her** *(Columbia DB-4096)*	11			
9	Kathie Kay - **A House With Love In It** *(H.M.V. POP-265)*			5	13
9	Frankie Vaughan - **Kewpie Doll** *(Philips PB-825)*	★			
11	Perry Como - **Kewpie Doll** *(R.C.A. RCA-1055)*	★			
11	Terry Dene - **The Golden Age** *(Decca F-10977)*				
11	Marino Marini & His Quartet - **The Pansy** *(Durium DC-16629)*				
11	Hank Williams - **SONGS FOR A BROKEN HEART** *(M.G.M. MGM-EP-639)* **EP**				
15	Owen Bradley Quintet - **Big Guitar** *(Brunswick 05736)*				
15	Peter Miles - **My Little Girl** *(Columbia DB-4117)*	13	8		
15	Slim Whitman - **A Very Precious Love** *(London HLP-8590)*	5	15		13
	Terry Dene - **Stairway Of Love** *(Decca F-11016)*	3	★		
	Michael Holliday - **Stairway Of Love** *(Columbia DB-4121)*	5	★		
	Bill Haley & His Comets - **Skinny Minnie** *(Brunswick 05742)*	7	15	3	
	David Whitfield - **On The Street Where You Live** *(Decca F-11018)*	7	★		
	Ricky Nelson - **Believe What You Say / My Bucket's Got A Hole In It** *(London HLP-8594)*	9	10	1	6
	John Zacherle - **Dinner With Drac (Part 1)** *(London HLU-8599)*	9			
	Dean Martin - **Return To Me** *(Capitol CL-14844)*	12	2	2	
	Frankie Laine - **My Gal And A Prayer** *(Philips PB-821)*	13			
	Everly Brothers - **All I Have To Do Is Dream / Claudette** *(London HLA-8618)*		4	★	
	Ella Fitzgerald - **The Swingin' Shepherd Blues** *(H.M.V. POP-486)*		5	★	
	Andy Williams - **Are You Sincere** *(London HLA-8587)*		5		
	Gary Miller - **On The Street Where You Live** *(Pye Nixa 7N.15140)*		9		3
	Jimmy McCracklin & His Band - **The Walk** *(London HLM-8598)*		11	18	
	Ella Fitzgerald - **Ev'ry Time We Say Goodbye** *(H.M.V. POP-373)*		12	8	19
	David Seville & His Orch. - **Witch Doctor** *(London HLU-8619)*		12	★	
	Marion Ryan - **Stairway Of Love** *(Pye Nixa 7N.15138)*		15	15	
	Gene Vincent & His Blue Caps - **Baby Blue / True To You** *(Capitol CL-14868)*		15	9	
	Alma Cogan - **Stairway Of Love / Comes Love** *(H.M.V. POP-482)*		19		
	Don Lang & His Frantic Five - **Witch Doctor** *(H.M.V. POP-488)*		19	★	

3   <<< MAY 1958 >>>   **10** **17** **24** **31**

7		14	21	28
★	Chuck Berry - **Johnny B. Goode** *(London HLM-8629)*			
★	Mudlarks - **Book Of Love** *(Columbia DB-4133)*			
1	Four Preps - **Big Man** *(Capitol CL-14873)*	★		
2	Dean Martin - **Return To Me** *(Capitol CL-14844)*	★		
3	Doris Day - **A Very Precious Love** / **Teacher's Pet** *(Philips PB-799)*	★		
3	Ted Heath & His Music - **Tom Hark** *(Decca F-11025)*	2		
5	Marino Marini & His Quartet -			
	MARINO MARINI & HIS HAPPY MUSIC (VOL. 1) *(Durium U-20007)* **EP**			
6	Tommy Steele - **It's All Happening** *(Decca F-11026)*	8	10	17
7	Don Gibson - **Oh, Lonesome Me** *(R.C.A. RCA-1056)*	10	5	
7	Ronnie Hilton - **On The Street Where You Live** *(H.M.V. POP-479)*	16		
7	Spokes Mashiyane - **Boys Of Jo'burg** / **Jika Spokes** *(Oriole CB-1441)*			6
10	Johnny Cash - **Ballad Of A Teenage Queen** *(London HLS-8586)*	10		
10	Jimmie Rodgers - **Secretly** / **Make Me A Miracle** *(Columbia DB-4130)*			9
10	Frank Sinatra and Keely Smith - **How Are Ya' Fixed For Love?** *(Capitol CL-14863)*	1		
13	Lord Rockingham's XI - **Fried Onions** *(Decca F-11024)*			17
13	Johnny Mathis - **Chances Are** *(Philips PB-749)*			
	Monotones - **Book Of Love** *(London HLM-8625)*	2	2	14
	Frank Sinatra - **SINATRA!** *(Capitol EAP1-1013)* **EP**	2	1	1
	Eddie Calvert - **Little Serenade** *(Columbia DB-4105)*	5	★	
	Fats Domino - **Sick And Tired** *(London HLP-8628)*	5	2	9
	Bridie Gallagher - **Take This Message To My Mother** / **The Girl From Donegal** *(Beltona BE-2696)*	5		14
	Frank Sinatra - **THIS IS SINATRA (VOL. 2)** *(Capitol LCT-6155)* **LP**	8	★	
	Kathie Kay - **The Secret Of Happiness** *(H.M.V. POP-485)*	10		
	Sheb Wooley - **The Purple People Eater** *(M.G.M. MGM-981)*	10	★	
	Eartha Kitt - **African Lullaby** / **Monotonous** *(H.M.V. B-10803)*	14		
	Johnny Luck - **Play Rough** *(Fontana H-110)*	14		
	Renato Carasone - **Torero – Cha Cha Cha** *(Parlophone R-4433)*	16		6
	Southlanders - **Torero** *(Decca F-11032)*	16		3
	Rosemary Clooney - **I Could Have Danced All Night** *(Philips PB-800)*		2	6
	Aquatones - **You** *(London HLO-8631)*		5	9
	Nat 'King' Cole - **Looking Back** *(Capitol CL-14882)*		5	5
	Ferlin Husky - **The Drunken Driver** *(Capitol CL-14883)*		8	17
	Johnny Mathis - **Wild Is The Wind** *(Fontana H-103)*		8	
	Pat Boone - **Sugar Moon** *(London HLD-8640)*		10	★
	Jackie Dennis - **The Purple People Eater** *(Decca F-11033)*		10	★
	Mal Perry - **Make Me A Miracle** *(Fontana H-133)*		10	
	Joe 'Mr. Piano' Henderson - **Trudie** *(Pye Nixa 7N.15147)*			2
	Slim Whitman - **A Very Precious Love** *(London HLP-8590)*			3
	Bridie Gallagher - **At The Close Of An Irish Day** *(Beltona BE-2697)*			9
	Kaye Sisters - **Torero** *(Philips PB-832)*			9
	Guy Mitchell - **Hangin' Around** *(Philips PB-830)*			14
	Winifred Atwell - **Streets Of Sorento** *(Decca F-10924)*			17
	Dave King - **I Suddenly** *(Decca F-11012)*			17
	Julius LaRosa - **Torero** *(R.C.A. RCA-1063)*			17
	Little Richard - **Ooh! My Soul** *(London HLO-8647)*			17
	Larry Williams - **Dizzy Miss Lizzy** *(London HLU-8604)*			17
	Link Wray & His Ray Men - **Rumble** / **The Swag** *(London HLA-8623)*			17

5			12	19	26
★	Renato Carasone - **Torero – Cha Cha Cha** *(Parlophone R-4433)*				
★	Fats Domino - **Sick And Tired** *(London HLP-8628)*				
★	Ted Heath & His Music - **Tom Hark** *(Decca F-11025)*				
★	Julius LaRosa - **Torero** *(R.C.A. RCA-1063)*				
★	Frank Sinatra - **SINATRA!** *(Capitol EAP1-1013)* 🖽				
★	Art & Dotty Todd - **Chanson d'Amour** *(London HLB-8620)*				
1	Little Richard - **Ooh! My Soul / True, Fine Mama** *(London HLO-8647)*	★			
2	Jimmie Rodgers - **Secretly / Make Me A Miracle** *(Columbia DB-4130)*	3		12	
3	Diamond Accordion Band - **Irish Medley [M]** *(Beltona BE-2694)*				
4	Ella Fitzgerald - **St. Louis Blues / Beale Street Blues** *(H.M.V. POP-499)*	8	2	11	
4	Lord Rockingham's XI - **Fried Onions** *(Decca F-11024)*				
6	Joe 'Mr. Piano' Henderson - **Trudie** *(Pye Nixa 7N.15147)*		3	★	
7	Tommy Steele - **It's All Happening** *(Decca F-11026)*				
8	Aquatones - **You** *(London HLO-8631)*			17	
8	Nat 'King' Cole - **Looking Back** *(Capitol CL-14882)*	1	7	17	
8	Bobby Helms - **Jacqueline** *(Brunswick 05748)*				
8	Chuck Willis - **What Am I Living For** *(London HLE-8635)*				
12	Ferlin Husky - **The Drunken Driver** *(Capitol CL-14883)*			9	
12	Tommy Steele & The Steelmen - **The Only Man On The Island** *(Decca F-11041)*	★			
14	Bobby Freeman - **Do You Want To Dance** *(London HLJ-8644)*	4			
14	Ronnie Hilton - **On The Street Where You Live** *(H.M.V. POP-479)*				
14	Southlanders - **Torero** *(Decca F-11032)*			7	
17	Bridie Gallagher - **Take This Message To My Mother / The Girl From Donegal** *(Beltona BE-2696)*				
18	Dion & The Belmonts - **I Wonder Why** *(London HLH-8646)*				
18	Bobby Helms - **Fraulein** *(Brunswick 05711)*				
18	Dave King - **I Suddenly** *(Decca F-11012)*				
18	Spokes Mashiyane - **Boys Of Jo'burg / Jika Spokes** *(Oriole CB-1441)*				
18	Link Wray & His Ray Men - **Rumble** *(London HLA-8623)*				
23	Rosemary Clooney - **I Could Have Danced All Night** *(Philips PB-800)*				
23	Lonnie Donegan - **DONEGAN ON STAGE** *(Pye Nixa NEP-24075)* 🖽				
23	Kathie Kay - **Hillside In Scotland** *(H.M.V. POP-498)*			6	
23	Jack Marshall, His Orch. & Chorus - **Thunder Road Chase** *(Capitol CL-14888)*				
23	Pérez Prado & His Orch. - **Patricia** *(R.C.A. RCA-1067)*	5	6	★	
23	Chuck Willis - **That Train Has Gone** *(London HLE-8489)*				
	Frankie Vaughan - **Wonderful Things / Judy** *(Philips PB-834)*	2	1	17	
	Norrie Paramor & His Orch. - **I Could Have Danced All Night** *(Columbia DB-4119)*	5		21	
	David Whitfield - **The Right To Love / That's When Your Heartaches Begin** *(Decca F-11039)*	5	7	9	
	Monotones - **Book Of Love** *(London HLM-8625)*	8	3		
	Champs - **El Rancho Rock** *(London HL-8655)*		3	12	
	Chris Barber's Jazz Band - **When The Saints Go Marching In** *(Pye Nixa 7NJ-2023)*			7	
	Nancy Whiskey - **I Know Where I'm Goin' / Hillside In Scotland** *(Oriole CB-1452)*			1	
	Fats Domino - **Little Mary** *(London HLP-8663)*			2	
	Neville Taylor - **House Of Bamboo / Mercy, Mercy Percy** *(Parlophone R-4447)*			3	
	Coasters - **Yakety Yak** *(London HLE-8665)*			4	
	Five Chestnuts - **Teenage Love** *(Columbia DB-4165)*			4	
	Gene Kelly - **A Very Precious Love** *(R.C.A. RCA-1068)*			7	
	Glen Mason - **I May Never Pass This Way Again** *(Parlophone R-4415)*			12	
	Johnny Cash - **Guess Things Happen That Way** *(London HLS-8656)*			15	
	Bobby Darin - **Splish Splash** *(London HLE-8666)*			15	
	Alma Cogan - **Fly Away Lovers** *(H.M.V. POP-500)*			17	
	Russ Conway - **Got A Match** *(Columbia DB-4166)*			21	

2		9	16	23	30
★	Coasters - **Yakety Yak** (London HLE-8665)				
★	Bobby Darin - **Splish Splash** (London HLE-8666)				
★	Bobby Helms - **Jacqueline** (Brunswick 05748)				
★	Frankie Vaughan - **Wonderful Things** (Philips PB-834)				
1	Southlanders - **Torero** (Decca F-11032)		11		
2	Kathie Kay - **Hillside In Scotland** (H.M.V. POP-498)		8		
3	Peggy Lee - **Fever** (Capitol CL-14902)	1	★		
4	Nancy Whiskey - **I Know Where I'm Goin'** / **Hillside In Scotland** (Oriole CB-1452)	4	5		
5	Aquatones - **You** (London HLO-8631)	6	11		
6	Johnny Cash - **Guess Things Happen That Way** (London HLS-8656)	9	18		
6	Neville Taylor - **House Of Bamboo** / **Mercy, Mercy Percy** (Parlophone R-4447)				
8	Ella Fitzgerald - **St. Louis Blues** / **Beale Street Blues** (H.M.V. POP-499)			7	
8	Bridie Gallagher - **I'll Forgive But I'll Never Forget** (Beltona BE-2704)				
8	Frank Gallup - **Got A Match?** (H.M.V. POP-509)	6			
11	Norrie Paramor & His Orch. - **I Could Have Danced All Night** (Columbia DB-4119)				
11	David Whitfield - **The Right To Love** (Decca F-11039)	★			
11	Chuck Willis - **What Am I Living For** (London HLE-8635)		8		
14	Russ Conway - **Got A Match** (Columbia DB-4166)				★
14	Ronnie Hilton - **Her Hair Was Yellow** (H.M.V. POP-497)				
16	Nat 'King' Cole - **Come Closer To Me** (Capitol CL-14898)				
16	Charlie Drake - **Hello, My Darlings** / **Splish Splash** (Parlophone R-4461)	★			
	Bobby Freeman - **Do You Want To Dance** (London HLJ-8644)	2	6	1	2
	OBC - **MY FAIR LADY (VOL. 1)** (Philips BBE-12251) **EP**	3	4		
	Various Artists - **Lord's Taverners Star Band Hit Parade** (Decca F-11043)	4	10		
	Playmates - **Don't Go Home** (Columbia DB-4151)	6			
	Jan & Arnie - **Jennie Lee** (London HL-8653)	9			
	Gene Kelly - **A Very Precious Love** (R.C.A. RCA-1068)	9	11		
	Max Bygraves - **Gotta Have Rain** / **Little Train** (Decca F-11046)	12		★	
	Ella Fitzgerald - **Manhattan** (H.M.V. POP-373)	12			
	Frank Holder - **Nor The Moon By Night** (Parlophone R-4459)	12			
	Ricky Nelson - **Poor Little Fool** (London HLP-8670)	12	1	★	
	Duane Eddy - **Rebel-Rouser** (London HL-8669)		2	2	1
	Buddy Holly - **Early In The Morning** (Coral Q-72333)		2	★	
	Julie Andrews and Philippa Bevans - **I Could Have Danced All Night** (Philips PB-846)		6		
	Alma Cogan - **Fly Away Lovers** (H.M.V. POP-500)		11		
	Lord Melody - **The Devil** (Melodisc 45/1440)		11		
	Bridie Gallagher - **Hillside In Scotland** (Beltona BE-2705)		16		
	Russ Hamilton - **Little One** (Oriole CB-1404)		16		
	Nat 'King' Cole - **Looking Back** (Capitol CL-14882)		18		
	Jimmie Rodgers - **Secretly** (Columbia DB-4130)			★	
	Don Lang & His Frantic Five - **The Bird On My Head** (H.M.V. POP-510)			3	
	Malcolm Vaughan - **Ev'ry Hour, Ev'ry Day Of My Life** / **Miss You** (H.M.V. POP-502)			4	
	Mario Lanza - **Seven Hills Of Rome** (R.C.A. RCA-1045)			5	
	Gene Vincent & His Blue Caps - **Rocky Road Blues** (Capitol CL-14908)			5	3
	Marino Marini & His Quartet - **Come Prima** / **Volare** (Durium DC-16632)				4
	Poni-Tails - **Born Too Late** (H.M.V. POP-516)				4

6		13	20	27
★	Duane Eddy - **Rebel-Rouser** *(London HL-8669)*			
1	Connie Francis - **My Sailor Boy** *(M.G.M. MGM-932)*			
1	Gene Vincent & His Blue Caps - **Rocky Road Blues** *(Capitol CL-14908)*			
3	Bridie Gallagher - **The Boys From County Armagh** / **Killarney And You** *(Beltona BE-2679)*			3
3	Eydie Gormé - **You Need Hands** *(H.M.V. POP-493)*			
3	Hank Snow - **COUNTRY GUITAR (VOL. 4)** *(R.C.A. RCX-116)* **EP**			2
6	Johnny Mathis - **A Certain Smile** *(Fontana H-142)*		★	
7	Ferlin Husky - **I Saw God** *(Capitol CL-14916)*			
8	Ferlin Husky - **The Drunken Driver** *(Capitol CL-14883)*			
9	Connie Francis - **Eighteen** *(M.G.M. MGM-962)*			
9	Elvis Presley - **KING CREOLE (VOL. 1) [OST]** *(R.C.A. RCX-117)* **EP**	4	1	1
	Poni-Tails - **Born Too Late** *(H.M.V. POP-516)*	1	★	
	Lonnie Donegan - **Lonesome Traveller** / **Times Are Gettin' Hard Boys** *(Pye Nixa 7N.15158)*	2	★	
	Marino Marini & His Quartet - **Come Prima** / **Volare** *(Durium DC-16632)*	3	★	
	Chuck Berry - **Vacation Time** *(London HL-8677)*	4		
	Tom Lehrer - **SONGS BY TOM LEHRER** *(Decca LF-1311)* **LP**		2	9
	Malcolm Vaughan - **Ev'ry Hour, Ev'ry Day Of My Life** / **Miss You** *(H.M.V. POP-502)*			4
	Jack Scott - **My True Love** *(London HLU-8626)*			5
	Jerry Lee Lewis - **Break-Up** *(London HLS-8700)*			6
	Paul Robeson - **ROBESON'S HERE!** *(Topic TOP-32)* **EP**			6
	Marty Wilde & His Wildcats - **My Lucky Love** *(Philips PB-850)*			8

Ferlin Husky

Jack Scott

Duane Eddy

Marty Wilde

4		11	18	25
1	Elvis Presley - **KING CREOLE (VOL. 1) [OST]** (R.C.A. RCX-117) **EP**	4		
2	Frankie Avalon - **Ginger Bread** (H.M.V. POP-517)	★		
2	Bridie Gallagher - **The Boys From County Armagh** / **Killarney And You** (Beltona BE-2679)			6
4	Tom Lehrer - **SONGS BY TOM LEHRER** (Decca LF-1311) **LP**	10	2	5
4	Jack Scott - **My True Love** (London HLU-8626)	★		
4	Hank Snow - **COUNTRY GUITAR (VOL. 4)** (R.C.A. RCX-116) **EP**			
7	Shirley Bassey - **Hands Across The Sea** / **As I Love You** (Philips PB-845)			
7	Faron Young - **I Hate Myself** / **That's The Way I Feel** (Capitol CL-14930)			
9	Boots Brown & His Blockbusters - **Cerveza** (R.C.A. RCA-1078)	3		1
9	Four Aces - **Hangin' Up A Horseshoe** (Brunswick 05758)	10		
9	Debbie Reynolds - **This Happy Feeling** (Coral Q-72324)		5	
12	Eddie Cochran - **Summertime Blues** (London HLU-8702)	10	3	
12	Jerry Lee Lewis - **Break-Up** (London HLS-8700)	4		
12	Marty Wilde & His Wildcats - **My Lucky Love** (Philips PB-850)	14		
	Jodie Sands - **Someday (You'll Want Me To Want You)** (H.M.V. POP-533)	1	★	
	Malcolm Vaughan - **More Than Ever** (H.M.V. POP-538)	2	★	
	Tommy Dorsey Orchestra - **Tea For Two Cha Cha** (Brunswick 05757)	4	★	
	Johnny Cash- **The Ways Of A Woman In Love** (London HLS-8709)	7		
	Robin Luke - **Susie Darlin'** (London HLD-8676)	7	★	
	Elvis Presley - **KING CREOLE (VOL. 2) [OST]** (R.C.A. RCX-118) **EP**	7		
	Paul Anka - **Midnight** (Columbia DB-4172)	10		★
	Bobby Helms - **Fraulein** (Brunswick 05711)	14		
	Jim Backus - **Delicious (The Laughing Song)** (London HLJ-8674)	16		
	Lord Rockingham's XI - **Hoots Mon** (Decca F-11059)		1	★
	Ruby Murray - **Real Love** (Columbia DB-4192)		3	
	Robert Earl - **More Than Ever** (Philips PB-867)		6	★
	Kathie Kay - **Old Scotch Mother** (H.M.V. POP-167)			2
	Ferlin Husky - **Terrific Together** (Capitol CL-14922)			3
	Ferlin Husky - **The Drunken Driver** (Capitol CL-14883)			4
	Tommy Collins - **It Tickles** (Capitol CL-14894)			6
	Jim Dale - **Tread Softly Stranger** (Parlophone R-4424)			6
	Kalin Twins - **Forget Me Not** (Brunswick 05759)			6
	Jimmie Rodgers - **Are You Really Mine** (Columbia DB-4175)			6
	Johnny Cash - **I Walk The Line** (London HL-8358)			11
	Connie Francis- **I'll Get By** / **Fallin'** (M.G.M. MGM-993)			11
	Marino Marini & His Quartet - **I Could Have Danced All Night** (Durium DC-16634)			11

	1	8	15	22	29
Eddie Cochran - **Summertime Blues** (London HLU-8702)	★				
Connie Francis - **I'll Get By** / **Fallin'** (M.G.M. MGM-993)	★				
Tom Lehrer - **SONGS BY TOM LEHRER** (Decca LF-1311) **LP**	1	★			
Perry Como - **Love Makes The World Go 'round** / **Mandolins In The Moonlight** (R.C.A. RCA-1086)	2	★			
Kalin Twins - **Forget Me Not** (Brunswick 05759)	2	1		10	
Toni Dalli - **More Than Ever** (Columbia DB-4195)	4				
Ricky Nelson - **Someday** / **I Got A Feeling** (London HLP-8732)	4	★			
Bobby Day - **Rockin' Robin** (London HL-8726)	6	★			
Eddie Fontaine - **Nothin' Shakin'** (London HLM-8711)	6	2			17
Don Gibson - **Blue Blue Day** (R.C.A. RCA-1073)	6	7			
Roger Williams - **Near You** (London HLR-8690)	6	4			
Duane Eddy - **Ramrod** / **The Walker** (London HL-8723)		2	3		9
Crickets - **It's So Easy** (Coral Q-72343)		4	1	★	
Georgia Gibbs - **The Hula Hoop Song** (Columbia DB-4201)		4			
Bobby Darin - **Queen Of The Hop** (London HLE-8737)		7		10	
Tommy Steele - **Come On, Let's Go** / **Put A Ring On Her Finger** (Decca F-11072)		7	★		
Boots Brown & His Blockbusters - **Cerveza** (R.C.A. RCA-1078)		10	11		
Coasters - **Sorry But I'm Gonna Have To Pass** (London HLE-8729)		10			
Ken Mackintosh & His Orch. - **That Old Cha Cha Feeling** (H.M.V. POP-543)		10	8	10	
Cliff Richard & The Drifters - **High Class Baby** (Columbia DB-4203)			2	★	
Johnny Cash - **All Over Again** / **What Do I Care** (Philips PB-874)			4		
Jimmie Rodgers - **Woman From Liberia** (Columbia DB-4206)			4		8
Pat Boone - **Gee, But It's Lonely** / **For My Good Fortune** (London HLD-8739)			6		4
Champs - **Chariot Rock** (London HL-8715)			6	10	
Kingsmen - **Week-End** (London HLE-8735)			8	3	
Mike Preston - **My Lucky Love** (Decca F-11053)			8		
Peter Sellers - **I'm So Ashamed** / **A Drop Of The Hard Stuff** (Parlophone R-4491)				1	7
Hank Thompson & His Brazos Valley Boys - **Squaws Along The Yukon** (Capitol CL-14945)				2	2
Ferlin Husky - **I Saw God** (Capitol CL-14916)				3	
Ferlin Husky - **All Of The Time** (Capitol CL-14954)				3	
Ruby Murray - **Real Love** (Columbia DB-4192)				3	4
Southlanders - **The Mole In A Hole** (Decca F-11067)				7	9
Big Bopper - **Chantilly Lace** (Mercury AMT-1002)				8	19
Kathie Kay - **Old Scotch Mother** (H.M.V. POP-167)				8	9
Gordon MacRae - **The Secret** (Capitol CL-14920)				10	
Diamonds - **Walking Along** (Mercury AMT-1004)				15	
Ferlin Husky - **The Drunken Driver** (Capitol CL-14883)					1
Bridie Gallagher - **Goodbye Johnny** (Beltona BE-2707)					3
Harry Belafonte - **The Son Of Mary** (R.C.A. RCA-1084)					4
Cozy Cole - **Topsy** (London HL-8750)					9
Glen Mason - **The End** (Parlophone R-4485)					9
Ted Taylor Four - **Son Of Honky Tonk** (Oriole CB-1464)					9
Teresa Brewer - **The Hula Hoop Song** (Coral Q-72340)					15
Hank Snow - **COUNTRY GUITAR (VOL. 4)** (R.C.A. RCX-116) **EP**					15
Bridie Gallagher - **The Boys From County Armagh** / **Killarney And You** (Beltona BE-2679)					17
Franchito & His Orch. - **Eso Es El Amor** (Oriole CB-1467)					19

DECEMBER 1958

6		13	20	27
★	Pat Boone - **Gee, But It's Lonely** / **For My Good Fortune** (*London HLD-8739*)			
★	Cozy Cole - **Topsy** (*London HL-8750*)			
1	Edmund Hockridge - **More Than Ever** (*Pye Nixa 7N.15160*)			
1	Ferlin Husky - **The Drunken Driver** (*Capitol CL-14883*)			
3	Martinas & His Music - **Cha Cha Momma Brown** (*Columbia DB-4223*)	1	★	
4	Southlanders - **The Mole In A Hole** (*Decca F-11067*)			
5	Ruby Murray - **Real Love** (*Columbia DB-4192*)	★		
5	Jimmie Rodgers - **Woman From Liberia** (*Columbia DB-4206*)		★	
7	Hank Thompson & His Brazos Valley Boys - **Squaws Along The Yukon** (*Capitol CL-14945*)			
8	Harry Belafonte - **The Son Of Mary** (*R.C.A. RCA-1084*)	★		
8	Big Bopper - **Chantilly Lace** (*Mercury AMT-1002*)			
8	Ricky Nelson - **Lonesome Town** (*London HLP-8738*)		6	5
11	Peter Sellers - **I'm So Ashamed** (*Parlophone R-4491*)			
12	Harry Belafonte - **Silent Night** / **The Twelve Days Of Christmas** (*R.C.A. RCA-1085*)	7	10	8
12	Earl Grant - **The End** (*Brunswick 05762*)			
12	Rikki Price - **Tom Dooley** (*Fontana H-162*)		12	10
15	Steve Allen - **Almost In Your Arms** (*London HLD-8742*)			
15	Eddie Fontaine - **Nothin' Shakin'** (*London HLM-8711*)	7		
15	Franchito & His Orch. - **Eso Es El Amor** (*Oriole CB-1467*)	7	12	10
15	Buddy Holly - **Heartbeat** (*Coral Q-72346*)	2	★	
19	Bridie Gallagher - **Goodbye Johnny** (*Beltona BE-2707*)			
	Toni Dalli - **Catari, Catari** (*Columbia DB-4173*)	3		
	Duane Eddy - **Cannonball** (*London HL-8764*)	4	2	1
	Shirley Bassey - **As I Love You** (*Philips PB-845*)	5	★	
	Peggy Lee - **Sweetheart** (*Capitol CL-14955*)	5		
	Max Bygraves - **My Ukelele** (*Decca F-11077*)	7	6	5
	Tommy Dorsey Orchestra - **I Want To Be Happy Cha Cha** (*Brunswick 05769*)	7		
	Elvis Presley - **ELVIS SAILS** (*R.C.A. RCX-131*) 〔EP〕	7		
	Connie Francis - **You Always Hurt The One You Love** (*M.G.M. MGM-998*)		1	★
	Russ Conway - **'My Fair Lady' Pops [M]** (*Columbia DB-4191*)		2	1
	Dick James - **Daddy's Little Girl** (*Parlophone R-4498*)		4	3
	Little Richard - **Baby Face** (*London HLU-8770*)		5	4
	Shirley Bassey - **Kiss Me, Honey Honey, Kiss Me** (*Philips PB-860*)		6	★
	Gene & Eunice - **The Vow** (*Vogue Pop V-9126*)		6	5
	Glenn Miller & His Orch. - **GLENN MILLER SPECIAL** (*H.M.V. 7EG-8204*) 〔EP〕		11	9
	Bobby Darin - **Queen Of The Hop** (*London HLE-8737*)		12	10
	Slim Dusty - **A Pub With No Beer** (*Columbia DB-4212*)		12	10

3		10	17	24	31
★	Max Bygraves - **My Ukelele** (Decca F-11077)				
★	Duane Eddy - **Cannonball** (London HL-8764)				
★	Little Richard - **Baby Face** (London HLU-8770)				
1	Valerie Shane - **Meet Me Tonight In Dreamland** (Philips PB-879)				
	Big Bopper - **Chantilly Lace** (Mercury AMT-1002)	★			
	Bobby Darin - **Queen Of The Hop** (London HLE-8737)	★			
	Four Aces - **The World Outside** (Brunswick 05773)	1	2	★	
	John Barry Seven - **Farrago / Bee's Knees** (Parlophone R-4488)	2	4		
	Russ Conway - **The World Outside** (Columbia DB-4234)	3	★		
	Chipmunks - **The Chipmunk Song** (London HLU-8762)	4			
	Jimmy Shand & His Band - **Memories O' Rabbie Burns [M]** (Parlophone R-4512)	5			
	Ruth Brown - **This Little Girl's Gone Rockin'** (London HLE-8757)	6			
	Diamonds - **Walking Along** (Mercury AMT-1004)	6	7		4
	Franchito & His Orch. - **Eso Es El Amor** (Oriole CB-1467)	6			
	Ricky Nelson - **Lonesome Town** (London HLP-8738)	6		3	1
	Poni-Tails - **Seven Minutes In Heaven** (H.M.V. POP-558)	6			
	Big Ben Banjo Band - **Be Happy** (Columbia DB-4233)	11			
	Fats Domino - **Whole Lotta Loving** (London HLP-8759)	11	1	1	2
	Platters - **Smoke Gets In Your Eyes** (Mercury AMT-1016)	11	★		
	Slim Dusty - **A Pub With No Beer** (Columbia DB-4212)		3	2	★
	Edmund Hockridge - **Tonight** (Pye Nixa 7N.15167)		3		8
	Jerry Lee Lewis - **High School Confidential** (London HLS-8780)		5	★	
	Pinky & Perky - **Tom Dooley** (Decca F-11095)		5		
	Charlie Drake - **Tom Thumb's Tune** (Parlophone R-4496)		7		
	Billy Eckstine - **Gigi** (Mercury AMT-1018)		9		
	Joan Regan - **Love Like Ours** (H.M.V. POP-555)		9		
	Joni James - **There Must Be A Way** (M.G.M. MGM-1002)			5	★
	Eddie Calvert - **Trumpet Cha Cha Cha** (Columbia DB-4221)			6	
	Johnny Mathis - **Call Me** (Fontana H-163)			7	4
	Eartha Kitt - **Just An Old Fashioned Girl** (R.C.A. RCA-1087)			8	
	Paul Anka - **My Heart Sings** (Columbia DB-4241)			9	★
	Hugh O'Brian - **The Legend Of Wyatt Earp** (H.M.V. POP-539)			9	
	Playmates - **Beep Beep** (Columbia DB-4224)			9	
	Cyril Stapleton & His Orch. - **Nick Nack Paddy Wack** (Decca F-11094)			9	
	Big Bopper - **Big Bopper's Wedding** (Mercury AMT-1017)				3
	Eddie Cochran - **C'mon Everybody** (London HLU-8792)				4
	Clyde McPhatter - **A Lover's Question / I Can't Stand Up Alone** (London HLE-8755)				7
	Billy Fury - **Maybe Tomorrow** (Decca F-11102)				8
	Lord Rockingham's XI - **Wee Tom** (Decca F-11104)				8
	Jimmie Rodgers - **Bimbombey** (Columbia DB-4235)				8

Bobby Darin

Ricky Nelson

Paul Anka

The Big Bopper

7		14	21	28
★	Lord Rockingham's XI - **Wee Tom** *(Decca F-11104)*			
1	Fats Domino - **Whole Lotta Loving** *(London HLP-8759)*			
2	Eddie Cochran - **C'mon Everybody** *(London HLU-8792)*	9	1	4
3	Robert Earl - **The Wonderful Secret Of Love** *(Philips PB-891)*	★		
3	David Whitfield - **Willingly** *(Decca F-11101)*	3	3	
5	Johnny Mathis - **Call Me** *(Fontana H-163)*	10		
5	Ricky Nelson - **Lonesome Town** *(London HLP-8738)*			
7	Monograms - **The Greatest Mistake Of My Life** *(Parlophone R-4515)*	1		
7	Neil Sedaka - **No Vacancy** *(R.C.A. RCA-1099)*			
9	Ruth Brown - **This Little Girl's Gone Rockin'** *(London HLE-8757)*			
10	Billy Fury - **Maybe Tomorrow** *(Decca F-11102)*		5	★
10	Lloyd Price - **Stagger Lee** *(H.M.V. POP-580)*	★		
12	Avon Sisters - **Jerri-Lee (I Love Him So)** *(Columbia DB-4236)*			
12	Diamonds - **Walking Along** *(Mercury AMT-1004)*			
14	Chipmunks - **The Chipmunk Song** *(London HLU-8762)*			4
14	Billy Eckstine - **Gigi** *(Mercury AMT-1018)*	★		
14	Bobby Freeman - **Shame On You Miss Johnson** *(London HLJ-8782)*			
17	John Barry Seven - **Farrago / Bee's Knees** *(Parlophone R-4488)*			
17	Big Bopper - **Big Bopper's Wedding** *(Mercury AMT-1017)*			
	Valerie Shane - **Meet Me Tonight In Dreamland** *(Philips PB-879)*	2		
	Chuck Miller - **The Auctioneer** *(Mercury AMT-1026)*	3		2
	Playmates - **Beep Beep** *(Columbia DB-4224)*	5	11	★
	Peggy Lee - **Alright, Okay, You Win** *(Capitol CL-14984)*	6		
	Russ Conway - **Side Saddle** *(Columbia DB-4256)*	7	★	
	Cyril Stapleton & His Orch. - **Nick Nack Paddy Wack** *(Decca F-11094)*	7	6	4
	Vera Lynn - **Vera Sings Today's Pop Hits [M]** *(Decca F-11106)*		2	
	Michael Flanders - **The Little Drummer Boy** *(Parlophone R-4528)*		4	★
	Gene Vincent & His Blue Caps - **Say Mama** *(Capitol CL-14974)*		7	
	Edmund Hockridge - **Tonight** *(Pye Nixa 7N.15167)*		8	
	Bill Parsons & His Orch. - **The All American Boy** *(London HL-8798)*		8	1
	Reg Owen & His Orch. - **Manhattan Spiritual** *(Pye International 7N.25009)*		10	★
	Les Chakachas - **Eso Es El Amor** *(R.C.A. RCA-1097)*			3
	Crests - **16 Candles** *(London HL-8794)*			4
	Nat 'King' Cole - **Madrid** *(Capitol CL-14987)*			8

REG OWEN "MANHATTAN SPIRITUAL"

7N 25009 (45 & 78)

		7		14	21	28
★	Eddie Cochran - **C'mon Everybody** (*London HLU-8792*)					
1	Domenico Modugno - **Ciao Ciao Bambina** (*Oriole CB-1489*)				1	★
1	Dickie Valentine - **Venus** (*Pye Nixa 7N.15192*)			★		
3	Chuck Miller - **The Auctioneer** (*Mercury AMT-1026*)					
4	Les Chakachas - **Eso Es El Amor** (*R.C.A. RCA-1097*)					
5	Johnny Cash - **Don't Take Your Guns To Town** (*Philips PB-897*)					
6	Teresa Brewer - **The One Rose** (*Coral Q-72354*)			13		
6	Bobby Darin - **Plain Jane** (*London HLE-8815*)					
	David Whitfield - **Willingly** (*Decca F-11101*)			1		
	Vic Damone - **Gigi** (*Philips PB-889*)			2		10
	Jane Morgan - **If Only I Could Live My Life Again** (*London HLR-8810*)			3	4	
	Coasters - **Charlie Brown** (*London HLE-8819*)			4	2	★
	Bill Parsons & His Orch. - **The All American Boy** (*London HL-8798*)				3	2
	Duane Eddy - **The Lonely One** (*London HLW-8821*)				5	1
	Bernard Bresslaw - **Charlie Brown** (*H.M.V. POP-599*)				6	
	Brenda Lee - **Bill Bailey, Won't You Please Come Home** (*Brunswick 05780*)				7	
	Ricky Nelson - **It's Late** (*London HLP-8817*)				7	
	Fats Domino - **Telling Lies** (*London HLP-8822*)				9	
	Enrico Leandros & His Orch. - **Take Me Dreaming** (*Oriole CB-1487*)				10	
	Marty Robbins - **The Hanging Tree** (*Fontana H-184*)				10	
	Tommy Steele - **Hiawatha** (*Decca F-11117*)				10	6
	Tommy Edwards - **Please Mr. Sun** (*M.G.M. MGM-1006*)				13	
	Joe 'Mr. Piano' Henderson - **Mr. Piano Plays – Volume 1 [M]** (*Pye Nixa 7N.15186*)				13	
	Joe 'Mr. Piano' Henderson - **Chick** (*Pye Nixa 7N.15187*)				13	
	John Barry Seven - **Long John** (*Parlophone R-4530*)					3
	Max Bygraves - **Napoli – Napoli** (*Decca F-11119*)					4
	Poni-Tails - **Early To Bed** (*H.M.V. POP-596*)					4
	Little Richard - **By The Light Of The Silvery Moon** (*London HLU-8831*)					6
	Frankie Avalon - **Venus** (*H.M.V. POP-603*)					8
	Jimmie & The Night Hoppers - **Night Hop** (*London HLP-8830*)					9
	Joan Regan - **May You Always** (*H.M.V. POP-593*)					10
	Johnny Cash - **JOHNNY CASH SINGS HANK WILLIAMS** (*London RE-S-1193*) **EP**					12
	Tommy Dorsey Orchestra - **Dinah – Cha Cha** (*Brunswick 05784*)					12
	Arlene Fontana - **I'm In Love** (*Pye International 7N.25010*)					12
	Frankie Vaughan - **The Lady Is A Square** (*Philips PB-896*)					12
	Frank Sinatra - **French Foreign Legion** (*Capitol CL-14997*)					16
	Gene Vincent & His Blue Caps - **Over The Rainbow** (*Capitol CL-15000*)					16

4		11	18	25
★	Duane Eddy - **The Lonely One** (London HLW-8821)			
★	Little Richard - **By The Light Of The Silvery Moon** (London HLU-8831)			
1	Arlene Fontana - **I'm In Love** (Pye International 7N.25010)	7		
2	Jack Scott - **Goodbye Baby** (London HLL-8804)			
3	Champs - **Gone Train / Beatnik** (London HLH-8811)		18	
3	Jane Morgan - **If Only I Could Live My Life Again** (London HLR-8810)	2	2	
5	Pat Boone - **With The Wind And The Rain In Your Hair / There's Good Rockin'Tonight** (London HLD-8824)		★	
5	Frankie Vaughan - **The Lady Is A Square** (Philips PB-896)		7	
7	Valerie Shane - **Meet Me Tonight In Dreamland** (Philips PB-879)	5		
8	John Barry Seven - **Long John** (Parlophone R-4530)		18	
8	Jimmy Isle - **Diamond Ring** (London HLS-8832)			
10	Frankie Avalon - **Venus** (H.M.V. POP-603)		★	
10	Chuck Miller - **The Auctioneer** (Mercury AMT-1026)	5		
10	Ricky Nelson - **It's Late / Never Be Anyone Else But You** (London HLP-8817)	7	★	
10	Dick Shane - **Don't Come Back Again** (Decca F-11122)			
14	Nat 'King' Cole - **Madrid** (Capitol CL-14987)			
14	Neil Sedaka - **I Go Ape** (R.C.A. RCA-1115)	9	6	★
	Bill Parsons & His Orch. - **The All American Boy** (London HL-8798)	★		
	Poni-Tails - **Early To Bed** (H.M.V. POP-596)	★		
	Frank Sinatra - **French Foreign Legion** (Capitol CL-14997)	★		
	Joan Regan - **May You Always** (H.M.V. POP-593)	1	9	6
	Alma Cogan - **Pink Shoe Laces** (H.M.V. POP-608)	2	7	
	Dodie Stevens - **Pink Shoe Laces** (London HLD-8834)	2	9	
	Frankie Vaughan and the Kaye Sisters - **Come Softly To Me** (Philips PB-913)		1	★
	Connie Francis - **If I Didn't Care** (M.G.M. MGM-1012)		2	6
	Crickets - **Love's Made A Fool Of You** (Coral Q-72365)		4	★
	Jerry Lee Lewis - **Lovin' Up A Storm / Big Blon' Baby** (London HLS-8840)		4	★
	Anthony Newley - **IDLE ON PARADE [OST]** (Decca DFE-6566) EP		9	8
	Johnny Mathis - **You'd Be So Nice To Come Home To** (Fontana H-186)		12	
	Marty Robbins - **The Hanging Tree** (Fontana H-184)		12	15
	Fleetwoods - **Come Softly To Me** (London HLU-8841)		14	★
	Bruce Forsyth - **I'M IN CHARGE** (Parlophone GEP-8807) EP		14	
	Richard Barrett with the Chantels - **Come Softly To Me** (H.M.V. POP-609)		16	
	Teresa Brewer - **Fair Weather Sweetheart** (Coral Q-72364)		16	
	Shirley Bassey - **Crazy Rhythm** (Philips PB-917)			1
	Johnny Cash - **Luther Played The Boogie / Thanks A Lot** (London HLS-8847)			2
	George Jones - **White Lightning** (Mercury AMT-1036)			3
	Dale Hawkins - **Yea-Yea** (London HLM-8842)			4
	Jimmie Rodgers - **I'm Never Gonna Tell** (Columbia DB-4281)			4
	Impalas - **Sorry (I Ran All The Way Home)** (M.G.M. MGM-1015)			8
	Rosemary June - **With You Beside Me** (Pye International 7N.25015)			8
	Johnny O'Neill - **Wagon Train** (R.C.A. RCA-1114)			8
	Tommy Steele - **Hiawatha** (Decca F-11117)			8
	Tommy Edwards - **Please Mr. Sun / The Morning Side Of The Mountain** (M.G.M. MGM-1006)			13
	Frankie Ford - **Sea Cruise** (London HL-8850)			13
	Lonnie Donegan - **RELAX WITH LONNIE** (Pye Nixa NEP-24107) EP			15
	Craig Douglas - **Come Softly To Me** (Top Rank JAR-110)			15
	Kingston Trio - **The Tijuana Jail** (Capitol CL-15002)			15
	Johnny Maddox - **Old Fashioned Love** (London HLD-8826)			15
	Anthony Newley - **I've Waited So Long** (Decca F-11127)			15
	Gene Vincent & His Blue Caps - **Over The Rainbow** (Capitol CL-15000)			15
	Andy Williams - **Hawaiian Wedding Song** (London HLA-8784)			15

2		9	16	23	30
★	Craig Douglas - **Come Softly To Me** (Top Rank JAR-110)				
★	Anthony Newley - **I've Waited So Long** (Decca F-11127)				
★	Anthony Newley - **IDLE ON PARADE [OST]** (Decca DFE-6566) **EP**				
★	Joan Regan - **May You Always** (H.M.V. POP-593)				
1	Lonnie Donegan - **RELAX WITH LONNIE** (Pye Nixa NEP-24107) **EP**				
1	Lloyd Price - **Where Were You** (H.M.V. POP-598)		★		
3	Chuck Berry - **Almost Grown** (London HLM-8853)				
3	Jimmy Lloyd - **I Kneel At Your Throne** (Philips PB-909)				
5	Rosemary June - **With You Beside Me / I Used To Love You But It's All Over Now** (Pye International 7N.25015)				
6	Bing Crosby - **Gigi** (Brunswick 05770)				
6	Marty Robbins - **The Hanging Tree** (Fontana H-184)				
6	Jack Scott - **I Never Felt Like This** (London HLL-8851)				
9	Johnny Cash - **Luther Played The Boogie / Thanks A Lot** (London HLS-8847)				
9	Slim Dusty - **The Answer To A Pub With No Beer** (Columbia DB-4294)	11			
9	Connie Francis - **If I Didn't Care** (M.G.M. MGM-1012)		6		8
9	Joe Gordon Folk Four - **Barnyards O' Delgaty / Bonnie Wee Jeannie McColl** (H.M.V. POP-591)				
13	Mr. Acker Bilk - **MR. ACKER BILK SINGS** (Pye Nixa NJE-1067) **EP**				
13	Frankie Ford - **Sea Cruise** (London HL-8850)	1	1	5	
13	Al Martino - **I Can't Get You Out Of My Heart** (Top Rank JAR-108)	11			
13	Jane Morgan - **If Only I Could Live My Life Again** (London HLR-8810)	11	★		
13	Larry Williams - **Bad Boy' / She Said 'Yeah'** (London HLU-8844)				
	Russ Conway - **Roulette** (Columbia DB-4298)	1	★		
	Impalas - **Sorry (I Ran All The Way Home)** (M.G.M. MGM-1015)	3			
	Nat 'King' Cole - **You Made Me Love You** (Capitol CL-15017)	4			★
	Travis & Bob - **Tell Him No** (Pye International 7N.25018)	4			
	Johnny Cash - **COUNTRY BOY** (London RE-S-1212) **EP**	6			
	Joe Medlin - **I Kneel At Your Throne** (Mercury AMT-1032)	7	8		
	Johnny Mathis - **Let's Love / You'd Be So Nice To Come Home To** (Fontana H-186)	8			4
	Betty Miller - **Pearly Gates / Old Time Religion** (Top Rank JAR-115)	8			
	Jackie Wilson - **That's Why** (Coral Q-72366)	8	3	5	
	Jimmie Rodgers - **I'm Never Gonna Tell** (Columbia DB-4281)	11			
	Billy Grammer - **Bonaparte's Retreat** (Felsted AF-121)		1		
	Chico Holiday - **Young Ideas** (R.C.A. RCA-1117)		3		
	Jackson Brothers - **Tell Him No** (London HLX-8845)		3		
	Steve Lawrence - **Only Love Me** (H.M.V. POP-604)		6		2
	Buddy Knox - **I Think I'm Gonna Kill Myself** (Columbia DB-4302)		8		
	Lorie Mann - **A Penny A Kiss, A Penny A Hug** (Top Rank JAR-116)		8	2	
	Johnny Mathis - **THERE GOES MY HEART** (Fontana TFE-17088) **EP**		11		
	Dave 'Baby' Cortez - **The Happy Organ** (London HLU-8852)			1	
	Kathy Linden - **Goodbye Jimmy, Goodbye** (Felsted AF-122)			2	
	Thomas Wayne - **Tragedy** (London HLU-8846)			4	
	Platters - **Enchanted** (Mercury AMT-1039)			5	11
	Derry Hart & The Hartbeats - **Nowhere In This World** (Decca F-11138)			8	
	Johnny O'Neill - **Wagon Train** (R.C.A. RCA-1114)			8	
	Dodie Stevens - **Pink Shoe Laces** (London HLD-8834)				★
	Lord Rockingham's XI - **Ra-Ra Rockingham** (Decca F-11139)				1
	Champs - **Caramba** (London HLH-8864)				2
	Dion & The Belmonts - **A Teenager In Love** (London HLU-8874)				5
	Johnny Kidd & The Pirates - **Please Don't Touch** (H.M.V. POP-615)				5
	Trio Los Paraguayos - **TRIO LOS PARAGUAYOS** (Philips BBE-12176) **EP**				5
	Paul Anka - **I Miss You So** (Columbia DB-4286)				8
	Brook Benton - **Endlessly** (Mercury AMT-1043)				8
	Alyn Ainsworth & His Orch. - **Bedtime For Drums** (Parlophone R-4533)				11
	Bud Flanagan - **Strollin'** (Columbia DB-4265)				11
	Sonny James - **Talk Of The School** (Capitol CL-15022)				11

6	Artist - Title	13	20	27
1	Johnny Kidd & The Pirates - **Please Don't Touch** (H.M.V. POP-615)	★		
2	Billy Fury - **Margo** (Decca F-11128)	3	8	★
3	Lloyd Price - **Personality** (H.M.V. POP-626)	★		
4	Rockin' R's - **The Beat** (London HL-8872)	6		
5	Dion & The Belmonts - **A Teenager In Love** (London HLU-8874)	1		★
6	Travis & Bob - **Tell Him No** (Pye International 7N-25018)			
7	Craig Douglas - **A Teenager In Love** (Top Rank JAR-133)	★		
7	Lena Horne - **A New Fangled Tango** (R.C.A. RCA-1120)	13		
7	Platters - **Enchanted** (Mercury AMT-1039)	6		
7	Dickie Valentine - **A Teenager In Love** (Pye Nixa 7N.15202)			
11	Dave 'Baby' Cortez - **The Happy Organ** (London HLU-8852)	2		
12	Tommy Dee - **Three Stars** (Melodisc 45/1516)			
12	Thomas Wayne - **Tragedy** (London HLU-8846)	14		
14	Johnny Cash - **Frankie's Man, Johnny / You Dreamer You** (Philips PB-928)	5		
14	Cliff Richard & The Drifters - **SERIOUS CHARGE [OST]** (Columbia SEG-7895) EP			
16	Bachelors - **Please Don't Touch** (Parlophone R-4547)			
16	Frankie Ford - **Sea Cruise** (London HL-8850)	9	8	8
16	Connie Francis - **If I Didn't Care** (M.G.M. MGM-1012)			
16	Ferlin Husky - **Draggin' The River** (Capitol CL-15027)			
16	Johnny Mathis - **Let's Love / You'd Be So Nice To Come Home To** (Fontana H-186)			
16	Frankie Vaughan - **The Heart Of A Man** (Philips PB-930)	9	4	4
22	Shirley Bassey - **Love For Sale** (Philips PB-917)			
22	Wilbert Harrison - **Kansas City** (Top Rank JAR-132)	4		
	Larry Williams - **Bad Boy / She Said 'Yeah'** (London HLU-8844)	6		
	Connie Francis - **Lipstick On Your Collar** (M.G.M. MGM-1018)	9	1	1
	Buddy Holly - **Midnight Shift** (Brunswick 05800)	9	1	1
	Fiestas - **So Fine** (London HL-8870)	14		
	Brook Benton - **Endlessly** (Mercury AMT-1043)	16		
	Dale Wright - **That's Show Biz** (Pye International 7N.25022)	16		
	Impalas - **Sorry (I Ran All The Way Home)** (M.G.M. MGM-1015)	18	10	9
	Duffy Power - **Dream Lover** (Fontana H-194)	18		
	Gene Vincent & The Blue Caps - **Summertime** (Capitol CL-15035)	18		
	Freddy Cannon - **Tallahassee Lassie** (Top Rank JAR-135)		3	3
	Coasters - **Along Came Jones** (London HLE-8882)		4	4
	Tommy Edwards - **My Melancholy Baby** (M.G.M. MGM-1020)		6	6
	Preston Epps - **Bongo Rock** (Top Rank JAR-140)		6	6
	Billy Grammer - **Bonaparte's Retreat** (Felsted AF-121)		10	9
	Kathy Linden - **Goodbye Jimmy, Goodbye** (Felsted AF-122)		10	9

Record Mirror was not published on 27 June, during the whole of July, or on 1 and 8 August. For all these dates, the positions of 20 June have been repeated, except for those records which charted.

Lena Horne

Dion & The Belmonts

Johnny Kidd

Cliff Richard

4		11	18	25
★	Connie Francis - **Lipstick On Your Collar** (M.G.M. MGM-1018)			
1	Buddy Holly - **Midnight Shift** (Brunswick 05800)	1	1	1
2	Freddy Cannon - **Tallahassee Lassie** (Top Rank JAR-135)	2	2	2
3	Coasters - **Along Came Jones** (London HLE-8882)	3	3	3
3	Frankie Vaughan - **The Heart Of A Man** (Philips PB-930)	3	3	★
5	Tommy Edwards - **My Melancholy Baby** (M.G.M. MGM-1020)	5	5	4
5	Preston Epps - **Bongo Rock** (Top Rank JAR-140)	5	5	4
7	Frankie Ford - **Sea Cruise** (London HL-8850)	7	7	6
8	Billy Grammer - **Bonaparte's Retreat** (Felsted AF-121)	8	8	7
8	Impalas - **Sorry (I Ran All The Way Home)** (M.G.M. MGM-1015)	8	8	7
8	Kathy Linden - **Goodbye Jimmy, Goodbye** (Felsted AF-122)	8	8	7
	Brook Benton - **Endlessly** (Mercury AMT-1043)	★		

Record Mirror was not published on 27 June, during the whole of July, or on 1 and 8 August. For all these dates, the positions of 20 June have been repeated, except for those records which charted.

Freddy Cannon / The Coasters / Preston Epps / Tommy Edwards

1		8	15	22	29
★	Buddy Holly - **Midnight Shift** (Brunswick 05800)				
1	Freddy Cannon - **Tallahassee Lassie** (Top Rank JAR-135)	1	★		
2	Coasters - **Along Came Jones** (London HLE-8882)	2			
3	Tommy Edwards - **My Melancholy Baby** (M.G.M. MGM-1020)	★			
3	Preston Epps - **Bongo Rock** (Top Rank JAR-140)	3			
5	Frankie Ford - **Sea Cruise** (London HL-8850)	4			
6	Billy Grammer - **Bonaparte's Retreat** (Felsted AF-121)	5			
6	Impalas - **Sorry (I Ran All The Way Home)** (M.G.M. MGM-1015)	★			
6	Kathy Linden - **Goodbye Jimmy, Goodbye** (Felsted AF-122)	5			
	Al Saxon - **Only Sixteen** (Fontana H-205)		1		★
	Ray Peterson - **The Wonder Of You** (R.C.A. RCA-1131)		2	9	
	Platters - **Remember When** (Mercury AMT-1053)		2	6	★
	Jerry Keller - **Here Comes Summer** (London HLR-8890)		4		★
	Carl Dobkins Jr. - **My Heart Is An Open Book** (Brunswick 05804)		5		4
	Manuel and the Music of the Mountains - **The Honeymoon Song** (Columbia DB-4323)		6	4	★
	Megatrons - **Velvet Waters** (Top Rank JAR-146)		6		
	Drifters - **There Goes My Baby** (London HLE-8892)		8		
	Fabian - **Tiger** (H.M.V. POP-643)		8	14	
	Ritchie Valens - **That's My Little Suzie** (London HL-8886)		8		
	Kingston Trio - **M.T.A.** (Capitol CL-15040)		11		
	Johnny & The Hurricanes - **Crossfire** (London HL-8899)		12	14	
	Nina & Frederik - **Listen To The Ocean** (Columbia DB-4332)		13		
	OLC - **THE MERMAID THEATRE PRESENTS 'LOCK UP YOUR DAUGHTERS'** (Decca LK-4320) 🇱🇵			1	
	Trio Los Paraguayos - **Bell Bird** (Philips PB-947)			1	
	Ray Charles - **What'd I Say?** (London HLE-8917)			3	
	Skip & Flip - **It Was I** (Top Rank JAR-156)			5	
	Barbara Evans - **Souvenirs** (R.C.A. RCA-1122)			6	
	Sammy Turner - **Lavender Blue** (London HLX-8918)			6	8
	Mystics - **Hushabye** (H.M.V. POP-646)			9	
	Poni-Tails - **Moody** (H.M.V. POP-644)			9	
	Inadequates - **Audie** (Capitol CL-15051)			12	
	Gene Vincent & The Blue Caps - **Summertime** (Capitol CL-15035)			12	
	Ella Fitzgerald - **Ev'ry Time We Say Goodbye** (H.M.V. POP-373)			16	
	Johnny Gentle - **Milk From The Coconut** (Philips PB-945)			16	
	Frank Sinatra - **High Hopes** (Capitol CL-15052)			16	★
	Dee Clark - **Just Keep It Up** (London HL-8915)				1
	George Jones - **Who Shot Sam** (Mercury AMT-1058)				2
	Sarah Vaughan - **Broken-Hearted Melody** (Mercury AMT-1057)				2
	Arthur Lyman Group - **Taboo** (Vogue Pop V-9153)				5
	Miki & Griff - **Hold Back Tomorrow** (Pye Nixa 7N.15213)				5
	Mudlarks - **Waterloo** (Columbia DB-4331)				5
	Chris Barber's Jazz Band - **Lonesome** (Columbia DB-4333)				8
	Chubby Checker - **The Class** (Top Rank JAR-154)				10
	Bill Haley & His Comets - **Shaky** (Brunswick 05805)				10
	Marilyn Monroe - **I Wanna Be Loved By You** (London HLT-8862)				10
	Jane Morgan - **I Can't Begin To Tell You** (London HLR-8925)				10

Record Mirror was not published on 27 June, during the whole of July, or on 1 and 8 August. For all these dates, the positions of 20 June have been repeated, except for those records which charted.

		5	12	19	26
★	Ray Peterson - **The Wonder Of You** (R.C.A. RCA-1131)				
1	Sammy Turner - **Lavender Blue** (London HLX-8918)		7		
2	Carl Dobkins Jr. - **My Heart Is An Open Book** (Brunswick 05804)				
3	Jane Morgan - **I Can't Begin To Tell You** (London HLR-8925)		2	8	
4	Dee Clark - **Just Keep It Up** (London HL-8915)		★		
4	Sarah Vaughan - **Broken-Hearted Melody** (Mercury AMT-1057)		★		
6	Arthur Lyman Group - **Taboo** (Vogue Pop V-9153)			12	5
7	Browns - **The Three Bells** (R.C.A. RCA-1140)		★		
7	Ronnie Carroll - **The Wonder Of You / Wonderful You** (Philips PB-944)				
7	George Jones - **Who Shot Sam** (Mercury AMT-1058)		9		
7	Knightsbridge Strings - **Cry** (Top Rank JAR-170)		1	4	
11	Chris Barber's Jazz Band - **Lonesome** (Columbia DB-4333)				12
12	Lloyd Price - **I'm Gonna Get Married** (H.M.V. POP-650)		★		
12	David Whitfield - **A Million Stars** (Decca F-11144)				
	Frankie Vaughan - **Walkin' Tall** (Philips PB-931)		2	★	
	Johnny Restivo - **The Shape I'm In** (R.C.A. RCA-1143)		4	10	
	Dean Martin - **Maybe** (Capitol CL-15064)		5		
	Michael Holliday - **My Heart Is An Open Book** (Columbia DB-4216)		6		
	Phil Phillips with the Twilights - **Sea Of Love** (Mercury AMT-1059)		7		3
	Fats Domino - **I Want To Walk You Home / I'm Gonna Be A Wheel Some Day** (London HLP-8942)			1	2
	Playmates - **What Is Love?** (Columbia DB-4338)			2	10
	Marty Wilde - **Sea Of Love** (Philips PB-959)			3	★
	Johnny Cash - **I Got Stripes / Five Feet High And Rising** (Philips PB-953)			5	5
	Johnnie Ray - **I'll Never Fall In Love Again / You're All That I Live For** (Philips PB-952)			5	
	Jerry Lee Lewis - **Let's Talk About Us** (London HLS-8941)			5	
	Brook Benton - **Thank You Pretty Baby** (Mercury AMT-1061)			8	
	Johnny Cash - **Katy Too** (London HLS-8928)			10	10
	Trio Los Paraguayos - **Bell Bird** (Philips PB-947)			12	
	Miki & Griff - **Hold Back Tomorrow** (Pye Nixa 7N.15213)				1
	Eddie Cochran - **Somethin' Else** (London HLU-8944)				4
	Bobby Rydell - **Kissin' Time** (Top Rank JAR-181)				5
	Tommy Steele - **You Were Mine** (Decca F-11162)				5
	Petula Clark - **Adonis** (Pye Nixa 7N.15220)				9
	Don Lang & His Frantic Five - **A Hoot An' A Holler** (H.M.V. POP-649)				13
	Clinton Ford - **Old Shep** (Oriole CB-1500)				14
	Santo & Johnny - **Sleep Walk** (Pye International 7N.25037)				14
	Gerry Mulligan Combo - **I Want To Live – Theme** (London HLT-8901)				16
	Tradewinds - **Furry Murray** (R.C.A. RCA-1141)				16

3		10	17	24	31
★	Miki & Griff - **Hold Back Tomorrow** (*Pye Nixa 7N.15213*)				
1	Eddie Cochran - **Somethin' Else** (*London HLU-8944*)	15	★		
2	Tommy Steele - **You Were Mine** (*Decca F-11162*)	10	16	11	7
3	Johnny Cash - **I Got Stripes** / **Five Feet High And Rising** (*Philips PB-953*)	10			
4	Brook Benton - **Thank You Pretty Baby** (*Mercury AMT-1061*)	19			
4	Phil Phillips with the Twilights - **Sea Of Love** (*Mercury AMT-1059*)		8	7	
6	Johnny & The Hurricanes - **Red River Rock** (*London HL-8948*)	★			
7	Fats Domino - **I Want To Walk You Home** (*London HLP-8942*)	1	2	★	
8	Clinton Ford - **Old Shep** (*Oriole CB-1500*)	6	14	★	
9	Ken Morris - **Copper Knob** (*H.M.V. POP-647*)		8	3	16
9	Dickie Valentine - **One More Sunrise** (*Pye Nixa 7N.15221*)			★	
11	Joyce Shock - **Cry, Baby, Cry** (*Philips PB-957*)				
12	Arthur Lyman Group - **Taboo** (*Vogue Pop V-9153*)	19			
12	Ken Mackintosh & His Orch. - **Morgen** (*H.M.V. POP-656*)			13	
12	Billy Vaughn & His Orch. - **Morgen** (*London HLD-8952*)	22	8	7	3
15	Don Lang & His Frantic Five - **A Hoot An' A Holler** (*H.M.V. POP-649*)				
16	Johnny Restivo - **The Shape I'm In** (*R.C.A. RCA-1143*)	★			
16	Chan Romero - **The Hippy Hippy Shake** (*Columbia DB-4341*)	3	1		10
18	LaVern Baker - **So High, So Low** (*London HLE-8945*)				
18	Bobby Rydell - **Kissin' Time** (*Top Rank JAR-181*)		8		10
18	Santo & Johnny - **Sleep Walk** (*Pye International 7N.25037*)	★			
21	Fred Buscaglione & His Asternovas - **Guarda Che Luna** (*Cetra SP-4011*)				
21	Sammy Turner - **Lavender Blue** (*London HLX-8918*)				
23	Shirley Bassey - **Count On Me** (*Columbia DB-4344*)			20	21
23	Fred Buscaglione & His Asternovas - **Carina** (*Cetra SP-4010*)				
23	Johnny Cash - **Katy Too** (*London HLS-8928*)				
23	Vince Eager - **Makin' Love** / **Primrose Lane** (*Top Rank JAR-191*)			7	
23	Ella Fitzgerald - **But Not For Me** (*H.M.V. POP-657*)	★			
23	Billy Fury - **Angel Face** (*Decca F-11158*)	19	16		21

	10	17	24	31
23 Johnny & The Hurricanes - **Crossfire** (London HL-8899)	10			
23 Anthony Newley - **Someone To Love** (Decca F-11163)	4			
23 Stephanie Voss and Terence Cooper - **Lovely Lover** (Decca F-11165)				
Chris Barber's Jazz Band - **Lonesome** (Columbia DB-4333)	★			
Floyd Robinson - **Makin' Love** (R.C.A. RCA-1146)	1	★		
Robert Earl - **The Test Of Time / The Key** (Philips PB-960)	4		16	
Bo Diddley - **Crackin' Up** (London HLM-8913)	7			
Joe 'Mr. Piano' Henderson - **Treble Chance** (Pye Nixa 7N.15224)	7	8	★	
Don Gibson - **Don't Tell Me Your Troubles** (R.C.A. RCA-1150)	9		21	
Clovers - **Love Potion No. 9** (London HLT-8949)	10			
Bob Summers - **Rattle Rhythm** (Capitol CL-15063)	14			
Adam Singers - **Morgen** (Pye International 7N.25033)	15			
Eddie Hickey - **Lady May** (Decca F-11153)	15			
Homer & Jethro - **The Battle Of Kookamonga** (R.C.A. RCA-1148)	15	16		
Ronnie Hawkins & The Hawks - **Mary Lou** (Columbia DB-4345)	22			
Jerry Lee Lewis - **Let's Talk About Us** (London HLS-8941)	22			
Faron Young - **I Hear You Talkin'** (Capitol CL-15050)	22			
Jerry Wallace - **Primrose Lane** (London HLH-8943)		3	7	
Mike Preston - **Mr. Blue** (Decca F-11167)		4	★	
Crests - **The Angels Listened In** (London HL-8954)		5		
Hank Snow - **Old Shep** (R.C.A. RCA-1151)		5	4	2
Paul Anka - **Put Your Head On My Shoulder** (Columbia DB-4355)		7	13	★
Roy Young - **Hey Little Girl** (Fontana H-215)		8		
Eugene Church - **Miami** (London HL-8940)		14		
Tony Brent - **Forever, My Darling** (Columbia DB-4357)		16		
Sanford Clark - **New Kind Of Fool** (London HLW-8959)		16		
Craig Douglas - **Wish It Were Me / The Riddle Of Love** (Top Rank JAR-204)		16	★	
Emile Ford & The Checkmates - **What Do You Want To Make Those Eyes At Me For?** (Pye Nixa 7N.15225)		16	23	★
Coasters - **Poison Ivy** (London HLE-8938)			1	★
Mel Robbins - **Save It** (London HLM-8966)			1	5
Guy Mitchell - **Heartaches By The Number** (Philips PB-964)			4	10
Ivo Robić & The Song-Masters - **Morgen** (Polydor NH-23923)			4	7
Johnny October - **Growin' Prettier** (Capitol CL-15070)			11	
Sandy Nelson - **Teen Beat** (Top Rank JAR-197)			13	★
Dee Clark - **Hey Little Girl** (Top Rank JAR-196)			16	
Johnnie Ray - **I'll Never Fall In Love Again** (Philips PB-952)			17	
David MacBeth - **Mr. Blue** (Pye Nixa 7N.15231)			17	★
Wink Martindale - **Deck Of Cards** (London HLD-8962)			17	
Fleetwoods - **Mr. Blue** (Top Rank JAR-202)			20	4

TWO ORIGINALS FROM THE TOP
OF THE AMERICAN HIT PARADE

No 1 Come softly to me
HL 8841
THE FLEETWOODS

No 3 Pink shoe laces DODIE STEVENS
HLD 8834

RECORDS MAGAZINE 16 pages of pictures and features. Complete details of all Decca-group stereo and mono releases. Full colour. Your monthly guide to good record buying. Sixpence from your dealer or newsagent.

LONDON RECORDS DIVISION OF THE DECCA RECORD COMPANY LTD DECCA HOUSE ALBERT EMBANKMENT LONDON SE11

7		14	21	28
★	Ivo Robić & The Song-Masters - **Morgen** (Polydor NH-23923)			
1	Guy Mitchell - **Heartaches By The Number** (Philips PB-964)	4	2	★
2	Neil Sedaka - **Oh! Carol** (R.C.A. RCA-1152)	★		
3	Johnny Cash - **You Tell Me / Goodbye, Little Darlin', Goodbye** (London HLS-8979)			
4	Sammy Turner - **Always** (London HLX-8963)	★		
5	Pinky & Perky - **Party Sing-Song [M]** (Decca F-11174)	15		
6	Chet Atkins - **Boo Boo Stick Beat** (R.C.A. RCA-1153)			
6	Frankie Avalon - **Just Ask Your Heart** (H.M.V. POP-658)	15		
6	Fleetwoods - **Mr. Blue** (Top Rank JAR-202)	11	7	
6	Bobby Rydell - **Kissin' Time** (Top Rank JAR-181)			
10	Bo Diddley - **Say Man** (London HLM-8975)			
10	Platters - **My Blue Heaven** (Mercury AMT-1066)	5		20
10	Jerry Wallace - **Primrose Lane** (London HLH-8943)			
13	Isley Brothers - **Shout** (R.C.A. RCA-1149)			
13	Frankie Laine - **Rawhide** (Philips PB-965)	★		
15	Shirley Bassey - **Count On Me / If You Love Me** (Columbia DB-4344)	★		
15	Paul Evans and the Curls - **Seven Little Girls Sitting In The Back Seat** (London HLL-8968)	13	21	★
15	Billy Vaughn & His Orch. - **Morgen** (London HLD-8952)	18	10	
18	Jerry Lordan - **I'll Stay Single** (Parlophone R-4588)	6	19	14
18	Bert Weedon - **Nashville Boogie / King Size Guitar** (Top Rank JAR-221)	2	★	
20	Doris Day - **The Tunnel Of Love** (Philips PB-949)			
20	Wade Flemons - **Slow Motion** (Top Rank JAR-206)			
20	Wailers - **Tall Cool One** (London HL-8958)			
23	Dee Clark - **Hey Little Girl** (Top Rank JAR-196)	20		
23	Knightsbridge Chorale - **Eton Boating Song** (Top Rank JAR-220)			
23	Johnny Mathis - **The Best Of Everything** (Fontana H-218)	9	1	★
23	OST - **THE FIVE PENNIES** (London HA-U-2189) LP		19	
23	Cliff Richard & The Drifters - **SERIOUS CHARGE [OST]** (Columbia SEG-7895) EP	20		
23	Mel Robbins - **Save It** (London HLM-8966)			26
23	Hank Snow - **Old Shep** (R.C.A. RCA-1151)	9	21	
23	Tommy Steele - **You Were Mine** (Decca F-11162)	13		
	Rock-A-Teens - **Woo-Hoo** (Columbia DB-4361)	1	2	20
	Adam Faith - **What Do You Want?** (Parlophone R-4591)	3	★	
	Russ Conway - **More And More Party Pops [M]** (Columbia DB-4373)	6	★	
	Johnnie Ray - **I'll Never Fall In Love Again** (Philips PB-952)	6	7	18
	Bert Weedon - **Teenage Guitar** (Top Rank JAR-136)	11		

7	<<< NOVEMBER 1959 >>>	14	21	28
Stevie Marsh - **If You Were The Only Boy In The World** (Decca F-11181)	15		4
Pat Boone - **A Fool's Hall Of Fame** (London HLD-8974)	18	13	26
Don Gibson - **Don't Tell Me Your Troubles / Heartbreak Avenue** (R.C.A. RCA-1150)	20		10
Beverley Sisters - **Little Donkey** (Decca F-11172)	23	★	
Lonnie Donegan - **San Miguel / Talking Guitar Blues** (Pye Nixa 7N.15237)	23	13	3
Jerry Fuller - **Tennessee Waltz** (London HLH-8982)	23	7	1
Brook Benton - **So Many Ways** (Mercury AMT-1068)		4	
Wink Martindale - **Deck Of Cards** (London HLD-8962)		4	★
Jack Scott - **There Comes A Time** (London HLL-8970)		6	
Winifred Atwell - **Piano Party [M]** (Decca F-11183)		10	★
Addrisi Brothers - **It's Love** (Columbia DB-4370)		12	
Larry Lawrence & The Band of Gold - **Bongo Boogie** (Pye International 7N.25042)		13	
Alma Cogan - **The Train Of Love** (H.M.V. POP-760)		16	4
Fireballs - **Torquay** (Top Rank JAR-218)		16	20
Tommy Steele - **Little White Bull** (Decca F-11177)		16	★
Bobby Comstock & The Counts - **Tennessee Waltz** (Top Rank JAR-223)		21	
Jerry Keller - **If I Had A Girl** (London HLR-8980)		21	26
Drifters - **Dance With Me** (London HLE-8988)			2
Connie Francis - **Among My Souvenirs** (M.G.M. MGM-1046)			4
Peter Sellers - **My Old Dutch / Puttin' On The Smile** (Parlophone R-4605)			4
Johnny Wells - **Lonely Moon** (Columbia DB-4377)			4
Marty Wilde - **Bad Boy** (Philips PB-972)			4
Don Costa & His Orch. - **I Walk The Line** (London HLT-8992)			10
Ernie Field's Orchestra - **In The Mood** (London HL-8985)			10
Leroy Holmes & His Orch. - **Alice Blue Gown** (M.G.M. MGM-1044)			10
Crickets - **When You Ask About Love** (Coral Q-72382)			14
Frank Sinatra - **Talk To Me** (Capitol CL-15086)			14
Conway Twitty - **Rosaleena** (M.G.M. MGM-1047)			14
Jerry Lee Lewis - **Little Queenie** (London HLS-8993)			18
Atmospheres - **The Fickle Chicken** (London HLW-8977)			20
Kalin Twins - **The Meaning Of The Blues** (Brunswick 05814)			20
Lana Sisters with Al Saxon - **(Seven Little Girls) Sitting In The Back Seat** (Fontana H-221)			20
E.C. Beatty - **Ski King** (Felsted AF-127)			26
Lloyd Price - **Come Into My Heart** (H.M.V. POP-672)			26

5		12	19	26
★	Lonnie Donegan - **San Miguel** (Pye Nixa 7N.15237)			
★	Connie Francis - **Among My Souvenirs** (M.G.M. MGM-1046)			
★	Stevie Marsh - **If You Were The Only Boy In The World** (Decca F-11181)			
★	Johnnie Ray - **I'll Never Fall In Love Again** (Philips PB-952)			
★	Marty Wilde - **Bad Boy** (Philips PB-972)			
1	Joan Regan - **Happy Anniversary** (Pye Nixa 7N.15238)	1	9	
2	Conway Twitty - **Rosaleena** (M.G.M. MGM-1047)	8		
3	Jerry Fuller - **Tennessee Waltz** (London HLH-8982)	10	2	13
4	Pat Boone - **A Fool's Hall Of Fame** (London HLD-8974)	10	5	
5	Ernie Field's Orchestra - **In The Mood** (London HL-8985)	3	9	★
5	Ronnie Hilton - **Happy Anniversary** (H.M.V. POP-684)	8		
5	Various Artists - **A FESTIVAL OF EDINBURGH** (Waverley LLP-1001) **LP**		14	3
8	Max Bygraves - **Jingle Bell Rock** (Decca F-11176)	3	★	
8	Alma Cogan - **The Train Of Love** (H.M.V. POP-760)	2	★	
10	Pinky & Perky - **Party Sing-Song [M]** (Decca F-11174)	14		
11	Kestrels - **In The Chapel In The Moonlight** (Pye Nixa 7N.15234)			16
11	Rock-A-Teens - **Woo-Hoo** (Columbia DB-4361)			
11	Wailers - **Dirty Robber** (London HL-8994)			
14	Chet Atkins - **Boo Boo Stick Beat** (R.C.A. RCA-1153)			
14	Freddie Cannon - **Way Down Yonder In New Orleans** (Top Rank JAR-247)	13	17	
14	Jerry Lordan - **I'll Stay Single** (Parlophone R-4588)			
14	Peter Sellers - **My Old Dutch / Puttin' On The Smile** (Parlophone R-4605)			
18	Crickets - **When You Ask About Love** (Coral Q-72382)	14		
18	Lena Horne - **A New Fangled Tango** (R.C.A. RCA-1120)	3		
18	Nash Lorraine - **The Ways Of Love** (Pye Nixa 7N.15235)			
18	Marty Robbins - **Cool Water / Big Iron** (Fontana H-229)			
18	Frank Sinatra - **Talk To Me** (Capitol CL-15086)	6		
	Fats Domino - **Be My Guest** (London HLP-9005)	6	★	
	Michael Holliday - **Starry Eyed** (Columbia DB-4378)	10		2
	Billy Fury - **My Christmas Prayer** (Decca F-11189)	14	12	
	Johnny & The Hurricanes - **Reveille Rock** (London HL-9017)		1	★
	Lorie Mann - **So Many Ways** (Top Rank JAR-237)		3	
	Tiny Lewis - **Too Much Rockin'** (Parlophone R-4617)		4	7
	Adriano - **The Happy Hobo** (Parlophone R-4602)		6	
	Bill Black's Combo - **Smokie** (Felsted AF-129)		6	
	Donald Peers - **Roses From Venice** (Columbia DB-4369)		6	
	Don Gibson - **I'm Movin' On** (R.C.A. RCA-1158)		9	
	Atmospheres - **The Fickle Chicken** (London HLW-8977)		12	
	Jerry Lee Lewis - **Little Queenie** (London HLS-8993)		14	
	Sandy Nelson - **Drum Party** (London HLP-9015)		14	7
	Julian - **Sue Saturday** (Pye Nixa 7N.15236)		17	6
	Gary Stites - **Starry Eyed** (London HLL-9003)		17	
	Gene Vincent - **Wild Cat / Right Here On Earth** (Capitol CL-15099)		17	16
	Drifters - **Dance With Me** (London HLE-8988)			1
	Johnny Cash - **Little Drummer Boy** (Philips PB-979)			3
	Bill Forbes - **Too Young** (Columbia DB-4386)			3
	Browns - **Scarlet Ribbons** (R.C.A. RCA-1157)			7
	Dale Hawkins - **Liza Jane** (London HLM-9016)			7
	Andy Williams - **Lonely Street** (London HLA-8957)			11
	Jackie Wilson - **Talk That Talk** (Coral Q-72384)			11
	Mr. Acker Bilk - **Summer Set** (Columbia DB-4382)			13
	Lou Monte - **Santa Nicola** (R.C.A. RCA-1161)			13
	Bell Sounds - **Marching Guitars** (H.M.V. POP-685)			16

2		9	16	23	30
★	Freddie Cannon - **Way Down Yonder In New Orleans** *(Top Rank JAR-247)*				
★	Michael Holliday - **Starry Eyed** *(Columbia DB-4378)*				
1	Little Tony & His Brothers - **Too Good** *(Decca F-11190)*	★			
2	Gene Vincent - **Wild Cat / Right Here On Earth** *(Capitol CL-15099)*	★			
3	Drifters - **Dance With Me** *(London HLE-8988)*	★			
4	Don Costa & His Orch. - **I Walk The Line** *(London HLT-8992)*				
5	Browns - **Scarlet Ribbons** *(R.C.A. RCA-1157)*	6	5		
5	Bill Forbes - **Too Young** *(Columbia DB-4386)*	3	★		
	Jerry Lordan - **I'll Stay Single** *(Parlophone R-4588)*	★			
	Cliff Richard & The Drifters - **SERIOUS CHARGE [OST]** *(Columbia SEG-7895)* 🅴🅿	★			
	Ricky Nelson - **I Wanna Be Loved / Mighty Good** *(London HLP-9021)*	1	★		
	Anthony Newley - **Why** *(Decca F-11194)*	2	★		
	Jerry Fuller - **Tennessee Waltz** *(London HLH-8982)*	4	11		1
	Crickets - **When You Ask About Love** *(Coral Q-72382)*	5	★		
	Frankie Avalon - **Why** *(H.M.V. POP-688)*	6	★		
	Sandy Nelson - **Drum Party** *(London HLP-9015)*	6			5
	Craig Douglas - **Pretty Blue Eyes** *(Top Rank JAR-268)*		1	★	
	Toni Fisher - **The Big Hurt** *(Top Rank JAR-261)*		2	1	1
	Marty Robbins - **El Paso** *(Fontana H-233)*		3	2	★
	Eddie Cochran - **Hallelujah, I Love Her So** *(London HLW-9022)*		4	★	
	Jimmy Clanton - **Go, Jimmy, Go** *(Top Rank JAR-269)*		5		
	Maureen Evans - **The Big Hurt** *(Oriole CB-1533)*		5	★	
	Peggy Lee - **You Deserve** *(Capitol CL-15103)*		5	2	
	Paul Anka - **It's Time To Cry** *(Columbia DB-4390)*		9	8	
	Andy Williams - **Lonely Street** *(London HLA-8957)*		9		
	Sanford Clark - **Son-Of-A-Gun** *(London HLW-9026)*		11		
	Joan Regan - **Happy Anniversary** *(Pye Nixa 7N.15238)*		11		
	Carl Perkins - **I Don't See Me In Your Eyes Anymore** *(Philips PB-983)*		14		
	Mr. Acker Bilk - **Summer Set** *(Columbia DB-4382)*			★	
	OST - **THE FIVE PENNIES** *(London HA-U-2189)* 🅻🅿			★	
	Johnny Preston - **Running Bear** *(Mercury AMT-1079)*			2	
	Applejacks - **Circle Dance** *(Top Rank JAR-273)*			5	
	Frankie Vaughan - **What More Do You Want** *(Philips PB-985)*			5	★
	Lance Fortune - **Be Mine** *(Pye 7N.15240)*			7	
	Bobby Freeman - **Sinbad** *(London HLJ-9031)*			8	
	Elvis Presley - **STRICTLY ELVIS** *(R.C.A. RCX-175)* 🅴🅿			8	★
	Sarah Vaughan - **Smooth Operator** *(Mercury AMT-1071)*			8	
	Carl Dobkins - **Lucky Devil** *(Brunswick 05817)*			12	
	Jack Scott - **What In The World's Come Over You** *(Top Rank JAR-280)*			12	5
	Kay Starr - **Riders In The Sky** *(Capitol CL-15105)*			12	
	Marv Johnson - **You Got What It Takes** *(London HLT-9013)*				1
	Fabian - **Hound Dog Man** *(H.M.V. POP-695)*				4
	Frank Ifield - **Lucky Devil** *(Columbia DB-4399)*				5
	Danny Valentino - **Stampede** *(M.G.M. MGM-1049)*				5
	Vince Eager - **El Paso** *(Top Rank JAR-275)*				9
	Kalin Twins - **The Meaning Of The Blues** *(Brunswick 05814)*				9

6		13	20	27
★	Johnny Preston - **Running Bear** *(Mercury AMT-1079)*			
★	Joan Regan - **Happy Anniversary** *(Pye Nixa 7N.15238)*			
1	Marv Johnson - **You Got What It Takes** *(London HLT-9013)*	★		
2	Eddie Smith with the Hornets - **Upturn** *(Top Rank JAR-285)*		5	
3	Everly Brothers - **Let It Be Me** *(London HLA-9039)*	★		
4	Toni Fisher - **The Big Hurt** *(Top Rank JAR-261)*	★		
5	Fabian - **Hound Dog Man** *(H.M.V. POP-695)*			
6	Jack Scott - **What In The World's Come Over You** *(Top Rank JAR-280)*		1	2
7	Bruce Forsyth - **My Little Budgie** *(Parlophone R-4620)*			
7	Ernie Freeman - **Big River** *(London HLP-9041)*			
9	Viscounts - **Rockin' Little Angel** *(Pye 7N.15249)*			
	Lance Fortune - **Be Mine** *(Pye 7N.15240)*	★		
	Sanford Clark - **Son-Of-A-Gun** *(London HLW-9026)*	1	15	
	Danny Valentino - **Stampede** *(M.G.M. MGM-1049)*	1		
	Brook Benton - **So Many Ways** *(Mercury AMT-1068)*	3		
	Billy Fury - **Collette** *(Decca F-11200)*	3		
	Frank Ifield - **Lucky Devil** *(Columbia DB-4399)*		★	
	Percy Faith & His Orch. - **The Theme from 'A Summer Place'** *(Philips PB-989)*		2	1
	Champs - **Too Much Tequila** *(London HLH-9052)*		3	
	Steve Lawrence - **Pretty Blue Eyes** *(H.M.V. POP-689)*		3	
	Joe Brown & The Bruvvers - **The Darktown Strutters' Ball** *(Decca F-11207)*		5	
	Johnny Duncan - **Any Time** *(Columbia DB-4415)*		5	11
	Mark Dinning - **Teen Angel** *(M.G.M. MGM-1053)*		8	
	Ray Smith - **Rockin' Little Angel** *(London HL-9051)*		8	
	Malcolm Vaughan - **Oh, So Wunderbar** *(H.M.V. POP-700)*		8	
	Knightsbridge Strings - **Ring Ding** *(Top Rank JAR-272)*		11	
	Jerry Lordan - **Who Could Be Bluer?** *(Parlophone R-4627)*		11	★
	Josh MacRae - **Talking Army Blues** / **Talking Guitar Blues** *(Top Rank JAR-290)*		11	
	Gene Vincent & The Blue Caps - **Summertime** *(Capitol CL-15035)*		14	
	John Barry Seven Plus Four - **Hit And Miss** *(Columbia DB-4414)*		15	★
	Perry Como - **Delaware** *(R.C.A. RCA-1170)*		15	★
	Brenda Lee - **Sweet Nuthin's** *(Brunswick 05819)*		15	
	Paul Anka - **It's Time To Cry** *(Columbia DB-4390)*			★
	Freddie Cannon - **California Here I Come** / **Indiana** *(Top Rank JAR-309)*			3
	Conway Twitty - **Lonely Blue Boy** *(M.G.M. MGM-1056)*			3
	Ray Bryant Trio - **Little Susie (Parts 2 & 4)** *(Pye International 7N.25052)*			5
	Dale Hawkins - **Hot Dog** / **Our Turn** *(London HLM-9060)*			6
	Bryan Johnston - **Looking High, High, High** *(Decca F-11213)*			6
	Jimmy Jones - **Handy Man** *(M.G.M. MGM-1051)*			6
	Nellie Lutcher - **My Mother's Eyes** *(Capitol CL-15106)*			9
	Spencer Ross - **Tracy's Theme** *(Philips PB-992)*			9
	Ella Fitzgerald - **Like Young** *(H.M.V. POP-701)*			11
	Don Webb - **Little Ditty Baby** *(Coral Q-72385)*			11
	Alex Murray - **Teen Angel** *(Decca F-11203)*			14
	Robert Earl - **Oh, So Wunderbar** *(Philips PB-986)*			15

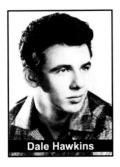
Dale Hawkins

Everly Brothers

Billy Fury

Brenda Lee

5		12	19	26
★	Joe Brown & The Bruvvers - **The Darktown Strutters' Ball** *(Decca F-11207)*			
★	Freddie Cannon - **California Here I Come** / **Indiana** *(Top Rank JAR-309)*			
★	Percy Faith & His Orch. - **The Theme from 'A Summer Place'** *(Philips PB-989)*			
★	Billy Fury - **Collette** *(Decca F-11200)*			
★	Jack Scott - **What In The World's Come Over You** *(Top Rank JAR-280)*			
1	Jimmy Jones - **Handy Man** *(M.G.M. MGM-1051)*	★		
2	Bobby Rydell - **Wild One** *(Columbia DB-4429)*	★		
3	Josh MacRae - **Talking Army Blues** / **Talking Guitar Blues** *(Top Rank JAR-290)*	1		
4	Conway Twitty - **Lonely Blue Boy** *(M.G.M. MGM-1056)*	2		
5	Chet Atkins - **Teensville** *(R.C.A. RCA-1174)*		★	
6	Max Bygraves - **Fings Ain't Wot They Used T' Be** *(Decca F-11214)*	★		
7	Bryan Johnston - **Looking High, High, High** *(Decca F-11213)*	★		
7	Little Richard - **I Got It** *(London HLU-9065)*			
7	Gene Vincent - **My Heart** *(Capitol CL-15115)*	★		
10	Johnny Horton - **The Same Old Tale The Crow Told Me** *(Philips PB-995)*			
11	Fabian - **Hound Dog Man** *(H.M.V. POP-695)*	★		
12	Richard Allan - **As Time Goes By** / **Only One** *(Parlophone R-4634)*	4		★
12	Winifred Atwell - **Tops In Pops [M]** *(Decca F-11208)*		3	
12	Dion & The Belmonts - **Where Or When** *(London HLU-9030)*	8		
12	Mudlarks - **Candy** *(Columbia DB-4417)*			
12	Frank Sinatra - **It's Nice To Go Trav'ling** / **Brazil** *(Capitol CL-15116)*	9	7	5
	Mark Dinning - **Teen Angel** *(M.G.M. MGM-1053)*	★		
	Nina & Frederik - **Listen To The Ocean** *(Columbia DB-4332)*	★		
	Johnny Cash - **Straight A's In Love** *(London HLS-9070)*	2		
	Chuck Berry - **Too Pooped To Pop** / **Let It Rock** *(London HLM-9069)*	5	1	2
	Pat Boone - **New Lovers** *(London HLD-9067)*	6		
	Johnny Ferguson - **Angela Jones** *(M.G.M. MGM-1059)*	7		
	Champs - **Too Much Tequila** *(London HLH-9052)*	9	★	
	Fireflies - **I Can't Say Goodbye** *(London HLU-9057)*	9		
	Guy Mitchell - **The Same Old Me** *(Philips PB-998)*	9		
	Paul Evans - **Midnite Special** *(London HLL-9045)*	13		
	Brenda Lee - **Sweet Nuthin's** *(Brunswick 05819)*		★	★
	Jim Reeves - **He'll Have To Go** *(R.C.A. RCA-1168)*		2	★
	Johnny Bachelor - **Mumbles** *(London HLN-9074)*		4	
	Steve Lawrence - **Footsteps** *(H.M.V. POP-726)*		5	
	Lloyd Price - **Lady Luck** *(H.M.V. POP-712)*		5	
	Shirley Bassey - **With These Hands** *(Columbia DB-4421)*		7	1
	Frankie Avalon - **Don't Throw Away All Those Teardrops** *(H.M.V. POP-727)*		9	
	Bobby Bare - **I'm Hanging Up My Rifle** *(Top Rank JAR-310)*		10	
	Russ Conway - **MY CONCERTO FOR YOU** *(Columbia 33SX-1214)* **LP**		10	★
	Mr. Acker Bilk - **ACKER'S AWAY** *(Columbia SEG-7940)* **EP**			★
	Davy Jones - **Amapola** *(Pye 7N.15254)*			2
	Bobby Comstock & The Counts - **Jambalaya** *(London HLE-9080)*			4
	Fabian - **String Along** *(H.M.V. POP-724)*			5
	Lyn Vernon - **Woodchoppers Ball** *(Top Rank JAR-323)*			7

Frankie Avalon

Johnny Cash

Fabian

Jim Reeves

	2	9	16	23	30
Shirley Bassey - **With These Hands** (Columbia DB-4421)	★				
Carl Dobkins - **Lucky Devil** (Brunswick 05817)	★				
Paul Evans - **Midnite Special** (London HLL-9045)	★				
Steve Lawrence - **Footsteps** (H.M.V. POP-726)	★				
Édith Piaf - **Milord** (Columbia DC-754)	1	1			
Jerry Lee Lewis - **I'll Sail My Ship Alone** (London HLS-9083)	2				
Don Gibson - **Just One Time** (R.C.A. RCA-1183)	3				
Dennis Lotis - **Love Me A Little** (Columbia DB-4432)	4				
Drifters - **This Magic Moment** (London HLE-9081)	5				
Johnny Bachelor - **Mumbles** (London HLN-9074)	6				
Frank Sinatra - **It's Nice To Go Trav'ling** (Capitol CL-15116)	6	★			
Royal Rockers- **Jet II** (Top Rank JAR-329)	8				
Annette - **O Dio Mio** (Top Rank JAR-343)		2			
Barrett Strong - **Money (That's What I Want)** (London HLU-9088)		3			
Dorsey Burnette - **Tall Oak Tree** (London HLN-9047)		4			
Milton Grayson - **Forget You** (London HLU-9068)		5			9
Floyd Robinson - **I Believe In Love** (R.C.A. RCA-1179)		6			
Clyde McPhatter - **Think Me A Kiss** (M.G.M. MGM-1061)		7	8		12
Anthony Newley - **Someone To Love** (Decca F-11163)		7			
Bill Black's Combo - **White Silver Sands** (London HLU-9090)		9			
Stan Freberg - **The Old Payola Roll Blues** (Capitol CL-15122)		9	3		
Teen Beats - **Slop Beat / Califf Boogie** (Top Rank JAR-342)			1	3	
Sanford Clark - **Go On Home** (London HLW-9095)			2		6
The Big Sound of Don Ralke - **77 Sunset Strip** (Warner Bros. WB-2)			4		
Frankie Avalon - **Don't Throw Away All Those Teardrops** (H.M.V. POP-727)			5	★	
Billy Bland - **Let The Little Girl Dance** (London HL-9096)			5		
Craig Douglas - **The Heart Of A Teenage Girl** (Top Rank JAR-340)			5	★	
Preston Epps - **Bongo Boogie** (Top Rank JAR-345)			8		
Fabian - **String Along** (H.M.V. POP-724)			10		
Lance Fortune - **This Love I Have For You** (Pye 7N.15260)			10	1	9
Buddy Holly - **Heartbeat** (Coral Q-72392)			10	★	
Lloyd Price - **Lady Luck** (H.M.V. POP-712)				★	
Billy Mure & His Orch. - **Jambalaya** (Top Rank JAR-344)				2	
Brothers Four - **Greenfields** (Philips PB-1009)				3	2
Ernie Fields & His Orch. - **Chattanooga Choo Choo** (London HL-9100)				5	★
Cliff Adams Orch. - **The Lonely Man Theme** (Pye International 7N.25056)				6	★
Johnny Cash - **Seasons Of My Heart** (Philips PB-1017)					1
Jody Gibson - **So You Think You've Got Troubles** (Parlophone R-4645)					2
Rosco Gordon - **Goin' Home** (Top Rank JAR-332)					2
Charlie Rich - **Lonely Weekends** (London HLU-9107)					2
Edward Byrnes and Connie Stevens - **Kookie Kookie (Lend Me Your Comb)** (Warner Bros. WB-5)				7	
Fireballs - **Foot-Patter** (Top Rank JAR-354)					7
Nat Kendrick & The Swans - **Mashed Potatoes** (Top Rank JAR-351)					11
Mike Preston - **A Girl Like You** (Decca F-11222)					12
Conway Twitty - **What Am I Living For** (M.G.M. MGM-1066)					12
Andy Williams - **Wake Me When It's Over** (London HLA-9099)					12
Gene Vincent & The Blue Caps - **Summertime** (Capitol CL-15035)					16
Norman Wisdom - **Follow A Star** (Top Rank JAR-246)					16

MAY 1960

	7	14	21	28
Brothers Four - **Greenfields** (Philips PB-1009)	★			
Edward Byrnes and Connie Stevens - **Kookie Kookie (Lend Me Your Comb)** (Warner Bros. WB-5)	★			
Lance Fortune - **This Love I Have For You** (Pye 7N.15260)	★			
Jody Gibson - **So You Think You've Got Troubles** (Parlophone R-4645)	1	5	7	
Brooks Brothers - **Green Fields** (Top Rank JAR-349)	2			
Crickets - **Baby My Heart** (Coral Q-72395)	3	12	2	★
Johnny Cash - **Seasons Of My Heart** / **Smiling Bill McCall** (Philips PB-1017)	4			
Édith Piaf - **Milord** (Columbia DC-754)	4	★		
Lyn Cornell - **Like Love** (Decca F-11227)	6			
Browns - **The Old Lamplighter** (R.C.A. RCA-1176)	7			
Amos Milburn - **Bad Bad Whiskey** (Vogue Pop V-9163)	7			
Billy Bland - **Let The Little Girl Dance** (London HL-9096)	9	★		
Rosco Gordon - **Goin' Home** (Top Rank JAR-332)	9	9		
Kemal Rachid et ses Ottomans - **Mustapha** (Philips 370.280F (French))	9			
Neville Taylor - **Dance With A Dolly** (Oriole CB-1546)	9			
Teen Beats - **Slop Beat** / **Califf Boogie** (Top Rank JAR-342)	9			
Stan Freberg - **The Old Payola Roll Blues** (Capitol CL-15122)		★		
Bo Diddley - **Road Runner** (London HLM-9112)		1		
Sir Chauncey & His Exciting Strings - **Beautiful Obsession** (Warner Bros. WB-9)		2		
Freddy Cannon - **The Urge** / **Jump Over** (Top Rank JAR-369)		3	★	
Skip & Flip - **Cherry Pie** (Top Rank JAR-358)		3	2	4
Harold Dorman - **Mountain Of Love** (Top Rank JAR-357)		5		
Milton Grayson - **Forget You** (London HLU-9068)		5		
Bill Black's Combo - **White Silver Sands** (London HLU-9090)		8	6	11
Frankie Avalon - **The Faithful Kind** (H.M.V. POP-742)		9		
Jerry Wallace - **You're Singing Our Love Song To Somebody Else** (London HLH-9110)		9	5	7
Chris Barber's Jazz Band - **Bill Bailey, Won't You Please Come Home** (Pye Nixa 7NJ-2030)		13		
Four Preps - **Got A Girl** (Capitol CL-15128)		13	2	★
Dave Sampson and the Hunters - **Sweet Dreams** / **It's Lonesome** (Columbia DB-4449)		13	★	
Norman Wisdom - **FOLLOW A STAR [OST]** (Top Rank JKP-2052) **EP**		13		
Jerry Lordan - **Sing Like An Angel** (Parlophone R-4653)			1	11
Anita Bryant - **Paper Roses** (London HLL-9114)			7	★
Clinton Ford - **Mustapha** (Oriole CB-1551)			7	8
Garry Mills - **Look For A Star** / **Footsteps** (Top Rank JAR-336)			7	
Charlie Rich - **Lonely Weekends** (London HLU-9107)			7	
Mr. Acker Bilk - **Marching Through Georgia** (Pye 7NJ-2029)			12	
Ricky Nelson - **Young Emotions** (London HLP-9121)			12	1
Marty Robbins - **Big Iron** (Fontana H-229)				★
Billy Gaye & The Gayetones - **Oh, Honey Love Me** (Waverley SLP-501)				2
Steve Perry - **Step By Step** (H.M.V. POP-745)				2
Sanford Clark - **Go On Home** (London HLW-9095)				5
Jack Scott - **Burning Bridges** / **Oh Little One** (Top Rank JAR-375)				6
Bobby Summers - **Little Brown Jug** (Capitol CL-15130)				9
Fats Waller - **Dinah** (R.C.A. RCA-1189)				9
Jeanne Black - **He'll Have To Stay** (Capitol CL-15131)				11
Edna Savage - **All I Need** (Parlophone R-4648)				11
Dick Jordan - **Little Christine** (Oriole CB-1548)				15
Kenny Lynch - **Mountain Of Love** (H.M.V. POP-751)				15
Dean Martin - **Who Was That Lady?** (Capitol CL-15127)				15

4		11	18	25
★	Jerry Lordan - **Sing Like An Angel** (Parlophone R-4653)			
★	Jack Scott - **Burning Bridges** (Top Rank JAR-375)			
1	Johnny Ferguson - **Angela Jones** (M.G.M. MGM-1059)		8	1
2	Jerry Wallace - **You're Singing Our Love Song To Somebody Else** (London HLH-9110)		6	★
3	Jerry Lee Lewis - **Baby, Baby, Bye Bye / Old Black Joe** (London HLS-9131)	★		
4	Billy Gaye & The Gayetones - **Oh, Honey Love Me** (Waverley SLP-501)	8	13	
5	Frank Ifield - **Happy-Go-Lucky Me** (Columbia DB-4464)			
6	Steve Perry - **Step By Step** (H.M.V. POP-745)	6		
7	Sally Kelly - **He'll Have To Stay** (Decca F-11238)		2	
7	Kenny Lynch - **Mountain Of Love** (H.M.V. POP-751)	14	16	★
7	Sammy Masters - **Rockin' Red Wing** (Warner Bros. WB-10)	★		
10	Sonny James - **Jenny Lou** (London HL-9132)			
10	Josh MacRae - **Talking Army Blues** (Top Rank JAR-290)	1	1	★
10	Charlie Rich - **Lonely Weekends** (London HLU-9107)			
10	Skip & Flip - **Cherry Pie** (Top Rank JAR-358)	14		
14	Brooks Brothers - **Green Fields** (Top Rank JAR-349)			
14	Johnny Russell - **Lonesome Boy** (M.G.M. MGM-1074)			
16	Jeanne Black - **He'll Have To Stay** (Capitol CL-15131)	4	4	★
16	Jane Morgan - **Romantica** (London HLR-9120)		★	
18	Clinton Ford - **Mustapha** (Oriole CB-1551)			
18	Staïffi et ses Mustafa's - **Mustafa** (Pye International 7N.25057)		16	9
20	Brook Benton - **The Ties That Bind** (Mercury AMT-1097)			
21	Al Brown's Tunetoppers - **The Madison** (Top Rank JAR-374)			
21	Ted Heath & His Music - **Madison Time No. 1** (Decca F-11232)			
21	Dick Jordan - **Little Christine** (Oriole CB-1548)	★		
21	Reivers - **The Wreck Of The John B.** (Top Rank JAR-244)			
	Mr. Acker Bilk - **MR. ACKER BILK SINGS** (Pye Nixa NJE-1067) **EP**	★		
	David Kinnaird - **Mairi's Wedding / Northern Lights Of Aberdeen** (Top Rank JAR-385)	2	5	3
	Swe-Danes - **Scandinavian Shuffle** (Warner Bros. WB-7)	3		
	Bobby Rydell - **Swingin' School** (Columbia DB-4471)	4	18	★
	Temptations - **Barbara** (Top Rank JAR-384)	6		
	Jimmy Clanton - **Another Sleepless Night** (Top Rank JAR-382)	8		
	Ricky Nelson - **Young Emotions** (London HLP-9121)	8		
	Beau-Marks - **Clap Your Hands** (Top Rank JAR-377)	11		
	Jackie Rae - **Summer Place** (Fontana H-242)	12		
	Lana Sisters - **Someone Loves You, Joe** (Fontana H-252)	13		
	Brenda Lee - **Love You 'Till I Die** (Brunswick 05685)	14		
	Tommy Steele - **What A Mouth (What A North And South)** (Decca F-11245)		3	★
	Johnny Mathis - **Starbright / All Is Well** (Fontana H-254)		6	2
	Danny Davis - **You're My Only Girl** (Parlophone R-4657)		8	
	Ricky Wayne with the Fabulous Flee-Rakkers - **Chicka'roo** (Triumph RGM-1009)		10	9
	George Formby - **Happy Go Lucky Me / Banjo Boy** (Pye 7N.15269)		11	7
	Pat Boone - **Walking The Floor Over You** (London HLD-9138)		12	★
	Marke Anthony - **Why Didn't You Tell Me** (Decca F-11242)		13	★
	Avons - **We're Only Young Once** (Columbia DB-4461)		13	
	Enoch Kent - **The Smashing Of The Van** (Top Rank JAR-386)			3
	Johnny Carson - **Fraülein** (Fontana H-243)			5
	Marty Wilde - **Angry** (Philips PB-1037)			5
	Ken Dodd - **Love Is Like A Violin** (Decca F-11248)			8
	Laurel Aitken - **Boogie In My Bones** (Starlite ST.45-011)			11
	Fats Domino - **Tell Me That You Love Me** (London HLP-9133)			11
	Bobby Summers - **Little Brown Jug** (Capitol CL-15130)			11
	Sanford Clark - **Go On Home** (London HLW-9095)			14
	Four Lads - **Goona Goona** (Philips PB-1020)			15
	Valerie Masters - **Banjo Boy** (Fontana H-253)			15

		2	9	16	23	30
★	Ken Dodd - **Love Is Like A Violin** (Decca F-11248)					
1	Enoch Kent - **The Smashing Of The Van / Sean South Of Garryowen** (Top Rank JAR-386)	1	1	1	1	
2	David Kinnaird - **Mairi's Wedding / Northern Lights Of Aberdeen** (Top Rank JAR-385)	2	2	2		
3	Garry Mills - **Look For A Star** (Top Rank JAR-336)		★			
3	Ricky Wayne with the Fabulous Flee-Rakkers - **Chicka'roo** (Triumph RGM-1009)		9			
5	Joe Brown & The Bruvvers - **Jellied Eels** (Decca F-11246)		6			
6	Danny Davis - **You're My Only Girl** (Parlophone R-4657)			4	11	9
7	George Formby - **Happy Go Lucky Me / Banjo Boy** (Pye 7N.15269)			11	★	
8	Johnny Carson - **Fraülein** (Fontana H-243)					
8	Bobby Summers - **Little Brown Jug** (Capitol CL-15130)					
10	Sam Cooke - **Wonderful World** (H.M.V. POP-754)		★			
10	Bud Flanagan - **Strollin'** (Columbia DB-4265)					
10	Kaye Sisters - **Paper Roses** (Philips PB-1024)		★			
10	Little Tony & His Brothers - **Kiss Me, Kiss Me** (Decca F-21247)					
14	Johnny Ferguson - **Angela Jones** (M.G.M. MGM-1059)		★			
14	Buddy Greco - **The Lady Is A Tramp** (Fontana H-255)		★			
14	Frank Ifield - **Happy-Go-Lucky Me** (Columbia DB-4464)					
	Avons - **We're Only Young Once** (Columbia DB-4461)		★			
	Ricky Nelson - **Young Emotions** (London HLP-9121)		★			
	Fendermen - **Mule Skinner Blues** (Top Rank JAR-395)		3			9
	Dante & The Evergreens - **Alley-Oop** (Top Rank JAR-402)		4			
	Marty Wilde - **Angry** (Philips PB-1037)		5	★		
	Jimmy Clanton - **Another Sleepless Night** (Top Rank JAR-382)		7		★	
	Johnny Carson - **The Train Of Love** (Fontana H-259)		8	6	7	7
	Johnny Mathis - **Starbright** (Fontana H-254)		9	7	13	★
	Roy Orbison - **Only The Lonely** (London HLU-9149)		9			★
	John Barry & His Orch. - **Blueberry Hill / Never Let Go** (Columbia DB-4480)		12	★		
	Dinah Washington and Brook Benton - **A Rockin' Good Way** (Mercury AMT-1099)		12			
	Shirley Bassey - **As Long As He Needs Me** (Columbia DB-4490)		14			
	Sally Kelly - **He'll Have To Stay** (Decca F-11238)		14			
	Hank Thompson & His Brazos Valley Boys - **The Wild Side Of Life** (Capitol CL-13977)		14			
	Ian Menzies & His Clyde Valley Stompers - **The Fish Man** (Pye 7NJ-2031)			3	2	4
	Diamond Accordion Band - **Irish Medley [M]** (Beltona BE-2694)			4	7	17

6		13	20	27
★	Shirley Bassey - **As Long As He Needs Me** (Columbia DB-4490)			
★	Keith Kelly - **Listen Little Girl** (Parlophone R-4676)			
★	OST - **SEVEN BRIDES FOR SEVEN BROTHERS (PART 1)** (M.G.M. MGM-EP-513) EP			
★	Steve Perry - **Step By Step** (H.M.V. POP-745)			
1	Enoch Kent - **The Smashing Of The Van / Sean South Of Garryowen** (Top Rank JAR-386)	1	2	2
2	Ian Menzies & His Clyde Valley Stompers - **The Fish Man** (Pye 7NJ-2031)	2	1	1
3	Paul Hanford - **Itsy Bitsy Teenie Weenie Yellow Polka Dot Bikini** (Parlophone R-4680)	8	3	14
4	Johnnie Lee - **Cindy Lou** (Fontana H-257)			
4	Hank Locklin - **Please Help Me, I'm Falling** (R.C.A. RCA-1188)	★		
6	Danny Davis - **You're My Only Girl / Love Me** (Parlophone R-4657)	7	8	13
7	David Kinnaird - **Buttered Bannocks** (Top Rank JAR-414)		4	8
8	Bob Beckham - **Mais Oui** (Brunswick 05835)			
9	Brooks Brothers - **Please Help Me, I'm Falling** (Top Rank JAR-409)	★		
9	Kemal Rachid et ses Ottomans - **Mustapha** (Philips 370.280F (French))	12		
11	Johnny Carson - **The Train Of Love** (Fontana H-259)	4	11	
11	Dante & The Evergreens - **Alley-Oop** (Top Rank JAR-402)			
11	Craig Douglas - **Oh! What A Day / Why Why Why** (Top Rank JAR-406)	★		
11	Ferrante & Teicher - **Theme from 'The Apartment'** (London HLT-9164)		★	
11	Nina & Frederik - **Carnival** (Columbia DB-4486)			
	James Darren - **Because They're Young** (Pye International 7N.25059)	★		
	David Kinnaird - **Mairi's Wedding / Northern Lights Of Aberdeen** (Top Rank JAR-385)	3	5	9
	Donnie Brooks - **Mission Bell** (London HLN-9168)	5	5	10
	Ventures - **Walk Don't Run** (Top Rank JAR-417)	5		
	Mark Wynter - **Image Of A Girl** (Decca F-11263)	8	5	★
	Guy Mitchell - **Silver Moon Upon The Golden Sands** (Philips PB-1050)	10	8	14
	Mike Preston - **I'd Do Anything** (Decca F-11255)	11		★
	Carl Mann - **South Of The Border** (London HLS-9170)	13		
	Allan Bruce - **In All The World** (Fontana H-250)	14		
	Crests - **Trouble In Paradise** (H.M.V. POP-768)	14		
	Billy Williams - **I Cried For You** (Coral Q-72402)	14		
	Johnny Ashcroft - **Little Boy Lost** (H.M.V. POP-759)	17		
	Brook Benton - **The Ties That Bind** (Mercury AMT-1097)	17		
	Ron Goodwin & His Concert Orch. - **The Girl From Corsica** (Parlophone R-4649)	17		
	Fendermen - **Mule Skinner Blues** (Top Rank JAR-395)		★	
	Frank Weir & His Orch. - **Caribbean Honeymoon** (Oriole CB-1559)		8	3
	Johnny Angel - **You're Thrilling** (Parlophone R-4679)		12	
	Reivers - **The Wreck Of The John B. / The Wee Magic Stane** (Top Rank JAR-244)		13	
	Nelson Keene - **Image Of A Girl** (H.M.V. POP-771)		14	★
	Jack Scott - **Cool Water** (Top Rank JAR-419)		15	
	Four Lads - **The Sheik Of Chicago** (Philips PB-1051)		16	
	Wanda Jackson - **Let's Have A Party** (Capitol CL-15147)		16	4
	John Leyton - **Tell Laura I Love Her** (Top Rank JAR-426)		16	
	Richard Allen - **Doctor In Love** (Parlophone R-4673)			5
	Emile Ford - **Them There Eyes** (Pye 7N.15282)			5
	Bobby Rydell - **Volare** (Columbia DB-4495)			5
	Johnny Burnette - **Dreamin'** (London HLG-9172)			10
	Vince Taylor & His Playboys - **I'll Be Your Hero / Jet Black Machine** (Palette PG-9001)			10
	Chuck Berry - **Bye Bye Johnny** (London HLM-9159)			16
	Nat 'King' Cole and Stan Kenton - **My Love** (Capitol CL-15144)			16
	Miki & Griff - **Someday You'll Call My Name** (Pye 7N.15266)			16
	Renato Rascel - **Romantica** (R.C.A. RCA-1177)			16

3		10	17	24
★	Emile Ford - **Them There Eyes** (Pye 7N.15282)			
★	Wanda Jackson - **Let's Have A Party** (Capitol CL-15147)			
★	Bobby Rydell - **Volare** (Columbia DB-4495)			
★	Ventures - **Walk Don't Run** (Top Rank JAR-417)			
★	Frank Weir & His Orch. - **Caribbean Honeymoon** (Oriole CB-1559)			
1	Ian Menzies & His Clyde Valley Stompers - **The Fish Man** (Pye 7NJ-2031)	2	2	★
2	David Kinnaird - **Buttered Bannocks** (Top Rank JAR-414)	3	4	
3	Richard Allen - **Doctor In Love** (Parlophone R-4673)	5	10	11
4	Piltdown Men - **McDonald's Cave** (Capitol CL-15149)	★		
5	Jack Scott - **Cool Water** (Top Rank JAR-419)		8	
6	Johnny Angel - **You're Thrilling** (Parlophone R-4679)		15	8
6	Enoch Kent - **The Smashing Of The Van** / **Sean South Of Garryowen** (Top Rank JAR-386)	1	1	1
8	Johnny Carson - **The Train Of Love** (Fontana H-259)	6	12	
9	Paul Hanford - **Itsy Bitsy Teenie Weenie Yellow Polka Dot Bikini** (Parlophone R-4680)			
9	Vince Taylor & His Playboys - **I'll Be Your Hero** / **Jet Black Machine** (Palette PG-9001)		4	★
9	Hank Thompson & His Brazos Valley Boys - **The Wild Side Of Life** (Capitol CL-13977)			
12	Johnny Burnette - **Dreamin'** (London HLG-9172)	4	3	5
12	Fabian - **Strollin' In The Springtime** (H.M.V. POP-778)			
14	Bobby Freeman - **Shimmy Shimmy** (Parlophone R-4684)			
15	Al Saxon - **I've Heard That Song Before** (Fontana H-261)			
16	Grady Chapman - **Sweet Thing** (Mercury AMT-1107)			
16	John Leyton - **Tell Laura I Love Her** (Top Rank JAR-426)			
18	Nat 'King' Cole and Stan Kenton - **My Love** (Capitol CL-15144)			
18	Terry Dene - **Love Me Or Leave Me** (Oriole CB-1562)			
18	Ray Peterson - **Tell Laura I Love Her** (R.C.A. RCA-1195)	7	6	2
	Platters - **Red Sails In The Sunset** (Mercury AMT-1106)	8		
	Hank Ballard & The Midnighters - **The Twist** (Parlophone R-4688)	9		
	Danny Davis - **Love Me** (Parlophone R-4657)	9		
	Dave Sampson and the Hunters - **If You Need Me** (Columbia DB-4502)	9	18	
	Frankie Vaughan - **Kookie Little Paradise** (Philips PB-1054)	9		★
	Bill Black's Combo - **White Silver Sands** (London HLU-9090)	★		
	Various Artists - **THE EDINBURGH MILITARY TATTOO** (Waverley MLP-5001) **LP**		6	5
	Chubby Checker - **The Twist** (Columbia DB-4503)		8	★
	Johnny Cash - **Down The Street To 301** (London HLS-9182)		11	
	Don Gibson - **Far Far Away** (R.C.A. RCA-1200)		12	
	Frank Ifield - **Gotta Get A Date** (Columbia DB-4496)		14	★
	Chris Barber's Jazz Band - **Bohemia Rag** (Columbia DB-4501)		15	
	Clyde McPhatter - **Ta Ta** (Mercury AMT-1108)		15	
	Bobby Vee - **Devil Or Angel** (London HLG-9179)		18	
	Anita Bryant - **My Little Corner Of The World** (London HLL-9171)		20	
	Billy Fury - **Wondrous Place** (Decca F-11267)		20	★
	Robert Horton - **Wagon Train** (Pye 7N.15285)		20	
	Johnny & The Hurricanes - **Rocking Goose** (London HL-9190)			3
	Flee-Rakkers - **Sunday Date** (Pye 7N.15288)			4
	Johnny Bond - **Hot Rod Jalopy** (London HLU-9189)			5
	Fireballs - **Vaquero** (Top Rank JAR-507)			9
	Rhet Stoller - **Walk Don't Run** (Decca F-11271)			9
	Sammy Davis Jr. - **Eee-O Eleven** (H.M.V. POP-777)			11
	Robin Hall & Jimmy McGregor - **Football Crazy** (Decca F-11266)			11
	Johnny Ashcroft - **Little Boy Lost** (H.M.V. POP-759)			14
	Michael Cox - **Along Came Caroline** (H.M.V. POP-789)			14

	1	8	15	22	29
★ Johnny Burnette - **Dreamin'** (London HLG-9172)					
★ Sammy Davis Jr. - **Eee-O Eleven** (H.M.V. POP-777)					
★ Johnny & The Hurricanes - **Rocking Goose** (London HL-9190)					
1 Emmettones - **Johnson's Motor Car** (Beltona BL-2724)		2	4		
2 Enoch Kent - **The Smashing Of The Van / Sean South Of Garryowen** (Top Rank JAR-386)		13	7		
3 Johnny Angel - **You're Thrilling** (Parlophone R-4679)		7	4	5	6
3 Brook Benton - **Kiddio** (Mercury AMT-1109)		★			
5 Michael Cox - **Along Came Caroline** (H.M.V. POP-789)		★			
6 Fireballs - **Vaquero** (Top Rank JAR-507)					
7 Johnny Bond - **Hot Rod Jalopy** (London HLU-9189)		5			
8 Marty Robbins - **Is There Any Chance** (Fontana H-263)			4		
9 Emmettones - **Bold Robert Emmett** (Beltona BL-2722)				3	7
9 Flee-Rakkers - **Sunday Date** (Pye 7N.15288)			★		
9 Johnny Mathis - **My Love For You** (Fontana H-267)		★			
12 Jerry Lordan - **Ring, Write Or Call** (Parlophone R-4695)					
12 Garry Mills - **Top Teen Baby** (Top Rank JAR-500)		★			
14 Ray Peterson - **Tell Laura I Love Her** (R.C.A. RCA-1195)		★			
15 Ella Fitzgerald - **How High The Moon** (H.M.V. POP-782)		★			
15 Kenny Lynch - **Slowcoach** (H.M.V. POP-786)		7			
15 Austin Taylor - **Push Push** (Top Rank JAR-511)					
18 Richard Allen - **Doctor In Love** (Parlophone R-4673)					
18 Johnny Carson - **The Train Of Love** (Fontana H-259)					
20 Ronnie Carroll - **Chain Gang** (Philips PB-1060)					
20 David Kinnaird - **Mairi's Wedding / Northern Lights Of Aberdeen** (Top Rank JAR-385)					
20 Guy Mitchell - **Silver Moon Upon The Golden Sands** (Philips PB-1050)					
20 Ricky Nelson - **Yes, Sir, That's My Baby** (London HLP-9188)					
Anita Bryant - **My Little Corner Of The World** (London HLL-9171)		★			
Don Costa & His Orch. - **Never On Sunday** (London HLT-9195)		1	★		
Andy Stewart - **A Scottish Soldier** (Top Rank JAR-512)		3		3	8
Johnny Cash - **NOW, THERE WAS A SONG!** (Philips BBL-73580) 🄻🄿		4			
Faron Young - **There's Not Any Like You Left** (Capitol CL-15151)		5			
Galaxies - **The Big Triangle** (Capitol CL-15158)		9		12	
Johnny Cash - **Down The Street to 301** (London HLS-9182)		10			
Jim Gunner & The Echoes - **Hoolee Jump** (Decca F-11276)		11		2	4
Al Kasha - **Teardrops Are Falling** (Coral Q-72410)		11			
Hank Thompson - **She's Just A Whole Lot Like You** (Capitol CL-15156)		13			
Charlie Drake - **Mr. Custer** (Parlophone R-4701)			1	7	★

1 <<< OCTOBER 1960 >>>	8	15	22	29
Paul Chaplain & His Emeralds - **Shortnin' Bread** (London HLU-9205)	2			
Fats Domino - **Three Nights A Week** (London HLP-9198)	3	10	11	
Makadopulos & His Greek Serenaders - **Never On Sunday** (Palette PG-9005)	7	★		
The Big Sound of Don Ralke - **77 Sunset Strip** (Warner Bros. WB-2)	9			
Tommy Edwards - **Blue Heartaches** (M.G.M. MGM-1097)	9			
Milko Papayaki & His Orch. - **Never On Sunday** (H.M.V. POP-791)	9			
Lyn Cornell - **Never On Sunday** (Decca F-11277)	12	★		
Easy Riders - **Young In Love** (London HLR-9204)	12			
Steve Rossi - **Subito** (Philips PB-1061)	14			
Petula Clark - **Cinderella Jones** (Pye 7N.15281)	15			
Dalida - **Never On Sunday** (H.M.V. POP-793)	15	7		
Buddy Holly - **Learning The Game** (Coral Q-72411)	15	★		
Caterina Valente - **Secret Love** (Polydor NH-66816)	15			
Drifters - **Save The Last Dance For Me** (London HLK-9201)		1	★	
Marilyn Michaels - **Tell Tommy I Miss Him** (R.C.A. RCA-1208)		5	12	
Johnny Cash - **Loading Coal** (Philips PB-1075)		7		
Larry Verne - **Mr. Custer** (London HLN-9194)		10	1	
Craig Douglas - **Where's The Girl / My Hour Of Love** (Top Rank JAR-515)		13	2	
Mark Wynter - **Kickin' Up The Leaves** (Decca F-11279)		13	9	
Marty Gold & His Orch. - **Never On Sunday** (R.C.A. RCA-1205)		15		
Crazy Otto - **Glad Rag Doll** (Polydor NH-66634)		16		
Fendermen - **Don't You Just Know It** (Top Rank JAR-513)		16		
David MacBeth - **Pigtails In Paris** (Pye 7N.15291)		16		
Roy Orbison - **Blue Angel** (London HLU-9207)		16	★	
Elvis Presley - **It's Now Or Never** (R.C.A. RCA-1207)			2	
Brook Brothers - **Say The Word** (Pye 7N.15298)			4	
Laura Lee - **Tell Tommy I Miss Him** (Triumph RGM-1030)			9	
Dean Martin - **Just In Time** (Capitol CL-15155)			13	

5		12	19	26
★	Elvis Presley - **It's Now Or Never** (R.C.A. RCA-1207)			
1	Andy Stewart - **A Scottish Soldier** (Top Rank JAR-512)	4	19	2
2	Mark Wynter - **Kickin' Up The Leaves** (Decca F-11279)	★		
3	Umberto Bindi - **Il Nostro Concerto** (Oriole CB-1577)	★		
4	Johnny Angel - **You're Thrilling** (Parlophone R-4679)			
5	Dalida - **Never On Sunday** (H.M.V. POP-793)			
6	Laura Lee - **Tell Tommy I Miss Him** (Triumph RGM-1030)			
7	Brook Brothers - **Say The Word** (Pye 7N.15298)		3	5
7	David MacBeth - **Pigtails In Paris** (Pye 7N.15291)	7	21	16
7	Marilyn Michaels - **Tell Tommy I Miss Him** (R.C.A. RCA-1208)			
10	Johnny Bond - **Hot Rod Jalopy** (London HLU-9189)			
10	Bobby Darin - **Somebody To Love** (London HLK-9215)			
10	Craig Douglas - **Where's The Girl** / **My Hour Of Love** (Top Rank JAR-515)	7	4	5
10	Peter Sellers and Sophia Loren - **Goodness Gracious Me!** (Parlophone R-4702)	★		
10	Robb Storme - **One Thousand Nine Hundred And When** (Decca F-11282)		8	5
	Fats Domino - **Three Nights A Week** (London HLP-9198)	★		
	Emmettones - **Bold Robert Emmett** (Beltona BL-2722)	1	1	1
	Dennis Clancy with Johnstone's Scottish Accordion Band - **A Hundred Thousand Welcomes** (Waverley SLP-507)	2	10	
	Jim Gunner & The Echoes - **Hoolee Jump** (Decca F-11276)	3	6	25
	Jackie Wilson - **Alone At Last** (Coral Q-72412)	5		
	Simms/Wheeler Vintage Jazz Band - **Never On Sunday** (Polydor NH-66638)		6	
	Jimmy Jones - **Ready For Love** (M.G.M. MGM-1103)	7	★	
	Enoch Kent - **Sean South Of Garryowen** / **The Smashing Of The Van** (Top Rank JAR-386)	7	2	9
	Ray Conniff Singers - **Here Comes Santa Claus** (Philips PB-1071)	11		
	Johnny Preston - **Charming Billy** (Mercury AMT-1114)	11	21	5
	Mike Preston - **Togetherness** (Decca F-11287)	11		
	Club Quintet - **Caravelle** (Top Rank JAR-362)	14		
	Adam Faith - **ADAM** (Parlophone PMC-1128) **LP**	14	★	
	John Leyton - **The Girl On The Floor Above** (H.M.V. POP-798)	14		
	Valerie Masters - **Sweeter As The Day Goes By** (Fontana H-268)	14	21	
	Ted Taylor Four - **M.I.** (Oriole CB-1573)	14	17	
	Ventures - **Perfidia** (London HLG-9232)		4	★
	Joe Jones & His Orch. - **You Talk Too Much** (Columbia DB-4533)		6	
	David Kinnaird - **Mairi's Wedding** / **Northern Lights Of Aberdeen** (Top Rank JAR-385)		8	
	Johnny Carson - **You Talk Too Much** (Fontana H-277)		11	12
	Jack Scott - **Patsy** (Top Rank JAR-524)		11	

5   <<< NOVEMBER 1960 >>>   **12   19   26**

	12	19	26
Frankie Ford - **You Talk Too Much** (London HLP-9222)		13	3
Marty Robbins - **Ballad Of The Alamo** (Fontana H-270)		13	
Tony Dunning & The Tremolos - **Seventeen Tomorrow** (Palette PG-9006)		15	15
Joy & Dave - **My Very Good Friend The Milkman** (Decca F-11291)		15	
Johnny Horton - **North To Alaska** (Philips PB-1062)		17	
Day Brothers - **Angel / Just One More Kiss** (Oriole CB-1575)		19	
Russ Conway - **PARTY TIME** (Columbia 33SX-1279) **LP**		21	
Hunters - **Teen Scene** (Fontana H-276)			3
Emmettones - **Father Murphy** (Beltona BL-2723)			10
Firestones - **Party Cha [M]** (Decca F-11290)			10
Cowboy Copas - **Alabam** (Melodisc 45/1566)			12
Kalin Twins - **Zing! Went The Strings Of My Heart** (Brunswick 05844)			12
U.S. Bonds - **New Orleans** (Top Rank JAR-527)			16
Ernie Fields & His Orch. - **Raunchy** (London HL-9227)			16
Rockin' Saints - **Cheat On Me Baby** (Brunswick 05843)			16
Pete Chester & The Consulates - **Ten Swingin' Bottles** (Pye 7N.15305)			20
Iain Gregory - **Time Will Tell** (Pye 7N.15295)			20
Josh MacRae - **Let Ramensky Go** (Pye 7N.15307)			20
Jan Rohde - **Come Back Baby** (Qualiton Off Beat PSP-7128)			20
Gene Vincent - **Anna-Annabelle** (Capitol CL-15169)			20
Chubby Checker - **The Hucklebuck / Whole Lotta Shakin' Goin' On** (Columbia DB-4541)			25
Ken Dodd - **Dream That I Love You** (Decca F-11293)			25
David Kinnaird - **Auld Lang Syne** (Pye 7N.15311)			25
Jane Morgan - **Lord And Master** (London HLR-9210)			25
Shirelles - **Tonight's The Night** (London HL-9233)			25

Chubby Checker

The Shirelles

Craig Douglas

Adam Faith

3		10	17	24	31
★	Bing Crosby - **MERRY CHRISTMAS (VOL. 1)** *(Brunswick OE-9069)* **EP**				
1	Andy Stewart - **A Scottish Soldier** *(Top Rank JAR-512)*	1	1	2	7
2	Johnny Carson - **You Talk Too Much** *(Fontana H-277)*	7	★		
3	Brook Brothers - **Say The Word / Everything But Love** *(Pye 7N.15298)*	4	1	1	4
3	Pete Chester & The Consulates - **Ten Swingin' Bottles** *(Pye 7N.15305)*	13	1	★	
3	Iain Gregory - **Time Will Tell** *(Pye 7N.15295)*	★			
6	Hunters - **Teen Scene** *(Fontana H-276)*		8		
6	Robb Storme - **One Thousand Nine Hundred And When** *(Decca F-11282)*	15			
8	U.S. Bonds - **New Orleans** *(Top Rank JAR-527)*	9	8		
9	Guy Mitchell - **One Way Street** *(Philips PB-1084)*				
10	Craig Douglas - **Where's The Girl / My Hour Of Love** *(Top Rank JAR-515)*				
11	Cowboy Copas - **Alabam** *(Melodisc 45/1566)*	15			
11	Emmettones - **A Scottish Soldier** *(Beltona BL-2725)*		20		
11	Emile Ford & The Checkmates - **Counting Teardrops / White Christmas** *(Pye 7N.15314)*	★			
11	Johnny Preston - **Charming Billy** *(Mercury AMT-1114)*	★			
15	Eddy Arnold - **Just Out Of Reach** *(R.C.A. RCA-1212)*				
15	Frankie Ford - **You Talk Too Much** *(London HLP-9222)*				
15	Bridie Gallagher - **The Boys From County Armagh** *(Beltona BE-2679)*				
15	Ted Taylor Four - **M.I.** *(Oriole CB-1573)*	18			
19	Ken Dodd - **Dream That I Love You** *(Decca F-11293)*	25	16		16
19	Marty Robbins - **Ballad Of The Alamo** *(Fontana H-270)*				
19	Jack Scott - **Old Time Religion** *(Top Rank JAR-524)*				
22	Chubby Checker - **The Hucklebuck / Whole Lotta Shakin' Goin' On** *(Columbia DB-4541)*	9			11
22	Emmettones - **Father Murphy** *(Beltona BL-2723)*				
24	Maureen Evans - **Till** *(Oriole CB-1581)*				
24	Firestones - **Party Cha [M]** *(Decca F-11290)*		14		
26	Nelson Keene - **Teenage Troubles** *(H.M.V. POP-814)*				
26	Enoch Kent - **Sean South Of Garryowen / The Smashing Of The Van** *(Top Rank JAR-386)*	21	5	5	5
26	David MacBeth - **Pigtails In Paris** *(Pye 7N.15291)*				
	Emmettones - **Bold Robert Emmett** *(Beltona BL-2722)*	2	4	2	3
	Little Bobby Rey & His Band - **Rockin' 'J' Bells** *(Top Rank JAR-525)*	3			12
	Josh MacRae - **Let Ramensky Go** *(Pye 7N.15307)*	5			
	Bobby Rydell - **Sway** *(Columbia DB-4545)*	5	★		
	Johnny Cash - **RIDE THIS TRAIN** *(Philips BBL-7417)* **LP**	8			
	Al Saxon - **Blue-Eyed Boy** *(Fontana H-278)*	9	6	★	
	Faron Young - **Forget The Past** *(Capitol CL-15173)*	9	14		

3   **<<< DECEMBER 1960 >>>**   **10   17   24   31**

	10	17	24	31
Crazy Otto - **A Merry Christmas from Crazy Otto [M]** *(Polydor NH-66637)*	14			
Joe Jones & His Orch. - **You Talk Too Much** *(Columbia DB-4533)*	15	20		
Johnny Horton - **North To Alaska** *(Philips PB-1062)*	18	6	9	
David Kinnaird - **Auld Lang Syne** *(Pye 7N.15311)*	18	8	4	1
Johnny Cash - **Down The Street to 301** *(London HLS-9182)*	21			
Brook Benton - **Fools Rush In** *(Mercury AMT-1121)*	23			
Lou Smith - **Cruel Love** *(Top Rank JAR-520)*	23			
Day Brothers - **Angel** *(Oriole CB-1575)*	25			
Paul Evans - **Hushabye Little Guitar** *(London HLL-9239)*	25			
Stan Freberg - **Green Chritma** *(Capitol CL-14966)*	25			
Russ Conway - **PARTY TIME** *(Columbia 33SX-1279)* **LP**		★		
Glenda Collins - **Take A Chance** *(Decca F-11280)*		8		
Fats Domino - **My Girl Josephine** *(London HLP-9244)*		8	7	12
Rhet Stoller - **Chariot** *(Decca F-11302)*		8		
Damita Jo - **I'll Save The Last Dance For You** *(Mercury AMT-1116)*		16		
Anita O'Day - **Tea For Two** *(H.M.V. POP-821)*		16	7	7
Tommy Steele - **Must Be Santa** *(Decca F-11299)*		16		★
Lyn Cornell - **The Angel And The Stranger** *(Decca F-11301)*		20		
Marion Ryan - **It's You That I Love** *(Columbia DB-4550)*		20	6	★
Caterina Valente - **Amour** / **Till** *(Decca F-11306)*		20		
Mike Preston - **Togetherness** *(Decca F-11287)*			★	
Jackie Wilson - **Alone At Last** *(Coral Q-72412)*			★	
Maurice Williams & The Zodiacs - **Stay** *(Top Rank JAR-526)*				2
Max Bygraves - **When You Come To The End Of A Lollipop** *(Decca F-11308)*				5
Olympics - **I Wish I Could Shimmy Like My Sister Kate** *(Vogue Pop V-9174)*				9
Verdi and Jimmy Silver & His Music - **PARTY TIME AT THE ASTOR CLUB** *(Decca LK-4290)* **LP**				9
LaVern Baker - **Bumble Bee** *(London HLK-9252)*				12
King Brothers - **Doll House** *(Parlophone R-4715)*				12
Jerry Butler - **He Will Break Your Heart** *(Top Rank JAR-531)*				16
Tony Dunning & The Tremolos - **Seventeen Tomorrow** *(Palette PG-9006)*				16
Bert Kaempfert & His Orch. - **Wonderland By Night** *(Polydor NH-66639)*				16

7		14	21	28
★	Fats Domino - **My Girl Josephine** (*London HLP-9244*)			
★	Rhet Stoller - **Chariot** (*Decca F-11302*)			
★	Maurice Williams & The Zodiacs - **Stay** (*Top Rank JAR-526*)			
1	Emmettones - **Bold Robert Emmett** (*Beltona BL-2722*)	9	3	
1	David Kinnaird - **Auld Lang Syne** (*Pye 7N.15311*)			
3	Bert Kaempfert & His Orch. - **Wonderland By Night** (*Polydor NH-66639*)	4		25
3	Mandrake - **Mandrake** (*Philips PB-1093*)		20	
5	Eddy Arnold - **Before This Day Ends / Just Out Of Reach** (*R.C.A. RCA-1212*)			11
5	Enoch Kent - **Sean South Of Garryowen / The Smashing Of The Van** (*Top Rank JAR-386*)	2		
7	Brook Benton - **Fools Rush In** (*Mercury AMT-1121*)			
7	Jerry Butler - **He Will Break Your Heart** (*Top Rank JAR-531*)	8		
9	Cowboy Copas - **Alabam** (*Melodisc 45/1566*)	4	5	17
9	King Brothers - **Doll House** (*Parlophone R-4715*)	★		
9	Jimmy Shand & His Band - **Sing In The New Year [M]** (*Parlophone R-4382*)			
12	Donnie Brooks - **Doll House** (*London HLN-9253*)		8	
13	Ferlin Husky - **Wings Of A Dove** (*Capitol CL-15160*)	24		18
13	Martin Slavin & His Gang - **Rock-A-Charleston** (*Oriole CB-1587*)			
15	Richard Allan - **Poetry In Motion** (*Parlophone R-4711*)			
15	David Kinnaird - **Northern Lights Of Old Aberdeen** (*Pye 7N.15317*)	20	8	22
15	Danny Rivers - **Can't You Hear My Heart** (*Decca F-11294*)	★		
18	Chubby Checker - **The Hucklebuck** (*Columbia DB-4541*)			
19	Brook Brothers - **Say The Word / Everything But Love** (*Pye 7N.15298*)	15	13	6
19	Billy `Crash' Craddock - **Good Time Billy** (*Philips PB-1092*)			
19	Josh MacRae - **WALKIN', TALKIN', SINGIN'** (*Pye NEP-24131*) **EP**			
22	Lorne Lesley - **We're Gonna Dance** (*Polydor NH-66956*)	17	15	
22	Jim Reeves - **Am I Losing You / I Missed Me** (*R.C.A. RCA-1214*)	11	20	8
24	Dion - **Lonely Teenager** (*Top Rank JAR-521*)	4	★	
24	Ken Dodd - **Dream That I Love You** (*Decca F-11293*)			
24	Simms/Wheeler Vintage Jazz Band - **Never On Sunday** (*Polydor NH-66638*)			
24	Faron Young - **Forget The Past / A World So Full Of Love** (*Capitol CL-15173*)		20	
	Johnny Horton - **North To Alaska** (*Philips PB-1062*)	★		
	Andy Stewart - **A Scottish Soldier** (*Top Rank JAR-512*)	★		
	Olympics - **I Wish I Could Shimmy Like My Sister Kate** (*Vogue Pop V-9174*)	1	★	
	Wanda Jackson - **Mean, Mean Man** (*Capitol CL-15176*)	2		★
	U.S. Bonds - **New Orleans** (*Top Rank JAR-527*)	4	★	
	Larry Marshall - **The Ballad Of Rob Roy** (*Parlophone R-4703*)	9		
	Ben E. King - **First Taste Of Love** (*London HLK-9258*)	11	1	★
	Hank Thompson - **It Got To Be A Habit** (*Capitol CL-15177*)	11	18	

7   **<<< JANUARY 1961 >>>**

	14	21	28
Crickets - **Don't Cha Know** (Coral Q-72417)	14	13	
Frank Ifield - **That's The Way It Goes** (Columbia DB-4568)	15	6	18
Marty Robbins - **MORE GUNFIGHTER BALLADS AND TRAIL SONGS** (Fontana TFL-5113) **LP**	17		
Marty Wilde - **Rubber Ball** (Philips PB-1101)	17	★	
LaVern Baker - **Bumble Bee** (London HLK-9252)	20		
Ray Conniff & His Orch. - **Smoke Gets In Your Eyes** (Philips PB-1048)	20		
Lolita - **Sailor** (Polydor NH-66818)	20		
Don Gibson - **Sweet Dreams** (R.C.A. RCA-1217)	24	4	11
Hunters - **Teen Scene** (Fontana H-276)	24		11
Manuel and the Music of the Mountains - **La Dolce Vita** (Columbia DB-4563)	24		18
Zacharias & His Magic Violins - **Never On Sunday** (Polydor NH-66635)	24		
Terry Lightfoot & His New Orleans Jazzmen - **The Old Pull 'n' Push** (Columbia DB-4567)	29		
Paul Evans - **Hushabye Little Guitar** (London HLL-9239)		2	6
Emmettones - **Father Murphy** (Beltona BL-2723)		6	2
Bobbejaan - **I'm Cryin' In My Beer** (Palette PG-9009)		10	
Joe Lynch - **Irish Soldier Boy** (Glenside EPW-108)		10	
Robb Storme - **Music / Five Minutes More** (Decca F-11313)		10	4
Petula Clark - **Sailor** (Pye 7N.15324)		15	★
Ricky Nelson - **Milk Cow Blues / You Are The Only One** (London HLP-9260)		15	8
Josh MacRae - **Messing About On The River** (Pye 7N.15319)		18	1
Sam Cooke - **Sad Mood** (R.C.A. RCA-1221)		20	
Lee Hazlewood with Duane Eddy - **Words Mean Nothing** (London HLW-9223)		24	
Josh MacRae - **Let Ramensky Go** (Pye 7N.15307)		24	
Packabeats - **Gypsy Beat** (Parlophone R-4729)			3
Bill Black's Combo - **Blue Tango** (London HLU-9267)			4
Conway Twitty - **C'est Si Bon** (M.G.M. MGM-1118)			8
Nat 'King' Cole - **The World In My Arms** (Capitol CL-15178)			11
Bernard Cribbins - **Folk Song** (Parlophone R-4712)			11
Buddy Knox - **Lovey Dovey** (London HLG-9268)			11
Bert Weedon - **Ginchy** (Top Rank JAR-537)			18
Neil Sedaka - **Calendar Girl** (R.C.A. RCA-1220)			22
Tommy Zang - **Hey Good Lookin'** (Polydor NH-66957)			22
Reivers - **The Wee Magic Stane** (Top Rank JAR-244)			25
Shirelles - **Will You Love Me Tomorrow** (Top Rank JAR-540)			25
Dick Jordan - **Angel On My Shoulder** (Oriole CB-1591)			28

4		11	18	25
★	Nat 'King' Cole - **The World In My Arms** (Capitol CL-15178)			
★	Josh MacRae - **Messing About On The River** (Pye 7N.15319)			
★	Neil Sedaka - **Calendar Girl** (R.C.A. RCA-1220)			
★	Shirelles - **Will You Love Me Tomorrow** (Top Rank JAR-540)			
★	Conway Twitty - **C'est Si Bon** (M.G.M. MGM-1118)			
★	Bert Weedon - **Ginchy** (Top Rank JAR-537)			
1	Emmettones - **Father Murphy** (Beltona BL-2723)		13	
2	Bert Kaempfert & His Orch. - **Wonderland By Night** (Polydor NH-66639)			
3	Hunters - **Teen Scene** (Fontana H-276)			
3	Packabeats - **Gypsy Beat** (Parlophone R-4729)	3		★
3	Lawrence Welk & His Orch. - **Calcutta** (London HLD-9261)	1	★	
6	M.G.M. Studio Orchestra, cond. Charles Wolcott - **Ruby Duby Du** (M.G.M. MGM-1115)			
7	Brook Brothers - **Say The Word** (Pye 7N.15298)	9		
8	Eddy Arnold - **Before This Day Ends** / **Just Out Of Reach** (R.C.A. RCA-1212)		10	15
8	Ferlin Husky - **Wings Of A Dove** (Capitol CL-15160)			
8	Reivers - **The Wee Magic Stane** (Top Rank JAR-244)			
8	Hank Thompson - **It Got To Be A Habit** (Capitol CL-15177)	12		
12	Cowboy Copas - **Alabam** (Melodisc 45/1566)			
12	David Kinnaird - **Northern Lights Of Old Aberdeen** (Pye 7N.15317)		16	18
12	Ronnie Love - **Chills And Fever** (London HLD-9272)			
12	Frankie Vaughan - **The Day It Happens To You** (Philips PB-1104)	8	16	
16	Ray Charles - **Ruby** (H.M.V. POP-825)			18
16	Frank Ifield - **That's The Way It Goes** (Columbia DB-4568)			
16	Buddy Knox - **Lovey Dovey** (London HLG-9268)			
16	Ricky Nelson - **Milk Cow Blues** / **You Are The Only One** (London HLP-9260)	12		
16	Conway Twitty - **The Flame** (M.G.M. MGM-1108)			
16	Viscounts - **Money (Is The Root Of All Evil)** (Pye 7N.15323)			
22	Browns - **Send Me The Pillow You Dream On** (R.C.A. RCA-1218)			
22	Johnny DeLittle - **Not Guilty** (Columbia DB-4578)			
	Emmettones - **Johnson's Motor Car** (Beltona BL-2724)	2		
	Simon Crum - **Enormity In Motion** (Capitol CL-15183)	4	6	
	String-A-Longs - **Wheels** (London HLU-9278)	5	13	★
	Floyd Cramer - **Last Date** (R.C.A. RCA-1211)	6		
	Jerry Murad's Harmonicats - **Cherry Pink And Apple Blossom White** (Philips PB-1105)	6	13	18
	Jeff Rowena Group - **Peanut Vendor** (Pye 7N.15328)	9	10	
	Dodie Stevens - **Yes, I'm Lonesome Tonight** (London HLD-9280)	9		
	Lolita - **Sailor** (Polydor NH-66818)	12		

MIRACLES

FUTURE STARS
OF THE 60s

MARK
WYNTER

THE TEENAGE STAR
OF '61

DREAM GIRL

45-F 11323

DECCA

4		11	18	25
★	Buzz Clifford - **Baby Sittin' Boogie** (*Fontana H-297*)			
★	Emile Ford & The Checkmates - **What Am I Gonna Do** (*Pye 7N.15331*)			
★	Mark Wynter - **Dream Girl** (*Decca F-11323*)			
1	Enoch Kent - **The Smashing Of The Van** (*Top Rank JAR-386*)			
2	Ventures - **Ram-Bunk-Shush** (*London HLG-9292*)	★		
3	Emmettones - **Bold Robert Emmett** (*Beltona BL-2722*)			
3	Bobby Rydell - **Good Time Baby** (*Columbia DB-4600*)			★
5	Craig Douglas - **The Girl Next Door** (*Top Rank JAR-543*)	3		
5	Miracles - **Shop Around** (*London HL-9276*)			
7	Bobbejaan - **I'm Cryin' In My Beer** (*Palette PG-9009*)			
7	Lonnie Donegan - **Beneath The Willow / Leave My Woman Alone** (*Pye 7N.15330*)	1		
9	Jim Reeves - **Whispering Hope** (*R.C.A. RCA-1223*)		★	
10	Gene Pitney - **Love My Life Away** (*London HL-9270*)	9		★
11	Skeeter Davis - **My Last Date** (*R.C.A. RCA-1222*)			
11	Royaltones - **Flamingo Express** (*London HLU-9296*)			
13	Brook Brothers - **Warpaint** (*Pye 7N.15333*)	1	★	
13	Krew Kats - **Trambone** (*H.M.V. POP-840*)	★		
15	Peggy Lee - **Till There Was You** (*Capitol CL-15184*)	9		★
16	Drifters - **I Count The Tears** (*London HLK-9287*)		★	
16	Max Harris & His Group - **Wheels** (*Fontana H-296*)	9		
16	Brenda Lee - **Emotions / I'm Learning About Love** (*Brunswick 05847*)	★		
19	Michael Cox and the Hunters - **Teenage Love** (*H.M.V. POP-830*)			
19	Ferlin Husky - **Wings Of A Dove** (*Capitol CL-15160*)			
19	Helen Shapiro - **Don't Treat Me Like A Child** (*Columbia DB-4589*)	7		★
19	Gene Vincent - **Mister Loneliness** (*Capitol CL-15185*)			
	Jack Scott - **Found A Woman** (*Top Rank JAR-547*)	3		
	Fats Domino - **Ain't That Just Like A Woman** (*London HLP-9301*)	5		
	Édith Piaf - **Non Je Ne Regrette Rien** (*Columbia DB-4596*)	6		
	Anthony Newley - **And The Heavens Cried** (*Decca F-11331*)	8	★	
	Dave Sampson and the Hunters - **Why The Chicken?** (*Columbia DB-4597*)	9		
	Chet Atkins - **THE OTHER CHET ATKINS** (*R.C.A. Victor RD-27194*) **LP**		★	

The last dealers' charts were published on 11 March.

SONG INDEX

This is an index of all singles listed in the *UK Bubbling Under Chart*, and the month and year in which they first bubbled under. It does not include non-bubbling flip-sides.

Re-entries are not shown unless they were reissues.

Recordings which subsequently became hits are marked ★

[M] after a title indicates that the recording was a medley.

For reasons of space, some artists' names have been abbreviated.

Records released under a pseudonym show the artist's name twice: the pseudonym first, followed by their main/usual name in square brackets. They are listed under the artist's main/usual name in the *Artists A-Z* section.

Titles such as 'M.T.A.', 'P.T.Q. Rag', etc, are listed at the beginning of each letter.

A Blossom Fell
1/55 ★ Ronnie Hilton
1/55 ★ Dickie Valentine
2/55 ★ Nat 'King' Cole
A Certain Smile
9/58 ★ Johnny Mathis
A Drop Of The Hard Stuff
11/58 Peter Sellers
A Fool's Hall Of Fame
11/59 Pat Boone
A Girl! A Girl!
7/54 Eddie Fisher
A Girl Like You
4/60 Mike Preston
A Handful Of Songs
8/57 ★ Tommy Steele
A Hoot An' A Holler
9/59 Don Lang & His Frantic Five
A House With Love In It
11/56 Kathie Kay
A Hundred Thousand Welcomes
11/60 Dennis Clancy
A Lover's Question
1/59 Clyde McPhatter
A Man Chases a Girl
2/55 Eddie Fisher
A Man On The March
2/57 Anne Shelton
A Merry Christmas from Crazy Otto [M]
12/60 Crazy Otto
A Million Stars
9/59 David Whitfield
A Mother's Love Is A Blessing
1/57 Bridie Gallagher
A New Fangled Tango
6/59 Lena Horne
A Peasant's Guitar
6/55 Mitchell Torok
A Penny A Kiss, A Penny A Hug
5/59 Lorie Mann
A Pub With No Beer
12/58 ★ Slim Dusty
A Rockin' Good Way
7/60 Dinah Washington and Brook Benton

A Rusty Old Halo
4/55 Bonnie Lou
4/55 Danny Purches
A Scottish Soldier
10/60 ★ Andy Stewart
12/60 Emmettones
A Sky-Blue Shirt And A Rainbow Tie
9/54 ★ Norman Brooks
10/54 Ray Ellington Quartet
A String Of Pearls
1/55 Glenn Miller & His Orchestra
A Sweet Old Fashioned Girl
7/56 ★ Teresa Brewer
A Tear Fell
5/56 Jill Day
A Teenager In Love
5/59 ★ Dion & The Belmonts
6/59 ★ Craig Douglas
6/59 Dickie Valentine
A Very Precious Love
4/58 ★ Doris Day
5/58 Slim Whitman
7/58 Gene Kelly
A White Sport Coat (And A Pink Carnation)
5/57 ★ Terry Dene
6/57 Marty Robbins
A Woman In Love
9/56 ★ Four Aces
9/56 Edmund Hockridge
A Wonderful Time Up There
3/58 ★ Pat Boone
A World So Full Of Love
1/61 Faron Young
Ace In The Hole
1/55 Humphrey Lyttelton & His Band
Addio Amore
2/55 Vera Lynn
Adelaide
8/56 Sammy Davis Jr.
Adonis
9/59 Petula Clark
African Lullaby
6/58 Eartha Kitt
African Waltz
2/61 ★ Johnny Dankworth & His Orchestra

After You've Gone
8/54   Frankie Laine
Ain't That A Shame
9/55   ★ Pat Boone
11/55   Southlanders
1/57   ★ Fats Domino
Ain't That Just Like A Woman
3/61   Fats Domino
Ain't You Glad
3/57   Vipers Skiffle Group
Alabam
11/60   Cowboy Copas
Alabama Jubilee
7/55   ★ Ferko String Band
8/55   Big Ben Banjo Band
Alice Blue Gown
11/59   Leroy Holmes & His Orchestra
All American Boy
2/59   ★ Bill Parsons [Bobby Bare]
All I Have To Do Is Dream
5/58   ★ Everly Brothers
All I Need
5/60   Edna Savage
All I Want Is Your Love
3/58   Johnny Otis Show
All Is Well
6/60   Johnny Mathis
All Of The Time
11/58   Ferlin Husky
All Over Again
11/58   Johnny Cash
All Shook Up
6/57   ★ Elvis Presley
All Star Hit Parade [M]
6/56   ★ Various Artists
Alley-Oop
7/60   Dante & The Evergreens
Almost Grown
5/59   Chuck Berry
Almost In Your Arms
12/58   Steve Allen
Alone
11/57   Brother Sisters
11/57   ★ Kaye Sisters
11/57   ★ Shepherd Sisters
Alone At Last
11/60   ★ Jackie Wilson
Alone Too Long
2/55   Nat 'King' Cole
Along Came Caroline
9/60   ★ Michael Cox
Along Came Jones
6/59   Coasters
Alright, Okay, You Win
2/59   Peggy Lee
Always
2/55   Jeff Chandler
11/59   ★ Sammy Turner
Always And Forever
3/58   Marion Ryan
Am I A Toy Or A Treasure
9/54   ★ Kay Starr

Am I Losing You
1/61   Jim Reeves
Amapola
3/60   Davy Jones
Among My Souvenirs
11/59   ★ Connie Francis
Amour
12/60   Caterina Valente
An Affair To Remember
11/57   ★ Vic Damone
An Irish Mother's Prayer
4/56   Paddy Carney
An Irish Waltz [M]
9/54   Jimmy Shand & His Band
And The Heavens Cried
3/61   ★ Anthony Newley
And This Is My Beloved
5/55   Sarah Vaughan
6/55   Jerry Vale
7/55   Eddie Fisher
Angel
11/60   Day Brothers
Angel And The Stranger, The
12/60   Lyn Cornell
Angel Face
10/59   Billy Fury
Angel On My Shoulder
1/61   Dick Jordan
Angel Smile
2/58   Nat 'King' Cole
Angela Jones
3/60   ★ Johnny Ferguson
Angels Listened In, The
10/59   Crests
Angry
6/60   ★ Marty Wilde
Anna-Annabelle
11/60   Gene Vincent
Another Sleepless Night
6/60   ★ Jimmy Clanton
Answer To A Pub With No Beer, The
5/59   Slim Dusty
Any Time
2/60   Johnny Duncan
Anyone Can Be A Millionaire
10/55   Johnny Brandon
Apache
7/60   ★ Shadows
Ape Call
3/57   Nervous Norvus
Apples, Peaches And Cherries
3/55   Peggy Lee
April Love
11/57   ★ Pat Boone
April Showers
8/54   Al Jolson
Are You Mine
11/55   Ginny Wright and Tom Tall
Are You Really Mine
10/58   Jimmie Rodgers
Are You Sincere
5/58   Andy Williams

Armen's Theme
1/57   Ted Heath & His Music
2/57   David Seville
Around The World
5/57 ★ Bing Crosby
5/57 ★ Ronnie Hilton
6/57   Ronnie Carroll
Arrivederci Darling
11/55   Lys Assia
11/55 ★ Edna Savage
1/56   Jo Stafford
As I Love You
10/58 ★ Shirley Bassey
As Long As He Needs Me
7/60 ★ Shirley Bassey
As Time Goes By
3/60 ★ Richard Allan
Ask For Joe
6/56   Joe 'Mr. Piano' Henderson
At The Close Of An Irish Day
6/58   Bridie Gallagher
At The Hop
1/58 ★ Danny & The Juniors
2/58 ★ Nick Todd
Auctioneer, The
6/57   Chuck Miller
2/59   Chuck Miller *(reissue)*
Audie
8/59   Inadequates
Auld Lang Syne
11/60   David Kinnaird
Autumn Concerto
9/56 ★ Melachrino Orchestra
10/56   Norrie Paramor & His Orchestra
11/56   Carmen Cavallaro
11/56   Ted Heath & His Music
Baby Baby
2/57 ★ Frankie Lymon & The Teenagers
Baby, Baby, Bye Bye
6/60 ★ Jerry Lee Lewis
Baby Blue
5/58   Gene Vincent
Baby Doll
3/57   Humphrey Lyttelton & His Band
Baby Face
12/58 ★ Little Richard
Baby Lover
2/58 ★ Petula Clark
Baby My Heart
5/60 ★ Crickets (post-Holly)
Baby Sittin' Boogie
2/61 ★ Buzz Clifford
Back In The Old Routine
8/54   Bing Crosby and Donald O'Connor
Back To Donegal
10/54   McNulty Family
Back Track
1/56   Sammy Davis Jr.
Bad, Bad Whiskey
5/60   Amos Milburn
Bad Boy (1)
5/59   Larry Williams

Bad Boy (2)
11/59 ★ Marty Wilde
Bad Man's Blunder
7/60   Kingston Trio
Ballad Of A Teenage Queen
4/58   Johnny Cash
Ballad Of Davy Crockett, The
1/56 ★ Max Bygraves
1/56 ★ Tennessee Ernie Ford
1/56 ★ Dick James
1/56 ★ Gary Miller
Ballad Of Rob Roy, The
1/61   Larry Marshall
Ballad Of The Alamo
11/60   Marty Robbins
Banana Boat (Day-O)
4/57   Stan Freberg
See also Banana Boat Song, The
Banana Boat Song, The
2/57 ★ Tarriers
3/57   Fontane Sisters
3/57   Freddy
3/57   Inia Te Wiata
3/57   Sarah Vaughan
See also Banana Boat (Day-O)
Band Of Gold
3/56   Petula Clark
3/56   Rosemary Squires
4/56   Rose Brennan
Bandera Waltz
9/55   Slim Whitman
Bandit, The
8/54   Henry Leca & His Orchestra
9/54   Johnston Brothers
9/54   Billy Shepard
10/54   Jack Parnell & His Orchestra
Banjo Boy
6/60 ★ George Formby
6/60 ★ Valerie Masters
Banjo's Back In Town, The
8/55 ★ Alma Cogan
Barbara
6/60   Temptations
Bark For Barksdale
12/54   Gerry Mulligan Quartet
Barnyards O' Delgaty
5/59   Joe Gordon Folk Four
Basin Street Blues
6/54   Louis Armstrong
Battle Of Kookamonga, The
10/59   Homer & Jethro
Be-Bop-A-Lula
7/56 ★ Gene Vincent
Be-Bop Baby
11/57   Ricky Nelson
Be Content
11/57   Kathie Kay
Be Good To Me
4/56   McGuire Sisters
Be Happy
1/59   Big Ben Banjo Band

Be Mine
  1/60 ★ Lance Fortune
Be My Girl
  10/57   Don Fox
Be My Guest
  12/59 ★ Fats Domino
Beale Street Blues
  7/58   Ella Fitzgerald
Beat, The
  6/59   Rockin' R's
Beatnik
  4/59   Champs
Beautiful Obsession
  5/60   Sir Chauncey & His Exciting
        Strings [Ernie Freeman]
Because
  10/59   Mario Lanza
Because Of You
  12/54   Sammy Davis Jr.
Because They're Young
  7/60 ★ James Darren
Bedtime For Drums
  5/59   Alyn Ainsworth & His Orchestra
Bee's Knees
  1/59   John Barry Seven
Beep Beep
  1/59 ★ Playmates
Before This Day Ends
  12/60   Eddy Arnold
Believe In Me
  10/56   Robert Earl
Believe What You Say
  4/58   Ricky Nelson
Bell Bird
  8/59   Trio Los Paraguayos
Bell Bottom Boogie
  9/54   Merrill Moore
Beloved
  1/55   Billy Eckstine
Beneath The Willow
  2/61   Lonnie Donegan
Best Behaviour
  9/54   Tony Kinsey Trio with Joe Harriott
Best Of Everything, The
  11/59 ★ Johnny Mathis
Between You And Me
  4/55   Charlie McGee
Beware (1)
  7/55   Toni Arden
Beware (2)
  11/55   Norman Wisdom
Big Beat, The
  3/58 ★ Fats Domino
Big Bopper's Wedding
  1/59   Big Bopper
Big Guitar
  3/58   Owen Bradley Quintet
  4/58   John Barry Seven
  See also Stranger Than Fiction
Big Hurt, The
  1/60 ★ Maureen Evans
  1/60 ★ Toni Fisher

Big Iron
  12/59 ★ Marty Robbins
Big Man
  5/58 ★ Four Preps
Big River
  2/60   Ernie Freeman
Big Triangle, The
  10/60   Galaxies
Bill Bailey, Won't You Please Come Home
  5/57   Clyde Valley Stompers
  3/59   Brenda Lee
  5/60   Chris Barber's Jazz Band
Billy
  4/58   Kathy Linden
Billy Goat
  7/57   Bill Haley & His Comets
Bimbombey
  1/59   Jimmie Rodgers
Bird On My Head, The
  8/58   Don Lang & His Frantic Five
Birds And The Bees, The
  6/56 ★ Alma Cogan
  8/56   Dave King
Birth Of The Blues, The
  3/55   Sammy Davis Jr.
Black Denim Trousers And Motorcycle Boots
  11/55   Vaughn Monroe
Black Hills Of Dakota, The
  8/54 ★ Doris Day
Black Mask Waltz, The
  2/55   Winifred Atwell
Bless Yore Beautiful Hide
  3/55   Howard Keel
Bloodshot Eyes
  10/54   Wynonie Harris
Blow The Wind Southerly
  1/55   Kathleen Ferrier
Blue Angel
  10/60 ★ Roy Orbison
Blue Bells Of Broadway, The
  6/54   Doris Day
Blue Blue Day
  11/58   Don Gibson
Blue Blue Heartache
  10/57 ★ Johnny Duncan
Blue-Eyed Boy
  12/60 ★ Al Saxon
Blue Heartaches
  10/60   Tommy Edwards
Blue Mirage
  4/55   Frank Chacksfield & His Orchestra
  4/55   Percy Faith & His Orchestra
Blue Monday
  2/57 ★ Fats Domino
Blue Moon
  11/56 ★ Elvis Presley
  1/58   Lynn Hope
Blue Pacific Blues
  See Sadie Thompson's Song
Blue Skies
  9/54   Earl Bostic Orchestra

Blue Star
9/55 ★ Charlie Applewhite
9/55 ★ Cyril Stapleton & His Orchestra
10/55 Ray Burns
10/55 Les Howard
11/55 ★ Eve Boswell
See also Medic Theme, The
Blue Suede Shoes
5/56 Boyd Bennett & His Rockets
5/56 ★ Carl Perkins
Blue Tango
1/61 Bill Black's Combo
2/61 Flee-Rekkers
Bluebell
4/56 Alma Cogan
Bluebell Polka
11/54 ★ Jimmy Shand & His Band
Blueberry Hill
11/56 ★ Fats Domino
7/60 ★ John Barry & His Orchestra
Bob's Yer Uncle
7/54 Guy Mitchell
Bobby Shafto
4/55 Chris Barber's Jazz Band
Body And Soul
11/54 George Shearing Quintet
Bohemia Rag
9/60 Chris Barber's Jazz Band
Bold Robert Emmett
10/60 Emmettones
Bonaparte's Retreat
5/59 Billy Grammer
Bongo Boogie
11/59 Larry Lawrence
4/60 Preston Epps
Bongo Rock
6/59 Preston Epps
Bonnie Blue Gal, The
1/56 Mitch Miller & His Orchestra
Bonnie Wee Jeannie McColl
5/59 Joe Gordon Folk Four
Boo Boo Stick Beat
11/59 Chet Atkins
Boogie In My Bones
6/60 Laurel Aitken
Book Of Love
5/58 Monotones
5/58 ★ Mudlarks
Boom Boom Boomerang
6/55 Billie Anthony
Born To Be With You
8/56 ★ Chordettes
10/56 Beverley Sisters
Born Too Late
8/58 ★ Poni-Tails
Boy Scout
2/55 Boy Scout Association
Boys From County Armagh, The
2/58 Bridie Gallagher
Boys Of Jo'burg, The
6/58 Spokes Mashiyane
Brass Buttons
10/55 Mantovani & His Orchestra

Brazil
3/60 Frank Sinatra
Break-Up
9/58 Jerry Lee Lewis
Breeze And I, The
8/55 Lois Winter
Bring Me A Bluebird
12/55 Ben Light
Broken-Hearted Melody
8/59 ★ Sarah Vaughan
Bumble Bee
12/60 LaVern Baker
Bumble Boogie
10/56 Winifred Atwell
Buona Sera
1/58 ★ Louis Prima
Burning Bridges
5/60 ★ Jack Scott
Bury My Body
3/56 Lonnie Donegan
But Not For Me
10/59 ★ Ella Fitzgerald
Buttered Bannocks
8/60 David Kinnaird
Butterfly
4/57 ★ Charlie Gracie
4/57 ★ Andy Williams
Buzz, Buzz, Buzz
2/58 Hollywood Flames
By Candlelight
10/54 Carlos Thompson
By The Fountains Of Rome
7/56 ★ Edmund Hockridge
By The Light Of The Silvery Moon
3/59 ★ Little Richard
Bye Bye Blackbird
10/54 Billy Daniels
Bye Bye Johnny
8/60 Chuck Berry
Bye Bye Love
6/57 ★ Everly Brothers
8/57 John Fraser
C.C. Rider
6/57 Chuck Willis
C'est La Vie
2/56 Dennis Lotis
C'est Magnifique
10/54 Teddy Johnson
10/54 Gordon MacRae
11/54 Irène Hilda & Edmund Hockridge
C'est Si Bon
1/61 ★ Conway Twitty
Calcutta
2/61 ★ Lawrence Welk & His Orchestra
Calendar Girl
1/61 ★ Neil Sedaka
Califf Boogie
4/60 Teen Beats
California Here I Come
2/60 ★ Freddy Cannon
Call Me
1/59 Johnny Mathis

377

Can I Steal A Little Love
3/57   Frank Sinatra
Can't Get Along Without You
3/58 ★ Frankie Vaughan
Can't You Hear My Heart
1/61 ★ Danny Rivers
Canadian Sunset
9/56   Ted Heath & His Music
11/56   Andy Williams
Candlelight
3/56   Mantovani & His Orchestra
Candy
3/60   Mudlarks
Cannonball
12/58 ★ Duane Eddy
Cara Mia
10/54   Ron Goodwin & His Concert Orch.
Caramba
5/59   Champs
Caravelle
11/60   Club Quintet
Caribbean
4/55 ★ Mitchell Torok
Caribbean Honeymoon
6/60 ★ Frank Weir & His Orchestra
Carina
10/59   Fred Buscaglione
Carnival
8/60   Nina & Frederik
Carousel Waltz, The
6/56 ★ Ray Martin & His Concert Orch.
7/56   Ray Bloch & His Orchestra
Cat Came Back, The
10/56 ★ Sonny James
Cat From Coos Bay, The
11/54   Wally Stott & His Orchestra
Catari, Catari
12/58   Toni Dalli
Cattle Call
3/55   Slim Whitman
Cerveza
10/58   Boots Brown & His Blockbusters
[Shorty Rogers]
Cha Cha Momma Brown
12/58 ★ Martinas & His Music
[Martin Slavin]
Chain Gang (1)
3/56 ★ Jimmy Young
Chain Gang (2)
10/60   Ronnie Carroll
Champion The Wonder Horse
8/56   Frankie Laine
Chances Are
11/57   Dave King
6/58   Johnny Mathis
Changing Partners
7/54   Patti Page
Chanson d'Amour
5/58 ★ Art & Dotty Todd
Chantez, Chantez
7/57   Eve Boswell
Chantilly Lace
11/58 ★ Big Bopper

Chapel Of The Roses
4/57   Dickie Valentine
4/57 ★ Malcolm Vaughan
Chariot
12/60 ★ Rhet Stoller
Chariot Rock
11/58   Champs
Charleston, The
6/54   Winifred Atwell
Charlie Brown
3/59   Bernard Bresslaw
3/59 ★ Coasters
Charming Billy
11/60 ★ Johnny Preston
Chattanooga Choo Choo
4/60 ★ Ernie Fields & His Orchestra
Cheat On Me, Baby
11/60   Rockin' Saints
Chee-Chee-Oo-Chee
5/55   Alma Cogan
5/55   Johnston Brothers
Cherokee
3/56   Stan Kenton & His Orchestra
Cherry Pie
5/60   Skip & Flip
Cherry Pink And Apple Blossom White
3/55 ★ Eddie Calvert
4/55   Xavier Cugat & His Orchestra
4/55   Edmundo Ros & His Orchestra
2/61   Jerry Murad's Harmonicats
Chick
3/59   Joe 'Mr. Piano' Henderson
Chicka'roo
6/60   Ricky Wayne
Chills And Fever
2/61   Ronnie Love
China Doll
8/54 ★ Slim Whitman
Chipmunk Song, The
1/59   Chipmunks [David Seville]
C-H-R-I-S-T-M-A-S
12/55   Rosemary Clooney
Christmas Alphabet
11/55 ★ Dickie Valentine
12/55   McGuire Sisters
Christmas And You
12/56 ★ Dave King
Christmas Medley [M]
12/55   Charlie Kunz
Church Bells May Ring
8/56   Willows
Ciao Ciao Bambina
3/59 ★ Domenico Modugno
Cinderella Jones
10/60   Petula Clark
Cindy Lou
7/60   Johnnie Lee
Cindy, Oh Cindy
12/56 ★ Vince Martin with the Tarriers
Cinnamon Sinner
9/54   Ted Heath & His Music
10/54   Frankie Vaughan

Circle Dance
1/60   Applejacks
Clap Your Hands
6/60   Beau-Marks
Clark Street
4/56   Elmer Bernstein Orchestra
Class, The
8/59   Chubby Checker
Claudette
5/58 ★ Everly Brothers
Click Clack
4/58   Dicky Doo & The Dont's
Close The Door
9/55 ★ Stargazers
Close Your Eyes
5/55 ★ Tony Bennett
Cloudburst
10/55   Ted Heath & His Music
10/55 ★ Don Lang
Cockles And Mussels
6/56   Eric Delaney Band
Cockney Capers [M]
1/55   Two Bills From Bermondsey
Coffee Bar Jive
8/57   Joe 'Mr. Piano' Henderson
Coffee Grinder
2/55   Humphrey Lyttelton & His Band
Cold, Cold Shower
4/57   Frankie Vaughan
Collette
2/60 ★ Billy Fury
Come Back Baby
11/60   Jan Rohde
Come Back My Love
9/56   Eve Boswell
Come Back To Sorrento
3/57   Harry Secombe
Come Closer To Me
8/58   Nat 'King' Cole
Come Go With Me
5/57   Dell-Vikings
Come Home To My Arms
12/56   Beverley Sisters
Come Into My Heart
11/59   Lloyd Price
C'mon Everybody
1/59 ★ Eddie Cochran
Come On, Come On, Come On
3/58   Tiny Topsy and the Charms
Come On, Let's Go
11/58   Tommy Steele
Come Prima
8/58 ★ Marino Marini & His Quartet
See also More Than Ever
Come Softly To Me
4/59   Richard Barrett with the Chantels
4/59 ★ Craig Douglas
4/59 ★ Fleetwoods
4/59 ★ Frankie Vaughan and the Kaye
        Sisters
Comes Love
5/58   Alma Cogan

Cookie
3/56   Eve Boswell
Cool Water
6/55 ★ Frankie Laine
12/59   Marty Robbins
8/60   Jack Scott
Copper Knob
10/59   Ken Morris
Count On Me
10/59 ★ Shirley Bassey
Count Your Blessings Instead Of Sheep
11/54 ★ Bing Crosby
11/54   Eddie Fisher
1/55   Rosemary Clooney
Counting Teardrops
12/60 ★ Emile Ford & The Checkmates
Crackin' Up
10/59   Bo Diddley
Crazy 'bout Ya Baby
9/54   Johnston Brothers
Crazy Dream
12/57 ★ Jim Dale
Crazy Girl
4/58   Charlie Gracie
Crazy Legs
3/57   Gene Vincent
Crazy Love
4/58 ★ Paul Anka
Crazy Man, Crazy
4/55   Bill Haley & His Comets
Crazy Otto Medley [M]
5/55   Johnny Maddox
Crazy Otto Rag, The
5/55   Big Ben Banjo Band
5/55   Petula Clark, etc.
5/55 ★ Stargazers
Crazy Rhythm
4/59   Shirley Bassey
Croce di Oro
1/56 ★ Joan Regan
Cross Over
4/58   Jimmy Bowen
Cross Over The Bridge
6/54   Patti Page
Crossfire
8/59   Johnny & The Hurricanes
Cruel Love
12/60   Lou Smith
Cry
9/59   Knightsbridge Strings
Cry Baby
8/56   Billy Williams Quartet
Cry, Baby, Cry
10/59   Joyce Shock
Cry Me A River
3/57 ★ Julie London
Cuckoo Waltz, The
7/55   Ken Griffin
Cuddle Me
9/54   Ted Heath & His Music
Cumberland Gap, The
3/57   Dickie Bishop & The Sidekicks
3/57 ★ Vipers Skiffle Group

Daddy's Little Girl
12/58   Dick James
Dam Busters (March), The
7/55 ★ Central Band of the Royal Air Force
8/55   Sidney Torch & His Orchestra
10/55   Concert Orchestra
10/55 ★ Billy Cotton & His Band
Dance With A Dolly
5/60   Neville Taylor
Dance With Me
11/59 ★ Drifters
Dance With Me Henry (Wallflower)
5/55   Georgia Gibbs
5/55   Suzi Miller
6/55   Jean Campbell
Dancing At The Tower No. 16 [M]
7/55   Reginald Dixon
Danny Boy
8/55   Slim Whitman
Dark Moon
8/57   Gale Storm
Darktown Strutters' Ball, The
2/60 ★ Joe Brown & The Bruvvers
D-A-R-L-I-N'
7/56   Hilltoppers
Darn That Dream
10/54   Gerry Mulligan Quartet
Day That It Happens To You, The
2/61   Frankie Vaughan
Dear Mary
10/56   Slim Whitman
Deck Of Cards
10/59 ★ Wink Martindale
Dede Dinah
4/58 ★ Frankie Avalon
'Deed I Do
8/54   Tommy Whittle w/Tony Kinsey Trio
Deep Purple
4/55   Earl Bostic & His Orchestra
11/57 ★ Billy Ward & His Dominoes
Deep Within Me
9/57   Tony Brent
Delaney's Delight
1/55   Eric Delaney
Delaney's Donkey
2/57   Joe Lynch
Delaware
2/60 ★ Perry Como
Delicious (The Laughing Song)
10/58   Jim Backus
Destiny (1)
7/54   Johnnie Ray
Destiny (2)
10/59   Henri René & His Orchestra
Devil, The
8/58   Lord Melody
Devil Or Angel
9/60   Bobby Vee
Devil Woman
10/57   Buddy Knox
Diamond Ring
4/59   Jimmy Isle

Dig Deep
1/55   Ted Heath & His Music
Diggin' My Potatoes
3/56   Lonnie Donegan
Dill Pickes
9/54   Winifred Atwell
Dim, Dim The Lights
1/55   Bill Haley & His Comets
Dinah
5/60   Fats Waller
Dinah – Cha Cha
3/59   Tommy Dorsey Orchestra
Ding Dong Rock-A-Billy Wedding
11/57   Marion Ryan
Dinner With Drac (Part 1)
5/58   John Zacherle
Dirty Robber
12/59   Wailers
Dixieland
9/54   Winifred Atwell
Dizzy Miss Lizzy
4/58   Larry Williams
Do, Do, Do
12/55   Johnny Maddox
Do The Bop
6/56   Hilltoppers
Do You Love Old Santa Claus
11/54   Max Bygraves
Do You Want To Dance
7/58   Bobby Freeman
Doctor In Love
8/60   Richard Allen [Richard Allan]
Doll House
12/60 ★ King Brothers
1/61   Donnie Brooks
Don't Be Angry
10/55   Nappy Brown
Don't Be That Way
3/56   Benny Goodman
Don't Cha Know
1/61   Crickets
Don't Come Back Again
4/59   Dick Shane
Don't Go Home
8/58   Playmates
Don't Go To Strangers
1/55 ★ Ronnie Harris
1/55   Al Martino
Don't Let Go
2/58 ★ Jim Dale
Don't Ring-a Da Bell
4/56   Alma Cogan
Don't Stay Away Too Long
9/55   Eddie Fisher
Don't Take Me For Granted
3/56   Joan Regan
Don't Take Your Guns To Town
3/59   Johnny Cash
Don't Tell Me Not To Love You
3/56   Lee Lawrence
Don't Tell Me Your Troubles
10/59   Don Gibson

Don't Throw Away All Those Teardrops
3/60 ★ Frankie Avalon
Don't Treat Me Like A Child
2/61 ★ Helen Shapiro
Don't Worry
6/55 ★ Johnny Brandon
7/55 Joy Nichols
Don't You Just Know It
10/60 Fendermen
Don't You Rock Me Daddy-O
1/57 Bob Cort Skiffle Group
1/57 ★ Vipers Skiffle Group
Donkey Cart, The
8/56 ★ Frank Chacksfield & His Orchestra
Donkey Tango
5/56 Ray Bloch & His Orchestra
Doomsday Rock
11/56 Tommy Steele
Doonaree
6/55 Vera Lynn
9/55 Carmel Quinn
10/55 Robert Wilson
Down By The Riverside
3/56 Ken Colyer's Jazzmen
Down By The Sugar Cane
7/56 Eve Boswell
Down The Street To 301
9/60 Johnny Cash
Draggin' The River
6/59 Ferlin Husky
Dream Girl
2/61 ★ Mark Wynter
Dream Lover
6/59 Duffy Power
Dream That I Love You
11/60 Ken Dodd
Dreamboat
5/55 ★ Alma Cogan
5/55 5 DeMarco Sisters
Dreamin'
8/60 ★ Johnny Burnette
Dreams Can Tell A Lie
2/56 Dickie Valentine
Drinking Song
10/54 ★ Mario Lanza
Drum Party
12/59 Sandy Nelson
Drunken Driver, The
6/58 Ferlin Husky
Dumplin's
4/58 Ernie Freeman
Dungaree Doll
3/56 Dickie Bennett
3/56 Eddie Fisher
Duvid Crockett
5/56 Mickey Katz & His Orchestra
Early Call (Bermondsey Bounce)
8/57 Humphrey Lyttelton & His Band
Early In The Morning
8/58 ★ Buddy Holly
Early To Bed
3/59 ★ Poni-Tails

Earth Angel
3/55 ★ Crew-Cuts
6/55 Penguins
7/55 Les Baxter & His Orchestra
Earthbound
9/56 Mario Lanza
East Of Suez
9/54 Charlie Ventura Septet
Ebb Tide
7/54 Jerry Colonna
Eddie And The Witchdoctor
5/55 Sauter–Finegan Orchestra
Eee-O Eleven
9/60 ★ Sammy Davis Jr.
Eighteen
9/58 Connie Francis
El Paso
1/60 Vince Eager
1/60 ★ Marty Robbins
El Rancho Rock
7/58 Champs
Elephant Tango
5/55 ★ Cyril Stapleton & His Orchestra
Elephants' Tango, The
6/55 Ray Martin & His Concert Orch.
Elevator Rock
11/56 Tommy Steele
Eleventh Hour Melody, The
3/56 Al Hibbler
Emotions
2/61 ★ Brenda Lee
Enchanted
5/59 Platters
End, The
11/58 Glen Mason
12/58 Earl Grant
Endless
8/54 ★ Dickie Valentine
Endlessly
5/59 ★ Brook Benton
Engagement Waltz, The
10/59 Dickie Valentine
Enormity In Motion
2/61 Simon Crum [Ferlin Husky]
Entertainer, The
9/55 Ken Colyer's Jazzmen
Eso Es El Amor
11/58 Franchito & His Orchestra
2/59 Les Chakachas
Eton Boating Song
11/59 Knightsbridge Chorale
Evermore
5/55 ★ Ruby Murray
5/55 Edna Savage
Every Day Is Mother's Day
4/57 Kathie Kay
Ev'ry Day Of My Life
6/55 ★ Malcolm Vaughan
8/55 Vera Lynn
Ev'ry Hour, Ev'ry Day Of My Life
8/58 Malcolm Vaughan

Ev'ry Street's A Boulevard In Old New York
  9/54   Dean Martin & Jerry Lewis
Ev'ry Time We Say Goodbye
  10/57   Ella Fitzgerald
Everything But Love
  11/60   Brook Brothers
Ev'rywhere
  4/55 ★ David Whitfield
Extra Day, The
  3/56   Dennis Lotis
Fabulous
  6/57 ★ Charlie Gracie
Fair Weather Sweetheart
  4/59   Teresa Brewer
Faithful Hussar, The
  6/56 ★ Ted Heath & His Music
  2/57 ★ Vera Lynn
Faithful Kind, The
  5/60   Frankie Avalon
Fallin'
  10/58 ★ Connie Francis
Fanagalo
  9/56   Frank Chacksfield Tunesmiths
  10/56   Zulu Rhythm Boys
Fanfare Boogie
  3/55   Eric Winstone & His Orchestra
Far Far Away
  9/60   Don Gibson
Faraway
  9/54   Eddie Calvert
Farewell, So Long, Goodbye
  8/55   Bill Haley & His Comets
Farrago
  1/59   John Barry Seven
Fascination
  9/57   Robert Earl
  9/57   Jane Morgan
Father Murphy
  11/60   Emmettones
Feel So Fine
  7/60 ★ Johnny Preston
Fever
  10/56   Little Willie John
  8/58 ★ Peggy Lee
Fickle Chicken
  11/59   Atmospheres
Fidgety Feet
  2/55   George Lewis
Finger Of Suspicion, The
  11/54 ★ Dickie Valentine
Fings Ain't Wot They Used T' Be
  3/60 ★ Max Bygraves
Fire Down Below
  5/57 ★ Jeri Southern
  8/57 ★ Shirley Bassey
First Taste Of Love
  1/61 ★ Ben E. King
Fish Man, The
  7/60 ★ Ian Menzies & His Clyde Valley
         Stompers [Clyde Valley Stompers]
Five Days, Five Days
  6/57   Gene Vincent

Five Feet High And Rising
  9/59   Johnny Cash
Five Foot Two, Eyes Of Blue
  11/55   Merrill Moore
Five Hundred Guys
  6/56   Frank Sinatra
Five Minutes More
  1/61   Robb Storme
5 Months, 2 Weeks, 2 Days
  4/58   Louis Prima
Flame, The (1)
  2/55   Anthony Steel
Flame, The (2)
  2/61   Conway Twitty
Flamingo
  8/54   Earl Bostic & His Orchestra
Flamingo Express
  3/61   Royaltones
Flip, Flop And Bop
  4/58   Floyd Cramer
Flip, Flop And Fly
  5/55   Johnnie Ray
Flowers Mean Forgiveness
  4/56   Frank Sinatra
Fly Away Lovers
  7/58   Alma Cogan
Flying Hickory
  8/55   Kirchin Band
Folk Song
  1/61   Bernard Cribbins
Follow A Star
  4/60   Norman Wisdom
Fools Rush In
  12/60 ★ Brook Benton
Foot-Patter
  4/60   Fireballs
Football Crazy
  9/60   Robin Hall & Jimmie MacGregor
Footprints In The Snow
  11/57 ★ Johnny Duncan
Footsteps
  3/60 ★ Steve Lawrence
  5/60   Garry Mills
For My Good Fortune
  11/58   Pat Boone
Forever, My Darling
  10/59   Tony Brent
Forget Me Not
  10/58   Kalin Twins
Forget The Past
  12/60   Faron Young
Forget You
  4/60   Milton Grayson
Forgotten Dreams
  8/57   Joe 'Mr. Piano' Henderson
Fortune In Dreams
  9/54   Kay Starr
Forty Cups Of Coffee
  4/57   Bill Haley & His Comets
Forty-Five Men In A Telephone Booth
  12/55   Four Tophatters
Found A Woman
  3/61   Jack Scott

Frankie And Johnny
2/55   George Melly
11/56   Sammy Davis Jr.
Frankie's Man, Johnny
6/59   Johnny Cash
Fraülein
7/58   Bobby Helms
6/60   Johnny Carson
Freddy
7/55   Eartha Kitt
Freight Train
3/57   ★ Chas McDevitt Skiffle Group
Freight Train Blues
4/57   2.19 Skiffle Group
French Foreign Legion
3/59   ★ Frank Sinatra
Fried Onions
6/58   Lord Rockingham's XI
Friends And Neighbours
7/54   Max Bygraves
Furry Murray
9/59   Tradewinds
Gal That Got Away, The
1/55   Frank Sinatra
Gal With The Yaller Shoes, The
5/56   Michael Holliday
6/56   Four Aces
Gang That Sang Heart Of My Heart, The
7/54   Four Aces
Garden Of Eden, The
1/57   Monty Norman
Gay Gordons [M]
10/54   Jimmy Shand & His Band
Gee But It's Lonely
11/58   ★ Pat Boone
Gee, But Ya Gotta Come Home
2/55   Guy Mitchell
Gentle Sex, The
1/55   Ray Martin & His Concert Orch.
Georgia On My Mind
10/55   Nat Gonella & His Trumpet
Georgia's Got A Moon
11/55   Betty Miller
Get A Job
3/58   Silhouettes
Get Along Home Cindy
11/57   Johnny Duncan
Gigi
1/59   ★ Billy Eckstine
3/59   ★ Vic Damone
5/59   Bing Crosby
10/59   Ronnie Hilton
Gilly Gilly Ossenfeffer Katzenellen Bogen By The Sea
8/54   ★ Max Bygraves
8/54   Four Lads
9/54   George Elrick and the Lumberjacks
Ginchy
1/61   ★ Bert Weedon
Ginger Bread
10/58   ★ Frankie Avalon

Girl Can't Help It, The
2/57   ★ Little Richard
Girl From Corsica, The
8/60   Ron Goodwin & His Concert Orch.
Girl From Donegal, The
6/58   Bridie Gallagher
Girl Next Door, The
3/61   Craig Douglas
Girl On The Floor Above, The
11/60   John Leyton
Girl With The Golden Braids, The
6/57   Perry Como
Give A Fool A Chance
9/55   Alma Cogan
9/55   Sammy Davis Jr.
Give Her My Love (When You Meet Her)
2/57   Jill Day
2/57   ★ Johnston Brothers
2/57   Anne Shelton
Give Me A Carriage With Eight White Horses
9/56   Guy Mitchell
Give Me The Moonlight, Give Me The Girl
3/55   Frankie Vaughan
Give Me Your Word
9/54   ★ Tennessee Ernie Ford
Give My Love To Rose
3/58   Johnny Cash
Glad All Over
3/58   Carl Perkins
Glad Rag Doll
10/55   Crazy Otto
10/60   Crazy Otto *(reissue)*
Go, Jimmy, Go
1/60   Jimmy Clanton
Go On By
10/55   Rosemary Clooney
Go On Home
4/60   Sanford Clark
Goin' Co'tin'
2/55   Ronnie Harris, Diana Decker,
              Ray Burns and Ruby Murray
Goin' Home
4/60   Rosco Gordon
Golden Age, The
5/58   Terry Dene
Gone
5/57   Ferlin Husky
5/57   Slim Whitman
Gone Train
4/59   Champs
Good And Lonesome
8/55   Kay Starr
Good Mornin' Life
1/58   Dennis Lotis
Good Rockin' Tonight
See There's Good Rockin' Tonight
Good Time Baby
2/61   ★ Bobby Rydell
Good Time Billy
1/61   Billy 'Crash' Craddock
Goodbye, Au Revoir, Adios
7/56   Johnnie Ray

Goodbye Baby
4/59   Jack Scott

Goodbye, Jimmy Goodbye
5/59   Kathy Linden

Goodbye Johnny
11/58   Bridie Gallagher

Goodbye, Little Darlin', Goodbye
11/59   Johnny Cash

Goodness Gracious Me!
11/60 ★ Peter Sellers and Sophia Loren

Goodnight, Sweetheart, Goodnight
5/55   McGuire Sisters

Goody Goody
9/57 ★ Frankie Lymon & The Teenagers

Goona Goona
6/60   Four Lads

Gordon Waltz , The [M]
11/54   Jimmy Shand & His Band

Got A Girl
4/60 ★ Four Preps

Got A Match?
7/58 ★ Russ Conway
8/58   Frank Gallup

Gotta Get A Date
9/60 ★ Frank Ifield

Gotta Have Me Go With You
3/55 Judy Garland

Gotta Have Rain
8/58 ★ Max Bygraves

Granada
9/54   Mario Lanza

Grand March [M]
10/54   Jim Cameron & His Band

Great Pretender, The
3/56 ★ Jackie Riggs
5/56   Stan Freberg
8/56 ★ Platters

Greater Sin, The
12/57   Frankie Laine

Greatest Mistake Of My Life, The
2/59   Monograms

Green Back Dollar
6/57 ★ Chas McDevitt Skiffle Group

Green Chritma
12/60   Stan Freberg

Green Door, The
11/56   Ray Ellington Quartet

Green Fields
5/60   Brook Brothers
See also Greenfields

Green Grows The Grass
5/56   Guy Mitchell

Green Tree Boogie
6/55   Bill Haley & His Comets

Greenfields
4/60 ★ Brothers Four
See also Green Fields

Greensleeves
3/57   Beverley Sisters

Growin' Prettier
10/59   Johnny October

Guarda Che Luna
10/59   Fred Buscaglione

Guess Things Happen That Way
7/58   Johnny Cash

Gunfight At The O.K. Corral
9/57   Frankie Laine

Gypsy Beat
1/61 ★ Packabeats

Ha! Ha! Ha!
1/58   Anne Shelton

Hajji Baba
12/54   Nat 'King' Cole

Hallelujah, I Love Her So
1/60 ★ Eddie Cochran

Hands Across The Sea
10/58   Shirley Bassey

Handy Man
2/60 ★ Jimmy Jones

Hangin' Around
6/58   Guy Mitchell

Hangin' Up A Horseshoe
10/58   Four Aces

Hanging Tree, The
3/59   Marty Robbins

Happiness Street
10/56   Tony Bennett

Happy Anniversary
12/59   Ronnie Hilton
12/59 ★ Joan Regan

Happy Days And Lonely Nights
11/54 ★ Suzi Miller
11/54 ★ Frankie Vaughan

Happy-Go-Lucky Me
6/60 ★ George Formby
6/60   Frank Ifield

Happy Guitar
3/58 ★ Tommy Steele

Happy Hobo, The
12/59   Adriano

Happy Is The Bride
3/58   Rosemary Squires

Happy Organ, The
5/59   Dave 'Baby' Cortez

Happy Wanderer, The
9/54   Frank Weir & His Saxophone
See also Val De Ri, Val De Ra

Happy Whistler, The
5/56 ★ Cyril Stapleton & His Orchestra

Hard Hearted Hannah
11/55   Ella Fitzgerald

Have You Ever Been Lonely
10/55   Pauline Shepherd

Hawaiian Wedding Song
4/59   Andy Williams

Hawk-Eye
11/55 ★ Frankie Laine

He
12/55   Al Hibbler
12/55   McGuire Sisters
1/56   Robert Earl

He Bought My Soul At Calvary
9/54   Jo Stafford

He Will Break Your Heart
12/60   Jerry Butler

He'll Have To Go
3/60 ★ Jim Reeves
He'll Have To Stay
5/60 ★ Jeanne Black
6/60 Sally Kelly
He's A Tramp
11/55 Peggy Lee
Heart
3/57 ★ Max Bygraves
3/57 Ronnie Hilton
3/57 McGuire Sisters
4/57 Four Aces
4/57 ★ Johnston Brothers
4/57 Ruby Murray
Heart Of A Man, The
6/59 ★ Frankie Vaughan
Heart Of A Teenage Girl, The
4/60 ★ Craig Douglas
Heartaches By The Number
10/59 ★ Guy Mitchell
Heartbeat (1)
11/54 ★ Ruby Murray
Heartbeat (2)
12/58 ★ Buddy Holly
4/60 ★ Buddy Holly *(reissue)*
Heartbreak Avenue
11/59 Don Gibson
Heartbreak Hotel
5/56 ★ Elvis Presley
7/56 ★ Stan Freberg
Hearts Of Stone
4/55 Charms
4/55 Fontane Sisters
Heaven Was Never Like This
9/54 Eddie Fisher
Hell Hath No Fury
4/56 ★ Frankie Laine
Hello Mrs. Jones
6/55 Vic Damone
6/55 Dickie Valentine
Hello, My Darlings
8/58 ★ Charlie Drake
Her Hair Was Yellow
8/58 Ronnie Hilton
Here Comes Santa Claus
11/60 Ray Conniff Singers
Here Comes Summer
8/59 ★ Jerry Keller
Here's To The Gordons
11/54 Robert Wilson
1/55 Kirk Stevens
Hernando's Hideaway
9/55 Ray Martin & His Concert Orch.
10/55 Archie Bleyer & His Orchestra
10/55 Alma Cogan
10/55 ★ Johnston Brothers
10/55 ★ Johnnie Ray
11/55 Ray Anthony & His Orchestra
Hey Brother Pour The Wine
8/54 Dean Martin
Hey Good Lookin'
1/61 ★ Tommy Zang

Hey, Jealous Lover
2/57 Lita Roza
3/57 Frank Sinatra
Hey Liley, Liley Lo
3/57 Vipers Skiffle Group
Hey Little Girl
10/59 Dee Clark
10/59 Roy Young
Hey Mr. Banjo
8/55 Big Ben Banjo Band
Hey There
9/55 ★ Sammy Davis Jr.
9/55 Barbara Lyon
10/55 ★ Johnnie Ray
10/55 ★ Lita Roza
11/55 Ronnie Hilton
11/55 Edmund Hockridge
Hey You!
10/57 ★ Tommy Steele
Hiawatha
11/56 Charlie McNair Skiffle Group
3/59 Tommy Steele
High And The Mighty, The
9/54 Les Baxter & His Orchestra
10/54 Leroy Holmes & His Orchestra
10/54 Pérez Prado & His Orchestra
10/54 Victor Young & His Singing Strings
11/54 Johnny Desmond
11/54 Harry James & His Orchestra
11/54 Gary Miller
11/54 Norrie Paramor & His Orchestra
12/54 Roland Shaw Orchestra
See also Theme from 'The High And The Mighty'
High Class Baby
11/58 ★ Cliff Richard & The Drifters
High Hopes
8/59 ★ Frank Sinatra
High School Confidential
1/59 ★ Jerry Lee Lewis
High Society
3/55 Jo Stafford and Frankie Laine
Highland Two-Step [M]
8/55 Bobby MacLeod & His Band
Hiking Song, The
5/58 Robert Wilson
Hillside In Scotland
7/58 Kathie Kay
7/58 Nancy Whiskey
8/58 Bridie Gallagher
Hippy Hippy Shake, The
10/59 Chan Romero
His Hands
7/55 Tennessee Ernie Ford
Hit And Miss
2/60 ★ John Barry Seven Plus Four
Hold Back Tomorrow
8/59 ★ Miki & Griff
Hold Me In Your Arms
5/55 Doris Day
Hold My Hand
11/54 Nat 'King' Cole
11/54 Ronnie Harris

Holy City, The
1/56   Eddie Calvert
Home
10/55   Johnny Brandon
Home Of The Blues
3/58   Johnny Cash
Homes Of Donegal
2/57   Joe Lynch
Homing Bird
10/57   Vipers Skiffle Group
Honestly
6/56   Joan Regan
Honestly, I Do
7/56   Ruby Murray
Honey Babe
9/55   Art Mooney & His Orchestra
9/55   Sauter–Finegan Orchestra
Honey Chile
1/57   ★ Fats Domino
Honey Love
12/54   Ted Heath & His Music
12/54   Vicki Young
Honeycomb
9/57   ★ Jimmie Rodgers
10/57   Marty Wilde
Honeymoon Song, The
8/59   ★ Manuel and the Music of the
            Mountains
Honky Tonk
1/57   Bill Doggett Combo
Honolulu Rock-A-Roll-A
7/56   Eartha Kitt
8/56   Moon Mullican
Hook, Line And Sinker
2/57   Bill Haley & His Comets
Hoolee Jump
10/60   Jim Gunner & The Echoes
Hootin' Blues
7/55   Sonny Terry Trio
Hoots Mon
10/58   ★ Lord Rockingham's XI
Hot Blues
8/54   Charlie Parker
Hot Diggity
5/56   ★ Michael Holliday
6/56   Glen Mason
6/56   ★ Stargazers
8/56   Marion Ryan
Hot Dog
2/60   Dale Hawkins
Hot Rod Jalopy
9/60   Johnny Bond
Hound Dog Man
1/60   ★ Fabian
House Of Bamboo
7/58   Neville Taylor
House Of Blue Lights, The
12/54   Merrill Moore
How Are Ya' Fixed For Love?
5/58   Frank Sinatra & Keely Smith
How Do You Speak To An Angel?
8/54   Eddie Fisher
9/54   ★ Dean Martin

How High The Moon
11/54   Stan Kenton & His Orchestra
10/60   ★ Ella Fitzgerald
How Important Can It Be?
4/55   Tony Brent
4/55   Mel Gaynor
4/55   Joni James
4/55   Sarah Vaughan
How Little We Know
7/56   Frank Sinatra
Hucklebuck, The
11/60   Chubby Checker
Hugged My Honey
9/57   Station Skiffle Group
Hula Hoop Song, The
11/58   Teresa Brewer
11/58   Georgia Gibbs
Hula Love
10/57   Buddy Knox
Humming Bird
9/55   Chordettes
9/55   ★ Frankie Laine
10/55   Beverley Sisters
Hushabye
8/59   Mystics
Hushabye Little Guitar
12/60   Paul Evans
I Am
8/57   Tony Bennett
I Am In Love
10/54   Nat 'King' Cole
I Am So Ashamed
11/58   Peter Sellers
I Believe In Love
4/60   Floyd Robinson
I Can't Begin To Tell You
8/59   Jane Morgan
I Can't Believe That You're In Love With Me
10/54   Micky Andrews
I Can't Get You Out Of My Heart
5/59   Al Martino
I Can't Say Goodbye
3/60   Fireflies
I Can't Stand Up Alone
1/59   Clyde McPhatter
I Can't Tell A Waltz From A Tango
11/54   ★ Alma Cogan
11/54   Patti Lewis
11/54   Patti Page
12/54   Lorrae Desmond
I Could Have Danced All Night
5/58   Mantovani & His Orchestra
6/58   Rosemary Clooney
7/58   Norrie Paramor & His Orchestra
8/58   Julie Andrews and Philippa Bevans
10/58   Marino Marini & His Quartet
I Count The Tears
2/61   ★ Drifters
I Cried For You
8/60   Billy Williams
I Don't Care If The Sun Don't Shine
11/56   ★ Elvis Presley

I Don't See Me In Your Eyes Anymore
  1/60   Carl Perkins
I Dreamed
  2/57   Billie Anthony
  2/57 ★ Jill Day
I Get A Kick Out Of You
  11/55   Frank Sinatra
I Get So Lonely
  7/54   Bing Crosby
I Go Ape
  4/59 ★ Neil Sedaka
I Got A Baby
  2/58   Gene Vincent
I Got A Feeling
  11/58 ★ Ricky Nelson
I Got It
  3/60   Little Richard
I Got Stripes
  9/59   Johnny Cash
I Gotta Go Home
  7/57   Gene & Eunice
I Hate Myself
  10/58   Faron Young
I Hear You Knocking
  1/56 ★ Gale Storm
I Hear You Talkin'
  10/59   Faron Young
I Heard The Angels Singing
  4/56   Frankie Laine
I Keep Her Picture Hanging Upside Down
  4/56   Jerry Lewis
I Kneel At Your Throne
  5/59   Jimmy Lloyd
  5/59   Joe Medlin
I Know I'm Home
  4/56   Ruby Murray
I Know Where I'm Goin'
  7/58   Nancy Whiskey
I Know You're Mine
  7/54   Betty Driver
I Love Paris
  10/54   Les Baxter & His Orchestra
  10/54   Ronnie Harris
  10/54   Tony Martin
  11/54   Georgia Gibbs
  11/54   Irène Hilda
  11/54   Patti Lewis
  12/54   Jan Rosol and Gwen Campbell
I Love To Love
  7/55   Lena Horne
I May Be Wrong
  8/54   Gerry Mulligan Quartet
I May Never Pass This Way Again
  3/58 ★ Robert Earl
  4/58 ★ Ronnie Hilton
  7/58   Glen Mason
I Met Him On A Sunday
  5/58   Shirelles
I Miss You So
  4/57   Johnnie Ray
  5/59   Paul Anka
I Missed Me
  1/61   Jim Reeves

I Need You Now
  9/54 ★ Eddie Fisher
  1/55   Stargazers
I Never Felt Like This
  5/59   Jack Scott
I Promise To Remember
  10/56   Frankie Lymon & The Teenagers
I Remember Mama
  6/55   Anne Shelton
I Saw God
  9/58   Ferlin Husky
I Shall Not Be Moved
  9/57   Jimmy Jackson's Rock 'n' Skiffle
I Should Care
  8/54   Jeff Chandler
I Speak To The Stars
  6/54   Doris Day
I Still Believe
  11/54   Johnnie Francis
  11/54 H Ronnie Hilton
  11/54   Al Martino
  12/54   I Still Believe
I Suddenly
  6/58   Dave King
I Think I'm Gonna Kill Myself
  5/59   Buddy Knox
I Understand Just How You Feel
  9/54   June Valli
  12/54   Jimmy Young
I Used To Love You But It's All Over Now
  4/59   Rosemary June
I Walk The Line
  10/58   Johnny Cash
  11/59   Don Costa & His Orchestra
I Wanna Be Loved
  1/60 ★ Ricky Nelson
I Wanna Be Loved By You
  8/59   Marilyn Monroe
I Want To Be Evil
  10/54   Eartha Kitt
I Want To Be Happy Cha Cha
  12/58   Tommy Dorsey Orchestra
I Want To Live – Theme
  9/59   Gerry Mulligan Combo
I Want To Walk You Home
  9/59 ★ Fats Domino
I Want You, I Need You, I Love You
  7/56 ★ Elvis Presley
I Want You To Be My Baby
  1/56   Don Lang
I Want You To Be My Girl
  8/56   Frankie Lymon & The Teenagers
I Went To Your Wedding
  11/54   Spike Jones & His City Slickers
I Wish I Could Shimmy Like My Sister Kate
  12/60 ★ Olympics
I Wonder
  4/55 ★ Jane Froman
  5/55   Ronnie Harris
  5/55 ★ Dickie Valentine
  6/55   Robert Earl
I Wonder Why
  7/58   Dion & The Belmonts

I'd Do Anything
8/60 ★ Mike Preston
I'd Like To Say A Few Words About Texas
11/56 Guy Mitchell
I'd Rather Have The Blues
7/55 Nat 'King' Cole
I'll Be Home
4/56 ★ Pat Boone
I'll Be Seeing You
11/56 Liberace
I'll Be True To You
4/56 Vera Lynn
I'll Be Your Hero
8/60 ★ Vince Taylor & His Playboys
I'll Buy You A Star
2/58 Edmund Hockridge
I'll Come When You Call
9/55 ★ Ruby Murray
I'll Forgive But I'll Never Forget
8/58 Bridie Gallagher
I'll Get By
10/58 ★ Connie Francis
I'll Never Fall In Love Again
9/59 ★ Johnnie Ray
I'll Never Stop Loving You
9/55 Slim Whitman
10/55 ★ Doris Day
10/55 David Whitfield
I'll Never Take You Back Again
10/55 Slim Whitman
I'll Sail My Ship Alone
4/60 Jerry Lee Lewis
I'll Save The Last Dance For You
12/60 Damita Jo
I'll Stay Single
10/59 Alfred Lynch
11/59 ★ Jerry Lordan
I'll Take You Home Again Kathleen
3/57 ★ Slim Whitman
I'll Walk With God
1/55 ★ Mario Lanza
I'm A Pilgrim
7/55 Tennessee Ernie Ford
I'm Beginning To See The Light
10/54 Gerry Mulligan Quartet
I'm Cryin' In My Beer
1/61 Bobbejaan
I'm Drowning My Sorrows
4/57 Teresa Brewer
I'm Feelin' Sorry
3/58 Jerry Lee Lewis
I'm Free
1/57 Robert Earl
I'm Gonna Be A Wheel Someday
9/59 Fats Domino
I'm Gonna Get Married
9/59 ★ Lloyd Price
I'm Gonna Live 'Till I Die
9/55 Frankie Laine
I'm Gonna Sit Right Down And Write Myself A Letter
7/57 ★ Billy Williams Quartet

I'm Hanging Up My Rifle
3/60 Bobby Bare
I'm In Favour Of Friendship
6/55 ★ Five Smith Brothers
I'm In Love
3/59 Arlene Fontana
I'm In Love Again
7/56 ★ Fats Domino
I'm In The Mood For Love
4/57 Fats Domino
I'm Learning About Love
2/61 Brenda Lee
I'm Movin' On
12/59 Don Gibson
I'm Never Gonna Tell
4/59 Jimmie Rodgers
I'm Not A Juvenile Delinquent
2/57 ★ Frankie Lymon & The Teenagers
I'm So Ashamed
11/58 Peter Sellers
I'm Starting To Go Steady
7/60 ★ Johnny Preston
I'm The Guy Who Found The Lost Chord
7/55 Jimmy Durante
I'm Walkin'
4/57 ★ Fats Domino
I've Been Thinking
7/55 Four Lads
I've Heard That Song Before
9/60 Al Saxon
I've Waited So Long
4/59 ★ Anthony Newley
If Anyone Finds This, I Love You
3/55 Kay Starr
If I Can Help Somebody
3/58 Billy Eckstine
If I Didn't Care
4/59 Connie Francis
If I Give My Heart To You
9/54 ★ Doris Day
9/54 ★ Joan Regan
11/54 Nat 'King' Cole
11/54 Denise Lor
If I Had A Girl
11/59 Jerry Keller
If Only I Could Live My Life Again
3/59 ★ Jane Morgan
If We Only Had Old Ireland Over Here
7/56 Sean Mooney & Trio
If You Ain't Lovin' (You Ain't Livin')
6/56 Faron Young
If You Believe
3/55 ★ Johnnie Ray
If You Ever Cease To Love
9/55 Ken Colyer's Jazzmen
If You Ever Go To Ireland
2/58 Margaret Barry
If You Love Me
10/59 Shirley Bassey
If You Love Me Baby
2/58 Johnny Duncan
If You Loved Me
4/58 Toni Dalli

If You Need Me
  9/60   Dave Sampson and the Hunters
If You Were The Only Boy In The World
  11/59   ★ Stevie Marsh
Il Nostro Concerto
  11/60   ★ Umberto Bindi
Image Of A Girl
  8/60   Nelson Keene
  8/60   ★ Mark Wynter
In A Little Spanish Town
  4/56   ★ Bing Crosby
In A Persian Market
  3/56   ★ Sammy Davis Jr.
In A Shanty In Old Shanty Town
  8/56   Somethin' Smith & The Redheads
In All The World
  8/60   Allan Bruce
In Old Lisbon
  1/56   Nelson Riddle & His Orchestra
In Port Afrique
  6/56   Ken-Tones
In The Beginning
  2/55   ★ Frankie Laine
In The Chapel In The Moonlight
  8/54   Kitty Kallen
  10/54   Four Knights
  12/54   Ken Griffin
  12/59   Kestrels
In The Middle Of A Dark, Dark Night
  7/57   ★ Guy Mitchell
In The Middle Of An Island
  8/57   Tony Bennett
In The Middle Of The House
  10/56   ★ Alma Cogan
  10/56   ★ Johnston Brothers and Keynotes
In The Mood
  11/59   ★ Ernie Fields & His Orchestra
In The Mood (For Mambo)
  2/55   Ted Heath & His Music
In The Wee Small Hours Of The Morning
  11/55   Frank Sinatra
Indian Love Call
  8/54   ★ Slim Whitman
Indiana
  6/54   Bud Powell Trio
  2/60   ★ Freddy Cannon
Innamorata
  2/56   ★ Dean Martin
Invention For Guitar And Trumpet
  3/56   Stan Kenton
Irish Marches No. 1 [M]
  6/56   Fred Hanna Band
Irish Medley [M]
  7/58   Diamond Accordion Band
          [Fred Hanna Band]
Irish Military Two-Step [M]
  6/44   Bobby MacLeod & His Band
Irish Soldier Boy
  9/54   Joe Lynch
  10/54   McNulty Family
Irish Waltz Medley No. 1 [M]
  7/56   Fred Hanna Band

Is A Blue Bird Blue
  7/60   ★ Conway Twitty
Is There Any Chance
  10/60   Marty Robbins
Island In The Sun
  6/57   ★ Harry Belafonte
Isle Of Capri
  8/54   Duke Ellington
It Got To Be A Habit
  1/61   Hank Thompson
It Isn't Right
  1/57   ★ Platters
It Only Hurts For A Little While
  10/56   Ronnie Carroll
It Takes A Worried Man To Sing A Worried Blues
  3/57   Bob Cort Skiffle Group
It Takes A Worried Man (To Sing A Worried Song)
  7/57   Chas McDevitt Skiffle Group
It Tickles
  10/58   Tommy Collins
It Was I
  8/59   Skip & Flip
It Worries Me
  11/54   Frank Sinatra
It's A Good Day
  6/54   Billy Daniels
It's A New World
  1/55   Judy Garland
It's A Sin
  9/55   Billy Valentine
It's A Woman's World
  1/55   Tony Brent
  1/55   Four Aces
  1/55   Ray Martin & His Concert Orch.
It's All Happening
  5/58   Tommy Steele
It's All In The Game
  6/57   Nat 'King' Cole
It's Almost Tomorrow
  1/56   ★ Dream Weavers
  3/56   Eve Boswell
It's Late
  3/59   ★ Ricky Nelson
It's Lonesome
  5/60   Dave Sampson and the Hunters
It's Love
  11/59   Addrisi Brothers
It's Nice To Go Trav'ling
  3/60   ★ Frank Sinatra
It's Now Or Never
  10/60   ★ Elvis Presley
It's So Easy
  11/58   ★ Crickets
It's Time To Cry
  1/60   ★ Paul Anka
It's You That I Love
  12/60   ★ Marion Ryan
Italian Theme, The
  3/56   ★ Cyril Stapleton & His Orchestra

Itsy Bitsy Teeny Weeny Yellow Polka Dot Bikini
7/60   Paul Hanford
Ivory Tower
5/56   Cathy Carr
Jacqueline
7/58 ★ Bobby Helms
Jambalaya
3/60   Bobby Comstock & The Counts
4/60   Billy Mure & His Orchestra
Jamie Boy
6/57   Kay Starr
Jellied Eels
7/60   Joe Brown & The Bruvvers
Jennie Lee
8/58   Jan & Arnie
Jenny, Jenny
9/57 ★ Little Richard
Jenny Lou
6/60   Sonny James
Jerri-Lee (I Love Him So)
2/59   Avon Sisters
Jeru
9/54   Gerry Mulligan Quartet
Jet II
4/60   Royal Rockers
Jet Black Machine
8/60 ★ Vince Taylor & His Playboys
Jig Along Home
10/57   Johnny Duncan
Jika Spokes
6/58   Spokes Mashiyane
Jilted
6/54   Joan Regan
Jim Dandy
3/57   Vipers Skiffle Group
Jimmy Unknown
2/56   Doris Day
2/56   Kathie Kay
Jingle Bell Rock
12/59 ★ Max Bygraves
John And Julie
7/55 ★ Eddie Calvert
Johnny B. Goode
5/58 ★ Chuck Berry
Johnny Concho Theme (Wait For Me)
8/56   Frank Sinatra
Johnny Guitar
8/54   Peggy Lee
Johnny Otis Hand Jive, The
5/58   Johnny Otis Show
Johnson's Motor Car
10/60   Emmettones
Join In And Sing [M]
12/54   Johnston Brothers
Join In And Sing No. 3 [M]
11/56 ★ Johnston Brothers
Join In And Sing No. 4 [M]
12/57   Johnston Brothers
Join In And Sing Again [M]
11/55 ★ Johnston Brothers
Join In The Chorus [M]
12/55   Billy's Banjo Band

Joker, The
2/58   Hilltoppers
Journey's End
3/56   Al Martino
Judy
7/58   Frankie Vaughan
Juke Box Baby
4/56 ★ Perry Como
Julie
1/57   Doris Day
Jump Over
5/60   Freddy Cannon
Jungle Dreams
8/54   Earl Bostic & His Orchestra
Just A Gigolo
8/54   Jaye P. Morgan
Just An Old Fashioned Girl
5/57   Eartha Kitt
1/59   Eartha Kitt *(reissue)*
Just Ask Your Heart
10/59   Frankie Avalon
Just Because
6/57   Lloyd Price
Just Born
12/57 ★ Jim Dale
Just In Time
10/60   Dean Martin
Just Keep It Up
8/59 ★ Dee Clark
Just One More Kiss
11/60   Day Brothers
Just One More Time
7/55   Eddie Fisher
Just One Of Those Things
2/55   Frank Sinatra
Just One Time
4/60   Don Gibson
Just Out Of Reach
12/60   Eddy Arnold
Just Say I Love Her
4/58   Toni Dalli
K.C. Moan
1/58   Delta Skiffle Group
Kansas City
6/59   Wilbert Harrison
Kansas City Special
8/57   Lorrae Desmond
Katy Too
9/59   Johnny Cash
Keep Right On To The End Of The Road
9/56   Clyde Valley Stompers
Kevin Barry
9/54   Joe Lynch
6/56   Myles O'Connor
7/60   Lonnie Donegan
Kewpie Doll
5/58 ★ Perry Como
5/58 ★ Frankie Vaughan
Key, The
10/59   Robert Earl
Ki Ri
7/54   Hélène Cordet

Kickin' Up The Leaves
10/60 ★ Mark Wynter
Kiddio
10/60 ★ Brook Benton
Killarney And You
6/57　Bridie Gallagher
King Size Guitar
11/59 ★ Bert Weedon
Kiss Me Again, Stranger
8/54　Doris Day
Kiss Me Another
6/56 ★ Georgia Gibbs
Kiss Me Big
3/55　Tennessee Ernie Ford
Kiss Me, Honey Honey, Kiss Me
12/58 ★ Shirley Bassey
Kiss Me, Kiss Me
7/60　Little Tony & His Brothers
Kissin' Time
9/59　Bobby Rydell
Kitty In The Basket
8/54　Diana Decker
Knock On Wood
7/54　Danny Kaye
Ko Ko Mo
3/55　Perry Como
3/55　Crew-Cuts
4/55　Hutton Sisters
Kookie, Kookie (Lend Me Your Comb)
4/60 ★ Edward Byrnes and Connie Stevens
Kookie Little Paradise
9/60 ★ Frankie Vaughan
La Dee Dah
3/58　Billy & Lillie
4/58　Bonnie Lou and Rusty York
La Dolce Vita
1/61　Manuel and the Music of the
　　　Mountains
Lady, The
8/55　David Whitfield
Lady Be Good
1/55　Gerry Mulligan Quartet
　　　with Lee Konitz
Lady Is A Square, The
3/59　Frankie Vaughan
Lady Is A Tramp, The
7/60 ★ Buddy Greco
Lady Luck
3/60 ★ Lloyd Price
Lady May
10/59　Eddie Hickey
Lady Of Madrid
10/55　David Whitfield
Lanigiro
2/55　Kirchin Band
Last Date
2/61　Floyd Cramer
Last Love
3/56　Ronnie Carroll
Last Resort
1/55　Tony Kinsey Trio with Joe Harriott
Last Train To San Fernando
7/57 ★ Johnny Duncan

Lavender Blue
8/59　Sammy Turner
Lay Down Your Arms
8/56 ★ Anne Shelton
Lazy Gondolier
1/55　Mantovani & His Orchestra
9/55　Dickie Valentine
Lazy Mary
4/58　Lou Monte
Learnin' The Blues
5/55 ★ Frank Sinatra
Learning The Game
10/60 ★ Buddy Holly
Leave My Kitten Alone
2/61　Little Willie John
Leave My Woman Alone
2/61　Lonnie Donegan
Left Bank, The
7/56 ★ Winifred Atwell
Legend Of Wyatt Earp, The
1/59　Hugh O'Brian
Lester Leaps In
7/54　Cyril Stapleton & His Orchestra
9/54　James Moody Sextet
　　　See also Lester Leaps The Mambo
Lester Leaps The Mambo
2/55　Kirchin Band
　　　See also Lester Leaps In
Let It Be Me
2/60 ★ Everly Brothers
Let It Ring
4/56　Doris Day
Let It Rock
3/60　Chuck Berry
Let Me Be Loved
10/57　Tommy Sands
Let Me Go, Lover
1/55 ★ Teresa Brewer
1/55　Peggy Lee
1/55　Patti Page
1/55 ★ Joan Weber
4/55　Jerry Colonna
Let Ramensky Go
11/60　Josh MacRae
Let The Bells Keep Ringing
4/58　Paul Anka
Let The Little Girl Dance
4/60 ★ Billy Bland
Let Us Be Sweethearts Over Again
8/55　Guy Mitchell
Let's All Rock Together
2/56　Jodimars
Let's Do It
8/54　Eartha Kitt
Let's Get Together No. 1 [M]
11/54 ★ Big Ben Banjo Band
Let's Get Together No. 2 [M]
11/54　Big Ben Banjo Band
Let's Get Together Again
11/55 ★ Big Ben Banjo Band
Let's Have A Ball
11/57 ★ Winifred Atwell

391

Let's Have A Party
8/60 ★ Wanda Jackson
Let's Love
5/59 Johnny Mathis
Let's Talk About Us
9/59 Jerry Lee Lewis
Light Still Shines In My Window, The
3/58 Johnny Otis Show
Like Love
5/60 Lyn Cornell
Like Young
2/60 Ella Fitzgerald
Linda Lu
10/59 Ray Sharpe
Lipstick On Your Collar
6/59 ★ Connie Francis
Listen Little Girl
7/60 ★ Keith Kelly
Listen To The Ocean
8/59 ★ Nina & Frederik
Little Bitty Pretty One
12/57 Thurston Harris and the Sharps
Little Boy Lost
7/60 Johnny Ashcroft
Little Brown Jug
9/54 Glenn Miller & His Orchestra
5/60 Bobby Summers
Little By Little
4/57 Nappy Brown
Little Child (Daddy Dear)
3/56 Danny Kaye and Dena Kaye
Little Christine
5/60 ★ Dick Jordan
Little Ditty Baby
2/60 Don Webb
Little Donkey
11/59 ★ Beverley Sisters
Little Drummer Boy, The
2/59 ★ Michael Flanders
12/59 Johnny Cash
Little Mary
7/58 Fats Domino
Little One
8/58 Russ Hamilton
Little Queenie
11/59 Jerry Lee Lewis
Little Serenade
6/58 ★ Eddie Calvert
Little Shoemaker, The
6/54 Frank Weir & His Saxophone
8/54 Alma Cogan
Little Susie (Parts 2 & 4)
2/60 Ray Bryant Trio
Little Things Mean A Lot
6/54 ★ Kitty Kallen
7/54 ★ Alma Cogan
8/54 Jimmy Young
Little Train
8/58 ★ Max Bygraves
Little White Bull
11/59 ★ Tommy Steele
Live Fast, Love Hard, Die Young
9/55 Faron Young

Liza Jane
12/59 Dale Hawkins
Lizzie Borden
2/56 Coronets
Loading Coal
10/60 Johnny Cash
Lollipop
4/58 ★ Chordettes
4/58 Gary Miller
4/58 ★ Mudlarks
Lonely Ballerina
1/55 ★ Mantovani & His Orchestra
Lonely Blue Boy
2/60 Conway Twitty
Lonely Little Robin
7/60 Browns
Lonely Man Theme, The
4/60 ★ Cliff Adams Orchestra
Lonely Moon
11/59 Johnny Wells
Lonely One, The
3/59 ★ Duane Eddy
Lonely Street
12/59 Andy Williams
Lonely Teenager
1/61 ★ Dion
Lonely Weekends
4/60 Charlie Rich
Lonesome
8/59 ★ Chris Barber's Jazz Band
Lonesome Boy
6/60 Johnny Russell
Lonesome Town
12/58 Ricky Nelson
Lonesome Train
4/57 Johnny Burnette Trio
Lonesome Traveller
9/58 ★ Lonnie Donegan
Long John
3/59 John Barry Seven
Long, Long Ago
5/55 Nat 'King' Cole and Dean Martin
Long Tall Sally
6/56 ★ Pat Boone
1/57 ★ Little Richard
Look For A Star
5/60 ★ Garry Mills
Looking Back
6/58 Nat 'King' Cole
Looking High, High, High
2/60 ★ Bryan Johnson
Lord And Master
11/60 Jane Morgan
Lord's Taverners Star Band Hit Parade [M]
8/58 Various Artists
Losing You
6/55 Tennessee Ernie Ford
Lost John
4/56 ★ Lonnie Donegan
Love And Kisses
7/55 Tony Brent

Love And Marriage
1/56   Alma Cogan
1/56   Joan Regan
1/56 ★ Frank Sinatra
Love Bug Crawl
3/58   Jimmy Edwards
Love For Sale
6/59   Shirley Bassey
Love Is A Golden Ring
3/57   Dave King
3/57 ★ Frankie Laine
Love Is A Many Splendo(u)red Thing
10/55 ★ Nat 'King' Cole
10/55   Don Cornell
10/55   Four Aces
11/55   David Hughes
3/56   Frank Chacksfield & His Orchestra
Love Is Like A Violin
6/60 ★ Ken Dodd
Love Like Ours
1/59   Joan Regan
Love Makes The World Go 'round
10/58 ★ Perry Como
Love Me
7/60   Danny Davis
Love Me A Little
4/60   Dennis Lotis
Love Me Forever
1/58 ★ Four Esquires
1/58 ★ Eydie Gormé
Love Me Or Leave Me
9/54   Gerry Mulligan Quartet
6/55 ★ Sammy Davis Jr.
7/55   Billy Eckstine
8/55   Lena Horne
9/55 ★ Doris Day
9/60   Terry Dene
Love My Life Away
3/61 ★ Gene Pitney
Love Potion No. 9
10/59   Clovers
Love You 'Till I Die
7/57   Brenda Lee
Love's Made A Fool Of You
4/59 ★ Crickets (post-Holly)
Lovely Lover
10/59   Stephanie Voss and Terence
          Cooper
Lovey Dovey
1/61   Buddy Knox
Lovin' Up A Storm
4/59 ★ Jerry Lee Lewis
Loving Machine
1/55   Wynonie Harris
Lua Bonita
8/54   Zé do Norte
Lucky Devil
1/60 ★ Carl Dobkins Jr.
1/60 ★ Frank Ifield
Lullaby Of Birdland
5/55   Ella Fitzgerald
Lulu's Back In Town
8/56   Mel Tormé

Luther Played The Boogie
4/59   Johnny Cash
M.I.
11/60   Ted Taylor Four
M.T.A.
8/59   Kingston Trio
Ma (He's Making Eyes At Me)
11/57 ★ Johnny Otis Show
Madagascar
5/57   Ted Heath & His Music
Madison, The
6/60   Al Brown's Tunetoppers
Madison Time No. 1
6/60   Ted Heath & His Music
Madonna, Madonna
11/54   Johnnie Francis
Madrid
2/59   Nat 'King' Cole
Magic Tango, The
9/54   Tony Brent
Main Title (The Man With The Golden Arm)
4/56 ★ Billy May & His Orchestra
    See also Man With The Golden Arm
Mairi's Wedding
6/60   David Kinnaird
Mais Oui
8/60   Bob Beckham
Majorca
1/55 ★ Petula Clark
2/55   Johnston Brothers
Make Her Mine
8/54 ★ Nat 'King' Cole
Make Him Jealous
4/56   Ruby Murray
Make It A Party [M] (1)
12/55   Coronets
Make It A Party [M] (2)
10/56 ★ Winifred Atwell
Make Love To Me
6/54   Alma Cogan
Make Me A Miracle
6/58   Mal Perry
6/58   Jimmie Rodgers
Make Yourself Comfortable
1/55   Sarah Vaughan
Makin' Love
10/59   Vince Eager
10/59 ★ Floyd Robinson
Malagueña
9/55   Jane Forrest
9/55   Caterina Valente
10/55   Ted Heath & His Music
Mama
4/55 ★ David Whitfield
8/55   Danny Purches
Mama Doll Song, The
11/54   Beverley Sisters
11/54   Patti Page
Mama Don't Allow It
8/54   George Lewis
    See also Mamma Don't Allow
Mama From The Train
1/57   Lynne Allison

Mama Looka Boo Boo
6/57   Harry Belafonte
Mama Teach Me To Dance
10/56   Alma Cogan
Mambo Italiano
1/55   ★ Dean Martin
2/55   Alma Cogan
Mambo Macoco
2/55   Kirchin Band
Mambo Rock
3/55   ★ Bill Haley & His Comets
Mambolino
9/54   Earl Bostic & His Orchestra
Mambostic
11/54   Earl Bostic & His Orchestra
Mamma Don't Allow
7/56   Sid Phillips Band
See also Mama Don't Allow It
Man And Woman
8/54   Rosemary Clooney and Guy
         Mitchell
Man I Love, The
9/54   Wardell Gray
Man In The Raincoat, The
9/55   Lita Roza
Man On Fire
12/57   Bing Crosby
Man That Got Away, The
2/55   ★ Judy Garland
Man Who Plays The Mandolino, The
2/57   ★ Dean Martin
Man With The Golden Arm
3/56   Sammy Davis Jr.
See also Main Title
Manchester United Calypso
4/57   ★ Edric Connor
Mandolin Serenade
7/57   Mantovani & His Orchestra
9/57   Murray Campbell
Mandolino
11/54   Les Paul
Mandolins In The Moonlight
11/58   ★ Perry Como
Mandrake
1/61   Mandrake
Mandy The Pansy
See Pansy, The
Mangos
4/57   Stargazers
Manhattan
9/57   Ella Fitzgerald
Manhattan Spiritual
2/59   ★ Reg Owen & His Orchestra
March Hare, The
5/56   Joseph McNally
Marching Guitars
12/59   Bell Sounds
Marching Through Georgia
5/60   Mr. Acker Bilk
Marching With Jimmy Shand [M]
3/56   Jimmy Shand & His Band
Margo
6/59   ★ Billy Fury

Marianne
3/57   Terry Gilkyson & The Easy Riders
3/57   ★ Hilltoppers
5/57   King Brothers
Martinique, The
5/55   Chris Barber's Jazz Band
Mary Lou
10/59   Ronnie Hawkins & The Hawks
Mary's Boy Child
12/57   Gracie Fields
Maryland, My Maryland
11/54   Kid Ory's Creole Jazz Band
Mashed Potatoes
4/60   Nat Kendrick & The Swans
Matchbox
11/57   Terry Wayne
May You Always
3/59   ★ Joan Regan
Maybe
9/59   Dean Martin
Maybe Baby
3/58   ★ Crickets
Maybe Tomorrow
1/59   ★ Billy Fury
McDonald's Cave
9/60   ★ Piltdown Men
Meadow Lane Stomp
12/56   Charlie McNair Skiffle Group
Mean, Mean Man
1/61   ★ Wanda Jackson
Meaning Of The Blues, The
11/59   Kalin Twins
Medic Theme, The
5/55   Les Baxter & His Orchestra
See also Blue Star
Meet Me On The Corner
10/55   ★ Max Bygraves
10/55   Coronets
Meet Me Tonight In Dreamland
1/59   Valerie Shane
Melodie d'Amour
11/57   Ames Brothers
Melody Of Love
4/55   ★ Ink Spots
4/55   Dinah Shore and Tony Martin
5/55   Earl Bostic & His Orchestra
5/55   Four Aces
Memories
12/54   Earl Bostic & His Orchestra
Memories Are Made Of This
2/56   ★ Dave King
3/56   Petula Clark
Memories O' Rabbie Burns [M]
1/59   Jimmy Shand & His Band
Memories Of You
2/56   Benny Goodman Trio with
         Rosemary Clooney
Mercy, Mercy Percy
7/58   Neville Taylor
Merrydown Rag
1/55   Chris Barber's Jazz Band
Messing About On The River
1/61   ★ Josh MacRae

Mezzy's Tune
1/55　Humphrey Lyttelton & His Band
Miami
10/59　Eugene Church
Midnight (1)
6/54　Eddie Calvert
Midnight (2)
10/58　★ Paul Anka
Midnight Shift
6/59　★ Buddy Holly
Midnight Sleighride
1/55　Sauter–Finegan Orchestra
Midnight Special
3/56　Lonnie Donegan
Midnite Special
3/60　★ Paul Evans
Mighty Good
1/60　Ricky Nelson
Milenberg Joys
6/57　Clyde Valley Stompers
Milk Cow Blues
1/61　Ricky Nelson
Milk From The Coconut
8/59　Johnny Gentle
Milord
4/60　★ Édith Piaf
Minor Mambo
1/55　Kirchin Band
Mirror, Mirror
7/55　Tony Brent
Miss Me Just A Little
2/58　Johnnie Ray
Miss You
9/58　Malcolm Vaughan
Mission Bell
8/60　Donnie Brooks
Mr. Blue
10/59　Fleetwoods
10/59　★ David MacBeth
10/59　★ Mike Preston
Mister Cuckoo
6/56　Edmundo Ros & His Orchestra
6/56　Frank Weir & His Orchestra
Mr. Custer
10/60　★ Charlie Drake
10/60　Larry Verne
Mr. Lee
11/57　Bobbettes
Mister Loneliness
3/61　Gene Vincent
Mr. Piano Plays – Volume 1 [M]
3/59　Joe 'Mr. Piano' Henderson
Mister Sandman
11/54　★ Max Bygraves
12/54　★ Four Aces
12/54　★ Dickie Valentine
1/55　Les Paul & Mary Ford
Mr. Wonderful
5/57　★ Peggy Lee
5/57　Ruby Murray
6/57　Marion Ryan
Mobile
1/55　★ Ray Burns

Moby Dick
6/56　Frankie Laine
Mole In A Hole, The
11/58　Southlanders
Mom-e-le
8/54　Billy Daniels
8/54　Issy Bonn
Moments To Remember
2/56　Four Lads
Money (Is The Root Of All Evil)
2/61　Viscounts
Money (That's What I Want)
4/60　Barrett Strong
Money Burns A Hole In My Pocket
10/54　Dean Martin
Monotonous
1/55　Eartha Kitt
Moody
8/59　Poni-Tails
Moonglow
5/56　Columbia Pictures Orchestra
Moonlight In Mayo
11/54　Jimmy Young
More
5/56　★ Jimmy Young
10/56　Robert Earl
More And More Party Pops [M]
11/59　★ Russ Conway
More Than Ever
10/58　★ Robert Earl
10/58　★ Malcolm Vaughan
11/58　Toni Dalli
12/58　Edmund Hockridge
See also Come Prima
Morgan Poisoned The Water Hole
10/59　Simon Crum [Ferlin Husky]
Morgen
10/59　Adam Singers
10/59　Ken Mackintosh & His Orchestra
10/59　★ Ivo Robić
10/59　Billy Vaughn & His Orchestra
See also One More Sunrise
Morning Side Of The Mountain, The
4/59　Tommy Edwards
Mountain Greenery
4/56　★ Mel Tormé
Mountain Of Love
5/60　Harold Dorman
5/60　★ Kenny Lynch
Move It Over, Baby
5/57　Gene & Eunice
Mule Skinner
6/56　Ken Colyer's Skiffle Group
Mule Skinner Blues
7/60　★ Fendermen
Mulher Rendeira
8/54　Coro Mixto
Mumbles
3/60　Johnny Bachelor
Music
1/61　Robb Storme
Music from 'Salad Days' [M]
11/54　Julian Slade

Muskrat Ramble
1/55   Yorkshire Jazz Band
9/55   Kid Ory's Creole Jazz Band
Must Be Santa
12/60 ★ Tommy Steele
Mustafa
6/60 ★ Staïffi et ses Mustafa's
See also Mustapha *and* Sheik Of Chicago
Mustapha
5/60   Clinton Ford
5/60   Kemal Rachid et ses Ottomans
See also Mustafa *and* Sheik Of Chicago
My Arms, My Heart, My Love
8/54   Eddie Fisher
My Blue Heaven
6/56   Fats Domino
11/59   Platters
My Bonnie Lassie
3/56   Robert Wilson
My Boy Flat Top
1/56 ★ Frankie Vaughan
My Bucket's Got A Hole In It
5/58   Ricky Nelson
My Christmas Prayer
12/59   Billy Fury
My Darling, My Darling
3/58   Sarah Vaughan
My Dream
9/57   Platters
My Dream Sonata
10/56   Nat 'King' Cole
'My Fair Lady' Pops [M]
12/58   Russ Conway
My Faith, My Hope, My Love
2/57   Jimmy Young
My Friend
8/54   Eddie Fisher
8/54   Frankie Laine
8/54   Vera Lynn
9/54   Issy Bonn
11/54   Edmund Hockridge
My Funny Valentine
11/55   Frank Sinatra
My Gal And A Prayer
5/58   Frankie Laine
My Girl Josephine
12/60 ★ Fats Domino
My Girl, My Girl
2/58   Jumpin' Jacks
My Heart
3/60 ★ Gene Vincent
My Heart Is An Open Book
8/59   Carl Dobkins Jr.
9/59   Michael Holliday
My Heart Sings
1/59 ★ Paul Anka
My Hour Of Love
10/60   Craig Douglas
My House Is Your House
4/57   Perry Como
My Last Date With You
2/61   Skeeter Davis

My Last Love
11/57   Kathie Kay
My Little Budgie
2/60   Bruce Forsyth
My Little Corner Of The World
9/60 ★ Anita Bryant
My Little Girl
5/58   Peter Miles
My Lonely Lover
7/55   Caterina Valente
My Love
8/60   Nat 'King' Cole and Stan Kenton
My Love For You
10/60 ★ Johnny Mathis
My Loving Hands
6/55   Ronnie Hilton
My Lucky Love
9/58   Marty Wilde
11/58   Mike Preston
My Melancholy Baby
6/59 ★ Tommy Edwards
My Mother's Eyes
2/58   Russ Hamilton
2/60   Nellie Lutcher
My Old Dutch
11/59   Peter Sellers
My One Sin
8/55 ★ Nat 'King' Cole
My Personal Possession
9/57 ★ Nat 'King' Cole
My Restless Lover
6/54   Patti Page
My Sailor Boy
3/57   Connie Francis
My September Love
3/56 ★ Robert Earl
12/56   Goons
My Son, My Son
9/54 ★ Vera Lynn and Frank Weir
10/54   Eddie Calvert
10/54   Robert Earl
10/54   Frankie Vaughan
My Special Angel
11/57 ★ Bobby Helms
12/57   Frank D'Rone
12/57   Robert Earl
My True Love
9/58 ★ Jack Scott
My Ukelele
12/58 ★ Max Bygraves
My Very Good Friend The Milkman
11/60   Joy & Dave
Napoli – Napoli
3/59   Max Bygraves
Nashvile Boogie
11/59 ★ Bert Weedon
Naughty Lady Of Shady Lane, The
1/55 ★ Ames Brothers
1/55   Archie Bleyer & His Orchestra
2/55   Beverley Sisters
2/55   Alma Cogan

Near You
10/58   Roger Williams
Nearness Of You, The
8/54   Bob Manning
10/54   Gerry Mulligan Quartet
Never Be Anyone Else But You
3/59 ★ Ricky Nelson
Never Do A Tango With An Eskimo
11/55 ★ Alma Cogan
Never Let Go
7/60   John Barry & His Orchestra
Never-Never Land, The
6/54   Frank Weir & His Saxophone
8/54   Diana Decker
Never On Sunday
10/60 ★ Lyn Cornell
10/60 ★ Don Costa & His Orchestra
10/60   Dalida
10/60   Marty Gold & His Orchestra
10/60 ★ Makadopoulos & His Greek
          Serenaders
10/60   Milko Papayaki & His Orchestra
11/60   Simms/Wheeler Vintage Jazz Band
1/61   Zacharias & His Magic Violins
New Juke Box Saturday Night
12/54   Modernaires
New Kind Of Fool
10/59   Sanford Clark
New Lovers
3/60   Pat Boone
New Orleans
11/60 ★ U.S. Bonds
Nick Nack Paddy Wack
1/59   Cyril Stapleton & His Orchestra
Nicolette
11/54   Tony Brent
Night And Day
7/55   Earl Bostic & His Orchestra
Night Hop
3/59   Jimmie & The Night Hoppers
Night Is Young And You're So Beautiful, The
12/56   Four Grads
Nights At The Turntable
1/55   Gerry Mulligan Quartet
Ninety-Nine Years
3/56   Guy Mitchell
No Man Is An Island
3/55   Don Cornell
No More
1/55   Stargazers
3/55 ★ McGuire Sisters
No, Not Much
4/56   Four Lads
4/56   Pauline Shepherd
No One But You
10/54 ★ Billy Eckstine
10/54   Carlos Thompson
12/54   Al Martino
No Other Baby
2/58   Bobby Helms
4/58   Vipers [Vipers Skiffle Group]

No Other Love
4/56 ★ Edmund Hockridge
5/56   Julius LaRosa
6/56   David Rose & His Orchestra
7/56   Ron Goodwin & His Concert Orch.
No Such Luck
8/55   Dickie Valentine
No Vacancy
2/59   Neil Sedaka
Noddy Is Naughty
4/57   Enid Blyton
Non Je Ne Regrette Rien
3/61   Édith Piaf
None Shall Sleep Tonight
3/56   Harry Secombe
Nor The Moon By Night
8/58   Frank Holder
Nora Malone
3/57 ★ Teresa Brewer
North To Alaska
11/60 ★ Johnny Horton
Northern Lights Of (Old) Aberdeen, The
11/54   Robert Wilson
6/60   David Kinnaird
1/61   David Kinnaird *(reissue)*
Not As A Stranger
8/55 ★ Frank Sinatra
Not Guilty
2/61   Johnny DeLittle
Nothin' Shakin'
10/58   Eddie Fontaine
Nothin' To Do
3/56   Max Bygraves
3/56 ★ Michael Holliday
Nothing In Common
5/58   Frank Sinatra and Keely Smith
Now You Has Jazz
11/56   Bing Crosby and Louis Armstrong
Nowhere In This World
5/59   Derry Hart & The Hartbeats
O Dio Mio
4/60   Annette
Offshore
10/54   Earl Bostic & His Orchestra
Oh Baby Mine I Get So Lonely
7/54   Bing Crosby
Oh! Carol
10/59 ★ Neil Sedaka
Oh, Honey Love Me
5/60   Billy Gaye & The Gayetones
Oh Julie
2/58   Sammy Salvo
Oh Little One
5/60   Jack Scott
Oh, Lonesome Me
4/58   Don Gibson
Oh, Mary Don't You Weep
10/57   Les Hobeaux
Oh-Oh, I'm Falling In Love Again
3/58 ★ Jimmie Rodgers
3/58   Marion Ryan

Oh, So Wunderbar
2/60   Robert Earl
2/60   Malcolm Vaughan
Oh! What A Day
7/60   ★ Craig Douglas
Ol' Saint Nicholas
12/55   Doris Day
Olay Olay
1/55   Billy Eckstine
Old Black Joe
6/60   Jerry Lee Lewis
Old Bog Road, The
6/56   Joe Lynch
Old Fashioned Love
4/59   Johnny Maddox
Old Lamplighter, The
5/60   Browns
Old Payola Roll Blues, The
4/60   ★ Stan Freberg
Old Pull 'n' Push, The
1/61   Terry Lightfoot
Old Rustic Bridge By The Mill
9/56   Clyde Valley Stompers
Old Scotch Mother
3/56   Kathie Kay
Old Shep
9/59   ★ Clinton Ford
10/59   Hank Snow
Old Time Religion
1/57   Clyde Valley Stompers
5/59   Betty Miller
12/60   Jack Scott
Olé Mambo
4/55   Edmundo Ros & His Orchestra
On A Christmas Day
11/59   Chris Barber''s Jazz Band
On My Word Of Honor
4/57   Platters
On The Street Where You Live
5/58   Ronnie Hilton
5/58   Gary Miller
5/58   ★ David Whitfield
On The Waterfront
11/54   Ron Goodwin & His Concert Orch.
11/54   Bill McGuffie & His Orchestra
On With The Motley
11/55   ★ Harry Secombe
Once In A While
2/61   Chimes
One For My Baby
8/57   Tony Bennett
One For The Road [M]
11/57   Freddie Mills
One In A Million
4/57   Platters
One More Sunrise
10/59   ★ Dickie Valentine
See also Morgen
One More Time
2/55   Dean Martin
One O'Clock Jump
9/54   Gene Norman's 'Just Jazz'

One Rose, The
3/59   Teresa Brewer
One Thousand Nine Hundred And When
11/60   Robb Storme
One Way Street
12/60   Guy Mitchell
Only Love Me
5/59   Steve Lawrence
Only Man On The Island, The
7/58   ★ Tommy Steele
Only One
3/60   ★ Richard Allan
Only Sixteen
8/59   ★ Al Saxon
Only The Lonely
7/60   ★ Roy Orbison
Only You
1/56   ★ Hilltoppers
8/56   ★ Platters
Ooh Bang Jiggilly Jang
12/55   Doris Day
Ooh! My Soul
6/58   ★ Little Richard
Open Up The Doghouse
6/55   Dean Martin and Nat 'King' Cole
Open Up Your Heart
4/55   Tony Brent and Anne Warren
4/55   Gail and Rosemary Clooney
4/55   Cowboy Church Sunday School
Oranges And Lemons
10/54   Eric Delaney & His Band
Ory's Creole Trombone
10/54   Bunk Johnson
Our Old Pi-anna
4/55   Marie Benson
Our Town
9/56   Frank Sinatra
Our Turn
2/60   Dale Hawkins
Out Of Town
5/56   ★ Max Bygraves
Over And Over
2/61   Bobby Day
Over The Rainbow
3/59   Gene Vincent
P.T.Q. Rag
9/55   Humphrey Lyttelton & His Band
Pansy, The
3/58   Marino Marini & His Quartet
Papa Loves Mama
7/60   ★ Joan Regan
Papa Loves Mambo
10/54   ★ Perry Como
10/54   Johnnie Ray
12/54   Nat 'King' Cole
Paper Kisses
2/55   Alma Cogan
Paper Roses
5/60   ★ Anita Bryant
7/60   ★ Kaye Sisters
Pardners
9/56   Dean Martin & Jerry Lewis

Party Cha [M]
11/60   Firestones
Party Doll
5/57   Steve Lawrence
Party Sing-Song [M] (1)
12/54   Vera Lynn
Party Sing-Song [M] (2)
11/59   Pinky & Perky
Party Time
11/57   Don Fox
Passing Strangers
9/57   ★ Sarah Vaughan and Billy Eckstine
Pat-A-Cake, Pat-A-Cake –
Three Blind Mice – Jingle Bells [M]
10/55   ★ Singing Dogs, The
Paths Of Paradise
4/55   ★ Johnnie Ray
Patricia
7/58   ★ Pérez Prado & His Orchestra
Patsy
11/60   Jack Scott
Peanut Vendor, The
3/56   Stan Kenton & His Orchestra
2/61   Jeff Rowena Group
Peanuts
1/58   Southlanders
Pearly Gates
9/56   Clyde Valley Stompers
5/59   Betty Miller
Peddler Man, The
10/54   Dean Martin
Peggy Sue
11/57   ★ Buddy Holly
Peggy's Love [M]
12/55   Jimmy Shand & His Band
Pendulum Song, The
5/55   Max Bygraves
5/55   Petula Clark
Perdido
2/55   Ronnie Scott Orchestra
Perfidia
9/54   Dave Brubeck
11/60   ★ Ventures
Perfume, Candy And Flowers
4/56   Guy Mitchell
Personality
6/59   ★ Lloyd Price
Pete Kelly's Blues
10/55   Ella Fitzgerald
12/55   Sid Phillips Band
Piano Medley No. 114 [M]
12/54   ★ Charlie Kunz
Piano Medley No. 115 [M]
2/55   Charlie Kunz
Piano Medley No. 116 [M]
3/55   Charlie Kunz
Piano Medley No. 117 [M]
5/55   Charlie Kunz
Piano Party [M]
11/59   ★ Winifred Atwell
Piano Pops No. 1 [M]
12/57   Russ Conway

Piano Pops No. 3 [M]
3/58   Russ Conway
Piccadilly Line
7/57   Jim Dale
Pick A Bale Of Cotton
1/57   Vipers Skiffle Group
Pigtails In Paris
10/60   David MacBeth
Pink Shoe Laces
4/59   Alma Cogan
4/59   ★ Dodie Stevens
Pink Sweater Angel
1/58   Johnnie Ray
Plain Jane
3/59   Bobby Darin
Plant A Kiss
10/57   Tommy Steele
Play Rough
6/58   Johnny Luck
Please Don't Touch
5/59   ★ Johnny Kidd & The Pirates
6/59   Bachelors
Please Help Me, I'm Falling
7/60   ★ Brook Brothers
7/60   ★ Hank Locklin
Please Mr. Sun
3/59   Tommy Edwards
Pledging My Love
See Forever, My Darling
Poetry In Motion
1/61   Richard Allan
Poison Ivy
10/59   ★ Coasters
Poor John
3/56   Les Baxter & His Orchestra
See also Poor People Of Paris, The
Poor Little Fool
8/58   ★ Ricky Nelson
Poor People Of Paris, The
3/56   Geraldo & His Orchestra
3/56   Norrie Paramor & His Orchestra
See also Poor John
Popular Medley No. 4 [M]
7/55   Vera Lynn
Por Favor
3/56   Dennis Lotis
Port-au-Prince
4/56   ★ Winifred Atwell
Portrait Of A Count
3/56   Stan Kenton & His Orchestra
Precious Lord, Lead Me On
10/55   Chris Barber's Jazz Band
Pretty Blue Eyes
1/60   ★ Craig Douglas
2/60   Steve Lawrence
Pride Of Erin No. 2 [M]
7/56   Fred Hanna Band
Pride Of Erin Waltz [M]
6/55   Bobby MacLeod & His Band
Pride Of Tipperary, The
3/56   Joe Lynch

Primrose Lane
  10/59   Vince Eager
  10/59   Jerry Wallace
Princess
  3/58 ★ Tommy Steele
Prize Of Gold
  2/55 ★ Joan Regan
Puh-leeze Mr. Brown
  11/57   Shirley Bassey
Purple People Eater, The
  6/58 ★ Jackie Dennis
  6/58 ★ Sheb Wooley
Push Push
  10/60   Austin Taylor
Put A Light In The Window
  1/58 ★ King Brothers
  2/58 ★ Southlanders
Put A Ring On Her Finger
  11/58   Tommy Steele
Put Your Head On My Shoulder
  10/59 ★ Paul Anka
Puttin' On The Smile
  11/59   Peter Sellers
Queen Of The Hop
  11/58 ★ Bobby Darin
Race With The Devil
  9/56 ★ Gene Vincent
Rain On My Window
  3/57   Nilsson Twins
Rain, Rain, Rain
  10/54 ★ Frankie Laine
Ra-Ra Rockingham
  5/59   Lord Rockingham's XI
Ram-Bunk-Shush
  3/61 ★ Ventures
Ramrod
  11/58   Duane Eddy
Rattle Rhythm
  10/59   Bob Summers
Raunchy
  1/58   Ernie Freeman
  1/58 ★ Ken Mackintosh & His Orchestra
  1/58 ★ Billy Vaughn & His Orchestra
  2/58   Winifred Atwell
  11/60   Ernie Fields & His Orchestra
Rawhide
  10/59 ★ Frankie Laine
Razzle Dazzle
  7/55 ★ Bill Haley & His Comets
Reach For The Sky
  9/56   Sidney Torch & His Orchestra
Ready For Love
  11/60 ★ Jimmy Jones
Ready, Willing And Able
  2/55 ★ Doris Day
Real Love
  10/58 ★ Ruby Murray
Rebel-Rouser
  8/58 ★ Duane Eddy
Reckless Blues
  3/55   Chris Barber's Jazz Band
Red Cat, The
  11/57   Russ Conway

Red House Reel, The [M]
  11/54   Jimmy Shand & His Band
Red River Rock
  10/59 ★ Johnny & The Hurricanes
Red Sails In The Sunset
  9/60   Platters
Red Wing
  9/55   Ken Colyer's Jazzmen
Reet Petite
  11/57 ★ Jackie Wilson
Relax-Ay-Voo
  11/55   Dean Martin and Line Renaud
Remember When
  8/59 ★ Platters
Remember You're Mine
  9/57 ★ Pat Boone
Return To Me
  5/58 ★ Dean Martin
Reveille Rock
  12/59 ★ Johnny & The Hurricanes
Rich In Love
  9/56   Pat Boone
Riddle Of Love, The
  10/59 ★ Craig Douglas
Riders In The Sky
  1/60   Kay Starr
Right Here On Earth
  12/59   Gene Vincent
Right To Be Wrong, The
  4/55   Johnston Brothers
Right To Love, The
  7/58 ★ David Whitfield
Ring Ding
  2/60   Knightsbridge Strings
Ring, Write Or Call
  10/60   Jerry Lordan
Rip It Up
  11/56 ★ Little Richard
  2/57 ★ Elvis Presley
River Of No Return, The
  9/54   Tennessee Ernie Ford
  11/54   Marilyn Monroe
Road Runner
  5/60   Bo Diddley
Roamin' In The Gloamin'
  4/55   Eric Delaney & His Band
Robert Wilson Medley [M]
  10/54   George Elrick
Robin Hood
  1/56 ★ Dick James
  1/56 ★ Gary Miller
  2/56   Nelson Riddle & His Orchestra
  3/56   Billy Cotton & His Band
Rock-A-Charleston
  1/61   Martin Slavin & His Gang
Rock And Cry
  1/58   Clyde McPhatter
Rock'n'Roll No. 1 [M]
  10/56   Big Ben Accordion Band
Rock'n'Roll Hit Parade [M]
  11/56   Voices
Rock And Roll Is Here To Stay
  4/58   Danny & The Juniors

Rock And Roll Music
2/58   Chuck Berry
Rock'n'Roll Party [M]
1/57   Dickie Valentine
Rock And Roll Rag
12/56   Art Baxter & His Rock'n'Roll
        Sinners
Rock And Roll Waltz
2/56 ★ Kay Starr
3/56   Ted Heath & His Music
Rock Around The Clock
10/54 ★ Bill Haley & His Comets
11/55   Deep River Boys
Rock Candy Baby
3/56   Frankie Vaughan
Rock Island Line
11/55 ★ Lonnie Donegan
7/56 ★ Stan Freberg
Rock The Joint
1/57 ★ Bill Haley & His Comets
Rock With The Caveman
10/56 ★ Tommy Steele
Rockin' At The Two I's
5/58   Wee Willie Harris
Rockin' 'J' Bells
12/60   Little Bobby Rey & His Band
Rockin' Little Angel
2/60   Ray Smith
2/60   Viscounts
Rockin' Red Wing
6/60 ★ Sammy Masters
Rockin' Robin
11/58 ★ Bobby Day
Rockin' Rollin' Rover
7/57   Bill Haley & His Comets
Rockin' Through Dixie
5/56   Geraldo & His Orchestra
Rocking Goose
9/60 ★ Johnny & The Hurricanes
Rocky Road Blues
8/58   Gene Vincent
Roll On Silvery Moon
7/55   Slim Whitman
Romantica
6/60 ★ Jane Morgan
8/60   Renato Rascel
Rosaleena
11/59   Conway Twitty
Rose And The Flame, The
12/55   Joan Regan
Rose Marie
9/54   Howard Keel
6/55 ★ Slim Whitman
Roses From Venice
12/59   Donald Peers
Roulette
5/59 ★ Russ Conway
Round And Round
4/57   Perry Como
4/57 ★ Jimmy Young
Royal Scots Polka
5/55   Jimmy Shand & His Band

Rubber Ball
1/61 ★ Marty Wilde
Ruby
2/61   Ray Charles
Ruby Duby Du
2/61   M.G.M. Studio Orchestra
Rudolph The Red-Nosed Reindeer
11/54   Smiley Burnette
12/54   Jimmy Boyd
1/55   Spike Jones & His City Slickers
Rum And Coca-Cola
4/57   Andrews Sisters
Rumble
5/58   Link Wray
Runnin' Wild
1/55   Firehouse Five + 2
Running Bear
1/60 ★ Johnny Preston
Sad Mood
1/61   Sam Cooke
Sadie Thompson's Song
6/54   Rita Hayworth [Jo Ann Greer]
Sail Along Silvery Moon
1/58   Billy Vaughn & His Orchestra
Sail Ho!
9/60   Robert Horton
Sailor
1/61 ★ Petula Clark
1/61   Lolita
St. Louis Blues
7/58   Ella Fitzgerald
St. Louis Blues March
12/55   751st U.S.A.F. Band
St. Therese Of The Roses
10/56 ★ Malcolm Vaughan
Salute To The Bandbox
6/54   Gigi Gryce–Clifford Brown Sextet
Same Old Me, The
3/60   Guy Mitchell
Same Old Saturday Night
11/55   Frank Sinatra
Same Old Tale The Crow Told Me, The
3/60   Johnny Horton
San Miguel
11/59 ★ Lonnie Donegan
Sand And The Sea, The
4/55   Nat 'King' Cole
Santa Baby
8/54   Eartha Kitt
Santa Bring My Baby Back
11/57 ★ Elvis Presley
Santa Nicola
12/59   Lou Monte
Santo Natale
10/54 ★ David Whitfield
11/54   David Hughes
Satin Doll
9/54   Duke Ellington
Save It
10/59   Mel Robbins
Save The Last Dance For Me
10/60 ★ Drifters

Savoy Scottish Medley
11/55   Will Starr
Say Mama
2/59   Gene Vincent
Say Man
11/59   Bo Diddley
Say The Word
10/60   Brook Brothers
Scandinavian Shuffle
6/60   Swe-Danes
Scarlet Ribbons
7/57   ★ Harry Belafonte
12/59   Browns
School Day
6/57   ★ Chuck Berry
7/57   Bob Cort Skiffle
7/57   'Big' Tiny Little
Scotland The Brave
9/54   Father Sydney MacEwan
11/54   Robert Wilson
3/56   Keynotes
8/56   Kenneth McKellar
'Scotlandia' Medley [M]
10/54   Felix Mendelssohn
Sea Cruise
4/59   Frankie Ford
Sea Of Love
9/59   Phil Phillips
9/59   ★ Marty Wilde
Sean South Of Garryowen
6/60   Enoch Kent
Searchin'
8/57   ★ Coasters
Seasons Of My Heart
4/60   Johnny Cash
Second Fiddle
7/56   Kay Starr
Secret, The
11/58   Gordon MacRae
Secret Love
10/60   Caterina Valente
Secret Of Happiness, The
6/58   Kathie Kay
Secretly
6/58   ★ Jimmie Rodgers
Selection of Marches [M]
9/55   Bowhill Colliery & District Pipe
        Band
Send For Me
9/57   Nat 'King' Cole
Send Me The Pillow You Dream On
2/61   Browns
Serenade
10/54   ★ Mario Lanza
4/56   ★ Mario Lanza *(remake)*
6/56   ★ Slim Whitman
Seven Days
3/56   ★ Anne Shelton
Seven Hills Of Rome
8/58   Mario Lanza
Seven Little Girls Sitting In The Back Seat
11/59   ★ Paul Evans and the Curls
11/59   Lana Sisters with Al Saxon

Seven Minutes In Heaven
1/59   Poni-Tails
Seventeen
10/55   ★ Boyd Bennett & His Rockets
10/55   ★ Fontane Sisters
10/55   Ella Mae Morse
10/55   ★ Frankie Vaughan
Seventeen Tomorrow
11/60   Tony Dunning & The Tremolos
Seventeen Tons
5/56   Max Bygraves
77 Sunset Strip
4/60   Big Sound of Don Ralke
Shake Me I Rattle
12/57   ★ Kaye Sisters
Shake, Rattle And Roll
11/54   ★ Bill Haley & His Comets
2/55   Deep River Boys
Shaky
8/59   Bill Haley & His Comets
Shame On You Miss Johnson
2/59   Bobby Freeman
Shape I'm In, The
9/59   ★ Johnny Restivo
Sh-Boom
8/54   ★ Crew-Cuts
8/54   Johnston Brothers
11/54   ★ Stan Freberg
12/54   Billy Williams Quartet
She Loves To Rock
10/56   Stargazers
She Said 'Yeah'
5/59   Larry Williams
She Sells Sea-Shells
1/58   Laurie London
She's Got It
2/57   ★ Little Richard
She's Just A Whole Lot Like You
10/60   Hank Thompson
Sheik Of Chicago, The
8/60   Four Lads
      See also Mustafa *and* Mustapha
Shifting, Whispering Sands, The
12/55   ★ Billy Vaughn & His Orchestra
1/56   ★ Eamonn Andrews
1/56   Monty Norman
Shimmy Shimmy
9/60   Bobby Freeman
Shiralee
6/57   ★ Tommy Steele
Shop Around
2/61   Miracles
Short Fat Fannie
9/57   ★ Larry Williams
Short Shorts
3/58   Royal Teens
Shortnin' Bread
10/60   Paul Chaplain & His Emeralds
Should We Tell Him
3/58   Everly Brothers
Shout
11/59   Isley Brothers

Shulie A Bop
6/54   Sarah Vaughan
Sick And Tired
6/58 ★ Fats Domino
Side Saddle
2/59 ★ Russ Conway
Silent Night, Holy Night
1/55   Beniamino Gigli
1/55   Mahalia Jackson
12/58   Harry Belafonte
Silhouettes
11/57   Rays
Silver Moon Upon The Golden Sands
8/60   Guy Mitchell
Sinbad
1/60   Bobby Freeman
Sincerely
3/55 ★ McGuire Sisters
Sing Boy Sing
3/58   Tommy Sands
Sing In The New Year [M]
1/58   Jimmy Shand & His Band
Sing It Again With Joe [M]
7/55 ★ Joe 'Mr. Piano' Henderson
Sing It With Joe [M]
5/55 ★ Joe 'Mr. Piano' Henderson
Sing It With Joe (Irish Medley) [M]
12/55   Joe 'Mr. Piano' Henderson
Sing It With Joe (Scottish Medley) [M]
12/55   Joe 'Mr. Piano' Henderson
Sing Like An Angel
5/60 ★ Jerry Lordan
Sing Song Time No. 1 [M]
10/55   Dick James
Sing With Jimmy Shand [M]
11/56 ★ Jimmy Shand & His Band
Singer Not The Song, The
2/61   Knightsbridge Strings
Singing In The Rain
9/54   Dabe Brubeck
Singing The Blues
12/56 ★ Tommy Steele
Sisters
1/55   Rosemary and Betty Clooney
Six Bridges To Cross
4/55   Sammy Davis Jr.
Six-Five Special
6/57   Bob Cort Skiffle
16 Candles
2/59   Crests
Sixteen Tons
1/56   Johnny Desmond
1/56   Michael Holliday
Sizzlin' Hot
10/57   Jimmy Miller & The Barbecues
        [Station Skiffle Group]
Ski King
11/59   E.C. Beatty
Skiffle Party [M]
11/57   Vipers Skiffle Group
Skinny Minnie
5/58   Bill Haley & His Comets

Skokiaan
10/54   Louis Armstrong
10/54   Four Lads
11/54   Alma Cogan
11/54   Ted Heath & His Music
11/54   Eric Jupp & His Orchestra
Sky Blue Shirt And A Rainbow Tie
See A Sky Blue Shirt And A Rainbow Tie
Sleep Walk
9/59 ★ Santo & Johnny
Sleeping Beauty
6/54   Nat 'King' Cole
Slievanamon
11/54   Maurice Keary
Slop Beat, The
4/60   Teen Beats
Slow Down
4/58   Larry Williams
Slow Motion
11/59   Wade Flemons
Slowcoach
10/60   Kenny Lynch
Sluefoot
6/55   Four Aces
7/55   Ray Anthony & His Orchestra
Small Talk
11/55   Al Martino
Smashing Of The Van, The
6/60   Enoch Kent
Smile
8/54   Frank Chacksfield & His Orchestra
8/54 ★ Nat 'King' Cole
8/54   Billy Daniels
8/54   David Whitfield
10/54   Petula Clark
10/54   Melachrino Orchestra
See also Theme from 'Modern Times'
Smiles
1/56   Crazy Otto
Smiling Bill McCall
4/60   Johnny Cash
Smoke Gets In Your Eyes
4/58   Dickie Barrett [Richard Barrett]
1/59 ★ Platters
7/60   Ray Conniff & His Orchestra
Smokie
12/59   Bill Black's Combo
Smooth Operator
1/60   Sarah Vaughan
So Fine
6/59   Fiestas
So High, So Low
10/59   LaVern Baker
So Long
4/57   Johnnie Ray
So Many Ways
11/59   Brook Benton
12/59   Lorie Mann
So You Think You've Got Troubles
4/60   Jody Gibson & The Muleskinners
Sobbin' Women
1/55   Howard Keel

Softly, Softly
2/55   Roland Shaw Orchestra
2/55   Alma Cogan
4/55   Mantovani & His Orchestra
Soho Fair
7/57   Russ Conway
Soldier's Song, The
9/55   John Feeney
Some Day
7/54   Frankie Laine
Some Day Soon
3/57   Eddie Fisher
Somebody
1/55 ★ Stargazers
3/55   Petula Clark
Somebody Bigger Than You And I
10/54   Tennessee Ernie Ford
Somebody To Love
11/60   Bobby Darin
Someday
11/58 ★ Ricky Nelson
Someday (You'll Want Me To Want You)
10/58 ★ Jodie Sands
Someday You'll Call My Name
8/60   Miki & Griff
Someone Loves You, Joe
6/60   Lana Sisters
Someone To Love
10/60   Anthony Newley
Somethin' Else
9/59 ★ Eddie Cochran
Something's Gotta Give
6/55   Billie Anthony
6/55 ★ Sammy Davis Jr.
Son-Of-A-Gun
1/60   Sanford Clark
Son Of Honky Tonk
11/58   Ted Taylor Four
Son Of Mary, The
11/58 ★ Harry Belafonte
Song Is You, The
9/54   Billy May & His Orchestra
Song Of The Barefoot Contessa
1/55   Philip Green & His Orchestra
1/55   Hugo Winterhalter's Orchestra
Song Of The Dreamer
11/55   Eddie Fisher
Song Of The Sea
2/55   Winfred Atwell
Song Of The Wild
11/55   Slim Whitman
Sorry (I Ran All The Way Home)
4/59 ★ Impalas
Sorry But I'm Gonna Have To Pass
11/58   Coasters
South Of The Border
8/60   Carl Mann
Souvenirs
8/59   Barbara Evans
Splish Splash
7/58 ★ Bobby Darin
8/58 ★ Charlie Drake

S'posin'
1/55   Jerry Allen
2/55   Don Cornell
Spring Is Here
6/54   George Shearing Quintet
Spring, Spring, Spring
4/55   Brothers and Girls [Howard Keel]
4/55   Ruby Murray, Ray Burns, Diana
           Decker and Ronnie Harris
Squaws Along The Yukon
11/58   Hank Thompson
Stagger Lee
2/59 ★ Lloyd Price
Stairway Of Love
5/58   Alma Cogan
5/58 ★ Terry Dene
5/58 ★ Michael Holliday
5/58   Marty Robbins
5/58   Marion Ryan
Stampede
1/60   Danny Valentino
Star O' Robbie Burns, The
11/54   Ian MacLeish
Starbright
6/60 ★ Johnny Mathis
Stardust
9/57 ★ Billy Ward & The Dominoes
Starry-Eyed
12/59 ★ Michael Holliday
12/59   Gary Stites
Stars Shine In Your Eyes
8/55   Edna Savage
Stay
12/60 ★ Maurice Williams & The Zodiacs
Step By Step
5/60 ★ Steve Perry
Stewball
4/56 ★ Lonnie Donegan
Stood Up
2/58 ★ Ricky Nelson
Story Of My Life, The
1/58 ★ Michael Holliday
1/58 ★ Dave King
2/58   Marty Robbins
Story Of Three Loves, The
6/54 ★ Winifred Atwell
Story Of Tina, The
8/54 ★ Ronnie Harris
9/54   Lee Lawrence
9/54 ★ Al Martino
Stowaway
6/55 ★ Barbara Lyon
6/55   Margaret Whiting
Straight A's In Love
3/60   Johnny Cash
Stranger In Paradise
4/55 ★ Tony Bennett
4/55 ★ Eddie Calvert
4/55 ★ Don Cornell
4/55 ★ Bing Crosby
4/55 ★ Four Aces
4/55   Ronnie Harris

4/55 ★ Tony Martin
7/55 Edmund Hockridge
Stranger Than Fiction
2/56 Bert Weedon
See also Big Guitar
Streamline Train
5/57 ★ Vipers Skiffle Group
Street Musician, The
8/56 Johnston Brothers
Street Symphony
9/56 Ray Martin & His Concert Orch.
Streets Of Sorrento
6/58 Winifred Atwell
String Along
3/60 Fabian
Stroll, The
1/58 Diamonds
Strollin'
5/59 Bud Flanagan
Strollin' Girl
4/58 Johnnie Ray
Strollin' In The Springtime
9/60 Fabian
Subito
10/60 Steve Rossi
Sucu-Sucu Party Cha
11/60 Firestones
Suddenly There's A Valley
11/55 ★ Petula Clark
11/55 ★ Julius LaRosa
11/55 ★ Lee Lawrence
11/55 ★ Jo Stafford
12/55 Gogi Grant
Sue Saturday
12/59 Julian
Sugar
11/55 Peggy Lee
Sugar Candy
7/57 Eve Boswell
Sugar Moon
6/58 ★ Pat Boone
Sugartime
2/58 ★ Jim Dale
Summer Place
6/60 Jackie Rae
Summer Set
12/59 ★ Mr. Acker Bilk
Summer Sing-Song
5/56 Dick James
Summertime
6/59 Gene Vincent
Summertime Blues
10/58 ★ Eddie Cochran
Summertime In Heidelberg
5/55 Mario Lanza and Elizabeth
Doubleday
Summertime In Venice
11/55 Rossano Brazzi
12/55 Ron Goodwin & His Concert Orch.
Sunday Date
9/60 ★ Flee-Rekkers [Flee-Rakkers]
Sundown Boogie
6/55 Bill Haley & His Comets

Susie Darlin'
10/58 ★ Robin Luke
Susie-Q
11/57 Dale Hawkins
Swag, The
5/58 Link Wray
Sway
7/54 ★ Dean Martin
8/54 Tony Brent
12/60 ★ Bobby Rydell
Sweet Adeline
11/54 Jerry Colonna
Sweet And Gentle
7/55 Eartha Kitt
8/55 Alan Dale
Sweet Dreams (1)
5/60 ★ Dave Sampson and the Hunters
Sweet Dreams (2)
1/61 Don Gibson
Sweet Little Sixteen
4/58 ★ Chuck Berry
Sweet Nuthin's
2/60 ★ Brenda Lee
Sweet Stuff
7/57 ★ Guy Mitchell
Sweet Thing
9/60 Grady Chapman
Sweeter As The Day Goes By
11/60 Valerie Masters
Sweetheart
12/58 Peggy Lee
Sweetheart Waltz [M]
2/61 Jimmy Shand & His Band
Swing House
9/54 Gerry Mulligan Quartet
Swingin' Daddy
3/58 Buddy Knox
Swingin' School
6/60 ★ Bobby Rydell
Swingin' Shepherd Blues, The
3/58 Johnny Pate Quintet
5/58 ★ Ella Fitzgerald
Ta Ta
9/60 Clyde McPhatter
Taboo
8/59 Arthur Lyman Group
Take A Chance
12/60 Glenda Collins
Take Me Dreaming
3/59 Enrico Leandros & His Orchestra
[Werner Müller & His Orchestra]
Take My Love
12/55 Mantovani & His Orchestra
Take This Hammer
11/55 Ken Colyer's Skiffle Group
Take This Message To My Mother
6/58 Bridie Gallagher
Taking A Chance On Love
6/55 Johnnie Ray
Talk Of The School
5/59 Sonny James
Talk That Talk
12/59 Jackie Wilson

Talk To Me
11/59   Frank Sinatra
Talking Army Blues
2/60 ★ Josh MacRae
Talking Guitar Blues
11/59   Lonnie Donegan
2/60   Josh MacRae
Tall Cool One
10/59   Wailers
Tall Oak Tree
4/60   Dorsey Burnette
Tallahassee Lassie
6/59 ★ Freddy Cannon
Tammy
9/57   Kathie Kay
10/57   Ames Brothers
Tap-Wood Polka
12/55   Will Starr
Tea For Two
10/54   Gerry Mulligan Quartet
12/60   Anita O'Day
Tea For Two Cha Cha
10/58 ★ Tommy Dorsey Orchestra
Teach Me Tonight
12/54   Nat 'King' Cole
12/54 ★ De Castro Sisters
Teach You To Rock
10/56 ★ Tony Crombie & His Rockets
Teacher's Pet
4/58   Doris Day
Teardrops Are Falling
10/60   Al Kasha
Teen Angel
2/60 ★ Mark Dinning
2/60   Alex Murray
Teen Beat
10/59 ★ Sandy Nelson
Teen Scene
11/60   Hunters
Teen-Age Crush
3/57   Tommy Sands
Teenage Dream
10/57   Terry Dene
Teenage Guitar
11/59   Bert Weedon
Teenage Love (1)
4/57   Frankie Lymon & The Teenagers
Teenage Love (2)
7/58   Five Chestnuts
3/61   Michael Cox and the Hunters
Teenage Troubles
12/60   Nelson Keene
Teensville
3/60 ★ Chet Atkins
Tell Him No
5/59   Jackson Brothers
5/59   Travis & Bob
Tell Laura I Love Her
8/60   John Leyton
9/60 ★ Ray Peterson
Tell Me, Tell Me
11/54   Tony Brent

Tell Me That You Love Me
6/60   Fats Domino
Tell Tommy I Miss Him
10/60   Laura Lee
10/60   Marilyn Michaels
Telling Lies
3/59   Fats Domino
Temptation
1/56   Caterina Valente
Ten Little Indians
11/55   Bill Haley & His Comets
Ten Swingin' Bottles
11/60 ★ Pete Chester & The Consulates
Ten Thousand Miles
9/56 ★ Michael Holliday
Tender Trap, The
1/56   Ella Fitzgerald
2/56   Debbie Reynolds
Tenderly
2/55   Oscar Peterson
Tennessee Waltz
11/59   Bobby Comstock & The Counts
11/59   Jerry Fuller
Tequila
3/58 ★ Champs
4/58   Johnny (The Gash) Gray
4/58 ★ Ted Heath & His Music
4/58   Stan Kenton & His Orchestra
4/58   Don Lang & His Frantic Five
Terrific Together
10/58   Ferlin Husky
Test Of Time, The
10/59   Robert Earl
Teviot Brig
12/54   Jimmy Shand & His Band
Texas Tambourine
1/58   Johnnie Ray
Thank You Pretty Baby
9/59   Brook Benton
Thanks A Lot
4/59   Johnny Cash
That Dear Old Gentleman
12/56   Max Bygraves
That Old Black Magic
9/55 ★ Sammy Davis Jr.
5/56   Billy Daniels
That Old Cha Cha Feeling
11/58   Ken Mackintosh & His Orchestra
That Train Has Gone
7/58   Chuck Willis
That'll Be The Day
9/57 ★ Crickets
That's All
4/56   Tennessee Ernie Ford
That's Happiness
11/57   Marion Ryan
That's How A Love Song Was Born
7/55 ★ Ray Burns
9/55   Frankie Vaughan
That's My Little Suzie
8/59   Ritchie Valens
That's Right
10/56 ★ Deep River Boys

That's Show Biz
6/59   Dale Wright
That's The Way I Feel
10/58   Faron Young
That's The Way It Goes
1/61   Frank Ifield
That's When Your Heartaches Begin
7/58   David Whitfield
That's Why
5/59   Jackie Wilson
Them There Eyes
8/60   ★ Emile Ford & The Checkmates
Theme from 'A Summer Place'
2/60   ★ Percy Faith & His Orchestra
Theme from 'Journey Into Space'
1/55   Frank Weir & His Saxophone
Theme from 'Medic'
See Blue Star *and* Medic Theme
Theme from 'Modern Times'
10/54   Ron Goodwin & His Concert Orch.
See also Smile
Theme from 'Picnic'
5/56   Columbia Pictures Orchestra
Theme from 'The Apartment'
8/60   ★ Ferrante & Teicher
Theme from 'The High And The Mighty'
11/54   Dimitri Tiomkin & His Orchestra
See also High And The Mighty, The
Theme from 'The Man With The Golden Arm'
See Main Title
Theme from 'The Threepenny Opera'
3/56   ★ Louis Armstrong
3/56   Joe 'Mr. Piano' Henderson
3/56   ★ Dick Hyman Trio
3/56   Norrie Paramor & His Orchestra
3/56   ★ Billy Vaughn & His Orchestra
See also Threepenny Opera, The
There Comes A Time
11/59   Jack Scott
There Goes My Baby
8/59   Drifters
There Goes My Heart
10/54   Nat 'King' Cole
3/55   Four Aces
There Must Be A Reason
7/54   ★ Frankie Laine
11/54   Vera Lynn
There Must Be A Way
1/59   ★ Joni James
There's A Blue Ridge Round My Heart Virginia
9/57   Betty Smith's Skiffle
There's A Gold Mine In The Sky
9/57   ★ Pat Boone
There's Good Rockin' Tonight
4/59   Pat Boone
There's No Business Like Show Business [M]
3/55   Big Ben Banjo Band
There's Not Any Like You Left
10/60   Faron Young
These Dangerous Years
8/57   ★ Frankie Vaughan

These Foolish Things
12/54   Earl Bostic & His Orchestra
They Can't Change The Name Of Ireland
7/56   Paddy Carney
They Were Doin' The Mambo
9/54   Ted Heath & His Music
10/54   Vaughn Monroe
Think It Over, Boys
4/58   Tommy Collins
Think Me A Kiss
4/60   Clyde McPhatter
This Happy Feeling
10/58   Debbie Reynolds
This Is My Story
7/57   Gene & Eunice
This Is The Night
3/56   Frankie Vaughan
This Little Girl Of Mine
3/58   Everly Brothers
This Little Girl's Gone Rockin'
1/59   Ruth Brown
This Love I Have For You
4/60   ★ Lance Fortune
This Magic Moment
4/60   Drifters
This Ole House
9/54   ★ Billie Anthony
10/54   ★ Rosemary Clooney
11/54   Joan Regan
Three Bells, The
9/59   ★ Browns
Three Coins In The Fountain
7/54   ★ Frank Sinatra
8/54   Tony Brent
Three Galleons
7/55   Robert Earl
1/56   Les Howard
365 Kisses
11/54   Stargazers
Three Nights A Week
10/60   ★ Fats Domino
Three O'Clock Jump
9/54   Gene Norman's 'Just Jazz'
Three Stars
6/59   Tommy Dee
3.10 To Yuma, The
9/57   Frankie Laine
Threepenny Opera, The
3/56   Norrie Paramor & His Orchestra
See also Theme from 'The Threepenny Opera'
Thunder Road Chase
7/58   Jack Marshall, His Orchestra and Chorus
Ticky Ticky Tick
7/56   Frankie Laine
Ties That Bind, The
6/60   Brook Benton
Tiger
8/59   Fabian
Tiger Rag
3/55   Kid Ory & His Creole Jazz Band
10/55   Chris Barber's Jazz Band

Tijuana Jail, The
    4/59   Kingston Trio
Tika Tika Tok
    5/55   Alma Cogan
Till
    12/60   Maureen Evans
    12/60   Caterina Valente
Till There Was You
    2/61 ★ Peggy Lee
Time Will Tell
    11/60 ★ Ian Gregory [Iain Gregory]
Times Are Gettin' Hard Boys
    9/58   Lonnie Donegan
Tina Marie
    10/55 ★ Perry Como
    11/55   Dennis Hale
Ting-A-Ling
    4/55   Eric Delaney & His Band
To Be Loved
    3/58 ★ Malcolm Vaughan
To Love Again
    8/56   Carmen Cavallaro
To The Ends Of The Earth
    1/57   Nat 'King' Cole
Togetherness
    11/60 ★ Mike Preston
Tom Dooley
    12/58   Rikki Price
    1/59   Pinky & Perky
Tom Hark
    5/58 ★ Ted Heath & His Music
Tom Thumb's Tune
    1/59   Charlie Drake
Tomato
    9/54   Marie Bryant
Tomorrow
    2/55 ★ Johnny Brandon
    3/55   Max Bygraves
Tonight
    1/59   Edmund Hockridge
Tonight's The Night
    11/60   Shirelles
Too Close For Comfort
    5/57   Sammy Davis Jr.
Too Good
    1/60 ★ Little Tony & His Brothers
Too Late
    8/55   Guy Mitchell
Too Many Heartaches
    3/55   Frankie Vaughan
Too Much
    5/57 ★ Elvis Presley
Too Much Rockin'
    12/59   Tiny Lewis
Too Much Tequila
    2/60 ★ Champs
Too Pooped To Pop
    3/60   Chuck Berry
Too Young
    12/59 ★ Bill Forbes
Too Young To Go Steady
    5/56   Nicky Kidd
    5/56   Anne Shelton

Toot
    9/60   Chubby Checker
Top Teen Baby
    10/60 ★ Garry Mills
Top Ten Special [M]
    10/57   Various Artists
Tops In Pops [M]
    3/60   Winifred Atwell
Topsy
    11/58 ★ Cozy Cole
Torero
    6/58   Kaye Sisters
    6/58 ★ Julius LaRosa
    6/58   Southlanders
Torero – Cha Cha Cha
    6/58 ★ Renato Carosone
Torquay
    11/59   Fireballs
Tracy's Theme
    2/60   Spencer Ross & His Orchestra
Tragedy
    5/59   Thomas Wayne
Train Of Love, The
    11/59 ★ Alma Cogan
    7/60   Johnny Carson
Trambone
    3/61 ★ Krew Kats
Tread Softly Stranger
    10/58   Jim Dale
Treasure Of Love
    7/56 ★ Clyde McPhatter
Treble Chance
    10/59 ★ Joe 'Mr. Piano' Henderson
Trouble In Paradise
    8/60   Crests
Trouble With Harry
    3/56 ★ Alfi & Harry [David Seville]
Truckin'
    1/55   Eric Delaney & His Band
Trudie
    6/58 ★ Joe 'Mr. Piano' Henderson
True, Fine Mama
    6/58   Little Richard
True Love
    11/56 ★ Bing Crosby and Grace Kelly
    12/56   Ruby Murray
True To You
    5/58   Gene Vincent
Trumpet Cha Cha Cha
    1/59   Eddie Calvert
Try Another Cherry Tree
    5/56   Max Bygraves
Trying
    7/56 ★ Hilltoppers
Tulips From Amsterdam
    4/58 ★ Max Bygraves
Tumbling Tumbleweeds
    2/56 ★ Slim Whitman
Tunnel Of Love, The
    10/59   Doris Day
Tutti Frutti
    4/56   Pat Boone
    1/57 ★ Little Richard

Twa Heids Are Better Than Yin
7/60   Joe Gordon Folk Four
Tweedle(e) Dee
3/55   Billie Anthony
3/55 ★ Frankie Vaughan
4/55   Alma Cogan
4/55 ★ Georgia Gibbs
12th Street Rag
1/55   Kid Ory & His Creole Jazz Band
Twelve Days Of Christmas, The
12/58   Harry Belafonte
20 Flight Rock
4/57   Eddie Cochran
26 Miles (Santa Catalina)
4/58   Four Preps
Twenty Tiny Fingers
10/55 ★ Coronets
10/55 ★ Stargazers
11/55   Marie Benson
12/55 ★ Alma Cogan
Twist, The
9/60   Hank Ballard & The Midnighters
9/60 ★ Chubby Checker
Two Different Worlds
1/57   David Hughes
Two Easter Sunday Sweethearts
4/55   Vera Lynn
Two Hearts, Two Kisses
5/55   Crew-Cuts
5/55   Doris Day
Two Hound Dogs
7/55   Bill Haley & His Comets
Two Step – Side Step
12/54   Bonnie Lou
Tyrolean Tango
10/54   Charles Williams & His Concert Orchestra
Uh-Huh
7/60   Keith Kelly
Unbelievable
12/54   Nat 'King' Cole
Unchain My Heart
4/58   Slim Whitman
Unchained Melody
4/55 ★ Al Hibbler
4/55 ★ Jimmy Young
5/55 ★ Les Baxter & His Orchestra
6/55   Don Cornell
6/55   Crew-Cuts
7/55   Roy Hamilton
Under The Bridges Of Paris
10/54 ★ Eartha Kitt
3/55 ★ Dean Martin
Unfaithful You
10/55   Vera Lynn
Union Maid
11/56   Arthur Baird Skiffle Group
Unsuspecting Heart
3/55   Kathy Lloyd
5/55   Terri Stevens
5/55   Frankie Vaughan
Upturn
2/60   Eddie Smith with the Hornets

Urge, The
5/60 ★ Freddy Cannon
Vacation Time
9/58   Chuck Berry
Val De Ri, Val De Ra
10/54   Beverley Sisters
See also Happy Wanderer, The
Valencia
2/56   Mario Lanza
Valley Of Tears
7/57 ★ Fats Domino
Vaquero
9/60   Fireballs
Velvet Glove, The
10/54   Jerry Colonna
Velvet Waters
8/59   Megatrons
Vendetta
10/54   Winifred Atwell
Veni – Vidi – Vici
11/54 ★ Ronnie Hilton
12/54   Gaylords
1/55   Dick James
Venus
3/59 ★ Frankie Avalon
3/59 ★ Dickie Valentine
Vera Sings Today's Pop Hits [M]
2/59   Vera Lynn
Very First Christmas Of All, The
11/55 ★ Ruby Murray
Victory Waltz [M]
4/55   Jimmy Shand & His Band
Voice, The
4/56   Dickie Valentine
Volare
8/58   Marino Marini & His Quartet
8/60 ★ Bobby Rydell
Vow, The
12/58   Gene & Eunice
Wagon Train
4/59   Johnny O'Neill
9/60   Robert Horton
Wait And See
12/57   Fats Domino
Wait For Me, Darling
8/54   Georgia Gibbs
8/54 ★ Joan Regan
11/54   Bonnie Lou
Waiting For The Robert E. Lee
7/60   Peter Elliott
Wake Me When It's Over
4/60   Andy Williams
Wake The Town And Tell The People
10/55   Les Baxter & His Orchestra
Wake Up, Irene
11/54   Hank Thompson
Wake Up Little Susie
11/57 ★ King Brothers
Walk, The
4/58   Jimmy McCracklin & His Band
Walk Don't Run
8/60 ★ Ventures
9/60   Rhet Stoller

Walk Hand In Hand
  6/56 ★ Jimmy Parkinson
  7/56   Vera Lynn
  7/56 ★ Tony Martin
Walker, The
  11/58   Duane Eddy
Walkin' After Midnight
  4/57   Jimmy Young
Walkin' Home From School
  2/58   Gene Vincent
Walkin' Shoes
  1/55   Gerry Mulligan Quartet
Walkin' Tall
  9/59 ★ Frankie Vaughan
Walking Along
  11/58   Diamonds
Walking The Floor Over You
  6/60 ★ Pat Boone
Wanting You
  5/56   Mario Lanza
Warpaint
  2/61 ★ Brook Brothers
Watching The World Go By
  6/56   Dean Martin
Water, Water
  6/57 ★ Tommy Steele
Waterloo
  8/59   Mudlarks
Watermelon Song, The
  3/57   Tennessee Ernie Ford
Way Down Yonder In New Orleans
  12/59 ★ Freddy Cannon
Ways Of A Woman In Love, The
  10/58   Johnny Cash
Ways Of Love, The
  12/59   Nash Lorraine
Wayward Wind
  6/56 ★ Gogi Grant
We Will Make Love
  5/57 ★ Russ Hamilton
  6/57   Kathie Kay
We'll Keep A Welcome
  7/56   Harry Secombe
We're Gonna Dance
  1/61   Lorne Lesley
We're Not Alone
  3/58 ★ Frankie Vaughan
We're Only Young Once
  6/60 ★ Avons
Wedding Bells
  2/55 ★ Eddie Fisher
Wee Magic Stane, The
  8/60   Reivers
Wee Tom
  1/59 ★ Lord Rockingham's XI
Week-End
  11/58   Kingsmen
West Of Zanzibar
  7/54 ★ Anthony Steel
What A Mouth (What A North And South)
  6/60 ★ Tommy Steele
What A Mouth, What A Mouth
  1/55   The Two Bills From Bermondsey

What Am I Doin' In Kansas City
  10/54   Guy Mitchell
What Am I Gonna Do
  2/61 ★ Emile Ford & The Checkmates
What Am I Living For
  7/58   Chuck Willis
  4/60   Conway Twitty
What Do I Care
  11/58   Johnny Cash
What Do You Do
  5/58   Tommy Steele
What Do You Want?
  11/59 ★ Adam Faith
What Do You Want To Make Those Eyes At Me For?
  10/59 ★ Emile Ford & The Checkmates
What In The World's Come Over You
  1/60 ★ Jack Scott
What Is A Wife?
  2/56   Steve Allen
What Is Life? (Che Faro?)
  1/55   Kathleen Ferrier
What Is Love?
  9/59   Playmates
What Is My Destiny
  9/57   Malcolm Vaughan
What More Do You Want
  1/60 ★ Frankie Vaughan
What More Is There To Say
  4/55   Billy Eckstine
What Will I Tell My Heart
  9/57   Fats Domino
What'd I Say?
  8/59   Ray Charles
Whatever Lola Wants
  3/57 ★ Alma Cogan
  3/57   Johnston Brothers
Whatever Will Be, Will Be
  6/56 ★ Doris Day
Wheels
  2/61 ★ String-A-Longs
  3/61   Max Harris with His Group
When I Grow Too Old To Dream
  6/55   Slim Whitman
When I Leave The World Behind
  3/55   Tony Brent
  2/57   Teresa Brewer
When I See You
  9/57   Fats Domino
When Mexico Gave Up The Rhumba
  9/56 ★ Mitchell Torok
When My Dream Boat Comes Home
  9/56   Fats Domino
When The Saints Go Marching In
  2/55   Saints Jazz Band
  5/55   Humphrey Lyttelton & His Band
  9/55   Dutch Swing College Band
  9/55   Kid Ory's Creole Jazz Band
  5/56   Teddy Buckner
  7/58   Chris Barber's Jazz Band
When Will I Be Loved
  7/60   Brook Brothers

When You Ask About Love
11/59 ★ Crickets (post-Holly)
When You Come To The End Of A Lollipop
12/60 Max Bygraves
When You Lose The One You Love
11/55 ★ David Whitfield
12/55 Dorothy Squires
1/56 Issy Bonn
When You're In Love
2/55 Joan Regan
3/55 Jane Powell and Howard Keel
Where Or When
3/60 Dion & The Belmonts
Where The River Shannon Flows
6/56 Mr. Acker Bilk
Where Were You
5/59 ★ Lloyd Price
Where Will The Dimple Be?
4/55 ★ Rosemary Clooney
5/55 Lorrae Desmond
6/55 Alma Cogan
Where's The Girl
10/60 Craig Douglas
Whiffenpoof Song, The
10/54 Louis Armstrong
10/56 Slim Whitman
Whispering Bells
9/57 Dell-Vikings
Whispering Hope
2/61 ★ Jim Reeves
Whistlin' Rufus
9/56 Chris Barber's Jazz Band
Whistling Gypsy, The
11/54 Patrick O'Hagan
White Christmas
11/54 Chris Barber's Jazz Band
11/54 Bing Crosby, Danny Kaye,
Peggy Lee and Trudy Stevens
11/54 Eddie Fisher
White Lightning
4/59 George Jones
White Silver Sands
9/57 Don Rondo
11/57 Don Lang & His Frantic Five
4/60 ★ Bill Black's Combo
Who Are We
4/56 ★ Vera Lynn
6/56 Gordon MacRae
8/56 Gogi Grant
Who Could Be Bluer?
2/60 ★ Jerry Lordan
Who Shot Sam
8/59 George Jones
Who Was That Lady?
5/60 Dean Martin
Who Will Shoe Your Pretty Little Foot
10/56 Tennessee Ernie Ford
Who's Afraid
11/54 Dickie Valentine
Who's Sorry Now
2/56 ★ Johnnie Ray
3/58 ★ Connie Francis

Whole Lotta Loving
1/59 Fats Domino
Whole Lotta Shakin' Goin' On
8/57 ★ Jerry Lee Lewis
11/60 Chubby Checker
Whole Lotta Woman
2/58 ★ Marvin Rainwater
Why
1/60 ★ Frankie Avalon
1/60 ★ Anthony Newley
Why Baby Why
4/57 ★ Pat Boone
Why Didn't You Tell Me
6/60 ★ Marke Anthony
Why Do Fools Fall In Love
6/56 ★ Frankie Lymon & The Teenagers
6/56 Gale Storm
7/56 ★ Alma Cogan
Why Don't They Understand
2/58 ★ George Hamilton IV
Why, Oh Why?
9/55 Tony Martin, Vic Damone, Russ
Tamblyn [actually Rex Dennis],
Jane Powell, Debbie Reynolds and
Ann Miller
Why The Chicken?
3/61 Dave Sampson and the Hunters
Why Why Why
7/60 Craig Douglas
Wild Cat
12/59 ★ Gene Vincent
Wild Cherry
5/56 Don Cherry
5/56 Nicky Kidd
Wild Colonial Boy, The
1/55 Patrick O'Hagan
Wild Is The Wind
2/58 Johnny Mathis
Wild One
3/60 ★ Bobby Rydell
Wild Side Of Life, The
7/60 Hank Thompson
Will You Love Me Tomorrow
1/61 ★ Shirelles
Willie Can
3/56 ★ Beverley Sisters
3/56 ★ Alma Cogan
3/56 Pauline Shepherd
4/56 Shirley Abicair
Willingly
2/59 David Whitfield
Wind In The Willow
6/57 Kathie Kay
Wings Of A Dove
1/61 Ferlin Husky
Winter Wonderland
6/54 Chet Baker Quartet
Wisdom Of A Fool, The
3/57 Ronnie Carroll
3/57 Ronnie Hilton
3/57 ★ Norman Wisdom
Wish It Were Me
10/59 Craig Douglas

Witch Doctor
5/58 ★ Don Lang & His Frantic Five
5/58 ★ David Seville

Witchcraft
1/58 ★ Frank Sinatra

With All My Heart
7/57 ★ Petula Clark
8/57   Buddy Greco
8/57   Dave King
8/57   Jodie Sands
8/57   Joan Savage
8/57   Judy Scott

With The Wind And The Rain In Your Hair
4/59 ★ Pat Boone

With These Hands
3/60 ★ Shirley Bassey

With You Beside Me
4/59   Rosemary June

With Your Love
12/55 ★ Malcolm Vaughan
1/56   Tony Brent
1/56 ★ Robert Earl
1/56   Vera Lynn

Without Him
5/57   Frankie Laine

Without Love
3/57   Rose Brennan
3/57   Ronnie Carroll

Woman From Liberia
11/58 ★ Jimmie Rodgers

Wonder Of You, The
8/59 ★ Ray Peterson
9/59   Ronnie Carroll

Wonderful Secret Of Love, The
2/59 ★ Robert Earl

Wonderful Things
7/58 ★ Frankie Vaughan

Wonderful, Wonderful
7/57 ★ Ronnie Hilton
7/57 ★ Gary Miller

Wonderful, Wonderful Day
4/55   Jane Powell

Wonderful World
7/60 ★ Sam Cooke

Wonderful You
9/59   Ronnie Carroll

Wonderland By Night
12/60   Bert Kaempfert & His Orchestra

Wondrous Place
9/60 ★ Billy Fury

Woodchoppers Ball
3/60   Lyn Vernon [B.B. Cunningham Jr.]

Woo-Hoo
11/59   Rock-A-Teens

Words Mean Nothing
1/61   Lee Hazlewood

World In My Arms, The
1/61 ★ Nat 'King' Cole

World Is Mine, The
3/57 ★ Malcolm Vaughan

World Is Waiting For The Sunrise, The
6/56   Chris Barber's Jazz Band

World Outside, The
1/59 ★ Russ Conway
1/59 ★ Four Aces

Wreck Of The John B., The
6/60   Reivers

Yakety Yak
7/58 ★ Coasters

Yaller, Yaller Gold
2/57   Michael Holliday

Yea-Yea
4/59   Dale Hawkins

Yellow Rose Of Texas, The
9/55   Billy Cotton & His Band
9/55 ★ Ronnie Hilton
9/55 ★ Mitch Miller & His Orchestra
10/55   Johnny Desmond
10/55   Michael Holliday
10.55 ★ Gary Miller
1/56 ★ Stan Freberg

Yes, I'm Lonesome Tonight
2/61   Dodie Stevens

Yes, Sir, That's My Baby
10/60   Ricky Nelson

You
6/58   Aquatones

You Always Hurt The One You Love
12/58 ★ Connie Francis

You Are My First Love
7/56 ★ Ruby Murray
3/57   Nat 'King' Cole

You Are My Sunshine
11/55   Ferko String Band

You Are The Only One
1/61   Ricky Nelson

You Can't Be True To Two
4/56 ★ Dave King

You Deserve
1/60   Peggy Lee

You Dreamer You
6/59   Johnny Cash

You Got What It Takes
1/60 ★ Marv Johnson

You Made Me Love You
8/55   Doris Day
5/59 ★ Nat 'King' Cole

You, Me And Us
1/57 ★ Alma Cogan

You My Love
2/55   Doris Day
2/55 ★ Frank Sinatra

You Need Hands
4/58 ★ Max Bygraves
9/58   Eydie Gormé

You Send Me
11/57 ★ Sam Cooke

You Talk Too Much
11/60 ★ Johnny Carson
11/60   Frankie Ford
11/60   Joe Jones & His Orchestra

You Tell Me
11/59   Johnny Cash

You Were Mine
9/59   Tommy Steele
10/59   Fireflies
You Win Again
3/58   Jerry Lee Lewis
You, You Romeo
8/57 ★ Shirley Bassey
You'd Be So Nice To Come Home To
4/59   Johnny Mathis
You'll Always Be My Lifetime Sweetheart
6/55   Perry Como
You'll Never Never Know
1/57 ★ Platters
You'll Never Walk Alone
6/56   Frank Sinatra
You're All That I Live For
9/59   Johnnie Ray
You're My Only Girl
6/60   Danny Davis
You're Sensational
2/57   Frank Sinatra
You're Singing Our Love Song To
Somebody Else
5/60 ★ Jerry Wallace
You're Thrilling
8/60   Johnny Angel
Young And Foolish
1/56 ★ Ronnie Hilton
2/56   Jo Stafford
Young At Heart
6/54 ★ Frank Sinatra
7/54   Bing Crosby
Young Emotions
5/60 ★ Ricky Nelson
Young Ideas
5/59   Chico Holiday
Young In Love
10/60   Easy Riders
Young Love
2/57 ★ Tab Hunter
2/57 ★ Sonny James
Your Cheatin' Heart
4/56   Hank Williams
Zambesi
1/56 ★ Lou Busch & His Orchestra
3/56   Stargazers
Zing! Went The Strings Of My Heart
11/60   Kalin Twins

ALBUM INDEX

This is an index of all 78 r.p.m., EP and LP albums listed in the *UK Bubbling Under Chart*, and the month and year in which they first bubbled under.

Re-entries are not shown unless they were reissues.

Albums which subsequently became hits are marked ★.

For ease of reference, some artists' names have been abbreviated.

Records released under a pseudonym show the artist's name twice: the pseudonym first, followed by their usual name in square brackets. They are listed under the artist's main/usual name in the *Artists A-Z* section.

78 r.p.m. Albums

BEETHOVEN – SYMPHONY NO. 5 IN C MINOR, OP. 67 [4-disc set]
11/54   N.B.C. Symphony Orchestra, *cond.* Arturo Toscanini
LOVE FROM JUDY [2-disc set]
1/55   Original London Cast
TCHAIKOVSKY – BALLET SUITE: 'THE SWAN LAKE', OP. 20 [2-disc set]
10/54   London Philharmonic Orchestra, *cond.* John Barbirolli
TCHAIKOVSKY – SWAN LAKE – BALLET MUSIC [4-disc set]
1/55   London Philharmonic Orchestra, *cond.* Antál Dorati

EPs

ACKER'S AWAY
10/59   ★ Mr. Acker Bilk
AMAZING BUD POWELL TRIO, THE
2/55   Bud Powell Trio
AMONG MY SOUVENIRS (PART 1)
5/58   Al Jolson
ARTISTRY OF STAN GETZ, THE
10/55   Stan Getz
BACKSTAIRS SESSION
10/55   Lonnie Donegan
5/56   Lonnie Donegan *(reissue)*
BUNDLE OF JOY [OST]
3/57   Eddie Fisher
BUNK JOHNSON & HIS NEW ORLEANS BAND
11/56   Bunk Johnson
CALYPSO
4/57   Harry Belafonte
CARMEN McRAE (PART 1)
9/56   Carmen McRae
CHET BAKER QUARTET
2/55   Chet Baker Quartet
CHRIS BARBER PLAYS SPIRITUALS
1/55   Chris Barber's Jazz Band
CHRIS BARBER SKIFFLE GROUP, THE
2/57   Chris Barber's Skiffle Group
CHUBBY JACKSON'S ALL STARS
11/54   Chubby Jackson's All Stars
CLIFFORD BROWN & ART FARMER WITH THE SWEDISH ALL STARS (VOL. 2)
6/54   Clifford Brown & Art Farmer with the Swedish All Stars
COLEMAN HAWKINS
2/55   Coleman Hawkins

COUNTRY BOY
5/59   Johnny Cash
COUNTRY GUITAR (VOL. 4)
3/58   Hank Snow
COUNTRY GUITAR (VOL. 13)
2/61   Jimmie Driftwood
DAVE BRUBECK QUARTET
11/54   Dave Brubeck
DEDICATED TO YOU
10/56   Billy Eckstine and Sarah Vaughan
DONEGAN ON STAGE
7/58   Lonnie Donegan
ELLA SINGS 'PAL JOEY'
5/58   Ella Fitzgerald
ELVIS PRESLEY
10/57   Elvis Presley
ELVIS SAILS
12/58   Elvis Presley
ERROLL GARNER
8/54   Erroll Garner
FABULOUS PLATTERS, THE
11/56   Platters
FLAMINGO
1/55   Earl Bostic & His Orchestra
FOLLOW A STAR [OST]
5/60   Norman Wisdom
GEMS OF JAZZ NO. 1
1/55   Dutch Swing College Band
GENE NORMAN PRESENTS 'JUST JAZZ'
11/54   Gene Norman's 'Just Jazz'
GENE NORMAN PRESENTS KAY STARR WITH BARNEY KESSEL
11/54   Kay Starr with Barney Kessel
GERRY MULLIGAN QUARTET, THE
2/55   Gerry Mulligan Quartet
GERRY MULLIGAN QUARTET (VOL. 1), THE
8/54   Gerry Mulligan Quartet
GERRY MULLIGAN QUARTET (VOL. 2), THE
9/54   Gerry Mulligan Quartet
GERRY MULLIGAN QUARTET (VOL. 3), THE
2/55   Gerry Mulligan Quartet with Lee Konitz
GIANTS OF MODERN JAZZ
7/56   Shorty Rogers
GLENN MILLER SPECIAL
12/58   Glenn Miller & His Orchestra
GOOD ROCKIN' TONIGHT
9/57   Elvis Presley
GUY MITCHELL
1/55   Guy Mitchell
GUYS AND DOLLS [OST]
10/56   ★ Marlon Brando / Jean Simmons
HANK
3/58   Hank Thompson
HAWK TALKS, THE
1/55   Coleman Hawkins
HERD FROM MARS (VOL. 1)
1/55   Woody Herman
HOWARD RUMSEY'S LIGHTHOUSE ALL STARS (VOL. 1)
1/55   Howard Rumsey's Lighthouse All Stars
I'M IN CHARGE
4/59   Bruce Forsyth
IDLE ON PARADE [OST]
4/59   ★ Anthony Newley

IT'S GREAT TO BE YOUNG
   6/56   Original Soundtrack
JAZZ AT THE ROYAL FESTIVAL HALL
   10/56   Chris Barber's Jazz Band
JIMMY DEUCHAR QUARTET WITH VICTOR FELDMAN, THE
   7/54   Jimmy Deuchar Quartet
JOHNNY CASH SINGS HANK WILLIAMS
   3/59   Johnny Cash
JOHNNY DUNCAN & HIS BLUE GRASS BOYS
   8/57   Johnny Duncan & The Blue Grass Boys
JOY NICHOLS
   1/55   Joy Nichols
KID ORY AND HIS CREOLE JAZZ BAND IN CONCERT
   5/55   Kid Ory & His Creole Jazz Band
KID ORY'S CREOLE JAZZ BAND
   6/54   Kid Ory's Creole Jazz Band
KID ORY'S CREOLE JAZZ BAND – 1953 (VOL. 1)
   12/55   Kid Ory's Creole Jazz Band
KING AND I, THE (PART 2)
   2/57   Original Soundtrack
KING CREOLE (VOL. 1) [OST]
   9/58   Elvis Presley
KING CREOLE (VOL. 2) [OST]
   10/58   Elvis Presley
KISMET
   4/56   Various Artists
LARS GULLIN QUINTET
   8/54   Lars Gullin Quintet
LITTLE RICHARD & HIS BAND (VOL. 1)
   2/57   Little Richard
LIVE IT UP (PART 1)
   8/56   Bill Haley & His Comets
LONNIE DONEGAN HIT PARADE
   2/57   Lonnie Donegan
LOVE ME TENDER
   1/57   Elvis Presley
MARINO MARINI & HIS HAPPY MUSIC (VOL. 1)
   5/58   Marino Marini & His Quartet
MERRY CHRISTMAS (VOL. 1)
   11/57 ★ Bing Crosby
MILT JACKSON MODERN JAZZ QUARTET
   8/54   Milt Jackson Modern Jazz Quartet
MR. ACKER BILK SINGS
   5/59 ★ Mr. Acker Bilk
MOONLIGHT SINATRA
   11/55   Frank Sinatra
MUGGSY SPANIER'S DIXIELAND BAND
   9/55   Muggsy Spanier's Dixieland Band
MUSIC FEATURED IN 'THE GLEN MILLER STORY'
   8/54   Louis Armstrong
MUSKRAT RAMBLE
   1/55   Louis Armstrong
MY FAIR LADY
   5/58   Various Artists
MY FAIR LADY (VOL. 1)
   8/58   Original Broadway Cast
NEW FACES
   1/56   Original Broadway Cast
NIGHT LIGHTS
   4/57   Nat 'King' Cole
OKLAHOMA! (PART 1)
   9/56   Original Soundtrack

OSCAR PETERSON PLAYS TENDERLY AND C JAM BLUES
2/55   Oscar Peterson Trio
PEACE IN THE VALLEY
6/57   ★ Elvis Presley
RELAX WITH LONNIE
4/59   Lonnie Donegan
ROBESON'S HERE!
9/58   Paul Robeson
ROCK AROUND THE CLOCK
9/56   Bill Haley & His Comets
ROCK 'N ROLL
9/56   Bill Haley & His Comets
ROMANCE IN SONG
10/55   Mario Lanza
SARAH VAUGHAN
5/56   Sarah Vaughan
SCOTTISH COUNTRY DANCES NO. 2
12/54   Jimmy Shand & His Band
SERIOUS CHARGE [OST]
6/59   ★ Cliff Richard & The Drifters
SEVEN BRIDES FOR SEVEN BROTHERS (PART 1)
3/55   ★ Original Soundtrack
SINATRA!
6/58   ★ Frank Sinatra
SKIFFLE SESSION
6/56   ★ Lonnie Donegan
SKIN DEEP
9/54   Duke Ellington
SO SMOOTH
7/56   Perry Como
SONGS FOR A BROKEN HEART
3/58   Hank Williams
SONGS FOR AND ABOUT MEN (PART 1)
4/56   Burl Ives
SONGS FOR AND ABOUT MEN (PART 2)
8/56   Burl Ives
SONGS FOR AND ABOUT MEN (PART 3)
8/56   Burl Ives
STRICTLY ELVIS
1/60   ★ Elvis Presley
SWEDISH-AMERICAN ALL STARS, THE
7/54   Swedish-American All Stars
SWEETHEARTS OR STRANGERS (PART 1)
11/57   Faron Young
SWEETHEARTS OR STRANGERS (PART 3)
3/58   Faron Young
TAKE IT SATCH!
5/56   ★ Louis Armstrong
TAKIN' IT EASY (VOL. 1)
1/55   Fawkes–Turner Sextet
THERE GOES MY HEART
5/59   Johnny Mathis
TONY KINSEY TRIO WITH JOE HARRIOTT
1/55   Tony Kinsey Trio with Joe Harriott
TRAGIC SONGS OF LIFE
3/58   Louvin Brothers
TRIO LOS PARAGUAYOS
5/59   Trio Los Paraguayos
WALKIN', TALKIN', SINGIN'
1/61   Josh MacRae
WEBB PIERCE (PART 1)
8/56   Webb Pierce

WEBB PIERCE (PART 3)
10/56   Webb Pierce
WILD ONE, THE [OST]
10/54   Shorty Rogers & His Orchestra
YOUNG AT HEART [OST]
9/56   Frank Sinatra
YOUNG LOVE
3/57   Tommy Steele & The Steelmen

LPs

A FESTIVAL OF EDINBURGH
12/59   Various Artists
A RECITAL OF BACH AND HANDEL ARIAS
1/55   Kathleen Ferrier with the London Philharmonic Orchestra, *cond.* Sir Adrian Boult
A STAR IS BORN [OST]
2/55   Judy Garland
ADAM
11/60   ★ Adam Faith
AL HAIG TRIO
11/54   Al Haig Trio
APRIL LOVE
4/58   Original Soundtrack
ART PEPPER QUARTET
6/54   Art Pepper Quartet
ART TATUM FROM GENE NORMAN'S 'JUST JAZZ'
9/54   Art Tatum
AT LAS VEGAS
10/56   Noël Coward
AT THE CRESCENDO
3/56   ★ Mel Tormé
AT THE LONDON PALLADIUM
8/54   Johnnie Ray
B.G. JAZZ CONCERT NO. 2
1/55   Benny Goodman
BACK TO THE DELTA
12/54   Ken Colyer's Jazzmen
BARNEY KESSEL
10/54   Barney Kessel
BEETHOVEN – SYMPHONY NO. 5 IN C MINOR, OP. 67
6/54   Concertgebouw Orchestra of Amsterdam, *cond.* Erich Kleiber
BEETHOVEN – VIOLIN CONCERTO IN D MAJOR, OP. 61
11/54   Yehudi Menuhin with the Philharmonia Orchestra, *cond.* Wilhelm Furtwängler
BILLIE HOLIDAY AND TEDDY WILSON ORCHESTRAS, THE
9/54   Billie Holliday and Teddy Wilson
BLACK COFFEE
6/54   Peggy Lee
CABARET NIGHT IN PARIS
11/54   Various Artists
CARMEN JONES
4/55   Original Soundtrack
CARNEGIE HALL JAZZ CONCERT
8/54   Benny Goodman
CAROUSEL
5/56   ★ Original Soundtrack
CHARLIE PARKER (VOL. 1)
7/55   Charlie Parker
CHRIS BARBER PLAYS (VOL. 2)
6/56   Chris Barber's Jazz Band
CHRIS BARBER PLAYS (VOL. 3)
2/57   Chris Barber's Jazz Band

CIMAROSA – IL MAESTRO DI CAPPELLA
11/54 Fernando Corena with Orchestra dei Pommeriggi Musicali di Milano, *cond.* Bruno Amaducci
COLE PORTER'S CAN-CAN
12/54 Original Broadway Cast
CONCERT AT THE LONDON PALLADIUM (VOL. 2)
2/55 Les Brown & His Band of Renown
COOL AND CRAZY
12/54 Shorty Rogers
COUNT BASIE / LESTER YOUNG
11/54 Count Basie / Lester Young
CUBAN FIRE!
11/56 Stan Kenton & His Orchestra
DAVE BRUBECK TRIO
12/54 Dave Brubeck
DOWN TO EARTHA
11/55 Eartha Kitt
DRUMMIN' MAN
1/55 Gene Krupa & His Orchestra
EARL BOSTIC, HIS ALTO SAX AND HIS ORCHESTRA
12/54 Earl Bostic & His Orchestra
EDINBURGH MILITARY TATTOO, THE
9/60 Various Artists
ELLA & LOUIS
12/56 Ella Fitzgerald and Louis Armstrong
ELLA SINGS GERSHWIN
6/54 Ella Fitzgerald
ELLINGTON '55
10/54 Duke Ellington
FIVE PENNIES, THE
11/59 ★ Original Soundtrack
GENE NORMAN PRESENTS 'JUST JAZZ'
1/55 Charlie Ventura Septet
GENE NORMAN PRESENTS 'JUST JAZZ' CONCERT
1/55 Lionel Hampton
GENE NORMAN PRESENTS THE CHASE AND THE STEEPLECHASE
6/54 Wardell Gray and Dexter Gordon
GENE NORMAN PRESENTS THE GERRY MULLIGAN QUARTET
9/54 Gerry Mulligan Quartet
GEORGE LEWIS & HIS NEW ORLEANS STOMPERS
1/55 George Lewis & His New Orleans Stompers
GERRY MULLIGAN QUARTET (VOL. 2), THE
1/55 Gerry Mulligan Quartet
GERRY MULLIGAN QUARTET (VOL. 4), THE
9/54 Gerry Mulligan Quartet
GLENN MILLER STORY, THE [OST]
6/54 Glenn Miller & His Orchestra
GUSTAV HOLST – THE PLANETS, OP. 32
9/54 Philharmonic Promenade Orchestra, *cond.* Sir Adrian Boult
HERDMEN BLOW IN PARIS, THE
8/54 Herdmen
HERE IS DICKIE VALENTINE
4/55 Dickie Valentine
HIGH SOCIETY
11/56 ★ Original Soundtrack
HUMPH AT THE CONWAY
11/54 Humphrey Lyttelton & His Band
I LOVE PARIS
6/55 Michel Legrand & His Orchestra
IRISH SONGS OF RESISTANCE (PART II) `8" Mini-LP`
2/58 Patrick Galvin with Al Jeffery

JAM SESSION
    9/55   Norman Granz
JAMMING WITH THE GREATS – NEW VOLUME 4
    3/56   Norman Granz' Jazz At The Philharmonic
JAZZ AT THE BLACKHAWK
    2/58   Dave Brubeck
JAZZ ON THE STREETS OF LONDON
    5/57   Happy Wanderers
JAZZ STUDIO 1
    10/54   Paul Quinichette, etc
JAZZ WORKSHOP (VOL. 1)
    6/54   J.J. Johnson, etc.
JUMPIN' AT THE WOODSIDE
    7/56   Buck Clayton
KAY CEE JAZZ
    12/54   Bennie Moten
KENTON PRESENTS JAZZ – BOB COOPER
    12/54   Bob Cooper Sextet
KENTON PRESENTS JAZZ – BILL HOLMAN
    12/54   Bill Holman Octet
KENTON PRESENTS JAZZ – FRANK ROSOLINO
    12/54   Frank Rosolino Sextet
KENTON PRESENTS JAZZ – CLAUDE WILLIAMSON
    12/54   Claude Williamson Trio
KENTON SHOWCASE: THE MUSIC OF BILL RUSSO / THE MUSIC OF BILL HOLMAN
    12/54   Stan Kenton & His Orchestra
KING AND I, THE
    9/56   ★ Original Soundtrack
KISMET
    4/55   Original Broadway Cast
LES GIRLS / THE PIRATE
    3/58   Original Soundtracks
LOVE ME OR LEAVE ME [OST]
    9/55   Doris Day
MAMBOS
    11/54   Pérez Prado & His Orchestra
MASTERPIECES
    10/54   Duke Ellington
MEL TORMÉ WITH THE MARTY PAICH 'DEK-TETTE'
    8/56   ★ Mel Tormé
MERMAID THEATRE PRESENTS 'LOCK UP YOUR DAUGHTERS', THE
    8/59   Original London Cast
MISS SHOW BUSINESS
    5/56   Judy Garland
MORE GUNFIGHTER BALLADS AND TRAIL SONGS
    1/61   Marty Robbins
MOZART ARIAS
    11/54   Hilde Gueden with the Vienna Philharmonic Orchestra, various conductors
MOZART – CONCERTO FOR PIANO AND ORCHESTRA NO. 15 IN B FLAT MAJOR, K. 450 / NO. 18 IN B FLAT MAJOR, K. 456
    9/54   Ingrid Haebler, Pro Musica Symphony Orchestra, Vienna
MUSIC FOR LOVERS ONLY
    12/54   Jackie Gleason
MUSIC IN THE MAKING
    11/54   Jo Hunter, etc.
MY CONCERTO FOR YOU
    3/60   ★ Russ Conway
NANCY WHISKEY SINGS `7" Mini-LP`
    3/58   Nancy Whiskey
NEW CONCEPTS OF ARTISTRY IN RHYTHM
    8/54   Stan Kenton & His Orchestra

NEW ORLEANS JOYS
12/54   Chris Barber's Jazz Band / Lonnie Donegan's Skiffle Group
NEW ORLEANS PARADE
1/55   George Lewis leading the Eureka Brass Band
NEW SOUNDS FROM EUROPE (VOL. 5: PARIS)
6/54   George Wallington Trio
1927
11/54   Louis Armstrong
NOW, THERE WAS A SONG!
10/60   Johnny Cash
OSCAR PETERSON PLAYS RICHARD ROGERS
6/56   Oscar Peterson Trio
OSCAR PETTIFORD SEXTET
11/54   Oscar Pettiford Sextet
OTHER CHET ATKINS, THE
2/61   ★ Chet Atkins
PAJAMA GAME, THE
10/55   Original Broadway Cast
PARTY TIME
11/60   ★ Russ Conway
PARTY TIME AT THE ASTOR CLUB
12/60   Verdi and Jimmy Silver & His Music
PERIOD – 1926
10/54   Louis Armstrong
PIRATE, THE
  See LES GIRLS / THE PIRATE
PLAYS IN A FIESTA FLAMENCA
11/54   Carlos Montoya
RIDE THIS TRAIN
12/60   Johnny Cash
RIMSKY-KORSAKOV – CAPRICCIO ESPAGNOL /
DEBUSSY – PRÉLUDE À L'APRÈS-MIDI D'UN FAUNE / CHABRIER – ESPAÑA
4/55   Hallé Orchestra, *cond.* Sir John Barbirolli
ROCK 'N ROLL
10/56   ★ Elvis Presley
ROCK 'N ROLL STAGE SHOW
10/56   Bill Haley & His Comets
SALAD DAYS
3/55   Original London Cast
SCOTS TRADITIONAL JAZZ CONCERT
12/56   Various Artists
SESSION FOR SEXTET NO. 2
1/55   Benny Goodman
SESSION WITH SINATRA
9/55   Frank Sinatra
SHELLY MANNE & HIS MEN
6/54   Shelly Manne & His Men
SHORTY ROGERS & HIS GIANTS
12/54   Shorty Rogers
SING AND DANCE WITH FRANK SINATRA
11/54   Frank Sinatra
SINGS FOR TWO IN LOVE
6/54   Nat 'King' Cole
SONGS BY TOM LEHRER
9/58   Tom Lehrer
SONGS FOR ROUNDERS
2/61   Hank Thompson
SONGS FOR YOUNG LOVERS
6/54   Frank Sinatra
SONGS FROM THE STUDENT PRINCE AND OTHER FAMOUS MELODIES
2/55   ★ Mario Lanza

SONGS FROM WALT DISNEY'S LADY AND THE TRAMP
9/57 Peggy Lee
STAN GETZ COLLATES
10/54 Stan Getz
STAN KENTON IN HI-FI
9/56 Stan Kenton & His Orchestra
SUMMER SONG
4/56 Original London Cast
SWEET AND HOT
5/56 Ella Fitzgerald
SWING EASY!
12/54 Frank Sinatra
SWING FROM PARIS
11/54 Quintet of the Hot Club of France
TCHAIKOVSKY – SYMPHONY NO. 4 IN F MINOR, OP. 36
4/55 Philharmonia Orchestra, *cond.* Herbert von Karajan
TCHAIKOVSKY – THE NUTCRACKER, OP. 71 `2-LP`
1/55 Minneapolis Symphony Orchestra, *cond.* Antál Dorati
THIS IS SINATRA (VOL. 2)
6/58 ★ Frank Sinatra
VOCAL GEMS FROM CAROUSEL
6/56 Original London Cast
VOICE OF YOUR CHOICE, THE
11/54 Frankie Laine
VOLUME 1: THE QUINTET
7/55 Lennie Niehaus
VOLUME 3
12/54 Lionel Hampton's Paris All Stars
WEDDING IN PARIS
6/54 Original London Cast
WEST COAST SOUND, THE
10/54 Shelley Mane & His Men
WHEN IRISH EYES ARE SMILING
12/55 Ruby Murray

OTHER TITLES FROM MUSIC MENTOR BOOKS

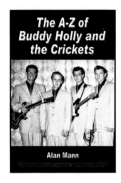

The A-Z of Buddy Holly and the Crickets
Alan Mann
ISBN-13: 978-0-9547068-0-7 *(paperback, 320 pages)*

The A-Z of Buddy Holly and the Crickets draws together a mass of Holly facts and info from a variety of published sources, as well as the author's own original research, and presents them in an easy-to-use encyclopaedic format. Now in its third edition, it has proved to be a popular and valuable reference work on this seminal rock'n'roller. It is a book that every Holly fan will want to keep at their fingertips. It is a book about a musical genius who will never be forgotten.

American Rock'n'Roll: The UK Tours 1956-72
Ian Wallis
ISBN-13: 978-0-9519888-6-2 *(paperback, 424 pages)*

The first-ever detailed overview of every visit to these shores by American (and Canadian!) rock'n'rollers. It's all here: over 400 pages of tour itineraries, support acts, show reports, TV appearances and other items of interest. Illustrated with dozens of original tour programmes, ads, ticket stubs and great live shots, many rare or previously unpublished.

The Big Beat Scene
Royston Ellis
ISBN-13: 978-0-9562679-1-7 *(paperback, 184 pages)*

Originally published in 1961, *The Big Beat Scene* was the first contemporary account of the teenage music scene in Britain. Written before the emergence of the Beatles, and without the benefit of hindsight, this fascinating document provides a unique, first-hand insight into the popularity and relevance of jazz, skiffle and rock'n'roll at a time when Cliff Richard & The Shadows were at the cutting edge of pop, and the social attitudes prevailing at the time. cover

Blues for Francis:
The Life and Work of Francis Wilford-Smith
Caroline Beecroft & Howard Rye
ISBN-13: 978-0-9562679-5-5 *(paperback, 404 pages)*

An internationally renowned cartoonist/illustrator, Francis Wilford-Smith was also one of the world's foremost collectors of blues and gospel 78s, and an acknowledged expert on piano blues. Naturally, this book focuses on the musical side of his life and includes all the scripts from his acclaimed BBC radio broadcasts (1970-95), the intriguing story of the historic private recordings he made of visiting blues pianists in 1960-61, and much more besides. Illustrated with dozens of unique photos and rare label shots.

British Hit EPs 1955-1989
George R. White
ISBN-13: 978-0-9562679-6-2 *(paperback, 320 pages)*

Fully revised and expanded second edition of the only chart book dedicated to British Hit EPs. Includes a history of the format, an artist-by-artist listing of every 7-inch hit EP from 1955 to 1989 (with full track details for each record), a trivia section, the official UK EP charts week by week, and much more. Profusely illustrated with over 600 sleeve shots.

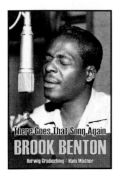

Brook Benton: There Goes That Song Again
Herwig Gradischnig & Hans Maitner
ISBN-13: 978-0-9562679-8-6 *(paperback, 434 pages)*

This first ever in-depth study of this magnificent singer's life and career is the result of a collaboration between two Austrian music experts and long-time Benton fans. The biographical part is based on an album of newspaper cuttings personally compiled by Benton and contains the singer's views on a wide variety of topics, as well as reviews of his work. The exhaustive discography by Hans Maitner identifies over 660 known recordings by Brook. Profusely illustrated with many rare photographs, vintage ads, record sleeves etc.

The Chuck Berry International Directory (Volume 1)
Morten Reff
ISBN-13: 978-0-9547068-6-9 *(paperback, 486 pages)*

For the heavyweight Berry fan. Everything you ever wanted to know about Chuck Berry, in four enormous volumes compiled by the world-renowned Norwegian Berry collector and authority, Morten Reff. This volume contains discographies for over 40 countries, plus over 700 rare label and sleeve illustrations.

The Chuck Berry International Directory (Volume 2)
Morten Reff
ISBN-13: 978-0-9547068-7-6 *(paperback, 532 pages)*

The second of four volumes in this extensive reference work dedicated to rock'n'roll's most influential guitarist and composer. Contains details of bootlegs; radio albums; movies; TV shows; video and DVD releases; international tour itineraries; hits, achievements and awards; Berry's songs, roots, and influence on other artists; tributes; Chuck Berry in print; fan clubs and websites; plus annotated discographies of pianist Johnnie Johnson (post-Berry) and the ultimate Berry copyist, Eddy Clearwater.

The Chuck Berry International Directory (Volume 3)
Morten Reff
ISBN-13: 978-0-9547068-8-3 *(paperback, 608 pages)*

The third volume in this award-winning reference work dedicated to rock'n'roll's most influential guitarist and composer. Contains details of over 4,500 cover versions of Chuck Berry songs including many rarities from around the world. Alphabetical listing by artist (brief biography, comprehensive details of recordings and relevant releases, illuminating commentary and critiques), plus dozens of label and sleeve illustrations.

The Chuck Berry International Directory (Volume 4)
Morten Reff
ISBN-13: 978-0-9547068-9-0 *(paperback, 546 pages)*

The fourth and final volume of this groundbreaking work contains an A-Z of cover versions of Chuck Berry songs, details of hit cover versions, cover versions in the movies and on TV, over 900 Berry soundalikes, a 'No Chuck' section (non-Berry songs with similar titles), games, and even a brief chapter on Chuck Berry karaoke! Also over 100 pages of additions and updates to *Volumes 1, 2* and *3*, plus useful indices of Berry's releases by title and by label.

Cook's Tours: Tales of a Tour Manager
Malcolm Cook
ISBN-13: 978-0-9562679-4-8 *(paperback, 324 pages)*

Throughout his 44 years in the entertainment industry, Malcolm Cook met and worked with some of the biggest names in show business. In this humorous, fast-paced biographical account, Cook lifts the lid on what it takes to keep a show on the road and artists and audiences happy. It's all here: transport problems, unscrupulous promoters, run-ins with East German police, hassles with the Mafia, tea with the Duke of Norfolk, the wind-ups, the laughter, the heartbreak and the tears. A unique insight into what really goes on behind the scenes.

Elvis & Buddy – Linked Lives
Alan Mann
ISBN-13: 978-0-9519888-5-5 *(paperback, 160 pages)*

The achievements of Elvis Presley and Buddy Holly have been extensively documented, but until now little if anything has been known about the many ways in which their lives were interconnected. The author examines each artist's early years, comparing their backgrounds and influences, chronicling all their meetings and examining the many amazing parallels in their lives, careers and tragic deaths. Over 50 photos, including many rare/previously unpublished.

The First Time We Met The Blues – A journey of discovery with Jimmy Page, Brian Jones, Mick Jagger and Keith Richards
David Williams
ISBN-13: 978-0-9547068-1-4 *(paperback, 130 pages)*

David Williams was a childhood friend of Led Zeppelin guitar legend, Jimmy Page. The author describes how they discovered the blues together, along with future members of the Rolling Stones. The climax of the book is a detailed account of a momentous journey by van from London to Manchester to see the 1962 *American Folk-Blues Festival*, where they got their first chance to see their heroes in action.

Jet Harris – In Spite of Everything
Dave Nicolson
ISBN-13: 978-0-9562679-2-4 *(paperback, 208 pages)*

As a founder member of the Shadows, and a chart-topper in his own right, bassist Jet Harris scaled the heights of superstardom in the 1960s. A helpless alcoholic for most of his adult life, he also sank to unimaginable depths of despair, leaving a string of broken hearts and shattered lives in his wake. In this unauthorised biography author Dave Nicolson examines his eventful life and career, and how he eventually overcame his addiction to the bottle.

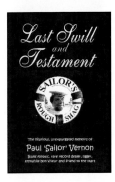

Last Swill and Testament
– The hilarious, unexpurgated memoirs of
Paul 'Sailor' Vernon
ISBN-13: 978-0-9547068-4-5 *(paperback, 228 pages)*

Born in London shortly after the end of World War II, Paul 'Sailor' Vernon came into his own during the 1960s when spotty teenage herberts with bad haircuts began discovering The Blues. For the Sailor it became a lifelong obsession that led him into a whirlwind of activity as a rare record dealer, magazine proprietor/editor, video bootlegger and record company director. It's all here in this one-of-a-kind life history that will leave you reaching for an enamel bucket and a fresh bottle of disinfectant!

Let The Good Times Rock!
– A Fan's Notes On Post-War American Roots Music
Bill Millar
ISBN-13: 978-0-9519888-8-6 *(paperback, 362 pages)*

For almost four decades, the name 'Bill Millar' has been synonymous with the very best in British music writing. This fabulous book collects together 49 of his best pieces – some previously unpublished – in a thematic compilation covering hillbilly, rockabilly, R&B, rock'n'roll, doo-wop, swamp pop and soul. Includes essays on acappella, doo-wop and blue-eyed soul, as well as detailed profiles of some of the most fascinating and influential personalities of each era.

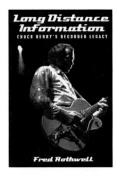

Long Distance Information
– Chuck Berry's Recorded Legacy
Fred Rothwell
ISBN-13: 978-0-9519888-2-4 *(paperback, 352 pages)*

The lowdown on every recording Chuck Berry has ever made. Includes an overview of his life and career, his influences, the stories behind his most famous compositions, full session details, listings of all his key US/UK vinyl and CD releases (including track details), TV and film appearances, and much, much more. Over 100 illustrations including label shots, vintage ads and previously unpublished photos.

Mike Sanchez: Big Town Playboy
Michael Madden (Foreword by Robert Plant)
ISBN-13: 978-0-9562679-7-9 *(paperback, 314 pages)*

The compelling story of one of the foremost exponents of authentic rhythm & blues and rock'n'roll in the world today. Author Michael Madden has been given full access to a vast archive of material charting Mike Sanchez's journey from his Spanish roots through an eventful 35-year musical career that has seen him progress through the ranks of the Rockets, the Big Town Playboys and Bill Wyman's Rhythm Kings to fronting his own band and performing with some of the biggest names of the rock world including Robert Plant, Eric Clapton, Mick Fleetwood and Jeff Beck.

More American Rock'n'Roll: The UK Tours 1973-84
Ian Wallis
ISBN-13: 978-0-9562679-3-1 *(paperback, 380 pages)*

The long-awaited follow-up to *American Rock'n'Roll: The UK Tours 1956-72*. Like its predecessor, it's crammed full of information about every American or Canadian rock'n'roller who visited Britain during the period covered. Dive into its pages and relive all those wonderful memories of nights spent in hot, sweaty clubs amongst the honking saxes, pounding pianos and twanging guitars.

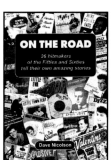

On The Road
Dave Nicolson
ISBN-13: 978-0-9519888-4-8 *(paperback, 256 pages)*

Gary 'US' Bonds, Pat Boone, Freddy Cannon, Crickets Jerry Allison, Sonny Curtis and Joe B. Mauldin, Bo Diddley, Dion, Fats Domino, Duane Eddy, Frankie Ford, Charlie Gracie, Brian Hyland, Marv Johnson, Ben E. King, Brenda Lee, Little Eva, Chris Montez, Johnny Moore (Drifters), Gene Pitney, Johnny Preston, Tommy Roe, Del Shannon, Edwin Starr, Johnny Tillotson and Bobby Vee tell their own fascinating stories. Over 150 illustrations including vintage ads, record sleeves, label shots, sheet music covers, etc.

On The Road Again
Dave Nicolson
ISBN-13: 978-0-9519888-9-3 *(paperback, 206 pages)*

Second volume of interviews with the stars of pop and rock'n'roll including Freddie Bell, Martin Denny, Johnny Farina (Santo & Johnny), the Kalin Twins, Robin Luke, Chas McDevitt, Phil Phillips, Marvin Rainwater, Herb Reed (Platters), Tommy Sands, Joe Terranova (Danny & The Juniors), Mitchell Torok, Marty Wilde and the 'Cool Ghoul' himself, John Zacherle.

Railroadin' Some: Railroads In The Early Blues
Max Haymes
ISBN-13: 978-0-9547068-3-8 *(paperback, 390 pages)*

This groundbreaking book, written by one of the foremost blues historians in the UK, is based on over 30 years research, exploration and absolute passion for early blues music. It is the first ever comprehensive study of the enormous impact of the railroads on 19th and early 20th Century African American society and the many and varied references to this new phenomenon in early blues lyrics. Includes ballin' the jack, smokestack lightning, hot shots, the bottoms, chain gangs, barrelhouses, hobo jungles and more.

**Music Mentor books are available from all good bookshops
or by mail order from:**

**Music Mentor Books
69 Station Road
Upper Poppleton
YORK YO26 6PZ
England**

Telephone: +44 (0)1904 330308
Email: music.mentor@lineone.net
Website: http://musicmentor0.tripod.com